PERSPECTIVES ON WRITING
Series Editor, Susan H. McLeod

M000285692

PERSPECTIVES ON WRITING

Series Editor, Susan H. McLeod

The Perspectives on Writing series addresses writing studies in a broad sense. Consistent with the wide-ranging approaches characteristic of teaching and scholarship in writing across the curriculum, the series presents works that take divergent perspectives on working as a writer, teaching writing, administering writing programs, and studying writing in its various forms.

The WAC Clearinghouse and Parlor Press are collaborating so that these books will be widely available through free digital distribution and low-cost print editions. The publishers and the Series editor are teachers and researchers of writing, committed to the principle that knowledge should circulate freely. We see the opportunities that new technologies have for further democratizing knowledge. And we see that to share the power of writing is to share the means for all to articulate their needs, interests, and learning into the great experiment of literacy.

Recent Books in the Series

Christy I. Wenger, *Yoga Minds, Writing Bodies: Contemplative Writing Pedagogy* (2015)

Sarah Allen, *Beyond Argument: Essaying as a Practice of (Ex)Change* (2015)

Steven J. Corbett, *Beyond Dichotomy: Synergizing Writing Center and Classroom Pedagogies* (2015)

Tara Roeder and Roseanne Gatto (Eds.), *Critical Expressivism: Theory and Practice in the Composition Classroom* (2015)

Terry Myers Zawacki and Michelle Cox (Eds), *WAC and Second-Language Writers: Research Towards Linguistically and Culturally Inclusive Programs and Practices*, (2014)

Charles Bazerman, *A Rhetoric of Literate Action: Literate Action Volume 1* (2013)

Charles Bazerman, *A Theory of Literate Action: Literate Action Volume 2* (2013)

Katherine V. Wills and Rich Rice (Eds.), *ePortfolio Performance Support Systems: Constructing, Presenting, and Assessing Portfolios* (2013)

Mike Duncan and Star Medzerian Vanguri (Eds.), *The Centrality of Style* (2013)

Chris Thaiss, Gerd Bräuer, Paula Carlino, Lisa Ganobcsik-Williams, and Aparna Sinha (Eds.), *Writing Programs Worldwide: Profiles of Academic Writing in Many Places* (2012)

FOUNDATIONAL PRACTICES OF ONLINE WRITING INSTRUCTION

Beth L. Hewett and Kevin Eric DePew, Editors
Elif Guler and Robbin Zeff Warner, Assistant Editors

The WAC Clearinghouse
wac.colostate.edu
Fort Collins, Colorado

Parlor Press
www.parlorpress.com
Anderson, South Carolina

The WAC Clearinghouse, Fort Collins, Colorado 80523-1052
Parlor Press, 3015 Brackenberry Drive, Anderson, South Carolina 29621

Printed in the United States of America

Library of Congress Cataloging-in-Publication Data Pending

Copyeditor: Don Donahue
Designer: Mike Palmquist
Series Editor: Susan H. McLeod

This book is printed on acid-free paper.

The WAC Clearinghouse supports teachers of writing across the disciplines. Hosted
by Colorado State University, it brings together scholarly journals and book series as
well as resources for teachers who use writing in their courses. This book is available
in digital format for free download at http://wac.colostate.edu.

Parlor Press, LLC is an independent publisher of scholarly and trade titles in print
and multimedia formats. This book is available in print and digital formats from
Parlor Press at http://www.parlorpress.com. For submission information or to find
out about Parlor Press publications, write to Parlor Press, 3015 Brackenberry Drive,
Anderson, South Carolina 29621, or email editor@parlorpress.com.

DEDICATION

This book is dedicated to the early pioneers in online writing instruction (OWI), who excitedly and doggedly explored the practices, pedagogies, and theories involved with moving composition to computer labs/classrooms and then into cyberspace. In particular, we wish to honor such innovators and thinkers as Cynthia Selfe; Gail Hawisher; Hugh Burns; Patricia Sullivan; Beth Kolko; Carolyn Handa; Deborah Holdstein; John Slatin; Fred Kemp and the entire Texas Tech crew that engaged computer technology for writing instruction in highly practical ways; the establishing creators and editors of *Kairos: A Journal of Rhetoric, Pedagogy, and Technology* (Mick Doherty, James Inman, Douglas Eyman, Cheryl Ball, and many other intrepid adventurers) who understood the creative and collaborative values of asking scholars to write in multimodal, online spaces; and the many other rhetoricians, technorhetoricians, scholars, and educators who have taken OWI from its earliest inceptions and brought it into the twenty-first century as a vital and nearly ubiquitous environment for teaching and learning writing.

CONTENTS

ACKNOWLEDGMENTS

CCCC Committee for Effective Practices in Online Writing Instruction

2007-2010: Beth Hewett, Keith Gibson, Michael Gos, Connie Mick, Geoffrey Middlebrook, Susan Miller-Cochran, Deborah Minter, Sushil Oswal, Christa Ehmann Powers, Carl Whithaus
2010-2013: Kevin Eric DePew, Beth Hewett, Diane Martinez, Lisa Meloncon, Deborah Minter, Webster Newbold, Leslie Olsen, Sushil Oswal, Christa Ehmann-Powers, Jason Snart, Scott Warnock
2013-2015: Kevin Eric DePew, Heidi Harris, Beth Hewett, Diane Martinez, Mahli Mechenbier, Lisa Meloncon, Leslie Olsen, Sushil Oswal, Jason Snart, Scott Warnock

Site Visit Hosts, Interviewees, and Other Educators

Indiana University-Purdue University of Illinois (IUPUI): Professors Steve Fox, Lynn Jettpace, Mary Sauer, Sharon Hendricks, and Dani Weber
Purdue University: Professors Richard Johnson-Sheehan, Samantha Blackmon, Shirley Rose, David Blakesley, Linda Bergmann, Tammy Conard-Salvo, Allen Brizee, and Dana Driscoll
Ball State University: Professors Web Newbold, Fred Thompson, Nikki Caswell, Jackie Grutsch McKinney, Rachel Baumgardner, Martha Payne, Mike Keefly, Linda Hanson, and Dani Weber
Montgomery College: Professors Samantha Veneruso, Dawn Downey, Tammy Peery, Ginny Streamer, and Emily Rosado
University of Maryland University College (UMUC): Professors Andrew Cavenaugh, Linda DiDesidero, Cindy Davis-Sbaschnig, Lisa Zimmerelli, David Taylor, Jean Dubro, Wendy McDonough, Jim Booth, Stephen Gladson, Jared Featherstone, Mark Parker
Expert/Stakeholder Panel: Kristine Blair, Linda Brender, Lee-Ann Kastman Breuch, Elizabeth (Beth) Carroll, Nancy Coppola, Steven Corbett, Laura DeSensa, Shareen Grogan, Heidi Harris, Heidi Hordis, Laura McGrath, Joanna Paull, Melody Pickle, Jim Porter, Rich Rice, Shelley Rodrigo, Todd Reuker, Peggy Sheehan, Melissa Shepherd, Jason Snart, Errol Sull, Angela Velez, Carl Whithaus, Daren Young, Sean Zednek
NCTE: Kent Williamson, Kristen Suchor
Others: Hundreds of practitioners and educators interested in OWI and OWLs who attended and provided feedback for panel and SIG presentations as well as the many respondents for the OWI Fully Online and Hybrid Surveys.

PREFACE

Webster Newbold
Ball State University

"Screeeeeeeech-squeeeeeeeek-squaaaaaaaawwk!" The 300-baud modems picked up the incoming calls from a half-dozen students who were then on the cutting edge of higher education, enrolled in my English composition class, which was taught via remote access to the Daedalus Integrated Writing Environment (DIWE) in our department's two local-area network (LAN) classrooms. The year was 1991. For some time we had been seeking to legitimize computer-assisted instruction (CAI) in language teaching areas by recasting its drill-and-practice reputation into potential for interactivity between writers—teachers and students—with real exchange and dialogue via networked machines. Several of us in the composition faculty had persuaded our university to invest in the possibilities for advancing writing instruction through network pedagogy. We had sensed the promise of digital technology for revolutionizing not only personal composing but also writing instruction, and we wanted to experiment to see what was possible.

As the dial-up students, or some of them, made the connection with computers on our LAN, they slowly—painfully—logged into the Daedalus system and began a real time written conversation in the Interchange conferencing application.

> "How are you today, Bob?" I sent out into the ether.
> "I'm ... fine ... Dr.... . Newbold ... how ... are ... you?" crept
> across the monochrome screen.
> "Steve, are you there too?"
> "I ... think ... so ... gosh ... this ... is ... slow"
> "Did everyone understand the reading for today?"
> "Kind ... of ... what ... is ... our ... assignment ... going ... to ...
> be?"

And so a long journey was begun with halting steps. It was a kairotic moment. Opportunity was at the threshold. Computer networks promised to bring people together, to erase barriers, to promote collaboration. We were riding the Third Wave and were energized by what we saw ahead. But serious hurdles stood in the way. What about access? Only some institutions could offer such facilities as we had, and few individuals outside the professional class owned personal computers. What about our technology? It often failed and was difficult for non-experts to navigate. What about professional legitimacy? Many of our colleagues were openly skeptical about teaching writing with computers. Still, the possibilities for extending and enriching our teaching, and for meeting needs of students, encouraged us. We knew that "technology was advancing" and attitudes toward online education were changing. We had a growing professional community to rely on and to learn from. So we went onward into the breach.

Recently, I was hurrying to an on-campus class clutching my Wi-Fi connected laptop, through which I had access via cloud storage to prearranged teaching content. Once in the classroom, I connected to the ceiling projector to show screen images of lesson concepts, examples, and websites, including our Blackboard learning management system (LMS). About three-quarters of my students had brought their own laptops with Internet access, and could pull up a Google doc that we would later use for group editing; students without laptops could use the classroom's own desktop stations. Most students knew what they were doing—many knew more than I did, in fact, about navigating devices and network pathways. In the middle of this buzz of activity, I suddenly thought "This has finally come together. This is what we were hoping for years ago. Now it's up to us to use it wisely."

IMPORTANCE OF THE OWI PRINCIPLES

Of course, writing educators have been working hard at doing just that—using digital technology wisely in writing instruction, but individual efforts and professional projects have not until now been able to draw on a comprehensive, research-based resource representing the potentially most effective practices in teaching writing online. The group of teacher-scholars behind this volume, past and current members of the College Conference on Composition and Communication (CCCC) Committee for Effective Practices in Online Writing Instruction (OWI) and members of their CCCC OWI Committee Expert/ Stakeholders' Panel, has attempted to provide that resource, under the charge of the CCCC Executive Committee. The 15 OWI principles articulated in *A Position Statement of Principles and Example Effective Practices for Online Writing Instruction (OWI)* provide a broad, research-based distillation of the problems, strategies, and conditions of postsecondary writing instruction online (CCCC OWI Committee, 2013).

Readers may be surprised that the first principle—the keynote of the document—deals not with pedagogy but with issues of inclusion and access—equity for all students who wish to study writing online, especially those with physical or learning disabilities, socioeconomic limitations, and multilingual challenges:

"Online writing instruction should be universally inclusive and accessible" (p. 7). But seeking greater opportunity for disabled students (sight- and hearing-impaired students come particularly to mind) can be seen as just the latest stage in a struggle to provide learning opportunities to all persons regardless of background or personal condition. The history of education in the past two centuries, in the United States and elsewhere, has been one of steady effort (although, admittedly, not in every quarter) to expand opportunity to students at all levels—to remove barriers of economic status, gender, ethnicity, and race. Now the focus is rightfully on those challenged by disability and similar disadvantages. Online teaching and learning presents some special problems in this ongoing struggle for access, problems that *A Position Statement of Principles and Example Effective Practices for OWI* addresses forthrightly in Principle 1 and implicitly in the other OWI principles. Not the least problem is the lack of awareness on the part of many about the difficulty blind students may face, for example, in merely reading screen text, or the issues that academic language presented onscreen may pose for the learning disabled. It is not only right that educators work to meet the needs of all of our students—indeed make it a first priority for OWI—but it is our institutions' legal responsibility and ours as employees to make appropriate accommodations under the Americans With Disabilities Act (ADA) of 1990 (see also Section 504 of the Rehabilitation Act of 1973). In addition to those protected by the ADA, OWI instructors have to proactively create opportunities and provide access to those who experience academic challenges due to socioeconomic and/or linguistic challenges. Until my work with the CCCC OWI Committee, I know that I had thought too little about the broad issue of access as I designed and carried out my own online classes. The CCCC OWI Committee hopes that OWI Principle 1 will provide an opportunity for many in our community to rethink and re-enact *access* in our teaching.

Writing pedagogy itself, whose basic theory is valid in any teaching-learning environment, is the focus of the first section of the document. The principles remind us of what have been widespread and implicit tenets in our profession: online writing courses (OWCs) should focus on writing rather than digital technology; teaching-learning strategies should make use of the affordances of the digital environment; and appropriate traditional theories, pedagogies, and strategies should be adapted to teaching online. Improving the skill of our students by retaining the value in proven methods, while adapting them to new forms of teaching-learning interactions, has always made sense. With elucidation of these general principles through examples of specific effective practices, the document points to practical steps that can be taken to support the quality and effectiveness of our teaching online.

Related concerns and interests of teachers and students also are focal points of the document. Teachers have a right to maintain reasonable control of their intellectual property as technologies enable "teaching" to be offered in a variety of ways that may benefit institutions more than instructors and their students. Materials being used in successive courses without the participation of the authoring teacher, stand-alone independent courses, and even massive online open courses (MOOCs) place stress on existing pedagogical and compensatory models. Those who teach online must not be put at a personal and professional disadvantage: appropriate compensation, workload, and training increase teachers' effectiveness and enrich students' learning. Teachers' satisfaction, often overlooked and undervalued, also is a core component of effective OWI.

Clearly, the needs of students should be understood and addressed. Online students should be prepared by both the institution and teacher for effective learning. This learning should take place in the context of online relationships involving peers and instructors, and general and technical assistance should be readily available both online and onsite. Helping students learn how to use any applicable hardware and software systems, and providing clear access to institutional resources such as library databases and research aids are other important components of student's success online. Major support for online writing students from writing centers and online writing labs (OWLs) has been increasingly available; writing programs and institutions need to ensure appropriate selection and training of tutors to make effective use of the online environment.

Those in charge—administrators, faculty, and tutors—have a special responsibility to coordinate and maximize the OWI enterprise within our institutions. This means not only proper oversight of classes and programs, but also organizing and conducting assessment and research with the goal of improving students' achievement and teachers' effectiveness and satisfaction. The whole writing instruction community can and should benefit from this shared knowledge.

THE URGENT NEED FOR PRINCIPLED OWI

All of us engaged in OWI have thought at one time or other about these obligations and challenges, but *A Position Statement of Principles and Example Effective Practices for OWI* focuses urgency in presenting them together as principles generated from survey, field, interview, and scholarly literature research. At several levels, the OWI principles can assist, support, and encourage teachers and administrators to engage in or offer quality, effective OWI as the number of enrolled students and teachers involved increases every year. In their Introduction to this book, Beth L. Hewett and Kevin Eric DePew report startling findings released by the Sloan Consortium: over the past ten years, the annual growth rates of online enrollments in all areas of higher education have varied from 9.3% to 17.3%, and total enrollments have leaped from 9.6% of all students in 2002 to 33.5% in 2012 (Allen & Seaman, 2014). These numbers alone should make all engaged in English education and writing instruction sit up and take notice of the need to meet this challenge.

The broad scope of the OWI principles and example effective practices presented in this volume makes them particularly valuable for starting discussions on campuses and within institutions where OWI is increasingly prevalent and important. The strong position that *A Position Statement of Principles and Example Effective Practices for OWI* and this book take regarding the need for access and inclusivity in OWI calls everyone to account in making this long-term goal of literacy education move closer to universal inclusion; students with disabilities and other socioeconomic and language-based challenges know best what they need, and, indeed, insist on in their education. Teachers, writing program and departmental leaders, and senior administrators now have a reasonable, research-based foundation for negotiating how best to meet needs on all sides and how to plan for expanding OWI and making it a strong part of the literacy curriculum.

We need OWI to succeed as part of the new culture-wide, digital landscape: individually, institutionally, and nationally, we must grow in positive ways, without overlooking the interests of any one group or our responsibilities as educators, including our obligations under the law. The 15 OWI principles explicated in this book can help us to make genuine and meaningful progress toward this goal.

REFERENCES

Allen, Elaine E., & Seaman, Jeff. (2014). Grade change: Tracking online education in the United States. *Babson Survey Research Group, Pearson, and the Sloan Consortium, 15*. Retrieved from http://www.onlinelearningsurvey.com/reports/gradechange.pdf

CCCC OWI Committee for Effective Practices in Online Writing Instruction. (2013). A position statement of principles and effective practices for online writing instruction (OWI). Retrieved from http://www.ncte.org/cccc/resources/93positions/owiprinciples

FOUNDATIONAL PRACTICES OF ONLINE WRITING INSTRUCTION

COMMONLY USED ABBREVIATIONS

ADA: Americans with Disabilities Act

AWE: Automated writing evaluation

BYOD: Bring Your Own Device

CAI: Computer-assisted instruction

CART: Communication Access Real-time Translation system for the deaf

CCCC: Conference on College Composition and Communication

CIO: Chief Information Officer

DIWE: Daedalus Integrated Writing Environment

dWPA: Distance writing program administrator

EC: CCCC Executive Committee

ELI: EDUCAUSE Learning Initiative

EPSS: Electronic performance support system

ET: Educational Technologist

FAQs: Frequently-asked questions

FYW: First-year writing

GED: General Education Development

HTML: HyperText Markup Language

ID: Instructional Designer

IM: instant messaging or text-based chat

IWCA: International Writing Centers Association

LAN: Local-area network

LDE: little distance education

LGBTQ: Lesbian, gay, bisexual, transgendered, and queer

LMS: Learning management system

MOOC: Massive open online course

MOOEE: Massive open online educational experience

NMC: New Media Consortium

OWC: Online writing course

OWI: Online writing instruction, inclusive of *both* the hybrid *and* the fully online settings

OWL: Online writing lab (or center)

PM: Project management

RAD: replicable, aggregable, and data-supported research

SMS: short-message service, also known as *texting*

TOEFL: Test of English as a Foreign Language

UDL: Universal Design for Learning

WAC: Writing across the Curriculum

WAI: Web Accessibility Initiative

WCAG 2.0: Web Content Authoring Guidelines 2.0

WCAG: Web Content Accessibility Guidelines

WPA: Writing program administrator

WYSIWYG: What You See is What You Get

A RESEARCH HISTORY OF THE CCCC OWI COMMITTEE

Beth L. Hewett
CCCC Committee for Effective Practices in OWI
Defend & Publish, LLC

Kevin Eric DePew
Old Dominion University

This introduction defines OWI and summarizes the research history behind the CCCC Committee for Effective Practices in OWI's *The State of the Art of OWI* (2011) and *A Position Statement of Principles and Example Effective Practices for OWI* (2013). To support these practices, this introduction briefly presents the CCCC OWI Committee's process for producing these findings is described and the key issues (i.e., the role of student inclusivity, OWLs, administrative concerns, and faculty and student preparation) that are discussed in detail throughout this collection.

Keywords: CCCC OWI Committee, committee charges, effective practice/s, expert practitioner/s, multimodal, national survey/s, observation, professional development, research, site visit, Sloan Consortium, stakeholder/s

The CCCC Committee for Effective Practices in Online Writing Instruction (OWI) was first constituted by the CCCC Executive Committee (EC) in March 2007. The members are a diverse group of OWI educators and scholars: those who work for traditional and for-profit four-year and two-year postsecondary institutions; part- and full-time composition educators; administrators and other stakeholders; specialists in multilingual writers,[1] disabilities-based OWI, and other learning needs/preferences; and online tutors and administrators.

The CCCC OWI Committee's original charges were to:

1. Identify and examine best strategies for online writing instruction in hybrid and distance-based composition classrooms.
2. Identify best practices for using various online media and pedagogies (e.g., networked classrooms, email and Internet-based conferences,

peer-reviewed papers) for the teaching of writing with both synchronous and asynchronous modalities while taking into consideration currently popular learning management environments.

3. Identify best practices for using online writing instruction for English language learners and students with disabilities.[2]
4. Identify best practices for training and professional development of OWI teachers.

When the CCCC OWI Committee was reconstituted and recharged in 2010, its responsibilities were updated to:

1. Identify and examine best strategies for online writing instruction using various online media and pedagogies primarily used for the teaching of writing in blended, hybrid, and distance-based writing classrooms, specifically composition classrooms, but including other college writing courses.
2. Identify best practices for using online instruction specifically for English language learners and individuals with disabilities in coordination with related CCCC committees.
3. Create a Position Statement on the Principles and Standards for OWI Preparation and Instruction. In consultation with the Assessment Committee and the Task Force on Position Statements, review and update the 2004 Position Statement "Teaching, Learning, and Assessing Writing in Digital Environments."
4. Share best practices in OWI with the CCCC membership in a variety of formats.

As of 2013, the CCCC OWI Committee's charges have evolved to:

1. Continue to identify, examine, and research online writing instruction (OWI) principles and effective strategies in online writing centers and in blended, hybrid, and distance-based writing classrooms, specifically composition classrooms but also including other college-writing or writing-intensive disciplinary courses.
2. Continue to identify, examine, and research effective practices for using OWI specifically for English language learners, individuals with physical and/or learning disabilities, and students with socioeconomic challenges in coordination with related CCCC committees.
3. Maintain and update the Position Statement on the OWI principles and effective practices.
4. In consultation with the Assessment Committee and other relevant groups, review and update the 2004 Position Statement "Teaching, Learning, and Assessing Writing in Digital Environments."

5. Identify and/or create instructional and professional development materials and strategies to be posted on the Committee's Web-based OWI Open Resource Web page.
6. Provide the writing instructional community with access to information about OWI-specific faculty and program development that can assist with legitimizing online teaching for professional development, remuneration, and advancement purposes.
7. Share effective practices in OWI with the CCCC membership in various formats, including instructional workshops at CCCC conferences and events as well as other professional venues.

In order to meet these charges, which always have been broad, deep, and challenging, the CCCC OWI Committee has undertaken extensive qualitative and quantitative research on student, instructional, and administrative OWI concerns and issues; compiled and analyzed the results; and composed a position statement outlining foundational principles that can lead to what we believe are potentially effective OWI practices. Currently, the CCCC OWI Committee is producing the *OWI Open Resource*, a Web-based source for OWI administrators, teachers, and tutors to submit their own effective practices grounded in the OWI principles for publication.

The primary results of all of these projects are the fifteen principles enumerated in *A Position Statement of Principles and Example Effective Practices for OWI* (CCCC OWI Committee, 2013) (an official educational statement approved by the CCCC Executive Committee) as well as in Chapter 1 of this book and considered in the rest of this book's chapters. *Foundational Practices of Online Writing Instruction* particularly responds to the CCCC OWI Committee's current seventh charge to share its knowledge by summarizing and explaining these principles and practices, and this book illustrates applications of these practices for administrators and instructors with varying degrees of OWI experience.

Foundational Practices of Online Writing Instruction, written by current and former CCCC OWI Committee members and acknowledged OWI experts and stakeholders, actually may pose more questions than it answers because so much remains unknown about OWI. Although the authors have tried to address their subjects with straightforward information and thoughtful guidance regarding the OWI principles enumerated in Chapter 1, they acknowledge that they remain curious and uncertain about many issues relative to OWI. This, we think, is a good thing. We anticipate that our audience will leave this collection with as many questions as they have answers. Some of these questions reflect the current state of OWI and the fact that there is still a lot more to learn about its practice (see Chapters 17 & 18). Other questions provide heuristics for administrators and instructors in local settings. Rather than approaching a local situation knowing exactly what practice to adopt, we want our audience of administrators and instructors to pose questions to themselves as they design their effective practices based on the grounded principles presented in this book. *Foundational Practices of Online Writing Instruction* has been developed to engage the nuances and complexities of OWI at a time when higher education is struggling with its historical bearings, contemporary reputation, financial challenges, and future goals. There is no question that OWI will be a part of higher education's future, but as Chapter 18 states, the future is *now*. When OWI is addressed in a principled manner, administrators and instructors will have reasonable guidance in sometimes murky waters—all to the benefit of writing students, who are flocking to online courses in unprecedented numbers and often with unrealistic expectations.

Take the issue of multimodality and its connections to online *writing* instruction (addressed in Chapter 15), for example. When thinking about multimodality as a subject for OWI, we must ask such questions as:

- What is writing as text, as discourse, as image, as audio, as video?
- Where alphabetic literacy has been primary—and, quite likely will remain primary—to our society's communication habits, how does OWI approach the teaching of multimodality? Or, should it leave such teaching to courses specializing in digital writing?
- Are these discourse approaches part and parcel of the same communicative need in the digital, twenty-first century?
- How does teaching multimodality in an OWI setting function versus teaching it in a traditional onsite setting?
- How do the complexities of having well-prepared teachers of multimodal OWI and sufficiently financed programs affect students from multilingual and socioeconomically challenged backgrounds, as well as for students with various physical or learning differences?

When thinking about multimodality as a means for improving inclusion and access of OWI students with different learning needs and for OWI instructors with particular teaching strengths, we must ask such questions as:

- How do OWI and multimodality work together (and against each other) when multimodality is one venue used to provide access for students and teachers?
- How do issues of access differ when multimodality is the subject of the writing course as well as one means for reaching students with different learning needs?

These kinds of questions complicate an already complex learning environment that is fraught with multiple levels of teaching and learning considerations.

Similar questions can be asked about the primary topics of each of *Foundational Practices of Online Writing Instruction's* chapters. Although we hope we have addressed readers' most pressing questions about OWI, we recognize that asking new questions may be even more important than articulating answers at this point in OWI's history—particularly given that no one answer will work in every institutional setting.

This Introduction outlines some of the questions and processes that have led to a clearer understanding of grounding principles for OWI and what we have chosen to call *effective practices* in keeping with the Sloan Consortium's Janet Moore (2011), who used this term to acknowledge the "rapid" changes occurring in online instruction overall (p. 93). The CCCC OWI Committee believes that such changes are ongoing, which suggests that effective practices for differing settings, institutions, administrators, faculty, and students will evolve continually.

WHAT IS OWI?

Online writing instruction, or OWI, can be defined as:

> writing instruction that occurs—at least partially if not fully—in a computer-based, Internet, or intranet instructional setting. It uses online/digital media to provide instruction; to talk about writing; or to distribute, share, and/or collect writing-related materials. OWI can occur in either the synchronous or asynchronous modality using a variety of electronic media, platforms, and technologies. (CCCC OWI Committee, 2011c, p. 2)

For some educators and scholars, OWI is a deficit model in comparison with the traditional, face-to-face (onsite) writing instruction undertaken from the time of Aristotle until about thirty years ago. As numerous articles attest, people worry that the loss of body/face/voice occurring in asynchronous settings particularly lead to a less humanly affective setting for courses that have come to be understood as social spaces for writing and sharing writing (DePew & Lettner-Rust, 2009; Gouge, 2009; Powers, 2010). Despite the potential for such misgivings, the CCCC OWI Committee (2011) determined in its *The State of the Art of OWI* that it recognized:

> a difference in a (currently) primarily text-based online instructional environment from one that traditionally occurs face-to-face. The Committee takes no position on the oft-asked question of whether OWI *should be* used and prac-

ticed in postsecondary settings because it accepts the reality that currently OWI *is* used and practiced in such settings. The Committee therefore believes that OWI needs its own study, theories, and practices. The Committee fundamentally believes that OWI has the potential to be an efficacious activity for postsecondary students and faculty. It recognizes, however, that some students and faculty will be better suited to the online educational environment than others. Further, it seems that there are certain conditions under which OWI can be implemented more effectively than others. Discerning and describing such conditions are part of this committee's charges. (p. 2)

Theories of OWI have been scarce, yet a few educators and scholars have posited new ideas, as shown in Chapter 17 of this book.

BEGINNING OF THE CCCC OWI COMMITTEE'S WORK

The CCCC OWI Committee's charges provided an exigency that prompted careful research into OWI. In our first face-to-face meeting, which occurred at the annual CCCC convention in 2007, CCCC OWI Committee members looked to one another and considered where to begin. None of us had any "best" practices ready to offer—particularly for so many different settings in any modality. Hence, we knew that in-depth research into the problems was needed. We began the research, as most people do, with a series of questions adapted at first from Sloan Consortium (2005) materials.

The Sloan Consortium identified the criteria of effective, or best, practices in online education, which we considered to be related to OWI and interdependent with it in that "practices in one area affect quality in another":

- *Innovation—the practice is inventive or original.* Of this particular criterion, we knew that innovation is important to working in the online setting; however, we wondered whether innovation is necessary for all of OWI. Although certainly innovative practices needed to be developed, we believed that at least some non-original practices in composition instruction could be adapted to OWI and would seem to be warranted by the context. This notion would later be folded into OWI Principle 4 (p. 17).
- *Replicability—the practice can be implemented in a variety of learning environments.* OWI is used in fully online (i.e., completely asynchronous and electronically synchronous) settings as well as with hybrid ones. It is used

for writing students in traditional and for-profit two-year and four-year institutions, as well as for learning support in the form of tutoring and other question/answer or advice settings. It is used with widely varied student populations in terms of ages, educational and economic backgrounds, learning needs and preferences, physical abilities, and linguistic contexts. While every OWI practice may not apply in all settings, many do transfer and can be adapted from a general practice to one that works in a specific institution or for a particular teacher's course.

- *Potential impact—the practice would advance the field if many adopted it.* We immediately saw a need for practices that would help the majority of instructors and students in OWI settings. At this point in our process, we had not realized that grounding principles might work better than a series of so-called best practices, but we did see that many educators and administrators in the field had been left to develop their own practices in isolation and, in effect, to reinvent the proverbial wheel. A more centralized or focused document would be helpful to move the field forward.

- *Supporting documentation—the practice is supported with evidence of effectiveness.* Although not every potentially effective practice has been researched empirically, many educators can point to evidence—anecdotal at a minimum—to argue for the effectiveness of their practices. We believed we could uncover some of these practices and find in the literature and in actual practice reasons for why they work. The need for supporting documentation framed the OWI research we outlined and conducted for our first six years.

- *Scope—the practice explains its relationship with other quality elements.* This notion of scope seems related to the idea that a practice grounded in principles holds in multiple settings and connects with other practices to create an effective OWI environment. We realized early that there needed to be connective tissue for the desired best practices document and later discovered that tissue in a series of OWI principles.

The Sloan Consortium also identified the elements of "quality pillars" in online learning as:

- *Learning Effectiveness: The provider demonstrates that the quality of learning online is comparable to the quality of its traditional programs.* OWI research into effectiveness was and is relatively slender given the challenges of conducting any replicable, aggregate, and data-supported (RAD) research in composition studies (Haswell, 2005). Yet, learning effectiveness is one significant measure of whether OWI is being developed in ways that help students learn to write sufficiently for their college settings.

- *Cost Effectiveness and Institutional Commitment: Institutions continuously improve services while reducing cost.* The CCCC OWI Committee remained aware of the need for cost effectiveness for institutions, but it was more conscious of actions that institutions might need to undertake to support their learners and teachers in OWI. Cost reduction is especially emphasized for contemporary education, but OWI is not necessarily the place to achieve it (DePew, Fishman, Ruetenik, & Romberger, 2006) and certainly not at the literal expense of teaching and learning.
- *Access: All learners who wish to learn online have the opportunity and can achieve success.* Although it was not within the CCCC OWI Committee's first set of charges, we learned that both access and the intention to provide it are crucial for any online communication—let alone OWI—to work. Even a PDF file that is not formatted for accessibility can be impossible for a blind individual's screen reader, and either text-heavy or image-heavy presentations can disinclude many students from learning. Likewise, institutions need to develop methods for making their online writing courses (OWCs) and online writing labs (OWLs)[3] available to students whose socioeconomic status limits their access to the technologies that mediate these opportunities. Moreover, administrators and instructors must not systemically limit the opportunities of students who produce different or non-standard varieties of English. It took us awhile, indeed far too long, but we came to realize that access is a first-degree concern, which eventually made it our overarching OWI principle (p. 7).
- *Faculty Satisfaction: Faculty achieve success with teaching online, citing appreciation and happiness.* Faculty need to feel comfortable in the online educational setting, and that means they need to experience their work as supported through training and professional development. OWI faculty often express a sense of feeling alone and overworked. We understood immediately that faculty satisfaction is critical to potentially effective OWI, and we set out to learn what could foster that sense of satisfaction in this newer teaching environment.
- *Student Satisfaction: Students are successful in learning online and are pleased with their experience.* Students, too, need to feel comfortable in the online educational environment. With annually increasing numbers of students entering the online educational arena—many born into the digital age—it might seem that they easily would find themselves experiencing success in OWI. However, the anecdotal evidence for failure and lack of persistence is high, possibly because students—while Internet and computer savvy—lack focused experience with educational uses of technology or, as Hewett (2015a) suggested, experience a literacy-cognition

gap when learning to write in online settings.

Using these criteria and elements of effective online practice as initial guides, the CCCC OWI Committee formulated the following initial questions for its research:

<u>Research questions based on elements of effective practices</u>

Learning effectiveness:
- What are the principles that ground effective student learning in an OWI environment?
- What conditions foster such learning?

Cost effectiveness and institutional commitment
- What are quality benchmarks for OWI?
- Costs:
  ◦ What are the financial costs of OWI?
  ◦ What are the hidden costs of OWI?
  ◦ How are these costs comparable to traditional writing instruction?
  ◦ How should institutions/administrators address these costs?
- What are the features of institutional support for an effective/successful OWI program?

Access
- What conditions foster student access to OWI?
- In what ways do administrators and faculty have similar and different responsibilities for fostering such access?
- Along these lines, what conditions foster faculty access to OWI?

Student satisfaction
- What are characteristics of student satisfaction in an OWI environment?
- What conditions foster student satisfaction?

Faculty satisfaction
- What are the characteristics of faculty satisfaction with OWI?
- What conditions foster faculty satisfaction with OWI?
- How should online instructors be evaluated, especially in comparison to existing evaluation structures used in tenure and promotion?

<u>Research questions based on specific elements of OWI</u>

Modality-specific questions
- What are the characteristics of synchronous technologies in an OWI program?
- What conditions foster successful synchronous OWI?
- What are the characteristics of asynchronous technologies in an OWI program?

- What conditions foster successful asynchronous OWI?
- How should faculty choose between these modalities when using these technologies to achieve writing course objectives?

Environment-specific questions
- What are the characteristics of hybrid learning environments for OWI?
- What conditions foster successful hybrid OWI?
- What are the characteristics of distance learning environments for OWI?
- What conditions foster successful distance OWI?
- How can content (learning) management systems be leveraged for OWI?
  - What are the differences in using large-scale, standardized content management systems (Blackboard, WebCT, etc.) vs. smaller, open-source systems (Moodle, etc.) for the delivery of OWI?
- How can collaborative environments like Wikis be leveraged for OWI?
- How can gaming simulations and other non-text-based environments be leveraged for OWI?

Pedagogy-specific questions
- What traditional learning strategies (e.g., collaborative learning and co-teaching), if any, are appropriate for OWI?
- How can we apply those strategies, if any, to an OWI environment?
- What learning strategies are distinctive to an OWI environment?
- How do we encourage and improve collaboration among students in OWI in distance-based classrooms?
- How do faculties stimulate student participation in OWI?
- What conditions foster student motivation in OWI environments?
- What are appropriate uses of new technologies in OWI? What conditions foster the funding and employment of such technologies?

Population-specific questions
- To what extent and in what ways can OWI accommodate certain learner groups other than native English speakers?
  - English language learners
  - Students with physical challenges
  - Students with learning challenges

Professional development-specific questions
- To what extent and in what ways should administrators (and, subsequently, faculty trainers) encourage new instructors to elect an OWI environment?
- How can instructors new to content management systems be supported to use those systems for OWI?
- What professional qualities and skills need to be emphasized in new

instructor training and on-going professional development relative to OWI?

- To what extent and in what ways do course material ownership issues discourage professors from developing online courses? How are these ownership issues best addressed?

<u>Future Research</u>

- What areas of OWI need to be addressed in future research?
- What are necessary "next steps" for CCCC's continued approach to OWI and its investigation?

These research questions became the CCCC OWI Committee's guide from which we constructed an annual research and action plan and began the process of learning more about OWI in order to determine potentially effective practices.

The CCCC OWI Committee has met face-to-face at the annual meeting of the CCCC and through regular teleconferences from 2007 to date. We made a commitment to each other that we would propose a panel and special interest group (SIG) for presentation at the annual conferences to share our findings and to listen to the needs of our colleagues interested in OWI.

RESEARCH INTO THE NATURE OF OWI

ANNOTATED BIBLIOGRAPHY

The first research project that the CCCC OWI Committee (CCCC OWI Committee, 2008) undertook was a review of the OWI literature deemed most likely to outline or address effective practices. We reasoned that scholarship already might have delineated some ideal practices for OWI that would serve our mission. The original nine committee members apportioned the literature from the 1980s through 2008 and began reading. We decided to write an annotated bibliography and publish it to the CCCC OWI Committee's CCCC Web page, using this intensive research to teach ourselves more about OWI and to make our efforts more broadly useful. Edited by Keith Gibson and Hewett, the bibliography's selected subject areas included OWI Pedagogy, OWI Technology, E-learning, and Online Writing Centers.

SITE VISITS AND OBSERVATIONS

While the annotated bibliography enabled an understanding of previous research, the CCCC OWI Committee quickly agreed that action-oriented and empirical research was needed. The CCCC OWI Committee's earliest solid data in 2008 emerged from three site visits[4] to closely located, postsecondary institutions using OWI. There, Connie Mick and Hewett saw an interesting range of availability, pedagogy, and support for and comfort level with OWI—all in a very small geographical region. Because our hosts scheduled the time primarily for faculty meetings and observations, the CCCC OWI Committee's visitors were not able to meet with students in any of these institutions.

At Ball State University, which at that time styled itself as the "most wired/wireless campus," Mick and Hewett met with faculty and graduate students who used technology regularly in their writing classes in a hybrid setting. The hybrid course meant that students and instructors met all of their hours in the computer lab and blended the technology and traditional teaching methods. Ball State teachers indicated that they were helping undergraduate students to navigate the rhetorical issues relative to technology and writing that they would face in their future working lives. Graduate students had many opportunities for professionalization regarding technology and writing instruction, and there were numerous English-dedicated computer classrooms.

At Indiana University-Purdue University Indianapolis (IUPUI), a school where instructors indicated they were in "competition" with Ball State for students, Mick and Hewett met with faculty that expressed a sense of being relatively untrained for using technology in writing courses. They stated a future intention to hire more teachers who were interested in and comfortable with OWI. They had two dedicated computer classrooms and encouraged the use of OnCourse, their learning management system (LMS) in a hybrid manner. For them, *hybrid* meetings comprised one day in computer classroom and one day in the traditional classroom, which the CCCC OWI Committee at first distinguished as a term from the more *blended* nature of the Ball State OWCs.

At Purdue University, Mick and Hewett met with faculty and graduate students who also were given technological opportunities that were supposed to make them "marketable." At that time, relatively little technology-based teaching was being done for first-year writing (FYW) students. Instructors taught in a hybrid setting using their computer classrooms; for Purdue, *hybrid* meant meeting one day in the computer lab and two days in a traditional, onsite classroom. The Purdue OWL, which had become famous for its numerous handouts available online, was in the process of revamping its platform based on empirical usability research; the new iteration was to be aimed at meeting the needs of a global readership that might use the OWL to fill teacher/textbook gaps. The OWL also was in the process of field-testing a home-grown asynchronous tutoring application, a practice the famed OWL previously had rejected.

Two additional site visits rounded out this stage of the research.

Hewett visited with administrators and faculty members of the University of Maryland University College (UMUC), who shared impressions of their program. About 70% of courses were taught in a fully online setting; attempts at hybrid instruction had only just begun there. Twelve writing courses at all student levels were taught online regularly. With well over 250 faculty members distributed across the United States and globally, a primary goal of administrators was to train faculty well; they accomplished this through a comprehensive two-week, financially uncompensated unit on online teaching; any attention to teaching *writing* online was accomplished in also uncompensated, asynchronous writing faculty meetings using a discussion board that teachers were expected to check and review regularly. Using a home-developed asynchronous LMS called WebTycho, instructors were provided teaching content through static modules; they taught actively through group discussions (called "conferences") and essay instruction. Site-visit participants stated that for students to be successful, they needed to be self-motivated, disciplined, and willing and able to read the modules and instruction.

Finally, Hewett visited Montgomery College, a prominent multi-campus, community college in Maryland. There, she met with administrators and faculty members, as well as students, who provided highlights of their OWI program. Fully online courses taught by both full-time and part-time instructors included their two-level first-year composition courses and business courses. These same courses were offered as hybrid models (which they called *blended*) and in onsite, networked computer classrooms. All OWCs were capped at 20 students while other writing courses had higher caps of 25 students (except for developmental writing, which was capped at 22 students). Students received a "mandatory" orientation to their OWCs in a face-to-face setting although not all students attended; however, the college was piloting online orientations for OWI. Students shared that they liked the ease of typing over handwriting (a sentiment echoed by one left-handed writer), the course structure, and a sense of the online course mirroring the business world. They expressed that they disliked the need to check online for instructor response and feedback and technology problems like computer crashes.

These site visits informed the CCCC OWI Committee on a number of issues. For example, faculty made clear that the CCCC should urge institutional support (i.e., financial compensation and course release) for training and acculturating existing faculty in OWI pedagogical processes (i.e., moving beyond familiarizing with the technology itself).

NATIONAL SURVEYS

The next research project that the CCCC OWI Committee undertook was to develop a trial survey to pilot at a special interest group (SIG) meeting at the CCCC 2009 convention. Its purpose was to query NCTE members about various OWI-focused concerns (i.e., administrative concerns, pedagogy, needed research, teaching issues, and student needs) and to provide the data needed for a final CCCC OWI Committee report. Questions for the pilot survey emerged from the original research questions developed by the CCCC OWI Committee and the previous two research steps of reviewing and annotating the published literature and questioning and observing administrators, faculty, and students during the site visits. The pilot revealed gaps in the survey and language issues that needed to be corrected.

The resulting survey was extensive, and NCTE's Executive Director Kent Williamson personally helped the CCCC OWI Committee to revise it. Revision led to the survey being separated into two different questionnaires, one addressing fully online OWI and the other addressing hybrid OWI. Because of the scope of the CCCC OWI Committee's charges and because we did not want to overtax our disciplinary colleagues by asking them to complete multiple surveys over a period of months, the surveys remained comprehensive with an estimated time of 45-60 minutes required to complete. They were fielded on the NCTE website using Zoomerang in March, 2010 with 139 respondents for the hybrid survey (CCCC OWI Committee, 2011b) and 158 for the fully online one (CCCC OWI Committee, 2011a). The resulting analysis of these surveys comprised a report the CCCC OWI Committee called the *State of the Art of OWI* (CCCC OWI Committee, 2011c) because we realized that the survey was not yielding anything that could be called "best" or "effective" practices. Instead, it was providing the then-baseline understanding of OWI. While the Executive Summary and the entire report can be read online, the following excerpt of emergent themes summarizes its results:

1. *Pedagogy:* Teachers and administrators, to include those in writing centers, typically are simply migrating traditional face-to-face writing pedagogies to the online setting—both fully online and hybrid. Theory and practice specific to OWI has yet to be fully developed and engaged in postsecondary online settings across the United States.

2. *Training:* Training is needed in pedagogy-specific theory and practice in both fully online and hybrid settings, but particularly in fully online settings because of its unique complete mediation by computers. In most cases, it appears that "writing" and how to achieve strong writing and identifiable student results are left out of online writing instructional training.

3. *Supplemental Support:* Online writing centers are not developed by enough institutions to handle the needs of students in both fully online

and hybrid online settings. To that end, training is insufficiently developed to the unique setting as it is, re: above, migrated primarily from the face-to-face setting.

4. *English Language (EL2) Users:* The needs of EL2 learners and users are vastly unknown and insufficiently addressed in the online setting—both fully online and hybrid.

5. *Students with Disabilities:* The needs of students with various kinds of disabilities have not received sufficient and appropriate consideration in light of writing courses in online settings, although the hybrid setting indicates somewhat of a beginning. Teachers and administrators do not know what they are responsible to do or how to do it for any particular variation of learning or physical disabilities relative to the Americans with Disabilities Act (ADA) or to a particular student's specified needs.

6. *Satisfaction:* Instructors are dissatisfied with the levels of support they receive regarding technology, course caps, training, pay, and professional development/interactions relative to OWI in both the fully online and hybrid settings. Such dissatisfaction can lead to poor teaching, low expectations for students and for an online course, and insufficient retention of experienced instructors at a time when OWI continues to grow. (CCCC OWI Committee, 2011c, p. 7)

In sum, among other early findings, we learned that educators have a wide range—from minimal to extensive—of preparation and training for their online instruction. It appeared that much of the training had an extremely tactical focus on how instructors can engage the technology used in a course. There appeared to be less of an emphasis on the pedagogy of teaching with technology. Along those lines, the issue of actually teaching *writing* as the disciplinary subject appeared to be treated somewhat inconsistently at representative institutions. Some of the respondents expressed a lack of ability to speak to a theory and pedagogy of OWI. Their responses suggested that discerning effective practices in areas other than the superstructure and infrastructure of OWI courses might be the biggest challenge this CCCC OWI Committee would face. These themes and considerations set the stage for another necessary action research project.

SEEKING GUIDANCE FROM EXPERT PRACTITIONERS AND STAKEHOLDERS

A final stage of the action research involved developing a panel of as many OWI expert practitioners and stakeholders as possible. The CCCC OWI Committee needed their guidance to cull potential strong or effective practices from *The State of the Art of OWI* (CCCC OWI Committee, 2011c) and other research. We reasoned that by learning the successful practices of expert practitioners and stakeholders, we could compare them with the needs revealed through previous research and develop a Position Statement that best reflected our more thorough understanding of OWI.

The CCCC OWI Committee recruited members for this expert/stakeholders panel using professional contacts and requests via listserv and private email. After receiving nominations, we conducted email conversations with nominated individuals to gather their academic resumes and gather statements of interest. Then each applicant was individually interviewed by phone and follow-up email; more than 30 total interviews occurred in August and September 2011. Twenty-five people were selected, and two left the panel due to schedule conflicts. Panelists included educators and administrators from a variety of academic settings (i.e., traditional university, four-year, and two-year colleges, as well as for-profit colleges and writing center settings). Skills, interests, and areas of expertise included:

1. first-year courses through graduate instruction;
2. genres like FYW through business/tech writing;
3. community college through the research university settings;
4. public, private, and for-profit institutions;
5. writing addressed both in courses and writing centers;
6. fully online and hybrid OWC experience;
7. accessibility issues regarding disabilities[5] and EL2 learners; and
8. expressed preferences for either asynchronous or synchronous modalities.

Using synchronous, Web-conferencing software, we met three times with the expert and stakeholder panel during the 2011-2012 academic year. Each meeting included a scripted series of questions intended to determine the effective practices and recommendations of these individuals. We continued these conversations asynchronously through online discussion media throughout the same time period.

In the first meeting, participants discussed OWI pedagogy. They outlined their most effective instructional strategies for the OWI classroom/environment. This conversation revealed a number of pedagogies, many of which drew from extensive knowledge of onsite composition instruction. Expert practitioners and stakeholders expressed that they needed, for example, to provide ground rules and clear interaction guidance for students, to address the importance of group work and participation (in opposition to online courses that required individual activities alone), to develop and achieve realistic expectations of the course, and to explain procedures for teacher feedback allowing flexibility for student learning needs. An example comment was:

One of the things that I am realizing that is the most effective strategy for me is to make teaching more of an active verb for myself whether it is completely online or the online portion of the hybrid class. So that the discussion to this point [is] to try to get students involved in laying ground rules for example or talking about expectations. I just love that idea of having them buy into what is happening. To try to represent myself in the online environment as actively teaching the course, rather than what I think a lot of students feel like it is there waiting for them laid out front to back. As sort of static or one long document that happens to be broken up into a lot of different units or sections. (CCCC OWI Committee, 2011d)

We learned more from a question asking how participants knew these were the most effective instructional strategies for their particular students. One participant indicated that retention numbers were the "proof of the pudding" and that they would count increasingly in the near future. Another emphasized that her active presence in the course led to comparable presence from students. One teacher similarly explained that his own enthusiasm was the key to strong online teaching and that he received from his students what he gave to them:

In listening to everyone, one thing that comes across that is really needed in any online course is the enthusiasm of the instructor/faculty member. When that enthusiasm is not there, then no matter how much effort we put into the class, in terms of what we load the class with, no matter how much software, no matter how many pieces of material, the students are not going to be involved. What I get to see from my students in whether or not something is working for me is a combination of what I do in terms of a strategy and the enthusiasm I try to inject in it—I get this back from my students. My enthusiasm and my involvement in the course in trying to give them the materials above and beyond perhaps the course's mission is loaded with comes back to me with my students emails, more engaged, wanting to be more involved, wanting to ask more questions, which is exciting to me and exciting to the students as well. It shows up in the discussion; it shows up in the students wanting to learn more in why something is right or not right in writing. (CCCC OWI Committee, 2011d)

The other primary focus of the first meeting regarded training. We asked OWI experts and stakeholders about the training they received (if, indeed, they received any) when they initially prepared for OWI, what elements they had to teach themselves, what effective training methods for OWI are, and how they would advise people developing a training program for beginning OWI teachers. One teacher mentioned the quality of the UMUC online teaching training program (outlined above) and another mentioned Sloan Consortium training. Other responses ranged from the institution providing no training for online instruction (which, admittedly seemed to be rare) to no training for OWI particularly (which seemed common) to creative training methods like online play rooms. The "trial and error" method of training—or self-teaching—was fairly frequently mentioned.

The primary topics of the second teleconference were student and instructor experiences of OWI. We asked expert practitioners and stakeholders about their most effective instructional strategies for their particular students, the relative benefits and disadvantages of OWI for students, and what types of students benefit most and least from OWI contexts. Regarding instructors, we were concerned with the conditions under which they teach most and least effectively in OWI contexts, the benefits and disadvantages of OWI for instructors, and the types of instructors that benefit most and least from OWI contexts.

In the third meeting, we discussed such administrative issues as reasonable and appropriate OWI course loads and class sizes, course preparation and weekly grading time, and instructor pay. We also asked for participants' thinking about what CCCC as an organization could do to help them with OWI. Their overwhelming response involved publishing a position statement and having free resources like a website with examples of strong instructional strategies and professional development through workshops and Webinars.

When all the research was completed, we had a better understanding of what a set of OWI effective practices might look like.[6] The advice and insight of these experts/stakeholders was instrumental in helping the CCCC OWI Committee create *A Position Statement of Principles and Example Effective Practices for OWI* (CCCC OWI Committee, 2013).

ORGANIZATION OF THE BOOK

Foundational Practices of Online Writing Instruction is an admittedly lengthy book written to approach the OWI principles and practices comprehensively. Because of this intention, we are pleased to be publishing in the *Perspectives on Writing* series with the WAC Clearinghouse and Parlor Press. Their hybrid model of providing texts either in free digital form or at-cost printed copy enables readers to access the book as a whole or piecemeal in digital or print forms as suited to their unique needs. To assist readers who download or purchase the book as a whole, we offer a commonly used abbreviations list, chart of OWI principles addressed in each chapter, and an index for easy search. To assist readers who prefer to download or use only those chapters of interest to them, we offer each chapter as a self-contained discussion that provides its own abstract, keywords, and references list. To assist readers who are interested in reading about particular ways to use the OWI principles, Table Intro.1 provides a cross-referenced chart of chapters to OWI principles discussed in those chapters. Finally, despite the number of authors involved in the project whose unique voices we strived to honor, we have cross-referenced each chapter and sought to develop a consistent OWI-focused voice.

Table Intro.1. Chapter and OWI principles reference

Chapter	OWI Principle														
	1	2	3	4	5	6	7	8	9	10	11	12	13	14	15
1	•	•	•	•	•	•	•	•	•	•	•	•	•	•	•
2	•	•	•	•	•	•	•	•		•	•		•		
3	•	•	•				•				•		•		•
4	•	•	•	•	•	•									
5	•	•	•	•			•			•			•	•	
6	•		•	•		•	•	•	•	•	•		•		
7	•		•	•	•		•	•	•		•				
8	•							•							•
9	•	•	•	•			•		•	•	•		•	•	•
10	•	•								•			•		
11	•		•	•			•							•	
12	•	•	•	•	•	•	•	•	•	•	•	•	•	•	•
13	•	•	•	•			•	•	•	•	•		•	•	•
14	•	•					•			•	•	•			
15	•	•	•	•											
16	•	•	•				•			•	•	•	•		•
17	•	•	•	•	•	•		•							•
18	•						•		•				•		

Divided into five sections, *Foundational Practices of Online Writing Instruction* is guided by the primary principles of OWI. It demonstrates above all the CCCC OWI Committee's belief that inclusivity and accessibility must be considered at the inception of any program's online writing instructional venture. To that end, the book includes issues of inclusivity, access, and accessibility in every chapter while addressing different OWI concerns through the lens of the OWI principles.

Part 1, "An OWI Primer," guides writing program administrators (WPAs) and instructors through the OWI principles and the choices they have regarding course infrastructure and environment. Every WPA and OWI teacher's first step should be to determine the course outcomes when developing or revising an OWI program or designing a course; such outcomes should be decided respective of the course's primary modality and delivery media. Hewett, in the first chapter "Grounding Principles of OWI," explains the key principles that the CCCC OWI Committee believes undergird OWI, why they are foundational, and how they position OWI similar to and different from traditional composition. She emphasizes how accessibility issues are central to all principles for OWI given the need for inclusivity in a sometimes faceless environment and given the CCCC OWI Committee's view that an OWI program needs to address inclusivity and access proactively. Hewett provides some examples of effective practices or strategies for these principles. The next two chapters discuss OWI infrastructure in terms of the hybrid versus fully online environments and the asynchronous versus synchronous modalities. Jason Snart's Chapter 2, "Hybrid and Fully Online OWI," examines the OWI principles and effective practice strategies for hybrid and fully online OWI. Snart describes such issues as how these environments differ for teachers and for students—especially regarding seat time, the kinds of strategies that appear best to foster student learning (to include sharing of writing), and what it means to work in a hybrid setting versus that of a completely distributed one. Similarly, in Chapter 3, "Asynchronous and Synchronous Modalities," Connie Mick and Geoffrey Middlebrook examine the OWI principles and effective practice strategies in light of determining whether synchronous or asynchronous modalities—or a combination—will work in a particular course, class, level, and institution. Mick and Middlebrook consider the strengths and weaknesses of these modalities from an effective practices perspective.

Part 2, "OWI Pedagogy and Administrative Decisions," is developed to assist readers with the design of OWI in both OWCs and OWLs. In Chapter 4 "Teaching the OWI Course," Scott Warnock explores some of the foundational principles that ground instructional presence, conversational strategies, response to student writing, class management and organization, course assessment, and classroom technologies. Because of rapidly changing technologies, Warnock particularly considers understanding new technologies from their foundations before introducing them to the OWC. In Chapter 5, Diane Martinez and Leslie

Olsen's "Online Writing Labs" provides similar guidance about OWLs, emphasizing that online writing support is an integral component of the OWI infrastructure that should be informed by similar principles and effective practices. Martinez and Olsen examine how OWL practices and fundamentals are similar to and different from traditional, face-to-face ones. Other logistical decisions that they address are how to select and train OWL tutors and what to consider when thinking about modalities of synchronous and asynchronous settings. Part 2 concludes with two chapters about programmatic decisions that WPAs have to make about OWI. In "Administrative Decisions for OWI," the sixth chapter, Deborah Minter surveys the OWI principles and effective practice strategies for determining optimal class sizes, reading/writing literacy load on teachers and students, and methods for increasing retention. Minter also addresses strategies for assessing OWI programs and courses that adhere to the OWI principles outlined in this book. Building upon this discussion in Chapter 7's "Contingent Faculty and OWI," Mahli Mechenbier acknowledges that many OWCs are taught by contingent and adjunct faculty who typically have little institutional power. After establishing the institutional realities of such instructors, Mechenbier describes the issues that contingent faculty often face when asked to or volunteer to teach OWCs; she provides recommendations about how WPAs can protect these faculty and ensure that their students receive the best quality of instruction. Likewise, she suggests how contingent faculty can protect and advance themselves professionally in the OWI context.

As with the traditional, onsite classroom, OWCs enroll many nonmainstream students, such as student populations with various learning and physical disabilities, those from different socioeconomic backgrounds, and those who have limited access to appropriate online connectivity. Additionally, there are multilingual student populations who communicate in varieties of English outside of the academic standard but for whom OWI presents the most realistic venue for continuing education. Part 3, "Practicing Inclusivity in OWI," includes three chapters supporting the argument that if an educational institution is going to admit these students, then it must develop strategies for incorporating them in all aspects of the academic experience, including appropriate access to OWI. Sushil Oswal, in Chapter 8's "Physical and Learning Disabilities in OWI," examines the unique concerns that students with physical disabilities and learning challenges have when taking OWI courses; he offers suggestions for addressing these challenges. Oswal positions OWI Principle 1 (p. 17) in legal and ethical ramifications for such students. Susan Miller-Cochran raises concerns about inclusion and access based on linguistic production in Chapter 9, "Multilingual Writers and OWI." Charting nearly unknown territory, Miller-Cochran uses OWI Principle 1 to support practical suggestions for addressing these challenges. Likewise, Michael Gos' Chapter 10, "Nontraditional Student Access to OWI," considers the challenges that nontraditional (e.g., adult, remotely rural, urban, military, and incarcerated) students may experience when taking an OWC or trying to access an OWL. Gos provides practical suggestions for addressing these challenges within the rationale of OWI Principle 1.

While OWI inevitably will have its complications, institutions can design methods to prepare and professionalize the faculty and orient the students that anticipate problems and help stakeholders navigate them. In Part 4, "Faculty and Student Preparation for OWI," the authors challenge the trope that instructors and students simply are migrating the writing course to online technologies; on the contrary, OWI requires extensive and specialized preparation on both participants' behalf. Faculty not only must learn how to teach using effective and appropriate methods for OWI contexts, they also need to professionalize while immersed in the practice of this instruction. In Chapter 11, "Faculty Preparation for OWI," Lee-Ann Kastner Breuch examines how the training for an OWC differs from general distance learning training and why this difference is important for writing instructors nationwide. To this end, Breuch outlines five primary focal points for designing training that moves beyond merely familiarizing educators with technology. Rich Rice's Chapter 12, "Faculty Professionalization for OWI," addresses professionalization as it is tied to labor and compensation. He uses the metaphor of software design to consider course ownership, adaptable course shells, and pay for course preparation time. To consider students as important stakeholders in the OWC, Lisa Meloncon and Heidi Harris' Chapter 13, "Preparing Students for OWI," examines how administrators and instructors can assess students' readiness for hybrid and fully online settings. It also explicates OWI principles and effective practices for adequately preparing students for technology-based courses and for learning to write in such settings. To the end of empowering students to succeed, Meloncon and Harris provide strategies for student self-assessment and decision making in OWCs. In Chapter 14, "Preparing for the Rhetoricity of OWI," Kevin Eric DePew argues that OWI Principle 2 (p. 11) opens up an opportunity for both faculty and student preparation; he addresses OWI as a digital rhetoric with all of the political and ideological dimensions of a rhetoric. This aspect of OWI preparation is not simply about learning the nuts and bolts of the technology and composition pedagogies, but it also is about how to read them rhetorically. DePew considers the rhetorical features of which OWI instructors should be aware and how they reasonably can impart this awareness to their students.

Part 5, "New Directions in OWI," brings this book to a conclusion by examining more leading-edged OWI-focused composition instruction and technologies. In Chapter 15's "Teaching Multimodal Assignments in OWI Contexts,"

Kristine Blair provides effective practices for instructors who want or need to move beyond alphabetic, linguistic-based assignments into teaching multimodal discourse forms. Blair provides examples of multimodal technologies and writing assignments and explains how they can be taught in OWI contexts. Examining another new trend in Chapter 16, Shelley Rodrigo's "OWI on the Go" acknowledges that some students' access to online connectivity comes through such mobile devices as cellphones or tablets. These technologies, which offer both unique affordances and challenges for students and teachers, complicate the OWI principles and enrich effective practices. Finally, because *Foundational Practices of Online Writing Instruction* contributes to a much broader, ongoing conversation, the book concludes with two chapters that guide both OWI and writing studies in general toward new iterations. First, in Chapter 17's "OWI Research Considerations," Christa Ehmann and Hewett consider the complications of and critical need to study distance education in the OWI context. They explain how to engage in consistent and useful investigation of one's program, factors to consider, and how to measure and assess one's program. Then, in Chapter 18, "The Future of OWI," Hewett & Warnock express their belief that the future already is here, suggesting that OWI is emblematic of increasingly digital composition and, as such, has much to offer writing studies scholars and educators who teach writing in any venue.

The contexts of writing instruction inevitably will change with the evolution of online writing and digital communication technologies as well as new ways of imagining writing instruction. To this end, we hope that the guidance provided in the final two chapters, the questions that the previous sixteen chapters raise, and the desire to apply foundational practices for OWI in one's own context will encourage readers to join this conversation by designing practices, contributing to the data about OWI, and reshaping its theory.

NOTES

1. *Multilingual* is a term currently used by scholars in fields that study writers who speak, read, and write in multiple languages and who may be continuing to learn the mechanics and expectations of writing in English. Although we use the term *multilingual* in common in this book, at times these writers are referred to as *ESL students* or *English language learners* to reflect language actually used by the CCCC OWI Committee during a historical time.

2. Addressing students with disabilities was added to the charges after the first two years of the OWI Committee's work together.

3. An online writing lab, or OWL, also is called an online writing center, or OWC, in many institutions. In this book, we use *OWL* to designate a writing tutoring

service and *OWC* to designate an online writing course.

4. This research was funded by the CCCC Executive Committee.

5. As evidence of the critical need to address access issues, only one respondent indicated interest or expertise with this area.

6. It is important to acknowledge, however, that students were the OWI stakeholders we researched the least thoroughly. We believe that the needs of the learner are paramount, and that students need to be more actively included as a voice in future investigation, as indicated in Chapter 17.

REFERENCES

CCCC OWI Committee for Effective Practices in Online Writing Instruction. (2008). *Annotated bibliography on online writing instruction 1980-2008.* Committee for Best Practices on Online Writing Instruction. (Keith Gibson & Beth L. Hewett, Eds.). Retrieved from http://www.ncte.org/library/NCTEFiles/Groups/CCCC/Committees/OWIAnnotatedBib.pdf

CCCC OWI Committee for Effective Practices in Online Writing Instruction. (2011a*). Fully online distance-based courses survey results.* Retrieved from http://s.zoomerang.com/sr.aspx?sm=EAupi15gkwWur6G7egRSXUw8k-pNMu1f5gjUp01aogtY%3d

CCCC OWI Committee for Effective Practices in Online Writing Instruction. (2011b). *Hybrid/blended course survey results.* Retrieved from http://s.zoomerang.com/sr.aspx?sm=%2fPsFeeRDwfznaIyyz4sV0qxkkh5Ry7O1NdnGH-CxIBD4%3d

CCCC OWI Committee for Effective Practices in Online Writing Instruction. (2011c). *The state of the art of OWI.* Retrieved from http://www.ncte.org/library/NCTEFiles/Groups/CCCC/Committees/OWI_State-of-Art_Report_April_2011.pdf

CCCC OWI Committee for Effective Practices in Online Writing Instruction. (2011d). [Transcript of expert/stakeholders' panel virtual meeting of 10/27/2011.] Unplublished raw data.

CCCC OWI Committee for Effective Practices in Online Writing Instruction. (2012a). [Transcript of expert/stakeholders' panel virtual meeting of 01/12/2012.] Unpublished raw data.

CCCC OWI Committee for Effective Practices in Online Writing Instruction. (2012b). [Transcript of expert/stakeholders' panel virtual meeting of 02/17/2012.] Unpublished raw data.

CCCC OWI Committee for Effective Practices in Online Writing Instruction. (2013). *A position statement of principles and effective practices for online writ-*

ing instruction (OWI). Retrieved from http://www.ncte.org/cccc/resources/positions/owiprinciples

DePew, Kevin Eric & Lettner-Rust, Heather. (2009). Mediating power: Distance learning interfaces, classroom epistemology, and the gaze. *Computers and Composition, 26,* 174-189.

DePew, Kevin Eric, Fishman, Teddi, Ruetenik, Bridget Fahey & Romberger, Julia E. (2006). Designing efficiencies: The parallel narratives of distance education and composition studies. *Computers and Composition, 23*(1), 49-67.

Gouge, Catherine. (2009). Conversation at a crucial moment: Hybrid courses and the future of writing programs, *College English, 71*(4), 338-362.

Haswell, Richard. (2005). NCTE/CCCC's recent war on scholarship. *Written Communication 22*(2), 198-223.

Hewett, Beth L. (2015). *Reading to learn and writing to teach: Literacy strategies for online writing instruction.* Boston: Bedford/St. Martin's Press.

Moore, J. C. (2011). A synthesis of Sloan-C effective practices. *Journal of Asynchronous Learning Networks, 16*(1), 91-115.

Powers, Christa Ehmann. (2010). A study of online writing instructor perceptions. In Beth L. Hewett (Ed.), *The online writing conference: A guide for teachers and tutors* (pp. 163-171). Portsmouth, NH: Heinemann.

Sloan Consortium. (2005). Retrieved from http://www.aln.org/publications/books/v9n3_moore.pdf; see also http://www.seo-li.com/synthesis-of-sloan-c-effective-practices-the-sloan.html

PART 1. AN OWI PRIMER

CHAPTER 1

GROUNDING PRINCIPLES OF OWI

Beth L. Hewett
CCCC Committee for Effective Practices in OWI
Defend & Publish, LLC

This chapter lists and explains the key principles that ground both hybrid and fully online OWI. It discusses why they are foundational and how they inform OWI similar to and different from traditional composition. The chapter emphasizes how accessibility issues are central to all principles for OWI given the need for inclusivity and access in a sometimes faceless environment and given the Committee's view that an OWI program should address them proactively.

Keywords: access, accessibility, ADA, asynchronous, committee charges, fully online, hybrid, inclusion, inclusivity, learning disability (style, challenge), multilingual, CCCC OWI Committee, OWI principle, persistence, physical disability, RAD, socioeconomic, synchronous

My 21-year old relative recently failed her fully online, first-year writing (FYW) course. This young woman is bright and motivated as evidenced by five years of employment with a prominent fast food company where she had worked her way up to full-time assistant manager. Her accomplishment stems from self-discipline, an ability to meet deadlines and schedules, and hard work. Quite frankly, most people simply cannot last long in that work environment. Although I confess that I have no idea how strong her writing is because she wanted to do the course without my tutorial, she expressed her failure as a semester where the teacher "didn't care" and "didn't communicate—it took two weeks to get a response email any time I emailed!" She complained that the teacher did not teach and she did not learn anything. She also expressed that the information for where to go for the monitored final exam did not get posted until too late to get a space at a testing center where she could schedule it to match her work and other test schedules. So she gave up, did not call each testing center, and did not take the exam.

Did everything happen exactly this way? The teacher has her own story that might indicate other or additional reasons for this failed OWI experience. Nonetheless, my young relative makes points that many students have expressed; furthermore, many students fail their OWCs through lack of persistence, a sense of not learning, failure to post essays on time or in the right portal, dropping out without properly withdrawing, or giving up at the last minute. The problem of failed OWI students is the mirror image of the failures expressed by faculty and administrators. OWI is not an easy way to learn to write, yet it is absolutely a legitimate, do-able, and often a necessary option for taking a writing course or a writing-intensive disciplinary course.

As the Introduction indicates, the CCCC OWI Committee was tasked with understanding OWI from a variety of angles. Our first charge was, "Identify and examine best strategies for online writing instruction using various online media and pedagogies primarily used for the teaching of writing in blended, hybrid, and distance-based writing classrooms, specifically composition classrooms, but including other college writing courses." In addition, we originally were charged to consider online tutoring and students with multilingual student experiences and, given what we learned from working with a disabled committee member, we also considered those with physical and learning disabilities. These broad charges led us to examine the published literature; observe practices at various institutions; survey the composition community's perspectives; and tap the experiences of expert practitioners, administrators, and stakeholders to come to some notion of effective practices in OWI.

One of the biggest surprises in this process was discovering just how little information existed relative to OWI and practices that might possibly be called "effective," let alone "best." In fact, although the CCCC OWI Committee's intensive, six-year research projects suggest that OWI is, indeed, receiving attention, scholars appear to be working so much from their local settings that a global teaching and learning perspective is difficult to achieve. This local focus has led to publication of some interesting practices that potentially are adaptable, but these practices do not transfer broadly to two-year and four-year college settings and with widely varied student populations. We needed to understand OWI from a more universal perspective, allowing scholarship to provide informed guidance from which educators can address their local concerns.

Furthermore, most OWI research tends not to be replicable, aggregable, and data-supported (RAD) (Haswell, 2005). As such, the literature provides great ideas to try out in individual course settings and some thoughts about strategies to avoid, but it fails to provide theory-based or theory-generating guidance that can be applied more broadly to OWI and writing studies' needs. Thus, there remains too much practitioner lore surrounding OWI (North, 1987), and the writing studies field passes on much of that lore along in scholarship, conferences, and online chats. Anecdotally speaking, when I meet with faculty from different institutions, I see a lot of wheel reinvention because people do not know how others have addressed similar concerns.

Additionally, in some places, although thankfully fewer than in the past, scholars still are arguing the relative value of using OWI over onsite teaching, sometimes viewing it as a deficit model for teaching a skill so intimately communicative as writing. Perhaps my young relative now would agree since she claims she will never again take an online course, but I do not believe the deficits are in the model itself or even in the students. The deficits, if any, are in our understanding of how to teach students to write through primarily written material—particularly in asynchronous settings but also in synchronous ones. Boiled down, that is the essential problem for which the CCCC OWI Committee was formed and charged. Yet, the CCCC OWI Committee also was formed and charged with understanding OWI from the faculty and administrative perspectives. One cannot provide excellent instruction to students in the online (or any) environment without also providing excellent support to those who teach and administer the program.

Once we completed research—knowing there was so much more to do—we found our first major writing challenges when we tried to draft a position statement of best practices. We quickly realized that (1) there can be no "best" in such a rapidly changing field, and (2) none of the practices that we had learned from our research would transfer to all the settings we were asked to address. For those reasons, we agreed to use the term "effective" practices as the Sloan Consortium did (Moore, 2011). Lacking sufficient theories of OWI particularly, we also realized we needed to rely on common educational principles that could be articulated and adapted in view of OWI's particulars. Indeed, colleagues have told us repeatedly that they needed foundational guidelines for potentially successful OWI. After those decisions, writing became more natural and the research fell into place. For each of the OWI principles, example effective practices emerged from our research, and these seemed to be both general and specific enough that they could be adapted to various settings and teacher/student populations. Additionally, as much as possible, we refrained from naming, supporting, or promoting any particular technology or software, which inevitably will change. Although technology change is certain, there is relative stability in modality (e.g., asynchronous and synchronous) and media (e.g., text, images, audio, and audio/video) on which OWI teachers can count.

Some respondents to *A Position Statement of Principles and Example Effective Practices for OWI* (CCCC OWI Committee, 2013) have remarked that the principles and example effective practices are "nothing new" or "not surprising." That is a good thing, we believe. It signals that OWI is, indeed, a familiar form of writing instruction to which common disciplinary knowledge and familiar educational philosophies about strong teaching, learning, and support strategies apply. If *A Position Statement of Principles and Example Effective Practices for OWI* was overly shocking in content, it would indicate that educators have been doing things all wrong! On the contrary, the very familiarity of the OWI principles and example effective practices demonstrates that most WPAs and teachers are on the right track, which may reassure educators who experience OWI as a long, lonely trek through uncharted territory.

Some words about definition and language are important here.

First, merely using a word processing program to write does not constitute being online or working through computer mediation. OWI occurs by using computer technology to learn writing from a teacher, tutor, or other students and by using it to communicate about that writing, to share writing for learning purposes, and to present writing for course completion purposes. Being *online* can mean working at a geographic distance or even in an onsite computer lab using technology that enables the learning about and sharing of writing; in essence, the computer technology facilitates the communication about writing, often through an LMS. With this definition in mind, *A Position Statement of Principles and Example Effective Practices for OWI* (CCCC OWI Committee, 2013) and this book refer to *OWI* as including *both* the hybrid *and* the fully online settings unless otherwise stated. We consider the hybrid course setting, often called *blended* or *mixed mode*, to include any OWI that is not fully online. An OWC is hybrid if any of the course interactions occur in computer-meditated settings, whether distance-based or in Internet/intranet-enabled, traditional onsite classrooms or computer labs. Fully online courses occur entirely "online and at-a-distance through the Internet or intranet" and students respond from geographically distributed sites whether they meet from "short (i.e., campus-based) or long (i.e., across state/international borders) distance" (Hewett, 2013, p. 196). If face-to-face interactions among teachers and students are scheduled (and "scheduled" is a key part of the definition being advanced here) parts of the course, however, and the course includes computer-mediated interaction, then the OWC is hybrid.[1] Pedagogically, both hybrid and fully online OWCs make use of similar teaching and learning strategies; yet the hybrid OWC, as discussed in Chapter 2, has significantly different administrative conditions relative to seat- and face-time; in meeting those conditions, the timing and deployment of selected OWI-based pedagogies will differ in various ways. These considerations are important to remember when reading and using this book because the CCCC OWI Committee was tasked with addressing both hybrid and fully online settings, and we quickly realized that although each course setting has basic similarities, they differ vastly in how individual institutions will define, imagine, and organize the OWC.

Second, because we envisioned the principles as foundational to potentially effective OWI, we decided that using the word *should* "indicates that among several possibilities one is recommended as particularly suitable, without mentioning or excluding others; or that a certain course of action is preferred but not necessarily required (*should* equals *is recommended that*)" (IEEE, 2012, p. 9). This use of *should* can be contrasted with our decision not to employ the words *shall* ("equals *is required to*") or *must* (used "to describe unavoidable situations") (IEEE, 2012, p. 9). While we have received understandable criticism that *A Position Statement of Principles and Example Effective Practices for OWI* (CCCC OWI Committee, 2013) reads as a prescriptive set of rules, our goal was to develop more descriptive guidelines for all involved in OWI. We had to balance the desire to present these guidelines such that stakeholders could adapt them to their settings with the need to provide the kinds of language that educators and administrators have requested—language that would enable them to argue at their institutions for fairness, equity, and educationally sound conditions and teaching and learning expectations. In essence, the principles are an ideal, but certainly an attainable ideal that writing programs should work toward. We hope that readers of this book will appreciate the semantic challenges that these crossing purposes revealed, and that you will use these principles and effective practices as guidelines to support OWI in your particular settings.

This chapter tells the story of how the 15 OWI principles were determined by the CCCC OWI Committee, leading to effective practices that provide examples of the principles. It is a microhistory born of the exigency outlined above and of the research detailed in this book's Introduction. It is, as well, a story that admits of uncertainty and a need for *A Position Statement of Principles and Example Effective Practices for OWI* to be organic; changing with research, scholarship, and experience; and one to which the practitioners in the field can contribute as well as from which they can benefit.[2] Finally, the discussions in this chapter—and the book as a whole—should not be read as presenting universal rules but as grounded guidance about sound OWI instructional practices regardless of the particular technologies. In the following sections, each OWI principle is reproduced with its rationale from *A Position Statement of Principles and Example Effective Practices for OWI* and is followed by an additional explanatory discussion.

OWI PRINCIPLE 1

As articulated in *A Position Statement of Principles and Example Effective Practices for OWI* (CCCC OWI Committee, 2013), OWI Principle 1 is overarching, and the CCCC OWI Committee believes that those who use these principles should consider inclusivity and access at every step of planning and implementing OWI.

OWI Principle 1: Online writing instruction should be universally inclusive and accessible.

RATIONALE FOR OWI PRINCIPLE 1

The primary ideas driving the OWI principles outlined in this document are inclusivity and accessibility. Hence, OWI Principle 1 supersedes and connects to every principle in this document. In particular, the CCCC OWI Committee believes that the needs of learners with physical disabilities, learning disabilities, multilingual backgrounds, and learning challenges related to socioeconomic issues (i.e., often called the digital divide where access is the primary issue) must be addressed in an OWI environment to the maximum degree possible for the given institutional setting. Furthermore, given that OWI typically is a text-intensive medium where reading is a necessary skill, addressing the accessibility needs of the least confident readers increases the potential to reach all types of learners.

The CCCC published in 2006 and reaffirmed in 2011 its statement regarding disability issues for educators, staff, and students. This statement recognizes that fully inclusive environments are necessary for the equitable and appropriate teaching of writing at the postsecondary level. The CCCC statement regarding disability issues strongly indicates that a proactive approach to physical and pedagogical access is superior to one that includes "added on" or retrofitted alternatives. It further states that:

> Making writing classrooms and curricula inclusive and accessible to those with disabilities means employing flexible and diverse approaches to the teaching of reading and writing to ensure pedagogical as well as physical access; using multiple teaching and learning formats; welcoming students with disabilities in course syllabi; and including disability issues or perspectives in course content and faculty development workshops.

Additionally, this statement specifically addresses electronic environments: "CCCC is committed to accessible online environments, including making the CCCC website accessible, as well as working to teach others about ways to make their program and course websites fully inclusive."

Such inclusivity must be a fundamental part of any initiative that includes OWI, given its inherent connection to technology; patterns of exclusion have too often resulted from an uncritical adoption of digital technology and an indifference to how it could be used by persons with various disabilities and learning challenges. The CCCC OWI Committee therefore posits that no statement of OWI principles and practices can be appropriate if it does not fully recognize and accommodate educators and students with varying physical, learning, linguistic, and socioeconomic challenges.

We specifically include multilingual learners who may have a different working knowledge of academic English and/or different cultural backgrounds.[3] The *CCCC Statement on Second Language Writing and Writers* (2009) advocates that all writing teachers should be prepared to address pedagogically the linguistic and cultural diversity of the multilingual students in their classes.

Thus, both the CCCC Committee for Second Language Writing and Writers (2009) and the CCCC Committee on Disability Issues in College Composition (2011) agree that such teachers' and writers' needs must be addressed at all levels of writing courses to include such concerns as content, teacher training, and administrative actions. To this end, the CCCC OWI Committee holds that—to the degree possible—all of its OWI principles and effective practices should adhere to the need for inclusivity and accessibility at all levels of pedagogy, student satisfaction, faculty satisfaction, and administrative concerns, including selection of the technological modality and software for OWI.

Some of the guidelines presented below are adapted from Burgstahler and Cory's (2008) principles of universal design while others are developed primarily for this document:

- *Equitable use:* The course and its digital designs should be usable by all students and teachers to include those with physical, visual, hearing, learning, attention, and communication differences (inclusive of multilingual students whose first language may or may not be English).
- *Technological equality:* The technology should be financially accessible to all students and teachers in the course.
- *Flexibility in use:* The course and its digital design should accommodate a wide range of individual preferences and abilities.
- *Simple and intuitive use:* Use of the course materials and the digital design should be comprehensible regardless of the user's experience, knowledge, language skills, or current concentration level.
- *Perceptible information:* The course materials and the digital design should communicate necessary information effectively to the user, regardless of ambient conditions or the user's sensory abilities.
- *Tolerance for technological error:* The course materials and the digital design in particular should minimize the potential for failure based on accidental or unintended actions such as a technological crash. They should, for example, provide automatic protection of data entered and simple means for recovering such data.

- *Tolerance for mechanical error in writing:* Teacher response and assessment of writing should reflect an awareness of the relatively low value to be placed on mechanical and usage errors in student writing particularly for multilingual and physically and learning-challenged writers. Although grammar, mechanics, and usage need to be taught, evaluation should focus primarily on how well ideas are communicated and secondarily on sentence-level errors.
- *Low physical effect:* The OWC's digital design should be usable efficiently, comfortably, and with a minimum of fatigue.
- *Size and space for approach and use:* The physical design of the computer- or other classroom should be of the appropriate size and space for approach, reach, manipulation, and use regardless of the user's body size, posture, or mobility.

We must note that adhering to the principles of universal design "reduces, but does not eliminate, the need for accommodations for students with disabilities" (Burgstahler & Cory, 2008, pp. 24-25). Therefore, there will be times when—regardless of how well prepared an OWI program is for faculty and students with different needs—some accommodations may need to be made (Burgstahler & Cory, 2008).

DISCUSSION

The CCCC OWI Committee decided that access and inclusivity should comprise the overarching principle for all of OWI in part because educators never really have thought that way. While this decision was critiqued by one CCCC EC reviewer as "political," making a political statement was not our goal—although we can see how it has political ramifications. Our goal was to make a moral and ethical statement with respect to a significant legal issue upon which thoughtful educators could ground OWI. This decision was prompted by several considerations.

One consideration emerged from responses to questions about access in our hybrid and fully online surveys. What we discovered shocked us. Closed-ended responses regarding access, disabilities, and the ADA in the fully online survey were especially disheartening because in hybrid courses, presumably, teachers and students may have shared more information about disabilities:

> In FO-Q51,[4] 50% of respondents indicated that they had
> taught students with either disclosed or obvious disabilities in
> their fully online courses, while 23% said they had not taught
> such students and 28% did not know. The number of nega-
> tive responses to earlier FO-Q 49, 50 and 51 also raises some

red flags about the lack of preparation for delivering accessible online writing instruction. Out of overall 158 respondents, eight did not respond to FO-Q49, seven did not provide an ADA-compliant course, and 39 did not know whether or not their courses were ADA compliant. Likewise, responses to FO-Q50 about the availability of ADA training at their institution indicates that out of 152 respondents, 43 did not even know whether or not their institution provided this training. In another 24 cases, the institution lacked arrangements for educating its instructors in ADA and disability issues. In FO-Q51, the ratio of instructors who did teach disabled students—85 as compared the 41 who did not know whether they did or did not—is worrisome. (CCCC OWI Committee, 2011c, p. 30)

In open-ended questions about what they wanted to know about access and OWI, respondents on the whole demonstrated a poor understanding of the ADA and of their responsibilities to students, as well as challenges in working with their administration and offices of disabilities. Some respondents, like the three cited below (see CCCC OWI Committee, 2011a, and 2011b), were oddly lackadaisical and expressed willingness to bar students needing accommodations from their OWCs:

- "How different disabilities react to online environments—are certain disabilities necessarily prohibitive to being successful online, or can any environment be adapted?"
- "What's a reasonable accommodation in the online environment and when should you just refuse and declare that the student must take the class in the face-to-face setting? (I have a dyslexic student this term and have been required to post audio files of every single text file or website that is required reading in the course, as well as audio versions of the textbooks and essays.)"
- "If they have a disability it is good to know, but, really, legally I don't think we are to make accommodations."

I cite these statements here because I think many—*many*—educators have thought these very thoughts, especially in regard to OWI but also regarding composition education generally. The frustration expressed by the second-cited respondent may resonate with faculty who have not had successful dealings with the institution's office of disability where students and teachers both can receive assistance and from whom online instructors especially should receive training. Without appropriate professional development around access and the ADA's legal rulings, it can feel impossibly overwhelming to have to account for inclusion and access when a student self-discloses a need or otherwise self-advocates. Indeed, I have seen educational institutions take a legalistic stance and deny those needs if the student has not been tested formally for a learning challenge. For example, testing for dyslexia or auditory processing disabilities after public high school graduation tends to be the student's responsibility, and it can be prohibitively expensive and possibly shaming in a culture where learning abilities still are measures of self-worth. Similarly, multilingual writers may not want to admit they have problems learning something—whether culturally or otherwise—given already considerable linguistic challenges, and those who have limiting socioeconomic backgrounds also may not want to admit additional difficulties.

To be sure, from a common retroactive perspective, once a course has been developed, it is disconcerting and strategically challenging to adjust it for students who self-disclose a need for special access or inclusive materials. In such cases, one must re-plan to address the problem and find ways to help the student, which may require additional and creative work to make online material accessible and more time on the teacher's part. Such situations are highlighted by such legal cases as the recent lawsuit against Harvard and MIT, where these institutions have provided online material freely to the public but have failed to make it accessible through closed captioning to the deaf, for example (Lewin, 2015). Scratching the surface likely would reveal other ADA problems in these courses that have been otherwise generously offered. This difficulty is one reason the CCCC OWI Committee strongly recommends taking the access and inclusivity "problem" and turning it into a proactive mindset that welcomes all enrolled students from the inception of the class to its ending. I like to call this a *spirit of generosity* toward all of our students. Traditionally, inclusion and access have been handled with retrofit, but if they become part and parcel of our thinking about teaching online, we will be able to accommodate more students with more varied challenges than we might imagine—without them even having to self-disclose their issues. Although hopefully students will recognize an inclusive environment and will be willing to share their abilities and disabilities to the goal of achieving success in their OWCs, educational research reveals that students' particular learning needs, while not necessarily disabilities, may be difficult for them to name let alone disclose (Hewett, 2015a).

Another consideration that prompted us to rethink issues around access and inclusivity regarded a series of the CCCC OWI Committee's communication failures with one committee member who is a professor of some note in his work with technical communication and digital accessibility. He also happens to be blind. Perhaps because he once was sighted, he understands and eloquently conveys the difficulties of a blind or otherwise physically challenged person. A professor with a disability like blindness has daily challenges that sighted people cannot imagine. The time it takes me to draft and revise an article, for example, is exacerbated in a blind person's life because he has to read everything that has been produced with only able-bodied readers in mind. On the one hand, online instruction is a boon for blind faculty and students because it solves the eternal problem of arranging transportation to get from one point to another in an automobile-oriented culture. On the other hand, screen readers used by blind computer users can only process information that is designed following international standards for Web accessibility. When instructional designers and faculty ignore these standards or are ignorant of them, the average eight hours of a typical work day can be expanded to many more for people with serious disabilities like blindness, and we should remember that disabled individuals like my committee colleague still have the rest of their family lives to live in the given 24-hour day.

In purposeful ways, our blind colleague prodded the CCCC OWI Committee to become more aware of access issues, and that was useful. Just as important, however, the CCCC OWI Committee members have embarrassed ourselves repeatedly over the years as we have communicated via email with attached documents and through Wikis, file sharing software, and Internet-based synchronous meetings. More times than I can count, we unintentionally dis-included this colleague from the conversation by perfectly natural (read *learned*) actions like sending email in colors unreadable by his screen reader, using marginal comments in Microsoft Word that his screen reader could not access, choosing inaccessible Wiki or file-sharing software tools without consulting him, and setting up synchronous meetings without sending him meeting information sufficiently early to check out the accessibility of the connections to the screen reader. We are not mean people, but we are all a part of a thoughtless academic culture that considers access for the disabled as a retrofit, an afterthought, a proviso that should take place when the disabled faculty or student is knocking at our door. Our mutual embarrassment provided ample teachable moments and opportunities to challenge our natural-sounding, able-bodied thinking and to change our behaviors. If online technology access was such an issue in a CCCC committee where we were *charged* to consider access for OWI, surely it is a greater issue in the classroom.

In 2012, the CCCC OWI Committee gave a workshop at the CCCC convention. While it was not as successful as we would have liked, the 30 attendees who stayed for the entire workshop sent our committee an encouraging message by rating the final access-related component of the workshop as the best part of the experience. Interestingly, we had done what everyone else does about accessibility—we had placed it last on the agenda, and we had done that every single year in our conference panel presentations, too. It suddenly dawned on me after this workshop that access is not just *something* that OWI needs to address; it is *the key concern* with which we should be engaged at every step. As a result, the CCCC OWI Committee drastically changed our thinking about inclusivity and access. In 2013, by giving our drafted OWI principles a green light, the CCCC EC, the top leaders of our profession, also recognized that it is time to place inclusivity and accessibility in the interface of our online pedagogy and not let it trail as an add-on or save-it-for-later application like a Band-Aid.

Additionally, we must acknowledge other populations needing inclusion and access. The CCCC OWI Committee has had specialists in multilingual learning and those who know socioeconomically challenged populations well. Multilingual students, for example, often are placed into separate classes for both onsite and online writing. Those who have taught such students realize that they may have writing markers signaling their first language, dialect, or spoken language other than English. Some students are not selected for such homogenous online courses because they enter OWCs under the radar or because only heterogeneous courses are offered. Additionally, some institutions do not separate multilingual and typical native English speakers in their writing courses. Given varied student language abilities, faculty need to be able to accommodate some of the primary writing differences multilingual students may exhibit—particularly in a setting where reading and writing are the primary teaching and interpersonal communicative means. In keeping with their institutions' administrative decisions about working with students who have language-learning concerns, *all* OWI teachers should be prepared to help multilingual students with their writing using potentially effective online technology and strategies.

Similarly, students from various socioeconomic backgrounds elect online courses in part because of family requirements, outside jobs, and the illusion that OWI will more easily address those concerns. Many of these students will not be familiar with online learning strategies—some may not even own the required technology (Hewett, 2015a) and others may use cellular phones as the sole technology for their OWI courses (see Chapter 16). Regardless of one's opinion about such technology uses for educational purposes, we must prepare for these students' specific needs. When an OWC is developed with inclusivity and access at the front instead of the backend, teachers are better prepared to help the socioeconomically challenged writing student to succeed.

The CCCC OWI Committee includes faculty and administrators with students as stakeholders in the legal need and ethical imperative for inclusivity and access. Faculty should consider how OWI Principle 1 can be used to improve the learning needs of a wide variety of students as opposed to, for example, one self-disclosing vision-impaired student. However, administrators have an equal responsibility to set faculty up for success. Unquestionably, just as students have different learning styles, teachers have different learning and teaching styles for OWI that should be accommodated in an ethical workplace.

Finally, I want to acknowledge a growing cohort of writing scholar teachers who are involved in a new field of Rhetoric and Disability. They have advocated for, worked in, and led efforts at integrating accessibility in writing studies pedagogy and scholarship. Many of these colleagues either themselves have a disability or are related to someone with a disability. Despite their path-breaking work, however, accessibility is practiced and felt only in isolated pockets of writing studies. We could say that we have some individuals who practice accessibility, and then we have some other individuals and groups who support the cause of accessibility, but as a discipline we still see it as an exception, an add-on, or a problem to solve. In this book, the authors employ OWI Principle 1 to endorse and explore a more wide-ranging and complex understanding of inclusion, access, and accessibility that aims to change the status quo for students and teachers with disabilities, linguistic diversity, and place-boundedness in our writing programs, particularly in our online instruction, which always has been sold as a panacea for these groups.

Access is about being inclusive at all levels of the educational pyramid, and although providing access is not necessarily cost-effective, the onus is on higher educational institutions to serve out their missions of helping their entire student bodies to learn and their faculty to teach. This effort and its costs should be seen as an investment—and an ethical and moral imperative—not as a burden. A spirit of generosity goes a long way.

OWI PRINCIPLE 2

The second OWI principle is the first of five principles outlined regarding pedagogical practices. It addresses the primacy of writing instruction over technology.

> OWI Principle 2: An online writing course should focus on writing and not on technology orientation or teaching students how to use learning and other technologies.

RATIONALE FOR OWI PRINCIPLE 2

Unlike a digital rhetoric course an OWC is not considered to be a place for stretching technological skills as much as for becoming stronger writers in various selected genres. To this end, it is important to recall the access and inclusivity issues found in OWI Principle 1. Students should use the provided technology to support their writing and not the other way around. It must be clear that OWI teachers and students alike do not need to be technology experts, computer programmers, or Web designers to accomplish the instructional purposes of an OWC.

DISCUSSION

The CCCC OWI Committee acknowledges that, as with OWI Principle 1, OWI Principle 2 has controversial implications (see Chapter 14, for example). Scholarship in computers and writing (e.g., Journet, Ball, & Trauman, 2012; Prior et al., 2007; Selber, 2004; Selfe, 2009, 1999) frame the writing done with digital technologies as rhetorical acts; the CCCC OWI Committee endorses this framing. However, the responses from the CCCC OWI Committee research revealed that there is both an absence of experts in digital writing at many institutions and of administrators and instructors familiar with this scholarship (CCCC OWI Committee, 2011d, 2012a, & 2012b). Moreover, administrators and instructors at some of these institutions support efficient, correction-based writing instruction and see the digital technology merely as a tool for achieving these ends. These issues must be considered in light of the fact that many OWI instructors are underprepared instructors and under-supported contingent faculty (see Chapter 7), who are much more versed in writing instruction than they are in teaching with technology or theorizing the technology's role in their own teaching. While these conditions do not comply with the ideals of writing studies' scholarship, they are the reality at many institutions, and *A Position Statement of Principles and Example Effective Practices for OWI* (CCCC OWI Committee, 2013) has been articulated in its current form to acknowledge the contemporary realities while pushing institutions *toward* the ideal practices.

Unquestionably, contemporary students live in a digital age where the world seems to shrink with the speed of connectivity and constant communication. College graduates should leave their education with a broad understanding of various technologies, their functional effects, and rhetorical implications, as well as with experience in using technologies in settings that may assist them in workplace and home environments (Selber, 2004). However, such goals are not the *primary* function of OWCs and of most writing-intensive disciplinary courses.

This statement might seem to be obvious, but teachers and other stakeholders shared with the CCCC OWI Committee their concerns about their perceived need to constantly learn newer and different technologies and software in order to keep up with student uses of those technologies outside the classroom. We realized that the pull of increasingly new technologies could create the impression that newer is better or that what students use in their daily lives must be used in their educational lives. Certainly, cogent arguments have been made for that kind of thinking (Alexander, 2006; Jukes, McCain & Crockett, 2010; Selfe & Hawisher, 2007; Small & Vorgon, 2008).

Nonetheless, a *writing* course should be primarily about *writing*—whether that writing is an alphabetic essay or a multimodal composition. When essay writing instruction is supported through technology, then only the selected technology is necessary for the course and students need to become functionally and rhetorically literate in it alone. When the writing instruction teaches a multimodal composition, again only the selected technology is necessary for the course and students need to become functionally and rhetorically literate in it alone. Practically speaking, if they are to use particular word processing software, students might be required to learn certain features of that software such as setting margins, using spell checkers, creating automatic tables of contents, and the like. In some classes, instructors may introduce students to different types of writing technologies (e.g., blogs, Wikis, slideware, and audiocasting) and give them the opportunity and choice—keeping issues of access in mind—to fulfill the assignment using the most appropriate writing technology for its purpose. But even in these cases, the assignment should focus on writing—composing, if you will—and not on *proficiency with the technology*. In the LMS, students might be required to learn how and where to post completed essays; how to reach their instructors privately or publicly; how to meet peer groups, if used, and so on.

Furthermore, teachers and students should not *need* to be particularly technologically astute to interact through the selected technologies for an OWC. For example, teachers should be trained and enabled to use the institution's LMS to build out the writing course components, but they should not need to learn how to create a separate Web page to teach the writing course.[5] Despite the deficiencies of any one LMS (and every LMS has them, albeit some worse than others), teachers should be enabled to use it and only it for fulfilling their course outcomes and optimal pedagogical strategies. Similarly, students may be asked to use a Wiki in the LMS if that is a component of the writing course, but they should not have to learn how to design and create unique Wiki pages. The focus should be on the writing in the Wiki and not the HyperText Markup Language (HTML) or even "what you see is what you get" (WYSIWYG) construction of it unless the instructor or writing program can pedagogically justify learning these type of skills in light of the rhetorical focus of the writing course (e.g., technical writing course, FYW for engineers and computer science majors).

Interestingly, two members of the CCCC OWI Committee Expert/Stakeholder Panel clarified this idea for the CCCC OWI Committee when they recommended the opposite approach—going outside the LMS for additional technology that would (1) connect students to the "real" world and (2) vary the technologies to keep student interest levels high. While these goals are laudable, their focus on the technology over the writing itself seem more likely to risk the necessary emphasis on student writing rather than to enhance it. Especially when keeping inclusivity and accessibility in mind, the writing needs to drive the technology choices and not the other way around (Hewett, 2013).

In this way, the CCCC OWI Committee believed that OWI Principle 2 also addressed inclusion and access. Institutions typically provide an LMS of some sort that the institutional information technology (IT) department ideally will have chosen for a high degree of access. In a leveling of the playing field, all online writing students—and many onsite students—will need to navigate that LMS in some way; it is part of their common educational experience determined by institutional choice. Students with particular disabilities, such as sight or sound, should be enabled to use that LMS as part of the institution's responsibility to meet the ADA's legal requirements. However, when outside game, role play, or social networking software is added to the writing course, the playing field no longer is level. Even when access to these technologies is free of financial cost, there may be high costs in terms of students' time and efforts. Downloading software for entertainment is different from being required to do so for educational purposes. Writing instruction easily can become lost— for uncounted precious hours—to the potential confusions surrounding using such outside software in educational settings. If an instructor or WPA is going to adopt any of these programs—which we do not recommend—the resulting writing course should be taught by someone who can effectively and efficiently teach the software to potential new users of all learning styles and abilities in that course. More importantly, such instructors need to be able to pedagogically theorize and explain why these students would benefit from this pedagogical approach to writing and how to induce required learning outcomes for student writers using the respective technology. Courses that employ these programs should never be taught by casual users or instructors who merely know how to functionally use the program without being taught why they are using it and how to effectively use it to teach writing.

To these ends, the CCCC OWI Committee believes that technologies outside the LMS should be reserved for courses that specialize in them—such as digital writing or technology-focused, multimodal courses—and should not be required of teachers or students of such primary OWI courses as FYW, advanced composition, or writing-intensive disciplinary courses. Even then, we believe that inclusion and access should drive the technological choices. To be sure, this issue is complex, as Chapter 14 aptly discusses. There is a fine line to be walked when a course addresses the highly metacognitive issues involved in composing with technology. When students are asked to rhetorically assess the technologies with which they are asked to write and to deliver their compositions—both alphabetic and image-based texts—they also may need to learn and use different technologies. In such cases, the CCCC OWI Committee recommends thoughtful, balanced application of both OWI Principles 1 and 2 when developing the course and selecting digital technologies.

OWI PRINCIPLE 3

The CCCC OWI Committee's research suggested that traditional writing instruction requires some changes of habits, thought, and even of theory to accommodate an online environment.

> OWI Principle 3: Appropriate composition teaching/learning strategies should be developed for the unique features of the online instructional environment.

RATIONALE FOR OWI PRINCIPLE 3

Some changes in traditional composition pedagogy are necessary for teaching writing in the OWI setting, an environment that is by nature text-centric and reading-heavy and that requires intensive written communication. Educators who develop and teach OWCs should use pedagogical theories and strategies that account for the distinctive nature and opportunities provided by the online setting. New pedagogies should be explored and implemented to leverage the inherent benefits of the electronic environment in relation to composition instruction (e.g., discussion boards and blogs that allow students to exchange thoughtful claims and support in writing or private messaging that allows students to communicate with one's teacher through writing).

OWI-specific pedagogies can address the diverse learning needs of students, who can benefit from the different ways writing can be taught online. Such approaches foster a culture of learning and knowledge creation—rooted in the multimodal online environment—that opens up new opportunities for student thought and expression and prepares students for the 21st-century skills and modalities that will help them thrive as citizens and workers.

DISCUSSION

As its first emergent theme in the Executive Summary of *The State of the Art of OWI* (CCCC OWI Committee, 2011c), the CCCC OWI Committee found, "Teachers and administrators, to include those in writing centers, typically are simply migrating traditional face-to-face writing pedagogies to the online setting—both fully online and hybrid. Theory and practice specific to OWI has yet to be fully developed and engaged in postsecondary online settings across the United States" (CCCC OWI Committee, 2011c, p. 7). In later research with the CCCC OWI Committee Expert/Stakeholder Panel, panelists told us about such instructional strategies for OWI that included building clear online communication expectations, scaffolding assignments in specific ways, and providing repetition and redundancy of information. What neither the survey respondents nor the panelists addressed in any depth were theoretical explanations and unique strategies that consider OWI's particular characteristics. We believe that reality stems from rather sparse OWI theory-making.

Some migration of contemporary theories and practices from onsite to online settings is necessary and appropriate as the discussion in OWI Principle 4 below should make clear. Writing instruction maintains certain goals in both settings. Good composition instruction is necessary for OWI, and the online setting is not alien to education. Indeed, one might consider OWI Principle 3 to be the yin to the yang of OWI Principle 4 in that most OWCs reflect traditional onsite writing pedagogy, but the medium in which instruction is set also changes the approach to writing instruction. More importantly, because the medium also may affect both student writing and student learning about writing, it makes sense to search for new composing theories for a digital instructional environment.

In previous publications, I have called for theories of OWI, stating that there is something different about OWI from onsite writing instruction that incorporates yet goes beyond the technology (Hewett, 2001, 2004-2005, 2006, 2010, 2013, 2015a, 2015b; Hewett & Ehmann, 2004). This request for theorizing OWI is not so much about providing new teaching strategies; strategizing is a natural part of educational expertise where we would link our pedagogies to available technologies that enable the instruction (Warnock, 2009, p. xiv). Instead, it is about providing fundamental explanations for the unique qualities and challenges of OWI, which then will lead naturally to new strategies. Two theories for OWI have emerged in my own research: (1) a need for semantic integrity[6] in the teacher's writing to the student (Hewett, 2010, 2015b) and (2) the complex needs for different of literacy strategies for students and teachers in text-rich settings (Hewett, 2015a).

In this light, research (see Chapter 17) helps educators to articulate what happens in the OWI setting. Theorizing helps to synthesize and explain what happens and it grounds appropriate instructional strategies as well as helps educators to discern the relative benefits of existing strategies that can be adapted to OWI settings. Current research offers tiny pieces of a much larger puzzle. Although general online instructional theory, which is relatively robust, can help, it is important to learn more about OWI specifically. The fact that writing is both the subject under study and the textual venue for reading about and learning to write makes OWI significantly challenging. Questions that OWI theory should address include:

- If in any way at all, how does affect change among students and teachers when moving from onsite to online settings and the concomitant loss of real-time, non-mediated body/face/voice?
- If such change exists, how does it influence writing growth, development, and improvement if in any way at all?
- Given the media of text, audio, and audio/video, what are the effects of such mediation on writing instruction and learning if in any way at all?
- If in any way at all, how does the loss of body/face/voice affect:
  - Student cognition of what is being taught about writing?
  - Student reading of related fiction or nonfiction for the course, of instructional content, of response to writing, or of interpersonal communications?
  - Student writing interests, practice, growth, or maturity?
- How does the loss of body/face/voice affect teachers' instructional methods regarding writing about writing if in any way at all?
- How does the loss of body/face/voice affect instructional response to student writing whether the response is text-based or audio/video enhanced if in any way at all?
- How, if in any way at all, does the loss of body/face/voice affect the interactions between teachers and students with different learning styles, disabilities, multilingual histories, or challenged socioeconomic backgrounds?

Such theorizing would help OWI educators to move beyond old perceptions that online instruction is naturally inferior to onsite instruction, which can open the field to a better understanding of how people learn to read and write in a digital age and in technologically enhanced settings. This movement is crucial because hundreds of thousands of students are learning to write using digital technologies and in OWI settings, and educators can benefit them more with composition theories that match currently used modalities and media. Such theorizing would help to address the loss of body/face/voice connection in most OWI settings and explain the relative benefits of different ways to communicate online. Finally, it would help to address whether and how the heavily text-centric nature of both asynchronous and synchronous OWI affects learning and requires different or stronger reading skills, leading to practical ways of understanding student reading and writing challenges in contemporary digitally enhanced settings.

OWI PRINCIPLE 4

Through our research, the CCCC OWI Committee realized that many of the contemporary theories, pedagogies, and strategies of onsite composition courses apply to OWI, which is reflected in OWI Principle 4.

> **OWI Principle 4: Appropriate onsite composition theories, pedagogies, and strategies should be migrated and adapted to the online instructional environment.**

RATIONALE FOR OWI PRINCIPLE 4

OWI Principle 3 explains that those teaching OWCs should think of ways to maximize the distinct opportunities of the electronic environment. However, one impediment to those moving their instruction online is the unfounded belief that *everything* about their teaching will have to change.

Composition studies has a rich research and teaching history, and the CCCC OWI Committee recognizes that many core pedagogies of onsite writing instruction can and should remain in OWI. Many pedagogical theories and strategies that have not been designed with OWI in mind can be adapted to the online setting. Indeed, various foundational rhetorical and writing theories and their connected onsite pedagogies and strategies can be migrated online successfully. Teachers should seek opportunities to use their established practices when moving online while seeking alternative ways of offering those practices within digital spaces and using electronic tools.

DISCUSSION

OWI Principle 4 presents the yang to OWI Principle 3's yin. Both the Fully Online and Hybrid OWI surveys (CCCC OWI Committee, 2011a & 2011b) strongly supported the belief that OWI is an extension venue for contemporary writing instruction. Although to differing degrees and with different emphases, both surveys indicated participant beliefs that writing is a process; writing should attend to audience, purpose, and occasion; writing is a social process; and/or writing and revising are generative and recursive acts (CCCC OWI Committee, 2011c, pp. 21-24, 48-52). Participants also included common instructional philosophies such as the necessity of peer feedback for writing improvement and that face-to-face interaction is important even in OWI, a belief expressed heavily in the hybrid participant group.

Our research taught the CCCC OWI Committee that such common composition theories as social construction, writing process, Aristotelian rhetoric, and expressivism all continue to fit the beliefs that OWI teachers have about writing instruction in the online environment. The only contemporary belief that participants almost universally indicated would contraindicate OWI is that writing is not teachable and it can only receive reader response; only 7 of 297 total respondents indicated agreement with that statement. One survey respondent stated:

> I do not agree entirely with the first clause; however, my experience has been that student needs vary to such a great extent that most writing instruction needs to be greatly individualized. I find the discussion forums allow students to work with other students' texts and to develop a sense of what their writing practices are and how their practices affect the response to and perceived quality of their work. (p. 52)

Scott Warnock (2009) also presented a strong case for migrating strategies stemming from contemporary composition theory into the online setting (pp. xiii-xv). Among those familiar strategies are transferring peer and teacher discussions online using asynchronous text-based conversation forums, assigning small peer groups in a similar forum for peer review of drafts and other tasks, requiring multiple drafts of essays, asking students to read books and modules about writing, assessing portfolios, and using teacher response—both text-based and audio-based—as part of the learning experience. Such strategies work in OWI because they speak to core composing theories that have proven value for writing instruction overall.

The key to migrating theory and strategies that originated in onsite composition instruction to OWI seems to be a willingness to adapt and to be creative. Adaptation requires that one consider the nature of an asynchronous discussion, for example, to be as legitimate a way to talk as in-class, face-to-face, oral talk. Creativity engages this modality as an educational bonus because it offers students additional opportunities to write for real audiences and to practice critical reading (often of imperfect text) for thinking and response purposes (Palmquist, 1993).

Inclusivity and access can be addressed in this migration of theories and strategies in highly practical ways. With text-based discussion, for example, the LMS should have been selected such that screen readers can read the discussion, enabling the sight impaired to respond. The asynchronous setting means that students with such challenges as writing disabilities, dyslexia, and physical differences can take more time to keyboard their responses. Students who cannot use the keyboard for whatever set of reasons or who need to take a break from physically writing can use speech-recognition software and still complete the assignment. Students with varied learning styles, skill levels, and personality types (e.g., slow readers, poor typists, and shyer students) all can participate.

In terms of presenting instructional modules or texts for students to read, as would be done through textbooks and handouts in most onsite writing courses, the online setting invites the visual additions of photographs, drawings, charts, tables, brainstorming diagrams, and such audio/video media as YouTube movies. Such variety again can appeal to a wide variety of student learning styles. Access, however, should be addressed further by providing captions to images and transcripts of audio/video pieces.

OWI PRINCIPLE 5

Teacher satisfaction is important as described in OWI Principle 12, but so is student progress. This OWI principle speaks to conditions for instruction that should promote both goals.

> **OWI Principle 5: Online writing teachers should retain reasonable control over their own content and/or techniques for conveying, teaching, and assessing their students' writing in their OWCs.**

RATIONALE FOR OWI PRINCIPLE 5

Particularly in FYW courses, a tension can exist between institutional/programmatic instructional requirements and outcomes and the flexibility that experienced educators need to teach effectively. Within the context of institutional/programmatic outcomes, online writing teachers should have the freedom to develop their OWCs with content, methods, and technologies that best suit their purposes, expertise, and teaching style. Because achieving advanced levels of fluency in writing requires the complex integration of different kinds of skills and knowledge (e.g., rhetorical awareness, linguistic competency, and genre literacy), highly qualified writing teachers not only are "content experts" in rhetorical, linguistic, and genre literacy but also are knowledgeable about composing and assessing learning situations in response to their specific students.

This principle speaks to the larger issue that faces many institutions with vast numbers of OWC writing sections. The pressures of these large programs lead to unified (and often restrictive) course templates and core syllabi and sometimes even more restrictive course shells. These features often are the result of programs that rely heavily on contingent faculty; it is well known that institutions turn to uniformity of method and materials in lieu of hiring, training, and retaining expert, full-time writing teachers.

Online writing teachers do their best work when they retain some control over their courses, and OWI effective practices should be accounted for in helping to balance necessary institutional pedagogical goals with teacher flexibility. This recommendation (and every listed effective practice for this principle) strongly relies on teachers having received the training, professional development, and assessment described in OWI Principle 7.

DISCUSSION

One of the quality pillars in online learning is faculty satisfaction as indicated by a sense of being appreciated and of professional happiness (Sloan Consortium, 2005). When we asked field interviewees, CCCC panel audiences, SIG participants, survey participants, and the CCCC OWI Committee Expert/ Stakeholder Panelists about this issue, one concern emerged repeatedly: Teachers wanted the autonomy to develop their courses per their expertise and personal preferences. People expressed that they did not like being made to use predesigned or shell-based courses, yet they also expressed worries about the amount of work that free-form course development requires in online settings.

For example, in the CCCC OWI Committee (2011a & 2011b) surveys, in response to open-ended questions, teachers claimed they had wanted "teacher autonomy"; the CCCC OWI Committee found it interesting that "those who tended to see their teaching as isolated (negative) also tended to see their academic freedom as more limited" (CCCC OWI Committee, 2011c, pp. 36, 66). There seemed to be a correspondence between having little sense of an association with other OWI teachers and a sense of being able to develop their courses as they saw fit. Furthermore, the survey respondents saw "consistency/ inconsistency among sections (this concern seems to contradict concerns about academic freedom, which tended to suggest a common syllabus and rigid course structure)" as a major issue (CCCC OWI Committee, 2011c, pp. 37, 67). In this case, the CCCC OWI Committee sensed that both WPAs and teachers were expressing that courses were not necessarily consistently robust or rigorous for students when they were not predesigned. Indeed, Andrew Cavenaugh, Director of Writing at UMUC, confirmed that concern from a WPA's perspective (personal communication, July 17, 2012).

In a survey-based open-ended statement, one professor working in a five-week FYW format stated, "I think student learning is very much affected by the compressed format coupled with online. Changing the course to incorporate new technology and pedagogical ideas is attractive and responsible but seriously daunting. And I'd have to undertake it pretty much alone" (CCCC OWI Committee, 2011c, p. 38). This statement seemed to suggest that having independence to redevelop portions of a writing course is desirable but challenging in potentially energy-sapping ways. In the second online meeting with the CCCC

OWI Committee Expert/Stakeholder Panel, one professor raised the issue of using predesigned course shells several times: "Adjunct or not, I prefer a choice and opportunity for academic freedom, but the first time I've taught for any institution, I've preferred having a predesigned course, just to start" (CCCC OWI Committee, 2013a, p. 42).

The CCCC OWI Committee understood the feedback we were receiving to represent a mixed concern of (1) desiring to be an autonomous teacher of writing, (2) understanding the occasional need for predesigned course formats, and (3) needing to balance the two to achieve a reasonable potential for positive student outcomes and professional satisfaction. To this end, OWI Principle 5 strives to recognize that experienced *and appropriately trained* teachers of OWI should have as much control as possible over their course content, instructional techniques, and assessment methods. This need for training, addressed in OWI Principle 7, takes into account the tension between consistency of courses and the autonomy to make one's own professional choices.

However, OWI Principle 5 also recognizes that institutions have the responsibility of ensuring equally robust OWI courses regardless of the individual teachers' pedagogical preferences. Sometimes course shells are necessary to develop that baseline equality for which the institution and/or writing program is responsible. To that end, we think that the first time newly trained OWI teachers instruct an OWI course or the first time experienced OWI teachers instruct for the institution, they should be provided a predesigned course; such a course enables them to both gain and demonstrate expertise and may provide needed breathing space to settle into the OWI and institutional environment. We recognize the complexity of seeing OWI Principle 5 as a guideline and not a rule, however; WPAs might adapt this recommendation wholesale or to individual teachers based on their unique backgrounds and strengths.

This issue concerns inclusion and accessibility, of course. Students (and their teachers) have a right to expect that their courses will fairly represent the outcomes dictated by the writing program. Yet, students also have a right to have their needs addressed individually so that they can learn writing using their strengths; such an inclusive attitude requires that teachers be free to bend elements of a predesigned course as they perceive necessary to meet all student needs and to support student learning optimally. At the same time, as we advocate for more agency for instructors, we also should acknowledge that these pre-designed shells offer an opportunity to OWI programs to develop accessible courses from bottom up without duplicating effort and with minimal investment in instructional design and curricular personnel.

This OWI principle, like most of them, reflects the recognition that there always is a balancing act among institutional, writing program, individual teacher, and student needs. To the greatest degree possible, we believe that experienced and trained teachers do their best work when given appropriate amounts of autonomy within the strictures of a developed and functional OWI program.

OWI PRINCIPLE 6

This OWI principle shows the CCCC OWI Committee's recognition that OWI takes more than the form of a writing course that has moved into online settings; indeed, it is an organic base for transitional and newly developing educational products and processes.

> OWI Principle 6: Alternative, self-paced, or experimental OWI models should be subject to the same principles of pedagogical soundness, teacher/designer preparation, and oversight detailed in this document.

RATIONALE FOR OWI PRINCIPLE 6

As emergent forms of online teaching increasingly are offered by many colleges and universities, and as these fall outside traditional onsite education models, some credit-bearing, online-supported, composition entities will receive less professional oversight and may fail to offer students adequate preparation for later work. OWCs listed as "self-paced" or "independent learning" frequently have a fixed syllabus that students work through at their own pace, with varying amounts of oversight from an educator, depending on the institution and the individual teacher. These self-paced OWCs are a component of OWI in the sense that they use digital technology, occur in online settings, and typically are geographically distributed. Hence, they are subject to many of the strengths and limitations of online teaching generally; they should reflect the principled approaches of OWI as outlined in this document. Similarly, experimental models for OWI, such as Massive Open Online Courses (MOOCs), are emerging. These, too, should reflect the principled approaches of OWI as described in this document.

DISCUSSION

OWI Principle 6 speaks to the essence of who is responsible—and in what ways—for the online learning of writing students. Studying alternative, self-paced, and experimental models of OWI was not a part of our committee's charges or major research given the need to address common FYW, advanced levels and genres of writing, and other writing-intensive disciplinary courses.

Instead, our interest in alternative, self-paced, and experimental OWI models emerged primarily from a "what about" series of questions regarding self-paced, credit-bearing writing courses that once were conducted through mail, then cassette tapes, then television, then email, and now the Internet. Who creates such courses? Who oversees their quality? Who are the teachers, and who prepares the teachers? How well do such courses prepare student writers? Any answers to our questions most likely vary by individual settings and participants. Sometimes the courses are certified by an academic institution and promoted by a corporate entity; other times, they are strictly in-house in the academic institution; and still other times, they are developed by a corporate entity and promoted as equal to that provided by a more traditional academic institution. Students may succeed, as they always seem to do, on a uniquely individual basis. Yet, such courses need a series of guiding principles, and the CCCC OWI Committee believes that *A Position Statement of Principles and Example Effective Practices for OWI* (CCCC OWI Committee, 2013) provides them.

Recently, in fact very close to the time for publishing *A Position Statement of Principles and Example Effective Practices for OWI*, an increasingly deliberated experimental form of online learning—the MOOC—gained headline reportage in a variety of daily educational publications such as *The Chronicle of Higher Education* and *Inside Higher Ed*, as well as scholarly journals (*College Composition and Communication,* 2013, pp. 688-703) and edited collection (Krause & Lowe, 2014). Most often, the deliberation about MOOCs involved a few humanities and science, technology, engineering, and mathematics (STEM) courses, but not OWI courses. For example, the three MOOC-participating scholars writing for *College Composition and Communication's* (2013) "Symposium on Massive Open Online Courses" were not taking writing classes *per se* although their music appreciation MOOC did include writing assignments to be commented upon and scored by peers. Some composition MOOCs were piloted and analyzed for potential benefits to student writers as of summer 2013 (i.e., Duke University, Georgia Tech University, Ohio State University, and Mt. San Jacinto College—all funded partially by The Bill & Melinda Gates Foundation[7]). Typically, however, the massive nature of a MOOC precludes teacher response to writing and, instead, promotes peer response as the primary feedback method both for content and writing process.

Of interest to the CCCC OWI Committee is a commitment to quality OWI and fairness to all stakeholders. While MOOCs are being touted theoretically for their ability to educate a great number of people, practically speaking they do not allow for individualized teacher instruction through response to writing (as opposed to individual peer response that is neither required nor moderated), which is a primary way of teaching writing online, as our research confirmed

(Head, 2013). In particular, CCCC OWI Committee Expert/Stakeholder Panelists indicated that written response to writing was a necessary and important part of their OWI work: "Yes ... part of it [amount of time spent in OWI] has to do with the amount of feedback we give students versus what we would give on physical assignments ... also, there is much discussion, versus nearly none in a face-2-face class" and "more attention to individual students with text feedback, etc. because one can't do that with nods and eye-contact, etc." (CCCC OWI Committee, 2012b, p. 49; also see Hewett, 2010 & 2015b). For the purposes of the CCCC OWI Committee's work, OWI primarily has been defined regarding credit-bearing writing courses of all levels and writing-intensive disciplinary courses. Therefore, we have been skeptical of how a MOOC can provide an adequate framework for OWI particularly given the inability of a teacher to connect with students individually. Much research needs to be done to determine whether peer response in the MOOC setting is sufficient to bring about writing development (Halasek et al., 2014). Chapter 17 offers key research questions about MOOCs to that end.

Just as important, the OWI principles were developed with inclusivity and accessibility as the overarching guiding theme. Alternative, self-paced, and experimental models may prove to be excellent ways to address the needs of particular students. For example, a student who cannot function intellectually or socially within the typical multi-student onsite or online course setting that requires collaborative work or discussions may excel in a self-paced OWI setting. Students who do not have the money to pay for the typical three-credit OWI refresher or developmental course may benefit from practicing rusty writing skills in a MOOC or an individualized course first. Nonetheless, we believe that even an experimental OWI model should be guided by a strong foundation in writing studies, specialized training in OWI (see OWI Principle 7), fair and equitable compensation for teacher's work (see OWI Principle 8), a reasonable course load for instructors that enables instruction by essay response (see OWI Principle 9), and so on.

OWI PRINCIPLE 7

OWI Principle 7 is the first of three principles regarding teacher's concerns. It encompasses a wide variety of professional needs that should help to develop strong, confident, and satisfied OWI faculty.

OWI Principle 7: Writing Program Administrators (WPAs) for OWI programs and their online writing teachers should receive appropriate OWI-focused training, professional development, and assessment for evaluation and promotion purposes.

RATIONALE FOR OWI PRINCIPLE 7

This principle establishes an environment in which WPAs and their on-line writing teachers can develop, thrive, and meet OWI students' needs. Prior to supervising OWI teachers, WPAs need to have training and experience in OWI. Regarding faculty, OWI-teacher candidates should be selected first from a pool of experienced and proven writing teachers. Teachers—especially novice teachers (e.g., graduate student teachers) and contingent faculty—should not be placed into OWCs until they have received appropriate training by their WPAs and institution. Although such a requirement places restrictions on the teaching pool, institutions should establish some way of training teachers and having them demonstrate their ability to teach writing online before they do so with an OWC.

WPAs and OWI teachers need proficiency in three specific areas. (1) They must be able to teach writing. (2) They must be able to teach writing specifically in a digital environment. (3) They must be able to teach writing in a course in which text is the primary communicative mode. Similarly, WPAs and OWI teachers need support through regular professional development opportunities and mentoring. As professional knowledge and theories change regarding OWI, active OWI teachers and WPAs who supervise them need to be educated and given opportunities to enact new ideas in their teaching and programs. Additionally, OWI programs and teaching should be assessed regularly and appropriately for the environment and in a manner comparable to traditional courses/writing program in the institution or unit.

DISCUSSION

The first requisite of this OWI principle is that teachers need training in OWI, not just in online technology or settings. To make such professional development fully useful, however, teachers first need WPAs who also have had adequate training and course experience in OWI. When teaching writing online is just an adjunct to a broader writing program and the WPA has little-to-no personal knowledge of it, then OWI teachers enter a situation where their work is not understood completely and may be underappreciated or—worse—not understood for its high-level skill requirements. Furthermore, WPAs with OWI training and experience more likely will understand the need for ongoing professional development opportunities for their OWI teachers. Perhaps most important, only WPAs with OWI training and experience are qualified to evaluate OWI teachers because the technology changes the pedagogy, as OWI Principles 3 and 4 point out; certainly, appropriate assessment is a cornerstone of a strong OWI program. Without training and course experience, WPA evaluators cannot understand how best to judge such factors of OWI course teaching and management as discussion facilitation and writing response; indeed, they do not know how best to help the teachers develop more effective skills. Hence, training WPAs first and then preparing their teachers for OWI is crucial.

In the CCCC OWI Committee's national surveys, respondents indicated that while training relative to the LMS was mandatory and other training included peer mentoring and instructional design as part of campus outreach and summer institutes, "training is inadequately developed at the level of online writing pedagogy and somewhat unevenly applied" (CCCC OWI Committee, 2011c, p. 34). Experts/stakeholders from the CCCC OWI Committee's panel, site visit interviewees, and survey respondents strongly agreed that not only should OWI teachers receive training relative to teaching writing online (as opposed to generic online instruction), but that they should be experienced teachers of writing from the outset. This concern stems from OWI teachers' almost universal need to understand student writing issues without body/face/voice connections. It means they should be able to read the writing, "listen" to students' written self-reflections, understand potential difficulties of an assignment, and decide how to help students using primarily written and asynchronous media. While some OWI courses are synchronous, anecdotal evidence suggests that many are fully online asynchronous courses. The ability to communicate *about writing using writing* is crucial (Hewett, 2010, 2015a, 2015b). This work cannot be done well by inexperienced writing teachers who do not have the fuller understanding of, or vocabulary for, describing writing. While it is not only fine but often incredibly helpful to pick up the telephone for a voice conversation or to use free audio/video software for connection, no teacher—regardless of experience—can manage the OWC load if every teaching interaction has to be accomplished as a scheduled voice conference. The CCCC OWI Committee offers this guidance with the full knowledge that following it may tie the hands of WPAs and graduate advisors seeking to flesh out their teaching pool or to educate their graduate students with OWI. However, a combination of experience with onsite writing teaching (environmentally familiar in some sense to all who have ever been in the onsite student seat) and training with mentoring or even co-teaching in hybrid and fully online settings is preferable to putting novice teachers in OWCs and expecting a strong outcome for the teachers or the students.

Professional development opportunities take time and energy, but OWI teachers have told the CCCC OWI Committee repeatedly that they crave them. In a written chat related to the second synchronous voice conference with experts/stakeholders, one respondent stated, "There is also an issue with the level of professional development with regard to elements of online instruction comes into play, too, right? [*sic*]" To this, another replied, "Institutions are all over the board in terms of training, support, development, mentoring" (CCCC OWI Committee, 2012b, p. 24). The "The State of the Art of OWI" (CCCC OWI Committee, 2011c) stated, "Instructors are dissatisfied with the levels of support they receive regarding technology, course caps, training, pay, and professional development/interactions relative to OWI in both the fully online and hybrid settings" (p. 7). The CCCC OWI Committee concluded, "Such dissatisfaction can lead to poor teaching, low expectations for students and for an online course, and insufficient retention of experienced instructors at a time when OWI continues to grow" (p. 7). Areas in which research revealed that professional development is needed include:

- Inclusion and accessibility, which means becoming educated about students with physical, learning, socioeconomic, and multilingual challenges in addition to being well-versed in writing studies (i.e., preparing the course, appropriate expectations for students with varying learning styles and needs, fair assessment and evaluation for OWI settings, communicating with students who have accessibility needs [including issues regarding those who have and have not self-disclosed such needs], ADA legal requirements, and educationally ethical requirements, among others.)
- Learning about and applying OWI theories and strategies that are unique to the digital environment.
- Migrating appropriate strategies from familiar onsite writing instructional settings to hybrid and fully online settings.
- Writing accessible and helpful essay response in time-saving ways.
- Communicating with students about writing in online settings.
- Encouraging critical reading of peer writing and discussions.
- Experiencing the OWI course from the student seat in order to learn the LMS, how long an assignment takes to complete, and the temptations of multitasking from the student view.

Professional development topics may be particular to an LMS or institutional setting, of course. For example, in an LMS that hosts what it calls a Wiki, OWI teachers benefit from technological familiarization with that Wiki feature from *both* the student *and* the instructor view; moreover, they benefit from training in how a Wiki may help (or hinder) certain types of writing development and how to match its benefits to their overall course goals. Undoubtedly, professional development is a key to strong OWI.

Finally, OWI teachers need fair and equitable assessment for evaluation and promotion purposes. Regular evaluation is crucial to an effective writing program in that it helps WPAs to match teachers to their courses and learn their program's strengths and weaknesses. Without adequate evaluation, it is difficult to guess at its success. Respondents at all levels shared with the CCCC OWI Committee a sense of feast or famine when it comes to OWI evaluation. Either they expressed a sense of being watched in a "big brotherly" fashion given the capability of a supervisor to log into their courses and read the interactions at any time or they received no feedback or formal evaluation—thereby receiving no help from a supervisor or mentor in improving their OWI teaching. To this end, the CCCC OWI Committee believes that assessment of OWI courses should occur at least as often as those for onsite teachers and no more often or rigorously. To view a teacher's OWC more often than onsite courses is akin to multiple evaluations. While ongoing views might help particular teachers to teach better or even reveal an exemplary teacher's strategies, it places onerous and unfair expectations on them versus their peers in onsite classrooms. However, if the WPA determines a need for more than one opportunity to review an OWI course *and* if an evaluative process is developed that is equitable with onsite writing courses and that keeps the OWI teacher informed, then different but equal evaluation may be effective. Furthermore, if OWI teachers are brought into their own assessment by, for example, allowing them to invite the evaluator to preview or review particular course components, the evaluative process may lose some of its high-stakes nature and engage a more collaborative spirit of cooperation and optimism for OWI improvement.

OWI PRINCIPLE 8

A second OWI faculty-level issue is the need for fair and equitable compensation.

> OWI Principle 8: Online writing teachers should receive fair and equitable compensation for their work.

RATIONALE FOR OWI PRINCIPLE 8

The work involved with OWI is new to some institutions and, as such, requires additional effort on the part of WPAs and faculty. At a minimum, the efforts involved in developing and teaching new OWCs should be presumed to represent intellectual and pedagogical labor equivalent to (and no less than) developing a new onsite writing course. Thus, also at a minimum, the compensation currently in place for teachers concerning the development of a new onsite course also should apply when asking teachers to develop an online course.

Other issues arise in terms of how much time and effort go into OWI-based teaching. For example, new research indicates that there is a quantifiably heavier reading load for teachers particularly in asynchronous settings, as well as a heavier reading and writing load for both teachers and students (Griffin & Minter, 2013). In the online writing setting, teachers need to build informational redundancy into a Web-based, LMS format. In other words, they often need to provide a syllabus in more than one form or in more than one online space. Assignments need to be written and distributed in more than one module or more than one format for ease of finding and retrieval. Furthermore, teachers need to provide content and instructional accessibility through redundant voice, visual, and text-based materials, in keeping with OWI Principle 1.

Altering course materials in these ways requires time and energy as well as thoughtful literacy approaches and knowledgeable language choices. Although some effective practice strategies can help to mitigate time load issues, they may add up for teachers. Therefore, the CCCC OWI Committee recommends additional compensation for first-time OWI teachers who are learning how to accommodate such necessary organizational and pedagogical strategies. Compensation in various forms (e.g., pay adjustments, course load modifications, and technology purchases) should be provided.

Discussion

Educators told the CCCC OWI Committee that fair and equitable compensation is important to their continuing interest in and development of OWI. In terms of importance of factors contributing to willingness to teach fully online courses, 62% of survey participants rated "time/money compensation for development of course" as "significant" or "very significant." Fifty-five percent similarly rated "time/money compensation for learning a sophisticated set of skills, theories, and technologies." In contrast, "Flexibility in teaching schedule," which some people consider to be a benefit of OWI, was rated highest in significance at 95% (CCCC OWI Committee, 2011c, pp. 37-38). For the same survey questions about hybrid courses, 57% of respondents rated "time/money compensation for development of course" as "significant" or "very significant" and 48% rated "time/money compensation for learning a sophisticated set of skills, theories, and technologies" similarly. (Presumably the difference is indicative of the hybrid course's often tricky similarity to traditional onsite courses; see Chapter 2 for a detailed discussion.) In response to open-ended questions, respondents also said:

- "Having time and/or compensation for course development would be another great plus, because it is very time consuming to develop an online or blended course, especially one that is as rigorous and pedagogically sound as a face-to-face course, and we don't have that, and, to be honest, I don't think our online courses are, in general, nearly as high of quality as our face-to-face courses." (CCCC OWI Committee, 2011c, p. 64)

- "Alert administrations to the need of adequate workload compensation for the difficulty of digitizing a course and a curriculum." (p. 70).

As stated in OWI Principle 8's rationale, equitable compensation for developing OWI courses and for new OWI teachers is important for a variety of reasons. Anecdotally, educators have shared how much time and energy they put into developing an OWC and how challenging it can be to teach OWI for the first time. For contingent faculty, as Chapter 7 discusses, compensation regarding time and money are incredibly important factors to achieving excellence in OWI courses.

While the CCCC OWI Committee takes the position that OWI is different from onsite composition instruction but not alien to it, OWI in a disciplinary sense is only about 30 years old, and relatively few teachers have had adequate training that would help them to develop sound new strategies and to migrate their most useful onsite strategies. The most experienced teachers have won their skills through trial and error. As newer writing teachers with different levels of involvement with digital tools engage students, they also will need to find the most effective ways to teach online despite their frequent uses of online media for social and even business settings (Hewett, 2015a). Educational uses of digital media in writing instruction are still relatively new and require much study (see Chapter 15). In addition to pay adjustments for newly developed courses, course load modifications, and technology purchases, other types of compensation may include stipends for training and professional development, financial assistance or grants for conferences, permission to work from home or alternative sites, official recognition of effort, and teaching assistants or co-teaching assignments to share the higher literacy load (Griffin & Minter, 2013; see also Chapters 11 & 12). Additionally, because not all teachers have the economic means to be technologically mobile in the anytime/anywhere nature of online instruction, they may be denied access to desired OWI courses. Finding creative ways to include such teachers can meet the needs of both OWI Principles 1 and 8. Finally, consideration of course "ownership," an issue bigger than this chapter's scope, also may lead to appropriate compensation venues.

OWI PRINCIPLE 9

This OWI principle considers how many students should be enrolled in an OWI course.

OWI Principle 9: OWCs should be capped responsibly at 20 students per course with 15 being a preferable number.

RATIONALE FOR OWI PRINCIPLE 9

The CCCC's Statement of Principles and Standards for the Postsecondary Teaching of Writing (1989), regarding the teaching conditions necessary for a quality education, stated that no more than 20 students (and preferably 15) should be in a college-level writing course. Further, it indicated that teachers should have no more than 60 students of writing in any one term. These guidelines were written in 1989 before the major onset of OWCs that continue to increase in number. Teaching writing through digital media is a text-intensive enterprise, even when voice and video are used. Text-heavy writing instruction leads to a high literacy load in terms of reading and writing for teachers and students, as noted in the rationale for OWI Principle 8. Because contemporary writing pedagogy encourages high-quality, individualized teacher-to-student interactions as well as peer reading and written discussion opportunities, the literacy load must be made manageable. Given these realities and the necessity to provide a robustly accessible teaching and learning environment (see OWI Principle 1) the maximum number of students in an OWC should adhere to these teaching conditions.

Coordinating the statement cited above with the principles of the *CCCC Statement on Second Language Writing and Writers* (2009) and with OWI Principle 1 of this document, any OWC solely comprised of physically-, learning-, linguistically-, or socioeconomically-challenged writing students (i.e., sometimes called "developmental" or "basic" writers) should have no more than 15 students. In such cases, teachers should be assigned a maximum of 45 such writing students per term. The added concerns of assisting students with basic reading and writing skills in a text-intensive online setting requires additional time and especially thoughtful writing on teachers' parts, as well as possible offline phone or in-person interventions. Fifteen students remains a reasonable number in these conditions.

DISCUSSION

A colleague recently described composition teaching in this way: teaching one course of 20 students is like teaching 20 courses of one student each. The simile describes the discipline's collective efforts to individualize writing instruction through conferences and written response to papers as well as personalized answers to students' individual questions. Personalization is an important skill when working with student writers, and it becomes still more important in hybrid and fully online courses where digital tools mediate the interactions. Loss of personalization can lead both to affect-based attrition (e.g., such as my young relative at the beginning of this chapter) and to cognitive reading and writing difficulties, as I theorize (Hewett, 2015a). Many teachers have multiple OWI courses of 20 or more students in each. When too many students are in any of those courses, teachers burn out, courses are depersonalized, and students fail to persist.

*A Position Statement of Principles and Example Effective Practices for OWI*s (CCCC OWI Committee, 2013) principle of capping OWI courses at 20 students with 15 as the optimal number might be considered by some to be a fantasy. Indeed, although the *CCCC Statement on Second Language Writing and Writers* (2009) has remained steady, the *CCCC's Statement of Principles and Standards for the Postsecondary Teaching of Writing* was updated after the publication of the OWI Principles to read simply "reasonable class sizes" (2013). The specific numbers have meaning to WPAs and teachers in writing studies, however, and the CCCC OWI Committee indicated as much in its November 2014 report to the CCCC EC. In December 2014, Howard Tinberg, then CCCC EC Chair indicated in an email to CCCC OWI Committee co-chairs that specific numbers likely would be reinstated in the near future through the CCCC position statement review process in response to requests by many CCCC members. Writing class size is a highly debated issue in the field because it is so critical; the realities of institutional contexts regarding financial decisions have to be weighed against varying factors, only some of which are whether teachers are fully prepared by their institutions to work with writers of varying skills—such as multilingual writers—and writers in online contexts. Anecdotal evidence suggests that many OWI courses are capped by their institutions in the low to high-twenties, yet some teachers of multiple courses describe as many as 100 OWI students in a semester. When asked about their institutions, CCCC OWI Committee Expert/ Stakeholder Panelists cited numbers that were:

- low (e.g., "Developmental: 10-15. First year: 15-18. Upper class: no more than 15"; "My tech comm UD class is capped at 15"; and "At my community college, it is 15 students for online or on ground"),
- high (e.g., "online writing classes have the same cap as our f2f classes: 24"; "26 students for composition"; and "it is 28 in the classroom, but it isn't unusual for half the class to drop"), and
- ideal (e.g., "15 to 20" and "Comp ideal 15-18") (CCCC OWI Committee, 2013a, pp. 5-6).

Text-rich courses require text-heavy work. Although more research should be conducted regarding retention in OWI, survey participants anecdotally reported that given the "same grading and feedback demands" in OWI as in onsite classes, "increases in student numbers would decrease feedback and ultimately effectiveness." A typical participant open-ended response was, "Frankly, online teaching should be called online writing. The sheer volume of interactive discussion posts and emails makes for a more labor intensive class than a face-to-face class. In addition, you can't simply speak to clarify a point. You must write and think even more carefully about how that writing will come across" (CCCC OWI Committee, 2011c, p. 44). On top of writing essay responses, respondents indicated that additional communications increased their workloads (e.g., commenting on discussion posts, crafting class announcements, responding to emails and questions)" (p. 44). One participant stated that while her institution's "face-to-face attrition rate is 2-4% in writing courses," the "State's online attrition rate is 50% in writing courses" (CCCC OWI Committee, 2011c, p. 45).

Although OWI is sufficiently different from onsite writing instruction to warrant new theories and strategies, the CCCC OWI Committee sees it as equal to onsite writing instruction in terms of course content, potential for quality, and credit-bearing nature. The CCCC OWI Committee decided to adhere to the reasoning provided by previously established CCCC committees regarding course caps because it could not find research that contraindicated them for either onsite or OWCs. This decision presented an interesting conundrum when a recent WPA-L listserv discussion (April 17, 2013) considered OWC caps in light of *A Position Statement of Principles and Example Effective Practices for OWI* (CCCC OWI Committee, 2013). Having cited deeper attrition rates for the online courses than for onsite ones, one writer questioned whether the CCCC OWI Committee would suggest higher caps for onsite courses in light of its recommendation of 15-20 students in online courses. As one of the interlocutors, I responded:

> ... it is true that we are not suggesting a lower cap for an online course than for an onsite one. Certainly, we are aware that most FY writing courses are capped too high to begin with, and we believe that many, many online courses are capped too high for the quality of instruction that needs to be conducted in an environment with a heavy literacy load. To be clear, we do not believe that a course cap of more than 20 student [*sic*] in an online FY writing course is advisable or effective.

Course caps also need to be developed with inclusion and access in mind. When students have special needs—be they learning, physical, multilingual, or socioeconomic—these needs should be addressed upfront with an inclusive course design. However, such needs also demand attention during the academic term as personalization and individualization requirements arise. Additionally, students who do not necessarily fit into the defined populations for accessibility may require attention when—for whatever reason they exist—literacy challenges arise in the online setting. OWI teachers who are teaching their courses actively will find themselves providing supplementary consideration to different students at various times with many of their interactions occurring through text. Unquestionably, lower course caps will assist OWI teachers with providing more accessible courses.

OWI PRINCIPLE 10

OWI Principle 10 is the first of five principles categorized as primarily a responsibility of the institution to WPAs, teachers, and students. This principle involves setting students up for success prior to taking an OWI course.

> **OWI Principle 10: Students should be prepared by the institution and their teachers for the unique technological and pedagogical components of OWI.**

RATIONALE FOR OWI PRINCIPLE 10

Adequate preparation is another issue of access, enabling students to succeed in a different learning environment by assisting them with technological and cognitive challenges. Any individual online course should include some form of orientation for students. Sometimes such orientation is left to general technology or advising units and is not provided within each course. Having been appropriately oriented to the institution's LMS (in keeping with Effective Practice 2.1), for example, students still need to understand what the OWC will be like. For this understanding, they need formal preparation particular to learning writing online. For instance, unlike some online courses, an OWC is not a self-paced or individually managed course in that regular and frequent student-to-group and student-to-teacher interactions are necessary within a well-defined time frame.

To this end, a clear OWI-orientation program should be provided at the institutional or unit level such that students are made aware of the unique requirements and technological opportunities of the OWC. Whether an institutional or unit trainer prepares and delivers such orientation, teachers should be primed to support and/or repeat elements of that training in the OWC to assist with student success. Neither institutional/unit administrators nor teachers should assume that because many students are frequent technology users, they will be successful with OWI. Indeed, the kind of online communicating that tech-savvy students do in their personal lives often is fast, frequent, and informal, which typically is not the kind of communicating they will need to do regularly to be successful in OWCs.

Discussion

In the CCCC OWI Committee's research, one of the most frequent comments that educators made about students and OWI regarded a general lack of preparedness for the online settings in which they were expected to learn. Such preparedness is necessary on two levels: (1) the institution's LMS and other prescribed technology and (2) using that technology for writing instruction. Preparing students for *using* technology in the course was mentioned more often than *learning writing with* technology. For example, in the nationwide surveys, the CCCC OWI Committee learned:

> The most important issues that respondents indicated students needed to be adequately oriented for OWI courses were technology orientation, time management skills, and the "ability to be successful." Admitting to the importance of all of these issues for success in any online course, none of these indicate successful indicators for an online *writing* course. Indeed, the expectation that students need to be able to read or write well to succeed in these courses fell at or below 6% response in both surveys. The differences between online courses and online writing courses, between online training and online writing instruction training, and online teaching and online writing teaching blur throughout this report, indicating that traditional ideas and strategies simply have migrated to the online setting without sufficient consideration of what the specific media mean for learning in a particular disciplinary area like writing. (CCCC OWI Committee, 2011c, p. 10)

These themes were repeated when talking with interviewees at site visits, audiences at CCCC panel and SIG presentations, and CCCC OWI Committee Expert/Stakeholder Panelists. The CCCC OWI Committee realized that students did, indeed, need technology orientation, yet they also needed preparation for using that technology in support of writing instruction. To this end, we wrote OWI Principle 10 to include both responsibilities and to indicate that the institution bears primary responsibility for the technology orientation as its absolutely minimal obligation.

The institution should develop basic orientation materials and strategies for helping students to learn the LMS. Site-visit interviewees suggested that such orientation might occur synchronously in an onsite computer lab with IT instructors or through an asynchronous, quiz-based delivery system. Such basic orientation is not a writing teacher's responsibility because the LMS is selected for students by the institution for multiple courses.

However, both the institution and the individual writing teacher might have responsibility for orienting writing students to the LMS for the purposes of writing instruction. The decision for responsibility should be made mutually among the institution, WPA, and IT department. All these stakeholders should understand that while an LMS can be used for delivering many courses, writing instruction is unique in the variety of LMS components students may be asked to use. Writing students typically are asked to:

- Post essays for teacher response, retrieving them when advised
- Post essays for peer response and respond to peers' essays
- Respond to discussion questions and to their peers' responses
- Work in small study groups, posting responses and document files
- Write private journals for teacher review and response
- Write publicly in Wikis or blogs for class review and response
- Write private IM-like chats to teachers and peers
- Write and respond to LMS-based emails
- Read instructional writing-focused modules and content
- Read announcements, class messages, and assignments from the teacher

These varied LMS uses differ from that of many disciplinary courses that limit LMS uses to posting completed assignments, reading modules and content, reading announcements and class messages, taking multiple choice or open-ended response quizzes, and using the LMS-based email. Writing courses, having been "flipped" for many years, are active work spaces, and students need to know how to use the LMS differently for this work. To this end, while the institution might have the best resources for developing and delivering an orientation to writing using the LMS at the overarching writing-course level, writing teachers also have some responsibility to help students succeed through early, carefully scaffolded orientation. One CCCC OWI Committee Expert/Stakeholder Panelist expressed:

> But also even scaffolding the learning of the technology ... .
> You got to give all the students training wheels to get through
> all that material. I think a lot of people underestimate how im-
> portant the first couple of weeks of getting started stuff are and
> hit the ground running. So bad practice is hitting the ground
> running without slowly, carefully articulated, carefully designed
> scaffolding assignments that hit both course design, course ad-
> aptation, technology, technology of how the course is delivered
> as well as the technologies they may be using within the course
> content. (CCCC OWI Committee, 2012a, pp. 16-17)

Because students have differing levels of ability for using technology and especially using technology for educational purposes, it will not hurt them to receive *both* institutional-level, general LMS/technology orientation *and* writing-specific LMS/technology orientation. Indeed, doing so will increase their potential to succeed in their OWI course as the expectations for how and why to use various LMS components will better match their experiences (see Chapter 13). Such orientation is an important way to keep accessibility upfront rather than retrofitted because it will enable the institution, WPA, teacher, and student to learn early whether accommodations or other changes will help individual students to succeed.

For example, when students have had adequate and timely orientation, they can make better decisions about whether their family situations, work schedules, and learning preferences will work for them in OWI. I learned about this during my dissertation research (Hewett, 1998). Two students were in settings not suited to their unique needs; one student was in the hybrid and the other in the onsite setting. The student in the hybrid class had a documented reading and writing disability; he was challenged consistently by the high literacy expectations of a primarily asynchronous content delivery, peer reading and response, and the need to communicate primarily through writing. The student in the onsite class had a documented auditory processing disorder that caused her frequent face-to-face peer group meetings to give her headaches as she struggled to deal with incomprehensible, competing voices in a primarily voice/auditory setting. Each student might have fared better in the other setting had they (and I) but known from appropriate orientation how to judge learning style against the literacy and communication loads of an OWC.

Finally, it is important to note that the CCCC OWI Committee differentiates OWI Principle 10 from OWI Principle 2, where we clearly state that writing should be the focus of the writing course and not technology orientation or teaching students how to use learning and other technologies that may or may not be useful in work and outside life. The goal of OWI Principle 10 is to ensure helpful orientation by the right parties, at the right time, and for the right purpose. The goal of OWI Principle 2 is to ensure that writing remains the focus of a writing course and that technology introduction and orientation should be for the purposes of such writing instruction.

OWI PRINCIPLE 11

A sense of aloneness easily can accompany OWI, and this principle seeks to help individuals—teachers and students—feel more connected to their OWI-related interactions within courses and among educators.

OWI Principle 11: Online writing teachers and their institutions should develop personalized and interpersonal online communities to foster student success.

RATIONALE FOR OWI PRINCIPLE 11

Students' motivation as learners often is improved by a sense of interpersonal connectedness to others within a course. Composition teachers long have practiced pedagogy of collaboration and individualization in which students are encouraged to see themselves as connected to their peers while being unique writers. It is believed generally that such writing courses inspire student success and satisfaction.

To that end, student investment is thought to be fostered when OWCs create community among teachers and students. Developing community is driven both by the institution and faculty interaction with students. Institutions not only must be committed to students and the delivery of highest quality OWI, but such a commitment should be communicated clearly by institutional leadership. It also should be fostered by an instructional practice of ongoing, student-centered evaluation of course work and learning.

DISCUSSION

Although in retrospect it could be expressed more clearly, OWI Principle 11 is about building student success by addressing the needs both teachers and students have for a sense of association among their peers. Regarding community building for teachers, in the CCCC OWI Committee's research, teachers often expressed a need to be connected to a broader online community, "a group of peers/mentors to build a teaching community for online teachers" (CCCC OWI Committee, 2011c, p. 34). More than 65% of surveyed teachers expressed this need (pp. 36, 65). One member of the CCCC OWI Committee Expert/Stakeholder Panel expressed that she was grateful to have a "community" when she had a faculty development experience with other teachers but that the community could not help her when she got into the classroom and had to "figure things out on my own to a large degree" (CCCC OWI Committee 2012a, p. 20; see also CCCC OWI Committee, 2012b, p. 11). To be truly helpful, then, it appeared that a teaching community should have experience that one can call upon when faced with actual work challenges.

Regarding community building for students, "how to create a community of learners in an online environment" was a concern that CCCC OWI Committee Expert/Stakeholder Panelists mentioned; particularly, community building was discussed regarding student retention and as an indicator for effective practices

(CCCC OWI Committee, 2012a, pp. 32-33). One of the ways that educators stated they responded to student needs was to "build community" among the disparate students, encouraging retention and helping to avoid the ghost student who fails to communicate yet remains on the roles (CCCC OWI Committee, 2011c, p. 10). One of the most popular of community-building activities that teachers indicated was "incorporating media that allow students to have some other encounters with each other (building personal Web pages so students can 'see' what classmates look like, for example)." Although no more than 26% of surveyed online writing teachers stated that they offered this option (pp. 28, 57), the idea was repeated in site-visit interviews, during CCCC panels and SIGs, and in expert/stakeholder meetings. The loss of body/face/voice seemed to inspire student and teacher biographies, postings of photos, and even the use of free conferencing technology outside the LMS to help people interact synchronously (CCCC OWI Committee, 2012a, p. 14). As one survey respondent stated, "Maybe I'm romanticizing online teaching a bit, but I don't think so. As a reluctant online teacher, I have been immensely gratified by my involvement with a broader (students are from all over the nation and the world) learning community" (p. 39).

The notion of an online community for teachers and students is fraught with challenge because it is romanticized to a degree. Will teachers spend leisure time communicating with their online communities? Should they? In such cases as tightly formed listserv groups, perhaps some will. Are students genuinely interested in developing "community" in the sense that composition instructors may desire? According to anthropologist Rebekah Nathan (2005), students construct their primary networks among smallish, ego-based groups of "two to six friends who formed their core university community" (p. 56). These relationships appear to occur early in one's school life and rarely include someone met in "an academic class or in an activity or club related to their major"; more frequently, the social networks develop "in some shared affiliation, whether voluntary or not, such as freshman dorm assignment, special freshman summer program, ROTC, ethnic club, or sorority and fraternity rush" (Nathan, 2005, pp. 57-58). Course-based "community" may need a different definition to make the work of OWI Principle 11 realistic. Indeed, such community may require concrete objectives on which all participants can agree (DePew, Spangler, & Spiegel, 2014).

In *Preparing Educators for Online Writing Instruction: Principles and Processes* (Hewett & Ehmann, 2004), the authors argued for a notion of community-building among educators that overtly recognizes the transactional versus social nature of academic groups. Their thesis was that teachers want to connect online because it can help them in their jobs by enabling them to share problems, solutions, challenges, frustrations, and successes. Called an "association" (Buber, 1923) to differentiate transactional from social communities, such connection can foster teacher and tutor satisfaction. Similarly, in OWI courses, when viewed as an association, student connections and course-based group interactions can be fostered to increase student satisfaction.

Whatever educators choose to call it, providing the possibility of online association among teachers, between teacher and students, and among students seems necessary to help people in the OWI setting see others as individuals with genuine writing needs and concerns. Online communities help to make the mediated interaction more human. In light of *A Position Statement of Principles and Example Effective Practices for OWI*s (CCCC OWI Committee, 2013) example effective practices for this OWI principle, it seems helpful here to remember that people will have different preferred methods of computer-mediated interaction (e.g., IM chat, email, lengthy posts, texting, phone and other voice-based media). Given that variety, teachers would do well to set expectations for a particular LMS-based medium that easily is used by the entire class for building some level of connections while understanding that students (and teachers) naturally will choose a preferred medium for various kinds of communications. Allowing that not all group-building interactions may occur using the course's preferred medium is one way of addressing inclusivity and accessibility for OWI Principle 11. Overall, the writing studies discipline still needs to consider how to overcome various access and inclusivity issues in order to enable the possibility of a sense of community.

Finally, a sense of being in the course together is fostered by teachers when they return student writing promptly, offer response to online discussions rather than asking students to conduct all conversations without them, request that students evaluate the course or module midstream (potentially leading to change during rather than after the term), and include students in decision making. Such affirmation of students as responsive people who can help to guide their OWC is an andragogical principle that may lead to a more bonded class (CCCC OWI Committee, 2012b, p. 10).

OWI PRINCIPLE 12

This OWI principle addresses the need for institutions to plan and engage support for OWI teachers.

> **OWI Principle 12: Institutions should foster teacher satisfaction in online writing courses as rigorously as they do for student and programmatic success.**

RATIONALE FOR OWI PRINCIPLE 12

Teacher satisfaction in an OWI environment is critical. Many teachers learned their craft in traditional, onsite settings, so they may experience anxiety and/or dissatisfaction in this newer educational setting. Teacher satisfaction is dependent on a number of affective factors, including being personally suited to teaching online and being comfortable communicating with students using digital/electronic means.

Teachers should be helped to understand the relative advantages and disadvantages of teaching an OWC in their institution, which includes such pedagogical factors as understanding how communication in the OWC environment differs and learning the benefits and challenges of the asynchronous and the synchronous modalities. Developing that understanding includes clearly describing any employment conditions specific to teaching an OWC course in the institution such as onsite and/or online office requirements; whether teaching an online course is understood to be equal in time or weight to a traditional onsite course; and how teaching an OWC is assessed for job retention, promotion, and tenure.

Time is a particularly sensitive issue for teachers, onsite as well as online. However, a standing misconception is that teaching and learning in an online environment is less time-intensive than teaching on campus because the teaching and learning often can be accomplished asynchronously and at one's own convenience. Research consistently has indicated that teaching online can be more time-intensive (Allen & Seaman, 2010; Seaman, 2009; Worley & Tesdell, 2009) because most communications and interactions (e.g., instruction, assignments, questions, answers, and grades) in OWCs are fully online. Teaching writing online involves focused teacher responses that are crafted to specific student compositions. Unlike what people might imagine can be done in other disciplines, most of these communications cannot be automated; there is no "leveraging" or "scalability" of these essentially unique interactions (as compared to, for example, providing the same content video to hundreds, if not thousands, of students). To that end, concerns about time management can be an issue that contributes to teacher dissatisfaction.

With their individual habits, logistics, time management, and personal career issues, teachers who are more suited to online modalities can engage the students and invest them in their own learning online, all of which contribute to teacher satisfaction.

DISCUSSION

Students are not the only ones whose satisfaction is important in OWI. According to the Sloan Consortium (2005), faculty satisfaction leads to online instructional success, and it is fostered by appreciation and happiness with their institutions and instructional settings. OWI Principle 12 was articulated to suggest ways to achieve such satisfaction, which we believe can lead to retaining strong OWI teachers and, ultimately, to student success.

In the CCCC OWI Committee's surveys of OWI teachers, we were dismayed but not surprised to learn that many participants were dissatisfied in their OWCs and online instructional opportunities. Among the problems leading to such unhappiness were "the levels of support they receive regarding technology, course caps, training, pay, and professional development/interactions relative to OWI in both the fully online and hybrid settings" (CCCC OWI Committee, 2011c, p. 7). Survey analysis suggested that "such dissatisfaction can lead to poor teaching, low expectations for students and for an online course, and insufficient retention of experienced instructors at a time when OWI continues to grow" (p. 7). As a result of their general unhappiness, respondents expressed "ambiguity" about "recommend[ing] their online setting to other writing instructors[;] only 58% of the fully online respondents and 46% hybrid respondents said they would" (p. 13).

The respondents also indicated that they were more interested in logistical (e.g., technical support, increased training, off-campus office hours, and lower course caps) and intrinsic (e.g., mentoring and companionship while teaching online, expressed student appreciation, and student success through reading the online materials) rewards more than additional financial remuneration (pp. 37, 38, 66). These interests relate directly to OWI Principles 8 and 9. The CCCC OWI Committee determined that "concerns among respondents would seem to be connected directly to perceived lack of administrative and technical support, as well as desires for ongoing training in terms of both technology and course design" (p. 66).

OWI Principle 12 outlined some specific, reasonable strategies for helping teachers to find more satisfaction in OWI. Most of them revolve around respecting the teacher's need to learn about what constitutes effective OWI: a need to know about OWI practically and theoretically; a need to connect with other OWI teachers at the institution and across the nation; a need to have regular, compensated professional development; a need to be informed about institutional OWI-based outlook and the forecasted teacher pool; and so on. Once enumerated, these needs may seem self-evident, but teachers across the nation have informed us that they are not so evident to their WPAs or their institutions. Steady nationwide increases in OWI courses strongly suggest that more teachers will be needed, but without frank discussions for and among an institution's OWI teaching pool, those most involved in increasing *effective* OWI courses will not know what to expect.

Such an issue of respect also is one of inclusivity and access. Just as not every student will do well in OWI, not every teacher is well-suited to it. Teachers need to know whether their teaching preferences suit them to OWI, which is an issue of appropriate access to the OWI course. Teachers who prefer to teach online over onsite writing courses should be given fair opportunities to do so because they more likely will excel in their preferred setting. Frank discussions about preferred media for communicating, theories of writing instruction, and notions of student learning and success can help teachers to place themselves appropriately in online and onsite settings. Teachers who are not good candidates for OWI should not be made (or allowed) to teach such courses; inclusivity, in this case, does not mean that everyone should be teaching OWI equally often regardless of skill and ability. (However, as Warnock and I discuss in Chapter 18, given the future of OWI, we believe that all *new* teachers should be prepared for OWI in such ways as to help them find their strengths in the online teaching environment.) Finally, mentoring, appropriate hand-holding, regular assessment, and thoughtful communication also can foster teacher satisfaction. Without satisfied and competent OWI teachers, the program is dead in the water; student success levels will confirm that reality.

OWI PRINCIPLE 13

OWI Principle 13 addresses the need for institutions to provide online students with online support services.

> **OWI Principle 13: OWI students should be provided support components through online/digital media as a primary resource; they should have access to onsite support components as a secondary set of resources.**

RATIONALE FOR OWI PRINCIPLE 13

Writing instruction that is conducted online requires online support systems. Such support should take the form of online writing labs (OWLs; also known as online writing centers) as well as online libraries, online accessible IT support, and distance-based student counseling. Such reinforcing programs provide student access to the same support components that students in traditional, onsite courses receive. This issue is one of access and inclusivity (see OWI Principle 1), but it also is one of enabling students to use the digital educational environment more fully (see OWI Principle 10). When students are in a "learn-anytime" environment, they should have broad access to support services.

OWLs, for example, support the process-oriented elements of writing as well as its social nature. As do brick-and-mortar writing centers, OWLs foster one-to-one relationships between tutors and writers and provide tailored feedback and assistance to students as a complement to in-class, faculty-led instruction. Tailored, personalized feedback from peer or professional tutors can afford invaluable learning opportunities for student writers. With institutional and faculty support, students must be prepared to use OWLs as sites of interaction and dialogue and not as linear "drop-off" points to "fix" papers. OWLs can further benefit OWI students by strategically modeling asynchronous or synchronous interactions within the writing process.

DISCUSSION

The CCCC OWI Committee quickly learned through its research that online writing students need online support systems. That tenet might seem to be self-evident, but when OWI still carries some stigma of being a deficit model in comparison with traditional onsite writing instruction, it follows that support services also lag in valuing online components. OWI Principle 13 addressed the need for consistently available online library, IT assistance, and student counseling, but it focused primarily on the need for OWL support.

Even though useful literature exists that supports OWL development (see, for example, (Driscoll, Brizee, Salvo, & Sousa, 2008; Hewett, 2002, Inman & Sewell, 2000; Hobson, 1998; IWCA, 2002; Karper & Stolley, 2007; Wolfe & Griffin, 2013;), the writing center field has not yet embraced OWLs as equal to traditional writing centers. Chapter 5 addresses some of the underlying issues.

The CCCC OWI Committee's nationwide surveys supported information gained through our field visit interviews; most students who took their writing courses in hybrid or fully online settings did not have access to OWL services:

> The survey assumed that online tutoring would be available
> to students in both fully online and hybrid settings given that
> their instruction was occurring at least part time in an online
> setting. In the fully online setting, barely 50% of the respon-
> dents reported such availability; asynchronous tutoring was
> more often available to these students than synchronous. The
> vast majority of supplemental support was available through
> static online materials with a text-based nature. The results for
> the hybrid setting were remarkably similar with the exception
> that outsourced online tutoring was made available to 2-year
> community college students more often than for other fully
> online students. Quite a few respondents in both settings in-
> dicated either no access to online writing center assistance or a

> need for students to come in to a traditional brick-and-mortar writing center *if* one was available. The possibility that some students, particularly those in fully online settings, could not access the campus-based writing center did not emerge in open-ended "other" responses. The lack of supplemental support for students in online settings is worrisome. (CCCC OWI Committee, 2011c, p. 9)

Students who did have online tutoring available typically did not receive instruction in how to access or use those services: "as many as 30% (fully online) and 47% (hybrid) reported that students did not receive any instruction for using those tutoring services" (CCCC OWI Committee, 2011c, p. 9). Most instruction that they received was text-based, which can be inaccessible to many students because of physical or learning challenges, difficulties with educational technology, or because they simply do not read instructional text well.

OWLs that did exist were primarily asynchronous (50.3% for fully online respondents and 51% for hybrid respondents), with fewer synchronous tutorials provided (25.8% for fully online respondents and 23% for hybrid respondents). Interestingly, 22% of fully online respondents indicated they had outsourced tutoring available and 8% of hybrid respondents indicated outsourced tutoring (pp. 24-25, 52). The higher number of outsourced tutoring in fully online settings had a clear connection to the inability to require students to use an onsite writing center; from a logistical standpoint, hybrid students who met at least some of their classes on campus could be required to use the onsite writing center instead of providing online support. Hence, writing tutorial services were overwhelmingly provided in traditional onsite centers with text-based, module-like resources available online.

Although most online tutorials were accomplished asynchronously according to the surveys, the CCCC OWI Committee Expert/Stakeholder Panel indicated a preference for synchronous tutorials, which anecdotally are preferred most often by tutorial providers on the national writing center listserv (WCenter) as evidenced by posts. One panelist expressed the preference challenge as, "I think it is a big question, an important question and the idea of comparing versus just saying they are different, one is not better than the other. I think this a huge discussion that we can talk about for a long time" (CCCC OWI Committee, 2012a, p. 25). This open-mindedness about modality was countered by a distinct preference for synchronicity in the discussion:

> So, we don't have the young super tech savvy students necessarily. So what we find works the best for synchronous online tutoring is using Adobe Connect to share documents so we

can be looking at it together or chatting. But we don't always
use the audio feature along with it; we use the telephone,
because of bandwidth issues mainly. We also use the phone
with email; if they email the paper we are both looking at the
paper and talking on the phone. (CCCC OWI Committee,
2012a, p. 13)

To date, the CCCC OWI Committee has not found evidence that synchronous online tutorials are superior to asynchronous ones although there are some studies suggesting student preference for audio and audio/video feedback (Moore & Filling, 2012; Sommers, 2012, 2013); more research certainly needs to be engaged. It does not seem reasonable, however, to develop tutoring based on the tutor's or OWL administrator's modality preference alone.

Indeed, contrary to a general sense among research participants that synchronous tutorials were superior to asynchronous ones given their likeness to traditional onsite tutorials, the CCCC OWI Committee realized that students needed to have access to tutoring that mirrored their course technology and its typical modality. To that end, we recommend providing high quality tutoring in the same modality and using the same media that students have available for class. If the course is provided asynchronously through the LMS, then it makes sense to use the LMS to address one-to-one tutoring; if the LMS is inappropriate to the task, then it makes sense to do so through similar software that would be familiar to students because of their educational uses of the LMS. If the course is provided synchronously, then it makes the most sense to provide synchronous tutorials. When it is possible to provide both modalities, then students can choose the modality based on their personal learning preferences, which engages the spirit of generosity to which I referred earlier in the chapter. Similarly for the medium: If the course uses text primarily, it is helpful to use text-based tutorials; when the course uses audio/visual response primarily, then such response makes sense for tutorials. Certainly, to address all learning styles, both modalities and media could be offered for student choice.

Finally, the CCCC OWI Committee learned that some educators were considering accessibility issues in developing their OWL services:

From a tutoring perspective, I mean tutor presence is also
important but also what someone mentioned, about teaching really being adaptable to the student needs and using
whatever technology works with the students, whether that is
texts, email ... that we are prepared to go where the student
is comfortable, technologically and with their learning styles.
We really tried to do that in the writing center. So that we are

working with voice, over the phone or in Adobe Connect like
this meeting is. Whatever we need to do to help the student
focus on their writing [*sic*] and not so much on the environment that might be strange to them. (CCCC OWI Committee, 2012a, p. 12)

Another panelist expressed, "Now in the writing center, we produce a lot
of different resources including movies or tutorials; we have to make sure all of
those are accessible, sometimes including a transcript or a PDF needs to be accessible" (CCCC OWI Committee, 2012a, pp. 27-28). This awareness of accessibility appeared to be higher among those involved directly in providing writing
tutoring than among OWI teachers more generally; the heightened awareness
possibly stemmed from the writing center field's attention to students' individual needs in their traditionally one-to-one setting.

When OWI Principle 1 is held as the overarching principle, then inclusivity
and access are the most critical considerations for OWI Principle 13. Providing
inclusion and access means selecting the tutoring modality and media with students' course modality and media in mind—making the interaction as simple
and familiar as possible. It also means providing OWL access despite an institution's current capability (or lack thereof) to build and house an OWL; when
an OWL cannot be developed in-house or when doing so may take months
or years, then students should be provided interim tutorial support through
connections with other educational institutions or by outsourcing to other providers. When inclusivity and accessibility are the first principle, the decision to
have OWL-based tutoring support is automatic; how to provide high-quality
tutoring is the only question left.

OWI PRINCIPLE 14

If OWLs are to be upheld as necessary sites for OWI-based tutoring support,
then they require high-quality, environment-specific tutor selection, training,
and professional development.

> **OWI Principle 14: Online writing lab administrators and
> tutors should undergo selection, training, and ongoing pro-
> fessional development activities that match the environment
> in which they will work.**

RATIONALE FOR OWI PRINCIPLE 14

As it is with writing instructors, tutor (peer or professional) training and ongoing professional development are paramount. Such training and orientation must address the distinctive nature of online writing tutoring in asynchronous and synchronous venues.

The OWL coordinator should be well-versed in both traditional writing center and OWL pedagogy and theory. This individual should be experienced with the environments and modalities in which the tutoring occurs. To this end, the coordinator should select online tutors for their (1) writing tutoring potential and/or experience; (2) strengths in expressing writing instruction in writing; and (3) comfort level with online technologies, which can be developed further in training. For OWL tutors to model technology use for students, it is crucial that they be trained through and with the settings, modalities, media, and technologies in which they will tutor. Further, they should receive individualized mentoring as well as any group training. All tutors should be trained to interact with students using diverse media—print and electronic text, audio, and video—and they should be prepared to work with students with diverse abilities and learning styles, in line with OWI Principle 1.

The OWL's commitment to screening, training, and professional development will yield higher quality tutorial sessions that ultimately benefit all students. For peer and professional tutors alike, such commitment ultimately will refine and hone their practice and understanding of OWL tutoring.

DISCUSSION

Online tutors should be selected for their suitability and desire to teach online, need environment-specific training in OWI, and require on-going professional development for the same reasons that online writing teachers need these, as outlined and discussed under OWI Principles 7 and 12. The CCCC OWI Committee's research strongly indicated that contemporary online tutors are not yet receiving such assistance.

Our national surveys, for example, showed that the training provided typically is not occurring in the setting in which the tutoring is to occur, which is a foundational educational principle for teacher and tutor preparation (Hewett & Ehmann, 2004). When asked "to check all applicable responses to a question about how tutors were trained for online writing center work," "up to 47%" of fully online respondents "indicated that the tutors received the same training as face-to-face tutors, while 31% indicated that their tutors received non-credit bearing training dedicated to online tutoring" (CCCC OWI Committee, 2011c, p. 25). Furthermore, "only 1% indicated that their tutors had some kind of credit-bearing online-specific tutor training, while 7% reported that tutors received credit-bearing training in non-online specific processes and 9% reported that their tutors received credit-bearing training on technology and online pedagogies" (pp. 25-26). Of the hybrid-focused respondents:

> Up to 60% indicated that the tutors received the same training as face-to-face tutors, while 25% indicated that their tutors received non-credit bearing training dedicated to online tutoring. Zero percent indicated that their tutors had some kind of credit-bearing online-specific tutor training, while 8% reported that tutors received credit-bearing training in non-online specific processes and 8% reported that their tutors received credit-bearing training on technology and online pedagogies. (CCCC OWI Committee, 2011c, p. 54)

In reviewing these numbers, the CCCC OWI Committee expressed concern that "the 'same training' as face-to-face tutors may account for some common tutoring principles, but not the particular strategies and/or principles necessary for a text-based tutoring asynchronous or synchronous (chat) setting, nor for the faceless telephone synchronous setting" (p. 54).[8]

Selecting suitable tutors for the online environment is important because they have to be able and willing to work primarily in text for asynchronous settings and without facial or body language for most synchronous settings. Many tutors and their writing center administrators train and conduct their work from traditional, onsite theories and practices that are not necessarily helpful in online settings. As a result, they express a sense of working in a less viable environment (Ehmann Powers, 2010). Moving a one-to-one writing tutorial to an online environment can be off-putting and can cause tutors to lose track of their goals. One respondent in the CCCC OWI Committee Expert/Stakeholder Panel discussions stated:

> And I actually did a research project on this a few years ago and what I found specifically was that these wonderful face to face tutors didn't have to be explicitly told who their student was. When they got online, all of a sudden they forgot their role and they started fixing papers instead of providing recommendations and suggestions, and so I had to go and create some new online strategies for this faculty. (CCCC OWI Committee, 2012a, p. 25)

This respondent saw the problem as a "disconnect between online strategies and face-to-face strategies" (p. 25). Unfortunately, the published literature often does not address the specific differences between online and onsite strategies for tutoring (Bruce & Rafoth, 2009; Ryan & Zimmerelli, 2010; see Hewett,

2015b, 2010, 2011 for research and strategies that do address these differences). Additional research can expand knowledge about how online tutoring shapes student understanding and writing perceptions (see Wolfe & Griffin, 2013, for example).

As indicated in the discussion regarding OWI Principle 13, inclusivity and accessibility demand that online writing students have online tutoring. That tutoring is most accessible in the online environment in which students are learning although it is reasonable and inclusive also to offer another online modality or medium or to welcome (but not force through lack of other options) online students to onsite settings. Nonetheless, online tutoring differs drastically from onsite tutoring; using asynchronous text to explain and intervene, for example, is quite different from orally talking a student through writing strengths and weaknesses or encouraging change while never touching the student's paper with a pen. These very differences place inadequately trained tutors in the position of going against what they believe to be tutoring best practices and can leave the online student with less than the best assistance and feedback. Genuinely accessible online tutoring will meet students at their points of need rather than allowing what the tutor is comfortable or familiar with to be the guiding factor. Appropriate tutor selection, online training, and ongoing professional development can mitigate these problems.

OWI PRINCIPLE 15

This final OWI principle is in a category of its own, which is research.

> OWI Principle 15: OWI/OWL administrators and teachers/
> tutors should be committed to ongoing research into their
> programs and courses as well as the very principles in this
> document.

RATIONALE FOR OWI PRINCIPLE 15

Emerging from the CCCC OWI Committee's work is a repeatedly articulated need for professional development in the area of OWI and OWLs (see OWI Principle 12 and OWI Principle 14). To be sure, there is urgent need to educate the writing community on OWI and OWLs and to help direct the teaching and learning of our students with what is known about state of the art and effective practices. Advances in OWI and OWLs should be grounded in valid and reliable research findings and systematic information dissemination. OWI and OWLs are particularly well positioned as sites of ongoing research in that almost all interactions are saved and archived (e.g., via email, platform communication, online group discussion, writing revisions), enabling empirical analysis.

Therefore, to bolster the theoretical and pedagogical frameworks for OWI and OWLs, OWI and OWL administrators and teachers/tutors alike should be committed to ongoing research of their courses, students, and programs. Such research should draw directly from these courses, students, and programs when appropriate. Such pedagogically driven research must be validated both by the scholarly community and administrators in composition studies. Empirical, repeatable, and longitudinal research that addresses questions regarding the phenomena of OWI and OWLs will drive a deeper understanding of OWI and OWLs, ultimately benefiting students and the teaching and learning of writing in online contexts. Both qualitative and quantitative methodological designs can be employed to address key questions surrounding OWI and OWL outcomes, processes, and participant perspectives.

DISCUSSION

We simply do not know enough about OWI, OWCs, OWLs, and all the ways that students learn and fail to learn to write through digital technologies. That is the point of OWI Principle 15, which is addressed in great depth in Chapter 17. The ongoing need for research also is addressed to some degree in the rest of the chapters in this book. The research conducted by the CCCC OWI Committee in support of developing these 15 OWI principles and their example effective practices offers a beginning. Without additional research, however, as education moves more firmly into the digital arena, our collective gut feelings, anecdotal experiences, and guesses will not be enough. The CCCC OWI Committee's annotated bibliography and the research gathered for various CompPile documents (see Warnock, 2013, for example) help us to learn and understand OWI more. Inclusivity and accessibility concerns are among the least well-understood of all OWI issues. Mainstream students are more often studied than those with physical, learning, multilingual, or socioeconomic challenges. Necessary research would examine student writers with such concerns to improve and advance our understanding of OWI teaching and learning overall, as well as to better enable OWI access to all students who want or need it.

Clearly, a new generation of research is necessary. OWI Principle 15 urges scholars and educators to address that need.

NOTES

1. There are differences between the pedagogical aspects and the institutional/administrative aspects of how writing courses are delivered. When is *homework* just

homework, and when does that work constitute a hybrid experience? Does *hybrid* always mean digital, out-of-class experiences? As we completed this book, we realized that the definitions and terminology inherent to our work likely will need to undergo some change to better depict what is happening in OWCs across various institutional contexts.

2. The OWI Committee expects to reconsider and revise as needed the particulars of *A Position Statement of Principles and Example Effective Practices for OWI* triennially.

3. Multilingual learners are not conflated here with students who have disabilities although some certainly may have such needs. On the contrary, their needs stem primarily from linguistic and cultural concerns that may inhibit their learning in online environments. Similarly, students from impoverished or "different" socioeconomic backgrounds require an inclusive setting that recognizes their challenges in OWI.

4. "FO" is shorthand for "Fully Online" as opposed to "H" for "Hybrid" survey respondents. "Q" indicates "question."

5. In the CCCC OWI survey of fully-online faculty and administrators, respondents rated their need for advanced Web design skills at 20% in comparison with, for example, the ability to respond to student needs in a timely manner at 100% (CCCC OWI Committee, 2011c, p. 36). In the survey regarding hybrid OWI, they rated advanced Web design skills at 22% (p. 65). For both cases, these ratings were the lowest and revealed that instructors were less concerned with technological proficiency than with other aspects of composition instruction. These results also may reflect who institutions hire to teach writing, the limited scope some teachers bring to writing instruction, and the limited preparation they receive to teach writing.

6. Semantic Integrity theory indicates that the teacher's message is written in a straightforward, linguistically direct manner and that it matches her intention and that the intention can be read and correctly interpreted by the average student.

7. English Composition 1: Achieving Expertise, developed by Denise Comer (Duke). 12 weeks, launched March 18, 2013; Writing 2: Rhetorical Composing, developed by Kay Halasek, Scott DeWitt, Susan Delagrange, Ben McCorkle & Cindy Selfe (Ohio State), 10 weeks, launched April 22, 2013; Crafting an Effective Writer: Tools of the Trade, developed by Larry Barkley, Ted Blake, & Lorrie Ross (Mt. San Jacinto), 5 weeks, launched May 13, 2013; First Year Composition 2.0, developed by Karen Head (Georgia Tech), 8 weeks, launched May 27, 2013.

8. From the CCCC OWI Committee Expert/Stakeholder Panel, although this topic was not fully aired, one educator indicated that an "entire training is an online training because we are dealing with virtual employees" when developing

a training scenario for a distributed workplace other than tutoring (CCCC OWI Committee, 2011d, p. 21).

REFERENCES

Alexander, Jonathan. (2006). *Digital youth: Emerging literacies on the World Wide Web*. Kresskill, NJ: Hampton Press.

Bruce, Shanti & Rafoth, Ben. (2009). *ESL writers: A guide for writing tutors* (2nd ed.). Portsmouth, NH: Heinemann.

Buber, Martin. (1923). *I and thou*. (Walter Kaufmann, Trans.). 1970. New York: Scribner.

Conference on College Composition and Communication (CCCC). (2009). *CCCC statement on second language writing and writers*. Retrieved from http://www.ncte.org/cccc/resources/positions/secondlangwriting

CCCC OWI Committee for Effective Practices in Online Writing Instruction. (2008). *Annotated bibliography on online writing instruction 1980-2008*. Committee for Best Practices on Online Writing Instruction. (Keith Gibson & Beth Hewett, Eds.). Retrieved from http://www.ncte.org/library/NCTE-Files/Groups/CCCC/Committees/OWIAnnotatedBib.pdf

CCCC OWI Committee for Effective Practices in Online Writing Instruction. (2011a). *Fully online distance-based courses survey results*. Retrieved from http://s.zoomerang.com/sr.aspx?sm=EAupi15gkwWur6G7egRSXUw8k-pNMu1f5gjUp01aogtY%3d

CCCC OWI Committee for Effective Practices in Online Writing Instruction. (2011b). *Hybrid/blended course survey results*. Retrieved from http://s.zoomer-ang.com/sr.aspx?sm=%2fPsFeeRDwfznaIyyz4sV0qxkkh5Ry7O1NdnGH-CxIBD4%3d

CCCC OWI Committee for Effective Practices in Online Writing Instruction. (2011c). *The state of the art of OWI*. Retrieved from http://www.ncte.org/library/NCTEFiles/Groups/CCCC/Committees/OWI_State-of-Art_Report_April_2011.pdf

CCCC OWI Committee for Effective Practices in Online Writing Instruction. (2011d). [Transcript of expert/stakeholders' panel virtual meeting of 10/27/2011.] Unpublished raw data.

CCCC OWI Committee for Effective Practices in Online Writing Instruction. (2012a). [Transcript of expert/stakeholders' panel virtual meeting of 01/12/2012.] Unpublished raw data.

CCCC OWI Committee for Effective Practices in Online Writing Instruction. (2012b). [Transcript of expert/stakeholders' panel virtual meeting of 02/17/2012.] Unpublished raw data.

CCCC OWI Committee for Effective Practices in Online Writing Instruction. (2013). *A position statement of principles and effective practices for online writing instruction (OWI)*. Retrieved from http://www.ncte.org/cccc/resources/positions/owiprinciples

CCCC Committee for Principles and Standards for the Postsecondary Teaching of Writing. (1989). *Statement of principles and standards for the postsecondary teaching of writing*. Retrieved from http://www.ncte.org/cccc/resources/positions/postsecondarywriting

CCCC Task Force to Revise the CCCC Principles and Standards for the Teaching of Writing. (2013). *Statement of principles and standards for the postsecondary teaching of writing*. Retrieved from http://www.ncte.org/cccc/resources/positions/postsecondarywriting

DePew, Kevin E., Spangler, Sarah, & Spiegel, Cheri L. (2014). Getting past our assumptions about Web 2.0 and community building: How to design research-based literacy pedagogy. In Marohang Limbu & Binod Gurung (Eds.), *Emerging pedagogies in the networked knowledge society: Practices integrating social media and globalization* (pp. 120-143). Hershey, PA: IGI Global.

Driscoll, Dana, Brizee, Allen, Salvo, Michael, & Sousa, Morgan. (2008). Usability and user-centered theory for 21st century OWLs. In Pavel Zemliansky & Kirk St.Amant (Eds.), *Handbook of research on virtual workplaces and the new nature of business practices (pp. 614-631)*. Hershey, PA: IGI Global.

Griffin, June & Minter, Deborah. (2013). The rise of the online writing classroom: Reflecting on the material conditions of college composition teaching. *College Composition and Communication, 65*(1), 140-161.

Halasek, Kay, McCorkle, Ben, Selfe, Cynthia L., DeWitt, Scott Lloyd, Delagrange, Susan, Michaels, Jennifer & Clinnin, Kaitlin. (2014). A MOOC with a view: How MOOCs encourage us to reexamine pedagogical doxa. In Steven D. Krause & Charles Lowe (Eds.), *Invasion of the MOOCs: The promise and perils of massive open online courses* (pp. 156-166). Anderson, SC: Parlor Press.

Head, Karen. (2013). Inside a MOOC in progress. *The Chronicle of Higher Education*. Retrieved from http://chronicle.com/blogs/wiredcampus/inside-a-mooc-in-progress/44397

Hewett, Beth. L. (2000). Characteristics of interactive oral and computer-mediated peer group talk and its influence on revision. *Computers and Composition, 17*(3), 265-88.

Hewett, Beth. L. (2001). Generating new theory for online writing instruction. *Kairos: Rhetoric, Technology, and Pedagogy, 6.2*. Retrieved from http://english.ttu.edu/kairos/6.2/index.html

Hewett, Beth. L. (2002). Theoretical underpinnings of online writing labs (OWLs). *The OWL maintenance and development guide*. Retrieved from http://defendandpublish.com/OWL_Theory.pdf

Hewett, Beth L. (2004-2005). Asynchronous online instructional commentary: A study of student revision. *Readerly/Writerly Texts: Essays in Literary, Composition, and Pedagogical Theory (Double Issue), 11 & 12*(1 & 2), 47-67.

Hewett, Beth L. (2006). Synchronous online conference-based instruction: A study of whiteboard interactions and student writing. *Computers and Composition, 23*(1), 4-31.

Hewett, Beth L. (2010). *The online writing conference: A guide for teachers and tutors.* Portsmouth, NH, Boynton/Cook.

Hewett, Beth L. (2011). *Instructor's study guide for the online writing conference: A guide for teachers and tutors.* Portsmouth, NH: Heinemann.

Hewett, B. L. (2013). Fully online and hybrid writing instruction. In H. Brooke Hessler, Amy Rupiper Taggart, & Kurt Schick (Eds.), *A guide to composition pedagogies* (2nd ed.) (pp. 194-211). Oxford, UK: Oxford University Press.

Hewett, Beth L. (2015a). *Reading to learn and writing to teach: Literacy strategies for online writing instruction.* Boston: Bedford/St. Martin's Press.

Hewett, Beth L. (2015b). *The online writing conference: A guide for teachers and tutors* (Updated). Boston: Bedford/St. Martin's Press.

Hewett, Beth L. & Ehmann, Christa. (2004). *Preparing educators for online writing instruction.* Urbana, IL, National Council of Teachers of English.

Hobson, Eric H. (Ed.). (1998). *Wiring the writing center.* Logan, UT: Utah State University Press.

The Institute of Electrical and Electronics Engineers. (2012). *IEEE standards style manual.* Retrieved from https://development.standards.ieee.org/myproject/Public/mytools/draft/styleman.pdf

International Writing Centers Association (IWCA). (2002). *OWL construction and maintenance guide.* International Writing Centers Association Press. (CD).

Inman, James & Sewell, Donna (Eds.). (2000). *Taking flight with OWLs: Examining electronic writing center work.* New York: Erlbaum.

Journet, Debra, Ball, Cheryl E., & Trauman, R. (Eds.). (2012). *The new work of composing.* Logan, UT: Computers and Composition Digital Press/Utah State University Press. Retrieved from http://ccdigitalpress.org/nwc

Jukes, Ian, McCain, Ted, & Crockett, Lee. (2010).*Understanding the digital generation: Teaching and learning in the new digital landscape.* Kelowna, BC, CA: 21st Century Fluency Project.

Karper, Erin & Stolley, Karl. (2007). New wings for an old OWL: Database solutions for small and large-scale writing center Web sites. *Databases in higher education: New media discourse in composition and rhetoric.* Rich Rice & Jeffrey White, Eds. New York: Hampton Press.

Krause, Stephen D. & Lowe, C Charles. (2014). *Invasion of the MOOCs: The promises and perils of massive open online courses.* Anderson, SC: Parlor Press.

Lewin, Tamar. (2015, February 15). Harvard and M.I.T. are sued over lack of closed captions. *The New York Times.* Retrieved from http://www.nytimes.com/2015/02/13/education/harvard-and-mit-sued-over-failing-to-caption-online-courses.html?_r=0

Meloncon, Lisa. (Ed.). (2014). *Rhetorical access-ability: At the intersection of technical communication and disability studies.* Amityville, NY: Baywood Publishing.

Moore, J. C. (2011). A synthesis of Sloan-C effective practices. *Journal of Asynchronous Learning Networks, 16*(1): 91-115.

Moore, Noreen S. & Filling, Michelle L. (2012). iFeedback: Using video technology for improving student writing. *Journal of College Literacy and Learning, 3*–14.

Nathan, Rebekah. (2005). *My freshman year: What a professor learned by becoming a student.* Ithaca, NY: Cornell University Press.

North, Stephen M. (1987). The making of knowledge in composition: Portrait of an emerging field. Portsmouth, NH: Heinemann.

Palmquist, Michael. (1993). Network-supported interaction in two writing classrooms. *Computers and Composition, 10*(4), 25-57.

Powers, Christa Ehmann. (2010). A study of online writing instructor perceptions. In Hewett (Ed.), *The Online Writing Conference: A Guide for Teachers and Tutors* (pp. 163-171). Portsmouth, NH: Heinemann.

Prior, Paul, Solberg, Janine, Berry, Patrick, Bellwoar, Hannah, Chewing, Bill, Lunsford, Karen K., ... Walker, Joyce. (2007). Re-situating and re-mediating the canons: A cultural-historical remapping of rhetorical activity. *Kairos: A Journal of Rhetoric, Technology, and Pedagogy, 11*(3). Retrieved from http://kairos.technorhetoric.net/11.3/index.html

Ryan, Leigh & Zimmerelli, Lisa. (2010). *Bedford guide for writing tutors* (5th ed.). Boston, MA: Bedford.

Selber, Stuart A. (2004a). *Multiliteracies for a digital age.* Carbondale, IL: Southern Illinois University Press.

Selber, Stuart. (2004b). Reimagining the functional side of computer literacy. *College Composition and Communication, 55*(3), 470-503.

Selfe, Cynthia L. (1999). *Technology and literacy in the twenty-first century: The importance of paying attention.* Carbondale, IL: Southern Illinois University Press.

Selfe, Cynthia L. & Hawisher, Gail E. (Eds.). (2007). *Gaming lives in the twenty-first century: Literate connections.* New York, NY: Palgrave Macmillan.

Selfe, Cynthia L. (2009). The movement of air: The breath of meaning: Aurality and multimodal composing. *College Composition and Communication, 60*(4), 616-663.

Sloan Consortium. (2005). *Effective practices.* Retrieved from http://www.aln.org/publications/books/v9n3_moore.pdf; see also http://www.sloan-c.org/effective/

Small, Gary & Vorgon, Gigi. (2008). *iBrain: Surviving the technological alteration of the modern mind.* New York: Harper Collins.

Sommers, Jeff. (2012). Response rethought ... again: Exploring recorded comments and the teacher-student bond. *Journal of Writing Assessment, 5*(1). Retrieved from http://www.journalofwritingassessment.org/article.php?article=59

Sommers, Jeff. (2013). Response 2.0: Commentary on student writing for the new millennium. *Journal of College Literacy and Learning, 39,* 21–37.

Warnock, Scott. (2009). *Teaching writing online: How and why.* Champaign, IL: National Council of Teachers of English.

Warnock, Scott. (2013). Studies comparing outcomes among onsite, hybrid and fully online writing courses. *WPA CompPile Research Bibliographies, 21.* Retrieved from http://comppile.org/wpa/bibliographies/Bib21/Warnock.pdf

Wolfe, Joanna & Griffin, Jo Ann. (2013). Comparing technologies for online writing conferences: Effects of medium on conversation. *Writing Center Journal, 32*(2), 60-92.

Yergeau, Melanie, Brewer, Elizabeth, Kerschbaum, Stephanie, Oswal, Sushil K., Price, Margaret, Selfe, Cynthia L., Salvo, Michael J., & Howes, Franny. (2013). Multimodality in motion: Disability and kairotic spaces. *Kairos: A Journal of Rhetoric, Technology, and Pedagogy.* Retrieved from http://kairos.technorhetoric.net/18.1/coverweb/yergeau-et-al/index.html

CHAPTER 2

HYBRID AND FULLY ONLINE OWI

Jason Snart
College of DuPage

This chapter outlines key similarities and differences between hybrid and fully online writing instruction. Both instructional settings offer challenges and opportunities and neither is necessarily preferable to the other in all circumstances. Nor should these instructional settings be understood as mere variants of the imagined norm of fully face-to-face instruction. In fact, creating and delivering effective writing classes requires grounding in basic principles of sound pedagogy regardless of instructional setting.

Keywords: accessibility, blended, fully online, hybrid, institutional planning, instructional design, instructional setting, professional development, scheduling, student engagement, student success, student support

Early in my teaching career, I had a situation that highlighted some of the perils of teaching a hybrid FYW course. It was final exam week, and I was headed to the classroom where my hybrid composition class was scheduled to take its final exam, an in-class reflective essay. Lo and behold, the room was already occupied by another class taking its final exam. My students were waiting nervously in the hallway. I started to get nervous, too. I double-checked the exam schedule and, yes, this was where we were supposed to be. We were a Tuesday/Thursday class and this room was where we were to meet for our final exam and this was the right time... . Now what? Luckily, there was an available room not too far away, so my students and I moved there and they wrote their essays.

Later, I tried to figure out the mix up. Were two classes accidentally scheduled into the same room at the same time during finals week? I reread the final exam schedule and this time saw when our final was *supposed* to have occurred. I realized that the error was mine and that it was a revealing one.

I had mistakenly assumed that my FYW class, a hybrid that met face-to-face on Tuesday but *not* on Thursday, would still be treated as a "Tuesday/Thursday" class for final exam scheduling purposes. Despite everything I thought I knew about effective hybrid course design, I still basically understood my class as a Tuesday/Thursday class that just did not meet face-to-face on Thursdays throughout the term. For some reason, I seemed to have thought of my course as just a variation, maybe even a deficit model, of face-to-face instruction since it "skipped" a part of its physical meeting time every week. The result was that I instructed the class to meet in the wrong room for the exam.

It is hard to pinpoint exactly where or how this notion arose for me. As for many writing teachers, it may have emerged from a lack of institutional support for hybrid learning, at least in its earliest existence at my campus, in the form of professional development opportunities and cross- or inter-disciplinary conversations. Interestingly, in order to teach a hybrid course at my institution, faculty must complete an administrative form. The first question asks for a descriptive paragraph indicating "the differences between the traditional format offering of this course and the proposed hybrid format" ("Request to Teach Hybrid Delivery Course"). Why did this form not ask simply for a descriptive paragraph about the "proposed hybrid format"? Why was the hybrid positioned immediately as a variant?

While the language on the form may not be ideal, some sort of administrative process for distinguishing the hybrid course certainly was important because it ideally ensured that the course would be identified *as hybrid* in the registration system, enabling students to know (and *choose*) the course setting in advance. Additionally, faculty certainly had to think about course design at some point, and doing so at the outset has its advantages. My point, however, is that the hybrid proposal form positioned the hybrid setting only relative to the traditional, onsite course setting, inviting faculty to think about the hybrid OWC as relational alone. In considering my mistake with the hybrid course's final exam, I simply may have lost sight of the fact that my hybrid OWC could be—even needed to be—understood as in a unique setting and not just relative to an established or implicitly normative instructional setting.

As I have studied hybrid learning and now become its spokesperson for the CCCC OWI Committee (Snart, 2010), I realized that a hybrid is its own unique kind of course. It is not face-to-face learning with a piece missing—not a deficit model. Nor is it a "class and a half," with all the instructional material I normally would present face-to-face, somehow compressed into half the time, in addition to an online component.[1] Similarly, a fully online OWC is not just a digital mirror of the traditional onsite course. Both the hybrid and fully online OWCs are as unique to their electronically mediated environments as they are similar to what many experienced teachers still consider the norm of a brick-and-mortar classroom.

This chapter addresses hybrid (sometimes called *blended*) and fully online educational environments as course settings both in terms of what they share in common and how they differ. *Foundational Practices of Online Writing Instruction* is explicitly about teaching writing in the online setting, which of course is where the hybrid and fully online settings implicitly are most alike. The hybrid OWC, however, is a balance of onsite and online environment and pedagogical strategies in nuanced ways. This chapter therefore gives hybrid OWCs more explicit consideration as a primary way of addressing the similarities and differences. In particular, I emphasize access, seat time, course organization, and course design, especially in terms of engaging students and allowing for both students and instructors to become invested and to see learning, fully online or otherwise, as at least to some degree a personality driven endeavor rather than an isolated, mechanical set of tasks to be completed.

HYBRID AND FULLY-ONLINE OWCS

For the purposes of this book, the term *hybrid* describes an environment where traditional, face-to-face instruction is combined with either distance-based or onsite computer-mediated settings. Sometimes, hybrid courses are conducted through computer-mediation while face-to-face in an onsite computer lab (Hewett, 2013, p. 197; see also Chapter 1). This definition of hybrid course settings allows for the wide variety of ways in which instructional settings can be combined in the hybrid format. A *fully online* course setting describes classes with no onsite, face-to-face components. It occurs completely "online and at-a-distance through an Internet or an intranet"; students can connect to the course from short distances such as the campus or longer geographic distances such as across national or international borders (p. 196). When inclusivity and equitable access are factored into the equation, fully online instruction may make use of—while not requiring—alternative communicative venues such as the phone or onsite conferences (when geographically possible and amenable to both student and teacher).

I often hear from colleagues that institutions considering moving their curricula online will envision a face-to-face course that might become a hybrid class that might then become a fully online class. Although each of these courses will share something in common given that they ostensibly cover the same material, to imagine instructional settings as mere variations of one another is unlikely to produce either good hybrid or good fully online OWCs. Scott Warnock (2009) noted that some teachers may be able to "view [their] move into the online teaching environment as a progression that will begin with teaching a hybrid first" (p. 12). Yet, even though hybrid instruction may appear to be a middle ground or even a step between tradition and fully online instruction, such a perspective misses the nuances and challenges of hybrid learning for OWI as well as the need to design both hybrid and fully online OWCs with the instructional setting in mind from the ground up.

Finally, because hybrid and fully online OWI already occur in higher education, their potentially effective practices need to be addressed. In other words, this chapter will not debate the merits of hybrid and fully online OWI in terms of whether they should or should not exist at all. To be sure, this debate is hardly settled; a 2013 *Inside Higher Ed* survey of faculty attitudes toward online learning indicated that fewer than half of those surveyed believe that online courses are as effective as face-to-face courses (Lederman & Jaschik, 2013). Nonetheless, to debate the value of instructional settings that already are a mainstay at many institutions does not seem productive, as the CCCC OWI Committee observed in *The State of the Art of OWI* (CCCC OWI Committee, 2011c, p. 2).

SIMILARITIES BETWEEN HYBRID AND FULLY ONLINE OWCS

Hybrid and fully online OWCs are similar in that they both involve instructional time mediated by technology. Even though a hybrid OWC meets at least part of the time in a traditional face-to-face setting, it uses the electronic environment for similar activities and teaching purposes. In both settings, the computer or other devices are used for such activities as:

- Word processing
- Paper submission and reposting to the student
- Peer review activities
- Discussion forums
- Journal and other writing
- One-to-one and one-to-group/class communications such as instant messages, email, and message board[2] postings
- Wiki/collaborative writing development

Chapter 4 particularly enumerates some of these activities as pedagogical strategies for writing instruction.

In the fully online setting, which remains new to many students and teachers, activities typically occur asynchronously, making time one of the key distinctions of fully online OWCs from both hybrid and traditional learning (see Chapter 3 for a discussion of asychronicity and synchronicity). Both teachers and students need to learn to use the technology for activities that they previously have experienced as synchronous, oral, and aural. Thus, writing becomes a way of speaking and reading a way of listening (Hewett, 2010, 2015a, 2015b), which means that the literacy load increases exponentially (Griffin & Minter, 2013; Hewett, 2015a) leading potentially to stronger writing skills through sheer amount of text as well as focused communicative effort and, of course, attempting to meet course goals (Barker & Kemp, 1990; Palmquist, 1993). In a hybrid setting, on the other hand, some unique concerns arise—consequently, my focus on the differences among hybrid, fully online, and face-to-face learning in this chapter. Many of the issues that arise for hybrid learning are pertinent to fully online OWCs, but hybrid OWI also involves a balance with traditional writing instruction that fully online instruction does not.

DIFFERENCES BETWEEN HYBRID AND FULLY ONLINE OWCS

The primary difference between hybrid and fully online OWCs, at least in their most basic forms, is the degree of physical face-time, or seat time, involved (see Table 2.1).

Table 2.1. Primary differences between hybrid and fully online OWCs

Hybrid Writing Course	Fully Online Writing Course
Some face-to-face classroom interaction	No face-to-face classroom interaction
Some distance-based online learning as determined by institutional needs	Completely distance-based online learning

This distinction of face-time may seem elementary, but it is essential. Educators need to understand hybrid and fully online course settings as unique because, from a design perspective, no instructional setting should be understood as so much a *version* or *variation* of another that the job of the instructional designer or teacher is simply to migrate learning materials from one setting to the other. Indeed, given the potential dilemma of trying to see instructional settings as both deeply related but necessarily unique, two key OWI principles should be coordinated. OWI Principle 3 stated that "appropriate composition teaching/learning strategies should be developed for the unique features of the online instructional environment" (CCCC OWI Committee, 2013, p. 12). OWI Principle 4, on the other hand—and seemingly contradictorily—indicated that "appropriate onsite composition theories, pedagogies, and strategies should be migrated and adapted to the online instructional environment" (p. 14). As Chapter 1 revealed, there remains a need to develop strategies and theories unique to the online setting while using the most appropriate of current strategies developed from traditional, onsite learning.

Migration is a pedagogical approach that OWI Principle 4 acknowledges and that Warnock (2009) advocated, yet migration alone may lead to poorly designed courses and low teacher and student satisfaction. The notion of adaptation is crucial to understanding the practicality behind OWI Principle 4. Even where basic pedagogies can be *applied* across instructional settings, they invariably will need to be *adapted* to suit the new context. Migration of strategies and theories to either online setting necessitates adaptation because it ultimately requires that the learning strategy or pedagogy be reimagined relative to what is happening in a course as a whole. Although it may seem counterintuitive, such is especially true for hybrid instruction, where onsite composition strategies are transferred from the fully face-to-face instructional setting to one that includes an onsite, face-to-face component but has an equally important online component. In other words, just because a teaching strategy from an onsite, face-to-face class is migrated into the face-to-face portion of a hybrid class does not mean that that strategy will function equivalently in both settings. That teaching strategy will bear a new relationship to what is going on around it.

For example, I have often used a peer group technique in my fully onsite composition classes in which students work in teams of three or four to develop a set of relevant questions about a text we are reading. Although I transferred this technique into my hybrid writing class, it exists differently in that setting. In the fully onsite context, the questions that the students develop are then posed orally, in real-time, to other student teams in the class. Oral discussion continues as we narrow our set of questions to one or two key approaches for writing about what we have read. In the hybrid setting, students take their group questions from the oral portion of the class and then post them to their online discussion board. All students then evaluate and respond to each group's questions using writing. It is not until a later face-to-face class period that we return orally to the initial questions that students developed in class *and* the response material that has been generated online. Thus, the initial group activity exists in both the face-to-face and hybrid iterations of the writing class, but it exists *differently* because of how it interacts with other environmental elements in the course. Transferring the same activity to a fully online course typically means that no oral discussion occurs, making all discussion about the readings text-based, with the activity occurring perhaps in two separate discussion forums. Students become responsible for listening to their classmates through reading their remarks and then for talking through written responses; the process can lead to thoughtful discussions if well handled (Warnock, 2009), but the give-and-take of the discussions differs considerably from that of the oral ones (Hewett, 2004-2005). That said, because an LMS might offer synchronous conferencing, it is possible (yet likely uncommon) to return some of the traditional oral discussion to the process.

One practical difference regarding how this activity functions concerns the quality of the developed questions. Because students in the hybrid writing course ultimately post their questions in text to a discussion board, those questions tend to be more refined and focused relative to what is generated and then shared immediately in their real-time, face-to-face setting—the setting that they have in common with onsite courses. The quality of these initial questions has implications for how students' writing process unfolds, since those in the hybrid setting tend to start writing with questions that already are somewhat refined and focused, as they might be in the fully online setting as well. In the fully onsite setting, to achieve a similar quality of initial questions, one must build writing time into the class meetings such that students can work textually, rather than just orally, to refine the questions generated in the initial inquiry period.

With this sense of migration as necessitating adaptation, educators can see both the hybrid and fully online OWI settings as unique from the traditional onsite one rather than as distortions of other instructional settings, transitional steps from one setting to another, or somehow as lesser relatives of an imagined norm. But even as unique instructional settings, both hybrid and fully online OWI share the same need for grounding in solid pedagogy and effective practice, and in both cases educators will need to provide opportunities for student engagement and success.

Therefore, while certain onsite, face-to-face teaching and learning strategies naturally will find their way into hybrid and fully online OWCs, OWI Principle 3 requires consideration (p. 12) as described in Chapter 1. New strategies may require new theory to explain why and how they can work effectively in online settings. Such strategies may include teaching students using a combination of text and audio/video media and providing text in visually appealing (hence, more readable) ways.

Ultimately, some obvious differences between these two technologically enhanced teaching settings notwithstanding, they share the need to be grounded in effective pedagogical practices, as described in the OWI principles. Furthermore, regardless of instructional setting, faculty need to be supported by their institutions when working in either course setting. What makes for a successful learning experience is not the technology or any particular personality type working within a given setting, but rather accessible tools to engage students' creativity and ingenuity and to help them realize an intellectual and emotional presence in the learning environment, digital or otherwise.

NUANCES THAT DEFINE INSTRUCTIONAL SETTING

INSTITUTIONAL DEFINITIONS

There can be many variables at work in defining the parameters of hybrid and fully online OWCs, such that the relatively straightforward comparison presented in Table 2.1 quickly becomes more nuanced with each variation presenting new implications for design and teaching. For example, in some cases, institutions might require limited onsite meeting times in what they *call* fully online instruction to meet institutional desires or perceived needs. Students might be required to take major tests or complete timed writing assignments in a proctored environment, be it a campus testing center or other designated testing site, for example. This scenario begs the question of exactly what is a fully online setting, while it illustrates how policies designed for all online instruction may not be universally applied and in some cases may be detrimental to the ways that courses in certain disciplinary material, like OWI, can be taught.

Many institutions have developed course classification guidelines such that a course that is entirely distance-based is defined as fully online (although as indicated earlier, in certain cases this setting might still require physical trips to campus, belying its classification as *fully online*). In the case of hybrid OWCs, there always will be both a physical classroom component and an online component, but the exact ways in which these two instructional settings are combined is dependent on individual instructor choices and on institutional requirements that mandate a minimum or maximum time for one instructional setting relative to the other. A course that is predominantly face-to-face, but trades some limited seat time for online work may be called Web-enhanced (or another equivalent term), yet its needs are similar to the hybrid course.

There being no single definition, the hybrid OWC appears to be the most nuanced in terms of how it is defined and structured within various institutions. One institution's hybrid course description read, "You will periodically meet on campus for face-to-face course sessions with your instructors" (Kirtland Community College, 2014). For another institution, the hybrid OWC was defined a little more specifically: "at least 30% of the course content is delivered through the Internet" (Ozarks Technical Community College, 2014). The "Hybrid Courses" website for the College of DuPage (2013) indicated that "hybrid courses integrate 50 percent classroom instruction with 50 percent online learning." Unfortunately, even this description is not exact, as anybody who teaches a Monday/Wednesday/Friday class in the hybrid format will realize, since that type of class is unlikely to split classroom and online time fifty-fifty each week. The Sloan Consortium defined a "blended" course—another term for the hybrid course—as one for which the online component comprises from 30% to 79% of a course (Allen, Seaman, & Garrett, 2010). Each of these definitions leads to a somewhat different course setting where the oral and written features of the course play out differently and uniquely.

With increasingly accessible and usable technological affordances available to higher education, there has grown a new diversity of instructional settings that can be bundled within one course. There are fully online classes during which students experience no physical face-to-face time with peers or their instructors. Sometimes, though, fully online classes can involve a portion of class time that is conducted online synchronously, so there is face-time but instead of being physical, it is virtual. Such a synchronous online meeting requires that everyone be able to attend the course at the same time and day of the week; it must be so listed in the registration guide. Alternately, classes might be conducted entirely face-to-face onsite while also meeting in a computer lab such that while all class participants are physically together, in real-time, the class work occurs largely at the computer: students write, research, or collaborate digitally, all while synchronously, physically present. Still other classes might involve a mix of face-to-face time in a classroom with computer lab time. And, in so-called traditional classrooms, students may be asked to work with and present to peers using the enhanced technology of networked, digital tools. Finally, as Chapter 16 explains, mobile learning, which involves the use of handheld networked devices like smartphones, is becoming a feasible reality in some instructional settings, which means that teachers need to be aware of the kinds of hardware on which students might be learning.[3] It is hard to imagine what else might be on the horizon when it comes to technology and teaching.

Realistically, higher education institutions probably will not come to agreement on precise definitions for various course settings. On a practical level, overly standardized course setting definitions might cause institutions to lose the ability to adapt course settings to their own unique needs. However, defining course type clearly matters on several levels. Students who take classes at various institutions would benefit from knowing whether a hybrid class at one campus is roughly the same as a hybrid at another campus from which they might select a course. Additionally, broadly standardized definitions may help policy-making organizations across higher education speak to each other and to their member constituents in consistent ways. Ideally, some level of standardization will happen at the institutional level as individual campuses develop and refine their unique approaches to instructional design and delivery. Such standardization would enable local faculty, who have direct contact with a particular body of students, to have a voice at the table.

Perhaps most important regarding course setting definitions, students should be provided with as much information as possible about what a hybrid or fully online writing class might entail before registering, which means that academic advisors and counselors need to be fully versed in what these course types involve. Student preparedness for any online setting is, according to OWI Principle 10, an institutional responsibility primarily (p. 21). To this end, students should be informed about course setting and its requirements as part of the registration process. Many registration systems provide students with boiler plate language describing a hybrid course as involving some face-time and some online time but offer no further specifics. Therefore, a student might register for three separate hybrid courses, each of which coordinates onsite and online instruction differently, and each of which requires adjustments in the student's schedule and work habits. Setting student expectations accurately and appropriately is one way to help them avoid potentially unnecessary attrition or failure.

ACCESS ISSUES

Access concerns also play out in OWI with respect to how an OWC is defined institutionally, making OWI Principle 1, which calls for inclusivity and accessibility (p. 7), relevant to course description. Take the aforementioned *fully online* course that requires any kind of onsite meetings. In the strictest sense of the OWI environment, requiring onsite meetings means that the learning no longer is fully online, and using this terminology not only may confuse students and teachers but likely will limit access to some. For example, generally it would be impossible for a geographically distributed student in Colorado to attend a meeting at a Virginia institution in which she is enrolled as an online student. An accessible OWC would not ask such travel of its students. However, Texas is one state with state-mandated definitions for instructional settings, and it defined a "fully distance education course" as, "A course which may have mandatory face-to-face sessions totaling no more than 15 percent of the instructional time. Examples of face-to-face sessions include orientation, laboratory, exam review, or an in-person test" (Texas Administrative Code, 2010, RULE §4.257). Anecdotally, I have seen another interesting case occurring in Speech Communications. Since the majority of a student's grade is based on speeches delivered to the class, some programs have instituted a requirement that students taking a fully online class must be prepared to come to campus periodically throughout the term in order to speak in real-time in front of a live audience; it is easy to imagine similar scenarios with Technical Communication, multimodal writing, and even some FYW courses. Having online students record themselves speaking and then supplying that file to an instructor presents a number of difficulties, not least being how to manage large video files. In any case, when fully online classes are defined in this manner, they are neither one-hundred percent online nor fully accessible, which detracts significantly from the nature and benefits of a fully online course.

Transparent advertising of the kind described above also is a basic access issue. If students know that a particular course setting will require a certain amount of virtual and physical time in a classroom relative to time online courses, they can discern, self-disclose, and indicate necessary accommodations. Furthermore, with a good understanding of the learning settings available to them, students can make informed decisions about which instructional setting best suits their needs and abilities. Their decisions can help them to self-place into appropriate course sections that take advantage of useful onsite and online affordances. Without institutionally standardized language that defines various course settings, advertising to students becomes difficult and many will find themselves in classes that are not suited to their needs or abilities. I am frankly and consistently surprised to discover how many students arrive to my hybrid writing classes not knowing that the class is a hybrid and/or not knowing what that term means generally or for their writing work specifically.

In other cases, despite what the CCCC OWI Committee's effective practices research indicates, some institutions may not have fully developed student resources that are available *online*, including writing center/tutor (OWL), library, or IT support. So students might enroll in a fully online OWC, but if they need additional instructional or research support, or if they have basic IT issues, a trip to campus might be required. Such a campus visit can be impossible for some students; a lack of online support limits reasonable access to such resources as suggested by OWI Principle 13 (p. 26). Note that OWI Principle 13 emphasized digital access as *primary* for online learners as opposed to being merely an adjunct to it. How "online" is an online course for which most of the student support is only available onsite at a campus setting?

Table 2.2. Instructional settings, modality, and components

Instructional Setting	Synchronous	Asynchronous	Online Component	Face-to-face Component
Onsite	Yes	Maybe	Maybe	Yes
Fully Online	Maybe	Yes	Yes	Maybe
Hybrid	Yes	Maybe	Yes	Yes
Web-enhanced	Yes	Maybe	Yes	Yes

Table 2.2 illustrates the types of learning that might happen through digital tools in different instructional settings. These varied tools have ramifications for the socioeconomically challenged, for example. Given how education, and particularly writing instruction, has become increasingly technologized, the degree to which students have equal technology access also is diversified. *A Position Statement of Principles and Example Effective Practices for OWI* indicated that "learning challenges related to socioeconomic issues (i.e., often called the digital divide where access is the primary issue) must be addressed in an OWI environment to the maximum degree" (p. 7). To this end, while I note differences and similarities between hybrid and fully online OWI throughout this chapter, all students should have equitable access to learning resources regardless of instructional setting; therefore, students' learning needs, preferences, and general access

should inform decisions between hybrid and fully online course settings.

Furthermore, educators always must ask the costs of such necessary resources. Literally, what is their cost? The New Media Consortium's *Horizon Report* (2013) noted, for example, that "Tablets have gained traction in education because users can seamlessly load sets of apps and content of their choosing, making the tablet itself a portable personalized learning environment" (p. 15). Who buys the tablet? Who pays for the apps? Who provides the broadband Internet connection? And who buys the new tablet three years later when the old one is out of date? Indeed, while the digital divide might be shrinking, it has not disappeared. A recent Pew Research Center report (Zickhur, 2012) indicated that "While increased Internet adoption and the rise of mobile connectivity have reduced many gaps in technology access over the past decade, for some groups digital disparities still remain" (p. 1). Therefore, when thinking about questions of technology and the role it plays in effective hybrid and fully online writing instruction, we should not lose sight of educational equity and access to resources. This one aspect of instructional design and delivery perhaps unites *all* instructional settings.

Instructional Place and Time

Consider also the effect that digital student support availability has on instructional design. For example, if there is little-to-no research support offered online, to what degree can certain kinds of research or digital literacy projects be included in a fully online OWC? Or, when those types of assignments are included (since they are fundamental to many writing courses), how might lack of fully online support services negatively affect those students who need such support? Relative to OWI Principle 1, at-risk students or those in need of learning or technology accommodations are even more challenged in these cases (p. 7). Therefore, the assumption that a fully online course unfolds equally for all students and that it does so entirely online does not always bear out, which requires WPAs to consider its institution's resources and ability to support a fully online OWC before signing up its first teachers and advertising it to students.

Table 2.3 illustrates this challenge by presenting a range of contractually defined course types in terms of instructional setting for the College of DuPage, a two-year institution. From an instructional standpoint, teachers of writing need such information to make important decisions about how to manage class time and, in cases where multiple instructional settings are available for one course, about what activities might work best in what setting. Conceivably, a writing teacher could face a semester teaching just one course like FYW but be assigned a full load of four FYW classes in the form of one hybrid, one fully online, one onsite, and one Web-enhanced class. This undesirable situation is possible particularly for contingent faculty who teach at more than one institution (see Chapter 7), and it deeply affects the preparation and performance of teachers (and, subsequently, their students) faced with these differing settings.

Table 2.3. Course types defined by instructional setting(s) at the College of DuPage

Course type	Instructional setting(s)
Onsite	Instruction is entirely classroom-based
Fully Online	Instruction is entirely distance-based
Hybrid	Instruction is *at least* fifty percent classroom-based
Web-enhanced	Instruction is *at least* ninety percent classroom-based

In this example, despite the common FYW course, materials, and desired outcomes, the four different settings lead essentially to four course preparations—even though this situation would purport to protect teachers from an onerous number of separate course preparations. Consider the effect this variety of instructional settings has on faculty working conditions. For example, my contract stipulates that "class preparations for Faculty will normally be limited to three (3)" (College of DuPage, 2012). Notice that this preparation limitation is framed in terms of a "class," but with no acknowledgment of instructional setting. So my English composition hybrid, English composition fully online, and English composition in the onsite classroom are all counted as *one* preparation. This unrealistic understanding of my job presents both challenge and disincentive for those who wish to teach writing in a variety of course settings where the material is delivered and addressed differently. In fact, as an extension of OWI Principle 8, which argues that "online writing teachers should receive fair and equitable compensation for their work" (p. 19), I would add that part of a fair and equitable working environment should include institutional recognition that a single class, taught in a variety of environments and/or formats must be designed, taught, and managed—or prepped—differently.

OPPORTUNITIES AND CHALLENGES OF OWI SETTINGS

My early thinking about hybrids, as suggested in the anecdote that begins this chapter, revealed my sense, and maybe my institution's sense, of hybrid OWI as being somehow an alternative or distorted version of the traditional instructional setting. This distortion colored how I initially designed a hybrid OWC. Perhaps I unconsciously assumed that I should think in terms of a face-to-face course that fit instruction into one day a week, instead of the traditional two, and then *supplemented* that face-to-face work with online material, ancillary to the "real" work we did in the classroom. The result is that I probably did not integrate well the various instructional settings involved in a hybrid OWC and failed to position them as equals. Jay Caulfield (2011), a teacher of educational psychology, admitted something similar in *How to Design and Teach A Hybrid Course*: "For me, integrating the in-class and out-of-class teaching and learning activities ... was the toughest to learn. Sometimes I still don't get it right, yet I know it is an essential component of effective hybrid teaching" (p. 62).

I first began designing and teaching hybrids in 2007. While I think my earliest hybrid OWCs worked well, I simply was not able to see the hybrid setting in any way but relational to an onsite course, which may be the most common perspective. The final exam scheduling snafu that I described at the beginning of this chapter is an example of the degree to which I had not yet fully understood a hybrid course as existing as its own legitimate instructional setting. It also illustrates how my understanding did not necessarily align with administrative understandings of the hybrid setting. Indeed, neither was my thinking necessarily coordinated in any meaningful way with any other instructors who were designing and teaching hybrids.[4] We may have talked about such things casually and informally in hallway conversation, but there was no institutional mechanism to enable teachers who taught in the hybrid setting to meet and share challenges and successes.

Honoring the uniqueness of instructional settings is crucial to successfully teaching both hybrid and fully online OWCs, and in this way they are similar: Neither should be understood as an altered or deficit version of some other instructional setting, even though onsite instruction seems continually to be upheld as the standard of instruction and the normative measure to which all other instructional settings should be compared and to which all other instructional settings should aspire. Consider how often success, retention, and persistence rates are compared across instructional settings, often with fully online instruction on the low end of these measures. Such apples-to-oranges comparisons miss the important point that individual instructional settings come with their own unique opportunities and challenges. Furthermore, the conditions under which students register for classes can be vastly different depending on instructional setting. In many cases, for example, the student who would not otherwise have time to take an onsite class may register for that course online. In fact, students who might not have seen themselves as college students or who are unprepared for college work might take a fully online OWC, believing it to be easier than the onsite version of the course. This situation can be a recipe for student failure regardless of the quality and robustness of the course itself.

UNIQUE CONSIDERATIONS OF HYBRID OWI

INTEGRATION AND HYBRID OWI

Although this chapter focuses on the overall design and teaching challenges and opportunities shared by both hybrid and fully online writing instruction, one aspect of building a hybrid writing course is unique: integrating the face-to-face and online instructional settings. I use it here as an example of designing course time with OWI students to help readers understand the exigencies of developing hybrid *and* fully online courses. Aycock et al. (2012) asserted that "integration is the most important aspect of course re-design and because integration can be difficult and easily overlooked it is an aspect of course re-design that is often taken much too lightly."

In a hybrid course particularly, focus on integration needs to be intentional and persistent, from the earliest design efforts to enacting daily teaching activities. Particularly challenging might be students' (mis)understanding about how the hybrid setting operates, which is connected to the pervasive transactional language that surrounds hybrid course definitions and descriptions and that often works against instructors who are trying to clarify for students precisely what the hybrid setting entails. In other words, a hybrid often is defined as a course type that trades, replaces, or exchanges one instructional setting for another. For example, the University of Wisconsin at Milwaukee Hybrid Learning website (2013) reads, "'Hybrid' or 'Blended' are names commonly used to describe courses in which some traditional face-to-face 'seat time' has been replaced by online learning activities." Other institutional Web pages have used even more explicitly transactional language, as in this example from Aiken Technical College (2014): "A hybrid class trades about 50% of its traditional campus contact hours for online work."[5]

The College of DuPage (2013) provided a preferable definition in that it is less transactional: "Hybrid courses integrate 50 percent classroom instruction with 50 percent online learning." Even though this definition is too narrow—because, as noted earlier, some hybrids will not divide instructional time in a fifty-fifty split—it does focus productively on integration of instructional settings, rather than exchangeability between them. Even so, students in my hybrid classes often ask whether we trade classroom time for online time such that the online work must be done on Friday, in a fifty-minute block, or whenever the onsite meeting otherwise would occur. Students typically need help understanding that this block of learning time is integrated into a weekly plan and that it occurs online, perhaps distributed in chunks throughout the week. Furthermore, students and instructors alike are challenged by thinking in terms of learning *time*, as though each week we need to do activities online that would equate in some precise way with the amount of time we would otherwise be in the classroom. Indeed, this challenge is increased in the fully online setting where typically the instruction occurs asynchronously and no specific time is allotted to face-to-face meetings (see Chapter 3).

The transactional language surrounding hybrids probably persists because on some level instructors *do* need to imagine roughly how much work should occur online so that a three credit course remains a three credit course whether it exists in the hybrid or fully face-to-face instructional setting. The danger of adding too much or too little work outside of the face-to-face meeting exists. Beyond this need, any sense of a hybrid as a course type that trades instructional time in one setting for another can paint the wrong picture of how the hybrid actually works, as if a precise trade of fifty minutes per week of face-time for online time should lead to an equal, discrete, fifty-minute activity regardless of course setting.

PEDAGOGY AND HYBRID OWI

Consider this example of a straightforward hybrid OWC: A fifty-minute, onsite writing class at University X meets Monday, Wednesday, and Friday. The equivalent hybrid OWC meets Monday and Wednesday in the traditional classroom. The Friday session has various possibilities for instructional time. For instance, it could meet in a computer classroom where the teacher and students see each other face-to-face but use the computer terminals. Or, the hybrid nature of the OWC means that the Friday time might be integrated as online learning for which students complete the work independently. In either case, the setting should be the same weekly so students can build the course structure into their schedules, keeping them on track. The CCCC OWI Committee's *The State of the Art of OWI* (2011c) indicated that time management is one of OWI students' greatest challenges (p. 10). I stress to students that they should begin from week one to organize their schedules and make allowance for sufficient time to complete online work (which likely will need more than the fifty minutes they see in the onsite class trade-off), in the same way that they block out time for when they have to attend class in person. In fact, students taking fully online classes should be encouraged similarly to block out time specifically for course work, rather than letting it slide to the bottom of the to-do list, to be completed when "everything else" is done.

Although a weekly hybrid arrangement has some benefits, it is by no means the only way to effectively organize learning time in the hybrid format. In some cases, instructors might find it beneficial, and in keeping with their personal teaching style and pedagogy, to meet face-to-face for longer periods during the course—multiple weeks in a row, for example—and then to transition to a longer phase of online time. This arrangement might work particularly well if one is looking to integrate online writing conferences into a course. As Hewett (2010) stated in *The Online Writing Conference*, "the one-to-one online conference is an increasingly popular, vital, and viable way to teach writing" (p. xxii). Conducting such conferences online, rather than as part of the face-to-face component of a hybrid course, helps to keep the dialogue between instructor and student grounded in textual communication—a key component of the writing course itself.[6] It also affords students the opportunity to manage their time more flexibly, rather than being locked into blocks of onsite seat time. As writing instructors, we may find that we need more time with students and their writing individually rather than in the group classroom setting, especially as writing students take concepts and strategies we have introduced in the classroom and begin to apply them to produce their own, individual texts.

In relatively short order, the straightforward weekly division of hybrid learning time can morph into any number of forms. Is there a guiding principle regarding how much of a writing course should be conducted onsite and how much should be online and for how long at a stretch in each instructional setting? In a general sense, OWI Principle 5 provides important direction: Writing instructors "should retain reasonable control over their own content and/or techniques for conveying, teaching, and assessing their students' writing in their OWCs" (p. 15). In the case of teaching a hybrid OWC, OWI Principle 5 suggested that the instructor should be making decisions about how to best arrange instructional time. The hybrid design should *not* be automated by some kind of institutional scheduling system in an effort to maximize classroom space usage or haphazardly designed by a department chair or WPA who does not have a developed understanding of OWI and hybrid learning, in particular.

However, institutions may seek overly simplistic efficiencies by trying to capitalize on the hybrid learning model. Administrators may, for example, take two hybrid classes that in their fully onsite formats would meet twice per week, and pair them in a single classroom: Class A meets onsite Tuesday but not Thursday, while class B meets onsite Thursday but not Tuesday. This kind of administrative control over how a hybrid operates serves neither instructors nor students, nor am I convinced that efficiencies of this kind could ever be achieved on a scale that would have any measurable impact campus-wide. The degree to which faculty must give over curricular design to a centralized scheduling system in this scenario ultimately is unacceptable, particularly in terms of course goals and pedagogical strategies for meeting those goals. There is no one "right" division of learning time in the hybrid setting since an ideal arrangement for one instructor may not be ideal for another. Actually, the impact of hybrid design on student success is an area of much needed OWI-based composition research (see Chapter 17). But in keeping with OWI Principle 5 (p. 15), arranging instructional time should be within the instructor's curricular control, and as such can reflect his or her individual teaching style, personality, and pedagogical approaches.

Instructors wanting to explore how a hybrid writing course can be configured to best serve the students, however, probably will have to navigate a number of institutional constraints that potentially include mandates about exactly how a hybrid class must divide its time. Further, the instructor may have to sell the idea of a hybrid that does not divide its time on a weekly basis, in which case I advise presenting one's case with particular reference to established, disciplinary effective practice where or if those practices exist. In many ways, *A Position Statement of Principles and Example Effective Practices for OWI* (CCCC OWI Committee, 2013), which is this book's genesis, provides an ideal framework within which to situate individual teaching strategies.

Take the case of a faculty member who notices that in dividing her class time on a weekly basis, students are losing connection with their writing as process or they are responsible for returning to their online writing work without having accomplished much in a single weekly classroom session. Her students would seem to benefit from an extended set of classroom meetings to learn writing strategies in a real-time, onsite setting that allows for immediate interaction with peers and with the instructor. Then, having learned some strategies for invention and organization, an extended period of individualized online conferencing might seem most beneficial such that each student can apply material learned from those classroom meetings to produce a polished piece of writing. Conferencing online provides both teacher and student the opportunity to talk about the student's writing *in writing*, which can help students to clarify challenges they are facing as they express those challenges in writing rather than verbally (Hewett 2015b, 2010). A particular benefit of moving the learning online at this point in a writing course is that instruction can become much more adaptive and individualized since the instructor is no longer trying to deal with all her students as a group in the onsite setting. Rather, instruction can become much more specific to each student's needs. In this example, therefore, the instructional time for one-to-three weeks might be onsite and face-to-face. Then, the writing course would occur in a distance-based, online format for an equal period, featuring some or all of the following: asynchronous and/or synchronous online writing conferencing, online peer revision exchanges, and asynchronous instructor feedback on student drafts as they unfold.

Now let us extend this theoretical hybrid writing class design so that the week of onsite face-to-face meetings becomes a month or even two. Perhaps the hybrid writing class would meet every Tuesday and Thursday for the first half of a semester, just as a fully onsite writing course would (thus, requiring available classrooms and seats for this configuration). Then, perhaps all the work would be integrated to an online setting for the last half of the semester. This configuration still represents a 50% face-to-face/online split, adhering to at least the letter of the contractual law at the College of DuPage, for example. But will such a hybrid arrangement be supported by the administration? In most cases, this creative course design would be a hard sell in terms of seat space alone, but also in those cases where administrators are skeptical of (even resistant to) what are perceived to be "alternative" instructional settings. Like it or not, it will be incumbent on the teaching faculty member to establish sound pedagogy as the basis for dividing onsite and online time in the hybrid setting.

Perhaps, ultimately, OWI Principle 6 provides the guiding principle here, at least from the instructional perspective: "Alternative, self-paced, or experimental OWI models should be subject to the same principles of pedagogical soundness, teacher/designer preparation, and oversight detailed" in the position statement document (pp. 16-17). While hybrid writing instruction should not be understood as experimental or alternative, certain instructional designs that coordinate online and face-to-face time in seemingly unconventional ways are likely to be *perceived* as experimental or alternative. To that end, in Chapter 1, Hewett explains that experimental OWI models especially need to be developed and grounded by principles of rhetoric and composition. The instructor who wants to be creative with hybrid writing course design may have to demonstrate to administrators the sound pedagogy behind the design. But if the pedagogy is sound, *A Position Statement of Principles and Example Effective Practices for OWI* (CCCC OWI Committee, 2013) supports the assertion that hybrid writing instruction could take a number of successful forms.

DESIGNING HYBRID AND FULLY ONLINE OWI

THE SPECIAL NEED FOR ORGANIZATION IN OWI

Although effective organization of writing course content, assignments, grading—everything that goes into teaching writing in any setting—is important when teaching fully face-to-face, something about the regularity of the onsite meetings helps to make an onsite course feel unified and organized even when instructors have made no special design choices in this regard. The onsite instructional setting is probably the most natural for students and teachers in that both teachers and students are most familiar with it, and a potential sense of class continuity may emerge by virtue of that familiarity and the regular face-to-face meetings. A natural sense of organizational structure is not necessarily the case for either hybrid or fully online writing instruction, so the next section focuses on organizational strategies that can help both instructors and students navigate an OWC successfully. It will not surprise readers that a well-organized course is more likely to be effective than a poorly organized course, but such organization is a basic necessity in both fully online and hybrid writing courses. It is not something that will somehow take care of itself in either instructional setting, and developing a well-organized online course requires consciously thoughtful work on the instructor's part.

Organization suggests that course objectives are laid out clearly on the LMS and reiterated (repeated, as Warnock, 2009, and Hewett, 2015a suggested) in a number of website pages throughout a syllabus and the course itself. A course divided into units, modules, or weeks is likely to benefit from having each of those divisions introduced with learning goals, ones clearly linked to general course objectives. Basic organization of this kind (ideally) will help students to understand the *why* of what they are doing and, in turn, provide that important opportunity for intellectual and emotional presence. I have too often heard students complain about what they perceive to be busy-work in classes—including my own. In such cases, typically I learned that I had not made transparent enough the unit goals and how those were linked to course goals. For example, if we were writing paragraphs instead of full essays or creating outlines before starting rough drafts, it might have *felt* like busy-work disconnected from the supposedly real work of writing that was to be the focus of the course because I had not done a good job of connecting those activities to a bigger picture. Thoughtful course organization that includes reiteration of course and unit goals throughout can help give students a sense of why those small-scale activities are important.

Figure 2.1 is a screenshot of what students see in the Blackboard LMS in both my fully online and hybrid writing courses. Course and unit-specific goals help students to understand how pieces of the course are related and how or why materials are organized the way they are.

 Course Objectives and Goals

Upon successful completion of the course the student should be able to do the following:

- Apply a process approach to writing that incorporates independent research
- Develop and support a thesis in an essay incorporating research
- Apply strategies for organizing texts
- Analyze and respond critically and creatively to the ideas and strategies in the writing of others through reading a variety of texts, including academic discourse
- Use discourse appropriate for an academic audience
- Create more advanced, independent research projects and observe the conventions of documentation and citation

Figure 2.1. Course goals articulated in both fully online and hybrid OWI settings

As Figure 2.2 demonstrates, instructional units can be introduced with goals that help to outline what activities will be taking place. These unit-level goals in many cases can be tied back to course goals as a way of making course organization transparent. In other words, student are invited to see how what they do in an individual week, for example, is part of a larger overall structure.

The goals shown in these figures are not groundbreaking nor are they exhaustive for everything that we might cover in a given unit; indeed, some students may not even read them or, upon reading them may not comprehend them sufficiently (Hewett, 2015a). However, these statements provide the basic expected outcomes for the course and, by the end of a given OWC, I hope my students have done a lot more than accomplish the basic course objectives. Making these goals clear and reiterating them for students throughout a fully online or hybrid writing course can help to provide a sense of basic organization and purpose that might be missing for some learners when they are not meeting weekly with the same group of people in an onsite setting. These goals operate as textual reminders of what we are doing and why, whereas in the onsite, face-to-face course, I more likely would provide these reminders verbally in class.

One particular element of organization that is specific to the hybrid OWC is the coordination of the face-to-face and online instructional settings. In both settings, students should feel connected to the course and should feel they are participating in one, unified course whose onsite and online settings are equivalent in importance. In other words, the hybrid writing instructor should avoid giving students the sense that they are in a face-to-face class that is merely supplemented by online materials. Similarly, the hybrid writing instructor should create the course with such organizational unity that students do not feel that they are participating in two related, but ultimately separate, courses: a face-to-face course and a fully online course. Doing so can help prevent students from experiencing such courses as more than the credit-load for which they signed up (i.e., a three-credit course should not seem like a four-credit course just because

 Unit Objectives

In Unit 3 students will:

- analyze how general and specific statements work in essays and body paragraphs

- begin research using the library database system

- complete background reading and quiz on plagiarism

Figure 2.2. Sample unit-level learning goals statement

it is hybrid).

In addition to stating course and unit-level learning goals as clearly and as often as possible, another organizational strategy is to make sure that students understand how the syllabus (which lists weekly course activities and assignments) is coordinated with the course as it exists in the LMS. In my hybrid OWCs that divide time weekly, for example, I label each unit in the course the same way on the syllabus that is intended to be printed and that is designed for online presentation (e.g., "Unit 1 – Introductions"). Within each unit on the syllabus, I list days we will meet onsite and generally which readings or activities we will be doing (without being too exhaustive); additionally, I always include, in line with useful repetition, a reminder of the online component. Figure 2.3 provides a typical example.

Unit 1
Wed, Jan 14 – syllabus, explanations, expectations, and introductions
    - Remind.com|

Online – your Blackboard Homepage; online introductions

Unit 2
Mon, Jan 19 - no class meeting – MLK Jr. Day

Wed, Jan 21 – shape of an essay/paragraph
    - using databases
    - read "Araby"; "Gorilla, My Love"; "Girl"
(this means you have completed these readings prior to class)
    - class photo

Online – using database material

Unit 3
Mon, Jan 26 – read "Cathedral"; "Flight Patterns"
    - Padlet mobile assignment

Wed, Jan 28 - **Essay 1 assigned**
    - MLA citation
    - **sign up for student conferences**

Online – short story discussion

Figure 2.3. Example syllabus showing units and online work in a hybrid OWC

When students then go into the LMS, they know to look for the "Units" area of the course where they will find units that correspond with each of the units identified in the syllabus. Figure 2.4 provides an example. Basic coordination between the course schedule as revealed in the syllabus and the online component of the class helps students to see the two pieces of the class as connected rather than as two distinct endeavors.

Of course, the surface coordination that can be achieved through clear, redundant labeling will be part of a much deeper integration of what is occurring in the classroom and online. The work that students will find within each unit reflects what we have discussed in class. Sometimes the work that students complete online will then feed into what we cover in subsequent onsite meetings, which for fully online courses has to be accomplished digitally as well. For example, in the hybrid course, using student posts to online discussion boards as conversation starters for subsequent face-to-face discussion is an effective approach. Classroom discussion does not have to start from scratch, nor does the instructor have to put forward the first idea. Seeing their online work made present in the classroom also helps students to see the mixed instructional settings of their hybrid class as deeply related. In fact, making virtual discussion into physical and real-time onsite work also helps students to see themselves as members of a class both online and face-to-face.

Coordination between the online and face-to-face components of a hybrid writing course can be demonstrated in many ways. In the end, a hybrid writing

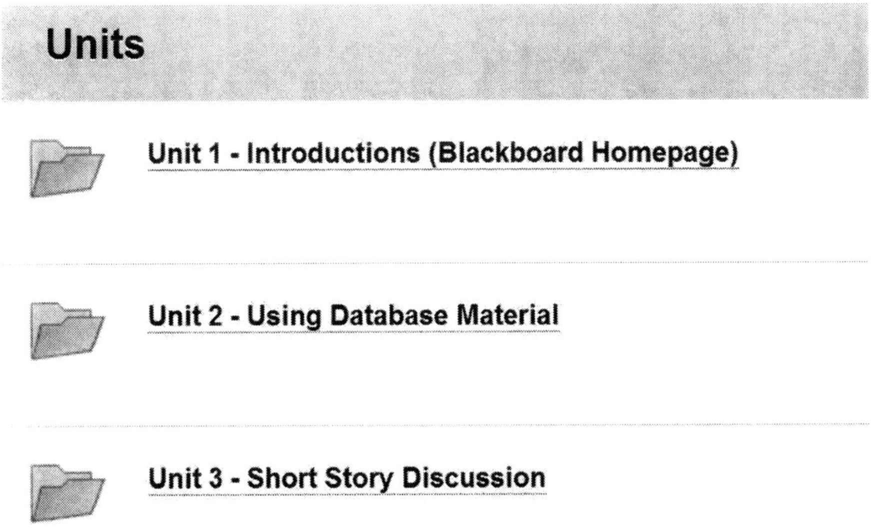

Units

Unit 1 - Introductions (Blackboard Homepage)

Unit 2 - Using Database Material

Unit 3 - Short Story Discussion

Figure 2.4. Example units area in Blackboard for a hybrid OWC

course will, ideally, feel like one learning experience. Through good integration, students will feel as present online as they do onsite.

BUILDING COMMUNITY

The need for social presence is shared by both hybrid and fully online OWI. By social presence, I mean the idea of people in a course together, even if that togetherness is virtual and not physical. Addressing presence means creating opportunities for learner engagement on the intellectual and the emotional levels. In other words, students are challenged, rewarded for creative thinking, and have the opportunity to demonstrate competency in a variety of ways. Furthermore, students need the opportunity to *care* about what is going on in a course. They ideally care about what they are doing but also what others are doing. They, again ideally, believe that they are part of a group of learners engaging in interesting and challenging material and they express a sense of pride in accomplishment. The course *matters* to them.

The term "ideal" is relative since I am talking largely about OWC design. That is, I am focused on what the instructor can control. Teachers can afford opportunities to students who in best-case scenarios will take advantage of them. But for whatever reason, some students will not take advantage of those opportunities or see the value in allowing themselves to be invested—intellectually or emotionally—in any given learning opportunity. These situations are not instructional failures on the part of the teacher (and may not be infrastructural failures of the LMS either). Writing teachers tend to provide well-organized and interesting opportunities for learner engagement and they encourage that engagement, but the teacher's work should not be judged on whether every single student becomes intellectually or emotionally connected to one particular writing course because it is, in all likelihood, an impossibility. Hence, the notion of "ideal" is just that—a generally unreachable goal of perfection.

OWI Principle 11 called for "personalized and interpersonal communities" (p. 23) to foster student success. Experience has shown that successful writing instruction *in both hybrid and fully online learning situations* is most likely to occur when instructors and students are given the opportunity to be present, to realize that both teaching and learning are, as Warnock (2009) asserted, "personality-driven endeavors" (p. 179). In other words, learning writing online (or in the traditional onsite setting, for that matter) should not be a solitary, passive experience. *A Position Statement of Principles and Example Effective Practices for OWI* makes abundantly clear that teachers and students alike need to be supported in the endeavor to make learning to write in the hybrid and fully online formats an engaging, challenging, and ultimately rewarding experience.

Creating opportunities for presence is one of the most important design guidelines for both hybrid and fully online OWI. In addition to scholarly research in this area (see, for example, Picciano, 2001; Savery, 2005; Whithaus & Neff, 2006), ultimately my personal experience as an educator causes me to see presence as crucial across instructional settings. The need for presence is grounded in OWI Principle 11, which stated, "Online writing teachers and their institutions should develop personalized and interpersonal online communities to foster student success" (p. 23).

When instruction shifts to the fully online environment, whether in the context of hybrid and fully online OWI, the learning situation can become isolating and even alienating for some students. It may feel like a correspondence course: each student works individually through material and communicates with a virtual "grader" who remains faceless. Being present as a virtual instructor—whether through photographs, text-based conversation, quirky posts, (Warnock, 2009), or personalized and problem-centered writing conferences and draft feedback (Hewett, 2010, 2015a, 2015b)—is an important part of building overall student engagement and success.

What happens when student and/or instructor presence is lacking in OWI? Every online educator likely knows the answer to this question from experience: Students are less likely to engage; they are prone to participate insufficiently in the course; and, in the worst situations, they lose focus, fall behind and either fail or withdraw. As Julia Stella and Michael Corry (2013) indicated, "Lack of engagement can cause a student to become at risk for failing an online writing course." They cited studies suggesting that "exemplary" online educators are those who challenge learners, affirm and encourage student effort, and who "let students know they care about their progress in the course as well as their personal well-being" (2013) To do any of this, let alone all of it, OWC instructors need to demonstrate presence in consciously purposeful ways. The hope is that when students experience the presence of others in a class with them (virtually or otherwise), they can feel supported in what they are doing.

The CCCC OWI Committee's *The State of the Art of OWI* (2011c) reported that writing teachers generally see writing as both a generative and a social process. One respondent cited in the report said, "My online writing courses are intensely social and collaborative—much more so than my face-to-face writing courses. Students collaborate to produce texts" (p. 22). Educators surveyed for this report also indicated that they viewed the "ability to establish a presence online" as very important (76%) or important (23%), indicating the degree to which OWI practitioners value being present for students (p. 90). These survey respondents were speaking from their experiences and belief systems as OWC instructors. Like them, my consistent experience has been that students who are familiar with each other work better together and are more engaged in what is happening in a class, regardless of whether those students know each other (and know me) online, onsite, or some combination of the two.

GOAL-BASED DESIGN

Effective hybrid and fully online OWC design often means taking what a teacher already does well in a writing class and adapting activities and assignments so that some or all of them occur online. Here is where the notion of migrating content and practices meets the needs for conscious adaptation and change for a different environment. However, as this chapter outlined earlier, the hybrid and fully online settings also present the opportunity to completely re-envision teaching and to start from the ground up, rather than thinking in relational terms alone. An effective approach to hybrid and fully online OWC design that seeks to honor both the uniqueness of the instructional settings while preserving what is already most effective about one's own teaching is to think in terms of course goals and learning objectives: in other words, goal-based design.

Ultimately, both using what is already available and starting fresh can work together. Many instructors can name a classroom activity that seems to work well for them. In such activities, students are engaged. Class time is enjoyable for the instructor. And students produce good writing. But taking that particular classroom activity and trying to migrate it verbatim to the online setting might not be possible or advisable. The onsite and online instructional settings simply are too different in many cases. To take advantage of a good onsite activity, it is necessary to take a step backward and consider what course goal or objective is achieved with it. Does the activity do a good job of getting students to think critically or creatively? Does it get students attuned to nuances of language? Does it get students actively working with sources and evaluating information effectively? These are important course goals in many writing classes.

Once an instructor has a sense of the goals that are being achieved effectively in the onsite setting and of what seems endemic to the activities that foster student success relative to those goals, he or she can begin course design from the ground up. In other words, instructors are not obliged to work from a completely clean slate when it comes to designing a hybrid or fully online OWC, but neither should they try to reconfigure every last classroom activity so that it can exist online.

For example, suppose that an instructor who typically teaches a fully onsite writing course wants to spur students to generate ideas about a text. To achieve this goal, she has her students work in groups for ten minutes at the start of class. In designing a similar activity for the online setting, however, it is difficult—and likely unproductive—to try to duplicate the face-to-face brainstorming activity by including a ten-minute chat-based synchronous session for her online students. First, that amount of time is probably too short a time for students to get situated online and to type meaningful ideas back and forth. Second, if the brainstorming activity includes shifting to synchronous conferencing software, there also is a likely time lag for getting students together; additionally, such software—even if available on the LMS—may introduce potential technical challenges (for both instructor and student) that can inhibit full participation by everybody in class and that may not meet the access needs suggested by OWI Principle 1 (p. 7). Indeed, although I have used Web-conferencing applications successfully in my own courses, their use simply to reproduce as closely as possible what happens in the onsite, face-to-face environment seems more complicated than necessary given what it is likely to achieve.

Instead, while the goal of having her students brainstorm together remains, the teacher would do well to change the activity. For example, students could be asked to collaborate through an asynchronous discussion board or a group Wiki located within the LMS. When multiplied across the various activities that are developed for a writing course, the goal-based design approach likely will produce an online course that looks drastically different from an onsite, face-to-face course—despite the fact that they share common basic learning goals.

Aycock et al. (2008) suggested that "performative learning activities may be best face-to-face" and "discursive learning activities may be best online" (p. 26). Similarly, instructors might find in the case of hybrid writing course design, as opposed to the fully online setting, that they ultimately think about which activities work best online and which work best face-to-face. Here, "best" can be quite subjective. Depending on a teacher's disposition and teaching style, he or she might believe that discussion is a good face-to-face activity that benefits from the dynamic, real-time give-and-take of classroom presence and non-verbal cues to engage students' interest. By the same token, much can be said for discussion enabled online, either asynchronously or synchronously. Especially with asynchronous discussion, students who might not otherwise be eager to participate in the face-to-face environment may be more at ease joining in, not to mention that the instructor can see readily who has participated and who has not, which can enable the teacher to draw out the students who fail to participate for whatever reasons. Additionally, asynchronous communication opportunities allow students to discuss ideas informally among themselves, but, unlike an informal oral discussion, students can reflect first about their contributions. They can write, edit, revise, delete, and post, taking more time than would ever be feasible in a real-time, oral situation.

If there is any conventional lore-like wisdom regarding hybrid course design in particular, it is probably that writing-based activities occur best online and that discussion-based activities occur best face-to-face. I would like to challenge this wisdom, however, not necessarily by claiming the reverse, but by emphasizing that instructors can vary which activities they use in any instructional setting. Variety is more useful than overly prescriptive approaches that dictate that *all* activities of one kind or another *always* must occur in a given instructional setting. To that end, thinking in terms of goals to be achieved is an important step away from the sense that the job of the educator in the fully online and hybrid settings is somehow to duplicate, however imprecisely, exactly what occurs in onsite teaching.

OWI SETTINGS ARE NOT ABOUT THE TECHNOLOGY

As described above, goal-based design asks writing instructors to take a broad view of their teaching, and it inevitably leads to specific questions about the technology involved. If instructors are not somehow trying to reproduce precisely online what happens onsite and they instead consider how learning goals can be achieved in new ways, the question of which digital tools can be used most effectively to achieve those goals inevitably will arise. Considering and selecting technology and software is one of the most challenging tasks that OWI teachers face. Especially regarding teaching writing online, educators often may think that technology and pedagogy are in a tense relationship with one another. Which comes first? And which ends up requiring the majority of our energy and attention?

Hewett (2013) argued that "to let the technology drive the educational experience" for OWI is ultimately to "abandon instructional authority to the technology" (p. 204). She recommended that instructors first examine course setting (i.e., hybrid or fully online), pedagogical purpose (i.e., course type, genre, and level), digital modality (i.e., asynchronicity versus synchronicity), the desired media (i.e., text, voice, audio/video), and student audience (i.e., age, expectations, and capabilities, as well as physical disabilities, learning challenges, socioeconomic backgrounds, and multilingual considerations) before considering technology—available or desired. It is well and good for instructors to consider technology last, yet the reality remains that technology may be what is most emphasized institutionally. Often, for example, professional training and support for those desiring to teach hybrid or fully online OWCs (when such support exists) come almost exclusively in the form of IT training: how to use the latest tools in the LMS, how to master the gradebook, how to develop a test bank, and so on (OWI Committee, 2011c).

To be sure, it is hard to separate thinking about hybrid or fully online writing instruction from technology, since what seems to differentiate these settings from a fully onsite writing class is the technology. And, certainly, practical training in an LMS is crucial for teachers, but that is only one aspect of what training needs to be, as OWI Principle 7 indicated (p. 17; see also Chapter 11). There also must be ample discussion and training regarding the underlying pedagogy. *A Position Statement of Principles and Example Effective Practices for OWI* provided important guidance in this regard in that it asserted the primacy of pedagogy over technology. OWI Principle 2 stated, "An online writing course should focus on writing and not on technology orientation or teaching students how to use learning and other technologies." Furthermore, it said, "Unlike a digital rhetoric course an OWC is not considered to be a place for stretching technological skills as much as for becoming stronger writers in various selected genres" (p. 11).

It is important for OWI teachers to have these OWI principles at their disposal because so often we find ourselves being asked, explicitly or otherwise, to be technology experts when we teach writing in the hybrid or fully online settings. We also are asked routinely to make good writing instructional use of LMSs or other institutionally supported technologies that are not well suited to OWI because they were not designed with writing instruction in mind.

Yet, while we always want to foreground the pedagogy of our work and not technology, there really is no escaping the fact that OWI is mediated through technology in ways that fully face-to-face writing instruction is not. In fact, OWI Principle 13 asserted that "students should be prepared by the institution and their teachers for the unique technological and pedagogical components of OWI" (p. 26). Thus, while OWI Principle 2 indicated that the writing course is not the place to teach technologies per se, the writing instructor, *along with* the institution, retains some responsibilities for orienting and assisting students in OWCs to use the technology for writing course purposes (p. 11). As many OWI educators probably have discovered, regardless of the setting, a student who has technical trouble tends to go to the teacher first for technology help—and with complaints.

The technology-pedagogy question is not an easy one to parse, even as instructors seek to emphasize pedagogy. For example, the *Horizon Report* (2013) stated, "Adoption of progressive pedagogies ... is often enabled through the exploration of emerging technologies" (p. 10). However, the report also affirmed, "Simply capitalizing on new technology is not enough ... new models [of education] must use these tools and services to engage students on a deeper level" (p. 10). In some ways, these two statements encapsulate the tension many educators experience between writing pedagogy and technology. Technology can enable, and is sometimes necessary, in realizing creative new pedagogy. Yet, that technology left on its own, no matter how flashy, hyped, or slick, ultimately will fall flat in its efforts to engage students. On the contrary, such technology is likely to become a barrier to learning—a chore for students to use, a headache for instructors to troubleshoot—and in the end not worth the effort at all.

As educators, especially those who teach writing using technology, we often find ourselves trying to balance an interest in exploring new technology tools with the need to ground the use of those tools in sound pedagogy. It is easy, though often exhausting, to chase the latest technology trend as that final solution needed to solve teaching challenges. But technology is ephemeral. What is here one semester is gone the next. To this end, pedagogy ultimately must ground use of technology, as Hewett (2013) indicated.

In addition to keeping OWI Principle 2 (p. 11) in mind, thinking about design as framed by learning goals, as is discussed above, also can help avoid the pitfall of techno-centrism into which hybrid and fully online writing instruction can fall. A good design-based process might be:

1. I have outlined a learning goal I would like to achieve.
2. What online tool can I use to accomplish that goal?
3. What barriers, if any, is that technology likely to produce?

Alternatively, a technology-centered version of this same process might be:

1. I have this technology tool.
2. How can I make students use it online?
3. Which of my learning goals might apply?

In this latter scenario, the cart is before the horse, or, to use a more twenty-first century version of the adage, it is a solution (the technology) in search of a problem (the learning goal).

Staying fundamentally goal- rather than technology-focused also can help to mitigate a common assumption about students and technology, which is the belief that since students (of all ages) often are familiar and savvy with certain technologies for social networking—be it Facebook or their phones—they will be equally savvy when it comes to using LMS digital tools in an OWC. In my experience, students' facility in one digital environment is not a predictor of facility in a different one (see also Hewett, 2015a). I have seen little correlation, in fact, between students' proclivity toward technology in their daily lives and their ability to perform well within the digital piece of a writing course. In fact, much of what writing teachers ask students to do online is precisely the opposite of what they usually do online. As writing instructors, we might ask for students' considered reflection about a reading, for example, and that they communicate in language that has been carefully crafted and revised. What we receive may appear to be quickly written and off-the-cuff, which usually is appropriate for a text message to a friend, but that writing style does not translate well into an OWC.

In the end, though, as Hewett (2010) noted, "without adequate preparation and understanding about OWI, educators do not control the most basic of their online pedagogies; instead their teaching is mediated by the online environment" (p. 159). Instead of teaching *with* technology, instructors end up teaching *to* technology, which is unlikely to benefit students and is almost certain to exhaust educators.

CONCLUSION AND RECOMMENDATIONS

Certainly hybrid and fully online writing instruction are different in many ways. But despite how different these instructional settings look on the surface, they share fundamental design and effective practice realities in common. Somewhat paradoxically, they share uniqueness in common. In other words, it is important to think about each setting as its own, free-standing learning model. Neither hybrid nor fully online writing instruction should be understood as a modification of another instructional setting like classroom-based instruction. As unique environments with countless possible configurations, the design of effective hybrid and fully online OWCs should happen from the ground-up, with attention to what learning objectives are to be met and with a focus on pedagogy before technology.

Furthermore, in both hybrid and online settings, teachers can work to cultivate opportunities for presence for themselves and their students in order to combat what Hewett called that "sense of aloneness" that can accompany OWI (Chapter 1). As OWI Principle 11 (p. 23) asserted and Mick and Middlebrook address in Chapter 3; "Online writing teachers and their institutions should develop personalized and interpersonal online communities to foster student success."

In conclusion, let us return to Table 2.1, which presented hybrid and fully online writing instruction as, at least on the surface, quite different. Here, let us revise that table as Table 2.4 to present the similarities between the instructional settings instead.

Table 2.4. The similarities between hybrid and fully online OWCs

Instructional Elements	Fully Online Writing Instruction	Hybrid Writing Instruction
Opportunities for presence	Yes	Yes
Opportunities for interaction	Yes	Yes
Opportunities for engagement	Yes	Yes

Those who teach in either the hybrid or fully online environment would benefit from the following recommendations:

- Understand that educational settings are unique in that neither the hybrid nor the fully online modality is a variant of some imagined norm or theoretical standard; yet each of these settings shares the need for grounding the OWC in effective pedagogy.
- Highlight opportunities for students to be intellectually, socially, and emotionally present in face-to-face, hybrid, and fully online settings.
- Emphasize core educational aims like critical and creative thinking equally across educational settings, be they hybrid, fully online, or face-to-face.
- Ground teaching in effective pedagogy and allow that pedagogy to guide instruction rather than letting technology dictate what does, or does not, happen in the class.

NOTES

1. Aycock et al. (2008) discussed the problem of hybrid courses sometimes becoming "a course and a half" when teachers "take everything from the face-to-face course and add online work on top" (p. 30).

2. Message boards also are commonly known as discussion boards; the authors in this book use these terms interchangeably.

3. The New Media Consortium's *Horizon Report* (2011) noted:, "Mobiles continue to merit close attention as an emerging technology for teaching and learning." See also earlier works like Liz Kolb's (2008) *Toys to tools: Connecting student cell phones to education.*

4. Since 2007, I have been part of many formal and informal professional development opportunities at my institution related to hybrids as we look to inform the various stakeholders across campus about what hybrids are, how they can work, and how they need to be supported. In Spring of 2014, I offered an 8-week Teaching and Learning Center workshop on campus (delivered as a hybrid, of course), which marked an important step *on the institutional level* to facilitate good hybrid course design, delivery, and administrative support going forward.

5. I unfortunately used such transactional language throughout *Hybrid Learning: The Perils and Promise of Blending Online and Face-to-face Instruction in Higher Education* (2010). This oversight reminds me of how much I am continuing to learn about designing, teaching, and even talking about hybrid courses, as well as how embedded this transactional language is within our academic culture.

6. Hewett (2010) noted, "Teaching through text is the essence of teaching in online settings" (p. 161). This premise is threaded throughout Hewett's work, includ-

ing *Reading to Learn and Writing to Teach: Literacy Strategies for OWI* (2015a). She stressed that even while multimodal texts and media become more accessible and easier to use, the teaching of writing should stay grounded in text as its fundamental mode of communication.

REFERENCES

Aiken Technical College. (2014). Student Handbook: *Definition of online, hybrid, and supplemental courses.* Retrieved from http://www.atc.edu/Catalog/handbook/S4.aspx

Allen, I. Elaine, Jeff Seaman, & Richard Garrett. (2007). *Blending in: The extent and promise of blended education in the United States.* The Sloan Consortium. Retrieved from http://sloanconsortium.org/sites/default/files/Blending_In.pdf

Aycock, Alan, et al. (2008). *Faculty development for blended teaching and learning: A sloan-c certificate program.* The Sloan Consortium.

Aycock, Alan, et al. (2012). *Strategies for integrating online and face-to-face in blended learning.* The Sloan Consortium. Retrieved from https://uwm.courses.wisconsin.edu/d2l/lms/content/viewer/main_frame.d2l?ou=302428&tId=2072451

Barker, Thomas T., & Kemp, Fred O. (1990). Network theory: A post-modern pedagogy for the writing classroom. In Carolyn Handa (Ed.), *Computers in society: Teaching composition in the twenty-first century* (pp. 1-27). Upper Montclair, NJ: Boynton/Cook.

Caulfield, Jay. (2011). *How to design and teach a hybrid course: Achieving student-centered learning through blended classroom, online and experiential activities.* Sterling, VA, Stylus Publishing.

CCCC Committee for Effective Practices in Online Writing Instruction. (2011c). *The state of the art of OWI.* Retrieved from http://www.ncte.org/library/NCTEFiles/Groups/CCCC/Committees/OWI_State-of-Art_Report_April_2011.pdf

CCCC OWI Committee for Effective Practices in Online Writing Instruction. (2013). *A position statement of principles and effective practices for online writing instruction (OWI).* Retrieved from http://www.ncte.org/cccc/resources/positions/owiprinciples

College of DuPage. (2012). *Contractual agreement between the Board of Trustees of College of DuPage and College of DuPage Faculty Association IEA/NEA 2012/2015.* Retrieved from http://www.cod.edu/about/humanresources/pdf/codfa_agreement.pdf

College of DuPage. (2013). *Hybrid courses.* Retrieved from http://www.cod.edu/academics/hybrid.aspx

Dobbs, R. R., Waid, C. A., & del Carmen, A. (2009). Students' perceptions of online courses: The effect of online course experience. *The Quarterly Review of Distance Education, 10* (1), 9-26.

Griffin, June & Minter, Deborah. (2013). The rise of the online writing classroom: Reflecting on the material conditions of college composition teaching. *College Composition and Communication, 65*(1), 140-161.

Hewett, Beth L. (2004-2005). Asynchronous online instructional commentary: A study of student revision. *Readerly/Writerly Texts: Essays in Literary, Composition, and Pedagogical Theory, (Double Issue) 11 & 12*(1 & 2), 47-67.

Hewett, Beth L. (2010). *The online writing conference: A guide for teachers and tutors.* Portsmouth, NH, Boynton/Cook.

Hewett, Beth L. (2013). Fully online and hybrid writing instruction. In H. Brooke Hessler, Amy Rupiper Taggart, & Kurt Schick (Eds.), *A guide to composition pedagogies*(2nd ed.) (pp. 194-211). Oxford, UK: Oxford University Press.

Hewett, Beth L. (2015a). *Reading to learn and writing to teach: Literacy strategies for online writing instruction.* Boston: Bedford/St. Martin's Press.

Hewett, Beth L. (2015b). *The online writing conference: A guide for teachers and tutors.* (Updated). Boston: Bedford/St. Martin's Press.

Horizon Report. (2013). *New Media Consortium.* Retrieved from Kirtland Community College. (2014). *Online and hybrid courses.* Retrieved from http://www.kirtland.edu/online-learning/online-and-hybrid-courses

Lederman, Doug & Scott Jaschik. (2013). *Survey of faculty attitudes on technology.* Inside Higher Ed. Retrieved from http://www.insidehighered.com/news/survey/survey-faculty-attitudes-technology

New Media Consortium/EDUCAUSE Learning Initiative. (2013). *Horizon report.* Retrieved from http://www.nmc.org/pdf/2013-horizon-report-HE.pdf

Palmquist, Michael. (1993). Network-supported interaction in two writing classrooms. *Computers and Composition, 10*(4), 25-57.

Picciano, A. G. (2001). *Distance learning: Making connections across virtual space and time.* Upper Saddle River, NJ: Prentice-Hall.

Ozarks Technical Community College. (2014). *OTC online: Online vs. hybrid courses.* Retrieved from http://www.otc.edu/online/10390.php

Savery, John. (2005). BE VOCAL: Characteristics of successful online instructors. *Journal of Interactive Online Learning, (4)*2.

Snart, Jason Allen. (2010). *Hybrid learning: The perils and promises of blending online and face-to-face instruction in higher education.* Santa Barbara, CA: Praeger.

Stella, Julia & Michael Corry. (2013, Summer). Teaching writing in online distance education: Supporting student success. *Online journal of distance learning administration, 16*(2).

Texas Administrative Code, RULE §4.257. (2010). Retrieved from http://info.sos.state.tx.us/pls/pub/readtac$ext.TacPage?sl=R&app=9&p_dir=&p_rloc=&ptloc=&p_ploc=&pg=1&p_tac=&ti=19&pt=1&ch=4&rl=257

United States Department of Education. (2010). *Transforming American education: Learning powered by technology.* Retrieved from http://www.ed.gov/technology/netp-2010

University of Wisconsin–Milwaukee. (2013). *Hybrid courses.* Retrieved from http://www4.uwm.edu/ltc/hybrid/about_hybrid/index.cfm

Warnock, Scott. (2009). *Teaching writing online: How and why.* Champaign, IL: National Council of Teachers of English.

Whithaus, Carl & Joyce Magnotto Neff. (2006). Contact and interactivity: Social constructionist pedagogy in a video-based management writing course. *Technical Communication Quarterly (15)*4: 431-456.

Zickhur, Katherine & Aaron Smith. (2012). *Digital differences.* Pew Internet and American life project. Retrieved from http://www.pewinternet.org/~/media//Files/Reports/2012/PIP_Digital_differences_041312.pdf

CHAPTER 3

ASYNCHRONOUS AND SYNCHRONOUS MODALITIES

Connie Snyder Mick
University of Notre Dame

Geoffrey Middlebrook
University of Southern California

Along with formulating specific, observable, and measurable learner outcomes, one of the basic decisions that OWI administrators and instructors must confront involves course design and delivery, and more specifically, choosing from among the many tools and techniques available for OWI. That decision-making process inevitably requires managing the questions of digital modality: when, why, and how to deploy asynchronous (non-real time) and synchronous (real time and near-real time) modalities. This chapter addresses those questions along with the dimensions of inclusivity and accessibility, technical viability and support, and pedagogical rationale.

Keywords: accessibility, asynchronous, impact, inclusivity, modality/ies, near-real time, non-real time, pace, permanence, scale, social presence, synchronous, technical viability

There are the two digital modalities through which OWI is conducted, the asynchronous and the synchronous. Sometimes one modality alone is used and sometimes they are mixed. This chapter addresses the digital modalities used in both hybrid and fully online OWI settings described in Chapter 2.

Asynchronicity occurs in a different time setting in that interactions occur with a time lag between and among them. Participants can be geographically distributed or even in the same room, but if they interact in "non-real time," their communication and work is asynchronous. Almost all writing instructors already engage in asynchronous instructional practices when they post course materials to an LMS or respond to individual student emails. Asynchronous OWCs typically enable teachers and students to interact over a longer period of time such as, for example, two days or a week, and they provide wide latitude with scheduling coursework and interactions. They use such media as text, images, recorded audio, and recorded audio/video.

Synchronicity, on the other hand, occurs in the "same time" setting in that interactions transpire without a time lag in "real time" or with a very short one in "near-real time" (indicating a very short time between interactions as with text-based instant messaging [IM] or short-message service [SMS]). Again, participants can be geographically distributed or located in the same room. Synchronous OWCs typically require teachers and students to be communicating with immediacy, and they must meet at a particular scheduled time for the activity to be genuinely synchronous and equally accessible to all in the course, much as in a traditional onsite course setting. They use such media as text and live audio/video where the participants talk and see each other in real time. However, synchronous OWCs typically also take advantage of asynchronous media for distributing and collecting assignments, providing content, and requiring text-based discussions (Hewett, 2013).

The scholarly literature suggests that successful online teaching and learning are facilitated by "high authenticity ... , high interactivity, and high collaboration" (D'Agustino, 2012, p. 148). These components are especially salient in OWI, where vibrant virtual writing communities must thrive in order to meet the requirements of all students for timely and effective feedback together with a sense of real audience, regardless of participant differences in cognition or personality. Phrased another way, in addition to formulating specific, observable, and measurable learner outcomes, when it comes to course construction and implementation, the question that OWI decision makers should ask is not whether either the asynchronous or synchronous option is intrinsically better but rather, as Stefan Hrastinski (2008) stated, "when, why, and how" to deploy both (p. 52). In order to address those deployment questions, this chapter examines the discrete and combined implications of asynchronous and synchronous modalities in the domain of OWI. In so doing, the most relevant OWI principles serve as framing devices and instruments of analysis.

MODALITY OPTIONS, EXPECTATIONS, AND RESOURCES

To set the stage for making informed choices in OWI, we begin with a brief delineation of asynchronous and synchronous modalities in terms of the media and tools they typically use.[1]

Commonly used tools for the asynchronous modality include email, discussion boards, blogs, Wikis, social networking sites, e-lists, and streaming audio or video. Among the frequently identified advantages of using asynchronous technology in OWI are (1) higher levels of temporal flexibility, (2) increased cognitive participation because of the time allowance for amplified reflection, (3) higher potential to use the increased allowable time for processing information, (4) multiple opportunities to write and read, and (5) the existence of an archival record for transactions conducted in the environment. Yet, asynchronous platforms lack immediacy and thus may contribute to a sense of participant isolation, or what the online education literature would call loss of social presence. Asynchronous pedagogy includes asking students to read the syllabus, assignments, and content for the OWC—in their own timeframe and at their own speed. Students also are asked to write their thinking out in whole-class and peer-group discussions that teachers will read and, hopefully, to which teachers also will respond. Teacher-to-student conferences about the course or as response to written papers tend to happen asynchronously, requiring teachers to construct readable and cogent text and requiring students to read with care to understand the messages (Hewett, 2015a, 2015b). Both students and teachers must go online fairly often to interact; instructors may need to go online more often given their responsibilities to read texts from and write texts for multiple students.

Synchronous tools, by contrast, involve media relative to meeting concurrently through text and voice (i.e., live chat), live document sharing, live audio or video conferencing (both one-to-one and one-to-group), meetings in virtual worlds, and white board sharing. Some synchronous work can occur through the institution's LMS depending on its built-in capabilities, but sometimes outside software are brought to the classroom for this work. Synchronous media's primary advantage typically is identified as interpersonal rather than cognitive, ostensibly owing to participants' feelings of intimacy and real-time engagement, which tend to be associated with student satisfaction, student learning, and lower rates of attrition. Such synchronous interactions can help to avoid miscommunications and to address problems when miscommunication has occurred. Nevertheless, synchronous media can create significant scheduling challenges particularly if the teacher wants to speak with the entire class, but even for one-to-one interactions. Additionally, synchronous media/software can be costly and may require significant bandwidth to be efficient and effective. Relative to OWI Principle 1 (p. 11), they may be challenging to provide in terms of student access unless the LMS offers the necessary accessible portals; even then, some students will not have the video or audio capacity using their home computers and on-campus computer labs.

Table 3.1 outlines some of the tools that the asynchronous and synchronous modalities use in OWI settings. It is worth noting that asynchronous OWCs by their nature typically take advantage only of asynchronous media while synchronous OWCs may take advantage of both asynchronous and synchronous media.

Table 3.1. Example asynchronous and synchronous tools

Asynchronous Tools	Synchronous Tools
• Email	• Text-based chat
• Discussion/message boards	• Voice-based chat, to include the phone
• Blogs	• Audio and/or video conferencing
• Social media sites	• Web conferencing
• Listservs	• Virtual worlds
• Streaming audio or video	• Whiteboards
• Wikis	• Real-time document sharing (e.g., Google Documents)
• Non-real-time document sharing (e.g., Google Documents)	

Presently, asynchronous resources seem to be more widely used with online learning, in large part because the implementation barriers are lower. According to empirical evidence, that preference apparently holds true for OWI, but it seemingly varies with the selected tool. For instance, the fully online distance-based survey results gathered by the CCCC OWI Committee in 2011 indicated that 93.8% of the surveyed faculty relied on asynchronous discussion; regarding the asynchronous tools used, however, only 10.1% employed blogs, 7.9% took advantage of Wikis, and 5.3% used social media sites, some of which have synchronous affordances (CCCC OWI Committee, 2011a). For the OWI hybrid survey findings, the figures were 78% for asynchronous discussion, together with 13.9% for blogs, 10.3% for Wikis, and 3.5% for social networking sites (CCCC OWI Committee, 2011b). Those survey data suggest that asynchronous modalities are more frequently used in OWI, but not why. Possible reasons include the general capabilities of most LMSs as they are configured for higher education disciplines, which may be an issue of cost, and the degree to which teachers value or are prepared to use asynchronous tools in their OWCs. The potential for choosing and using one modality over *or* with the other is nuanced. In *Preparing Educators for Online Writing Instruction*, Beth L. Hewett and Christa Ehmann (2004) observed that "asynchronous writing instruction looks very familiar to instructors," in terms of their experience with providing written response to student papers whereas "synchronous writing instruction can be highly useful," yet "tricky in that it requires highly developed verbal teaching skills and vocabulary about writing along with strategies for encouraging students to commit to writing out their thinking" (pp. 116-117). A few years later, Scott Warnock (2009) noted in *Teaching Writing Online* that "having an asynchronous textual presence" is foundational in OWI (p. 2).

In the early stages of OWI course formulation, it is essential to consider the ramifications of multiple variables, not the least of which are the choice to use asynchronous and synchronous modes. To do so well requires closely interrogating the expectations and resources of stakeholders in order to balance practical and pedagogical concerns, with the key cohorts being students, instructors, WPAs, and relevant information technology (IT) representatives from the institution. For instance, data gathering and discussions could help course designers determine the feasibility and thus allocation of asynchronous and synchronous tools. On this point it is worth noting that the CCCC OWI Committee's nationwide surveys (2011a & 2011b) indicated that many OWI teachers inherited a course design or interface, while others worked to configure their own course—typically within the confines of a previously selected LMS. Yet, in the interests of outcomes, orientations and workshops could facilitate conversations about pedagogical expectations and available resources. For example, if instructors or WPAs think it is essential for students to share full drafts of their papers while conversing about them in real time, but the IT personnel state that campus infrastructure will not reliably support Web conferencing or that students may not have such access, then text-based chat may become the necessary synchronous platform of choice. This decision and others like it should be reinforced by a clearly articulated rationale for how a modality enhances the teaching of writing as well as how such a choice enhances access and inclusivity, per OWI Principle 1 (p. 7).

Selecting a modality for an OWC could be facilitated by surveying the students as the course's primary audience. According to Janet C. Moore (2011), Chief Knowledge Officer at the Sloan Consortium, "clear expectations help manage the volume and quality of interaction" that promote effective learning online (p. 97). With that in mind, surveys could invite students to share information about their own resources and levels of expertise that would assist in selecting an institution's LMS or choosing between asynchronous and synchronous modalities when creating an OWC, while sessions and materials that outline policies, processes, rights, and responsibilities would provide a touchstone for support before and throughout a course. Such training is entirely consistent with OWI Principle 10, which stated that "students should be prepared by the institution and their teachers for the unique technological and pedagogical components" of online writing (p. 21). Taking all stakeholder groups into account, the following are fundamental questions to help identify expectations and resources related to choosing asynchronous and synchronous modes for teaching and learning writing online. Only after gathering and assessing this information can one make solid decisions about specific media, tools, and online instructional techniques.

1. **Students:** To what extent do you need technical assistance accessing asyn-

chronous materials from the institution's LMS? Do you own a computer camera and/or microphone for participating in synchronous chat, video, or audio exchanges? To what extent would you need additional access or technical assistance for participating fully in synchronous chat, video, or audio exchanges? Describe the technical profile of your primary and secondary connectivity sources. If you use assistive technology, please describe what it is and what you know about its connectivity to the campus chat, audio, and video.

2. **Instructors:** To what extent do you need technical assistance accessing asynchronous materials from the institution's LMS? Do you own or have available a computer camera and/or microphone for participating in synchronous chat, video, or audio exchanges? To what extent would you need additional access or technical assistance for participating fully in synchronous chat, video, or audio exchanges? Describe the technical profile of your primary and secondary connectivity sources.

3. **Institution:** To what extent are you able to provide access to asynchronous and synchronous modalities through the institution's LMS? To what extent are you able to offer an initial technological orientation and ongoing 24/7 technical support to students and instructors in both hybrid and fully online OWCs? To what extent are you able to offer workshops on key techniques for teaching and learning writing online? To what extent are you able to provide additional access to students with physical disabilities, learning challenges, multilingual backgrounds, or socioeconomic challenges? Do you have resources for describing asynchronous videos for visually challenged students? What arrangements do you have for live captioning in synchronous meetings?

INTERACTION AND COMMUNITY

Chapters 1 and 2 made clear the importance of connectedness among participants in an online writing environment. Connection, in fact, is at the core of OWI Principle 11, which asserts the need to develop "personalized and interpersonal online communities to foster student success" (p. 23). As scholars have suggested, digital connectedness is correspondingly accompanied by challenges (see, for example, DePew, Spangler, & Spiegel, 2013). However, with a teaching focus on process and revision, writing instruction even in onsite environments has always confronted the dynamic nature of knowledge construction through alphabetic text, and writing instructors, therefore, bring a wealth of disciplinary knowledge that can help inform community-building online. Indeed, the recent focus on flipping the classroom for more interactivity and individualization is a relatively old practice in writing pedagogy, and many writing faculty have years of experience designing activities that enhance interaction; these activities include group tasks that balance guided, scaffolded prompts with the need to allow for wandering and depth in discourse. Administrators responsible for OWI training, then, would be well advised to foreground and tap into that existing knowledge, as it will help instructors to make effective choices about how to employ asynchronous and synchronous modalities that lead to online interconnectedness, while emphasizing the pedagogical nature of such choices over mere technological feasibility.

Despite such experience, as reports amass documenting and sometimes championing the swift shift toward online learning in higher education (Allen & Seaman, 2013), instructors may experience uncertainty about their ability to adjust to new modalities for delivery, and as a result, they may feel breathlessly squeezed by this convergence. WPAs who shepherd OWI teachers from "face-to-face" to hybrid or fully online environments not surprisingly may encounter a range of attitudes and levels of preparation for that shift.

Veteran writing faculty who express anxiety about moving to OWI should be reassured that they already possess a foundational familiarity with asynchronous and synchronous modes. By definition, face-to-face teaching is primarily synchronous because onsite classroom activities happen in real time, and instructors accordingly develop methods and preferences for managing such exchanges informed by their training and course learning objectives. Such synchronicity and onsite, face-to-face interactions are a significant part of hybrid OWI, as Jason Snart discusses in Chapter 2. Beyond face-to-face interactions, digital synchronicity also uses the common qualities of talk and turn-taking whether accomplished through oral talk or text-based chat. Moreover, these same instructors use asynchronous communication increasingly often through their institution's LMS to exchange such digital products as syllabi, assignment descriptions, essays, and assessments. This experience means that writing faculty can by default follow the recommendation outlined in OWI Principle 4 that "appropriate onsite theories, pedagogies, and strategies should be migrated and adapted to the online instructional environment" (p. 14). The challenge is to transfer that experience with an awareness of the nuances of the online medium.

On the other end of the spectrum, less-seasoned writing teachers might possess competence with asynchronous and synchronous digital technologies, yet they may not have thought critically about how to transfer that aptitude for teaching purposes. In this case, teachers with technological expertise run the risk of assuming that students share that fluency and access. OWI administrators might, as a precaution, require these teachers to articulate a clear rationale for each technology they propose to use and to run an assessment that lists the risks of those tools given the potential challenges to students, along with possible adaptations and accommodations. The imperative to anticipate and thus avoid frustrations over digital technology that can spread from instructors to students—breeding discontent and distraction in online settings—is part of what animates OWI Principle 7, which stated that "online writing teachers should receive appropriate OWI-focused training, professional development, and assessment for evaluation and promotion purposes" (p. 17). While it might not be feasible to consider all potential challenges and solutions, thinking through these possibilities will better prepare instructors for their online teaching duties.

In considering challenges and solutions, OWI instructors would be well advised to consider the implications of shifting from asynchronous to synchronous modalities or vice versa. Even when an LMS offers primarily asynchronous over synchronous media, for example, it is possible to switch modalities in the interest of assisting students, individually or collectively. For example, if a student is in danger of failure or if she expresses uncertainty or frustration, the teacher can connect with her synchronously via text (IM chat) on the LMS, in a Web conference using the LMS or free software, or with the telephone, which is accessible to almost all students. Switching modality and/or medium enables reconnection and forward movement. Considering when to reverse modalities or when to use both modalities in order to meet different learning styles and objectives is probably the best way to prepare for all students to participate fully and fairly in online coursework. Not only that, but instructors should work with their institutions to compose documentation for novice student users of required course technologies; if, in so doing, they conclude that possible discomfort among students is of a certain magnitude, the problematic tools should be abandoned for ones that requires less knowledge or management.

Kevin Eric DePew & Heather Lettner-Rust (2009) posited that if synchronous communication is the default delivery mode in the onsite classroom, the asynchronous mode plays that role online. They observed that historically, distance education was designed primarily to allow students to pace themselves, asynchronously interacting with instructors through the postal service initially and through digital tools more recently. But champions of distance education, then and now, have sometimes been motivated by efficiencies and not pedagogical value, and OWI stakeholders should be cautious of approaches that do not align with the recommendations of such leaders in the field as the Sloan Consortium. With that said, while the asynchronous modality is currently dominant in OWI, a movement to develop more affordable, reliable, and efficacious synchronous tools suggests that the latter could become a more significant feature on the OWI landscape. Synchronous platforms may well offer new pedagogical opportunities and challenges, which teachers and researchers should continue to explore and research. This exploration is part of OWI Principle 3's message: "Appropriate composition teaching/learning strategies should be developed for the unique features of the online instructional environment" (p. 12). Nevertheless, mere access to tools should not be the guiding force in using them. On the contrary, understanding the advantages and limitations of asynchronous and synchronous resources for teaching writing is a *sine qua non* for OWI stakeholders, who are the focus of the next section.

ACROSS THREE DIMENSIONS

The emerging consensus regarding the choice of asynchronous and synchronous modes is that neither is inherently better, but that they complement one another and should be employed after considering the instructional and rhetorical situation of each activity in an OWC (Hewett, 2013). This observation invokes the previously mentioned questions of when, why, and how to deploy these modalities to advance OWI. The following discussion examines three dimensions across which asynchronous and synchronous options can be compared to determine which are suited for a particular situation: inclusivity and accessibility, technical viability and IT support, and pedagogical rationale. The order is significant here for the first two are practical and must be addressed before moving on to the third. To state the obvious, if students or instructors cannot participate fully in the life of the course or if the technology sets up access roadblocks the IT support cannot address, that course should be redesigned until the obstructions are removed. Table 3.2 and the following discussion provide a comparative overview given these dimensions.

Inclusivity and Accessibility

OWI Principle 1 rightly declared that "online writing instruction should be universally inclusive and accessible" (p. 7). This overarching need has profound implications for course design and execution, and Section 3, "Practicing Inclusivity," offers extensive theoretical and practical insight on the issue. In this chapter, however, the emphasis is on inclusive and accessible design as a dimension of asynchronous and synchronous modalities. Broadly speaking, asynchronous approaches afford students time to use adaptive technologies that remediate physical, cognitive, or linguistic challenges. For example, research suggests that persons with Autism spectrum disorders might work best in such asynchronous modes as email (Wyatt, 2012). Similarly, Hewett (2000, 1998) suggested that students with audio-processing disorders might fare better in online, text-based peer groups, while students with certain kinds of writing disabilities might

Table 3.2. Modality dimensions, strengths, and challenges for OWI

Modes	Dimensions	
Dimension One: Inclusivity and Accessibility	STRENGTHS	
	• Typically text-based interactions use common literacy skills. • Research available on how to ensure that OWI works for everyone, minimizing disparities due to technological access. • Time lag affords students the opportunity to employ assistance related to disabilities, such as typing aides or submitting responses in approved alternative media.	• Enables voice and live video connections to accompany an environment that typically is text-rich. • Accommodates learning styles that rely on immediate feedback and real-time visuals. • Many tool types available through universal access or embedded institutional cost structures, meaning that no additional fee/s required.
	CHALLENGES	
	• Typically text-based interactions require strong reading and writing skills, which may be problematic for students with particular learning or physical disabilities. • Instructors and designers must have access to the latest research on design for inclusivity and must be able to use platforms that support the deepest accommodations. • Instructors and designers must receive information on accessibility issues from students with enough time to address solutions, so cooperation with institutional partners addressing accessibility needs is essential.	• Some versions require voice and live video connections that may impede students who interact more comfortably through text or who cannot afford such connections. • Speed of communication could impede participation of students or instructors with disabilities. • Speed of communications could impede participation by those challenged by low-bandwidth and connectivity. • Certain communication interfaces are not designed to interact well, if at all, with software that facilitates communication for students or instructors with physical disabilities.
Dimension Two: Technical Viability and IT Support	STRENGTHS	
	• Technical support is typically built into the major providers on campus and in the public domain; platforms have been around long enough that crowdsourcing and on-campus assistance can often address concerns.	• If using popular institutional or universal access platforms, IT support should be familiar with common problems.

Dimension Two: Technical Viability and IT Support	CHALLENGES	
	• Timely, skilled technical support from institutional IT and software designers is essential to maintaining reliable service with full capabilities.	• IT support might not be available when assistance is needed if students and teachers interact outside business hours or if funding for support services does not meet demand.
Dimension Three: Pedagogical Rationale Permanence Pace Scale Social Impact	STRENGTHS	
	• Most LMS and public platforms have recording tools to capture exchanges for future consideration. • Intermittent communication process allows time for deeper thought and construction of response at pace determined by instructor and students. • Exchanges are easily scalable to individual, whole class, or targeted group; scale is flexible from one-on-one to thousands in a MOOC. • Social exchanges related to building relationships and addressing concerns can be carefully constructed as participants have time to consider and compose such interactions.	• In a smaller class or within small groups, accommodates time-sensitive social and relational functions such as: (1) exchanges that help establish identity and personal connection, and (2) exchanges that facilitate planning for such activities as group work.
	CHALLENGES	
	• Pace does not easily allow for fluid, time-sensitive social and relational acts, such as (1) exchanges that help establish identity and personal connection, and (2) exchanges that facilitate planning for such activities as group work.	• Exchanges might not be recordable due to limitations in technology or storage capacity; therefore, they may not be reviewable for deeper consideration or ongoing use. • Privileges speed over care for grammatical correctness or depth of thought. • Capacity for direct participation is limited with multiple students. • Ability to respond quickly could facilitate uncensored and careless comments that degrade social fabric.

accomplish peer group work more efficiently and effectively in synchronous or onsite settings. Likewise, in an especially text-rich setting like the asynchronous modality where nearly all exchanges are text-based, students can benefit from consistently reading and writing, but students with particular learning styles may flounder when their reading or writing skills—although rightly challenged by the mode—are weaker than needed (Hewett, 2015a). In such cases, real-time talk may provide students with necessary relief and added capacity for understanding. Although researchers need to continue to research the access issues related to asynchronous tools, there remains a potentially greater challenge in reaching full and fair standards for OWI participation with synchronous options. The synchronous modality can provide a vehicle for meaningful student involvement in OWI, such as oral discussion and real-time document sharing to complement less dynamic textual interchange. This potential notwithstanding, in terms of socio-economic stratification, to raise just one dynamic, the continuing digital divide confirms that many students still have hardware, software, and bandwidth impediments that make more advanced connections such as Web conferencing difficult if not impossible for taking an OWC.

TECHNICAL VIABILITY AND IT SUPPORT

The second dimension is technical viability and IT support, which resonates with OWI Principle 2 that an "online writing course should focus on writing and not on technology orientation or teaching students how to use learning and other technologies" (p. 11). OWI Principle 13 also is relevant in stating the "students should be provided support components through online/digital media as a primary resource; they should have access to onsite support components as a secondary set of resources" (p. 26). That is, course expectations and learning objectives need alignment to available infrastructure, with IT staff available to address students' and instructors' difficulties directly. This need can be appreciated in the CCCC OWI Committee survey (2011a) of fully online distance-based courses, where instructors named "technical problems" as one of their most challenging areas. It is reasonable to conclude that robust asynchronous and synchronous training and—in particular—IT support would free instructors to focus their priorities on teaching or tutoring writing. Even so, Hewett and Ehmann (2004) noted that "asynchronous instruction tends to be less costly and simpler to develop than synchronous instruction" (p. 69). With that understood, the attempt to minimize expenses and technical problems may manifest in the form of avoiding synchronous tools in the teaching and learning of writing online, as these are typically associated with more technical problems—or at least more panic-inducing problems. Yet, if time and experience are helping to address issues with asynchronous tools, the same will in all likelihood eventually arrive for synchronous feature sets as well. Until then, WPAs or instructors seeking to reduce uncertainties in OWI will probably continue to use well-established asynchronous tools for the majority if not all of their course needs. Although understandable, this represents a concern to the field if, as discussed in the next section, there are pedagogical reasons for using both modalities.

PEDAGOGICAL RATIONALE

Issues of inclusivity and accessibility together with technical viability and support must be resolved in order for OWI to be successful. However, these two dimensions will be of dramatically less consequence if OWI instructors and administrators do not ascertain the pedagogical merits of asynchronous and synchronous modalities. Below, therefore, are comparative analyses of those modes according to four metrics: permanence, pace, scale, and impact.

Permanence

As noted earlier, asynchronous communication entails the intermittent exchange between sender and receiver during which the receiver, at a time of his or her choosing, actively retrieves the former's message to complete the communication thread. Given the nature of asynchronous tools, in particular those housed in a course LMS such as discussion boards, these interactions are more likely to create an archived record of exchanges, which can be highly useful for participants to refer to later. For instance, from the students' perspective, that archive assists with essay revision by permitting a return to teacher, peer, and tutor recommendations on an earlier version of the document. With regard to OWI faculty, the record created through automatic saving and digital archiving offers, among other things, information on student engagement with one another as well as with the course materials, which may be pedagogically useful for identifying outliers who are not fully invested in or perhaps are unclear about the nature of course assignments and processes. While quantity of time spent is no substitute for quality of time, and one cannot be certain that these measures of quantity are precisely accurate, such elements do add information to an instructor's understanding of students' asynchronous performance.

In contrast, synchronous communication can be defined as the near immediate (with simultaneous potential), interactive exchange of messages between sender and receiver. Not surprisingly, creating permanence in this mode is often far more complicated than in asynchronous discourse. Typically, participants must turn on recording devices for synchronous exchanges and ought to have the permission of all parties to do so since recording might not be the default setting. Furthermore, while some chat, whiteboard, and voice conferencing tools have the option of recording, a challenge may be the generally large synchronous file size that requires capture and storage capacity. If synchronous interactions in OWI cannot be recorded, participants are obliged to rely on notes and memories, which is the very method they would employ in an onsite classroom. What might be gained from a technologically mediated synchronous interchange that facilitates robust, expressive interaction—complementing communicative intentions through such kinetic acts as body gestures, facial reactions, and tone of voice—could be offset by the inability to revisit these encounters for future review. That is obviously consequential when, for example, it comes to feedback during an essay writing invention session online. Analyzing recorded text-based chat in their class on argumentation, Leena I. Laurinen and Miika J. Marttunen (2007) noted that "chat debates in computerised [*sic*] learning environments can easily be stored, which opens up a possibility for reflecting on debates later on, and students can use them as source material for the further development of their ideas," such as by using the text of the chat to create "argumentation diagrams" (p. 244).

Pace

The conventional dynamic in asynchronous communication is, broadly speaking, self-paced, thereby both accommodating learning differences and allowing cognitive room for the careful construction and understanding of content. Pace represents a core affordance for online instructors of writing who teach and assess a variety of written student products, for it gives students the opportunity to draft and revise in ways that reflect their deepest understanding of writing and rhetorical precepts. Whether the task is a two-hundred word post at a course blog or a two-thousand word thesis-driven argument, the students' asynchronous tempo for writing and talking through writing can be conducive to thoughtfulness and polish.

Regarding synchronous communication, on the other hand, pace is both its strength and challenge. Hrastinski (2008) asserted that the synchronous modality is especially suited to secondary, lighter objectives, including "discussing less complex issues, getting acquainted, and planning tasks" (p. 54), but he explained that students are nonetheless highly motivated to participate in synchronous discussions because they know that responses happen rapidly. Hewett (2006) and Hewett and Ehmann (2004) indicated differently that synchronous conferences represent an ideal modality for discussing singular issues of importance like brainstorming an idea or taking a concept and working it into a thesis.

Of course, synchronous interactions can be equated with "quick" responses (Hrastinski, 2008), and such immediate responses are not always carefully considered. The OWI setting is no exception. Poorly prepared or unfiltered "knee-jerk" answers easily could diminish the value of a lively session on any facet of the writing process. Pace is moderated by medium, as well. For example, synchronous voice interactions are more quickly responsive than text-based IM chat. The latter becomes threaded and convoluted even between two participants who think and type at different rates. With that said, many students who have grown up immersed in online communication are likely to be at least familiar with, if not thoroughly comfortable at, a synchronous pace, and instructors should consider how those exchanges could be integrated into the class ecology.

Scale

A seminal aspect of asynchronous modalities is that they allow instructors the latitude to scale the provision of material to individuals, groups, or the whole class. Simply stated, email and other documents are as readily delivered to one student as to every student. Warnock (2009) described how years of experience have led him to rely on asynchronous communication for its reliability and inclusivity, allowing even quieter students to be involved, in contrast to synchronous discourse, which he describes as "fairly linear, almost always meaning that not everyone can participate" (pp. 69-70).

In comparison, perhaps the most restrictive aspect of synchronous resources is the criterion of scalability. Just as large class size inhibits active participation by all members in onsite settings, digital synchronous tools have an inherent ceiling for authentic interaction. Instructional technologists, however, are playing with the power of synchronicity in promising ways. Such play can be innovative, if dicey for OWI, as one Coursera MOOC designed for a composition course demonstrated.[2] Its purpose was to offer a sense of simultaneity to its hundreds of participants who nevertheless could not all interact with the instructor at once. A strategy was to schedule live lectures that students could attend in real time or watch recorded thereafter. This synchronous experience was one-directional as students could not insert questions into the lecture; they could, however, join in the course's chat-based discussion areas while watching the lecture. Another synchronous experience for this group was a series of live video-conference writing workshops comprised of the instructor and a handful of students who were selected from a pool of course applicants; the rest of the MOOC students could watch the workshops live or recorded later. OWI Principle 15 calls for "ongoing research" by administrators and teachers (p. 31), and that is very much needed if synchronous options are to be made scalable for purposes of OWI.

Impact

One of the most significant critiques of online learning is that too often neither instructors nor students indicate that they have forged satisfying relationships with one another. In relation to this phenomenon, the CCCC OWI Committee (2011a) found in its research that instructors in fully online distance-based courses emphasized the importance of actively nurturing engagement with students, noting that "courses do not run by themselves," but instead require careful attention to connection and community. The symptoms of low levels of impact are clear in, among other ways, the high attrition rates associated with online courses compared to their face-to-face or blended counterparts (Dziuban, Hartman, & Moskal, 2004). Many scholars have addressed this issue, and it is the reason why OWI Principle 11 asks instructors and their institutions to attend to the potential associative power of online communities (p. 23). Asynchronous modalities can and do contribute to the ties that bind course participants, in ways such as reflective blog postings shared in class space, member profiles, and open discussion areas that invite more playfulness and self-sponsored participation (Kear, 2011). Instructors, too, can and should perform "immediacy behaviors" (Arbaugh, 2001, p. 43) by, for instance, stepping into student discussions at appropriate times to confirm they, too, are part of that constitutive community.

Even so, it is probably in the area of impact that synchronous resources hold the greatest promise for shaping the quality of future OWI, as these platforms are especially vital in helping to establish and sustain an immediacy of "social presence," a feeling among course participants that real people are connecting even though they are geographically distributed. Synchronicity in OWI most naturally echoes the call and response of face-to-face conversation and animates, according to Hewett (2010), the "turn-taking, spontaneity, and relatively high degrees of interactivity" that forge social connectedness (p. 25). In peer review, to cite one example, a student-to-student chat can facilitate the critique through shared greetings that personalize the activity and establish goodwill and camaraderie in a difficult task. Proponents and practitioners of OWI alike should take note that many comprehensive strategies for developing deeper relationships in online courses include some type of synchronous communication, whether it is through phone calls, chat, or face-to-face meetings. Indeed, the CCCC OWI Committee (2011a) survey of fully online courses found that faculty at every position level agreed that "even with OWI, face-to-face interaction with students is important" (p. 8). Thus, while synchronous communication might constitute a smaller percentage of course time, it is nonetheless an integral component to developing a successful pedagogical strategy in the online teaching and learning of writing.

CONCLUSION AND RECOMMENDATIONS

While asynchronous feature sets have been and currently remain dominant with regard to OWI course infrastructure, under certain conditions, the evolution of hardware and software makes synchronous platforms a desirable option for particular OWI purposes (e.g., facilitating rapid conversational exchanges that establish the social presence necessary for honest but encouraging peer writing workshops online). In the future, advances in bandwidth and increases in access to greater connectivity are likely to make synchronous activities more accessible to OWI teachers and students, but OWI instructors and administrators still will need to assume responsibility for ensuring adequate access for all students.

Although the two modalities and their ability to be used separately or together in an OWC may not change, the media and tools developed for asynchronous and synchronous uses will continue to develop. To this end, the advantages of differentiated instruction means that instructors should continue to use available media and tools from both modalities thoughtfully and with access as an upfront value, just as they should do in the traditional face-to-face classroom. Furthermore, instructors should have a clear pedagogical rationale for using asynchronous or synchronous communication in OWI (Hewett, 2013). The following list of recommendations may help WPAs and teachers in making their decisions about digital modality for their OWCs.

- For accessibility purposes, survey students, instructors, and institutions about available modality and media.
- Survey students regarding their comfort levels with any social media and interactions built into the course, enabling those with invisible disabilities to express their social needs.
- Ensure 24/7 or otherwise sufficient IT support of both asynchronous and synchronous modalities for all instructors and students.
- Use asynchronous tools for a wide range of course-critical tasks, and take advantage of synchronous tools as needs and resources permit.
- Upon confirming student access, use asynchronous and synchronous modes to appeal to different learning styles and for specific pedagogical purposes.
- Ensure that the students and instructor have backup access on campus or elsewhere (or another backup plan) in case connectivity is lost or severely downgraded.
- Confirm that synchronous tools have recording capacity and ensure that students use that feature to document course interactions.
- Create a course "social contract" that identifies expectations for civil discourse to be followed by the students and instructor, and convey whether those expectations differ according to modality.

ACKNOWLEDGMENTS

The authors would like to express their gratitude to John Bonham at the University of Southern California, who completed essential research to lay the foundation of this chapter.

NOTES

1. For more information, see the Rogers et al., 2009, *Encyclopedia of Distance and Online Learning*; see also Hewett, 2013.

2. Hosted at Duke University, "English Composition I: Achieving Expertise" was taught by Denise Comer. The course ran roughly March-June, 2013, and it was attended by Connie Snyder Mick.

REFERENCES

Allen, Elaine & Seaman, Jeff (2013). *Changing course: Ten years of tracking online education in the United States*. The Sloan Consortium. Retrieved from http://sloanconsortium.org/publications/survey/changing_course_2012

Arbaugh, J. Ben. (2001). How instructor immediacy behaviors affect student satisfaction and learning in Web-based courses. *Business Communication Quarterly, 64*(4), 42-54.

CCCC OWI Committee for Effective Practices in Online Writing Instruction. (2011a). *Fully online distance-based courses survey results*. Retrieved from http://s.zoomerang.com/sr.aspx?sm=EAupi15gkwWur6G7egRSXUw8k-pNMu1f5gjUp01aogtY%3d

CCCC OWI Committee for Effective Practices in Online Writing Instruction. (2011b). *Hybrid/blended course survey results*. Retrieved from http://s.zoomerang.com/sr.aspx?sm=%2fPsFeeRDwfznaIyyz4sV0qxkkh5Ry7O1NdnGH-CxIBD4%3d

Conference on College Composition and Communication. (2004). *CCCC Position statement on teaching, learning, and assessing writing in digital environments*. Retrieved from http://www.ncte.org/cccc/resources/positions/digitalenvironments

D'Augustino, Steven. (2012). Toward a course conversion model for distance learning. *Journal of International Education in Business, 5*, 145-162.

DePew, Kevin E. & Lettner-Rust, Heather. (2009). Mediating power: Distance learning, classroom epistemology and the gaze. *Computers and Composition, 26*, 174-189.

DePew, Kevin E., Spangler, Sarah, & Spiegel, Cheri L. (2013). Getting past our assumptions about Web 2.0 and community building: How to design research-based literacy pedagogy. In Marohang Limbu & Binod Gurung (Eds.), *Emerging pedagogies in the networked knowledge society: Practices integrating social media and globalization* (pp. 120-143). Hershey, PA: IGI Global.

Dziuban, C., Hartman, J., Moskal, P., Sorg, S., & Truman, B. (2004). Three ALN modalities: An institutional perspective. In John Bourne & Janet C. Moore (Eds.), *Elements of quality online education: Into the mainstream* (pp. 127-148). Needham, MA: Sloan Center for Online Education.

Hewett, Beth L. (2006). Synchronous online conference-based instruction: A study of whiteboard interactions and student writing. *Computers and Composition, 23*(1), 4-31.

Hewett, Beth. L. (2010). *The online writing conference: A guide for teachers and tutors.* Portsmouth, NH: Boynton/Cook.

Hewett, Beth L. (2013). Fully online and hybrid writing instruction. In H. Brooke Hessler, Amy Rupiper Taggart, & Kurt Schick (Eds.), *A guide to composition pedagogies* (2nd ed.). (pp. 194-211). Oxford, UK: Oxford University Press.

Hewett, Beth L. (2015a). *Reading to learn and writing to teach: Literacy strategies for online writing instruction.* Boston: Bedford/St. Martin's Press.

Hewett, Beth L. (2015b). *The online writing conference: A guide for teachers and tutors.* Updated. Boston: Bedford/St. Martin's Press.

Hewett, Beth L. & Ehmann, Christa. (2004). *Preparing educators for online writing instruction: Principles and processes.* Urbana, IL: National Council of Teachers of English.

Hrastinski, Stefan (2008). Asynchronous & synchronous e-learning. *EDUCAUSE Quarterly, 4*, 51-55.

Johnson, Genevieve Marie (2006). Synchronous and asynchronous text-based CMC in educational contexts: A review of recent literature. *TechTrends, 50*, 46-53.

Kear, Karen L. (2011). *Online and social networking communities: A best practice guide for educators.* New York: Routledge.

Laurinen, Leena I. & Marttunen, Miika J. (2007). Written arguments and collaborative speech acts in practising the argumentative power of language through chat debates. *Computers and Composition, 24*(3), 230–246.

Moore, Janet C. (2011). A synthesis of Sloan-C effective practices. *Journal of Asynchronous Learning Networks, 16*(1): 91-115.

Rogers, Patricia, Berg, Gary, Boettcher, Judith, Howard, Caroline, Justice, Lorraine, & Karen Schenk, Karen (Eds.). (2009). *Encyclopedia of distance and online learning* (2nd ed.). Hershey, PA: IGI Global.

Warnock, Scott (2009). *Teaching writing online: How and why.* Urbana, IL: National Council of Teachers of English.

Wyatt, Christopher S. (2010). Online pedagogy: Designing writing courses for students with autism spectrum disorders (Doctoral dissertation, University of Minnesota). Available from ProQuest Dissertations and Theses database. Retrieved from http://search.proquest.com.libproxy.usc.edu/docview/597211269?accountid=14749 (597211269)

PART 2. OWI PEDAGOGY AND ADMINISTRATIVE DECISIONS

CHAPTER 4

TEACHING THE OWI COURSE

Scott Warnock
Drexel University

This chapter examines some foundational principles that ground instructional presence, conversational strategies, response to student writing, class management and organization, course assessment, and classroom technologies. Because of the rapid changes to technologies, the chapter pays particular attention to how to understand new technologies from their foundations before introducing them to the OWI course, or OWC.

Keywords: assessment, asynchronous, composition, conversation, hybrid, message board, OWI, presence, redundancy, response, teaching, teacher training

While there are many nuanced sub-positions within it, the CCCC OWI Committee's (2013) *A Position Statement of Principles and Example Effective Practices for OWI* is, in essence, about teaching writing online effectively. Even the most teaching-centric principles, the ones discussed in this chapter, do not offer a template because there are so many ways to teach writing online effectively. Like onsite teaching, OWI works or not based on context and the specific dynamics of an instructor and students—and institutions, of course. As Wilbert McKeachie (2002) pointed out, teachers must consider the various cultures and subcultures of their instructional environment (p. 4). The general "problem" that the pedagogy-specific principles address, though, is simple to articulate: *How do instructors teach writing online well?*

Framed by that question, this chapter attempts to cover a lot of ground. It discusses the five OWI principles focused on pedagogy (OWI Principles 2-6), examining such aspects of online instruction as:

- teacher presence
- strategies for building and encouraging conversation in OWCs
- responding to student writing and how, if at all, that might differ in OWI than it does in onsite courses
- class management and organization
- course evaluation and assessment
- class[room] technologies

This chapter does not and cannot serve as a stand-in for a full instructional guide for teaching writing online. Other publications have done that essential work, and they are addressed throughout this chapter. Instead, I look at these five OWI principles and accompanying effective practices and how they consider certain obstacles, issues, and challenges that instructors will encounter in both hybrid and fully online courses. In fact, the problems teachers face can in many cases be articulated as an inversion of these instructional OWI principles. For many reasons, writing teachers are placed and/or pressured into teaching situations and scenarios that may not enable them to offer their best teaching selves, perhaps preventing them, as Peter Filene (2005) said of teaching practice, from being "true to yourself" (p. 12). The challenge may be finding ways to hold onto teaching persona and voice while cultivating and sharing good pedagogical ideas and practices. These are the issues that the instructionally driven practices discussed in this chapter are designed to address.

OWI PRINCIPLE 2

An online writing course should focus on writing and not on technology orientation or teaching students how to use learning and other technologies.

Many writing courses, and FYW in particular, have a history of becoming a catch-all for college students; Wendy Bishop (2003), for example, wrote of finding composition's "pedagogical roots" (p. 65). Teachers find themselves doing everything in these courses—geographical orientation, technological orientation, psychotherapy, library skills—and the course can become so divided with these other activities that it only tangentially discusses writing. That situation, while common, is not effective for any kind of teaching; yet, technology complicates the issue in particular ways. As Diana G. Oblinger and James L. Oblinger (2005) expressed, students respond to learning activities more than they respond to any specific use of technology (p. 12). OWI teachers must use technology in the service of the compositional/pedagogical goals of their courses.

This curricular atomization can be a particular issue online, the CCCC OWI Committee's Expert/Stakeholders' panelists noted repeatedly during the research into *A Position Statement of Principles and Example Effective Practices for OWI* (CCCC OWI Committee, 2013). Even though composition has changed and shifted from applied rhetoric to a variety of writing studies' approaches (see Downs & Wardle [2007]), when writing instruction occurs in digital environments, the OWI teacher's goal is clear: "Whatever we need to do to help the student focus on their writing and not so much on the environment" (Shareen

Grogan, CCCC OWI Committee, 2011d). Because an OWC is facilitated with technology and FYW instructors in particular are often at the front line of interaction with an institution's students, teachers can turn into a regular (and, if they are not careful, all-hours) contact point for student technology woes. OWI Principle 2 (p. 11) is explicit: Teachers need to make sure their efforts are focused on teaching writing, and they need multi-level support to maintain that focus. Teachers will support students with all of the material and technological conditions in which they compose because those types of concerns often are inextricable from writing/composing itself, but they cannot be placed in the role of technology expert/support person.

This stance may seem obvious in terms of larger technological applications. Teachers may want to help students with issues like securing their LMS accounts. But on the practical level, this activity quickly becomes complicated. For instance, years ago an FYW student sent me this email:

> I'm having trouble viewing the syllabus because i deleted my
> microsoft word on accident. I know that as drexel students we
> can download it for free but it does not allow me to log in.
> I'm doing the whole drexel\userid thing.

Teachers, especially those new at their school, could be drawn into many well-meaning hunts to help students like this. Instead, the institution should provide clear, easily accessible help through IT departments and 24/7 (or reasonably accessible) help desks.

OWI Principle 2's example effective practices support that a teacher's focus on the writing of the course must be articulated and reinforced throughout a program and even an institution. Effective Practice 2.1 stated, "The requirement for the institution's initial technology orientation should be handled by the institution's information technology (IT) unit and not the OWI teacher of any OWC" (p. 11), and this practice is followed by 2.2: "An OWI teacher should not be considered a technology point person" and "reasonable technical assistance should be available to teachers" as well as students in person (if onsite) and by phone, email, or instant messaging during all instructional hours (p. 11).

In case of technology failure, teachers also should have an alternate lesson plan when the technology cannot be fixed on the spot. Since my earliest use of digital instructional technology, I have always used a risk-benefit-type analysis structure, accepting, as David Jonassen (2012) said in an article about educational decision making: "Risk assessment decisions assume that consequences are not in the hands of the decision maker but rather depend on chance, nature, and luck" (p. 346). I introduce or use tools and technology because I think the benefit justifies it. This decision is no different than anything we introduce to our courses. A simple onsite teaching analogy: If I invite a guest speaker to my onsite course, I think the benefit to students outweighs the risk that the speaker may get a flat tire (which happened to me once, resulting in no speaker). Teachers do not abandon chalkboards because one day the chalk might be missing. But teachers should have a back-up plan so that when something does not go right—say the conferencing software crashes—they can still do what they need to: Maybe, in this case, use the phone. Technology opens up teaching opportunities, but the challenge is to prevent the experience from hinging on the function of a few irreplaceable tools. Sometimes, perhaps, it is best just to stay simple. CCCC OWI Committee Expert/Stakeholders Beth Carroll and Lee-Ann Kastman Breuch said that a *least* effective practice for them and their colleagues was using anything too technology-heavy: Simple technology like Microsoft Word documents, GoogleDocs, and even telephones are good tools (CCCC OWI Committee, 2012a).

The excessive focus on technology can be a problem not just in terms of students emailing or phoning teachers because they cannot get their LMS working or a teacher's overreliance on breakable apps. Online environments by nature lend themselves to multimedia and Web-based/focused assignments and work. This nature provides tremendous opportunities for students to work with a mindset toward the capabilities and affordances of the digital writing environment (see also Chapter 14). Of course, composition broadly conceived includes images, sounds, and other media, but FYW and most other writing teachers and students do not and should not have to know the technological and rhetorical nuances of HTML code, for instance—especially now, when so many tools provide easy ways to do everything from design work to video recording. According to Effective Practice 2.3, the instructional focus should be on "the rhetorical nature of writing for the Web," on the *compositional* aspects of using technology to create writing (p. 11). Aside from access obstacles—outlined thoroughly in OWI Principle 1—most students, despite technological skill, can create a blog in a minute. Asking them to create a blog is well within the scope of many writing courses because blogs are a contemporary genre with teachable writing conventions for reaching particular audiences. In asking students to write a blog, however, as Effective Practice 2.3 emphasized, students should "focus on learning composition and not on learning technological platforms or software" (p. 11). In other words, students should not have to create a homepage or specialized Web page outside the affordances of their institutional LMS in order to accomplish a typical writing assignment. Significant access and inclusivity concerns arise when students are required to learn such technological skills in the typical writing course without training in the tool's use. In other circumstances, these tools themselves might lack accessibility or might be incompatible with the student's adaptive technology. Worse yet, such technology might not be suitable for certain students due to particular learning styles and abilities. Note, however, that if instructors—and, more importantly, their writing programs—want to incorporate a rhetorical exploration of platforms and tools, particularly in advanced writing courses, they should do so while conscientiously taking on the responsibility for providing access and inclusivity, as well as necessary teacher and student preparation. *A Position Statement of Principles and Example Effective Practices for OWI* (CCCC OWI Committee, 2013) was developed not to forbid changes in composition studies but to protect those who may have such instruction forced upon them without essential technical support and training.

Of course, planning always helps maintain course focus. According to Effective Practice 2.4 (p. 11), a teacher's focus on writing can be aided significantly if the teacher receives institution-supported professional development *before* the course starts (also see Chapters 11 & 14). The real world of staffing involves pressure to get things done quickly and sometimes without adequate planning, particularly when contingent faculty are hired late (see Chapter 7), but ideally teachers would have a full semester or more *before teaching online* to become trained in the necessary pedagogies and technologies.

Ultimately, this conversation is centered in *access*. As Larry LaFond (2002) stated more than a decade ago, many have viewed distance learning as a way to broaden access, but the promise of access also brings problems; the digital divide still prevents many students—and even teachers—from full access to OWI. By being mindful of access and overall composition goals, teachers are better positioned to maintain an environment that is inclusive for all.

OWI PRINCIPLE 3

Appropriate composition teaching/learning strategies should be developed for the unique features of the online instructional environment.

OWI courses are writing courses, first and foremost, but, as I have argued elsewhere (Warnock 2009), teaching writing with digital technology tools opens up incredible opportunities. Technologies should not control what teachers do, but teachers would be remiss not to take advantage of the *affordances* of educational technologies for writing courses. In fact, after using digital tools, most teachers develop new approaches that influence their core pedagogy. Susan Lowes (2008) called teachers who move back and forth from face-to-face to online platforms "trans-classroom teachers." She stated:

> And as a teacher moves, either simultaneously or serially, from one environment to the other, the course being taught will

> also be transformed as it is shaped and reshaped to fit first
> one context and then the other. Much like immigrants who
> leave the cultural comfort of their home societies and move to
> places with very different cultures and social practices, those
> who teach online leave the familiarity of the face-to-face class-
> room for the uncharted terrain of the online environment,
> whose constraints and affordances often lead to very different
> practices. (para. 2)

These "different practices" can—and probably should—compel teachers to look closely at their teaching selves, helping them find new ways to work with and engage students.

However, the astonishing rapidity of digital technology change means teachers must think about technologies in foundational ways before introducing them to an OWI course. This point returns us to how teachers conceptualize themselves: They should consider what they are trying to accomplish and then think about ways that technology complements those goals and philosophies, as discussed to some degree in Chapters 2 and 3. Doing so may require some earnest (and perhaps painful) self-reflection. Teachers do not want to become pigeon-holed into particular, highly specific types of technology; instead, they should think about how various applications help them accomplish their course goals.

STRAIGHTFORWARD COMMUNICATION AND CLEAR TEXTUAL TEACHING PRACTICES

Online courses put more pressure on teachers' communication skills (Hewett, 2015a) because most of what is communicated and taught is mediated by technology. In asynchronous courses, almost all instruction, content, and teaching through feedback to student writing is done with text and provided to students without the certainty of future in-person meetings. In synchronous courses, which are rarer, the same largely holds true. When spoken language is used in real time or in audio and audio/video recordings, for example, specificity of language and what Beth Hewett calls semantic integrity (i.e., fidelity between the writer's intention and the reader's inference) also are crucial (Hewett, 2010, 2015a, 2015b). Effective Practice 3.1 provided overt guidance in this way: OWI teachers should use "written language that is readable and comprehensible," and the many written instructions should be "straightforward, plain, and linguistically direct" (p. 12).

Teachers should re-consider how their messages appear to their students, beginning with the initial design and practices in course documents. CCCC OWI

Committee Expert/Stakeholder Jim Porter said:

> Early on I was too reliant on emails and long narratives on
> description of things and that just wasn't very effective [for]
> presenting information. But I think shorter, more compact
> things, shorter presentations, shorter videos, shorter agenda
> […] I think focusing and cutting the extra verbosity and
> making the information design really sharp helps students to
> understand what's due when and what the main principles
> are. (CCCC OWI Committee, 2011d).

OWCs need various new "ground rules," Porter said, about things like "How are we going to communicate with one another? How are we going to have discussions?" (CCCC OWI Committee, 2011d), and the articulation of the rules themselves must be clear. CCCC OWI Committee Expert/Stakeholder Rich Rice said that "a best practice" he applies is to create an "expanded" syllabus with lots of hyperlinks "to lead individual students to different things, giving them more active practice" (CCCC OWI Committee, 2012a).

As Hewett (2015a) argued extensively in *Reading to Learn and Writing to Teach: Literacy Strategies for Online Writing Instruction*, cultivating good OWI practices also requires developing a culture of reading and re-reading in the course—for both teacher and students. Text-rich settings also are text heavy, as Hewett says in Chapter 1. Indeed, the reading for students in OWI can be incredibly different than in comparable onsite courses. June Griffin and Deborah Minter (2013) compared the required reading of students in one fully online and two traditional onsite writing courses, finding that "the reading load of the online classes was more than 2.75 times greater than the face-to-face classes" (p. 153). Given this reading load, a teacher's incomplete or underdeveloped thought in an email or discussion post can lead to multiple problems of student comprehension and teacher *ethos*. Instructors must carefully proofread their own work for content and clarity; this work places them in the role of *modeling* communication behavior *and strong writing skills*, a key point for me (Warnock, 2009) and for Hewett (2010, 2015a, 2015b). It is interesting how such modeling can change practice; for instance, in my message board conversations, I ask students to use cited evidence whenever possible. Online, with search engines at your fingertips, there is little excuse to say, "I once heard about a study." Of course, as a teacher I am pressed for time occasionally and want to say, "I once heard about a study," but I just cannot say that and expect students not to do so, too. Everything I write in an OWC provides a model—strong or weak—for student writers. These points all connect with issues of instructor *presence*. CCCC OWI Committee Member Jason Snart[1] said in a meeting of expert/stakeholders: "So

157

I think from my perspective on the instructor side of it, is the more I can make my involvement obvious to the students on a regular basis, the more effective that seems to be for me to get them to feel like they need to be involved with the class, with each other, with me on a regular basis as well" (CCCC OWI Committee, 2011d).

In asynchronous, text-based courses, the pressures of heavy reading and writing loads and the need for clarity and teacher modeling increase. The course is primarily, if not exclusively, textual. As we mention throughout this book, this text-centric nature of the asynchronous course (and of many features in online synchronous writing courses as well) provides many opportunities to help students learn to write. However, teachers must step back and think in a usability-centered way (see Redish, 2012) about the documents as well as the communication experiences in the course. Access issues are monumental when writing is taught through text primarily and students, some of whom are poor readers of instructional text, must teach themselves through what they read (Hewett, 2015a).

Time is a factor in OWI, and time is necessary to communicate well with students. Initially, the time to teach an OWC can be daunting, as many argue. But I have found that teachers will (or *should*) develop a vast pool of carefully crafted communications. I have files of easily searchable message board prompts, general pieces of advice, even course announcements, and I believe teachers can *leverage* their time rapidly in online environments if they use these tools well. While OWI teachers may not have the onsite room of students with whom to discuss general issues in a writing project, they can create a document or post of such observations, which students can revisit as often as they want. There is a quality of thoughtful repetition in OWI that gives online students, who cannot line up outside the office after class asking for a repeat performance of the "General issues with Project 1" speech, opportunity to access needed answers to their questions.

USING AUDIO AND VISUAL TECHNOLOGY

While technology can be integral to response, in line with broader OWI principles, the *strategies* are what matter. This *thinking digitally* also means that teaching writing online, interacting with students' documents, and writing in ways that are exclusively digital open up communication opportunities teachers might not have considered onsite. Using audio/video is one way technology can enhance communications, whether the course is text-centric and asynchronous or live video-based and synchronous, as Effective Practice 3.2 suggested. Those audio/video technologies can be used either asynchronously in recorded form in response to student writing (J. Sommers, 2002; Warnock, 2008) or as a means of facilitating synchronous conferences. In line with other key ideas in *A Position Statement of Principles and Example Effective Practices for OWI* (CCCC OWI Committee, 2013), as long as access issues have been addressed adequately, using these modalities helps learners in various ways while also providing crucial communicative *redundancy* in course lessons.

Because of modeling and other text-centric teaching philosophies, WPAs and instructors can make strong arguments to use text-based writing as the core of course communications, but in the interest of clarity, textual experiences in the course can be enhanced significantly by multimedia. The barriers that might impede the use of audio and video are dropping precipitously, so instructors can more easily and effectively incorporate audio/video technologies into their courses. Nonetheless, it is crucial to remember that although teachers' communications may be in audio and video as well as text, even audio/video technologies do not relieve instructors of the challenges of conciseness and clarity. Audio and video—even synchronous, video dialogue— still rely on clear and unambiguous messages, as even the best technologies obstruct common in-person cues of facial and body language.

RESPONDING TO STUDENT WRITING

In OWI, teachers may have to think differently in the area of the classic writing teacher communications to students—response to student writing projects. As any writing teacher knows, responding to writing is one of the most significant aspects of our interaction with students, and we do much individualized teaching in this process. Although response once was dominated by teachers' (mostly) one-way interactions with students' major written projects, OWI teachers and students are in a constant cycle of response that can be much more dialogic and complex (Hewett, 2015a). Researchers have long described patterns of vagueness, terseness, and sometimes outright meanness in teaching response (N. Sommers, 1982)—the product of writing thousands of words about similar problems in a short period of time. Writing is difficult, no matter who you are, and that does not change at all—at all!—when teachers write to students. In fact, an audience of developing students seeking advice for writing may be the most challenging audience a writer can face.

Teachers have to consider the use of stylistic approaches such as rhetorical questions, idioms, and metaphorical/figurative language. Will they work? In many cases, Hewett thinks they will not (2010, 2015b), advocating linguistically direct (not necessarily *directive*) response instead. Is it better to be as direct as possible? How much does a teacher balance prescriptive advice with Socratic questions? Is certain redundancy necessary in these stylistic and rhetorical choices to accommodate the cognitive needs of students with differing learning abilities? How helpful will it be for comments to be anchored to a rubric? Effective Practice 3.5 suggests one approach, a problem-centered approach to write to students. As Hewett (2015a) indicated, such a problem-centered approach could include asking open-ended questions; demonstrating; illustrating; and, again, modeling (specifically modeling at the level "being required of the student"). Teachers cannot assume that the ambiguity inherent in open-ended questions is appropriate for all learners, and they should provide additional scaffolds for those who might process information differently. Teachers need to think about the clarity of writing vocabulary and other instructional terms (Hewett, 2011, p. 12). Developing revision strategies is integral, and teachers must think about such strategies differently than in onsite instruction. CCCC OWI Committee Expert/Stakeholder Panelist Errol Sull said a top problem students cite in OWI courses is "that they get lack of instructor feedback or get lack of instructor's feedback in time"; to maintain the student-teacher connection, he indicated "that custom feedback has to be there" (CCCC OWI Committee, 2011d).

While strategy matters most, technologies exist to make written response to student writing more efficient *and* effective. CCCC OWI Committee Expert/Stakeholder Angela Solic revealed that "another best practice is using software to help grading" (CCCC OWI Committee, 2012a). Such technologies are not exclusive to online learning, of course; their use simply represents another way writing instruction in general can be inflected by digital environments.

RESPONDING TO SMALL ASSIGNMENTS

In an OWC, teachers often will look at many smaller writing assignments as well as multiple essay drafts, so that classic teacher response to larger projects may change. CCCC OWI Committee Expert/Stakeholder Rich Rice said in his technical writing course he does not grade many papers but he sees lots of message board posts: "A best practice would also be realizing as an instructor you do not have to read every single post or grade every single thing to be effective. The point is they are contributing; the point is not that you are grading everything that they are contributing." CCCC OWI Committee Expert/Stakeholder Melody Pickle, elaborating on that point, indicated that looking at and grading "discussion boards and things like that" are "significantly going to change the grading time or time in the class" (CCCC OWI Committee, 2012b). In fact, responding to these small assignments might not be best thought of as grading, as CCCC OWI Committee Member Web Newbold said: "Perhaps 'assessment' would be a good term to use" (CCCC OWI Committee, 2012b).

Interestingly, even though evaluating a stack of projects is time consuming, teachers quickly understand the time expectations. Working with small assignments, especially in a dialogic way, can disrupt those expectations. CCCC OWI Committee Member Heidi Harris cautioned that instructors might supplant large projects with "a bunch of small assignments" and then "they can't get student feedback there on time and this pushes that feeling that students have to constantly be doing something to be constantly connecting with the class" (CCCC OWI Committee, 2012a). Such actions actually are counter-productive, as Snart indicates in Chapter 2. It is too easy to think students need to be online more hours per week than they would when engaging onsite course work, and such tasks can become busy work both to students and teachers.

TEXT-WISE, MEDIUM MEETS MESSAGE

Many writers decry the use of emoticons, and exclamation point overuse is rampant; yet, word processing and HTML writing environments offer a variety of communication and rhetorical opportunities that OWI teachers should consider. Although instructors may not want to create an intricate, layered hypertext narrative every time they write a course announcement, they can take advantage of those tools. Effective Practice 3.3 addressed teachers' uses of different writing tools if for no other reason than "to mirror the types of online writing students most often read" (p. 12) This practice is in line with the central pedagogical principle that OWI is about writing instruction, not Web design, and using the various text-production capabilities can help clarify a message. Such tools include such simple strategies as emphasizing text by strike-through, highlighting, and graphics and drawing. As writers and rhetoricians themselves, OWI teacher-writers should make the most of the opportunities and tools available for textual communication with students.

REDUNDANCY AND SUPPORT

OWI teachers should employ *redundancy* in their OWCs—in the content, instructional texts, and any documents students must read or ideas that are crucial to their writing growth. In line with Effective Practice 3.6 (serendipitously also expressed in Effective Practice 4.6), it is important to consider that strategic redundancy provides students with various ways of receiving the same information (p. 15). In *Teaching Writing Online* (2009), one of my own guidelines is that "Redundancy is crucial when you deliver information in your OWcourses"; for example, I suggested that teachers provide information about the due date of a final project using the syllabus, specific project instructions, course announcements, and even email (pp. 56-57). If teachers provide information in different ways using various tools *and* media, they can help students—especially those who may have a disability impeding their comprehension in one medium—to understand both the information and its importance to the course. (By the way, this type of redundancy is different from the "Redundancy Principle" of Ruth C. Clark and Richard E. Mayer [2011], which advised against *simultaneous* redundancy in multimedia, such as the triple-presentation [e.g., text on slide, spoken, hand-out] of information in a presentation).

Teachers can use electronic tools to replicate—and I believe strengthen—their communicative approaches in the course. This redundancy is not nagging because it provides all learners, and perhaps particularly those with disability-based obstacles to textual comprehension, with a better chance to succeed. Most institutional LMSs offer multiple "places" for teachers to give students information, such as individual pages for the digital syllabus and a static downloadable syllabus, discussion post spaces, class announcement spaces, individualized spaces like email or journals, and the like. It is standard practice for many teachers to provide library modules, connections to student support services (in line with OWI Principles 1 and 13), and other helpful materials. Students should have particular places to discuss assignments (and not just with the teacher but with each other), to pose questions (my "Questions about the course" thread often is the most high-traffic thread in a class), and to provide meeting spaces for students, whether synchronous or asynchronous. Such variety lends itself to teachers posting messages, assignments, and comments redundantly.

Finally, teachers also will want to think about ways that digital tools can replicate behaviors they perhaps do not even think about as part of teaching. For instance, the end-of-class onsite verbal assignment reminder may be a common practice, but education technology can provide other, sometimes better ways to keep students on track, such as a weekly video assignment reminder.

REMEMBER TO CONNECT VIA WRITING

Again, a great—and perhaps revolutionary—thing in OWI is that students will engage in most course interactions via writing, and, although plenty of technologies exist to connect students and teachers without writing (including the humble phone), OWI teachers may want to encourage students deliberately to pose logistical questions via writing. In doing so, students can learn by practicing the "how to" variety of exposition while seeing how teachers and peers explain step-by-step directions. After all, students can learn from these transactional written interactions, including simple things like how to provide a good subject line or how to name documents effectively. While teachers all have amusing teaching anecdotes of receiving emails with subjects like "Yo dude" or receiving a pool of student project files and discovering 50 of them are named "Essay1," there are deeper rhetorical ideas at work in such practices—especially in terms of providing students with reflective moments in fast-paced digital communications.

Hybrid Articulation Between Onsite and Online Activities

As Snart addresses in Chapter 2, it is crucial to plan what onsite and online activities will occur, particularly in hybrid courses. I like teaching hybrid courses and try to do a good job when I do. But something that continues to bedevil me is how teachers can maximize the articulation between onsite and online experiences. Teachers should seek ways to "expand" the class[room] productively, using the differentiation among modalities not only to help students write and learn but to conduct arguments and discussions using the different skills demanded by different communication modalities—all of which can improve their overall digital communication skills. Teachers certainly can have conversations face-to-face and online to complement and draw on the strengths of different environments. They can develop an invention exercise for a major project as an in-person group, drawing on brainstorming and frenetic discussion, and then productively take the conversation onto a message board in which the individual authors describe their ideas more formally in writing.

Teachers should be thinking along those lines. Effective Practice 3.9 stated, "From a writing instructional perspective, teachers should take full advantage of the flexibility of electronic communications in the planning and guiding of projects and activities" (p. 13). To this end, teachers should conceive their use of electronic tools around the general concept of "expanding the classroom." The notion of a "flipped classroom" currently is in vogue. A quick Internet search of "flipped classroom" provided numerous perspectives on this teaching strategy (EDUCAUSE, 2012, offered a good summary), but in essence, this is a new term/frame for an old teaching approach: Have students do their passive learning (which might include listening to a lecture) outside of the class[room] and use the onsite/in-class time to collaborate, write, or work in a lab. Hybrid teaching, as Snart (2010) said in *Hybrid Learning,* "does present the opportunity for truly re-imagined teaching" (p. 112).

To experienced OWI teachers, it may seem rudimentary to read in Effective Practice 3.9 that "The concept of the 'classroom' can be expanded productively to include time when students and teacher are not physically present in a room" (p. 13). Nonetheless, a complex notion underlies this idea—learning is continuous. "Continuous" is a deliberate word choice because it invites students into an ongoing relationship with their learning experiences, a relationship that helps them challenge the idea that learning takes place exclusively "in" school settings. This notion helps set up undergraduate students for the goal of lifelong learning that we see most often in effective adult learners and workers.

MODERATION IS AN ART

Moderating a good conversation in any venue is both art and craft, but online moderation, whether asynchronous or synchronous, introduces additional challenges. In my observation of OWCs and reading student evaluations associated with them, a common disappointment that students voice is the lack of engagement in the asynchronous discussions by their teachers. Effective Practice 3.10 stated, "Teachers should moderate online class discussions to develop a collaborative OWC and to ensure participation of all students, the free and productive exchange of ideas, and a constant habit of written expression with a genuine audience" (p. 14). Fortunately, teachers can respond to this practice by learning more about moderating conversations online. George Collison et al. (2000) wrote an excellent book about teaching in these environments (*Facilitating Online Learning: Effective Strategies for Moderators*), as did Tisha Bender (2003) (*Discussion-Based Online Teaching to Enhance Student Learning: Theory, Practice and Assessment*) and Gilly Salmon (2000) (*E-Moderating: The Key to Teaching and Learning Online*).

Teachers unaccustomed to the dynamics of a group of students having a textual discussion will need to be ready for something quite different from their typical onsite experience. I mentioned in *Teaching Writing Online* (2009):

> In synchronous or onsite environments, the conversation is
> fairly linear, almost always meaning that not everyone can
> participate. With message boards, conversations can build in
> parallel fashion. Some students may be shy about speaking
> their minds in a classroom conversation or even a fast-paced
> chat setting, where by the time you respond, the rest of the
> group is on to another topic. (pp. 69-70)

Teachers can capitalize on the anonymity (or at least suppressed presence) of messages boards, which two decades ago Gail Hawisher (1992) found open to more equitable participation (p. 88). The class conversation forum is in theory an open place with opportunity for "talking" that students may especially enjoy because, even though they are experienced with texting and Facebooking, they may have never been pushed to have a serious conversation about something that does not involve their personal lives (and personal affinities). Remember, though, that students' "digital nativeness" can be an impediment in this way, leading some to respond to formal discussion requests with informal language, a lack of thoughtfulness, and too much personal information. The technology of threaded conversations itself can be a barrier for others with neurological or visual disabilities who might miss social cues or who might experience confusion when confronted with a volley of little-structured, impromptu verbal exchanges.

Effective Practice 3.10 suggested that teachers should find ways to capitalize on the positive traits of the digital dialogic environment (p. 14). Teachers can push students in ways they may not be comfortable doing in class. For instance, I find that I am more effective at calling students out in constructive ways when working with them online. If they make an unsupported assertion, I am quick to ask them for necessary support in online conversations. Onsite, if students struggle to make a point, to articulate their perspective, I sometimes find myself shying away from pressing them in the interest of avoiding embarrassing them. Online, my class culture allows for this kind of pushing: *"What do you mean?— and being clear about what you mean is a natural part of the course."*

Teachers can take advantage of the gaps in online dialogue, which occur in part because reflection time is built-in and is particularly conducive to asynchronous environments, to ask highly difficult questions. In a way, that also is a kind of class flipping. In an onsite class, teachers might be concerned about having a room full of students turning pages or scrolling in an effort to mine texts for specific concepts, but online, I assume they have the space and time to hunt and reflect. I *want* them to do so. The use of research represents a major shift in my expectations for students' communications practices. I can ask them for research in ways I could not do onsite *because every student in the conversation has the Web immediately available.* But teachers need to find out when to query, to prod, to challenge—all while having built a structure that keeps students engaged. This type of teaching does not come easy, but the opportunities are rich.

META LEARNING

Teachers should maximize the inherently archival nature of OWI as much as possible. *Students in an OWC have virtual piles of their own low-stakes writing to work with and analyze,* and teachers should think rhetorically and metacognitively to help students write more effectively. Effective Practice 3.11 suggested that metacognitive activities are ideal opportunities for process-based work and even for approaches like writing portfolios:

> The inherently archival nature of the online environment
> should be used for learning. To this end, teachers should use

the digital setting to encourage students to rhetorically and metacognitively analyze their own learning/writing processes and progress. Such strategies can identify growth areas and points for further assistance. (CCCC OWI Committee, 2013, p. 12)

Why is low-stakes writing important in encouraging students to work on meta aspects of writing? Consider this in-class exercise, which I admit to cruelly administering to my students. Students come to an onsite class with a hard-copy paper to turn in, and, right before they do so, I ask them to pair up and read the paper aloud to each other. Ouch. Of course, the well-meaning teacher only does this to demonstrate the power of collaborative proofing, but singed students who really engage with the exercise find errors in a paper that *is about to be turned in for a grade.* The high-stakes nature of the project—an essay due that day—could undermine the endeavor. Using the vast amount of low-stakes materials assembled in most asynchronous courses, teachers can achieve similar meta/reflective practices while students can do what we really hope they do: look at their own work critically but without too much pressure that can *obstruct their ability to see the text as it is.* When I write on deadline, I know I will myself into believing my text is error-free because that is what I need to believe at that time; students should learn that all writers have this need and editing still may be necessary.

TIMING OF RESPONSE AND FEEDBACK

Responding to students is crucial teaching work because feedback provides students with their most individualized teaching experience in online settings. It also is time-intensive and time-sensitive. Remember that in an OWC, teachers are *not* spending that three hours or more a week in a classroom, even if some of their time is spent in synchronous interactions via virtual classrooms or onsite for hybrid courses. The interactions they do have often are presented in a written form to students, and teachers will need to define with some care and precision the parameters of that response. Effective Practice 3.12 indicated, "The feedback loop both for essay response and question/issue response as well as the expected timing for these processes should be well-defined in any OWC" (p. 14). One reason for establishing feedback timing is to aid students in their writing and planning, but another important reason is for the teachers' benefit. OWI teachers do not want students to have unreasonable (maybe on a human endurance level) expectations of response. As CCCC OWI Committee Expert/Stakeholder Joanna Paul said simply, "I think it's important not to overload ourselves with graded writing to review" (CCCC OWI Committee, 2012a). Whether OWI teachers provide response windows or give students timing expectations in days or hours, they should create an understanding of expectations of how issues might be resolved; in the language of Effective Practice 3.12, "Doing so builds appropriate boundaries, trust, and a sense of relationship" (p. 12).

Timeframes for essay, journal, and discussion post responses might best be set program-wide by the WPA, but, in keeping with OWI Principle 5, individual teachers should retain reasonable control over the amount of time they spend and when they write those responses (p. 15).

OWI PRINCIPLE 4

Appropriate onsite composition theories, pedagogies, and strategies should be migrated and adapted to the online instructional environment.

In line with remembering they are teaching a *writing* course—albeit online—and that there are nuances to OWI that lend themselves to new theories and strategies, OWI teachers also need to foreground, perhaps in a more fundamental way, their role as *teacher*. Many teachers still come to online teaching from onsite teaching. Migration of pedagogy is key. In other words, OWI teachers—particularly novice instructors—should begin with what they do best onsite and adapt those strategies to online settings. I remember, while working on my dissertation in 2000, sitting down with a senior faculty member. Our conversation turned to education technologies. In a pleasant conversation, he told me that his concerns about educational technology took this form: While he was well regarded as a teacher and took his teaching seriously, he believed there was an assumption that he would change to accommodate educational technologies. In short, he expressed that he felt "colonized" by teaching technologies. I think it is important not just for teachers but also for those involved with faculty development and instructional design to understand this thread of colonization.

OWI Principle 4 (p. 14) highlights the concept of *migration*, or taking what we know of writing pedagogy and "moving" it to an online setting, albeit with adaptation, as OWI Principle 4 indicated and Snart explains in Chapter 2. The world of educational technology offers much that is new. But it does not mean that dedicated teachers have to abandon what has made them effective. Instead, this principle recognized prior effectiveness and encouraged: "Teachers should seek opportunities to use their established practices when moving online while seeking alternative ways of offering those practices within digital spaces and using electronic tools" (p. 14). While shifting to OWI can be a heady experience, modality, media, and technology change should offer opportunity and promise, not chaos and anxiety.

BUILDING ASSIGNMENTS

For many writing instructors, building assignments piecemeal, in components, is integral to good instruction. As many chapters in this book describe, technology facilitates division of work into process components. Some simple asynchronous technologies—message boards, blogs—facilitate the kinds of conversations that help build dialogue around course projects and assignments.

In my own courses, I have always felt good about having open, in-class, onsite conversations about topics for major projects. These have been lively and productive, and I often end up listing the topics on the board and providing every student with an opportunity to contribute. In moving online (both hybrid and fully online), I realized that this useful in-class discussion practice could be even better. Providing a message board on which students can openly discuss project topics through text has proven excellent; in this case, they are writing their responses, providing additional time to reflect and offer substantive commentary. Meanwhile, I also have the time provided by asynchronous environments to look at all of the topics *in toto* and to generate, in addition to focused responses to individual students, a collective message—with quoted evidence—to the whole group. All our work becomes an artifact for the course that we refer to through the process of developing the writing project, which is a useful way for teaching students how to scaffold their own thinking and writing.

BUILDING COURSE KNOWLEDGE

Long-standing ideas about knowledge creation and rhetorical theory make for tremendous partners with online writing environments. Electronic platforms and conventional modalities and tools provide strong opportunities for students to think about their own composing processes and thinking processes together (see Bruffee, 1984).

For instance, message boards—a simple way to enable students to have asynchronous written conversations—provide many meta-writing opportunities to help students think through their writing process and practices as well as those of other students. As I described in "The Low-Stakes, Risk-Friendly Message Board Text?" (2010), I have asked students to "share your secrets" about research:

> "Where do you start? How do you do it? What techniques do
> you use? How do you stay organized? How do you remem-
> ber how to incorporate quotes? ... Let us know some of your
> research tricks." Although one might think students would

respond tepidly to a post about research process, that has not been the case. In fact, they have revealed so many interesting aspects of their research process that I have abstracted the best of these responses into one file and provided them as a "gift" to the whole class at the term's end. (p. 103)

Through these types of practices, we rip through the silence surrounding many student writing practices. Rather than just learning "best practices" from me—one voice—they see strategies their peers use. Some of these practices are sophisticated, and peers immediately remark on that. They learn a whole crowd-sourced array of research practices. While teachers could do this kind of work onsite, the asynchronicity and lack of face-to-face immediacy seem to provide opportunities for students to have deep online conversations that might fall flat onsite.

Teachers certainly can use the vast amount of student-generated writing to ask students to proof their own work, to reread and re-evaluate their arguments, and even to think through how they converse rhetorically in an online forum versus a similar argument made in a "formal" project. At the 2007 Penn State Conference on Rhetoric and Composition, I discussed my student "Nick," who wrote a superb message board counterargument to several classmates during a debate about intelligent design. After I suggested he convert this counterargument into a major project, he *deflated* his writing. In the presentation, I pointed out changes from the message board conversation to Nick's "official" paper: "'Thesis statement' runs on grammatically; voice is strained: seems afraid to say, 'In my opinion,' giving the prose a contrived, inflated sense of objectivity" (Warnock, 2007, July). Somehow, the writing changed—perhaps to Ken Macrorie's (1970) "Engfish"—and it lost its edge, but in our discussions about the post, Nick seemed to realize that his writing could have power.

Using the Technology to Facilitate Dialogue

Many onsite teachers may wonder what will happen to their course interactions when they move to OWI. But teachers have an opportunity to, as Effective Practice 4.4 pointed out, "extend the reach of classroom interactions" (p. 14), while helping students at all times to be cognizant of the rhetorical nuances of the electronic realm. As I mentioned earlier regarding moderating online discussions, electronic tools for writing and thinking provide opportunities to create a collaboration- and writing-centered course experience.

Leslie Blair (2005) wrote about the potential of message boards for students' writing: "The practice they receive through writing to communicate with their instructor and peers can be as influential to their writing skills as major essay assignments." When students begin to communicate online, Blair said, "Their perception of audience begins to shift," as the instructor and other students create a multifaceted audience and "they begin to recognize the biases, opinions, and preconceived notions of their audience, which allows them to practice writing for the addressee." Also, quiet students now "are much more likely to make their opinions known in an online environment where they can contemplate their words before the rest of the group has access to them" (sect. 2, para. 5). Blair suggests the ideal of what can happen in an OWC, making the digital environment a cornerstone of a good composition course.

OWI PRINCIPLE 5

> **Online writing teachers should retain reasonable control over their own content and/or techniques for conveying, teaching, and assessing their students' writing in their OWCs.**

As writing teachers, let us acknowledge that our teaching may not be ours to control fully. The CCCC OWI Committee developed OWI Principle 5 (p. 15) to account for this teaching reality; it provides WPAs and their OWI teachers with language that might prevent teaching from morphing into a mass-produced good or service.

In the CCCC OWI Committee's conversations with CCCC OWI Committee Expert/Stakeholder Panelists, a recurring theme arose about teaching from prescribed syllabi: it is not a recommended practice, to say the least. CCCC OWI Committee Expert/Stakeholder Angela Solic said, "The least effective strategy for me has been to use content that another instructor created." CCCC OWI Committee member Web Newbold said, "I strongly support Angela's point about using someone else's course. It's often tempting (or required) to use pre-packaged content, and some may be able to do that well, but it hasn't worked for me." CCCC OWI Committee Expert/Stakeholder Melody Pickle reinforced this thought, saying, "I think a best practice would allow the teacher to have some of his or her own content" (CCCC OWI Committee, 2012a). CCCC OWI Committee Expert/Stakeholder Rich Rice took the conversation a pedagogical step further, pointing out that even teaching one's own "core syllabus" can be a problem: "One of the least effective strategies has always been if I just copy and paste a previous course into a new semester and then don't leave room to change the nature of the course based on where students take it without taking into consideration the students and what their interests are, reading and writing assignments, [and] things like that" (CCCC OWI Committee, 2012a).

The experts strongly expressed that there was a responsibly to personalizing courses, in line with what D. Randy Garrison and Terry D. Anderson (1999) called "little distance education" (LDE), a structure reducing industrialization and maximizing aspects like interaction, meaningful learning outcomes, and active learning. LDE is considered to be "flexible in design," and "course materials are created [...] and stored such that they can easily be modified, augmented, annotated" by students and teachers (p. 54). These CCCC OWI Committee Expert/Stakeholders seem to be pointing to a similar model.

WHEN A TEMPLATE OR CORE MIGHT BE USEFUL

The word "reasonable" appears in OWI Principle 5 because the CCCC OWI Committee recognized, particularly with FYW, that many institutions and programs have some understandable levels of uniformity or standardization in their syllabi and outcomes. Students travel through the writing requirements and courses in some progression, and most teachers would agree that Technical Writing II should extend logically from the work in Technical Writing I. I think back to a thought-experiment conversation I had with one of the best teachers I know. We were talking about sequencing a FYW program, and, in defending a core syllabus and outcomes for such an approach, I asked, "What if students took an English 101 that featured *War and Peace* and then they took an English 102 and discovered that instructor also wanted to use *War and Peace*?" My colleague said she could envision a situation in which students would learn a tremendous amount from two such courses. Perhaps she was right (especially if she were one of the teachers), but in most situations, students in required course sequences have expectations that they will build on knowledge they acquired in the previous course and will not be reliant on a kind of super-teacher who can make the most of repeated content. This expectation seems obvious in a math curriculum (where Algebra I content would mostly not be retaught in an Algebra II course), and it seems obvious for writing courses if outcomes are clearly defined. Hence, the idea of reasonable control for an instructor of a given OWC, we understand, has to exist in the context of program and course requirements.

Certainly, a writing program should encourage that core syllabi may contain supports, structures, and pacing that can work for students with disabilities, different learning styles, challenged socioeconomic backgrounds, multilingual skills, and the like. WPAs rightly can expect some standardization and uniformity with issues of access and inclusivity, as OWI Principle 1 indicated. These are reasonable areas where template language can be helpful.

Such templates and core requirements also provide areas of certainty for teachers—in other words, some boundaries and well-defined limits are helpful.

For example, while having some teaching independence was widely supported in CCCC OWI Committee Expert/Stakeholder conversations, several panelists discussed how templates can be useful, especially for first-time OWI instructors. For instance, CCCC OWI Committee Expert/Stakeholder Shareen Grogan said, "It's really nice to have a parameter so that you know, maybe a template that helps you decide how much is appropriate for a given week in an online course, but then with a lot of freedom to add, to embellish, to adapt to tweak the assignments" (CCCC OWI Committee, 2012a). What appeared important was not just the freedom to do whatever one wishes for the sake of freedom, but a sense that independence of choice is better for teaching and, thus, for OWI students.

As an inherent part of teaching, OWI instructors still need to conduct courses in ways allowing them to provide the best of themselves, and the example effective practices associated with OWI Principle 5 attempt to reflect that through a focus on flexibility, as discussed below.

WORKING WITH TEACHERS AND FLEXIBILITY

Good communication is a key practice in which flexibility is critical. Teachers must be informed about alterations to their programs, for example, via reliable communications. Embedded in this idea of flexibility is the quality of *trust*: Teachers need to be trusted to provide quality OWI. WPAs and institutions must work *with* teachers and should communicate with them about the shape, progress, and direction of OWI initiatives. WPAs should work closely with faculty in their programs to design curricula that account for expected and anticipated OWI aspects of these programs. Faculty and administrators also must have a clear means of communication about OWI, as indicated in OWI Principle 11 (p. 23) and explored in Chapters 11 and 12.

Interviews with the CCCC OWI Committee Expert/Stakeholders suggested concerns that any standardization in online learning may lead to teachers losing their freedom to create and deliver writing courses that match their strengths and educational philosophies. However, nothing inherent to OWI leads to such an outcome; administrations and institutions that want standardized education will seek it regardless of the course learning environment. Additionally, the threat posed by some online models, in which teachers could lose control of the intellectual property of a first-time-generated course and then be replaced in subsequent semesters, seems more difficult to enact in writing courses, since the subject matter is so different from "content" courses (a key point about OWI made throughout this book).

Flexible teaching takes shape in many different ways, and the CCCC OWI

Committee focused on articulating some of these ways in the example effective practices for OWI Principle 5 in a "while/should" structure that addresses strategies for retaining reasonable instructional control in relation to institutional realities:

- Effective Practice 5.2: While institutions and programs should have clear-cut ways of providing accommodations for all students, teachers should still have flexibility in offering help, such as, if necessary, moving outside an LMS to provide a more accessible environment.
- Effective Practice 5.3: While it is reasonable that programs have unified textbook choices (maybe for cost relief alone), teachers should have some choice in their own subject matter and be able to focus text-driven conversation in the way that best suits their teaching. This is especially relevant in OWI courses; a link is an easy thing to share with students, and teachers need to be able to engage in perhaps one of the most enjoyable aspects of OWI: Providing an "aha" moment in the term when they come across a reading that they think ties in beautifully with what they are teaching.
- Effective Practice 5.4: While many teachers must work with core assignments, OWI teachers should have flexibility in assignment specifics. Teachers should be able to embed assignments within the particular "class culture" of their course. For writing courses in particular, this flexibility has a practical side: It enables programs to avoid the problem of having hundreds and maybe thousands of similar student writing submissions at the same time, a heterogeneity that discourages plagiarism.
- Effective Practice 5.5: While programs should develop methods of collecting teaching materials, teachers should also have ways not only of individually adding and sharing such materials. Again, communication is invaluable.
- Effective Practice 5.6: While programs should provide ways of consistent response to student writing, OWI teachers should have the room to explore ways of engaging and communicating with students. Like moderating, interpersonal contact is one of the great arts of teaching, and this only increases in written forums or through audio/video-type synchronous discussions, which require different approaches.
- Effective Practice 5.7: While programs should have consistent grading and assessment practices, OWI teachers need flexibility in grading and course-level assessment. Teachers might answer to an overall grading approach—e.g., As, Bs, and Cs—but still should be able to establish methods of grading online discussions and weighting various course components. Programs should encourage program-wide conversations about

grading. (Warning!: From my faculty development experience, these conversations might be hotly contested.) (p. 16).

A culture of reasonable control and flexibility gives an OWI program the best chance of doing what it is there to do: teach students to write more effectively.

OWI PRINCIPLE 6

Alternative, self-paced, or experimental OWI models should be subject to the same principles of pedagogical soundness, teacher/designer preparation, and oversight detailed in this document.

Readers will have heard a great deal about Massive Open Online Courses (MOOCs), a highly touted experimental educational platform. In preparing for a conference in 2013, I compiled over 100 news stories about MOOCs in less than six months. Yet, in delivering MOOCs or the next greatest teaching innovation, OWI teachers should not forego what makes great teaching and what makes institutions of higher education work.

Of course, as Patrick Deneen (2013) said, institutions and their faculty are having trouble articulating the logic against MOOCs because we in higher education have long been complicit in many practices that discourage good teaching and student-teacher interactions. How many students have sat in a class of 600 and/or taken a course with an adjunct who was not provided professional development opportunities and was paid a mere $1,500 for that course? (see Chapter 7). By their actions, institutions have said, "We will stick you in a huge lecture hall and let you gawk at the oak trim while hoping you would not notice that you could get this kind of education in many other ways"—other ways that include, astonishingly enough, *reading a book, having your friends read the same book, and then talking to them about it.* Some MOOCs have been shown to be effective, and why not? People who want to learn are pretty good at doing so, and that is something all institutions of higher education should think about. The real challenge may not be getting the stuff into learners' heads, but in *motivating* them in the first place. I probably should not admit this, but one of my children had the recurring issue of having his elbow pop out of the socket when he was little. Using Web instructions from an orthopedics journal, I once re-set his arm. Please do not extrapolate too much from my quackery, but people can learn specialized things from the Web. If higher education thinks its forte is guarding and disseminating that knowledge, it is in big trouble.

Soon after publishing *A Position Statement of Principles and Example Effective Practices for OWI,* one of the first requests the CCCC OWI Committee received was to take a stronger stance specific to MOOCs. While OWI Principle 6 does address these alternative forms, we state our case more overtly regarding such delivery systems in OWI Principle 9: "OWCs should be capped responsibly at 20 students per course with 15 being a preferable number" (pp. 20-21). There is an interesting kind of logic at work here. While OWI Principle 9 was written inductively based on the experiences of many writing teachers, extrapolating its use for MOOCs or other teaching structures, we hope, will be a deductive exercise. Thus, a 60,000-person digital experience is not a *course* and does not fit any reasonable description of one. In fact, Hewett and I believe our conversations regarding MOOCs actually should be about MOOEEs: Massive Open Online *Educational Experiences*. Can people learn to write in such an environment? Sure. As mentioned, the time of the autodidact is upon us. But such an experience should not be confused with the disciplinary concept of a *writing* course, in which interaction with the instructor is integral. Because, for better or worse, many content courses onsite have already been instructor-less in many ways, those involved cannot complain about MOOCs. But that situation does not fit the composition community, and we must consider such experimental forms differently.

WPAs AND WRITING INSTRUCTORS NEED TO APPROVE EVEN EXPERIMENTAL WRITING COURSES

Decisions about online writing curricula (and, of course, all writing curricula) need to be made by writing teachers. In some institutions, there may be a temptation or even overt desire by administrators to suggest the way that a writing course curriculum will be developed and taught. Many of the effective practices associated with OWI Principle 6 are designed to support and empower WPAs to make decisions crucial to writing programs. To this end, the CCCC OWI Committee also believes WPAs "should have final approval of alternative, self-paced, or experimental OWI models integrated into the online curriculum." These courses and structures should not just emerge from administrators who have little understanding of writing studies and then be foisted upon the writing program. Similarly, WPAs should be able to select teachers for OWI courses—experimental and otherwise—in ways that make sense for the pedagogy and philosophy of that writing program.

WPA- AND TEACHER-CENTRIC TRAINING

Faculty training is a big, underappreciated—certainly it is under-*discussed*—problem in OWI, as OWI Principle 7 (p. 17) and Chapter 11 reveal. WPAs need to have a clear, ever-present voice in how writing program faculty not only are selected but are trained to teach writing courses. A primary consideration in this area, which is addressed more fully in Chapter 11, is how administrations must provide space and support for training and ongoing professional development.

Effective Practice 6.3 makes clear that teachers of any OWI course, experimental or otherwise, should be offered the same professional training and development opportunities as other OWI faculty (p. 17). Because that strategy assumes a more functional training structure for onsite, face-to-face writing programs than perhaps is occurring in many institutions, the CCCC OWI Committee hopes OWI Principle 6 may be extended to writing instruction more generally.

WPA- AND TEACHER-CENTRIC ASSESSMENT AND EVALUATION

Another weak point in OWI and some onsite writing programs is assessment and evaluation of teachers. In particular, writing programs may not observe and assess teachers adequately. Effective Practice 6.4 stated that any "alternative, self-paced, or experimental" OWC should be observed regularly by a WPA or teaching peer and assessed based on quality markers of online instruction (p. 17). These evaluators and the evaluations they are using cannot just come out of nowhere. As Vincenza Benigno and Guglielmo Trentin (2000) said, evaluation of online courses often is based on faulty comparisons to onsite instruction and/or is conducted by teachers who do not have OWI training or experience; indeed, sometimes they do not even have training or experience in *writing instruction* itself. Effective Practice 6.5 could be helpful for assessment of writing instruction in general: "Alternative, self-paced, or experimental OWI course teachers should be evaluated/assessed by a peer or supervisor who has similar training and equal or superior abilities/experience in writing instruction generally and OWI particularly" (p. 17). The onus, thus, is placed on programs and perhaps institutions to find quality people who understand the theories and pedagogies of OWI and provide them with reasonable and fair means to evaluate such courses.

Cristie Cowles Charles (2002), in "Why We Need More Assessment of Online Composition Courses: A Brief History," indicated that the complexity and sometimes rigidity of OWI makes the need for fair and adequate evaluation even more important: "For example, the more funding, administration, programming, video production, graphic design, and structured curriculum go into creating a course, the harder it is to change that course's content." Furthermore, "In fact, I submit that the more fixed a course's content and environment become (whether the course is traditional or online), the more evaluation becomes absolutely necessary because the instructor and students become increasingly restricted in their ability to adapt the course to their needs" (sect. 2, para. 3). Charles' words have particular meaning under OWI Principle 6 because even experimental OWI structures can be seen as written in stone after a semester or two of teaching, making the experimental course's efficacy and its teachers' abilities less well understood even while they become standardized and fixed.

As a final point on evaluation, Effective Practice 6.6 (p. 17) emanated from the idea that often OWI courses are subjected to a kind of evaluative scrutiny and rigor that few onsite courses have (see, for example, Warnock, 2007). There are various reasons for this unbalanced assessment, including institutions' and particular administrators' poor understanding of educational outcomes and the difficulty of measuring educational cause-and-effect. At times, when asked about the effectiveness of online and hybrid courses, as a WPA, I have responded with: "Well, where is our outcome data about our onsite courses?" Or, I have said: "Where is our ironclad and empirical outcome data about the usefulness of attending this institution over the one across town or about students taking the 200k and *not going to college*?" My words have been spoken in the spirit of what Peter Thiel (n.d.) was attempting with his Thiel Fellowships (The Thiel Foundation). At some point, teachers have to believe in what they are doing as educators despite the astonishing pressure driven by standardized assessments and testing.

Pedagogically sound OWCs, even experimental ones, should not be subjected to a gauntlet of assessment that an institution's onsite writing courses have not been subjected to. Effective Practice 6.6 helps steer writing teachers in this way; if teachers want information to stave off such assessments, they might look to a CompPile bibliography prepared about such comparisons (Warnock, 2013). They also can view the extensive *No Significant Difference* website. Although the CCCC OWI Committee certainly wants alternative courses to be good, we also want standard online and onsite courses to be good. Teacher evaluation is one area that requires a broader conversation about a program's pedagogy, and online writing programs should encourage that type of dialogue and self-reflection.

CONCLUSION AND RECOMMENDATIONS

Readers will have noted that this chapter is not about the nuts and bolts of an OWC; they also will have noted that the OWI principles, even with their associated effective practices, do not represent an out-of-the-box recipe for teaching composition online. OWI is a vast, open mission such as befits any writing instructional setting. Recommendations and ideas are good, but it is impossible to say generally, "Yes, this is the one way to be successful." The adventure and diversity of OWI and of teaching in higher education provide more opportunities and challenges than that simplistic statement would allow.

The five instructionally-framed OWI principles addressed in this chapter were designed to create a structure upon which well-trained and knowledgeable OWI teachers can build specific instructional approaches and philosophies. They emphasize key concerns regarding writing in online settings to help WPAs and teachers to orient and direct themselves in the online setting. The effective practices offer details and examples to spur OWI faculty thinking for localized settings. Experienced onsite teachers moving into OWI need to think deeply about who they are as teachers and then work forward as they initially delve into electronic environments, being always mindful of the ways many students will access OWCs, as Chapter 16 addresses. Nonetheless, OWI teachers should take advantage of the many helpful tools and approaches facilitated and enabled by technology.

The CCCC OWI Committee has provided these guidelines to facilitate in-course OWI practice, not to dictate it. In short:

- The course is a writing course. Teachers should not let it slip into being something else, such as a course orienting students to institutional technologies.
- Teachers will want to develop new theory and pedagogy to account for the many exciting attributes and opportunities of digital tools ...
- ... and they also should migrate and adapt their best teaching practices and approaches from onsite to online teaching.
- Writing programs—and institutions themselves—should provide teachers with appropriate flexibility and independence in how they teach their courses.
- While OWI is inherently an innovative way to teach writing, teachers cannot abandon effective practices just because they have found a new technology platform or modality. OWCs should maintain core effective teaching practices.

I want to end this chapter with one final, admittedly redundant point: OWI WPAs and instructors always should remember that we are writing teachers first. If we do that, a world of teaching opportunity opens up in online settings. The pedagogy-focused OWI principles are designed to support teachers as they work to capitalize on that opportunity.

NOTE

1. At the time of these CCCC OWI Committee Expert/Stakeholder Panel meetings, both Jason Snart and Heidi Harris were panelists; they since have been invited to the CCCC OWI Committee. Herein, they are named simply as CCCC OWI Committee members.

REFERENCES

Benigno, Vincenza & Guglielmo Trentin. (2000). The evaluation of online courses. *Journal of Computer Assisted Learning 16*(3), 259–270.

Bender, Tisha. (2003). *Discussion-based online teaching to enhance student learning: Theory, practice and assessment.* Sterling, VA: Stylus.

Bishop, Wendy. (2003). Because teaching composition is (still) mostly about teaching composition. In Lynn Z. Bloom, Donald A. Daiker, & E. M. White (Eds.), *Composition Studies in the new millennium: Rereading the past, rewriting the future* (pp. 65-77). Carbondale, IL: Southern Illinois University Press.

Blair, Leslie. (2005). Teaching composition online: No longer the second-best choice. *Kairos 8*(2). Retrieved from http://english.ttu.edu/kairos/8.2/binder.html?praxis/blair/index.html

Bruffee, Kenneth A. (1984). Collaborative learning and the "conversations of mankind." *College English 46*(7), 635–52.

CCCC OWI Committee for Effective Practices in Online Writing Instruction. (2011d). [Transcript of expert/stakeholders' panel virtual meeting of 10/27/2011.] Unplublished raw data.

CCCC OWI Committee for Effective Practices in Online Writing Instruction. (2012a). [Transcript of expert/stakeholders' panel virtual meeting of 01/12/2012.] Unpublished raw data.

CCCC OWI Committee for Effective Practices in Online Writing Instruction. (2012b). [Transcript of expert/stakeholders' panel virtual meeting of 02/17/2012.] Unpublished raw data.

Charles, Cristie Cowles. (2002). Why we need more assessment of online composition courses: A brief history." *Kairos 7*(3). Retrieved from http://english.ttu.edu/kairos/7.3/coverweb/charles/

Clark, Ruth C., & Mayer, Richard E. (2011). *E-learning and the science of instruction: Proven guidelines for consumers and designers of multimedia learning* (3rd ed.). San Francisco, CA: John Wiley & Sons.

Collison, George, Bonnie Elbaum, Sarah Haavind, & Robert Tinker. (2000). *Facilitating online learning: Effective strategies for moderators.* Madison, WI: Atwood.

Deneen, Patrick J. (2013). We're all to blame for MOOCs. *The Chronicle of Higher Education.* Retrieved from http://chronicle.com/article/Were-All-to-Blame-for-MOOCs/139519/?cid=wc

Downs, Douglas & Wardle, Elizabeth. (2007). Teaching about writing, righting misconceptions: (Re)envisioning "first-year composition" as "introduction to writing studies." *College Composition and Communication 58*(4), 552–84.

EDUCAUSE. (2012). 7 things you should know about flipped classrooms.

EDUCAUSE Learning Initiative. Retrieved from http://net.educause.edu/ir/library/pdf/eli7081.pdf

Filene, Peter. (2005). *The joy of teaching*. Chapel Hill, NC: UNC Press.

Garrison, D. Randy & Anderson, Terry D. (1999). Avoiding the industrialization of research universities: Big and little distance education. *American Journal of Distance Education 13*(2), 48-63.

Griffin, June & Minter, Deborah. (2013). The rise of the online writing classroom. *College Composition and Communication 65*(1), 140-61.

Hawisher, Gail E. (1992). Electronic meetings of the minds: Research, electronic conferences, and composition Studies. In Gail E. Hawisher & Paul LeBlanc (Eds.), *Re-imagining computers and composition: Teaching and research in the virtual age* (pp. 81-101). Portsmouth: Boynton.

Hewett, Beth L. (2010). *The online writing conference: A guide for teachers and tutors*. Portsmouth, NH: Heinemann.

Hewett, Beth L. (2015a). *Reading to Learn and Writing to Teach: Literacy Strategies for online writing instruction*. Boston, MA: Bedford/St. Martin's Press.

Hewett, Beth L. (2015b). *The online writing conference: A guide for teachers and tutors* (Updated). Boston, MA: Bedford/St. Martin's Press.

Jonassen, David. (2012). Designing for decision making. *Educational Technology Research & Development 60*(2), 341-359.

LaFond, Larry. (2002). Learner access in the virtual classroom: The ethics of assessing online learning. *Kairos, 7*(3). Retrieved from http://technorhetoric.net/7.3/binder2.html?coverweb/LaFond/index.htm

Lowes, Susan. (2008). Online teaching and classroom change: The trans-classroom teacher in the age of the Internet. *Innovate, 4*(3). Retrieved from http://www.academia.edu/1106536/Online_Teaching_and_Classroom_Change_The_Trans-Classroom_Teacher_in_the_Age_of_the_Internet

Macrorie, Kenneth. (1970). *Uptaught*. Portsmouth, NH: Heinemann.

McKeachie, Wilbert. (2002). *McKeachie's teaching tips* (11th ed.). Boston: Houghton Mifflin.

No significant difference. (n.d.). Retrieved from http://www.nosignificantdifference.org/

Oblinger, Diana G. & Oblinger, James L. (Eds.). (2005). *Educating the net generation*. EDUCAUSE: Transforming Education Through Information Technologies. Ebook. Retrieved from www.educause.edu/educatingthenetgen/

Redish, Janice. (2012). *Letting go of the words* (2nd ed.). Waltham, MA: Morgan Kauffmann.

Salmon, Gilly. (2000). *E-moderating: The key to teaching and learning online*. London: Kogan.

Snart, Jason. (2010). *Hybrid learning: The perils and promise of blending online and face-to-face instruction in higher education.* Santa Barbara, CA: Praeger.

Sommers, Jeff. (2002). Spoken response: Space, time, and movies of the mind. In Pat Belanoff, Marcia Dickson, Sheryl I. Fontaine, & Charles Moran (Eds.), *Writing with Elbow,* (pp. 172-186). Logan, UT: Utah State Press.

Sommers, Nancy. (1982). Responding to student writing. *College Composition and Communication 33*(2), 148-156.

The Thiel Foundation. (n.d.). *The Thiel Fellowship.* Retrieved from http://www.thielfellowship.org/

Warnock, Scott. (2007). And then there were two: The growing pains of an online writing course faculty training initiative. *Proceedings of the Distance Learning Administration 2007 Conference.*

Warnock, Scott. (2007, July). Online writing instruction and the disappearing educational interface. *Rhetorics & Technologies: 20ᵗʰ Penn State Conference on Rhetoric and Composition.* Collegeville, PA.

Warnock, Scott. (2008). Responding to student writing with audio-visual feedback. In Terry Carter & Maria A. Clayton (Eds.), *Writing and the iGeneration: Composition in the computer-mediated classroom,* (pp. 201-227). Southlake, TX: Fountainhead Press.

Warnock, Scott. (2009.) *Teaching writing online: How and why.* Urbana: National Council of Teachers of English.

Warnock, Scott. (2010.) The class message board text: What is it and how can we use it to develop a student text-centered course? In Joseph Harris, John Miles, & Charles Paine (Eds.), *Teaching using student texts: Essays toward an informed practice* (pp. 96-107). Logan, UT: Utah State University Press.

Warnock, Scott. (2013.) *Studies comparing outcomes among onsite, hybrid, and fully-online writing courses. (WPA-CompPile Research Bibliographies, No. 21).* Council of Writing Program Administrators. Retrieved from http://comppile.org/wpa/bibliographies/Bib21/Warnock.pdf

Warnock, Scott. (n.d.) *Online writing teacher.* Retrieved from http://onlinewritingteacher.blogspot.com/

CHAPTER 5

ONLINE WRITING LABS

Diane Martinez
Western Carolina University

Leslie Olsen
Excelsior College

OWI should be supported by online writing centers, most often referred to as online writing labs or OWLs. Developing these support structures, however, can be a daunting endeavor for many institutions, as OWLs are plagued with issues related to the perception that it is a deficit model for tutoring, accessibility issues, appropriate tutor training, and technology. OWL administrators and tutors can use the OWI principles to overcome many of these obstacles in developing and delivering quality writing instruction through tutoring.

Keywords: access, asynchronous tutoring, online writing center, online writing instruction, online learning, online learning communities, online writing lab, online writing support, OWL, OWL administrator, synchronous tutoring, tutor/s, tutoring, tutor selection, tutor training

Online writing centers, also called online writing labs or OWLs, extend the reach of traditional writing centers and, in some cases, are developed independently of their onsite counterparts. An OWL can be considered an outgrowth of an onsite writing center in that it offers similar writing support services but in an online forum, and many times, to a new type of audience (Hewett, 2002; Moberg, 2010). With the surge of online courses being offered across the nation, the need for online writing support also is growing.

According to the International Writing Centers Association (IWCA) (2013), writing centers were established "in reaction to the 'literacy crisis' of the mid-1970s" (para. 11). While writing centers often were seen as supplemental support for writing courses, they were also mistakenly viewed as "drop off" centers where students could send or leave their papers for someone else to edit or "fix." Writing center staff have worked diligently to correct this perception by educating faculty and students about the writing center experience and creating a field of study through research and presentations that undergird writing center theories. As a result, many onsite writing centers now are recognized as valuable and integral components of writing programs and writing-across-the-curriculum efforts—serving students of all levels and in all types of courses where writing is assigned. While writing center directors and staff continue their struggle to educate faculty and students about the writing process and the collaborative role of the writing center in helping students become better writers, there is general acceptance about the usefulness of onsite writing centers; to date, thousands of onsite writing centers exist world-wide in postsecondary and secondary schools (IWCA, 2013). Interestingly, most likely because they are newer and use technology to reach students, OWLs are experiencing the same perception issues today that their onsite counterparts experienced not so many years ago.

OWLs vary in the services and resources they offer, but they generally provide students with online writing resources, such as PDF files or Web pages that relate to the writing process or grammar and mechanics. More technologically advanced OWLs tend to have interactive resources, allowing students the opportunity to apply new writing skills as they are learning how to use them. Some OWLs hire tutors to offer feedback on student writing through asynchronous means, such as email or Web-based software. Other OWLs have tutors or writing consultants who meet with students and offer synchronous, one-to-one consultations through text-based chat or voice-based conferencing software. The form of consultation and feedback is highly dependent on the technology available at the institution and in the OWL itself, as well as available technology among the student body. Whatever the makeup of the OWL, providing online writing support addresses issues of access and inclusivity for online students because, according to OWI Principle 13, "such reinforcing programs provide student access to the same support components that students in traditional, onsite courses receive" (CCCC OWI Committee, 2013, p. 26).

Like traditional writing centers, OWLs vary in their services and philosophy depending on the institution and the unique needs of its students (Breuch, 2005; Hewett, 2002). For instance, some small, private universities may use a Web page as their OWL, which only advertises the school's onsite writing center services because their entire student body resides on campus, there are no online courses offered, or students are expected to meet with tutors in person. Two-year community colleges, on the other hand, serve a student body that generally has more time constraints than students at private and traditional universities; thus, they are more likely to offer online resources and consultations (Neaderhiser & Wolfe, 2009). In addition, both onsite and online universities may outsource their tutoring to such privatized companies as Smarthinking, Inc. or NetTutor to meet the needs of the growing online student population ("Smarthinking," 2013; Thiel, 2010).

While Beth L. Hewett (2002) classified the functions of OWLs according to their relationship to the Current-Traditional, Neo-Classical, Neo-Platonic/Expressivist, and Social Constructivist schools of thought, Lee-Ann Kastman Breuch (2005) categorized OWLs according to writing philosophy. Her categories include: the "participant-observer model," which advances the idea that the goal of a writing center is to "produce better writers, not better writing" (p. 26); the "Storehouse Center," which is akin to a resource center; the "Garret Center," a place where students learn to find their individual voice and strengths; and, the "Burkean Parlor" that values collaboration in the writing process. The model that most writing centers and OWLs do not subscribe to is the fix-it shop, a place where students drop off or email their papers and allow tutors to revise, edit, and correct their writing for them. The fix-it shop model has been the source of many misperceptions garnered by students and faculty about what onsite writing centers do, and this misperception has been extended to OWLs. However, even for those OWLs that offer only asynchronous consultations, students are expected to be part of the writing process and responsible for their own revisions and corrections (Breuch, 2005; Dailey, 2004; Hewett, 2002; Neaderhiser & Wolfe, 2009; Wolfe & Griffin, 2013). In an OWL, just like in an onsite writing center, students should remain the agents of their own writing.

Whichever model is used, flexibility with teaching and learning at a distance helps to establish OWLs as the perfect support service for OWI—that is, if they actually are available. Results from the CCCC OWI Committee's national fully online and hybrid surveys indicated that fewer than half of the respondents in all categories reported the existence of an OWL or any asynchronous or synchronous tutoring available for online students at their institutions (CCCC OWI Committee, 2011a, 2011b). Offering OWCs without online writing support has serious implications for students because it creates inequity of available and accessible support services. Moreover, if an OWL is available, other issues may affect student learning and retention in online classes due to tutors and students being unfamiliar with how to use the technology, resources, and services of the OWL in ways that facilitate quality instruction and learning opportunities. Although OWLs have distinct differences among them, Eric Moberg (2010) identified several characteristics that successful OWLs have in common: ensuring access for all students, offering online consultations that focus on the writer and not the writing, providing tutor training, and using technologies that provide pedagogical value to the services of an OWL. These characteristics, however, do not always come about easily and many OWLs face serious challenges in these areas. While the issues associated with providing quality OWI through the services and resources of an OWL are complex, they are not insurmountable.

Technology has changed the way we read and write (Hewett, 2015a). OWLs can be considered places where "technology and writing have the ability to converge in the form of tutoring and collaboration" (Neaderhiser & Wolfe, 2009, p. 49). In this chapter, we argue that OWLs are integral to OWI as sites of tutoring and collaboration, just as onsite writing centers have been found to be integral to onsite writing instruction. First, we describe some of the challenges associated with developing and maintaining online writing center services and resources—access, consultations, training, and technology—and then we provide recommendations for how to address those issues at both the institutional and individual tutor levels. Central to our discussion are OWI Principles 1, 13, and 14 in their regard of OWLs as places of access and inclusivity (CCCC OWI Committee, 2013). Using the OWI principles as guidelines reveals solutions that institutions and individual tutors can implement to ensure that students receive a quality education in a distance setting.

OWI'S CHALLENGES AND OPPORTUNITIES FOR OWLS

Online students are like face-to-face students in that they, too, need feedback at multiple stages of their writing. Learning in a digital environment is different from learning in a face-to-face classroom, especially when it comes to writing instruction, because it is text-heavy (Griffin & Minter, 2013; Hewett, 2013, 2015a). Almost all communication is read and written including discussion boards, assignments, feedback, and grading. To best assist students in the online writing process, OWLs should have a pedagogically sound philosophy about teaching writing online, as indicated in OWI Principles 3 and 4. While some OWI-specific theories need to be developed, traditional composition theories, pedagogies, and strategies can be migrated from an onsite environment to an online environment, but they need to be modified or adapted to meet the unique challenges of online instruction and needs of online students (Breuch & Racine, 2000; Hewett, 2010, 2015b; Olsen, 2002; see also Chapters 1 & 4).

Before reviewing suggested strategies for developing OWLs and preparing tutors, it is helpful to have a full understanding of the challenges that OWL administrators and tutors face. These challenges include access and inclusivity, online consultations, training and professional development, and technology. Understanding the complexities of these issues helps administrators and tutors foresee potential problems, find solutions, and mitigate problems before they actually occur, before students are lost or not well served, or before money is spent.

ACCESS AND INCLUSIVITY

Primary considerations to developing an OWL should be to ensure that the services and resources of the OWL are accessible and inclusive of all students and offered in a modality that matches students' learning environments. Specifically, in OWI Principle 1, the CCCC OWI Committee recommended that all learners, regardless of their physical disabilities, learning challenges, language backgrounds (i.e., multilingual students), or socioeconomic status, should be supported in their educational endeavors. Along those same lines, access and inclusivity also pertain to the modality and medium in which support services and resources are offered. OWI Principle 13 explained that support for online students should be offered primarily online with onsite support as a secondary resource. Furthermore, in order to provide an equitable learning environment for all students, the CCCC Committee promoted a proactive approach in *A Position Statement of Principles and Example Effective Practices for OWI* (CCCC OWI Committee, 2013) to making all online resources and services accessible and inclusive. They encouraged institutions to address issues of inclusivity and accessibility at the forefront of any online educational endeavor, instead of as an afterthought as add-ons or retrofitted alternatives.

Accessibility and inclusivity address the different needs inherent to a widely diverse population, which include students, faculty, and staff with physical or learning disabilities, multilingual backgrounds, or socioeconomic challenges— the traditionally underserved. Currently, up to 45% of college and university students are underserved partly due to the lack of access to support services (Twigg, 2005). Underserved populations are "less likely to persist and graduate after enrolling in college" and are encouraged by faculty and advisors to choose a college that offers academic support services, including writing center access, that meet the needs of the student ("Maximizing," 2012, para. 1). In fact, Carol A. Twigg (2005) found that providing academic support helped create a learning community, a place where intellectual and social interactions integrate, thus increasing inclusivity, which "is critical to persistence, learning, and satisfaction" (p. 4).

The implications of OWI Principle 1 are that classrooms, curricula, and pedagogy should be flexible and employ alternatives for various learners. Taken further and with OWLs in mind, all resources—including websites and Web resources, services, and any technology being used—should be selected and developed with inclusivity and accessibility as primary guidelines. To this end, OWL administrators, tutors, and helpdesk personnel should be trained and comfortable serving all students—including multilingual and multicultural students— regardless of their disability, challenges, or background. OWL administrators should select technology that is financially available to all students—to enable them to have distance-based access—and that includes alternatives for sensory, size, and space preferences.

In *A Position Statement of Principles and Example Effective Practices for OWI* (CCCC OWI Committee, 2013), the CCCC OWI Committee encouraged developing materials and technology that use universal design, which embodies equitable and flexible features for simple and intuitive use. Even with universal design as a foundation for developing OWL services and resources, it should be noted that there is no way to foresee and prepare for all situations; universal design simply "reduces, but does not eliminate, the need for accommodations for students with disabilities" (Burgstahler & Cory, 2008, pp. 24-25). Accommodations may need to be made with various students, as new situations arise, and whenever new technologies are employed.

The principle of providing inclusivity and accessibility grounds all of the OWI principles and should be considered at the onset of developing solutions instead of as an afterthought. Accessibility often is considered in terms of disability, and while that certainly is one aspect and one reason that OWLs should be thoughtful of access, disabilities are not the only issues that can prevent students from receiving an equitable education. One's socioeconomic status may limit the ability to use synchronous tutoring, for example, in that lack of cameras/microphones or Web conferencing technology (i.e., technology that might otherwise be available in a campus lab) in one's home or public library may impede certain kinds of access for geographically distributed students. Varying learning styles and levels are other issues to consider when designing OWI materials. For example, some students may learn better with the time flexibility allotted in asynchronous tutoring; to limit tutoring to only synchronous settings would do a great disservice to such students.

As OWI Principle 1 "supersedes and connects to every [OWI] principle" (p. 7), any solutions and recommendations for OWL administrators begin with access. Accessibility and inclusivity are issues that all learners face, whether in an online or an onsite course, because they address the different needs inherent to a widely diverse population. Issues associated with access and inclusivity are more numerous than can be covered here, but an overarching guideline is that "OWI teachers should determine their uses of modality and media based not only on their pedagogical goals but also on their students' likely strengths and access" (p. 9). Instead of throwing a wide net of resources to an unknown audience, OWL administrators can take specific actions to get to know the student body better.

Recommendations for Access and Inclusivity

Increasing inclusivity and access in online writing instruction begins by working with the institution's disability office. Appropriate planning includes asking the right questions. For instance, asking about the types of accommodations already afforded to onsite students can inform how they might be adapted for online students. In addition, including IT support professionals in the conversation with staff from the disability office will help ensure that OWLs and the resources included in them are all ADA compliant and that the OWLs are accessible. These institutional partners can help determine which types of technologies can be used and which should be avoided, particularly when creating online learning communities.

A learning community—a place where the academic and social interests of students potentially can intersect—can increase inclusivity and assist in learning more about students' strengths and concerns. OWLs offer several opportunities to build learning communities online, which help to develop trust and rapport between students and tutors. Common software and familiar online platforms, such as the institution's LMS, can be used to create an open shell, where the discussion board invites focus groups with faculty and students to ask them about their online writing needs. This open forum allows students to get to know the tutors, become familiar with the online communication process, and know that their concerns are being heard. Scheduling weekly drop-in groups provides consistency to the conversations taking place in the discussion board. Additional forums include Wikis, blogs, and podcasts. An OWL Wiki can be open to everyone and serve as a place to hold and archive questions about writing, and with daily monitoring, the tutors can maintain an online presence in the community. Blogs written and monitored by the tutors about common writing issues will also increase their online presence. Podcasts with mini-lessons or OWL advertisements can place faces with names, which may encourage students who otherwise might be reluctant to seek the services. The key is to convey that the OWL and tutors are available and accessible in various online formats, and inclusive of all students, whether in fully online, hybrid, or fully onsite courses. Alternative technologies that assist students with disabilities also should be included when these learning communities/resources are established.

To sustain inclusive online learning communities, it is important to maintain easy access to and an online presence in the OWL. Online and onsite contact information, as well as availability information, should be prominent on the OWL homepage. Student expectations should be highlighted, including anticipated response times for answers to questions or feedback on papers. Responding to students within a reasonable, advertised timeframe of 24-48 hours has been an industry standard for returning emails and phone calls, but with faster technology, students are looking for faster ways to communicate. Depending on budgetary constraints and institutional needs, administrators might consider reducing the response time in keeping with student needs and expectations.

As technology progresses, so do the online literacy levels and expectations of the students. While the OWL discussion boards, Wikis, blogs, and podcasts offer multiple ways to transmit information, there should also be multiple ways for students to retrieve it. OWLs should enable student access through a variety of mobile devices, such as smartphones, tablets, laptops, and electronic notebooks (see Chapter 16). Finally, social media can provide access as well, including sending announcements, daily writing tips, OWL advertisements, or generalized writing advice. Be wary, however, that not all students subscribe to every form of online access, so redundant messages in alternate media can help reach a larger student body audience.

To develop more universally inclusive and accessible online writing support, OWI Principle 13 indicated that students who choose to take courses online should receive support services in the modality and medium in which their course meets with a secondary backup resource onsite (p. 26). This guideline suggests that students who meet asynchronously through the LMS should have asynchronous tutoring available, while students who meet synchronously should have synchronous tutoring available. When possible, having both modalities available is helpful to learners with varied preferences and access needs. Because having multiple venues to access writing support is essential to increasing retention in online learners, it is important not to assume that because tutors may be used to and/or prefer synchronous communication that it is either best for or preferred by students. When such assistance can occur using the same technologies as the OWC, the LMS may be called upon for double duty, thus saving the institution from purchasing or developing a separate OWL platform. When students can access and participate in various university intellectual and social circles, they become part of a new community, a learning community that promotes persistence. Thus, inclusivity and accessibility are foundational to the other OWI principles discussed in this chapter.

Online Consultations

Online consultations also are referred to as online tutoring or online conferences. According to Stephen Neaderhiser and Joanna Wolfe (2009), such "one-to-one interactions between a consultant and a writer ... can take place synchronously, in real time ... or they can take place asynchronously through technologies such as email" (p. 54). Online conferencing, however, is often viewed as being inferior to face-to-face conferences (Carlson & Apperson-Williams, 2003; Hewett, 2010, 2015b; Wolfe & Griffin, 2012). The online distance between tutor and student often is considered impersonal where the "tutoring table is replaced with a computer screen: cold, sterile, and, to many, uninviting" (Carlson & Apperson-Williams, 2003, p. 233). Even tutors who like their online tutoring work may express this concern (Ehmann Powers, 2010).

In addition, there is a common assumption among some scholars that online consultations lack the quality of instruction that comes from face-to-face tutoring, which often stems from a perceived lack of conversation (Wolfe & Griffin, 2012) and a perception that conversation is always superior to problem-centered instruction, a precept with which Hewett (2010, 2015b) disagreed given the text-heavy focus of online tutoring and OWI overall. Likewise, Wolfe and Griffin (2012) reported that there are innovative OWI methods that are just as effective as face-to-face consultations, and that in some instances were preferred by students over in-person tutoring sessions. In fact, while a majority of tutors surveyed preferred face-to-face consultations because they could work better from body language and facial cues, an overwhelming majority of students preferred the online environment. Students reported liking the convenience and time-saving aspects of online conferencing, as well as being able to make immediate changes to their papers during the tutoring sessions. Students especially liked sharing a screen and the audio aspect of some online conferencing.

Despite student preferences found in Wolfe and Griffin's (2012) research, Neaderhiser and Wolfe (2009) reported that from their survey, only about 10% of all online conferencing took place synchronously. This low percentage may be attributed to several possibilities including funding, unfamiliarity with more advanced types of software and how they can be used effectively for OWI, or, as mentioned previously, access needs of the student body. As Connie Mick and Geoffrey Middlebrook indicate in Chapter 3, asynchronous technologies are more commonly used in OWCs, which may be an issue of cost; similarly, they are more common for OWLs at this point in their development. Consequently, email is used about 90% of the time for online conferencing (Wolfe & Griffin, 2012), and online consultations can also take place on discussion boards.

Asynchronous and synchronous conferences offer different challenges with engaging students; however, there are ways to overcome those challenges that can be satisfying for students (Wolfe & Griffin, 2012). Whether using asynchronous or synchronous technology for online consultations, it is important to consider pedagogy. Traditional face-to-face classroom pedagogy often does not directly transfer to online environments (hence, the "yin" and "yang" of OWI Principles 3 and 4, per Chapter 1), and effective OWI requires online-focused training for tutors and students.

Asynchronous Tutoring

Asynchronous tutoring is a complex process that requires training to do it well. Hewett (2010) explained that "the roles of teacher and tutor naturally intersect" (p. 8), but one difference between the two is that tutors "listen, read, and provide formative feedback uninvolved with grading" (p. 8). The most common types of asynchronous tutoring include email and discussion boards. As Hewett (2010, 2015b) indicated, some critics argue that asynchronous consultations do not promote conversation between tutors and students because it is delayed communication and any interactions that may occur over email, for instance, are short-lived. Even though there is potential for students to email additional questions to a previous tutor, the dynamic often is criticized as being a question/answer session instead of a dialogue. Additionally, technology most often associated with asynchronous tutoring, such as email and discussion boards, often is seen as limiting conversation because there is no shared space for students and tutors to view papers together and discuss multiple questions that usually arise in face-to-face consultations (Neaderhiser & Wolfe, 2009). An additional challenge of asynchronous tutoring involves the funding to build or source it to begin with. Some institutions outsource feedback services to for-profit educational companies. Such services may be financially difficult for institutions to maintain, and there is concern (often expressed anecdotally on listservs) that the feedback received from personnel outside of an institution may counter what instructors expect at the students' institutions.

Opportunities to interact with online students in meaningful ways, however, are highly dependent on how tutors use the OWL technology and, of course, on how tutors are trained. For example, when providing asynchronous commentary, tutors should envision what happens after the student's paper has been returned. Is there opportunity for follow-up and interaction with the tutor? If so, how does a tutor continue a dialogue about a student's paper and engage the student to think through and write his or her own revisions? George Cooper, Kara Bui, and Linda Riker (2003) reported that such a relationship can take place, that "there are online strategies for establishing a relationship between the tutor and writer, for empowering writers to share in their own revision, and for dealing with specifics of grammar and mechanics—all done by relying on collaborative techniques and leading to a facilitated knowledge between tutor and client" (p. 257). Additionally, students benefit from training—either in class or through OWL-developed and provided videos—in how to read the tutorial so that they can make the best use of the advice they receive (Hewett, 2015b, 2010).

It may seem that providing written comments on student writing is fairly straightforward, but once again, the type of commentary should align with the philosophy of the OWL and the institution. Those philosophies can range from a holistic view, where writing from invention to proofreading is seen as an integrated, generative, circular process, to a more categorized approach, where writing is divided into content, style, format, and grammar and mechanics. If an OWL subscribes to a holistic philosophy of writing, then a tutor's strategies and comments should reflect that philosophy. Even when a student asks for help with only grammar and mechanics, there are ways to provide that assistance without correcting his or her paper. One of those ways is the 4-step intervention process developed by Hewett (2011, 2015b; see also Effective Practice 3.4), a problem-centered lesson approach that teaches students *what* the problem is, *why* it is a problem, *how* to address it or avoid it, and then asks them to *do* something about it. Such a process involves modeling different writing possibilities for the student using the student's writing, which should not be confused with doing for them. It is a teaching process that can be enacted for any level of problem from higher-to-lower order concerns.

Recommendations for Asynchronous Tutoring

All writers have their own strengths and weaknesses, as well as unique backgrounds, and it is important that tutors understand there is no one tried and true approach to writing. That said, there are some strategies for providing comments that are more helpful than others. Before commenting on a student paper, tutors should be familiar with various levels of writing competence and the challenges that go along with those levels, such as how novice writers often voice frustration with issues of control or being able to make the words on a page reflect their thinking. Novice writers also often mention that they are unsure about how to organize their thoughts enough to write them coherently. All of these factors can influence a tutoring session and tutors have to know when, where, and how to comment in ways that will help students better understand the process of writing versus getting an assignment *right* using any particular definition of that word. As with OWI overall, where the best online writing teacher is an experienced writing teacher, the best online tutors will understand writing regardless of setting.

Text-based asynchronous conferencing is both common and useful, but it also places stress on students' reading abilities (and, according to Hewett, 2015a, on teachers' and tutors' *writing* abilities). One way to help students is to contextualize the feedback within the student's writing and in connection to the assignment (when available) because the online setting often lacks the tutor's body language that a student might use to make sense of the response. Another way is to build redundancy into the feedback (a strategy outlined in Chapter 4) to enable the student to triangulate the communication's meaning and assess its value to the writing overall. These strategies have the additional benefits of addressing access concerns, such as those inherent to writers with neural processing disorders as well as those with weaker reading skills relative to instructional text.

To further help students with varied learning styles, asynchronous conferencing does not have to be entirely text-based. Successful OWLs use a variety of technologies, such as audio and audio/video feedback (for which students need speakers, an issue of access). Wolfe and Griffin (2012) reported on research that suggested "audio feedback was more effective than text-based feedback in conveying nuance and was associated with increased student involvement, content retention, and student satisfaction" (p. 63). They also stated that "audio feedback was associated with the perception that the instructor cared about the student" (p. 63). Although more research is needed on both text-based and audio feedback in asynchronous settings, it is not difficult for tutors to provide such feedback with adequate training on what kinds of feedback might be most helpful. Free software allows tutors to screen capture and narrate comments that students can see and hear when they receive their returned essays. Audio and audio/video comments also can be combined with written comments for a more comprehensive review that provides students with written next steps or other summary material. With some practice, audio and audio/video commentary does not take any more time than written comments alone. As a caution, however, unless the commentary is limited by time, it is easy to provide the student with an unfocused or overly lengthy response that may confuse their efforts to revise (Vincelette, 2013; Vincelette & Bostic, 2013).

Other ways to make asynchronous online conferences effective and satisfying include knowing how to use various technologies to draw out information from students and engage them in the writing process. First, it is important for tutors and students to establish goals or learning expectations (Hewett, 2010, 2015b; Ryan & Zimmerelli, 2010). Expectation and goal setting can be accomplished in several ways, such as having a student explain the assignment and concerns in an email or online form before submitting a paper to an online tutor. Furthermore, expectation and goal setting provides students with a moment of reflection about their writing in relation to the assignment, and it sets a common goal between student and tutor (Hewett, 2010, 2015b).

To create an asynchronous virtual relationship between tutor and student, tutors can provide personalized comments of the global and local kind (Cooper, Bui, & Riker, 2003; Crump, 2003; Hewett, 2010, 2011, 2015b; Ryan & Zimmerelli, 2010). Global comments, sometimes provided as opening comments, can appeal to students and may create a personal tone that prepares them for what follows, especially when a student's name is used and the tutor uses comments that are informal and friendly (Cooper, Bui, & Riker, 2003; Hewett, 2010, 2015b). Opening commentary can be used to get acquainted with the student and to introduce the student to what will follow by offering general observations of the paper that invite the student to continue reading and actively think through revisions.

For localized comments, dialogue, one of the main criticisms of asynchronous conferencing, can be promoted through carefully structured instructional comments. Cooper, Bui, & Riker (2003) suggested using questions to facilitate a Socratic approach to "engage the learner, not to manipulate him" (p. 259) in the online conference:

> Ideally, the tutor asks questions before giving directions and engages the client's own knowledge to solve a problem... . Writing [is] a dialogic process within the mind of the writer, especially to initiate, recognize, and cultivate the dialogic process used by experienced writers. Online tutors can also use questions to engage writers in this exercise. Because the tutor is not waiting for an answer, the writer is free to act as she wishes. The door to genuine contemplation is open and the writer remains in control. (p. 259)

In other words, the dialogue that may result from an asynchronous conference made possible through a tutor's written comments is "intended to create dialogue within the writer's mind" (p. 260). One common suggestion is that instructional comments should be structured by using praise or a compliment followed by a genuine question that considers a weak spot in the paper (Cooper, Bui, & Riker, 2003). Hewett (2010) recommended that tutors "offer clear, honest, critical responses to the writing. This strategy includes phrasing, such as: '*I'm awed by your strength in this situation*'" (p. 123), followed by critical feedback like "'*I'm confused by this entire paragraph. What did you want readers to understand?*'" (pp. 123-124). She also recommended using straightforward, linguistically direct language that has semantic integrity in terms of not asking rhetorical or closed ended questions or using linguistically indirect (conditional and suggestive) statements that students were unlikely to use in revising their writing. Hewett (2010, 2011, 2015b) considered so-called "genuine" questions to be *what, when, where, why, who,* and *how* because actually addressing them requires thoughtful answers that might lead to revisions when posed with some instruction.

When students ask for feedback on only grammar and mechanics, tutors may have a tendency to want to edit and correct student papers, but choosing patterns of errors is much more effective than marking every mistake in a student draft (Cooper, Bui, & Riker, 2003; Hewett, 2010, 2015b; Ryan & Zimmerelli, 2010). One reason for its effectiveness is that students can become overwhelmed with new information during conference. There is little value in pointing out 15 errors that a student cannot fully address; "students can only absorb so much feedback during one sitting" (Hewett, 2015b, 2010, p. 91), whether that is a synchronous or asynchronous event. Hewett also explained that "the student is being taught *through* the piece of writing" (2010, p. 91); therefore, when tutors point out patterns, they should also provide an explanation of the error using the student's own writing and how to fix it (Hewett, 2010, 2011, 2015b) similar to what would happen in a face-to-face interaction (Cooper, Bui, & Riker, 2003). This practice allows for use of the 4-step intervention process (Hewett, 2010, 2011, 2015b), for example, and hopefully leads to greater student engagement. With this strategy—useful for global, content-level issues as well—students are alerted of a persistent problem throughout their paper, and they are tasked with identifying similar errors and revising them on their own. Depending on their own time frames and on the OWL's policies, students typically can return to the OWL for additional help, but if they are under constraints, the response provides them with a starting point for analyzing their own writing and learning how to improve it.

By using a variety of tools and strategies, asynchronous conferences can be personalized and they can be an effective means of helping students improve their writing. Distance does not always equate to a cold, sterile communication despite educators' expressed fears. OWL technology affords many opportunities to create meaningful and helpful relationships in educational settings.

Synchronous Tutoring

In their research study on synchronous conferencing, Wolfe and Griffin (2012) found that "87% of student writers who participated in an online session either preferred the online environment or had no environment preference" (p. 81). The most common reasons cited for preferring online conferences were convenience and real-time editing—meaning students liked not having to be in a specific geographic place at a certain time—and being able to make changes to their papers during the session. Student criticisms of online tutoring in this same study were mostly about problems with technology, such as audio difficulties, but others noted that they had a hard time communicating their ideas in an electronic medium (Wolfe & Griffin, 2012). To add to that, Hewett (2006) noted that students who do not perform well when writing in instructional settings also may experience challenges with online conferences because they have to respond in real time and many times the writing they produce is immediately visible. Despite these challenges, synchronous online conferencing software is advancing in ways that will only increase how tutors and students can interact.

Some programs allow students and tutors to share a common virtual space where a student's paper can be viewed by both parties, a whiteboard that both student and tutor have access to, as well as audio and voice components to the platform. The conference, therefore, does not have to be entirely text-based when synchronous. Providing that they are accessible to students, these programs enable students to experience tutoring in a group situation where a tutor can work with one student, but other students who are waiting "in line" can see and potentially benefit from this instruction because they can hear the conversation taking place and all participants in the virtual conference "room" can see the whiteboard or student paper.[1] Conferences also can occur in a separate virtual room where the student and tutor have a one-on-one interaction away from other students' view and hearing. While these platforms are designed to replicate face-to-face interactions as closely as possible, Hewett (2006) cautioned that some instructors may "oversimplify the pedagogical transfer between traditional and synchronous writing instruction" (p. 6). She also emphasized that OWI "requires highly developed verbal teaching skills and vocabulary about writing along with strategies for encouraging students to commit to writing out their thinking as part of the conference" (p. 6). In other words, the OWL tutor not only needs to understand writing theoretically and pedagogically but also should have the vocabulary at hand for explaining the writing concerns at the student's level and in ways that encourage students to enact writing development or change while in the tutorial itself.

Recommendations for Synchronous Tutoring

One of the best things about the wide array of technologies today is just that—there is usually more than one way to do something. For instance, synchronous conferencing can take place using a variety of LMS or conferencing technologies, but also through IM or other chat programs. Chat-based technologies resemble the Burkean Parlor ideal, which is supposed to foster a more interactive conversation that is persistent; such technologies enable students to save and archive chats for later review. Other synchronous technologies available for online consultations include the telephone, audio and screen capture programs, and real-time screen sharing software. For students who do not do well in text-based synchronous environments, tutors can meet with students through free video programs, again, keeping access in mind regarding cameras and/or microphones (CCCC OWI Committee, 2013; Hewett, 2010, 2015a, 2015b).

As with any type of conference, setting goals for a tutoring session gives student and tutor direction and helps both use their time efficiently. Thus, tutors need to learn how to "assist their students in setting their own agendas for conferences and in making informed choices about how to apply the instruction" (Hewett, 2010, p. 50). Asynchronous online conferencing and text-based synchronous conferencing offer unique opportunities for students to use writing to talk about their writing, but they may not quite know how to do that. A good way to begin that conversation is to have students talk about the assignment and their process in completing the assignment followed by questions from the tutor about what the student liked best and least about his or her writing (Hewett, 2010). Again, this work requires practice, and as suggested in OWI Principle 14, tutors should practice this kind of scenario and dialogue using various types of technology from both the student and tutor perspectives (see also Hewett & Ehmann, 2004).

TUTOR SELECTION, TRAINING, AND PROFESSIONAL DEVELOPMENT

OWI is still a fairly new endeavor and requires new skills. While it may be partly true that anyone who teaches in a classroom can teach online, there are some qualifiers. According to OWI Principle 7 (pp. 17-19):

- Teachers should be carefully selected and then trained in OWI before they teach an online course.
- Experienced writing teachers—*who want to teach in a digital environment*—should be the first considered for teaching online.

This principle applies to OWL tutors as much as OWI teachers. Tutors who are familiar with tutoring onsite may not understand the nuances of tutoring online; furthermore, if they do not want to tutor online, their dissatisfaction may rub off onto the students with whom they interact. Online instruction does not fit every instructor's personality, and it is important that instructors understand the differences between classroom instruction and OWI and then decide where they would be better suited. Some educators may be comfortable and effective doing both online and face-to-face instruction, which should be encouraged, and these same principles apply to OWL tutors as well.

OWI Principle 14 emphasized the necessity for OWL tutor training and professional development that matches the environment in which tutors instruct writing (p. 28). As Chapter 1 discussed and Beth L. Hewett and Christa Ehmann (2004) argued, immersion into the environment in which one will teach or tutor is crucial to being prepared to assist students with and through that setting. Hence, tutor training—and this includes WPAs or OWL administrators who supervise or evaluate online tutors—needs to be scheduled and practiced in the technological modality and medium that enables tutors to experience what their students will experience and to practice helping their peers in that environment as well.

Tutor Selection

Tutor selection is an important consideration. Neaderhiser and Wolfe (2009) reported that some schools use graduate students or tutors with only one year of experience to conduct online consultations, while other schools carefully selected qualified and experienced faculty and staff who were familiar with online tutoring. And other schools may use relatively inexperienced undergraduate peer tutors for OWL tutoring. This split in tutor selection policies suggests that some OWI administrators see online tutoring as a regular duty that any writing center tutor can do and others see it as an area of expertise. Novice or untrained tutors cause problems for both OWLs and onsite writing centers (Hewett, 2015a, 2010; Moberg, 2010). However, as Moberg (2010) stated, "one key to the success of an online tutoring program is not the distance between tutor and student, but the training each receives" (p. 3).

According to OWI Principle 14, administrators should select online tutors based on their (1) tutoring potential and/or experience with writing; (2) strengths in expressing writing instruction *in writing*; and (3) comfort level with online technologies, which can be developed further in training (p. 28; Hewett, 2010, 2015b; Hewett & Ehmann, 2004). Furthermore, to assess their tutors well, OWL administrators should receive the same training. Effective practices for OWI Principle 14 indicated that:

- OWL supervisors should have "equal or superior" training and experiences in writing instruction *and* OWI than the tutors.
- OWI assessment should "occur in the setting and modalities that the teacher uses in the online writing course" (p. 19).
- OWI assessment should not be any more or less rigorous than traditional classroom assessment.

Each of these assessment recommendations is important to consider because instruction in an online environment has unique characteristics that are not part of the traditional classroom experience or at least do not match in any exact manner. A well-trained and experienced OWL supervisor will understand the complexities of online instruction, such as the challenges of engaging students at a distance in a primarily text-based venue and of providing effective feedback that encourages dialogue in this environment. Such administrators will be able to better assess the quality of instruction taking place in synchronous and asynchronous settings due to their experiences in the settings as both "student" and "tutor."

Training Tutors

According to OWI Principle 14, before tutors assist students in online conferences, they should have training appropriate to online tutoring (p. 28). The nature of the online conference, whether asynchronous or synchronous, presents challenges to tutors trained solely to do onsite, face-to-face writing center tutoring. According to Leslie Olsen (2002), "tutors accustomed to speaking directly with students when providing feedback must diagnose written work, establish conference priorities, and provide feedback—without the student" (p. 2). Lee-

Ann Kastman Breuch and Sam J. Racine (2000) contended that tutors typically had to accomplish this feat without much training directly related to OWI or negotiating online spaces. Training online tutors using online technology and strategies developed or adapted for OWI is essential because "training used in f2f centers does not translate easily to online writing centers" (Breuch & Racine, 2000, p. 246; see also Hewett, 2010, 2015b; Hewett & Ehmann, 2004).

OWL training should focus on three specific areas. Tutors must learn to (1) teach writing, (2) teach writing in an online environment, and (3) teach writing in a primarily text-based environment (CCCC OWI Committee, 2013, p. 17). Because OWI is fairly new and unexplored in many ways, and because technology constantly evolves and changes the way we read and write, OWI training for the course or a tutorial is not a one-time event, and it should be treated as ongoing professional development for tutors. For this reason, tutors should be trained to tolerate error with technology, as well as with student writing. Additionally, this training should be formal training developed by experts in OWI, and it is recommended that experienced online instructors mentor novice OWL tutors, as well.

As Hewett (2006) stated, there is still much to research on the subject of effective OWI (see Chapter 17); however, Wolfe and Griffin (2012), Hewett (2010, 2015b), and Hewett and Ehmann (2004) made strong cases for the need to train tutors with the technology they will be using. More importantly, tutors need to be trained to teach *about* writing in online environments because simply asking questions of students is insufficient (Hewett, 2006). Hewett and Ehmann (2004) outlined five common educational principles that are fundamental to training online writing tutors as well as OWI teachers: investigation, individualization, immersion, association, and reflection. Thus, as addressed through OWI Principles 7 and 14, there are several layers of necessary tutor training: technology, teaching, teaching writing, and teaching in an online environment (p. 17, 28). The point remains that tutoring online requires specialized skills, some of which were addressed by Hewett (2006) and Hewett and Ehmann (2004):

- Online tutors need to be able to recognize, name, and teach writing problems using appropriate writing-focused vocabulary written and spoken at levels students can comprehend.
- Online tutors need to understand the affordances and constraints of different technologies in learning environments, such as how and when to use a chat box, a whiteboard or shared space, and audio functions to encourage student participation.
- Students have varying levels of competence with technology, and a great deal of interaction between tutor and student can be spent on explaining the technology or instruction itself. It appears that both types of conversation are inevitable, and instructors need to be trained to incorporate

this functional dialogue into conversations about student writing and idea development. Likewise, tutors would benefit from knowing how to use various functions within a program for different types of dialogue, such as audio for instructional purposes and the chat box for more functional directions, such as how to use the whiteboard or other program features during a session.

- Time and space constraints can affect the quality of an online conference; thus, it would be advantageous for tutors to practice how to teach writing through writing within the typical online conference time set by the OWL administrator. For instance, tutors should know how to teach effective thesis development using a variety of media, such as audio, the whiteboard, and chat, and ensure students are part of that process and participate in the session.

Additional training considerations for tutors include learning how to address multiple issues within the same conversation. For instance, Hewett's (2006) empirical research study on using whiteboard technology for text-based, synchronous OWI indicated that "these whiteboard interactions were highly writing task-oriented ... and focused particularly on developing student writing and/or ideas" (p. 5). The interactions that took place demonstrated that students and tutors were having conversations about the writing under review and the writing process. About half of the conversations, however, also included dialogue "toward interpersonal connections, facilitating the tutorial process, and communicating about using the whiteboard" (Hewett, 2006, p. 5); thus, this study has implications for learning more about how to handle meta-conversations during a tutoring session as well as for understanding that a great deal of synchronous tutoring time may be focused interpersonally rather than on the writing itself.

Students come to online conferences with various levels of competency with technology; thus, tutors have to be prepared to address some technology concerns during a tutoring session. They also have to find ways to help students understand the type of instruction they are receiving especially when various types of technology are used, such as the combination of audio, text, and whiteboard in some conferencing programs. Hewett (2006) recommended that tutor training should include helping tutors find value and balance in these various types of necessary dialogue during tutoring sessions. While it may appear overwhelming to find balance between writing instruction and fielding questions about technology, there are training strategies where tutors can learn effective and efficient ways to do that. Role-playing that reflects scenarios that tutors will typically encounter is an effective training strategy (CCCC OWI Committee, 2013; Hewett & Ehmann, 2004). This is an important aspect of training because as Hewett (2006) explained, particularly "in a synchronous setting, online instructors must be able to think quickly about students' expressed needs and to flexibly adjust both their vocabulary and strategies while teaching students accurately" (pp. 6-7). Similar issues need to be addressed in asynchronous tutor training (Hewett, 2004-2005, 2011, 2015b).

Tutors need to practice how to ask students to write or talk about their writing using various forms of technology, and they must be able to discern what students want or need through their responses. Because some conferencing programs may include audio components, there is opportunity for this dialogue to take place orally; however, as mentioned earlier in this chapter, those who create the OWL should not assume that all students will have a microphone or speakers, so tutors need to be prepared to initiate the purpose of the conference using only writing in the text chat. This, too, requires practice because tutors have to learn how to engage the student immediately with appropriate, correct, and inviting language with which students are familiar and comfortable (Hewett, 2010, 2015b). According to Hewett (2010, 2015b), tutors also need practice with how to instruct students on their writing using only writing, which should use language that is straightforward and easy to understand on the student's end—language with semantic integrity. Ways to accomplish this include using common guidelines for online writing, such as chunking text into shorter paragraphs; using formatting tools when possible, such as bullets, numbering, and highlighting or word processing revision marks (strikethroughs to substitute words) on a whiteboard; and using graphics when appropriate and possible (CCCC OWI Committee, 2013; Hewett, 2011, 2015b).

Equally important is the idea that tutors need training in using pedagogically sound practices that teach writing according to the institution's philosophy. One way to accomplish this is to allow veteran online instructors who have a solid understanding of composition theory to mentor novice OWL tutors. Additionally, tutors need to understand the affordances and constraints of various technologies and how to use them in pedagogically sound ways. For instance, Hewett (2006) outlined the distinctions between a text-chat box and a whiteboard. Both are text-based tools; however, each one has unique instructional benefits that should be explained and understood by tutors. For instance, a whiteboard affords the opportunity for tutors and students to both view a paper and make immediate changes, whereas comments in a textbox may be more explanatory about a specific writing issue.

A challenge regarding OWL training and professional development is that many training programs focus primarily on the features of the institution's LMS or on functional training on the various programs used for tutoring, such as how to use track changes and comments features in the word processing program, how to use IM-chat, or how to use the whiteboard and shared Web spaces. Familiarity and comfort with technology is important; indeed, Wolfe and Griffin (2012) found functional literacy to be a key component in student satisfaction with online tutoring. However, technology should not be the singular focal point of OWL preparation, as one can extrapolate from OWI Principle 2 (p. 11). Tutors and OWI teachers should have a working knowledge of, and think critically about, various learning theories and how they apply to their work in the OWL, which necessitates some rhetorical understanding of the technology. The tools of technology allow tutors to connect with students at a distance and it is crucial to the job, but the writing instruction itself should be considered of greater importance and should be stressed differently from technology in OWL training.

Preparing Faculty and Students

Once an OWL is established, faculty need training on the support services available to students because they are the ones on the front line who can persuade students to seek support. In *The State of the Art of OWI* (CCCC OWI Committee, 2011c), some faculty reported not knowing whether their institution had a writing center or OWL. Other respondents reported knowing there was an OWL, but they did not know how tutoring took place, who the tutors were, or how they were selected. This vacuum of awareness can happen when the writing center is a separate entity from an English or composition department, but it also can be a consequence of not providing appropriate training. Subsequently, when faculty are unaware of the resources at their own institutions, students often are left without support; some faculty even may refer students to OWLs outside of their own institution in the belief that their own institution is not capable or set up to help their students.

Formal training programs in OWI should not be restricted to faculty only; students need adequate preparation to thrive in online environments, as well. Student preparation is linked to accessibility, and one way to ensure that all students succeed in an online learning environment is to provide training for them, most often accomplished through orientation. Students have perceptions about OWI, such as unfamiliarity with the time requirements, how to use the technology, and the necessary interactions that need to take place. These common misconceptions about online courses justify student training, even for an OWL. When using an OWL, students have to be made aware of the various resources and services, but, more importantly, they need to know how to use them effectively.

Findings from the CCCC OWI Committee surveys (2011a, 2011b) indicated that even when online tutoring was available, "as many as 30% (fully online) and 47% (hybrid) reported that students did not receive any instruction for using those tutoring services" (CCCC OWI Committee, 2011c, p. 9). Furthermore, when faculty were asked how students were prepared for using online tutoring services, some disturbing comments included:

- "Linked in courses"
- "I don't know"
- "No online tutoring is offered"
- "Again, not sure"
- "Again, it's a case-by-case basis: a bit more than nothing, but not much since we do not have the resources for this." (CCCC OWI Committee, 2011a & 2011b, Q29).

This lack of faculty knowledge about the institution's OWL—if it indeed existed—mirrors a lack of student preparation for using the OWL, and it suggests an assumption that online students are familiar and comfortable with technology or with using technology in educational settings, which may not be the case at all (CCCC OWI Committee, 2011c). Student orientation should cover more than the features of the LMS in use or the conferencing software of the OWL because students may not know how to use technology to learn to write. In other words, students may not know that asynchronous discussion, for example, affords them the opportunity to think through their responses and refine their writing before posting it to the board. Likewise, students should be given direction on how to use OWL handouts, such as how to study a particular sentence-level issue and then follow up with practice in a live tutoring session. When going into synchronous tutoring sessions, students should be prepared for the typical time online conferences take, how they are facilitated, what kinds of technology are used, how to use that technology, and what to do after they have completed an online conference (Hewett, 2010, 2015b).

During tutoring sessions, some students may not know how to ask for help or what to ask for, which is another reason that tutor training is so important. It takes skill to get students to talk about their writing and to articulate where they need help. Furthermore, once a tutoring session is over or a paper has been returned with comments, some students do not know what to do with the feedback. It is important, therefore, that tutors help students make sense of what they received in the various media used during the session. Lynn Anderson-Inman (1997) stated that OWLs that appear to work well are those that attempt to help students understand how to use the technology to improve their writing skills. In other words, tutors and instructors need to teach students "how to read and interpret any textual feedback or advice, and how to make decisions about the uses of that feedback in their writing" (p. 26). This kind of student preparation will help students understand that an OWL is not a drop-off center; rather it is a place where they can get help with their writing, which they own from beginning to end.

Student training and the ownership of writing that it should support also may help to assuage criticism that OWLs emphasize "drill and practice," where grammar is stressed over other aspects of writing (Dailey, 2004). Drill-and-practice certainly can become a focus for an OWL when only one or two less interactive technologies are used, such as providing handouts as only PDFs or hyperlinked pages. And if these handouts or Web pages cover only grammatical issues, then such a reputation probably has been earned. However, Claire Charlton (2006) said that more effective OWLs "go beyond grammar to offer brainstorming and editing self-help" (para. 5), and Muriel Harris and Michael Pemberton (1995) argued for a combination of asynchronous and synchronous technologies to be used for tutoring. These preferences return us to the definition of an OWL and the services it may offer.

While some institutions do offer student orientation, the CCCC OWI Committee noted problems with orientation that affect student preparation for OWI (CCCC OWI Committee, 2011c). For instance, almost half of all orientations offered were in a face-to-face environment instead of online. Providing face-to-face orientation for online learning is counter to the benefits students would receive from being immersed in the very environment in which they are expected to learn. This immersion would offer students a better sense of whether they are suited for online learning, or at least alert them to the type of experiences they can expect, a point explained in detail in OWI Principle 10. Such immersion, however, needs to occur at the institutional level so that students are familiar with the policies and procedures of a distance-based program at their school, as well as to teach them how to use the institutional LMS and deal with challenges or problems they may encounter with it. Students need LMS orientation because each course is set up somewhat differently, and they have to know where to find assignments and course materials, how to submit assignments, and how to access other portals used in instructor-specific preferences (CCCC OWI Committee, 2013). OWL administrators also should be aware of any institutional and classroom orientations so that their own orientation can complement and expand on what students already have been provided. Once students know what to expect and how to use the resources and services of the OWL, they may be more likely to use the OWL.

TECHNOLOGY

Online courses suggest an open learning environment where students can access the classroom 24/7; therefore, IT support systems should be in place to allow students to complete their work at any time as well. This issue, as addressed in OWI Principle 13 (p. 26), is one of access and inclusivity per OWI Principle 1 (p. 7), but it also is one of "enabling students to use the digital educational environment more fully" per OWI Principle 10 (p. 26). Since students are working in an online environment, support should be provided in that same manner. Such support includes an OWL for reading and writing instruction, online libraries, technical support, and even "distance-based student counseling" (p. 25). Results from the two OWI national surveys, however, indicated that fewer than half of the respondents in all institution-type categories reported the existence of an OWL or any asynchronous or synchronous tutoring available for online students at their institutions (CCCC OWI Committee, 2011a & 2011b).

When online tutoring was available, it was mostly asynchronous tutoring, which Wolfe and Griffin (2012) found in their study as well. In *The State of the Art of OWI* (CCCC OWI Committee, 2011c) it also was noted that "quite a few respondents in both settings indicated either no access to online writing center assistance or a need for students to come in to a traditional brick-and-mortar writing center *if* one was available" (p. 9). Once again, access was at the forefront of this disturbing statistic. Many students who take online courses are physically unable to come to campus for a wide variety of reasons. If institutions offer online courses, then distance students should get the support they need using distance technology as indicated in OWI Principle 13 (p. 26).

The versatility of various technologies is an added benefit when developing OWL resources. It can be helpful to use both the asynchronous and synchronous modalities along with a variety of accessible media, as discussed in this chapter. For instance, when creating materials about a particular writing issue, such as how to write a thesis statement, many instructors will create a handout usually in the form of a word-processed document or an accessible PDF. But there are other ways to reach students who have particular disabilities or learning styles. For instance, podcasts, screen-capture programs with audio, and videos are useful complements to text-based handouts, and they address students who have different learning preferences or strengths. Transcripts for audio-based tutorials (including pre-developed tutorial materials designed for a broader student audience) are a must, and such alternatives as Braille and large print should be offered as reasonable accommodations (p. 7).

CONCLUSION AND RECOMMENDATIONS

The development of an OWL is essential to academic success for online writing students, and any institution that offers online courses should provide such support for students. In short, online students should have adequate support for the unique issues they must deal with when writing and learning in an online environment (CCCC OWI Committee, 2013). Expecting online students—particularly those in fully online OWCs, but also those in hybrid OWCs—to use onsite resources is detrimental to their learning since they are not given the opportunity to take full advantage of the very technology that they are expected to use for their learning. This problem also is a crucial issue of accessibility since many online students are physically, logistically, or geographically unable to access onsite resources. If an institution does not provide online support by way of an OWL, online students who write for any course and at any level simply are not being served in an equitable fashion. To this end, we recommend the following:

- Issues associated with inclusivity and accessibility should be at the forefront of the design of any OWL.
- Faculty and tutors who conduct online conferences should be selected carefully to ensure they are comfortable working in an online setting and teaching writing through writing.
- All writing center administrators and tutors should attend formal training on how to teach writing in online writing environments and how to address different learning styles in online settings. Furthermore, they should also be trained to work with students with disabilities, varies learning styles, and multilingual learners.
- Writing center administrators and tutors should be trained to conduct synchronous and asynchronous tutoring conferences for a variety of learners.
- Students should be trained to use an OWL properly and in ways that best fit their learning styles.
- Writing center administrators and tutors should be trained to properly and skillfully use the hardware and software programs they will use during tutoring sessions. They should also be familiar enough with the technology to help students through basic maneuvers when first getting an online consultation started.

NOTES

1. Writing center directors should consult their campus administrators to see how these practices comply with local interpretations of the Family Educational Rights and Privacy Act (FERPA).

REFERENCES

Anderson-Inman, Lynn. (1997). OWLs: Online writing labs. *Journal of Adolescent & Adult Literacy 40*(8), 650-654.

Breuch, Lee-Ann. (2005). The idea(s) of an online writing center: In search of a conceptual model. *The Writing Center Journal, 25*(2), 21-38.

Breuch, Lee-Ann M. & Racine, Sam J. (2000). Developing sound tutor training for online writing centers: Creating productive peer reviewers. *Computers and Composition, 17*, 245-263.

Burgstahler, Sheryl & Cory, Rebecca. (2008). *Universal design in higher education: From principles to practice.* Cambridge, MA: Harvard Educational Press.

Carlson, David A. & Apperson-Williams, Eileen. (2003). The anxieties of distance: Online tutors reflect. In Christina Murphy & Steve Sherwood (Eds.), *The St. Martin's Sourcebook for Writing Tutors 2* (pp. 232-242). Boston, MA: Bedford/St. Martin's Press.

CCCC OWI Committee for Effective Practices in Online Writing Instruction. (2013). *A position statement of principles and effective practices for online writing instruction (OWI).* Retrieved from http://www.ncte.org/cccc/resources/positions/owiprinciples

CCCC OWI Committee for Effective Practices in Online Writing Instruction. (2011a). *Fully online distance-based courses survey results.* Retrieved from http://s.zoomerang.com/sr.aspx?sm=EAupi15gkwWur6G7egRSXUw8k-pNMu1f5gjUp01aogtY%3d

CCCC OWI Committee for Effective Practices in Online Writing Instruction. (2011b). *Hybrid/blended course survey results.* Retrieved from http://s.zoomerang.com/sr.aspx?sm=%2fPsFeeRDwfznaIyyz4sV0qxkkh5Ry7O1NdnGH-CxIBD4%3d

CCCC OWI Committee for Effective Practices in Online Writing Instruction. (2011c). *The state of the art of OWI.* Retrieved from http://www.ncte.org/library/NCTEFiles/Groups/CCCC/Committees/OWI_State-of-Art_Report_April_2011.pdf

Charlton, Claire. (2006). Just a click away: Online writing labs at universities offer free help with grammar, style, editing and other issues. *Writer 119*(9), 40-41.

Cooper, George, Bui, Kara, & Riker, Linda. (2003). Protocols and process in online tutoring. In Christina Murphy & Steve Sherwood (Eds.), *The St. Martin's Sourcebook for Writing Tutors 2* (pp. 255-266). Boston, MA: Bedford/St. Martin's Press.

Crump, Eric. (2003). At home in the MUD: Writing centers learn to wallow. In Christina Murphy & Steve Sherwood (Eds.), *The St. Martin's Sourcebook for Writing Tutors 2* (pp. 242-255). Boston, MA: Bedford/St. Martin's Press.

Dailey, Susan R. (2004). Linking technology to pedagogy in an online writing center. *Journal of the Legal Writing Institute*, 1-21. Retrieved from http://writingcenters.org

Griffin, June & Minter, Deborah. (2013). The rise of the online writing classroom: Reflecting on the material conditions of college composition teaching. *College Composition and Communication, 65*(1), 140-161.

Ehmann Powers, Christa. (2010). A study of online writing instructor perceptions. In Beth L. Hewett (Ed.) *The online writing conference: A guide for teachers and tutors* (pp. 163-171). Portsmouth, NH: Heinemann.

Harris, Muriel & Pemberton, Michael. (1995). Online writing labs: A taxonomy of options and issues. *Computers and Composition, 12*, 145-159.

Hewett, Beth L. (2002). Theoretical underpinnings of online writing labs (OWLs). *The OWL maintenance and development guide*. Portsmouth, NH: Heinemann. Retrieved from http://defendandpublish.com/OWL_Theory.pdf

Hewett, Beth L. (2004-2005). Asynchronous online instructional commentary: A study of student revision. *Readerly/Writerly Texts: Essays in Literary, Composition, and Pedagogical Theory (Double Issue) 11 & 12*(1 & 2), 47-67.

Hewett, Beth L. (2006). Synchronous online conference-based instruction: A study of whiteboard interactions and student writing. *Computers and Composition, 23*(1), 4-31.

Hewett, Beth L. (2010). *The online writing conference: A guide for teachers and tutors*. Portsmouth, NH, Boynton/Cook.

Hewett, Beth L. (2011). *Instructor's study guide for the online writing conference: A guide for teachers and tutors*. Portsmouth, NH: Heinemann.

Hewett, Beth L. (2013). Fully online and hybrid writing instruction. In H. Brooke Hessler, Amy Rupiper Taggart, & Kurt Schick (Eds.), *A guide to composition pedagogies* (2nd ed.) (pp. 194-211). Oxford, UK: Oxford University Press.

Hewett, Beth L. (2015a). *Reading to learn and writing to teach: Literacy strategies for online writing instruction*. Boston, MA: Bedford/St. Martin's Press.

Hewett, Beth L. (2015b). *The online writing conference: A guide for teachers and tutors* (Updated). Boston, MA: Bedford/St. Martin's Press.

Hewett, Beth L. & Ehmann, Christa. (2004). *Preparing educators for online writing instruction*. Urbana, IL: National Council of Teachers of English.

Institute for Higher Education Policy. (2012). *Maximizing then college choice process to increase fit & match for underserved students*. Retrieved from http://knowledgecenter.completionbydesign.org/sites/default/files/321%20Pathways%20to%20College%20Network%202012.pdf

International Writing Centers Association. (2013). *IWCA home page*. Retrieved from http://writingcenters.org

Moberg, Eric. (2010). The college writing center: Best practices, best technologies. *The College Writing Center*, 1-8.

Neaderhiser, Stephen & Wolfe, Joanna. (2009). Between technological endorsement and resistance: The state of online writing centers. *The Writing Center Journal, 29*(1), 49-77.

Olsen, Leslie. (2002). *A genre of its own: Training tutors for asynchronous online conferencing* (Unpublished manuscript, Department of English, University of Washington, Seattle, Washington). Retrieved from http://www.pnwca.org/files/UWBOWLTraining.pdf

Ryan, Leigh & Zimmerelli, Lisa. (2010). *The Bedford guide for writing tutors.* Boston, MA: Bedford/St. Martin's Press.

Smarthinking. (2013). *Capella University Graduate Writing Center.* Retrieved from http://www.capella.edu/writingcenter/smarthinking.aspx

Thiel, Teresa. (2010). *Report on online tutoring services (University of Missouri-St. Louis).* Retrieved from http://online.umsystem.edu/docspolicies/Report_on_Online_Tutoring_Services.pdf

Twigg, Carol A. (2005). *Increasing success for underserved students: Redesigning introductory courses.* National Center for Academic Transformation. Retrieved from http://www.thencat.org/Monographs/IncSuccess.pdf

Vincelette, Elizabeth. (2013). Video capture for grading: Multimedia feedback and the millennial student. In Ellen Smyth & John Volker (Eds.), *Enhancing instruction with visual media: Utilizing video and lecture capture* (pp. 107-127). Hershey, PA: IGI-Global.

Vincelette, Elizabeth & Bostic, Timothy. (2013). Show and tell: Student and instructor perceptions of screencast assessment. *Assessing Writing. 18*(4), 257-277.

Wolfe, Joanna & Griffin, Jo Ann. (2012). Comparing technologies for online writing conferences: Effects of medium on conversation. *Writing Center Journal, 32*(2), 60-92.

CHAPTER 6

ADMINISTRATIVE DECISIONS FOR OWI

Deborah Minter
University of Nebraska-Lincoln

Moving writing instruction online returns WPAs to many of the same questions they have faced historically, such as class size, appropriate support for teaching and learning, and equitable compensation. This chapter proposes that students and teachers are best served by informed WPAs who have developed an awareness of the challenges and opportunities unique to OWI. *A Position Statement of Principles and Example Effective Practices for OWI* (CCCC OWI Committee, 2013) and its OWI principles and example effective practices can help WPAs to conceptualize the work and resources required to mount effective online writing courses.

Keywords: budget, class size, compensation, literacy load, material conditions of teaching, resources, student preparation, writing program administration/administrator (WPA)

For WPAs, *A Position Statement of Principles and Example Effective Practices for OWI* (CCCC OWI Committee, 2013) will feel familiar in its call for attention to class size, equitable compensation, support for teacher development, and the availability of services that support developing writers such as OWLs and on-call reference librarians. These are not new concerns. Neither are attending to and advocating for writing teacher development, equitable compensation, fair and meaningful assessments of teaching effectiveness, and attending to and advocating for the kinds of broader institutional resources necessary for students' development as writers and learners, especially those resources that support contingent faculty (see Chapter 7). Still, as writing programs choose (or, in some cases, feel pressure) to move writing instruction online, *A Position Statement of Principles and Example Effective Practices for OWI* can help WPAs to conceptualize the work and resources required to mount the kind of OWCs that support teachers and students in doing their best work.

Arguably, the responsibility to make OWI an accessible and inclusive experience for both faculty and students rests with the institutions' WPAs, as OWI

Principle 1 advocated (p. 7). Although WPAs often have little direct access to necessary purse strings, they are positioned to make arguments to upper administrators (e.g., deans, division heads, and provosts) for resources that can increase access points of access for students and faculty. With these resources, WPAs have the power to engage in such activities as buying hardware and software for faculty to use to teach OWCs from their campus offices and potentially for teaching from remote locations, hiring Work Study students to compose documentation specific to OWI courses, and conducting research about the issues that faculty and students—especially because of disability, learning, linguistic, or socio-economic issues—have accessing OWI equipment. Similarly, WPAs or those administrators in charge of distance education need to conduct assessment of the program's writing courses; this assessment should help the administrator understand who is being well served by the program, which populations want to participate in OWCs but struggle to access them, and what issues prevent student access. Then, WPAs need to work with those involved with online education at their respective institutions to determine how best to address these issues. WPAs, as this chapter details, can proactively respond to OWI Principle 1 by addressing other principles in *A Position Statement of Principles and Example Effective Practices for OWI* (CCCC OWI Committee, 2013).

THE CRITICAL CONCERN OF CLASS SIZE

Among the 15 OWI principles for OWI, class size—maintaining an enrollment cap of 15-20—is identified as "the most effective practice the Committee can imagine." With OWI Principle 9 (pp. 20-21), this effective practices document takes its place among a number of position statements from professional organizations affiliated with the teaching of college-level English, all of which call for writing course caps in this range (see, for example, the CCCC's *Principles for the Postsecondary Teaching of Writing*, originally issued in 1966, updated in 1989, & revised in 2013; also see the Association of Departments of English's "ADE Guidelines for Class Size and Workload," first issued in 1974 and updated in 1992).

Alice Horning's (2007) "The Definitive Article on Class Size" is particularly useful for its overview of extant research to support the value of low student-faculty ratios in writing classes. Horning cited, for example, Richard Light's (2001) finding that the amount of writing required for a course is the best predictor of students' level of engagement with the course and argues that extensive writing "cannot reasonably be assigned, read, and responded to in large sections" (p. 12). She juxtaposed Light's study with Alexander W. Astin's (1993) *What Matters in College*, which reported that a low student-faculty ratio positively impacts student satisfaction and degree completion (p. 12). In addition to this sweeping look at contemporary qualitative accounts of practices that contribute to college student success, Horning (2007) provided a review of research focused specifically on class size in college writing courses. Perhaps the most provocative piece of evidence she provided was a brief overview of an institutional study conducted at Arizona State University (ASU), where they analyzed the impact of a reduced writing course cap of 19. In short, lowered class-sizes correlated with improved pass rates for ASU's FYW courses (i.e., English 101 and English 102), improved retention, reduced numbers of student withdrawals or failures from the courses, and "improved student evaluations for all ranks of faculty teaching ASU's 100-level courses" (Glau as cited in Horning, 2007). Thus, synthesizing extant research that demonstrates relationships among smaller class-size, college student success, and teaching effectiveness, Horning provided several lines of argument for the benefits of smaller class-sizes.

At a recent meeting of the CCCC, June Griffin and I (2012; see also 2013) offered an additional argument for the benefit of lower course caps in OWCs particularly. Reporting on our study of the sheer quantity of reading and writing required in a set of comparable FYW courses, we compared the quantity required in fully online versions of the course with the amount required in face-to-face versions of the course. We called this aspect of the writing course the "literacy load"—suggesting its relationship to other kinds of loads associated with the intellectual and material work of learning and teaching, such as "cognitive load" and "work load." Comparing the amount of reading required of students in four FYW courses—all governed by the same course guidelines with the same enrollments (although with different instructors and syllabi), we found that the reading load of the fully online classes was nearly triple that of the on-site, face-to-face classes. This finding is all the more remarkable considering that enrollment in the two OWCs averaged only 15 students while enrollment in the onsite courses averaged 21.

Although preliminary, this research underscores the need for careful attention not only to the amount of assigned reading (and writing, to the degree that it, too, must be read and addressed) in an OWC, but also to the amount of reading required to participate in class activities and embedded in the way the course is conducted online. Indeed, Scott Warnock (2009) estimated that he routinely writes more than 30,000 words per class (p. 6); he and the students are responsible for reading these words and many more. As we (Griffin & Minter, 2013) have written elsewhere: "These initial findings lead us to worry that the literacy load of online classes as they are often configured can overtax students, particularly academically underserved and ELL students" (p. 153). More specific to the concerns raised in this chapter, each additional student in an OWC functions like a multiplier in terms of other students' reading loads; and, when a majority of the course is conducted via text, an increase of only a few students can mean substantially more reading for both students and teachers. WPAs charged with overseeing OWCs as well as teachers interested in designing effective OWCs will want to attend to the literacy demands inherent in OWC design. As Beth L. Hewett (2015a) suggested in *Reading to Learn and Writing to Teach: Literacy Strategies for Online Writing Instruction*, strategic ways to address such literacy demands are through writing assignments that also address reading-to-learn skills, careful teacher-writing practices that attend to semantic integrity, and thoughtfully considered overall reading loads. Hence, OWI Principle 9 is worth serious discussion at any institution where OWI is used for teaching writing (pp. 20-21).

NEGOTIATING STUDENT PREPARATION

Reporting on the results of the Babson group's tenth annual survey of online learning for *Inside Higher Ed*, Doug Lederman (2013) noted that while enrollment in college-level online courses seemed to be slowing, growth in that segment of postsecondary education still outpaced growth in higher education more generally across the same period of time. In fact, the survey suggested that more than 6.7 million students (or nearly a third of all students enrolled in postsecondary education) in fall 2011 were enrolled in at least one online course for college credit. All of this comes as welcome news to those who see promise in online learning's potential to improve educational access for groups who have been traditionally underrepresented in college classrooms (see Chapter 10, for example).

If online instruction can alleviate a few of the practical challenges (e.g., lack of childcare and unreliable transportation) that interfere with some students' completion of face-to-face college courses, recent research suggests that online courses do not yet serve all populations of students equally well. Researchers Di Xu and Shanna Smith Jaggars (Community College Research Center, 2013) recently mined a dataset of more than 40,000 community and technical college students enrolled across 500,000 courses in the state of Washington. Analyzing correlations between student attributes such as gender, age, ethnicity, previous academic performance and students' ability to adapt to online classes, the researchers found that while students generally struggle in their efforts to adapt to online classes, "males, younger students, students with lower levels of academic skill, and Black students were likely to perform particularly poorly in online courses relative to their performance in face-to-face courses" (p. 19). In addition, analysis of student adaptability by discipline revealed the greatest negative effect for persistence and course grade in English classes (p. 20), the area in which OWI seeks to excel. The stakes of failing to deliver on the apparent promise of online learning only increase as post-secondary institutions come under increasing public scrutiny for disappointing retention and graduation rates.

Although poor retention and graduation rates can be trailing indicators—an aggregate after-the-fact indication that students were struggling academically—my own institution (University of Nebraska-Lincoln) along with many others attend to "D, F, W rates," a term that refers to the percentage of students who withdraw from a course or earn grades below a C in a given semester (see Lang & Baehr, 2012, whose essay detailed an administratively-mandated study of D, F, W rates in writing courses at their institution). A survey of online writing teachers conducted by the CCCC OWI Committee (2011a & 2011b) found 40 of 156 respondents reporting drop-out rates in their OWCs of between 21% and 40%—a finding that should concern any WPA or higher level-administrator poised to begin or expand offerings of OWCs. The percentages reported in these surveys were anecdotal and may have been made off the cuff, thus not reflecting the actual percentages, which easily could be higher for some institutions and student populations. Clearly, then, administrators need to give serious attention to the support required to ensure that teachers and learners are empowered to build successful OWCs to which students can commit and in which they can thrive.

OWI Principles 10 and 11 (pp. 21-24) addressed two important and often overlooked elements of support that are necessary as institutions press to capitalize on the prevalence and potential of online learning. Specifically, OWI Principle 10 advocates that Institutions (and the English or writing programs housed within them) should prepare students and teachers for the technological and pedagogical components that are unique to OWI (pp. 21-23). For example, while time management is a skill that many students have not yet mastered by the time they enter college, the particular challenges of time-management in online courses might surprise and disadvantage some students. As Warnock (2009) observed: "The lack of f2f time in an online class can be a danger for some students. They don't have to go to class several times a week, so they may allow course work to slide away ... and then find themselves in trouble" (p. 143). Careful course design can address this kind of challenge. Yet, if instructors—especially the ubiquitous contingent faculty (see Chapter 7) often charged with teaching FYW—are not included in professionalization opportunities, this careful design may not always occur. For example, teachers can learn how to space their major and minor assignments in ways that maintain a scaffold while engaging students with interesting, connected weekly or ongoing assignments (see Chapter 2). They also can build redundancy into the OWC that helps to keep students on track and teaches them ways of managing their time (see Chapter 4).

Many course developers opt for a general orientation to online learning, typically with the institution's LMS in mind. Online instructional design consultants at my own institution have developed an orientation to online learning that easily is customized at the program, course, or instructor levels. Such an orientation is designed to prepare students for online learning and to show them how to succeed with routine aspects of the course (e.g., accessing course assignments on the LMS, submitting formal writing to the instructor for response, communicating publicly with the class and privately with the instructor or individual class-members, and accessing technical support); this preparation acclimates students to the particular online environment they will be using. It clearly is important to have this orientation available in advance of the start of the semester because it can function to alert students who may have under-conceptualized the work of learning online or misunderstood the challenges of accessing the course through the computers or mobile devices available to them. It provides students with some information about potential access challenges, as detailed in OWI Principle 1 (p. 7; see also Chapters 1, 8, 9, 10, & 16), and (hopefully) it offers them hands-on education-based practice with the needed digital tools. With such an orientation, students can seek help, adjust schedules to give themselves sufficient time to do their online course work, or withdraw before such challenges negatively impact their finances or academic record.

Certainly, the orientation as a means of supporting students' success in OWCs is not the only available mechanism, but it provides a compelling example of how one practice—rarely a significant aspect of onsite, face-to-face writing classrooms—can have important implications as the course moves online. Second, it suggests how a WPA might leverage support for something the program needs by demonstrating its importance to student success and (depending on design) its capacity to be customized for other units across campus. Third, preparedness for full participation—and an opportunity for follow-up prior to the start of the course if a student identifies a barrier—is crucial to developing an online learning environment in which all students can participate fully. In that way, a general orientation to online learning also can support the development of a vibrant and participatory online community, as argued with OWI Principle 10 (pp. 21-23). To take an example from my own teaching, I prepared an online graduate course in the university's LMS, a central feature of which was going to be threaded discussion. Because the number of students was relatively small and I had worked with all of them in earlier onsite courses or professional development offerings, I did not think to include an orientation to the course. Early in the first week of the semester, one student with a visual impairment alerted me to the fact that her screen-reader was unable to accurately translate the threaded discussion as housed in the LMS. Working with the Services for Students with Disabilities Office on solving this problem was going to take some time—now, almost a week into the semester—and more time would impact her ability to join and shape the class' online community. We were able, as a class, to switch quickly to a social media tool that was accessible for this student and would allow most of the same work, but I could have eliminated what was a stressful experience for the student—a fundamental concern represented in OWI Principle 1— simply by adapting the online orientation and posting it in advance of the course (p. 7).

OWI Principle 10 asked for more than a general introduction to online learning for students however. It stated that OWI students should receive adequate preparation by both the institution and their teachers for the "unique technological and pedagogical components of OWI" (p. 21). To this end, it is the responsibility of WPAs to assist teachers in developing assignments or other orientation methods that help students see how to use the LMS, for example, in the OWC as opposed to in an online math or history course. The OWC often makes use of designated sites for placing course content, as would other disciplinary courses. It goes beyond posting content, however, by asking students to create content through their writing. Hence, the OWC might use such LMS sites as whole-class discussion areas that are public to the class and the teacher, private student-to-teacher writing spaces for such writing as journals or questions about an assignment or writing strategy, private/public spaces for peer response where both teacher and a small group might write and read, email for redundancy or class reminders, synchronous chat for time-sensitive consultations, and the like. Indeed, an OWC likely will more fully and possibly more creatively use the LMS than other disciplinary courses. With attention to access and inclusivity per OWI Principle 1 (p. 7), OWI teachers may even engage other software, as Chapter 14 argues, if the LMS simply cannot respond to a pedagogical/rhetorical need. For these reasons, students need to understand the online components of the OWC as writing course spaces and communicative venues beyond general online learning and time management strategies.

Outside of inadequate student preparation, an impediment to developing robust online classroom community that nourishes students' growth as writers is lack of access to the resources frequently available to on-campus students. According to the same CCCC OWI Committee surveys (2011a & 2011b), only 45% of the respondents indicated that online students at their institution had access to online, asynchronous appointments with a writing center or OWL tutor. The figure dropped to 20% for respondents whose institutions offered students the opportunity for an OWL appointment in real-time. OWLs provide support on multiple levels, as Chapter 5 discusses, and their presence is crucial to students in OWCs, particularly those in fully online settings.

In the same CCCC OWI Committee surveys, availability of librarians for students in OWCs was somewhat better but still troubling: 57% of respondents reported that online writing students at their institutions had access to asynchronous exchanges with a librarian—a figure that dropped to 38% for those offering access to libraries for real-time appointments. As OWI Principle 13 suggested, online writing students should have access to the same support resources as onsite students in the same program; and, they should have access to those resources through online/digital media as consistent with the online learning environment of the class (pp. 26-28). This means that WPAs need to allocate funds and other resources toward helping their online students achieve parity with their onsite peers. Certainly, as OWI Principle 13 stated, online students also should be eligible to use any of the on-campus or face-to-face support (just as onsite students should be allowed to access online support)—but resources that are only accessible for those who can physically walk into an onsite center disadvantages students who chose an online course precisely because of the challenges posed by a requirement to be physically present onsite.

ADMINISTRATIVE SUPPORT FOR OWI

Concerns for access to the kinds of resources that support developing writers and for the structures that sponsor productive writing communities and literacy education—these are not simply abstract questions for WPAs. Indeed, WPAs routinely map new developments in research on writing and literacy learning onto the specific features of their individual writing programs as housed within the specific institutional contexts of their colleges and universities. In considering a move to (or expansion of) OWI, WPAs might pose the following questions for programmatic or departmental discussion and resolution:

- What do we want to accomplish by moving writing courses from onsite to online settings? Would hybrid or fully online OWCs—or both—work best to meet such goals?
- What goals are specific to the writing curriculum at this institution and how might we move that work online effectively?
- What opportunities become available for students and teachers if the courses move online?
- What access and inclusivity concerns do our particular student populations bring to learning to write using digital technologies?
- What abilities and prior knowledge do students at this institution typically bring to the writing classroom? Conversely, what will they need to learn to succeed and thrive in online settings for writing instruction?

- What pedagogical challenges do teachers face as the writing course moves online? How will the WPAs learn what these specific challenges are?
- What support for online learning is this institution already prepared (or willing to commit) to offer students and teachers?

These questions connect intimately to the questions of OWI program development and faculty professionalization discussed in Chapter 12. As such, before moving to OWI or as a mid-course assessment or corrective, these two chapters can be read together.

While WPAs engage the kinds of questions posed above, focused predominantly on student learning, they necessarily are concerned with the material conditions of teaching—with the extent to which the institution supports and rewards teaching, writing teacher development, the issues of full-time versus part-time instructors, and the kind of sustainable and meaningful assessment practices that ensure quality instruction. This focus drives such related questions as:

- Does this institution provide reasonable compensation for the teaching of writing such that it is likely to provide reasonable compensation to teachers as they build-out online offerings for the institution?
- What challenges might teachers face as the writing classroom moves online?
- What support for online teaching does this institution offer? How would that support need to be modified to develop a strong OWI program?
- What is the ratio of full-time to part-time writing teachers, and how would that ratio be represented in a movement to OWI?
- What strategies are best suited to helping this program collect data on how readily students are reaching the learning goals of our program and/ or campus as instruction moves online?
- What assessment focus can provide meaningful insight on students' learning experience, bring the teachers in this program together and be cycled back on OWI in ways that will improve the experience and/or render visible the kinds of pedagogical support that would advance the goals of the program?

A Position Statement of Principles and Example Effective Practices for OWI (CCCC OWI Committee, 2013) called for equitable compensation spelled out by OWI Principle 8 (pp. 19-20), as well as appropriate professional development to grow pedagogies best suited for the online environment and teaching evaluation practices for the purposes of determining and rewarding high quality teaching as explained by OWI Principle 7 (pp. 17-19). To these ends, *A Position Statement of Principles and Example Effective Practices for OWI* took its place among a number of professional statements that have sought to articulate the intellectual and ethical principles at stake in compensating writing teachers for their labor, even as shifting technological landscapes have brought new possibilities and demands.

For WPAs, initiating or expanding OWI likely means revisiting and potentially re-evaluating the matter of workload and compensation. OWI Principle 8 urged that teachers should be compensated for time spent developing courses and for recognition that teaching writing online is initially time-consuming (pp. 19-20). One example of an effective practice, then, is to compensate first-time teachers with some form of additional pay or reduced teaching load. Equally important in minimizing the overload associated with starting up an online course is to be certain, as an administrator, that policies and support networks are in place to minimize additional and unhelpful pressures. For example, policies and practices that ensure the timely assignment of online courses to instructors and a clear articulation of how online courses count in the instructor's overall teaching load are critical to teachers' professional well-being. It is important to ensure that a network of support structures exists: IT, library, and OWL support should be available 24/7 for students and teachers while the class is underway. Such a network should be established in advance—versus identified on-the-fly using the code-and-fix approach identified and problematized in Chapter 12— allowing teachers to focus on conducting the course. In addition, writing programs should have clearly understood intellectual property policies governing ownership of the course site and teaching materials that individual instructors develop. Such consideration is especially important for part-time faculty, many of whom teach multiple online courses while seeking to establish themselves as marketable scholars (see Chapter 7). Although not always possible practically, a program's intellectual property policy ideally will have the collective agreement of the program's teachers.

Online writing teachers also should have opportunities for formative and summative assessment comparable to what onsite classroom teachers enjoy. So, for example, if onsite teachers can assume that their course materials are being read and assessed by experienced onsite classroom teachers, then online teachers also should have the opportunity to have their teaching materials and OWI interactions reviewed by experienced online writing teachers. However, while the archival nature of OWI interactions may make it seem like a good idea to review an OWC several times during a full semester, in reality such intense scrutiny—unless applied also to onsite writing courses or codified as the most effective strategy for assessing OWCs—can be intimidating to OWI teachers and onerous for the few people in the writing program considered experienced enough to do the evaluations (also see Chapter 4). The goal is to provide support for OWI teachers fully, equitably, but not punitively. To this end, course evaluations should be reviewed, if necessary, to ensure that the questions posed there provide insight into crucial elements of the OWC (e.g., disabled-accessible and effective course site design) as well as broader questions about pedagogical effectiveness. Processes for collecting student evaluations should not disadvantage online teachers. So, for example, if a WPA discovers differential rates of response in students' evaluations of onsite and online courses, efforts should be made to mitigate that difference as much as possible.

ADVOCATING FOR RESOURCES

One of the vexing truths of online courses at my own institution and others is that developing and offering them is incentivized financially. Thus, in addition to pedagogical or philosophical motivations to develop online courses, my institution has created a small financial incentive to do so. While course development grants (paid to faculty who are willing to develop and teach an online course) are no longer centrally funded, a small portion of the tuition generated by the course each time it is taught is returned to both the unit providing instruction and the college in which that unit is housed. Reporting on a study conducted by the Council of Colleges of Arts & Sciences (CCAS), Paul McCord (2013) suggested that some form of revenue-sharing on distance courses is fairly common. With 100 of its more than 700 member institutions responding to a survey on "Distributed Education: Status, Concerns and Consequences," roughly 40% reported a significant or critical concern with units' growing reliance on the money earned through distance course revenue (McCord, 2013, p. 19). This example of revenue-sharing illustrates, again, the ways in which issues that have historically concerned WPAs can take new forms as writing instruction moves online. In my home department, while onsite writing courses are budget-neutral, online courses generate revenue for the department. Moreover, at many institutions, revenue-sharing is only profitable if contingent faculty teach the course and/or it enrolls at least several dozen students. These ideal conditions can be difficult to achieve when most writing programs try to follow best practices and keep their class caps on their writing courses below 30 students, or ideally closer to 20 students, and when the most qualified faculty to teach OWCs are full-time and tenure-track faculty.

Questions of compensation, stipend-bound professional development, or paid programmatic assessment work quickly lead to questions of budget. How might WPAs, as a practical matter, prepare to seek additional funds from upper administration to support the cost of initiating or expanding online course offerings? The following are questions that I have used in preparing additional budget requests:

- What aspect of the college's mission is served by this work? How highly valued—in this moment—is this part of the mission?
- What strategic priorities are addressed by this work? Are those priorities of primary or secondary importance at this institutional moment?
- If successful, what noticeable impact will this work have?
- What is the potential for success? (Is there evidence of buy-in from those who are immediately involved in the work? Is there evidence of a sound, executable plan? Is there evidence of broad support from those inside and outside the program?)
- What will this initiative cost? What kind of money (i.e., one-time, short-term, or—the most difficult to commit—permanent money)? What is getting leveraged?
- What is the return on investment and what form will that return take (e.g., increased revenue, increased research opportunity, increased visibility within the institution, public recognition for progress toward its mission, and the like)? How long will it take to see that return?
- How is this responsibility substantially new—for teachers or for the program—not already accounted for in the unit's current budget?
- If this is a new responsibility, then given the budget model at this institution, how does one find money for new initiatives?

A Position Statement of Principles and Example Effective Practices for OWI (CCCC OWI Committee, 2013) carefully articulated with OWI Principle 3 the ways in which OWI represents substantially new work for writing programs, requiring developing some new pedagogies and theories and with OWI Principle 4 how to migrate and adapt existing pedagogies in significant ways to the OWC (pp. 12-15). It also addressed new forms of attention to learning in online environments and awareness of potential barriers to participation in online educational settings.

CONCLUSION AND RECOMMENDATIONS

Larry Johnson, Samantha Adams Becker, V. N. Estrada Cummins, A. Freeman, and Holly Ludgate (2013), in *The NMC Horizon Report: 2013 Higher Education Edition*, identified six emerging technologies or practices with the greatest potential for impact and uptake in the contexts of higher education. This report is the result of research jointly conducted by the New Media Consortium (NMC) and the EDUCAUSE Learning Initiative (ELI). The "six technologies to watch" are massive open online courses (MOOCs), tablet computing, games and gamification, learning analytics, and—on what the report terms "the far-term horizon ... four to five years away from widespread adoption"—3D printing and wearable technology (Johnson et al., 2013, pp. 4-5). Among the key trends identified in the report is the rise of "openness" (i.e., open content, open resources; easy access) as a value: "As authoritative sources lose their importance, there is need for more curation and other forms of validation to generate meaning in information and media" (p. 7). Additional key trends included increasing interest in "new sources of data for personalizing the learning experience and for performance measurement"; and, it included the authors' observation that "the role of educators continues to change": "Educators are providing mentorship and connecting students with the most effective forums and tools to navigate their areas of study" (p. 8). When these new and experimental forms of online instruction are extended directly to OWI, they require a WPA's attention. OWI Principle 6 addressed to this issue by placing them within the guidance of *A Position Statement of Principles and Example Effective Practices for OWI* regardless of their newness and lack of familiarity as writing pedagogies (pp. 16-17).

The NMC Horizon Report: 2013 Higher Education Edition (Johnson et al., 2013) report with its rhetoric of radical transformation returns us to the question at the opening of this chapter: Tasked with responsibility for developing effective and sustainable writing programs that are responsive to the needs of particular student-writers who are seeking educational opportunities from particular institutions, how might WPAs negotiate the needs of the program and the institution while navigating some of the heightened rhetoric surrounding online learning and the technologies that make it possible? Certainly *A Position Statement of Principles and Example Effective Practices for OWI* (CCCC OWI Committee, 2013) has been developed with a view toward supporting WPAs in this work. The following list of recommendations, summarized from this chapter, is provided to offer additional support for WPAs as they work to build and advocate for OWCs that are accessible and effective:

- Class-size remains a critical concern for OWI (as it has been for onsite, face-to-face classes). If instructors choose to move routine elements of a writing course such as explanations of assignments, class discussions and informal "in-class" activities online *as text*, the sheer quantity of required reading increases dramatically. And the workload for students (not just teachers) increases with each additional student. Navigating large amounts of text in a course-site can undermine students' chances of success, and some populations of students (those with less fluency in academic English; students with particular disabilities) are likely at higher risk.

- Student-writers need more than effective writing pedagogy to be successful in an online course. They require support for writing and research in the form of access to OWL tutors and librarians. They require support for navigating the technologies of writing and learning. They require guidance—in advance of the start of the course—regarding what technologies, capacities and time the course will demand.
- Student-writers have the greatest opportunity for success in online classes when teachers are well-supported—well trained, fairly compensated, and secure in the value of their intellectual work to the institution as demonstrated through fair and reasonable policies.
- In considering the move to OWI, WPAs should assess the educational and pedagogical value—*for their specific population of students and teachers*—of moving writing courses online. WPAs also should frankly assess the current level of support for online instruction on their campus and how that might need to be adjusted to address OWI on any scale.
- In advocating for the value of moving writing instruction online and for the resources necessary to do that work effectively, WPAs are well-served by the ability to explain how effective OWI contributes significantly to their institution's particular mission.

REFERENCES

Association of Departments of English. (1992). *ADE guidelines for class size and workload for college and university teachers of English: A statement of policy.* Retrieved from http://www.ade.org/policy/index.htm

Astin, Alexander W. (1993). *What matters in college? Four critical years revisited.* Hoboken, NJ: Jossey-Bass.

Conference on College Composition and Communication. (2013). *Principles for the Postsecondary Teaching of Writing.* Retrieved from http://www.ncte.org/cccc/resources/positions/postsecondarywriting

CCCC OWI Committee for Effective Practices in Online Writing Instruction. (2011a*). Fully online distance-based courses survey results.* Retrieved from http://s.zoomerang.com/sr.aspx?sm=EAupi15gkwWur6G7egRSXUw8k-pNMu1f5gjUp01aogtY%3d

CCCC OWI Committee for Effective Practices in Online Writing Instruction. (2011b). *Hybrid/blended course survey results.* Retrieved from http://s.zoomerang.com/sr.aspx?sm=%2fPsFeeRDwfznaIyyz4sV0qxkkh5Ry7O1NdnGH-CxIBD4%3d

CCCC OWI Committee for Effective Practices in Online Writing Instruction. (2013). *A position statement of principles and effective practices for online writ-*

ing instruction (OWI). Retrieved from http://www.ncte.org/cccc/resources/positions/owiprinciples

Community College Research Center. (2013, February). *Adaptability to online learning: Differences across types of students and academic subject areas.* (CCRC Working Paper No. 54). New York: Xu, Di & Jaggars, Shanna Smith.

Griffin, June & Minter, Deborah. (2012, March). Expert views from student voices regarding fully online and hybrid OWI. Paper presented at the Conference on College Composition and Communication, St. Louis, MO.

Griffin, June & Minter, Deborah. (2013). The rise of the online writing classroom: Reflecting on the material conditions of college composition teaching. *College Composition and Communication, 65*(1), pp. 140-161.

Horning, Alice. (2007). The definitive article on class size. *WPA: Writing Program Administration, 31*(1/2), 11-34.

Hewett, Beth L. (2015a). *Reading to learn and writing to teach: Literacy strategies for online writing instruction.* Boston, MA: Bedford/St. Martin's Press.

Johnson, Larry, Adams Becker, Samantha, Cummins, N. Estrada, V., Freeman, A. & Ludgate, Holly. (2013). *NMC horizons report: 2013 higher education edition. The New Media Consortium.* Retrieved from http://www.nmc.org/publications/2013-horizon-report-higher-ed

Lang, Susan & Baehr, Craig. (2012). Data mining: A hybrid methodology for complex and dynamic research. *College Composition and Communication, 64*(1), 172-194.

Lederman, Doug. (2013). Growth for online learning. *Inside Higher Ed.* Retrieved from www.insidehighered.com/news/2013/01/08/survey-finds-online-enrollments-slow-continue-grow#ixzz2cBTTcmFD

Light, Richard J. (2001). *Making the most of college: Students speak their minds.* Boston, MA: Harvard University Press.

McCord, Paul. (2013). *Distributed education: Status, concerns and consequences.* Retrieved from http://www.ccas.net/i4a/doclibrary/index.cfm?pageid=3667&showTitle=1

Warnock, Scott. (2009). *Teaching writing online: How and why.* Urbana, IL: National Council of Teachers of English.

CHAPTER 7

CONTINGENT FACULTY AND OWI

Mahli Mechenbier
Kent State University: Geauga

At a time when university budgets are being cut and faculty appointments increasingly are contingent (i.e., off the tenure track), WPAs must find ways to provide OWI-centered training, professional development opportunities, and mentoring to prepare contingent faculty to teach effectively online. Contingent faculty have limited contact with the university and often are classified as a money-saving solution to staffing online courses, especially writing courses in which contingent faculty are ubiquitous. As off-the-tenure-track faculty struggle to earn fair compensation, retain reasonable control over course content, and gain access to institutional technology, collaboration between WPAs and instructors regarding OWI concerns is essential.

Keywords: access, adjunct, contingent faculty, evaluation, intellectual property, ownership, part-time faculty, preparedness, retention, salary disparity

"Just get one of the adjuncts to teach it." How many times has an instructor heard an administrator casually solve a scheduling problem with these words and a wave of the hand? Contemporary adjuncts—the contingent faculty who teach on semester-to-semester contracts—often are used as "fillers" for undesirable courses such as FYW. They are the faceless many who teach (often) full-time loads for part-time pay, commuter professors who juggle course loads among multiple campuses,[1] and the default faculty to which the administration goes at the eleventh hour to complete department schedules.

According to the American Association of University Professors (AAUP) (2013), "by 2009—the latest year for which national data are available—75.6 percent of US faculty appointments were off the tenure track and 60.5 percent of US faculty appointments were part-time appointments off the tenure track, including graduate-student-employee appointments" (p. 1). The reality is that the majority of higher education faculty are contingent, and writing studies professionals are among these. "Adjunct"—once colloquially defined as "part-time"—has become an antiquated designation. In modern academia, distinctions have developed among the stratifications of contingent faculty:

1. Full-time, non-tenure-track lecturers (FTNTT) with renewable contracts
2. Visiting assistant professors (VAP), who have a one-year, full-time, non-continuing contract
3. Graduate teaching assistants (TA), who are on annual contracts presumably until they achieve their graduate degrees
4. Part-time faculty/adjuncts, who are term faculty with one-semester contracts
5. Post-doctoral fellows, who typically are limited to two-to-three years on contract

To further confound the contingent ranks, adjuncts can be (1) terminal (Ph.D. or MFA) or non-terminal (MA) regarding degrees, (2) legacy adjuncts (adjuncts who earned the BA and/or MA from the institution at which they currently teach), (3) retired teachers or professors who want to remain in education but have no desire to re-enter the full-time workforce, and/or (4) instructors who are seeking a full-time position and who teach part-time as a place-holder.

Contingent faculty often are the first line of defense at a university or college in that they are the faculty members who teach the introductory courses and the teachers new students meet first or most often. The majority of students take some form of FYW during their first or second year of postsecondary studies, and they are likely to be taking these courses from contingent faculty. The experiences and interactions these new students have with faculty often determine their success, dropout rates, and transfer decisions. Marina Micari and Pilar Pazos posit that "the relationship between college students and their teachers has been shown repeatedly to have an impact on the quality of students' experiences and learning" (2012, p. 41). However, despite their importance to new students, contingent faculty often are marginalized as lesser—not worth the resources of an already stretched departmental budget, the time of the tenure-line faculty, or professional development opportunities afforded to tenure-line faculty who instruct the same courses.

CONTINGENT FACULTY AND THE OWI COURSES

The contingent faculty pool at the typical higher education institution is open continually to new applicants; institutions add new adjunct faculty every semester as they experience attrition from previous adjuncts or dissatisfaction with those who are somehow underprepared or judged as low performing. The level of teaching preparedness among adjuncts varies significantly. There is an old joke, which is more real than funny, that at the beginning of a semester, anyone who meets minimal requirements and has a pulse will be hired to teach a writing class. Providing preparation for those newly hired faculty may not be a priority. Even when institutions hold an adjunct faculty orientation in the fall, those that are hired for spring semester often are left to fend for themselves. Knowing the name of the Administrative Assistant who processes payroll, learning how and where to make copies, gaining access to a university email address and LMS, figuring out where to park, *and* finding a desk and/or a phone onsite all are important for the new hire. An adjunct not familiar with institutional policies and procedures easily can be overwhelmed with must-do administrative checklists: The *teaching* becomes secondary. Indeed, a faculty orientation—however necessary—does not begin to meet the needs for a writing program orientation or a workshop on teaching writing for that particular institution. Adjuncts' needs are multi-faceted; meeting and creating professional relationships with colleagues, learning how to use the institution's LMS, determining grading polices, discovering where to send students for tutoring, and writing syllabi are competencies which are developed continually and not simply in a one-day faculty orientation.

OWI is one of the instructional areas for which contingent faculty are used in English and Writing departments. Although training contingent faculty both as the institution's writing teacher *and* as an online writing instructor is necessary to meet the needs of OWI students, one might wonder why an English or Writing Department—stamped by the institution as being a non-income generating member of the Humanities—would spend money on OWI-centered training and professional development for a group of contingent faculty who may or may not be teaching at the institution the following semester. Placing an adjunct into an OWC a few days before the semester begins is more common than the academy would care to admit; additional research might help to identify more precisely the frequency and resulting challenges for online writing students. For example, in discussions with the CCCC OWI Committee, CCCC OWI Committee Expert/Stakeholder Panelists pointed to the number of adjuncts their institutions used for OWI as, in one case, a way to keep full-time faculty available for onsite courses (CCCC OWI Committee Stakeholders' Meeting 3, 2012b).

The majority of this chapter will illustrate that how writing programs often interact with contingent faculty raises concerns about inclusivity and accessibility, as addressed in OWI Principle 1 of *A Position Statement of Principles and Example Effective Practices for OWI* (CCCC OWI Committee, 2013). Anecdotally speaking, contingent faculty rarely are included in departments' and writing programs' culture; as a result, many are systematically disempowered. Moreover, for many reasons—ranging from poor pay to an absence of office space to limited time on a single campus—adjuncts rarely have access to institutional resources necessary both for teaching and for their ongoing employment. The working conditions obviously hamstring the ways that contingent OWI instructors teach their courses. Their limited inclusion and access also affect how they work with their students. Assuming that a campus has resources to prepare instructors to work effectively with writers with physical and learning challenges, multilingual writers, or students affected socioeconomically by the "digital divide," contingent faculty rarely have the opportunities to access these resources and, therefore, often do not know what to do when confronted by these issues in their classes.

One of the issues connected to this limited access is contingent faculty's generally abysmal pay. Contingent faculty often are paid on a per-course/per-semester basis. According to the OWI Expert/stakeholders' panel, such pay tends to range from a low of about $1,200 to a high of $3,500 per course (CCCC OWI Committee Stakeholders' Meeting 3, 2012b). The Adjunct Project stated, "Adjuncts who teach English ... reported earning an average of $2,727 per course" (June & Newman, 2013, para. 14). Such low compensation for adjuncts results in an economic need for many to seek out and to teach more writing courses, many of which also have exceptionally high literacy loads. Logistically, teaching online is attractive to an adjunct who financially may need to teach at three different institutions yet cannot physically commute to three schools in a single work day. Even so-called "beltway fliers" have their limits, and online courses are a feasible solution to the location problem but not to the workload problem that accompanies most writing courses. Indeed, because OWCs particularly have high literacy loads, as discussed in Chapter 6, the adjunct's heavy teaching burden creates an untenable teaching situation and may lead to suboptimal learning conditions.

As this book has posited, while we still are teaching rhetoric and composition, OWI necessitates specialized knowledge of, and strategies for, using digital technology in writing instruction. To this end, the CCCC OWI Committee's research indicated that the level of training and mentoring that contingent faculty members receive often is insufficient to prepare them for teaching in an OWC. OWI Principle 7 stated, "Writing Program Administrators (WPAs) for OWI programs and their online writing teachers should receive appropriate OWI-focused training, professional development, and assessment for evaluation and promotion purposes" (p. 17). This principle was written to indicate the importance of such preparation for OWI—preparation that contingent faculty especially need. In the rationale for OWI Principle 7, the CCCC OWI Committee recommended that "teachers—especially novice teachers (e.g., graduate student teachers) and contingent faculty—should not be placed into OWCs until they have received appropriate training *by their WPAs and institution*" (p. 17; italics added). Training was listed as including peer-mentoring, assistance in syllabus development, tips regarding electronic asynchronous communication, and workshops to teach an instructor the technical aspects of the LMS or online classroom environment.

In Thomas J. Kramer's (2010) "The Impact of Economics and Technology on Changing Faculty Roles," the author analyzed the economic necessity of hiring contingent faculty for online courses for both financial and competitive reasons. As more and more tenure-track positions are replaced by instructors with non-tenure-track contracts, faculty responsibilities are shifting:

> One way to develop and staff online programs is to use contract and/or part time faculty, both to create the online courses and then deliver them. This also presents the opportunity to hire contract or part-time faculty who have particular content and technical expertise for such courses. At the same time, having full-time tenure-track faculty develop and deliver such courses and programs is also effective. However, it requires the willingness, motivation, and professional development support to do this effectively. If universities are not willing to provide incentives and professional development support, they will be more likely to turn to contract and part-time faculty. (p. 255)

Tenure-line faculty—concerned with research and publication requirements for tenure, promotion, and merit—may not be willing to learn such teaching tricks as developing an online course. Hence, ensuring that adjuncts have access to university resources and software for the OWCs they may be offered is imperative to the writing program's functioning and reputation. Too often, contingent faculty "tend to get compensated the least for their work, wield the least amount of institutional power, and can sometimes be the least prepared for their online work" (DePew, Fishman, Romberger, & Ruetenik, 2006, p. 59). CCCC OWI Committee Expert/Stakeholder Panelists expressed similar experiences (CCCC OWI Committee Stakeholders' Meeting 3, 2012). Because of the important contact that contingent faculty have with writing students and for their own professional development, WPAs need to accept responsibility for the training and professional development of OWI teachers.

To this end, *A Position Statement of Principles and Example Effective Practices for OWI's* (CCCC OWI Committee, 2013) Effective Practice 7.6 suggested that prospective OWI teachers should receive OWI-specific training including assistance in mastering both asynchronous and synchronous technological elements of the course, advice regarding accessibility, and training with media (pp. 18-19). Effective Practice 7.8 recommended that WPAs "should help teachers to progress into fully online teaching" through mentors and with initial experience in hybrid courses (p. 19). These suggested practices indicate that instructors cannot merely be shoehorned into OWCs with little or no training; as Chapters 1 and 4 reveal, there are new theories and skills necessary for OWI, and while it can work well to migrate and adapt some theories originally developed for face-to-face instruction, others are particular to OWI and its attendant environments (see OWI Principles 3 and 4). Just because instructors can teach an onsite course successfully does not mean they possess the skills to translate the course to an online venue. Technological skills aside, teachers of OWCs require knowledge of written communication skills and tone given the primarily text-based online teaching environment currently used in higher education. They require, as well, knowledge of how to engage the student in a Web-based classroom—as described in Chapter 4 particularly. As Deborah Minter indicates in Chapter 6, WPAs should argue for the necessary financial support to develop and field this specific kind of training, which goes beyond training for onsite instruction. It is unlikely that most adjunct instructors have had access to OWI training or professional development—of any kind—as a part-time faculty member; indeed, many full-time faculty anecdotally report having little-to-no OWI-specific training and professional development (CCCC OWI Committee, 2011c). Even with prior OWI training, contingent faculty members will benefit from additional access to professional development particular to each institution for which they work.

For the best results, the institution should ensure that all OWI faculty receive technical training and hands-on practice with both course content (in other words, with teaching *writing* online using the institution's preferred approaches) and the LMS itself at least one semester *prior* to teaching a writing course online. Kaye Shelton and George Saltsman (2006) stated, "The level and quality of the training faculty receive to enrich technical and instructional skills are also directly tied to the success of the faculty members' efforts in teaching online." To this end, faculty training for OWI should include both technical computer skills and classroom instructional skills. If a WPA asks a new adjunct, "Can you teach online?", the adjunct may answer, "Sure ... I have a laptop" without realizing that teaching online requires (among many other things) familiarity with the institution's LMS. (In fact, some contingent faculty may be so economically disadvantaged from low pay that they do not own sufficiently sophisticated technology to teach the course fluidly, potentially disenfranchising them from this professional teaching environment [CCCC OWI Committee Stakeholders' Meeting 3, 2012b].)

Funding these professional development opportunities is challenging in a climate of budget cuts, hiring freezes, and course cap increases. However, the importance of OWI-focused training strengthens a writing program in the long term. To have trained, competent, and experienced online faculty presupposes that they will become better instructors over time, thus improving the learning experience for students, increasing job satisfaction for the teacher, and solidifying a quality teaching pool for the writing program.

OWI-focused professional development does not always mean providing travel to a national conference with paid lodging and food although that certainly is a valid professional development opportunity. Rather, professional development can be a local opportunity with a mentoring program where a group of adjuncts observe a more experienced faculty member upload a course to a blank LMS or observe another online instructor teaching an asynchronous class. As Effective Practice 7.7 noted, mentorship and ongoing observation are important strategies for assisting teachers with a transition to OWI. They are useful, as well, for scalable training that develops an association among teachers, giving OWI teachers colleagues to whom they can turn for help. The WPA also can create opportunities for interaction through asynchronous discussions about the pedagogy of online teaching. The LMS is a perfect venue for this type of interaction as it facilitates the kinds of discussion that teachers will then expect of students in most OWCs. They can learn from each other and experience the valuable immersion that comes from being in the environment for real communicative purposes.

Adjuncts, especially those who teach FYW online, change—and *purposefully can change*—the dynamic of the writing program. However, they often are ignored by tenure-track faculty. Anecdotally, a sense that contingent faculty are a bother rather than a help can prevail. The fully employed faculty may think there are too many adjuncts to keep track of; tenure-line faculty often object to tenure-track lines being replaced with contingent lines; tenure-line faculty can resent having to mentor or perform classroom observations for adjuncts; and since adjuncts earn such a small amount, administering them may seem to be a waste of resources. In a way, contingent faculty who teach online courses are like commuter students while the tenure-line faculty are like on-campus, dormitory-residing students; institutions spend more time, resources, and attention in focusing on resident students (tenure-tracks) than it does on commuter students (adjuncts). Tenure-line faculty are positioned to secure a more valuable status at research universities because most are required to possess advanced terminal degrees, which often grants them access to resources that aid their ability to publish. On the other hand, contingent faculty who teach online, even those with terminal degrees, are "off-campus" in their relative geographical position even more so than the face-to-face adjunct—further marginalizing the online adjunct.

Adjunct faculty who teach hybrid OWCs spend at least partial time on campus while those who teach fully online OWCs have limited contact with the university because the physical need to be on campus is lessened by the nature of the online teaching venue. In some cases, contingent OWC instructors do not even reside in or near the states of the institutions for which they are teaching fully online courses. Holding writing courses online—particularly asynchronously—naturally means greater flexibility for both student and instructor. Similarly, online training (recommended by OWI Principle 7), provides that appropriate connective forum for OWI teachers, contingent or full-time. While synchronous online training sessions certainly can be developed and should be used in cases where immediacy of communication is necessary (see Chapter 3), it is challenging to schedule synchronous workshops that can be well attended by busy contingent faculty. Synchronizing the availability of adjuncts who teach at multiple institutions is almost impossible. WPAs must be inclusive and creative when extending mentoring and professional development opportunities to contingent faculty, making asynchronous training an especially useful venue.

Although their time on campus may be limited, OWI teachers need to know their supervisors. WPAs—and other administrators who hire faculty—should want to *meet* faculty who teach OWCs. WPAs should *know* and be able to speak to the teaching skills and personalities of their online faculty. Regina L. Garza Mitchell (2009) stated, "To avoid online education's being relegated to a lower tier, trust must be established regarding the quality and importance of this type of education. A lack of trust places faculty members who teach online at a disadvantage and may also affect teaching and learning in this setting." Undoubtedly, adjunct faculty who teach online should not be faceless members of the department, yet it is likely that they are in most cases. While meeting them may be a logistical challenge, it seems reasonable that unless the adjunct is geographically distributed in another area of the country, a one-time per semester meeting for all OWI teachers should be organized. My experience has been that contingent faculty members are hungry for face time with their WPAs and peers, even if that face time occurs synchronously online.

Assigning the Right Teachers to OWI

Having the right match of teacher to teaching environment is a key to effective OWI. In terms of hiring contingent faculty, especially last-minute hires, it may be difficult to see evidence of effective OWI teachers who are new to the institution; yet, finding such evidence is crucial particularly when appropriate orientation or training has not been or will not be provided. Evidence of ability to teach writing online helps to determine whether the online environment is a good fit for a prospective writing teacher. Adjunct teachers are judged swiftly on their course effectiveness and may lose their jobs from poor student evaluations while full-time tenured or tenure-line teachers may be given both more support and time to become fluent in online instruction. Effective Practice 7.4 stated that teachers "who would do better in traditional settings should be identified and assigned to such settings." Further, if "personality ... indicates a poor match for OWI," then other classroom arrangements can be made to maximize the success of the course and the learning experience of the students (p. 18). With little time to spare, it benefits both teachers and WPAs to understand the nature of good fit for OWI.

Determining effectiveness and fit prior to hiring a new adjunct for the OWI portion of the writing program may involve asking key questions about one's comfort level with online technology and digital teaching, in addition to questions about the instructor's philosophies and practices for the teaching of writing. Such questions can help both the adjunct teaching applicant and the WPA to discuss an apt fit with concrete terms:

- Have you taught writing online before? Where? How often? Which courses?
- What types of formal preparation have you received for OWI in the past? What types of ongoing professional development have you received from an institution or provided for yourself through other opportunities?
- What experience do you have teaching students with disabilities and multilingual speakers?
- Do you prefer teaching asynchronously or synchronously? Why?
- What LMSs have you used in the past? Which ones have worked best for you? Why?
- If you are given a pre-developed course to teach, what challenges do you anticipate? What kinds of help would you like from the WPA to this end?
- What is your favorite theory, book, or article regarding OWI?
- What do you like best about teaching writing online? How does this preference differ for you regarding teaching writing in a traditional, on-site setting?
- If you have not taught writing online before, what draws you to this choice now?
- What kinds of assistance to you anticipate needing as you move into an OWC for this institution?

Evaluating adjunct faculty once a year is central to the long-term success of a healthy writing program. Jill M. Langen, in her study on evaluation of faculty, maintained:

> With the dramatic increase in the use of adjunct faculty in higher education classrooms, it is critical that we understand how these faculty are being evaluated, and how these evaluation results are utili[z]ed. Without a clear and consistent process available to measure performance, it becomes increasingly difficult for administrators to ensure that quality learning opportunities are available in the classroom. (p. 185)

Assessment in online settings is both challenging and crucial. First, as Chapters 4 and 6 indicate, evaluation of any OWI teacher has not yet been standardized in any manner. Assessment for adjuncts is especially tenuous as it affects these teachers in significant financial ways; yet these effects are no more crucial than how contingent OWI faculty's teaching influences students and the writing program overall. Second, only through regular evaluation—but not more or less rigorous assessment than is conducted for onsite writing teachers, according to OWI Principle 7—can the WPA understand the potential for student writing development, particular teachers' ongoing professional development, and the writing program's health. To this end, on the most basic level, if department administrators and tenure-line faculty do not know their adjuncts, then how do contingent faculty establish professional contacts for their ongoing development as OWI teachers in the workplace?

Effective Practice 7.11 recommended that the evaluation of online writing teachers should be done by a "peer or supervisor who has similar training and equal or superior ... experience in ... OWI" (p. 19). WPAs should ensure that the mentors/evaluators of contingent online faculty possess experience in online pedagogy and are familiar with OWI principles. Many senior faculty who are respected for their teaching may have never taught online, let alone writing online. The CCCC OWI Committee believes that an instructor who has never taught online should not evaluate how another instructor teaches an OWC. That reasonable stance can be problematic for the adjunct who is seeking a full-time position, however. For contingent faculty, having a letter in their files that was written by a tenure-line faculty member—or even better, the WPA or department chair—may indeed assist them in a full-time job search. Yet, given that many online faculty *are* contingent, a letter written *by* a contingent faculty member *for* a contingent faculty member can be perceived as insignificant or inconsequential. Such recommendations can be dismissed by questions: Were the instructors friends? Couldn't the instructor get a tenure-line professor to observe the class? Is the part-timer not liked by the WPA? WPAs need to create standards for evaluating online adjunct faculty to ensure that knowledgeable peer-observers are applying online pedagogical principles to these courses and to the instructors. Assigning a tenure-line professor of Shakespeare to observe and evaluate an online FYW course is similar to asking an expert on Schubert to attend and evaluate a Lady Gaga concert. Indeed, tenure-line faculty may resent losing time they are asked to give to mentor or evaluate part-time faculty. Providing reasonable standards for assessment and adequate compensation—such as course releases—to those who do the evaluation may be helpful.

Engaging adjunct instructors on the campus and within the university community is focal to retaining quality contingent faculty. Kinga N. Jacobson (2013) stated, "Inviting adjunct faculty to instructional team meetings and college wide committees can build strong inter- and intradepartmental networks. These meetings develop mutually beneficial, peer-working relationships that lead to long-term retention of adjunct instructors." University service becomes problematic for many adjuncts due to their multiple-institution teaching schedules. Even if adjunct faculty are invited to serve, the tenure-line faculty have to be prepared to take the opinions of the adjuncts seriously despite their limited stake in the institution's mission. Even when "service" is not connected to the institution, however, it can be challenging for contingent faculty members to experience themselves as having a voice. One example emerged from the CCCC OWI Committee Fully-Online and Hybrid surveys (CCCC OWI Committee, 2011a & 2011b). As described in *The State of the Art of OWI*, (CCCC OWI Committee, 2011c), only 18% of the fully-online participants (p. 71) and 12% of the hybrid participants (p. 94) self-identified as adjunct faculty. This dearth of contingent voices in these two surveys indicates that the deeper understanding that adjuncts—who indeed may comprise the vast majority of OWI teachers—could provide is missing. While finding a universal solution that solves all contingent faculty needs may not be feasible due to the diversity of instructors in the adjunct pool, something must be done.

WPAs can begin by educating themselves about the adjuncts who teach in their programs. Such actions as maintaining open lines of communication and welcoming questions and conversations with contingent faculty address Effective Practice 12.3: "Individuals teachers should have adequate opportunity to discuss with the WPA how any changes relative to OWI may affect their careers" (p. 25). Online adjunct faculty should have the ability to speak to a reliable "go-to" regarding teaching-related concerns, and they should be able to do so without undue concern for their job security.

LOCATION, NEED, AND EXPERTISE

Part-time faculty often have different needs from full-time faculty, and it is the responsibility of WPAs to understand those needs. Some contingent faculty are part of a two-parent family, while others are single parents; some can only teach at night, while others can only teach on weekends; some have full-time employment elsewhere and are teaching to supplement income, and others cobble together part-time teaching positions as a "full-time" job, struggling to earn a living wage among several institutions. The culture of the campus is central in understanding—and working—the politics of a department: Are students predominantly commuters? Do they live in an on-campus dorm? Is the institution a community college? Is the institution a regional campus of a four-year university? Are the faculty subject to a collective bargaining agreement?

WPAs should recognize the special needs of managing contingent online faculty, especially regarding support and training for their futures as online writing teachers. The classification of contingent faculty member plus the type of institution combine to form the dynamic of how the instructor and university interact. For example, there are instructors who may teach more than six courses at multiple institutions to earn what-comes-close-to a living wage. Personal funds to attend conferences are non-existent; time to read current pedagogical journal articles is limited. Do adjuncts have time to send out applications for full-time positions? Do they have access and a password to the MLA's *Job Information List*?

Failure to provide online adjunct faculty with office space is an oversight that, while possibly understandable given the online nature of the teaching assignment, is significant for the faculty involved. The prevailing belief may be that the instructor is not on campus for class although this assumption would be wrong for hybrid course instructors. Therefore, some might believe that the adjunct would have no other reason to be present on campus. Yet, lack of an office is indicative of the bigger problem—a lack of resources that falls to the adjunct to replace. For example, without office space, the adjunct does not have an office phone; all phone calls to students will be placed on a personally owned device for which the adjunct pays the bill or uses personal, counted minutes. An absent-from-campus online adjunct will not have regular contact with fellow faculty and will not establish relationships with administrators. With provided office space, some OWC adjuncts may come to campus to make use of these resources and connect with others.

Indeed, online contingent faculty are fragmented. They exist on the periphery of the campus community, they often do not know each other personally, and they are competing with each other for courses (and income). Developing a community—even a virtual community—will promote collegiality and a sense of being *part* of the department. OWI Principle 11 speaks to the importance of student motivation which is driven by a "sense of interpersonal connectedness to others within a course" (p. 23). Contingent online faculty also will benefit from this sense of community and connection with other instructors; teacher satisfaction improves when faculty have a sense of contributing to the department. WPAs should want to protect the integrity of the adjunct pool while simultaneously promoting each instructor within the adjunct setting. Doing so can only be good for the students they teach. Furthermore, it is well known that part-time faculty make less money. They are the nomads of faculty—traveling to where they can make a living. They vary in skill and experience. However, WPAs should devote time and resources to the ethics of treating adjunct instructors appropriately, particularly in OWI, which is a new project for many institutions and for which fewer resources may be allotted.

To what degree do WPAs become involved with adjunct faculty? Do administrators ask an adjunct upon hiring or even in casual conversation, "Where else are you teaching?" or "How many courses total will you be teaching this term?" WPAs may not ask such questions because they do not want to know. Adjuncts' answers ("I teach nine online courses at three different institutions") may cause WPAs to question the quality of instruction within that university's online program, and *not asking* adjuncts direct questions regarding teaching load is promoting a culture of *not knowing*, thereby keeping the unattractive truths of the adjunct online writing instructor's professional life a secret. As one respondent to an OWI survey stated, "Often times, adjunct faculty teach the online courses, and while I am sure they are qualified and dedicated teachers, I know they have had the most minimal of training and many are teaching sections for a variety of campuses, so they have to keep things as simple as possible to manage the awful workload they carry" (CCCC OWI Committee, 2011c, p. 64). Such an "awful workload" may be difficult to minimize because of the sheer economics of many adjuncts' lives. As the section below on compensation reveals, low pay necessitates teaching multiple courses to survive. Even if an institution adopts OWI Principle 9's recommendation that "OWCs ... should be capped responsibly at 20 students per course," adjunct instructors who are teaching multiple online courses at multiple institutions—meaning multiple preparations, as indicated in Chapter 2—will not have a manageable literacy load.

The institutional structure has shifted with the addition of online courses. These have materialized rapidly as a way to balance the budget, to offer greater accessibility to college education, and to solve classroom space concerns. Now, departments are faced with the questions: How do we administrate these courses? How do we train and develop qualified faculty to teach them? How do we engage online faculty as part of the university community? Online education is the victim of its own success; it is the situation where a municipality builds a huge shopping mall, and then *after* the grand opening, the city sends in a construction crew to widen the road that leads to the mall. Online courses are here; now how do we ensure their success? It is crucial to prepare adjunct faculty to instruct

FYW and other writing-intensive courses they may teach by adopting OWI Principle 7 and offering "OWI-focused training, professional development, and assessment" (p. 17). Additionally, adjunct faculty deserve active support from instructional designers and WPAs to make their courses accessible to students with disabilities. Building accessibility into online courses requires significant time and labor, and instructors should be appropriately compensated for fulfilling this legal and ethical obligation on behalf of the institution. When WPAs are familiar with OWI and its strategies, they are in the leadership position necessary to share—and encourage—effective practices with their community of instructors.

COMPENSATION

"Contingent faculty are underpaid" has become a mantra for the adjunct. According to The Coalition on the Academic Workforce (2012), "Looking at all courses part-time faculty respondents reported on, the median pay per course, standardized to a three-credit course, is $2,700." More disheartening is that "respondents teaching on-site courses reported median pay per course of $2,850, [and] those teaching courses online reported $2,250" (Coalition, 2012, p. 12). Although these comparisons may not have been generated by examining the same types of institutions, the numbers are revealing. Members of the university administration may justify this disparity with the rationale that online adjuncts do not "have" to come to campus to teach, and therefore, they "save" on gas, parking costs, and even clothing. Yet, do students pay fewer tuition dollars for an online course than they do for a face-to-face class at the same university? No, they do not. Ethically, we know that the instructor should not be paid a reduced salary for an online course that appears on the student's academic transcript as "credit"—identical to the way a face-to-face class with the same course number would appear—just because the course was taught online. The salary disparity signifies that in some cases higher education *does* downgrade online adjunct instructors to an even more greatly reduced faculty status.

OWI Principle 8 stated, "Online writing teachers should receive fair and equitable compensation for their work." WPAs should uphold the value of OWCs—and those faculty who teach them—to the English or Writing Department as a whole. Once those adjunct faculty have been appropriately trained for their OWCs, it is only reasonable to want to keep them working. Fair compensation will help to ensure retention of capable, skilled, and trained online adjuncts who are committed to student success.

WPAs must understand the complexity of online instruction and argue for fair compensation. According to *A Position Statement of Principles and Example*

Effective Practices for OWI, "Altering course materials [to meet online students' needs] ... requires time and energy as well as thoughtful literacy approaches" (p. 19). Indeed, according to OWI expert/stakeholders, even pre-developed courses take additional time for adjunct faculty to manage. In one meeting, Jason Snart stated:

> I would like to see a dedicated paid-time offer for adjuncts who need to spend considerable time prepping what should be a pre-made course, in terms of fixing mistakes, changing names where their name has to be theirs instead of someone else's. Making sure page numbers are correct, just sort of an upkeep prior to a semester starting. So like a 2 hour paid— you can even call it a prep workshop time—something to that effect, because I think there is a lot of prep time that really goes uncompensated for adjuncts that are teaching these ready-made or pre made courses. (CCCC OWI Committee Stakeholders' Meeting 3, 2012b)

Compensation may include "pay adjustments, course load modifications, and technology purchases" (p. 20). To adjuncts being paid $2,250 a course, any compensation would be welcomed in recognition of their efforts.

The data tell a sad story, and in the never-enough university-budget-speak, it is unlikely that raising contingent faculty salaries is a priority. However, "fair and equitable compensation" goes beyond payment-per-course. Adjuncts often have to provide their own computers, laptops, and software when they teach OWCs. Even if a department is unwilling or unable to give adjuncts laptops, WPAs should implement a system where online adjuncts can sign-out laptops—with the necessary software installed—on a semester-long basis. Software is expensive for adjuncts who are teaching for $2,250 per course with no access to IT support. Such a measure speaks to issues of access and inclusivity as indicated in OWI Principle 1 (p. 7), and it addresses the concerns of OWI Expert/stakeholder Steven Corbett, who pointed out the inequities of impoverished adjunct faculty who do not own state-of-the-art computer technologies that would enable them to teach writing well online (CCCC OWI Committee Stakeholders' Meeting 3, 2012b).

Finally, compensation may include other "luxuries," as well. In the third meeting of the OWI Expert/stakeholders, Heidi Harris said:

> I know a lot of instructors who are teaching online are adjuncts and they get into that loop of not being able to really get really any publications because the traditional publishing

cycle is really intensive. They might have real expertise that they would like to share and that we can get quickly, through yes like an online journal for implementing processes like OWI that really talks about pedagogy, theory, research, connecting those points. I think we come up with a lot of best practices, but I don't see a lot of publications that can keep up with publishing current ideas that show how those practices are implemented. (CCCC OWI Committee Stakeholders' Meeting 3, 2012b)

In response to this suggestion, the CCCC OWI Committee has developed a peer-reviewed Online Resource (http://www.ncte.org/cccc/committees/owi) that enables the actual OWI practitioners—adjuncts in particular—to publish their OWI effective strategies. Adjunct faculty often teach with a great deal of passion and thoughtfulness; they, too, need publication opportunities that match their desire to communicate what they know to the disciplinary field.

CONTENT AND TEACHING STYLE

A first-time onsite writing instructor certainly will spend time developing a syllabus, selecting relevant texts, and writing exams and essay assignments. However, when that instructor walks into a classroom, little knowledge of technology is required in order to stand in front of a group of students and teach—even when the classroom is equipped with a computer-based projector.

Diametric to the traditional classroom approach, in order to successfully create a new online course, a collective effort is required. Rosemary Talab (2007) indicated that:

> Distance learning courses very often require teamwork, which "muddies" traditional definitions of intellectual property and course ownership. A faculty member developing a distance course might use a graphic artist, instructional designer, and a technical specialist for Web support, as well as institutional online course management tools. These are considerable expenses for an institution. Faculty control of content is of paramount importance. (p. 11)

As a result of such collaborative teamwork, the components of an online course are "divided and distributed to different administrative bodies—each with its own perception of what will be best for the students ... and what will be best for the university" (DePew et al., 2006).

Using Educational Technologists (ETs) and Instructional Designers (IDs) often denotes that the university has a proprietary interest in the online course. ETs and IDs are salaried employees of the institution, and tapping into university resources means the university has rights to the class. Full-time teachers may find themselves in a similar situation, which potentially makes sense—but remains debatable—given their fuller admission into the institutional community. However, adjunct faculty also may need to develop materials for their OWCs, materials that they cannot create collaboratively given their singularly migrant status. In such cases, if contingent faculty cannot transport an online class— or even small pieces of one developed to support an established or pre-made OWC—to another institution because of the originating institution's proprietary interests, why would these instructors want to expend time and energy in developing or improving an OWC?

OWI Principle 5 stated, "Online writing teachers should retain reasonable control over their own content and/or techniques for conveying, teaching, and assessing their students' writing in their OWCs" (p. 15). However, ownership of online course materials depends upon the policies at the institution. Most online adjuncts are accustomed to being independent workers; they may prefer to create their own materials and handouts for the course and to design the course themselves. The reality is that an online course may require IT department technological assistance. Even though the adjunct may be the content expert for the subject matter, the technology team may "tell [the instructor] what academic content will be. They tell you how your courses will operate, and so it becomes more of an execution" (Kelly, 2005). Online courses—unlike most traditional onsite classes—require the collegial collaboration of the instructor with out-of-department specialists.

Adjunct faculty need to be aware of both their rights and of the proprietary rights of the online course's home institution. If an adjunct teaches at more than one university, online course materials should be kept separate methodically. According to Douglas A. Kranch (2008), "Even with a contract that allots copyright to the faculty who produce a course, it may not be at all certain that those faculty also have the rights to ... transport it to another institution" (p. 354). Moreover, once the course or materials are in the LMS, practically speaking, they are archived and available to the institution for review, revision, or continued use.

It is the contingent faculty members' responsibility to familiarize themselves with institutional policies at every university where they are employed. It is the responsibility of administrators to direct adjuncts to policies related to intellectual property rights and copyright of online course materials. In a study of public and private Carnegie Doctoral Research-Extensive Universities (2007), "half of the universities gave control of syllabi, tests, and notes to faculty, only

31% of these institutions also included materials posted to the Web, and 36% of the universities claimed ownership of courseware and distance learning materials" (Loggie, et al.). Awareness and knowledge of institutional policies is fundamental to online adjunct faculty: Instructors must understand how to protect themselves and to identify what is theirs and what is owned by the university.

Shell (pre-fabricated or pre-made) courses are—and should be—troubling to contingent faculty. These courses have been pre-designed and, depending on institutional policy, may or may not be adapted to suit the instructor's individual teaching strengths. Adjuncts who teach writing online should be concerned with being able to engage their own teaching styles and the manners in which online course material is distributed. Helena Worthen (2013) posited, "Whether [an instructor] ... is allowed to change the class" is crucial regarding instructor autonomy (p. 30). The rationale for OWI Principle 5 explained:

> the pressures of ... large programs lead to unified (and often restrictive) course templates and core syllabi and sometimes even more restrictive course shells. These features often are the result of programs that rely heavily on contingent faculty; indeed, institutions may turn to uniformity of method and materials in lieu of hiring, training, and retaining expert, full-time writing teachers. (CCCC OWI Committee, 2013, p. 15)

WPAs who employ large numbers of adjuncts may find it easier to administrate and validate the program if online shell courses are standardized. However, this system of teaching removes control of content *and* style from instructors and forces them to "fit" into a microwaveable writing course which the instructor did not design. Instead of teaching, Bob Barber (2011) argued, "full-time faculty members are becoming managers in the framework of designing curriculum and then [are] handing [the course] off to part-timers to teach." Under this model of course design and dissemination, university models of education are transforming into corporate models of business industry where managers (i.e., tenured or tenure-track instructors) are delegating tasks to assembly line workers (adjuncts) to balance the need for administrative oversight.

JOB MARKET AND PROFESSIONAL IMPLICATIONS

There are job market implications associated with part-time education employment. If an instructor is an adjunct for too many years, then the items in one's vita start to blend together, giving the appearance of sameness with too many other contingent applicants; for example, it would seem that all writing adjuncts teach some version of FYW, and they do so in a repeated cycle. Adjuncts should strive to distinguish themselves so that they do not become "just one of the adjuncts" at an institution, and volunteering to teach OWCs can make an instructor stand out to writing programs that are establishing OWCs and are looking for full-time instructors to head the design or implementation of this new initiative. However, as indicated earlier, it may be challenging to find OWI-qualified and willing tenure-line faculty to observe the teaching of, or to mentor, an adjunct. Certainly, being recognized as a good teacher is positive. Being known as punctual and responsible is favorable to an adjunct's reputation. Having letters of reference from members of the profession who have observed one's teaching is crucial to the success of an application for a full-time position. Yet, how do adjuncts procure such helpful letters from tenure-line faculty?

Gaining one-on-one time with the WPA so that the adjunct is known not only will provide the opportunity to communicate about one's students and courses, but also will add a contact to one's professional references on the vita. Meeting colleagues and establishing face-to-face contacts is an issue of timing. Onsite or hybrid-based adjunct faculty may be forced to leave campus immediately after one class ends in order to drive to a second institution to teach another class. The multiple-location problem additionally affects service to the institution: Standing committees meet at certain times, and an adjunct teaching three courses at Institution #1 and two courses at Institution #2 may not be on the appropriate campus at the appropriate time to serve on the appropriate (high profile) committee in order to meet and to establish working relationships with tenure-line colleagues who may sit on future departmental hiring committees.

A common myth is that most adjuncts do not want a full-time position. Citing the 2004 *National Study of Postsecondary Faculty*, sponsored by the Department of Education and its National Center for Education Statistics, James Monks reported, "When part-time faculty were asked whether they would have preferred a full-time position at their current institution ... 35 percent reported that they would have preferred such a position" (2009, para. 9). Although these data suggest that *most* adjuncts are not seeking full-time employment, one-third of adjunct instructors—not a negligible number—desire to be hired full time. Additionally, since "many universities are averse to promoting their own adjunct faculty into tenure-track positions," internal adjunct faculty may have limited opportunities at the institutions most familiar with their teaching abilities (Fruscione, 2014, para. 2). A second myth is that most adjuncts do not possess the terminal degree. Again, the Coalition on the Academic Workforce offered an explanation: "At four-year institutions ... slightly more than half (54.2%) of respondents hold a doctoral or other terminal degree that would be considered the common qualification for tenure-track positions" (p. 8). Many adjuncts do possess the requisite educational pedigrees to be considered for tenure-line positions; however, due to inadequate mentoring or lack of resources, adjunct faculty may become discouraged or overwhelmed by the considerable effort and intricate process—letters of recommendation, teaching evaluations, publications, the ability to access and use the MLA *Job Information List*—required to apply for full-time lines.

There are rules. Larger economic forces are at work. Online courses are money-saving, paperless and classroom-less environments, and adjuncts are inexpensive labor. Adopting the mentality that "if I work here long enough, they will hire me" is not the way a part-time instructor can become qualified for a full-time position. Instead, learning more about one's writing program itself and meeting and conversing with the WPA may be the best places to start. However, while the academy is changing (moving into digital settings for instruction), teaching evaluations, service commitments, and research publications still count for full-time faculty hires. To this end, contingent faculty may find themselves in a never-ending adjunct loop unless they can develop full-time qualifications in these areas on a part-time salary and course overload scenario.

CONCLUSION AND RECOMMENDATIONS

Typically, adjuncts teach because they enjoy teaching. Many would like admission to the full-time ranks of their (otherwise) peers; many will try and most will not succeed. In class, an instructor may be thinking, "my job is great"—what is not to like about interacting with students, sustaining conversations about readings, and engaging eager minds in college-level topics? It is fulfilling work. However, out of class, an instructor may ask, "What happens next? How many classes will I get next semester? Can I make it another semester without health insurance? Will I get hired the next time there is a full-time position?" On the one hand, the teaching that contingent faculty do is satisfying, rewarding, and impacts the next generation. This mindset—albeit noble—diverts attention from the economic downside of the adjunct lifestyle. In the OWI setting, contingent faculty may be even more at a disadvantage. The following recommendations may help:

Online contingent faculty should:

- Implement Effective Practice 7.6 by knowing the WPA and finding time to communicate with the administration.
- Adopt OWI Principle 5 by becoming familiar with institutional policies regarding ownership of course materials.
- Stand for election and serve on committees.
- Use all technical support available to faculty and participate in training specific to online teaching as described in Effective Practice 7.5.

- Diversify the vita by gaining online teaching experience at two- and four-year institutions.
- Research and publish in appropriate venues—collaboratively or individually—about OWI practices and principles.

Administrators of OWI courses should:

- Be responsible and conscientious in providing online contingent faculty training and access to professional development as recommended by OWI Principle 7.
- Understand the various stratifications among contingent faculty in order to be prepared to advise adjuncts based upon their individual needs as online instructors.
- Follow Effective Practice 7.7 by assigning appropriate OWI mentors to adjunct faculty.
- Advocate for "fair and equitable compensation" for OWI teachers as defined in OWI Principle 8.
- Support the individual teaching styles of online adjunct faculty by encouraging flexibility in OWCs as endorsed by OWI Principle 5.

Both WPAs and contingent faculty are accountable for teaching writing in an online setting. WPAs have a special responsibility to adjuncts because of the unique circumstances—in rank, departmental economics, university politics, and intellectual property rights—associated with this group of instructors. Using the OWI principles as a guide will assist both administrators and contingent faculty in teaching writing online effectively.

NOTES

1. With some states' (e.g., Alabama, Virginia, New Hampshire, Maryland) interpretation of the Affordable Care Act (aka "Obamacare"), adjunct faculty are limited to 29 hours (i.e., the maximum to remain part-time labor) at all state public institutions; this rule allows the state to avoid the responsibility of paying them benefits. Additionally, these hours must be at a single institution. As a result, many adjunct instructors in these states cannot be "commuter professors"; consequently, however, neither can they make a living teaching as an adjunct for just one institution.

REFERENCES

American Association of University Professors. (2013). *The inclusion in governance of faculty members holding contingent Appointments (pp. 1-13)*. Retrieved from http://www.aaup.org/report/governance-inclusion

Barber, Bob. (2011). Faculty leadership and instructional technologies: Who decides? *New Directions for Community Colleges, 154,* 73-85.

The Coalition on the Academic Workforce. (2012). *A portrait of part-time faculty members (pp. 1-51).* Retrieved from http://www.academicworkforce.org/survey.html

CCCC OWI Committee for Effective Practices in Online Writing Instruction. (2011a). *Fully online distance-based courses survey results.* Retrieved from http://s.zoomerang.com/sr.aspx?sm=EAupi15gkwWur6G7egRSXUw8k-pNMu1f5gjUp01aogtY%3d

CCCC OWI Committee for Effective Practices in Online Writing Instruction. (2011b). *Hybrid/blended course survey results.* Retrieved from http://s.zoomerang.com/sr.aspx?sm=%2fPsFeeRDwfznaIyyz4sV0qxkkh5Ry7O1NdnGH-CxIBD4%3d

CCCC OWI Committee for Effective Practices in Online Writing Instruction. (2011c). *The state of the art of OWI.* Retrieved from http://www.ncte.org/library/NCTEFiles/Groups/CCCC/Committees/OWI_State-of-Art_Report_April_2011.pdf

CCCC OWI Committee for Effective Practices in Online Writing Instruction. (2012b). [Transcript of expert/stakeholders' panel virtual meeting of 02/17/2012.] Unpublished raw data.

CCCC OWI Committee for Effective Practices in Online Writing Instruction. (2013). *A position statement of principles and effective practices for online writing instruction (OWI).* Retrieved from http://www.ncte.org/cccc/resources/positions/owiprinciples

DePew, Kevin Eric, Fishman, T. A., Romberger, Julia E., & Ruetenik, Bridget Fahey. (2006). Designing efficiencies: The parallel narratives of distance education and composition studies. *Computers and Composition, 23,* 49-67.

Fruscione, Joseph. (2014). Moving up from the inside? *Inside Higher Ed.* Retrieved from https://www.insidehighered.com/advice/2014/03/24/two-adjuncts-discuss-career-paths-are-open-and-closed-them

Jacobson, Kinga N. (2013). Building the roadmap to adjunct faculty success. *Techniques, 88*(4) 10-11.

June, Audrey Williams & Newman, Jonah. (2013). Adjunct project reveals wide range in pay. *Chronicle of Higher Education, 59*(18) A1-A3.

Kelly, Rob. (2005). The benefits of being an online adjunct. *Online Classroom, 8.*

Kramer, Thomas J. (2010). The impact of economics and technology on changing faculty roles. *The Psychologist-Manage Journal, 13,* 251-257.

Kranch, Douglas A. (2008). Who owns online course intellectual property? *The Quarterly Review of Distance Education, 9*(4), 349-356.

Langen, Jill M. (2011). Evaluation of adjunct faculty in higher education institutions. *Assessment & Evaluation in Higher Education, 36*(2), 185-196.

Loggie, Kathryn Ann, Barron, Ann E., Gulitz, Elizabeth, Hohlfeld, Tina N., Kromrey, Jeffrey D., & Sweeney, Phyllis. (2007). Intellectual property and online courses: Policies at major research universities. *The Quarterly Review of Distance Education, 8*(2), 109-125.

Micari, Marina & Pazos, Pilar. (2012). Connecting to the professor: Impact of the student–faculty relationship in a highly challenging course. *College Teaching, 60*, 41-47.

Mitchell, Regina L. Garza. (2009). Ethics in an online environment. *New Directions for Community Colleges, 148*, 63-70.

Monks, James. (2009). Who are the part-time faculty? *Academe, 95*(4), 33-37.

Shelton, Kaye & Saltsman, George. (2006). Faculty issues in online education. University Business, 9(8), 74-76. Retrieved from http://www.nxtbook.com/nxtbooks/pmg/ub0806/

Talab, Rosemary. (2007). Faculty distance courseware ownership and the "Walmart" approach to higher education. *TechTrends, 51*(4), 9-12.

Worthen, Helena. (2013). What do we know about teaching online? *Academe, 99*(5), 28-33.

PART 3. PRACTICING INCLUSIVITY IN OWI

CHAPTER 8

PHYSICAL AND LEARNING DISABILITIES IN OWI

Sushil K. Oswal
University of Washington, Tacoma

OWCs are not fully accessible to students with physical disabilities and learning challenges at this time. *A Position Statement of Principles and Example Effective Practices for OWI* (CCCC OWI Committee, 2013) addresses these accessibility issues. This chapter interprets OWI Principle 1 while providing a rationale for the need for accessibility. Drawing on research in the fields of disability studies, writing studies, and technical communication for a rationale for disabled access, the author outlines the main points of the Universal Design for Learning Guidelines 2.0, discusses the key accessibility barriers for disabled students in OWI, proposes a disability and accessibility agenda for writing programs and illustrates how educators can employ the OWI effective practices to move toward an inclusive and accessible pedagogy. The chapter ends with suggestions for conducting further research in OWI and accessibility.

Keywords: access, Braille Display, Disability Services, Universal Design for Learning

In this digital era with promises of seamless, ubiquitous, and virtual technologies, more often than not we teach online courses that do not reach our students who have visual, hearing, physical, learning, and dozens of other disabilities. Educational institutions spend millions of dollars to purchase computer equipment that cannot be used by all students, and we publish research that does not even give a nod to this group although they are already a sizeable minority in our colleges. In 2008, for example, 11% of US college students reported having a disability (US Department of Education, 2012). Examples of failure to address disability in otherwise excellent publications on OWI include those by Kellie Cargile Cook and Keith Grant-Davie (2005; 2013); Beth L. Hewett (2010), and Scott Warnock (2009). Researchers in OWI have overlooked disability in their discussions even when they are considering the questions of access (see, for example, Gibson & Martinez, 2013) although Hewett has made considerable additions regarding access in her updated version of *The Online Writing Con-*

ference (2015b). While it may seem unnecessarily strident to call out scholars who are on the CCCC OWI Committee, their self-admitted previous failures in addressing inclusion and access for OWI and their determined goals of doing so in this book are hopeful for future OWC students and for OWI to become a morally, ethically, and legally just discipline.

The design of most online courses lags behind the innovative mainstream technologies and remains less than desirable for disabled students due to the inaccessibility of delivery tools or the content itself (Treviranus, n.d.) although many accommodations for students with print impairments or other disabilities can be accomplished with digital technology. We also cannot lose sight of the fact that "access to education provided by distance education is a necessity for all kinds of learners who are place-bound due to factors such as scarcity of public transportation, restricted employment possibilities, child-care demands, another family member's disability-related needs, or sheer remoteness of their domicile" (Rintala, 1998), issues addressed in more detail in Chapter 10.

College education can help disabled people become intellectually mature, acquire literacy skills to speak for themselves, and advocate for an equal place to live in the world. From a socioeconomic perspective, when a person with a disability or from any other underprivileged group is employed, the person's individual advantage also translates into benefits for the society in several sectors (Erisman & McSwain, 2006; Institute of Higher Education Policy, 1998). It takes them off the Disability Income rolls for financial support; improves the country's economic base through contributions to Social Security and other taxes, and offers greater opportunities to the disabled individuals to participate in the community's civic life. The benefits of the link between literacy and technology have been established in writing studies literature (for example, see Selfe, 1999). No doubt, with the added income, these meaningfully employed disabled college graduates also will have a higher consumption level and thus grow the national economy.

I am not making an essentialist argument about what online technology can do for the disabled and other place-bound students; rather, my arguments for accessible technologies regard the need to provide equitable educational tools to these populations so that they can have learning opportunities comparable to their non-disabled peers. Laura Brady (2001) cautioned about the dangers of essentializing contemporary digital tools, as well as OWI because access is not simply a matter of an up-to-date personal computer, an Internet connection, and enough funds to pay the college tuition. Exploring the questions of social and economic class in "Fault Lines in the Terrain of Distance Education," she mapped out three surface irregularities: access, students' perceptions of teachers' roles, and retention patterns in OWCs. She explained what she meant by these "irregularities" or "fault lines" by asserting that:

> distance education holds out the same hope as education in general (equal opportunity for all) and combines it with a popular belief in the transformative power of technology: it emphasizes the ideal of anyone learning anytime, anywhere. The result is a powerful ideology that explains and perpetuates existing social relationships and that makes an individual's place within that order seem natural. (2001, p. 353)

As I reflect on these facts of disparity in online teaching that Brady recorded more than a decade ago, I am reminded of a recent email exchange on the Discussions in the Field of Disability Studies and Rhetoric and Composition ListServ by a number of writing studies scholars about an online instruction study. A team of researchers from Columbia University had released the results of a longitudinal study of online instruction in community colleges they conducted in my state, Washington, in February 2013 (Xu and Jaggers, 2013). As expected, scholars invested in disability research and online instruction on this list had picked up the report to see whether this time disability had been included in a high-visibility study. In its results, the study reported that "males, younger students, Black students, and students with lower levels of prior academic performance had more difficulty adapting to online courses" (p. 6). These researchers expanded on these findings in the discussion and conclusion sections by extrapolating that "these patterns also suggest that performance gaps between key demographic groups already observed in face-to-face classrooms (e.g., gaps between male and female students, and gaps between White and ethnic minority students) are exacerbated in online courses" (p. 23). Xu and Jaggars stressed that these findings were troubling to them from an equity perspective and they worried that "online learning could strengthen, rather than ameliorate, educational inequity" (p. 23). What troubled the disability and rhetoric Listserv readers most from another angle of equity was that these researchers had studied Washington State's online instruction for years but the disabled students never appeared on their investigative radar. What has happened yet again is that the category of "disability" failed to make it into these researchers' population charts. The omission probably felt more irksome to some of us who teach writing because "English and social science" were on the top of the authors' list where a high proportion of even nondisabled students had more difficulty adapting to the online environment (p. 24).

Several members of this national discussion list inquired about this omission to understand whether this was reflective of the overall state of "things disabled" in Washington. The group also wanted someone from CCCC OWI Committee to voice this concern. I wrote back to say that:

> My suggestion is that any comments you send to CCCC
> should go both to all the members of the Executive Commit-
> tee of the organization and the Committee on Online Writing
> Instruction (COWI). Ultimately, it is the [Executive Com-
> mittee] EC that has the power to act and enact. I'm copying
> Beth Hewett on this message but a message from Brenda [Jo
> Brueggemann] to EC will be very helpful.

I further wrote:

> I'm on this committee and I'm pleased to note that Beth
> [Hewett, the Chair of the original CCCC Committee on On-
> line Writing Instruction and present Co-Chair] has listened
> to my constant harangues about accessibility very patiently.
> Based on the field research we have conducted on the state of
> Online Writing Instruction over the past six years, we as re-
> searchers and as a committee have a sense that writing faculty
> across the country are interested in accessibility, want to offer
> accessible online courses but they also sorely lack technical,
> training, and pedagogical support from administrators. (Feb-
> ruary 24, 2013)

In our national survey in 2011, I had formulated a set of disability-focused questions to capture the accessibility dimension of online teaching, and what we learned did not shock me as a person with some experience with disability and accessibility. We heard that people did not know whether they were teaching disabled students; if they knew they were doing so, then they did not know what they could do to support them and they did not know where they could themselves get training to help these students beyond giving them the phone number for the Disability Services Office on campus. Some respondents blatant-ly admitted that they did not believe they were obliged to help disabled students in any way at all.

In contextualizing the survey, I further reported to my peers on this Listserv that:

> Consequent to this survey, our committee has embraced the
> concept of accessibility at the interface level and endorsed the
> concepts of Universal Design for Learning with emphasis on
> both accessibility and usability for the disabled students and
> faculty. You will see that the long expected Effective Practices

for Online Writing Instruction document composed by our committee after six years of detailed academic research, including a nation-wide survey, interviews, focus groups, and of course, a thorough literature review, will reflect this disability and access focus. (February 24, 2013)

This is the baggage with which I enter into this conversation about OWI in this book, and, of course, in the CCCC OWI Committee, I wear the hat of so-called accessibility specialist. My goal in this chapter is to promote, explain, and exemplify OWI Principle 1: "Online writing instruction should be universally inclusive and accessible" and, whenever relevant in this meta-discussion of accessibility, wrap my fingers around some of the OWI issues in other chapters to provide further gloss on accessibility (p. 7). My point in providing the above anecdote about the Washington State report is to remind ourselves that disability and accessibility challenges are everywhere in America and, simultaneously, nowhere. We see disability as a fact of nature, but we do not recognize it as a fact of life, particularly of our academic work life, and even more crucially, our teaching life. Disability—and the concomitant need for access—still resides in that corner of the university, the college, and school where the Disability Services office is or where the disabled students' Resource Room is.

The purpose of this chapter is to interpret the OWI Principle 1 more completely to pull disability from the margins toward the center. Since this first principle is an overarching one, this chapter also should serve as a rationale for inclusivity and accessibility while enhancing our general understanding of accessibility issues. This chapter amply describes where we stand with the accessibility of OWI courses, but it aims at promoting accessibility practices and strategies for teaching writing online from various principles (See for example, Principles 1, 9, and 15). Other chapters in this collection contextually address other practices as a matter of designing inclusive pedagogy (particularly, see Chapter 11 by Lee-Ann Kastman Breuch.) I employ several programmatic and classroom scenarios throughout the chapter to substantiate the situations and problems I discuss so that WPAs and OWI instructors may consider how they can integrate disability inclusive thinking in their local settings. The chapter takes its bearings from research in the fields of disability studies, writing studies, and technical communication. In the remainder of this chapter, I explicate the first OWI principle in some detail, summarize the key points of the Universal Design for Learning (UDL) Guidelines 2.0 that further elucidate OWI Principle 1, discuss the key accessibility barriers for disabled students in OWI, and then explain how we can employ the OWI effective practices to move toward an inclusive and accessible pedagogy. In the concluding section, I speculate on some possible paths for accessibility and disability research in OWI.

A POSITION STATEMENT OF PRINCIPLES AND EFFECTIVE PRACTICES FOR OWI

The CCCC OWI Committee initially considered access in terms of the various constituencies: students faced with problems of technical and economic access to Internet technology, students who are developing linguistic proficiency in English, students living in remote rural areas confronted with an Internet connectivity gap, disabled students lacking access due to personal, technical, and institutional accessibility problems with technology, students lacking access to online writing pedagogy due to learning disabilities, and so on. As we mulled over these multifarious access issues and as we analyzed survey data from disability-related questions, we realized that many of the issues affecting disabled students also affected other constituencies. Our study of the fast-growing literature in the fields of disability and accessibility repeatedly informed us that the affordances provided by the flexibility and diversity of the disability-centered accessible pedagogy are equally beneficial for nondisabled students given various learning styles and approaches. We also realized that unless we moved these issues from the periphery to the center of OWI pedagogy, we could not address questions of access at the institutional and discipline level meaningfully. Some of this thinking also was based on our understanding of other findings of disability and accessibility research that repeatedly has proven that addressing these questions of accessibility after the fact (or from the periphery) results in temporary and generally poor fixes that provide only limited access and further marginalizes these constituencies.

While I do not subscribe to all the claims about accessibility made by the proponents of Universal Design, UDL, and interface-level design—numerous other social, market, institutional and other factors are equally responsible for the neglect of accessibility issues for these marginalized users—I believe that the frameworks afforded by these design and pedagogical perspectives offer a reasonable starting point to begin our systematic search for accessibility in OWI. For example, the principles of Universal Design, which originally were conceptualized in architecture for designing accessible edifices, are not adequate in educational settings because teaching and learning are dynamic interactions orchestrated by diverse actors. The contexts within which OWI pedagogical and learning acts occur are always fluid and they cannot be compared to building wheelchair ramps and placing Braille signs. Whereas the advocates of Principles for Universal Design might have some ground to claim that Universal Design is "the design of products and environments to be usable by all people, to the greatest extent possible, without the need for adaptation or specialized design," OWI pedagogy, or any other pedagogy for this purpose, cannot find a stable ground to make such a wide-ranging assertion (The Center for Universal Design, 1997). Likewise, the UDL goal of serving all students with a general framework for accessibility is simply unachievable because student disabilities can be so varied and the individual accessibility needs of each disability are so different (CAST, 2011).

Returning to *A Position Statement of Principles and Example Effective Practices for OWI* (CCCC OWI Committee, 2013) and its OWI principles and example effective practices for accessible pedagogy, I also want to emphasize that merely following the document will not make our OWCs accessible. Instead, we need a fundamental attitudinal shift in our field. While OWI Principle 1 recommended "using multiple teaching and learning formats; welcoming students with disabilities in course syllabi; and including disability issues or perspectives in course content and faculty development workshops" (p. 7), these practices are merely places *to begin* thinking about disability and accessibility. Our educational institutions and our pedagogies have thus far been conceptualized only for able-bodied students and those with typical learning abilities and preferences. As a result, this conceptualization of the purposes and practices of the academy has rendered disability invisible. To make room for these additional and different bodies, we will need to overhaul every aspect of our academic infrastructure. OWI is in an advantageous space to integrate this population because the online media are still in developing stages and the OWI field has yet not fully defined its philosophies and practices. The CCCC OWI Committee's commitment to an accessible online pedagogy is the first concrete evidence of the CCCC's delivering its earlier promises of inclusivity and accessibility as stated in its "Policy on Disability in CCCC" (2006, reaffirmed 2011). While the members of the CCCC Committee on Disability Issues in College Composition have promoted access in their activities, the CCCC OWI Committee's position statement is the first major, organization-wide initiative. Another important aspect of the CCCC OWI Committee's recommendations is in the recognition of the intersections of disability, multilingual learning, and basic writing in face-to-face, hybrid and fully online OWI.[1]

The twelve example effective practices written for OWI Principle 1 are an effort to draw the OWI community's attention to certain focal points for beginning to consider disability and accessibility inclusively, conceptually, and pedagogically. For example, in OWI Effective Practices 1.1, 1.4, 1.6, and 1.10 (pp. 9-10), when attention shifts from pedagogy to audience/students in choosing a modality, the CCCC OWI Committee urged educators to stop conceptualizing OWI pedagogy for the erstwhile stock audiences who were assumed to be able-bodied and enjoying all the access to technology that an institution of higher education offers. Likewise, OWI Effective Practices 1.2 1.3, 1.8, 1.9, and 1.11 draw attention to the reality that a sizeable segment of the student population (pp. 9-11), including disabled students, might not have had an opportunity to use the learning technologies and other resources educators might take for granted. These recommendations also draw attention to the institutional infrastructure that may or may not have any specialized technology available. Even if an institution has acquired this technology, it may not have a training program to assist students and faculty with such technology. The guidance about textbooks in OWI Effective Practice 1.3 pertains to the responsibility of instructors to choose only accessible textbooks (p. 9). While students cannot sue a publisher for offering inaccessible textbooks, they can take a college to court for assigning textbooks in inaccessible media. The textbook selection is one area where faculty have the power to choose accessible or inaccessible curricular materials. The Department of Justice's 2013 decision about the complaint against Louisiana Tech University has established that universities cannot pass on the responsibility of providing accessible curriculum materials to publishers (US Department of Justice, 2013).

OWI PRINCIPLE 1 AND THE UNIVERSAL DESIGN FOR LEARNING GUIDELINES 2.0

UDL Guidelines 1.0 were developed over time in the 1990s by David H. Rose and Jenna Wasson under the sponsorship of the Education Department at the Center for Applied Technology (CAST) and the National Center on Accessing the General Curriculum (NCAC) for secondary school settings; the guidelines began to be expanded to include higher education immediately (CAST 2008; Rose & Meyer, 2002; Rose & Meyer, 2006; Rose, Meyer, & Hitchcock, 2005). The UDL Guidelines 2.0 updated the earlier versions, particularly in the use of multi-modal means of representation and expression, and they have been applied broadly at all levels of education (CAST 2011). The UDL Guidelines 1.0 define Universal Design for Learning as "a process by which a curriculum (i.e., goals, methods, materials, and assessments) is intentionally and systematically designed from the beginning to address individual differences" (CAST, 2008). The Higher Education Opportunity Act of 2008 placed UDL in the legal domain by defining it inside the language of the act. According to this Act:

> the term Universal Design for Learning means a scientifically
> valid framework for guiding educational practice that: (A)
> provides flexibility in the ways information is presented, in

the ways students respond or demonstrate knowledge and skills, and in the ways students are engaged; and (B) reduces barriers in instruction, provides appropriate accommodations, supports, and challenges, and maintains high achievement expectations for all students, including students with disabilities and students who are limited English proficient. (122 STAT. 3088)

The UDL framework aims at short-circuiting the need for retrofits by employing contemporary technologies to provide access to diverse learners with varying skills, abilities, and aptitudes. The framework provides guidelines for accessible curricula under three categories: (1) "provide multiple means of representation" or the *what* of learning, (2) "provide multiple means of action and expression" or the *how* of learning, and (3) "provide multiple means of engagement" or the *why* of learning (CAST, 2011).

Although the twelve specific guidelines that UDL 2.0 presented are targeted at a whole array of disciplines ranging from mathematics to music, from the perspective of teaching writing online, many of the guidelines in each of the three categories are relevant. As it has been extrapolated to the OWI Principle 1, under the first category, OWI instructors should include options for "the display of information"; provide alternative representations of auditory and visual information for students with visual, hearing, and learning disabilities; use straightforward language to state ideas; and make underlying structural features of abstract ideas explicit using concrete examples in different modalities. Under action and expression, OWI instructors should assure full access to learning technologies to students with disabilities and make navigation of tools accessible, make physical action possible through multiple options for interacting with technology (e.g., mouse, keyboard, headpointers, and the like), employ a variety of media for communication, give students options to compose in multiple media, and provide sufficient technical support to execute the aforesaid. In terms of engagement, OWI instructors should give students enough autonomy to make our curriculum their own, applying diverse techniques and methods of knowledge acquisition and interaction. UDL Guidelines are in sync with the current goal-oriented, self-motivating, collaborative, and interactive writing studies pedagogy.

BARRIERS TO DISABLED ACCESS IN OWI AND HIGHER EDUCATION

The barriers to accessible education for disabled students in higher education are created by several internal and external factors. Academia's attitudes towards disability, non-inclusive institutional infrastructures, indifference of technology developers towards the accessibility of educational technologies, the stronghold of ableist pedagogy, and the relative small number of disabled students and faculty can be held primarily responsible for the current state of affairs.

INSTITUTIONAL AND DISCIPLINARY BARRIERS TO DISABLED ACCESS IN WRITING PROGRAMS

In 1995, disability theorist Lennard Davis declared, "Disability is an unavoidable outcome of living" (p. 8); in other words, all of us will be disabled in one way or another at some time of our lives. Yet, the academy continues to ignore that fact. Considering that the severely disabled still are woefully under-represented in the student body and faculty from this group remain few and far between, it is difficult to report meaningful progress in this arena. While writing studies and technical communication programs have registered great progress in preparing future professionals and college teachers, we still know little about disability, Disability Studies, and how to teach those students in our courses who happen to be disabled. Likewise, academic knowledge of teaching technical communication and composition to disabled students online has so far come from our own experiences, class observations shared at conferences, and a small body of published research for online settings—a great deal of which is also based on personal teaching experiences rather than empirical research (Lewiecki-Wilson & Brueggemann, 2008; Meloncon, 2013). Put together—OWI and the variegated disabilities of students (and teachers)—we know even less because we do not understand how we could make our knowledge and pedagogy accessible to all of them; nonetheless, these students keep arriving in our portals. In an online setting, this lacuna also might exist partially because we may not even know that we have disabled students in our courses unless they self-identify and partially because our discipline has hardly started to think of paying attention to disabled students in its conceptualization of pedagogical inclusivity and access (Oswal & Meloncon, 2014).

Why, so many years after the legislation of the ADA, is there not yet a long-term vision for accessible and usable OWI in this otherwise burgeoning field of education? We have not yet seen an LMS that offers multiple interfaces for interaction to users with diverse characteristics, learning styles, and adaptive devices (e.g., screen readers, headpointers, zoom software, and the like). We do not yet have a delivery tool that has truly adaptable parts and offers a range of features to cater to people who use digital technology differently. We do not think twice that a software package that can function perfectly only with a mouse might be a useless string of code to a high percentage of users who have not been considered by its designer (to a degree this problem is one of the rhetoricity that Kevin DePew speaks of in Chapter 14). We do not know what is entailed in the design and development of a digital learning environment system that would permit gainful interactions by people of different abilities employing diverse adaptive technologies. We know that digital technology in itself is plastic enough, the World Wide Web is open enough to render its interfaces accessible to each student in a writing course, and HTML, the language of the Web, is versatile enough to accommodate the needs of a variety of users, but we do not know how we could persuade the developers of these interfaces to implement this flexibility in their online learning tools (Cooper & Heath, 2009).

NEGATIVE ATTITUDES TOWARDS DISABILITY AND DIFFERENCE

Interesting parallels can be drawn between the view that cultural and racial differences are responsible for the English language "deficit" among multilingual students and the views about disability and the reasons for the success or failure of students with disabilities. Just as many times we fail to see that the English language reading and writing disciplines exclude anything that is not linguistically Anglo-Saxon, as able-bodied, highly intellectual professors, we also learn to design and teach courses for students who resemble our bodies and minds. We expect our students to perform the same functions with the same ease that we ourselves can exercise. Our convictions might have been validated in the past because a majority of our students succeeded in obtaining such competence. With the student demographics changing vastly because of the market demand for degreed workers, changing immigrant populations, the influx of disabled students, and the emerging historical research about the teaching of English during the past century, we are now learning that there always have been others who either are left to their own devices to fit themselves into the ableist mold or drop out of the higher education system. We should strengthen our own knowledge of linguistic differences, shed outdated teaching practices that were designed for an exclusionary era (Matsuda, 2006), and reinvent pedagogies and curricula to meet this different population. For example, efforts at educating deaf students so far have been concentrated on bridging the speech barrier between the hearing instructor and the ably-designed multimodal curricula through captioning, sound track transcripts, and interpreters. Very little research has been published in our field that proposes innovative pedagogies accounting for the linguistic differences between deaf and hearing learners. This research gap is particularly noticeable when it is a common knowledge that English is, at best, a second language for the deaf users of sign languages. Even the deaf-focused current research has not yet addressed this linguistic difference at the pedagogical level (Babcock, 2012).

To buck this historic trend in the American university, English Studies scholar Brenda Jo Brueggemann (2002) and Technical Communication researcher Jason Palmeri (2006) have made a call to resuscitate disability as an "enabling and transformative insight" in our discipline. They question the precarious location that disability presently occupies in higher education. The disabled students and faculty on most campuses remain emblematic of their wheelchairs, white canes, guide dogs, and hearing aids rather than as dues-paying, permanent members of the academic community. The argument I want to extend in step with Brueggemann (2002) and Palmeri's (2006) call is that we need to devise means to understand how to culturally deconstruct and reconstruct disability in order to move away from the outdated notions of disability as a stigmatized, decayed body requiring help or healing; it should be placed next to other accepted, strategically situated, and celebrated categories so that our disabled students and faculty/staff colleagues can enjoy the same privileges that we take for granted as a matter of our presence in the academy.

BARRIERS CREATED BY THE DIFFICULTY IN ENFORCING DISABILITY LAWS

Neither the ADA nor the other disability laws regulating education technologies restrict LMS manufacturers from introducing learning systems in the market without ascertaining their accessibility and usability for the disabled. Only the academic institutions have the power to enforce certain accessibility standards in their purchasing contracts; however, few colleges have yet taken this step to assure accessibility for their students, faculty, and staff. Most of the after-the-fact fixes provided by these developers fall way short of what a nondisabled user would find satisfactory from an ableist perspective. These retrofitted solutions rarely enable disabled students and faculty to perform at par with their peers and when it happens, it is only in selective pockets of the technology and lasts for only so long until the next system upgrade is implemented to undo the previous fix.

Even the proponents of adaptive system approach in the LMS industry, who draw upon the user data to design intelligent systems for driving the LMS, focus on the primary goal of efficiency rather than "to create an instructionally sound and flexible environment that supports learning for students with a range of abilities, disabilities, interests, backgrounds, and other characteristics" (Shute & Zapata, 2007). The problem with this last machine-centered approach of adapting LMS for individual users is that the users in this scenario are passive producers of data that gets scooped by the developers to figure out what the user want. The users otherwise have no direct say in defining what they need; rather, it is the developer who tells them what they need on the basis of the intelligent system's analyses of the user interactions with the LMS. Moreover, these intelligent systems flatten all user data to fit it into pre-defined categories and the possibilities of custom designed access go out of the window even before it has been conceptualized.

LEARNING MANAGEMENT SYSTEMS AND THEIR INHERENT ACCESSIBILITY BARRIERS

The next section expands on the chronic accessibility problems built into the design of latter-day content or LMSs, and it speculates on some of the classic causes for these problems to linger.

The History of Accessibility Problems in Early Online Delivery Tools

LMSs have had accessibility problems right from the beginning when they appeared on the academic market as bundles of tools built on diverse platforms lacking a foundational vision for interface-level access for a variety of users. Assembled from diverse sources, these commercially branded LMSs were targeted primarily at lecture classes, and their most attractive features for the instructors of these relatively large classes were the automated tools for quizzes. These LMSs eventually were to replace the faculty designed websites and hypertexts because of their greater interactivity. The university-based initiatives of this nature also started as an assemblage of tools and technologies suffering from the same accessibility gaps (see, for example, the University of Washington's home-grown assemblage of tools, Catalyst, which has otherwise been popular among faculty at a number of schools). We know through user experiences over the life history of these LMSs that the accessibility profile of these systems has not noticeably altered from that of their predecessors although they have many more contemporary tools available. Their developers have so far unrolled no master plans to amend the accessibility of these new tools (Oswal, 2013). Almost every one of the key players in the LMS market has implemented accessibility fixes from time to time under pressure from courts and organizations of the disabled, but an accessibility stalemate has so far lasted between what users need to learn or teach online and the commitment these developers are willing to make for this level of access. Their attention has remained on quickly adapting little-tested technologies and designs to compete in a trendy market rather than their pedagogical relevance.

From the perspective of Technical Communication and Composition Studies, even the innovative efficiency tools, such as Canvas SpeedGrader, do not exactly meld into the process or post-process pedagogy due to its focus on evaluating student work quantitatively. What I want to underscore here is the impact of such innovations on the already restricted access available to the disabled. Designing a new academic tool almost a quarter century after George H. W. Bush signed the ADA into a law, the Canvas developers paid little attention to its accessibility for the disabled and it remains only partially accessible to screen readers after applying sporadic fixes. I do not have to belabor the point that presently a major gap exists between what LMS designers conceptualize as accessible systems and what their users' needs are. Designed with visual interface as the primary mode of interaction, these LMSs sorely fall short of what is usable through other modalities. Their designers also conceptualize accessibility as a crude, one-on-one correspondence of everything visual into speech device-readable text with little accompanying contextual information. Since these environments have been designed for the human eye, they do not lend themselves well to other senses. All other senses do not respond to surroundings as quickly as the human eye does and they require more contextual support for making userly decisions. They also lack the instinctive interfaces for use that otherwise have become available in mass-marketed consumer technologies employing iOS interfaces developed for the day-to-day applications by users with a variety of abilities and preferences.

Speaking in the context of instructor and student agency, Jane Seale and Martyn Cooper (2010) pointed to another contextual lacuna in these LMS tools from the perspective of instructor-student learning relationship:

> It is highly probable that teachers will need to use their teaching experience and knowledge of learner needs to judge how exactly to respond to advice or conclusions derived from the application of [LMS] tools. This might be because the advice privileges certain aspects above others or because it does not take into account the varied and complex contexts in which e-learning must demonstrate accessibility. These contexts might relate to the relationship that the learner has with the teacher (e.g. types of conversations and interactions) or the relationship that the learner has with the educational institution (e.g. types of systems that an institution puts in place to facilitate personalization of the learning experience by learners). (p. 1115)

Hence, OWI teachers themselves need to become aware of their students' needs as learners to begin to address the access problems of an LMS that fails the students.

LMSs and Non-Inclusive Learning Models

What Seale and Cooper (2010) underlined is true even for exclusive learning contexts where instructors are forced to co-opt into specific structures imposed upon by particular tools while potentially compromising the integrity of their curriculum and pedagogy. In the context of inclusive learning, these restrictive structures can be doubly damaging to the distribution of even the most inclusively designed curriculum and pedagogy unless they have been well tested both for their technical accessibility and human usability by mostly novice disabled student users. The interactivity tools—the chat programs and discussion boards— have serious accessibility flaws because they have been designed only for ocular efficiency and ease requiring significantly greater effort and time investment on part of the keyboard users. Not only do they lack instinctive interfaces, but they also fail to provide any meaningful ecological information to non-visual users. This information is readily available to the sighted.

LMS Industry's Unwillingness to Adopt Inclusive Design

Working within a content-oriented approach to accessibility, Martyn Cooper and Andy Heath (2009) addressed this problem of missing user-centered ecological access through a new model for designing access that moves the authority to determine what type of access a user needs from the producer, supplier, or author of an E-learning system to the individual user and the technological and human agents supporting this user. In this model, instead of an LMS telling the users what they can have, the users tell the system what they need. These researchers believe that such a system is possible through an upfront collection of metadata from users that could then be employed to drive the system interface design and content development process so that the users can have what they need upon demand. If implemented, such a system could stand for an extreme example of participatory design where users truly contribute to the design based on what they really want or need rather than what the designers think they want. Their model overcomes some of the weaknesses of the current participatory process where designers bring in users after they have already narrowed down the options and want user participants to mainly validate one or other of their choices. Under this current design regime, even when developers invite participants to brainstorm the design concept, user ideas rarely get the same consideration as the expert perspectives do and the participants seldom see through the complete product development process. Thus far, no one has come forth to implement this participant-driven model, which would not only help with access issues generally but with OWI specifically given that most LMSs have not been designed with writing instruction in mind.

The Role of Higher Education in Perpetuating Inaccessible LMS Designs

On the other hand, imagining that our universities do not have a major role in determining the design of these academic tools of the trade is simply mind boggling. How could our institutions be both the power houses for educating top-notch computer scientists and also be silent witnesses to these LMS designs with at best a less-than-desirable accessibility and usability record for users with visual, physical, and learning disabilities? Irrespective of who has what certification from which disability organization, not a single LMS during the past decade has been fully accessible to all disabled students (Petri, Rangin, Richwine, & Thompson, 2012). The instructor-side accessibility record of these management systems is even worse because totally blind instructors, for example, are a rarity and universities have not expended any significant efforts to make the LMS developers aware of these problems. Nevertheless, these accessibility problems are a major barrier for blind faculty in providing their students the same technology-rich learning experience as their sighted colleagues do. This access gap is not only an issue for students to receive an equitable learning experience in a blind instructor's course, it also affects that instructor in how the students evaluate them in comparison with their able-bodied counterparts.

OTHER ACCESSIBILITY BARRIERS

Listed below are some of the other factors responsible for this accessibility-related techno stalemate in the United States:

- Lack of institutional policies for ensuring accessibility for the disabled
- Lack of implementation of disability policies when such policies exist
- Unwillingness of administrative departments—IT, libraries, student staff and faculty training, capital projects management, and purchasing and contracts—to view accessibility as their department's responsibility
- Leadership's own social attitudes towards disabled students, staff, and faculty
- Marginalization of disability and accessibility in almost every academic discipline in higher education

THE PROPOSED DISABILITY AND ACCESSIBILITY AGENDA FOR WRITING PROGRAMS

My practical purpose in composing this chapter has been to move educators—particularly OWI instructors—further along together so that those of us who are already committed to providing accessibility do not have to go on alone.

Speaking more directly, I would like WPAs—a hat I have worn—to know that full-time OWI teachers need your support in addressing this disability and accessibility agenda because nothing is more annoying than to hear on the disabled student discussion lists that they want to take online courses but these courses are simply not accessible to them if they are blind, deaf, or have hand-motor issues (see, for example, the archive of NABS-L, the Listserv of blind and visually impaired students run by the National Association of Blind Students). Within the local context, my appeal to WPA colleagues is that we should take the leadership role. We should act before online instruction gets set in a mold and becomes the new version of inaccessible face-to-face education. We should cry foul when our campus' IT czars adopt inaccessible LMSs. We should seek a seat at the table where these million-dollar decisions take place. We should argue for adequate training about adaptive technologies for our faculty so that they know what their students are using. We should invest resources in accessible content development from the start, and we should recruit disabled students actively. We also should hire disabled faculty so that we can cultivate a participatory atmosphere of accessibility for the disabled. OWI Principle 1 stated that we should adopt these measures as a matter of everyday academic life, not as a matter of legal expediency or an on-the-spot solution for providing "accommodations" because the disabled students are waiting at our campus gates (pp. 7-11).

NEED FOR WPAs TO ENGAGE IN THE TECHNOLOGICAL ACQUISITIONS BY UNIVERSITIES

Because technological and pedagogical barriers are intrinsically interlinked in online instruction from the standpoint of catering to students with disabilities, one cannot teach without a delivery tool that is inaccessible to this or any other population. We should insist on our institutions adopting well-considered accessibility guidelines for acquiring and deploying new technologies for delivering online instruction both to meet their legal obligations and provide equal learning opportunities to all students. Student complaints about the accessibility of LMSs and other online educational tools are common now. Most recently, University of Montana and Louisiana Tech University have been in the news for failing to provide access to these resources (Szpaller, 2012; Department of Justice, 2013).

TECHNOLOGY AND PEDAGOGY ARE INTERTWINED IN OWI

If we do not provide our faculty with accessible online interfaces to deliver curricula, whether it is our college's LMS, the online tutoring software, or just the websites, we cannot expect to fulfill disabled students' needs. Angela Owusu-Ansah, Patti Neill, and Michele K. Haralson (2011) reported that, in general, "faculty are not in favor of the acquisition of distance education technology before the identification of programs and appropriate pedagogy." Since the primary purposes of universities from faculty's perspective are teaching and knowledge production, the high-level administrators' "tendency to invest in technology first and pedagogy or content second causes problems" (para. 26). These researchers' diagnoses are on the mark because a technical tool-driven curriculum and pedagogy serves technology first and our students last, something that Hewett (2013) argued against. It begins to control the learning process from the start and lets the curricular and personal goals fall to the wayside.

In the current social and legal milieu, writing programs will be served better by moving to an inclusive approach to technology adoption at the IT planning stages. WPAs should press for accessible technology options from university leaders just as we ask for up-to-date and pedagogy-appropriate technologies because inclusive pedagogy cannot be separated from accessibility. Douglas Levin and Sousan Arafeh (2002) claimed that their research indicates that many administrators interested in integrating new technologies throughout their campuses also have invested in resources for implementing distance learning appropriate pedagogy. With consistent effort and legal reasoning, such administrators also can be convinced to invest in accessible technologies.

WRITING PROGRAMS BUILDING CAMPUS COALITIONS FOR PROMOTING THE ACCESSIBILITY GOALS

To achieve the goal of building an inclusive writing program that provides an accessible online learning experience for all students, designing an accessible institutional infrastructure is an imperative. To accomplish this task, the program leaders should work with administrative leaders across the campus to advocate for accessible technologies, library systems, tutoring services, and other academic infrastructure used by online students (see Chapters 5 & 6). Those WPA leaders who cannot develop such partnerships may have to opt for adopting simpler Web options for delivering online curriculum. The California State University system has tried to move in this direction by establishing university-wide accessibility standards for purchasing technology.

NEED FOR CLOSE INTERACTIVE RELATIONSHIP BETWEEN WRITING PROGRAMS AND DISABILITY SERVICES

WPAs with a disability-inclusive vision of their programs need to work with the student services administration to have their staff develop disabled students' orientation programs that will benefit not only OWCs but also all other online and onsite writing curricula as well as teacher training (see Chapters 11 & 12). Such programs will help Disability Services staff understand student needs, plan essential services, and assist these students to plan for themselves. Students with severe disabilities, such as blindness and deafness, require better-than-average skills to succeed at college. They do not only need to learn how to navigate the eclectic learning environments of American postsecondary institutions but also to learn to mix and match accessible and inaccessible technologies to get the school work done. Our nondisabled students acquire all this through regularly offered technology workshops, well-organized learning tutorials by most campus libraries, and of course, working with technologies that have been custom-designed for their psycho-physical profile, tested with users similar to them, employing ably conceptualized methodologies, and made fully accessible and usable.

While we should incorporate disabled audiences as we design skills workshops on our campuses, the Disability Services staff also can point students to other available learning resources outside the institution that would enable them to function effectively in a technology-pervasive college, and afterwards work, environment—online and off.

NEED FOR DEVELOPING FACULTY TRAINING IN THE AREA OF ACCESSIBILITY AND DISABILITY

WPAs also will find that as the pressure from the enforcement agencies grows on colleges to become compliant with online course content, on-campus Disability Services will pass on these tasks to faculty for making the content of their courses accessible (see Ingeno, 2013). As the case law in the area of disability builds, institutions will have a difficult time avoiding the questions of adequate accommodations for disabled students at curricular and pedagogical levels. A vast body of UDL-based research has shown that the faculty fears about the loss of academic freedom also have so far not proven true (see Konur, 2007 for an excellent summary of the relationship between providing access to the disabled and its effect on academic freedom and standards). In our own field of writing studies, Sharon Crowley (1998) explained that whenever a new population group is first admitted to the university, an academic crisis always is imagined or created in response to the threat posed by the newcomer to the existing structure. Providing accessibility to the disabled often results in greater access to the curriculum for all students. While reconceptualizing and redesigning accessibility-focused curricula and pedagogy require a major effort and involve a significant investment of time, in the long run the resulting improvements help WPAs and instructors meet their curricular goals much more effectively, increase student satisfaction, and raise retention levels. The Communication Access Realtime Translation system for the deaf (CART), for example, is for supporting deaf students, but it also can provide professionally finished class notes to all students when instructors deem it to be appropriate to share this information for later review.

OPTIONS FOR ADDRESSING ETHICAL AND INSTITUTIONAL EXIGENCIES

I am arguing not only that it is our ethical responsibility to be inclusive of the disabled students but I also want to stress that accessibility is no longer optional. Being prepared for this group of students is an exigency because our interpersonal interactions with our students in online settings are mediated by technology that neither favors, nor prejudices against, disability but certainly makes these students' differences invisible. On the student end, unless adopted with due care by institutions of higher education, this very technology might raise additional barriers in the path of learning for our students in onsite, hybrid, and fully online settings. While in onsite, face-to-face settings, faculty might accommodate a student's needs upon arrival or even mid-semester, in an OWI course, by the time a student comes forth to report the problem with a course component or requests for a special arrangement, it might be too late to work in the required changes without upsetting the overall design of the course. The definition of being "access ready" in legal terms is not to make "just-in-time" alterations; it is to be access ready even if we do not expect a single disabled student to enroll in the course.

The following heuristic, based on the earlier discussed UDL Guidelines 2.0, can assist WPAs and OWI instructors in their own planning tasks and shift the curricular focus to include accessibility at every level of the course design:

1. Do the course goals address students with disabilities?
2. Has the curriculum been developed to address these goals, serving the needs of all students including students with disabilities?
3. Has the course content been selected with prior consideration of disabled students? Are there other, more accessible content choices that could meet curriculum needs while serving this group a bit better?
4. Have the technology choices for delivering this curriculum been tested with actual disabled students? If the campus LMS is not fully-accessible, what other delivery choices have been considered? Can the writing instructors do more with less technology in order to make these courses

accessible to all the students?

5. Are the pedagogical methods and techniques differentiated enough through "multiple means of representation," "expression and action," and "engagement" as described by Universal Design for Learning?

6. Do these techniques match and support the learning goals of a range of abilities and skills, the selected delivery tools, and the chosen curriculum?

Here is a WPA scenario with one of many possible physical disabilities: *Tomorrow is the first day of classes and one of your faculty just realized that the online multimodal module they are using for the first unit of the five sections of their introductory OWC has no captions. Only this morning, the Disability Services have given them a heads up about a student with hearing disabilities being enrolled in one of these sections. If you post a message for captioning services help on one of the Disability Services discussion lists, the chances are that in response you will receive a link of this sort, www.automaticsync.com, with the warning that quick fixes are expensive. It is likely that your OWI instructor will not have the captioned module for the student for more than a week because many other instructors across the country have made similar discoveries at the same time.*

In writing studies, we have tried to confront the core issues underlying most of the problems we have addressed during the past three decades as a disciplinary community with an identity: basic writers, multilingual writers, gender, and more recently, plagiarism. Hence, I would argue that we take a more comprehensive approach to respond to this contingency as WPAs. After we have convinced the academic technologies boss to pay the enormous bill for this quick-fix captioning job described above so that the institution meets its legal obligations, we still will need to get to the core of the real problem. Writing program faculty seem to be unaware of the implications of the disability laws to their curricula and pedagogy. They do not seem to understand that "readiness" for disabled students means "being always ready" and not running around for fixes after the student's accommodations letter is in their Inbox. It is also possible that the textbook adoption policy in this program has not been revised since the passage of the ADA.

To be inclusive and persuasive to faculty in such a situation, the WPA can set up a conference call or Web conference with the entire writing studies faculty— not only those who currently teach with OWI—for the purpose of starting the formulation process to achieve a functional policy document spelling out a summary of the institution's and writing program's disability accommodations policy and how to implement it. Also, the WPA can set a deadline for submitting requests for such accommodations by instructors irrespective of whether they expect a disabled student in their courses, and the WPA can provide details on how the overall process works. Working with a smaller group of instructors on this all-inclusive outline of the document to produce a final draft, the WPA can produce a collaborative plan for responding to such contingencies in the future. Consulting the Disability Services and Special Education faculty for additional suggestions and verifications during this second phase can be helpful. Posting the document online and making time in the ensuing program meeting to walk everyone through the document for Q&A is an important step in getting the faculty to buy in. During this policy inaugural meeting, inviting the Disability Services and library accessibility staff to make quick presentations relating their accessibility services can get the faculty started with the process of updating their courses. Finally, producing a checklist from the program's newly minted policy implementation document for everyone to have in their teaching folders or to pin on the office wall can further reinforce the importance of accessibility.

To prevent this particular contingency in the future, it is crucial to write the textbook adoption policy to reflect the important curricular changes resulting from the influx of multimodal content in these writing courses. It also is necessary to describe the accessibility considerations that instructors should make before adopting any materials for their courses, including contacting the publishers and the college library for the status of captioning for hearing impaired on audio-visual items, audio description for the visually impaired on video content, availability of electronic text and/or recorded versions of your textbooks for students with learning and visual disabilities. On some campuses, these steps are performed by the Disability Services personnel as a routine function; so, faculty should first inquire if such help is there.

Faculty using complicated print textbooks with many visuals and graphs should check with the Disability Services about how to make such inaccessible book content accessible to disabled students (for a discussion of accessibility in technical communication textbooks, see Wilferth & Hart, 2005). Multimodality can be used constructively to solve such problems. Complicated graphs can be drawn tactilely employing a low-cost drawing kit from the American Printing House for the Blind, and the instructor can produce a transcript to describe each of the elaborate visuals and post them online for everyone's use. In a study of students receiving a mixture of asynchronous audio and text-based feedback, Philip Ice, Curtis Reagan, Perry Phillips, and John Wells (2007) recorded "extremely high student satisfaction with embedded asynchronous audio feedback as compared to asynchronous text only feedback" (p. 3). The authors suggested that what might be suitable for students with visual or learning disabilities might also serve others well, as is the contention in OWI Principle 1 as Hewett describes in Chapter 1 (see also Hewett, 2015a). Their interview data analyses revealed that the audio feedback was perceived to be more effective than text-based feedback for conveying nuanced comments. The students associated audio feedback with feelings of increased involvement, enhanced learning community interactions, increased retention of content, and with instructor being caring. How often do our students miss an important detail simply because their eyes have yet not become trained enough to pick those minutia? Christine Neuwirth, Chandhok Ravinder, Davida Charney, Patricia Wojahn, and Loel Kim's (1994) study of voice and written annotations in reviews also provided interesting findings about these modalities. Instructors of multimodal composition and technical communication also can develop full-fledged assignments around such inaccessible course materials where the combined abilities of the whole class can be put to work, including the disabled students.

We also need to understand who is responsible for the accessibility of third-party content. Suppose the campus is increasing the number of online classes and expanding the use of technology in the on-campus classes. Specifically, faculty are increasingly linking their course pages to third-party websites, video clips, old radio programs, and podcasts that they did not create. Offices of Distance Education often assist with access for only the course materials that they help faculty create. The issues arising out of the faculty-created course content often fall outside the purview of these instructional design departments. For example, often there is a streaming video with no captioning, or transcript of the sound track. What can WPAs do to educate faculty regarding their responsibilities? Simply speaking, we should make faculty responsible for generating accessible content through enforceable policies. Faculty interested in experimenting with multimodal composing of course content also must learn how to make this content accessible. Likewise, faculty who use wide-ranging third-party content are responsible for making it accessible to all students.

Here is another scenario designed to convey the ethical and legal obligations in the OWI classroom: *An OWI .instructor has a student who is blind in a hybrid OWC where multimodal composing is taught and expected. Six problems are presented with the appropriate actions for addressing the problems directly following each one.*

1. The instructor posts the homework on Canvas, but the student states that Canvas is not very accessible with JAWS screen reader.

The institution is responsible for adopting an accessible LMS, and it is the instructor's job to report the problem to the department chair. The student has the right to file a complaint with the Justice Department if the institution does nothing.

2. In the onsite, synchronous sessions of this course, the instructor gives in-class short writing assignments to inspire students with the assigned reading or writing tasks. The prompts for these short assignments are placed in front of the class on a PowerPoint slide, but the student's screen reader cannot read these slides.

The instructor can learn to make accessible slides that can be read by a screen reader. Another option is to email this prompt to the student at the same time or before the class. (See this inexpensive resource for learning to design accessible documents by TechVision at http://www.yourtechvision.com/).

3. The instructor writes on the electronic whiteboard during class discussions and brief lectures in these synchronous sessions so that visual learners can stay connected, but the blind student cannot read from this electronic board.

Most technical communication textbooks explain that visual presentation of information is not enough. Reading displayed information aloud assists all students in comprehension and assimilation (Johnson-Sheehan, 2012). Information Design research also explains that a combination of text and images serves all readers best and enables greater comprehension (Kahn, Tan, & Beaton, 1990; Sadoski & Paibio, 2001; Schriver, 2013).

4. The major multimodal assignments for this course require the use of audio-visual tools, particularly Flash, and the blind student doesn't know how to use it with the screen reader. The instructor also realizes that these assignments will require visual composing and the question is how the student will handle it.

In any of the situations described above, it is important to mind Gail Hawisher and Cynthia Selfe's (1991) repeated advice to critically appraise technologies before allowing them into our pedagogy. A simple answer is that OWI teachers cannot choose tools that are not accessible to certain learner groups. Flash is extremely difficult to use without sight although it now does have some accessibility features built into it. Students with other disabilities or health conditions also can react negatively to Flash; therefore, researching technology choices for their accessibility to the disabled before adopting them should be included in course planning. Students should have a few alternatives when multimodal tools are central to the curriculum. After the signing of the 2008 ADA Amendments Act, the Department of Justice has pursued universities when students complained about the choice of inaccessible technologies by their schools. (See, for example, the 2010 joint "Dear Colleagues" letter to all US college presidents about Amazon's Kindle ebook reader from Education and Justice Departments. Most recently, in February 2015, the National Association of the Deaf and other disability rights groups have sought class-action status in a lawsuit against MIT and Harvard, claiming that their failure to include closed captioning in their otherwise freely available online course offerings constitutes discrimination and violation of the ADA (Lewin, 2015).) In case students are expected to learn these multimedia tools on their own, OWI teachers should check beforehand that the learning resource's particular tools also are accessible for students with disabilities. If teaching these tools is part of the course content, pedagogical techniques should be tailored for disabled students even though OWI Principle

2 stated that educators are not responsible for teaching technology. In this case, the exigency is that teaching the technology to the disabled student is crucial to the student learning to write in the course. The legal concept of "equal opportunity" kicks in automatically in this situation because as instructors we chose to include this learning unit in our writing classes. The distinction holds up even in curricular terms because these multimedia tools then become a segment of the course content.

5. *The blind student is a fluent Braille reader, but the college Disability Services has only provided him with an audio-recorded version of the assigned text. The student claims that recorded books put him to sleep and he learns more by reading to himself in Braille. The instructor also believes that reading some of the sections closely in Braille is important, but the Disability Services states that Braille books are expensive to produce. After much cajoling on the instructor's part, they have found a tagged version of the E-text the other students use for the student to read on a Braille Display. Unfortunately, this student neither owns a Braille Display, nor does he have a Braille printer; so, he still cannot read this E-text in Braille.*

In the Argenyi v. Creighton University (2013) case appeal, the Eighth Circuit stated that both the ADA (1990) and Section 504 of the Rehabilitation Act (1973) require the provision of necessary auxiliary aids and services to individuals with disabilities. Turning to the case law, the Eighth Circuit further noted that a person is required to receive meaningful access to a University's program and activities. Although this "meaningful" access standard means that aids and services are not required to produce the identical result or level of achievement for persons with disabilities and those without disabilities, these aids and services still need to provide equal opportunity to the person with a disability in order to gain the same benefit. OWI instructors also should note that whatever services are available to on-campus students at an institution of higher education, the distance students also should have access to those resources.

Returning to the textbook issue, tagged E-text files, if done correctly, can facilitate reading with a screen reader. They also can be optimized for Braille Displays, but without a device to display or print Braille, a Braille copy is not possible. Since other students have an accessible E-text that does not require the purchase of a separate device, the college has the minimal obligation to lend a Braille Display to the student. Preferably, it should provide a hard copy of the book, which can be printed on a Braille printer in the Disability Services Office. Most Braille Displays offer only one line of text at time, so they do not allow a close study of a complete sentence or paragraph. Blind readers with the knowledge of the code often prefer to read the materials requiring close attention in hard copy Braille rather than listening with a screen reader. The claims about the cost of producing Braille copies often are exaggerated. Unless the institution's Disability Services has no one who can learn to operate a Braille printer, paper copies can be produced at a reasonable cost from the publisher-provided electronic text. The Braille production of books certainly does not cost any more than many other electronic software resources available to other students. The need for Braille is comparable to deaf students' need for interpreters and CART services, and on many campuses, deaf students also have to fight for these services.

6. The student owns a Perkins Brailler for taking notes, but he complains that the instructor explains concepts rather visually and he loses track of what is going on.

Multimodality is the forte of all twenty-first century writing professors; so, reaching OWI students using a variety of explanatory modes—visual, auditory, kinesthetic, and the like—is appropriate for this context.

In sum, the accessibility-related responsibilities in OWI can be divided into three categories:

1. Course delivery and student support infrastructure
2. Course curriculum and content development
3. Student-instructor interaction for content delivery and further content generation in the form of participative learning

While the WPA and the student service/technology personnel are obviously the point persons for arranging an accessible delivery and support infrastructure, the OWI instructor is in charge of both producing and delivering content that is accessible to everyone enrolled. If instructors have to work with an existing course template, they should work with the WPA on modifying this template to construct accessibility in the course without being inhibited by the idiosyncrasies of the template. If the institution provides pre-made courses to OWI instructors, then instructors should underscore the limitations of these canned courses to the WPA and play the role of an advocate for disabled students. In curricular matters, these disabled students, who might otherwise have gone through the struggle for access and accommodations with their parents during their earlier schooling, may not have the academic knowledge or intellectual maturity to represent their own problems as an instructor can do by advocating for them. We also can support students by teaching them how to advocate on one's own behalf through course content—readings, assignments, and class activities, pedagogical methods, and approaches that involve advocacy techniques, and by foregrounding the lessons of the aforesaid in other online spaces of courses.

Mary Lee Vance (2007) drew attention to the most challenging problem disabled students confront in the academy through a simple, generalized claim: "First-generation disabled individuals are forced into living in a world where able-bodied people have had generations of role models to assist them, and where the world is designed to address their needs" (p. 13). She continued, "Because society reinforces ableism, the first-generation disabled must carve out alternate paths to reach the same destinations, and on occasions the alternate paths may take longer to build, much less traverse" (p. 14). The point I want to emphasize is that contemporary disabled students have no reason to carve their paths all alone. The disability laws demand that education be inclusive and that pedagogy should reflect this inclusiveness in every aspect of the institution's functioning. We should not need reminders that this type of advocacy is not new to our colleges because we have gone through this process during the past five decades for accommodating women; racial minorities; lesbian, gay, bisexual, transgendered, and queer (LGBTQ); and various other minority students groups. Certainly, we should not forget that these dissatisfied disabled students are not good for the publicity of OWI programs.

Irrespective of what type of control WPAs and OWI instructors have over curriculum and content, they are in the driver's seat for making the student-instructor interaction accessible for content delivery and further content generation in the form of participative learning. Our task is not only to deliver this curriculum in an accessible manner but also to make sure that students have an amply accessible scaffold to interact with teachers and their peers, with the texts they generate in any of the modalities prescribed or elected, and with the overall delivery system—the ePortfolio software, the basic LMS tools, and those ubiquitous portable documents. It is an area of online learning where writing instructors can shine and literally make a huge contribution to online learning. The general research literature in distance education has not looked at the significance of such interactions in student knowledge-making processes as closely as the process theorists in face-to-face writing studies have done during the past four decades (Bazerman, 1988; Emig, 1970; Myers, 1985; Selzer, 1983). Again, OWI instructors can carve new paths for ourselves and disabled students by collaboratively devising innovative interactional techniques that would work both for disabled and nondisabled students for comprehending, analyzing, and synthesizing others' ideas. We can build accessible scaffolds for composing with our students and have them test these with one another and on themselves as they practice participatory learning and produce texts and iTexts for OWI-based writing assignments.

EXTENDING ACCESS TO STUDENTS WITH LEARNING DISABILITIES

While students with sensory disabilities face major challenges in accessing the current curriculum, we do not yet know the extent of challenges faced by students with learning disabilities and those who have different learning styles.

These students are entering postsecondary institutions in large numbers but we know very little about the different types of learning disabilities and how to address the needs of this highly diverse group. In addition to following UDL Guidelines 2.0, OWI instructors can benefit from knowing Web Content Authoring Guidelines 2.0 (WCAG 2.0) for curriculum content and interaction design, which provide useful information for addressing the needs of diverse learners. Beginning with the first three guidelines and eventually constructing a full repertoire of accessibility techniques, instructors can learn to integrate accessibility in their Web design, create accessible Web and PowerPoint presentations, and receive abundant guidance for making both dynamic and static content accessible even though the latter is not the purpose or focus of these guidelines.

Anne Meyer and David Rose (2005) stated that "more differentiated use of media for instruction reveals that individuals who are defined as learning disabled within print-based learning environments are not the same individuals who are defined as learning disabled within video- or audio-based learning environments" (24). Indeed, the range of learning challenges consists of difficulties with text (reading or writing), visual comprehension (reading or using images), hearing (auditory processing and comprehension), and the need for tactile/kinesthetic approaches to content and skills. There is much that this chapter cannot detail regarding learning disabilities, but OWI teachers, as Hewett pointed out in Chapter 1 (see also Hewett, 2015a) need to learn more about how their students learn and appeal to those styles through a variety of modalities and media. Those students who are classified as "disabled" may have more significant challenges than the average student, but most students have preferred learning styles to which OWI should provide inclusion and access.

CONCLUSION AND RECOMMENDATIONS

A need exists for a calculated effort at building institutional and programmatic research on disability, disabled students, and writing pedagogy. Kenneth Leithwood and Robert Aitken (1995) explained that a learning organization is "a group of people pursuing common purposes (individual purposes as well) with a collective commitment to regularly weighing the value of those purposes, modifying them when that makes sense, and continuously developing more effective and efficient ways of accomplishing those purposes" (p. 63). While WPAs and OWI instructors can learn from external research, local data about students' performance can be even more influential in evaluating mutual successes and failures (Peterson, 2001; Sullivan & Porter, 1997; see also Chapter 17). For this purpose, as OWI Principle 15 indicated, data gathering should be an ongoing process for all OWI administrators and instructors in the near future until a threshold of understanding about inclusive pedagogies for OWI is found. Developing pre- and post-semester surveys both for students and instructors can help to create a profile of the students' preparation for online learning as they enter OWI courses and the post surveys can indicate how efforts at inclusive learning are succeeding. These surveys should be geared to register details about students' abilities, technology use, technology proficiencies, learning styles, experiences with the inclusive course design and pedagogy, and the interactions with instructors and peers. OWI teachers also can begin their courses by asking students to compose a literacy narrative where they cover all the basic categories listed on their pre-course survey. Such a narrative can educate instructors about their students' learning preferences, skills, and needs while engaging them in a purposeful writing activity that naturally reveals writing strengths and weaknesses. These front-end information gathering activities can be followed by more intense feedback-gathering activities during the semester. Modified Small Group intake by a third-party instructor or administrator in online settings can be done without an interruption in the course schedule. Such a mid-semester evaluation can provide the instructor with feedback about their efforts at designing an inclusive course and give a chance to make changes with the same student group.

Underscoring the significance of Web accessibility for college students in face-to-face settings, Susanne Bruyere (2008) expressed that:

> Web-based technology can open or close doors to students
> with disabilities; admissions applications, financial aid in-
> formation, schedules, class assignments, bursar bills, and the
> like are typically posted on the Web. Inaccessible websites can
> pose significant barriers to people who are visually impaired
> or deaf or have learning disabilities. (p. 37)

WPAs and OWI teachers should be primary in removing—not in creating—barriers.

WPAs and writing faculty research writing, teach writing, tutor writing, and compose their own writing. As a group, we challenge the manufacturing model of instruction by arguing for small size classes for our students, as articulated in OWI Principle 9 (pp. 20-21), and we do so while remaining one of the lowest paid workforces in the academy. When our arguments lose in the face of administrative imperatives, we serve students anyway and always at the cost of our own economic, professional, and personal well-being. Our battles are not limited to confronting the administrative powers; we also regularly fight those unending battles on our campuses with colleagues in other disciplines about how to best improve students' writing. Likewise, in this age of New Media and multimodality, we should put up a stiff fight about which technologies to adopt and which ones to shun in favor of humane and student-centered pedagogies. We should engage ourselves in the campus-wide conversations on technology choices and technology services before the die is cast for the coming decades of online instruction and hard to reverse decisions are made on the behalf of our disabled students and faculty. We should not lose sight of the realities of the front of the room blackboards morphing into PowerPoint presentations with the instructor-centered pedagogies of the pre-1980s era returning to our face-to-face, hybrid, and fully online courses with a vengeance.

To establish a new model of college education for all, we should bring together OWI and UDL with the aim of designing an inclusive curriculum in the hands of ambitious instructors backed by an adequately accessible infrastructure to deliver OWI. If we employ these digital tools of distance learning with the awareness that they can be judged as better only if they can reach those who have previously been overlooked, ignored, or under-served, then we can move quickly beyond the novelty factor and become savvy adopters who concentrate on these tools' relevance to the task of teaching writing inclusively. We also may realize that rethinking our pedagogy through these accessibility-centered principles will initially demand additional work for preparing ourselves for such teaching, but, in the long run, our reconceptualized courses might offer much more in terms of content, pedagogy, and comprehensibility for all students.

The following are recommendations for WPAs and OWI teachers:

- WPAs should advocate to university administration for accessibility readiness for disabled students.
- Understand the legal and ethical obligations to provide equal access to our courses for all students, including students with disabilities.
- Keep in mind that accessibility does not stop with technology; it must become a part of all curricular and pedagogical thinking.
- Do not lose sight of the fact that reading and writing are even more important for disabled students because these literacy skills can help them become financially independent, prepare them to speak for themselves, and equip them to claim an equal place to live in the world.
- Do not forget that disabled students also have diverse needs and skill levels, and educators need to address their problems individually.
- Always place accessibility at the beginning of all planning; it should remain an integral part of all subsequent course design and delivery processes.
- Reach out to disabled students before or at the very beginning of the academic term so that all necessary arrangements for providing access can be made in time.
- Expand our repertoire of accessible teaching tools beyond the limits of

the UDL framework, even though it is a reasonable starting point for accessible course design and pedagogy.

The following are recommendations for readings that will help to equip WPAs and OWI teachers with the understanding and facts to argue for the rights of the disabled in policy meetings and in developing curricular changes:

Coombs, Norman. (2010). *Making online teaching accessible: Inclusive course design for students with disabilities*. San Francisco, CA: Jossey-Bass.

Jarrett, Caroline, Redish, Janice (Ginny), & Summers, Kathryn. (2013). *Designing for people who do not read easily*. In Lisa Meloncon (Ed.), *Rhetorical accessibility* (pp. 39-65). Amityville, NY: Baywood Publishing.

Kanter, Arlene S. & Ferri, Beth A. (Eds.). (2013). *Righting educational wrongs: Disability studies in law and education*. Syracuse, NY: Syracuse University Press.

Kleege, Georgina. (2005). Blindness and visual culture: An eyewitness account. *Journal of Visual Culture 4*(2), 179-190.

Seale, Jane K. (2006). *E-learning and disability in higher education*. Oxon, UK: Routledge.

Wyatt, Christopher Scott. (2010). *Online pedagogy: Designing writing courses for students with autism spectrum disorders* (Doctoral dissertation, University of Minnesota). Available from ProQuest Dissertations and Theses database. Retrieved from http://search.proquest.com/docview/597211269

Yergeau, Melanie. (2011). *Disabling composition: Toward a 21st-century, synaesthetic theory of writing* (Unpublished doctoral dissertation). The Ohio State University, Columbus, Ohio.

ACKNOWLEDGMENTS

I am thankful to Beth Kalikoff and Rich Rice for providing feedback on an early draft of this chapter.

NOTES

1. Regarding the text of *A Position Statement of Principles and Example Effective Practices for OWI*, this document leans heavily for its terminology on Sheryl Burgstahler and Rebecca C. Cory's (2008) research because our national surveys on OWI failed to locate a shared terminology among OWI instructors for discussing disability-related accessibility practices. Our own knowledge of the recommended practices has

been drawn from the cumulative disability literature in Education and Pedagogy, Accessible Computing, Human-Centered Design, and Disability Studies. As the discipline dedicates its pedagogical energies on these accessibility challenges across the country, I am confident that it will develop a set of writing-centered effective practices, as well as, a shared language to elucidate them.

REFERENCES

American Printing House for the Blind. (n.d.). Retrieved from www.aph.org

Americans with Disabilities Act (ADA). (1990). 42 U.S.C. § 12101 et seq (1993). Retrieved from http://www.ada.gov/pubs/adastatute08.htm

Argenyi v. Creighton University, 703 F.3d 441 (8th Cir. 2013). Retrieved from http://www.disabilityrightsnebraska.org/what_we_do/michael_argenyi_case.html

Babcock, Rebecca. (2012). *Tell me how it reads: Tutoring deaf and hearing students in the writing center.* Washington, DC: Gallaudet University Press.

Bazerman, Charles. (1988). *Shaping written knowledge: The genre and activity of the experimental articles in science.* Madison, WI: University of Wisconsin Press.

Brady, Laura. (2001). Fault lines in the terrain of distance education. *Computers and Composition, 18*(4), 347-357.

Brueggemann, Brenda Jo. (2002). An enabling pedagogy. In Sharon Snyder, Brenda Brueggemann, & Rosemarie Garland-Thomson (Eds.), *Disability studies: Enabling the humanities* (pp. 317-336). New York: The Modern Language Association.

Bruyere, Susanne. (2008). Total access: Making college web sites accessible to students with disabilities. *Community College Journal, 79*(1), 36-39.

Burgstahler, Sheryl & Cory, Rebecca C. (Eds.). (*2008*). *Universal design in higher education: From principles to practice.* Boston: Harvard Education Press.

CAST (2008). *Universal design for learning guidelines version 1.0.* Retrieved from http://www.cast.org/library/UDLguidelines/version1.html

CAST (2011). *Universal design for learning guidelines version 2.0.* Retrieved from http://www.udlcenter.org/aboutudl/udlguidelines

Cargile Cook, Kelli, & Grant-Davie, Keith. (2005). *Online Education.* Amityville, New York: Baywood Publishing.

Cargile Cook, Kelli, & Grant-Davie, Keith. (2013). *Online Education 2.0.* Amityville, New York: Baywood Publishing.

CCCC Committee on Disability Issues. (2015). Retrieved from http://www.ncte.org/cccc/committees/disabilityissues

CCCC Committee on Disability Issues in College Composition. (2006/2011). *A Policy on Disability in CCCC.* Retrieved from http://www.ncte.org/cccc/resources/positions/disabilitypolicy

CCCC OWI Committee for Effective Practices in Online Writing Instruction. (2011a). *Fully online distance-based courses survey results.* Retrieved from http://s.zoomerang.com/sr.aspx?sm=EAupi15gkwWur6G7egRSXUw8k-pNMu1f5gjUp01aogtY%3d

CCCC OWI Committee for Effective Practices in Online Writing Instruction. (2011b). *Hybrid/blended course survey results.* Retrieved from http://s.zoomerang.com/sr.aspx?sm=%2fPsFeeRDwfznaIyyz4sV0qxkkh5Ry7O1NdnGH-CxIBD4%3d

CCCC OWI Committee for Effective Practices in Online Writing Instruction. (2013). *A position statement of principles and effective practices for online writing instruction (OWI).* Retrieved from http://www.ncte.org/cccc/resources/positions/owiprinciples

The Center for Universal Design North Carolina State University. (1997). *The principles of universal design.* Retrieved from http://www.ncsu.edu/ncsu/design/cud/about_ud/udprinciplestext.htm

Cooper, Martyn & Heath, Andy. (2009). Access for all to e-learning. In A. Méndez-Vilas, A. Martín, J. A. Mesa González, & J. Mesa González (Eds.), *Research, reflections and innovations in integrating ICT in education* (pp. 1139-1143). Milton Keynes, UK: Open University Press.

Crowley, Sharon. (1998). *Composition in the university: Historical and polemical essays.* Pittsburgh: University of Pittsburgh Press.

Davis, Lennard. (1995). *Enforcing normalcy: Disability, deafness, and the body.* New York: Verso.

Emig, Janet. (1970). *The composing processes of twelfth graders.* Urbana, IL: National Council of Teachers of English.

Erisman, Wendy & McSwain, Courtney. (2006). *Expanding access and opportunity.* Washington, DC: Institute for Higher Education Policy.

Gibson, Keith & Martinez, Diane. (2013). From divide to continuum: Rethinking access in online education. In Kelli Cook, & Keith Grant-Davie, *Online Education 2.0: Evolving, adapting, and reinventing online technical communication* (pp. 197-212). Amityville, NY: Baywood Publishing.

Hawisher, Gail E. & Selfe, Cynthia L. (1991). The rhetoric of technology and the electronic writing classroom. *College Composition and Communication, 42*(1), 55-65.

Hewett, Beth L. (2010). *The online writing conference: A guide for teachers and tutors.* Portsmouth, NH: Boynton/Cook.

Hewett, Beth L. (2013). Fully online and hybrid writing instruction. In H. Brooke Hessler, Amy Rupiper Taggart, & Kurt Schick (Eds.), *A guide to composition pedagogies* (2nd ed.). (pp. 194-211). Oxford, UK: Oxford University Press.

Hewett, Beth L. (2015a). *Reading to learn and writing to teach: Literacy strategies for online writing instruction.* Boston, MA: Bedford/St. Martin's Press.

Hewett, Beth L. (2015b). *The online writing conference: A guide for teachers and tutors* (Updated). Boston, MA: Bedford/St. Martin's Press.

Houston, Lori. (n.d.). Working with learning disabled writers. Retrieved from http://compfaqs.org/LearningDisabledWriters/WorkingWithLearningDisabledWriters

Ice, Philip, Reagan Curtis, Perry Phillips, & John Wells. (2007). Using asynchronous audio feedback to enhance teaching presence and student sense of community. *Journal of Asynchronous Learning Networks, 11*(2), 3-25.

Ingeno, Lauren. (2013). Online accessibility a faculty duty. *Inside Higher Ed.* Retrieved from https://www.insidehighered.com/news/2013/06/24/faculty-responsible-making-online-materials-accessible-disabled-students

Institute for Higher Education Policy. (1998). *Assuring quality in distance learning: A preliminary review.* Washington, DC: The Council for Higher Education Accreditation.

Jarrett, Caroline, Redish, Janice, & Summers, Kathryn. (2013). Designing for people who do not read easily. In Lisa Meloncon (Ed.), *Rhetorical accessability: At the intersection of technical communication and disability studies* (pp. 39-66). Amityville, NY: Baywood Publishing.

Johnson-Sheehan, Richard. (2012). Preparing and giving presentations. In R. Johnson-Sheehan, *Technical Communication Today* (4th ed.) (pp. 573-610). New York: Pearson.

Kahn, Michael, Tan, Kay, & Beaton, Robert. (1990). Reduction of cognitive workload through information chunking. In D. Woods & E. Roth (Eds.), *Proceedings of the Human Factors and Ergonomics Society 34th Annual Meeting* (pp. 1509-1512). Santa Monica, CA:

Konur, Ozcan. (2007). Computer assisted teaching and assessment of disabled students. *Journal of Computer Assisted Learning,* 207-219. Retrieved from http://www.catea.gatech.edu/scitrain/kb/FullText_Articles/Konur_Computer-Assisted.pdf

Leithwood, Kenneth & Aitken, Robert. (1995). *Making schools smarter: A system for monitoring school and district progress.* Newbury Park, CA: Corwin.

Levin, Douglas & Arafeh, Sousan. (2002). *The digital disconnect: The widening gap between internet-savvy students and their schools.* Washington, DC: Pew Internet & American Life Project.

Lewiecki-Wilson, Cynthia, & Brueggemann, Brenda Jo (Eds.). (2008). *Disability and the teaching of writing: A critical sourcebook.* Boston, MA: Bedford/St. Martin's Press.

Lewin, Tamar. (2015, February 15). Harvard and M.I.T. are sued over lack of closed captions. *The New York Times.* Retrieved from http://www.nytimes.

com/2015/02/13/education/harvard-and-mit-sued-over-failing-to-caption-online-courses.html?_r=0

Matsuda, Paul K. (2006). The myth of linguistic homogeneity in US college composition. *College English, 68*(6), 637-651.

Meloncon, Lisa (Ed.). (2013). *Rhetorical accessability: At the intersection of technical communication and disability studies.* Amityville, NY: Baywood Publishing.

Meloncon, Lisa & Arduser, Lora. (2013). Communities of practice approach: A new model for online course development and sustainability. In Kelli Cook & Keith Grant-Davie, *Online education 2.0: Evolving, adapting, and reinventing online technical communication* (pp. 73-90). Amityville, NY: Baywood Publishing.

Meyer, Anne & Rose, David H. (2005). The future is in the margins: The role of technology and disability in educational reform. In David H. Rose, Anne Meyer, & Chuck Hitchcock (Eds.), *The universally designed classroom: Accessible curriculum and digital technologies,* (pp. 14-35). Cambridge, MA: Harvard Education Press.

Myers, Greg. (1985). The social construction of two biologists' proposals. *Written Communication, 2*(3), 219-245.

National Federation of the Blind. (n.d.). *Blindness statistics.* Retrieved from http://www.nfb.org/nfb/blindness_statistics.asp

Neuwirth, Christine, Ravinder, Chandhok, Charney, Davida, Wojahn, Patricia, & Kim, Loel. (1994). Distributed collaborative writing: A comparison of spoken and written modalities for reviewing and revising documents. *Proceedings of the Computer-Human Interaction '94 Conference* (pp. 55-62). New York: Association for Computing Machinery.

Oswal, Sushil K. (2013). Accessible eportfolios for visually-impaired users: Interfaces, design, & infrastructures. In Katherine Wills & Rich Rice (Eds.), *ePortfolio performance support systems: Constructing, presenting, and assessing portfolios* (pp. 133-152). Anderson, SC: Parlor Press.

Oswal, Sushil K. (2013, February 24). Online learning and disabled students [electronic mailing list comment]. Retrieved from https://lists.ucdenver.edu/cgi-bin/wa?A0=DS_RHET-COMP

Oswal, Sushil K. & Hewett, Beth L. (2013). Accessibility challenges for visually impaired students and their OWI teachers. In Lisa Meloncon (Ed.), *Rhetorical accessability: At the intersection of technical communication and disability studies* (pp. 135-156). Amityville, NY: Baywood Publishing.

Oswal, Sushil K. & Meloncon, Lisa. (2014). Paying attention to accessibility and disability in technical and professional communication online course design. *Journal of Business and Technical Communication, 28*(3), 271-300.

Owusu-Ansah, Angela, Neill, Patti, & Haralson, Michele. (2011). Distance education technology: Higher education barriers during the first decade of the twenty-first century. *Online journal of Distance Learning Administration, XIV*(II). Retrieved from http://www.westga.edu/~distance/ojdla/summer142/ansah_142.html

Palmeri, Jason. (2006). Disability studies, cultural analysis, and the critical practice of technical communication pedagogy. *Technical Communication Quarterly, 15*(1), 49-65.

Petri, Ken, Rangin, Hadi, Richwine, Brian, & Thompson, Marc. (2012). A comparison of Learning Management system accessibility. Paper presented at the EDUCAUSE Midwest Regional Conference, Chicago, IL.

Peterson, Patricia Webb. (2001). The debate about online learning: Key issues for writing teachers. *Computers and Composition, 18*(4), 359-370.

Rintala, Jan. (1998). Computer technology in higher education: An experiment, not a solution. *Quest, 50*(4), 366-378.

Rose, David H. & Anne Meyer (2002). Teaching every student in the digital age: Universal design for learning. Alexandria, VA: Association for Supervision and Curriculum Development.

Rose, David H. & Meyer, Anne. (2006). *A practical reader in universal design for learning*. Cambridge, MA: Harvard Education Press.

Rose, David H., Anne Meyer & Chuck Hitchcock (Eds.). (2005). *The universally designed classroom: Accessible curriculum and digital technologies*. Cambridge, MA: Harvard Education Press.

Sadoski, Mark & Paivio, Allan. (2001). *Imagery and text: A dual coding theory of reading and writing*. Mahwah, NJ: Erlbaum.

Schriver, Karen. (2013). What do technical communicators need to know about writing? In Johndan Johnson-Eilola & Stuart Selber (Eds.), *Solving problems in technical communication* (pp. 386-427). Chicago: University of Chicago Press.

Seale, Jane & Martyn, Cooper. (2010). E-learning and accessibility: An exploration of the potential role of generic pedagogical tools. *Computers and Education, 54*(4), 1107-1116.

Selfe, Cynthia. (1999). *Technology and literacy in the twenty-first century: The importance of paying attention*. Carbondale: Southern Illinois University Press.

Selzer, Jack. (1983). The composing processes of an engineer. *College Composition and Communication, 34*(2), 178-187.

Shute, Valerie & Zapata-Rivera, Diego. (2007). *Adaptive technologies*. Princeton, NJ: Educational Testing Service.

Sullivan, Patricia & James E. Porter. (1997). *Opening spaces: Writing technologies and critical research practices*. Greenwich, CT: Ablex.

Szpaller, Keila. (2012, September 18). Disabled UM students file complaint over inaccessible online courses. *Missoulian*. Retrieved from http://missoulian.com/news/local/disabled-um-students-file-complaint-over-inaccessi-ble-online-courses/article_d02c27ac-0145-11e2-bc26-001a4bcf887a.html

Treviranus, Jutta. (n.d.). *The electronic campus and equal access to higher education.* Retrieved from http://idrc.ocad.ca/index.php/resources/idrc-online/49-articles-and-papers/108-the-electronic-campus-and-equal-access-to-higher-education

US Census Bureau. (2011). *Disability.* Retrieved from http://www.census.gov/people/disability/

US Department of Education & Department of Justice. (2010). *Electronic book reader dear colleague letter.* Retrieved from http://www2.ed.gov/about/offices/list/ocr/letters/colleague-20100629.html U.S

Department of Education, Laws & Guidance. (2008). *Higher education opportunity act-2008.* Retrieved from http://www2.ed.gov/policy/highered/leg/hea08/index.html

US Department of Education, National Center for Education Statistics. (2012). *The 2012 Statistical abstract, table 285. Students' reported disability status by selected characteristics 2007 to 2008.* Retrieved from http://www.census.gov/compendia/statab/cats/education.html

U.S Department of Justice, Office of Public Affairs. (2013). *Justice Department Settles with Louisiana Tech University over inaccessible course materials.* Retrieved from http://www.justice.gov/opa/pr/2013/July/13-crt-831.html

US Equal Employment Opportunity Commission. (2008). *ADA amendments act of 2008.* Retrieved from http://www.eeoc.gov/laws/statutes/adaaa.cfm

Vance, Mary-Lee. (2007). *Disabled faculty and staff in a disabling society: Multiple identities in higher education.* Huntersville, NC: AHEAD.

Warnock, Scott. (2009). *Teaching writing online: How and Why.* Urbana, IL: National Council of Teachers of English.

Wilferth, Joe & Charles Hart. (2005) Designing in the dark: Toward informed technical design for the visually impaired. *Computers and Composition Online.* Retrieved from http://www.bgsu.edu/departments/english/cconline/wilferthhart/wilferthhart.htm

World Health Organization (WHO). (n.d.). *Disabilities.* Retrieved from http://www.who.int/topics/disabilities/en/#navigation

Web Accessibility Initiative. (n.d.). *Web content authoring guidelines 2.0.* Retrieved from www.w3c.org/wai/

Xu, Di, & Jaggars, Shanna Smith. (2013, February). *Adaptability to online learning: Differences across types of students and academic subject areas.* (CCRC Working Paper No. 54). New York: Community College Research Center. Retrieved from http://ccrc.tc.columbia.edu/media/k2/attachments/adaptability-to-online-learning.pdf

CHAPTER 9

MULTILINGUAL WRITERS AND OWI

Susan K. Miller-Cochran
North Carolina State University

Writing programs in higher education are enrolling increasing numbers of multilingual writers, introducing a unique set of considerations for inclusivity to the design and delivery of OWCs. Because so much communication in an OWC occurs through written English, and written English is exactly what a multilingual student is working to master, OWI teachers consistently face an inherent paradox of instructional design. This chapter places the OWI principles in conversation with other scholarship on multilingual writers, specifically the *CCCC Statement on Second Language Writing and Writers*, to provide recommendations for design and instruction in OWI environments that is inclusive of their needs.

Keywords: diversity, ESL, inclusive OWI design, inclusivity, language, multilingual student, second-language learner, second-language writer, universal user

Many of the guidelines that support effective OWI and provide universal access for all students (see especially Chapters 8 & 10) apply equally well to students who are multilingual writers, sometimes referred to as ESL or second-language writers. The specific linguistic challenges that multilingual writers face warrant additional attention, though, when considering how to interpret the OWI principles and to design effective approaches to OWI.

THE NEED FOR LINGUISTIC INCLUSIVITY

In this chapter, I use the term *multilingual* to refer to students who might speak a language other than English as their first language, speak multiple languages fluently, or perhaps speak multiple dialects of English. These students might be proficient in academic writing in their first languages or perhaps in multiple languages but probably not in English. By contrast, some students might not have developed written literacy in their first languages, of which English may be one.

Because of these vast differences in linguistic backgrounds and writing experiences, identifying students who might benefit from a pedagogical approach designed for language diversity can be incredibly difficult. Complicating this task are the many methods we use in higher education to admit and track students who come from a linguistically diverse background. Administrators and teachers in higher education often immediately think of international students when they hear the terms *multilingual, ESL,* or *second-language learners*, but multilingual writers also can be resident ESL students who are either citizens of the United States or permanent residents. Patricia Friedrich (2006) explained the importance of understanding these distinctions when she described the unique challenges faced by international ESL, resident ESL, and monolingual basic writers. Depending on how multilingual writers self-identify, they might not recognize the services an institution provides for students who come from linguistically diverse backgrounds as pertaining to them. Christina Ortmeier-Hooper's (2008) case study of three ESL writers complicated the field's understanding of how multilingual writers from varying backgrounds self-identify with or against these labels, and Todd Ruecker (2011) explored this complication further by reporting on multilingual writers' response to such labels in the placement process. A multilingual writer cannot solely be identified by a visa status, Test of English as a Foreign Language (TOEFL) score, skin color, or a spoken accent. Language diversity is present consistently in university writing classes and on college enrollment rosters, and teachers should design writing environments with this diversity in mind.

Paul Kei Matsuda (2006) challenged the assumptions prevalent in writing programs and rhetoric and composition studies scholarship that privilege a linguistically homogenous audience, asking the field to rethink those assumptions and understand that language diversity in writing classes, and on college campuses as a whole, is increasing. Writing programs consistently have ignored these differences, however, by designing courses that assume a threshold of common competency in written academic English (Matsuda, 2006) and hiring faculty who may have expertise in teaching writing but not in working with a linguistically diverse student population. This assumption of "linguistic homogeneity" (Matsuda, 2006) has led teachers (both online and in the classroom) to outsource language-specific help that students need in writing classes to other places such as Intensive English Programs, remedial courses, and writing centers. While such additional help certainly can aid student success in academic writing, especially when the class is taught as a hybrid or fully online OWC, it does not free the instructor of responsibility for designing and facilitating the class in a way that is inclusive of the needs of multilingual writers. Rather, instructors must know their students and understand the language diversity present in the class. The contextual cues that instructors might rely on to detect specific linguistic needs in an onsite classroom are sometimes absent in an online environment, although other cues might be present. For example, a multilingual writer in an onsite classroom might have a spoken accent or visibly struggle to complete an in-class writing activity on time. Likewise, the student might speak in another language with a classmate to ask for clarification on an assignment or use a translation dictionary to understand instructions or a reading assignment. In an online environment, these cues might be absent, but others might be present, such as transfer-related language issues in the student's writing or challenges with understanding organization and citation expectations in American academic writing. In all contexts, courses should be designed with the assumption that language variety will be present in the class. A linguistically-inclusive approach to OWI from the beginning of the design process can help students navigate a course effectively and prevent students from stumbling over elements of the course not essential to meeting the course objectives.

This chapter aims to bring some common educational principles related to multilingual writing instruction, specifically CCCC's *A Statement on Second Language Writing and Writers* (2009), into conversation with the *CCCC Position Statement of Principles and Example Effective Practices for Online Writing Instruction* (CCCC OWI Committee, 2013). Explicitly, this chapter outlines strategies to help writing programs and individual instructors design courses that uphold OWI Principle 1, that "Online writing instruction should be universally inclusive and accessible" (p. 7). Further, this chapter assumes, as Matsuda (2006) argued and others have reiterated (Miller-Cochran, 2010), that all college writing environments, even those online (Sánchez, 2013), include multilingual writers and must be designed to be inclusive and accessible to a linguistically diverse audience.

UNDERSTANDING THE NEEDS OF MULTILINGUAL WRITERS

If online writing specialists take cues from the scholarship on UDL (see Chapter 8), then OWI should be designed with the assumption that diversity is always present and that effective online courses take into consideration many elements of diversity in their design. Part of the challenge of implementing UDL principles into course design, however, is that the instructor/designer often thinks of a "universal user," essentializing the needs of a diverse group of users into a set of common traits. Jennifer Bowie (2009) encouraged teachers and course designers to think instead of a "universe of users," which allows for a multitude of diversity. This chapter argues that language diversity, especially in the context of writing classes, is an important element of that context, especially if we consider that individual students, such as the multilingual students with hearing impairment studied by Gary Long and his colleagues (2007), might need multiple accommodations in a class.

Because so much communication in an OWC occurs through written English, and written English is exactly what the multilingual student is working to master, OWI teachers consistently face an inherent paradox of instructional design. What must be acknowledged if a writing program or writing teacher seeks to design a course for a "universe of users" (Bowie, 2009) that takes into consideration the language variety present in American higher education writing classes? What needs do multilingual writers have that the teacher/designer must consider to design an effective OWC?

Understanding how multilingual writers use writing technologies provides an important piece to the puzzle if the field aims to respond to these questions. Several scholars in second language writing studies have explored how multilingual writers use a variety of technologies in their personal writing, in their academic writing, and in social media environments (e.g., Boas, 2011; DePew, 2011; DePew & Miller-Cochran, 2009; Shih, 2011). Developing a deep understanding of how multilingual writers use and navigate specific writing technologies can help teachers design and facilitate more effective writing classes generally and stronger OWCs specifically. This type of exploration and knowledge-building often is left to second language writing specialists, the "ESL Person" that Gail Shuck (2006) described, yet all teachers and writing program administrators (WPAs) need to develop awareness of the unique challenges and needs of multilingual writers (Miller-Cochran, 2010).

The *CCCC Position Statement on Second Language Writing and Writers* (2009) described the benefits to writing teachers of understanding the ways their multilingual students are using technology:

> For example, teaching writing with technology can give second language writing students an opportunity to build upon the literacy practices with which they are already familiar and comfortable. Those students who have access to technology can be relatively proficient with multiple applications, especially second language students who use the technology to keep in touch with home and reach out to people around the world. These students often demonstrate savvy rhetorical strategies, including the ability to communicate with others who write in other varieties of English. With the help of an instructor, second language writers can learn to bridge the strategies they

use to communicate socially through digital media to the expectations of the academy. Therefore, instructors need to learn how to proficiently work with the writing tools and within the writing contexts that will help second language writers create these bridges ... instructors need to be trained to work with various writing media (e.g., computer programs) so that they can take advantage of these pedagogical opportunities. (Part Four: Building on Students' Competencies)

Writing teachers have an opportunity during the design process to consider the kinds of technologies their students might already be familiar with, or they can leave open the technologies students can use to accomplish various writing tasks (if appropriate) to draw upon students' current literacy practices. Likewise, if a teacher believes it is important for students to master a specific technology, explicit instruction in the use of the technology should be a part of the course design for students who might not already be familiar with it. This need correlates with OWI Principles 2 and 10 (pp. 11, 21-23).

In addition to understanding how multilingual writers use writing technologies, teachers and course designers must understand the nature of the language learning process, realizing that "the process of acquiring syntactic and lexical competence" in a language does not happen in a semester or in a year (CCCC SLW Committee, 2009). Rather, it takes a significant amount of time to reach such competence, so a multilingual student may be mastering various aspects of written English throughout his or her college career. Multilingual writers also might struggle with other expectations in American academic writing contexts. As the *CCCC Statement on Second Language Writing and Writers* (2009) explained, "Some students may have difficulty adapting to or adopting North American discursive strategies because the nature and functions of discourse, audience, and rhetorical appeals often differ across cultural, national, linguistic, and educational contexts." For example, some multilingual students in online environments may struggle with unspoken expectations about participation in online discussions or the type of critiques they should offer classmates during peer review. For them—and to meet the needs of all students, frankly—OWI teachers should provide explicit expectations and instructions for how to participate in particular parts of the OWC. At the same time, other multilingual students already have had considerable exposure to written academic English and to American academic culture, and labels such as *ESL, multilingual,* or *international student* might inadvertently cause an instructor to make assumptions about the needs of multilingual students in the class that are not necessarily true. The bottom line is that OWI teachers should design the class to accommodate a variety of linguistic needs from the beginning—avoiding the need to retrofit the OWC—and make the expectations for course requirements clear, but they also should take the time to get to know individual students to be sure that their questions and needs are met.

To help meet the need for OWI teachers to understand the ways their multilingual writers might work best in an online, technology-rich environment, this chapter provides specific suggestions, drawn from the scholarship on OWI and on second language writing, to help with effective course design, especially in writing programs that enroll a significant number of multilingual writers. *A Position Statement of Principles and Example Effective Practices for OWI* (CCCC OWI Committee, 2013) provided a starting point from specific OWI principles by helping to raise questions particular to multilingual writers:

- What balance should an OWC strike between focusing on writing and providing support for technologies that might be unfamiliar to multilingual writers (OWI Principle 2, p. 11)?
- What unique strategies should be developed to help multilingual writers in an online writing environment (OWI Principle 3, pp. 12-14)?
- What theories of teaching writing should guide the design of a course that enrolls multilingual writers (OWI Principle 4, pp. 14-15)?
- How should faculty be prepared to work with multilingual writers in OWI environments (OWI Principle 7, pp. 17-19)?
- How many students should be allowed to enroll in a single section of an OWC (OWI Principle 9, pp. 20-21) when the course is entirely comprised of multilingual writers? When the course has both multilingual writers and those typically considered native writers?
- For what unique aspects of the technological and pedagogical components of OWI should multilingual writers be prepared (OWI Principle 10, pp. 21-23)?
- How should online communities be developed to foster student success for multilingual writers (OWI Principle 11, pp. 23-24)?
- What additional support—OWL, library, counseling, and the like—should be available for multilingual writers that might be essential to their success in an OWC (OWI Principle 13, pp. 26-28)?
- What selection, training, and ongoing professional development practices for OWL administrators and tutors would support multilingual writers' success (OWI Principle 14, pp. 28-30)?
- What ongoing research should the field pursue to understand the unique needs of multilingual writers in OWI environments (OWI Principle 15, pp. 31-32)?

The remainder of this chapter will respond to these questions by discussing the recommendations of the OWI principles in detail and relating them specifically to a multilingual writing context.

RECOMMENDATIONS FOR INCLUSIVE OWI DESIGN

The principles for OWI in *A Position Statement of Principles and Example Effective Practices for OWI* (CCCC OWI Committee, 2013) are equally applicable for classes enrolling multilingual writers, but a contextualized interpretation of some of the effective practices, paying specific attention to the needs of a linguistically diverse audience, helps guide effective course design. The following sections provide suggestions for effective practices tailored to a multilingual audience that draw on the instructional, faculty, institutional, and research principles provided in the statement.

INSTRUCTIONAL PRINCIPLES

Presenting Content and Choosing Technologies

What balance should an OWC strike between focusing on writing and providing support for technologies that might be unfamiliar to multilingual writers? As OWI Principle 2 reminded teachers, the focus of an OWC needs to remain on writing and not on teaching students to use technology unless a rhetorical knowledge of that technology is an integral part of the course outcomes (see Chapters 1 & 14).

> OWI Principle 2: An online writing course should focus on writing and not on technology orientation or teaching students how to use learning and other technologies (p. 11).

When working with multilingual writers, however, a teacher also must consider that some technologies may be unfamiliar to students, or they may be used to using similar but different technologies that are more popular in other social or cultural contexts than the technology the instructor assumes students would use. In such a case, the instructor has as least two options:

- Insist that the students use a specific technology because it achieves an important learning goal in the course.
- Provide students with the option of using a technology the instructor recommends or using a technology with which they are already familiar.

If the first option is chosen—such as the LMS—the instructor should provide information to help students learn to use the aspects of the technology that are most important for student success. This instruction could be provided in the form of links to videos or online help guides, access to IT support at the institution, or help from the instructor (in the form of instructions or guides created for the course). I recommend searching for resources already available online first before creating new help guides for students; many resources already are available online, but instructors might need to teach students how to find them.

Additionally, instructors should think broadly about the kinds of technologies they might allow students to use in an OWC, so they are using a familiar tool while mastering writing in a new language. For example, Debra Hoven and Agnieszka Palalas (2011) conducted a longitudinal study that investigated the use of mobile technology for language learning with multilingual students. Mobile technologies might provide a familiar anchor for multilingual students for some kinds of tasks, but the instructor must weigh the affordances of specific technologies with the goals of the course and assignment.

Facilitating the Course

What unique strategies should be developed to help multilingual writers in an online writing environment, and what theories of teaching writing should guide the design of a course that enrolls multilingual writers? OWI Principle 3 provided guidance in responding to these questions by reminding teachers that some strategies for OWI are unique to the instructional environment.

OWI Principle 3: Appropriate composition teaching/learning strategies should be developed for the unique features of the online instructional environment (p. 12).

A Position Statement of Principles and Example Effective Practices for OWI (CCCC OWI Committee, 2013) suggested that instruction in writing should be clear, and that oral and/or video supplements also should be provided. When designing an OWC for multilingual writers, providing instruction in multiple modalities is all the more important. As studies by such scholars as Joy Reid (1987) have shown, the learning preferences of multilingual writers can differ significantly from monolingual students and from each other. Providing multiple avenues for understanding instruction, especially when the language of instruction is not the students' first language, makes sense pedagogically. If a student has difficulty understanding written instructions, oral and/or video instruction might provide more clarity.

Furthermore, OWI Principle 4 reminded instructors that established effective pedagogical strategies, while they might need to be adapted for online instruction, are applicable in OWI environments.

OWI Principle 4: Appropriate onsite composition theories, pedagogies, and strategies should be migrated and adapted to the online instructional environment (p. 14).

In addition to considering the theories of teaching writing and teaching in online instructional environments mentioned in *A Position Statement of Principles and Example Effective Practices for OWI* (CCCC OWI Committee, 2013), instructors must consider established effective practices in second language writing studies. The *CCCC Position Statement on Second Language Writing and Writers* (2009) provided several principles for facilitating effective writing courses for multilingual writers. For example, course assignments should avoid relying on specific cultural knowledge to complete the assignment. When possible, an alternative assignment should be given for multilingual writers. When courses meet entirely or partially online, following such principles of course design are even more essential because important face-to-face contextual cues are absent that might indicate to an instructor when more information or an alternate assignment is needed. Multilingual students may not be comfortable from a cultural standpoint in signaling their confusion through direct questions.

FACULTY PRINCIPLES

Preparing Faculty to Work with Multilingual Writers

How should faculty be prepared to work with multilingual writers in OWI environments? OWI Principle 7 explained that instructors in online writing environments must have adequate preparation and professional development opportunities for teaching in online environments:

OWI Principle 7: Writing Program Administrators (WPAs) for OWI programs and their online writing teachers should receive appropriate OWI-focused training, professional development, and assessment for evaluation and promotion purposes (p. 17).

Just as teachers must be prepared to teach in an OWI environment, they also should be prepared to work with multilingual writers in an online setting. WPAs and writing teachers need to have adequate preparation for working with multilingual writers in all instructional environments (Miller-Cochran, 2010; Shuck, 2006). Gail Shuck (2006) described several strategies she used on her campus to strengthen awareness of the needs of multilingual writers across the curriculum. Two of her strategies included publishing multilingual student writing and conducting faculty development workshops for writing instructors across the curriculum (Shuck, 2006). The *CCCC Position Statement on Second Language*

Writing and Writers (2009) suggested the following topics for such faculty development workshops: cultural beliefs about writing, developing effective writing assignments, building on students' competence, and responding to multilingual writing. Workshops addressing these issues and incorporating effective practices for the online writing environment as well would help instructors design courses that are inclusive and accessible.

Course Caps

How many students should be allowed to enroll in a single section of an OWC? OWI Principle 9 provides a clear guideline for course caps in OWCs:

OWI Principle 9: OWCs should be capped responsibly at 20 students per course with 15 being a preferable number (p. 20).

The guideline provided for the OWCs in OWI Principle 9 matches the recommendation of the *CCCC Position Statement on Second Language Writing and Writers* for classes that enroll some multilingual writers in a course that also enrolls students who identify English as their first language (see Chapter 1). The recommendation for courses comprised *only* of multilingual writers, however, is a maximum enrollment of fifteen. Therefore, in a writing program that offers online courses designated only for multilingual writers, the maximum enrollment should be fifteen students. Additionally, institutions that enroll a significant number of multilingual writers in OWCs should consider setting a maximum enrollment of fifteen for all classes, given the preferred recommendation of OWI Principle 9 and the suggestion of the *CCCC Position Statement on Second Language Writing and Writers* (2009).

Fostering Student Success in the Course

For what unique aspects of the technological and pedagogical components of OWI should multilingual writers be prepared? OWI Principle 10 provided guidance for considering what preparation to offer all students who enroll in OWCs:

OWI Principle 10: Students should be prepared by the institution and their teachers for the unique technological and pedagogical components of OWI (p. 21).

In addition to the kinds of preparation described in the effective practices for OWI Principle 10 (see also Chapter 1), multilingual writers might need support to become familiar with technological and pedagogical expectations that are culturally specific. For example, an instructor might need to provide direct instruction with ample examples to students in an OWC about how to address correspondence to the instructor and to other students, what technology should be used to communicate, and what kinds of questions might be asked (and how frequently). Similarly, multilingual students may have different cultural conventions governing their understanding of such issues as plagiarism. While this is not an OWI-specific issue, it is certainly common in online settings where students do much of their research through the Internet. In such cases, explicit instruction that recognizes the cultural differences in notions of plagiarism would be appropriate pedagogy.

Teachers also should use care to construct online communities in a way that helps to foster success for multilingual writers. OWI Principle 11 underscored the value of online communities for student success:

OWI Principle 11: Online writing teachers and their institutions should develop personalized and interpersonal online communities to foster student success (p. 23).

When following the suggestions for effective practices for OWI Principle 11, however, OWI teachers should keep in mind the unique situation of multilingual writers. For example, Effective Practice 11.2 suggested using icebreakers and other writing activities to familiarize the students with the LMS and with each other (p. 23). While icebreakers can be quite effective, many such activities ask students to reveal personal information or be more familiar with colleagues in a class than some multilingual writers are used to or comfortable with. While it is certainly desirable to help acclimate students to expectations in an American academic setting, sensitivity to the students' familiarity with such activities, especially early in the semester, might help instructors choose activities that will not draw on expected common cultural knowledge or put students in an unnecessarily uncomfortable situation. Explaining the purpose of the activities and the importance of building a strong community in a writing course can also help foster multilingual student success.

Similarly, Effective Practice 11.7, which suggested providing informal spaces where students can discuss course content with or without teacher involvement, should be considered differently in a multilingual writing context (p. 24). Depending on the language backgrounds of the students in the course, instructors might consider whether or not they want to offer a space where students may converse in languages other than English to seek clarification or additional help. While scholars have written about the strategic and effective use of first languages in ESL classrooms (Yough & Fang, 2010), little has been written about the use of first languages in multilingual OWCs. This is a specific area of research that would be of use to the field (see Chapter 17).

Institutional Principles

Linking to Outside Help

The institution also bears responsibility to help foster online student success by providing appropriate resources to support their writing. What additional help should be available for multilingual writers that might be essential to their success in an OWI course? OWI Principle 13 provided a starting point for responding to this question:

> **OWI Principle 13: OWI students should be provided support components through online/digital media as a primary resource; they should have access to onsite support components as a secondary set of resources (p. 26).**

Because of the unique challenges that multilingual writers face in OWCs (that is, working to master written English in a course where nearly all of the instruction and communication is in written English), providing online/digital support for these students is all the more important. OWLs with appropriately trained tutors are especially important. As the *CCCC Position Statement on Second Language Writing and Writers* (2009) stated, multilingual writers use writing centers for a variety of reasons. They:

> often visit the writing center seeking support in understanding writing assignments, developing a piece of writing, and to gauge reader response to their writing. They may also seek input on interpreting teacher feedback or assessment and learning more about nuances of the English language. (para. 18)

Making such support available to students in the primary medium of instruction is essential to their success. Additionally, teachers should provide clear explanation to students about what to expect from writing centers/labs in American educational settings. As Shanti Bruce (2004) described, multilingual writers may experience anxiety about using the writing center because they do not know what their expectations should be. Multilingual writers may misunderstand the nature of what writing tutors will do to assist them because of differing cultural expectations, and preparing them for what to expect from a writing tutor can help facilitate a more useful session. Multilingual writers in OWCs should also have access to support in other modalities, especially if the challenge of communicating in written English about their learning of written English is proving difficult.

Preparing OWL Staff to Work with Multilingual Writers

Because the OWL can be so essential to multilingual writers' success, what selection, training, and ongoing professional development practices for OWL administrators and tutors will support these students' success? OWI Principle 14 outlined suggestions for the preparation of OWL administrators and tutors:

> **OWI Principle 14: Online writing lab administrators and tutors should undergo selection, training, and ongoing professional development activities that match the environment in which they will work (p. 28).**

In addition to receiving training for working in an online environment, OWL administrators and tutors should have access to training for working with multilingual writers. Because the OWL environment may involve both asynchronous and synchronous modalities (see Chapter 5) and because the needs of multilingual learners often differ from those of other students, various types of advice can be combined to develop a thorough training program. The *CCCC Position Statement on Second Language Writing and Writers* (2009) suggested hiring tutors with specific preparation in working with multilingual writers. Specific suggestions for tutors from the Statement included:

- Model and discuss effective approaches for working with second language writers in tutor training.
- Make available reference materials specific to language learners such as dictionaries on idiomatic English.
- Hire tutors with specialized knowledge in second language writing.
- Hire multilingual tutors who can provide second language writing students with first-hand writing strategies as well as empathy.

Beth L. Hewett and Robert Lynn (2007) offered context-focused recommendations for OWL tutors who would be meeting with multilingual students. Knowing that the meetings might occur in a text-based medium either asynchronously or synchronously, they recommended first that tutors should be immersed in the medium and modality as trainees because that would give them practice talking through text and in expressing their advice with precise language. Their first rule of thumb was to be correct in one's advice because being wrong or fuzzy about standard English practices would confuse the multilingual writer especially and might cause a lack of trust. The other ten recommendations were:

1. Know how to "give face"
2. Sell yourself as a tutor

3. Make an art of "clock watching"
4. Find out what the student wants
5. Learn how to talk to a particular student
6. Know what you're talking about
7. Proofread (your advice)
8. Contextualize the conference
9. Use clear language
10. Teach by doing

OWL websites also should be designed with consideration for the needs of multilingual writers. Fernando Sánchez (2013) examined the OWL websites of eight different institutions to determine how well they considered multilingual students' needs. His criteria provided a concise set of guidelines for OWL websites:

- *Intercultural Needs*: clear policies on what is expected of students as well as a description of their role in the tutoring session.
- *Writing Resource Needs*: exercises and handouts that deal with the composing process and which are addressed to ESL students.
- *Plagiarism Resource Needs*: a discussion of the cultural differences regarding the borrowing of other people's work and ideas.
- *Readability*: an average word count of 17 words per sentence. (Sanchez, 2013, p. 171)

CONCLUSION AND RECOMMENDATIONS

OWI Principle 15 asked the writing studies field to consider what kinds of ongoing research to pursue related to OWI:

> **OWI Principle 15: OWI/OWL administrators and teachers/ tutors should be committed to ongoing research into their programs and courses as well as the very principles in this document (p. 31).**

The suggestions in this chapter are derived from a combination of effective practices in OWI and in multilingual writing instruction, but very little systematic research has examined the unique environment of the multilingual OWC or OWL. Much work remains to be done. The field needs to discover what happens when teachers follow recommendations that combine the research in these areas. Who is included, and who has been left out? What remains to be considered?

To that end, this chapter recommends the following approaches for working effectively with multilingual writers in an OWC:

- Design the course to foster multilingual student success by suggesting additional resources already available online, providing instruction in multiple modalities, and avoiding course assignments that rely on specific cultural knowledge to complete the assignment.
- Provide support for students for technological and pedagogical expectations that are culturally specific; for example, explain the purpose of interpersonal activities to help foster multilingual student success.
- Prepare WPAs, teachers, OWL administrators, and OWL tutors both for teaching in an OWI environment and for working with multilingual writers.
- Set maximum course caps of fifteen students for OWCs composed *only* of multilingual writers.
- Consider whether or not to offer a space in the course (e.g., a designated discussion forum) where students may converse in languages other than English to seek clarification or additional help.
- Provide online/digital support for students through avenues such as OWLs, and give students a clear explanation about what to expect from writing centers/labs in American educational settings.
- Design and conduct systematic research examining the unique environment of the multilingual OWC to add to the field's knowledge base.

Michael Moore and Greg Kearsley (2004) have used the theory of transactional distance to describe the unique challenge in online teaching and learning of connecting students to the course, teacher, each other, and the content of the class. In an OWC with multilingual writers, language is an additional element that can create distance in the course because teachers often use language to build bridges intended to span the other gaps in transactional distance. Teachers cannot assume a homogenous level of competence in written or spoken English, so they must consider design elements, uses of technology, and pedagogical principles that can facilitate course objectives without further distancing multilingual writers. Ultimately, the effective practices I have described in this chapter are suggestions that could help facilitate the success of a variety of students, not just multilingual writers. This is the heart of UDL and designing for a universe of users; if teachers design for and teach to the possible needs of a variety of students, OWCs (and OWLs) will be more inclusive and accessible for all.

REFERENCES

Boas, Isabella Villas. (2011). Process writing and the internet: Blogs and Ning networks in the classroom. *English Teaching Forum, 2*, 26-33.

Bowie, Jennifer. (2009). Beyond the universal: The universe of users approach to user-centered design. In Susan Miller-Cochran & Rochelle L. Rodrigo (Eds.), *Rhetorically rethinking usability: Theories, practices, and methodologies* (pp. 135-163). Cresskill, NJ: Hampton Press.

Bruce, Shanti. (2004). Getting started. In Shanti Bruce & Bruce Rafoth (Eds.), *ESL writers: A guide for writing center tutors* (pp. 30-38). Portsmouth, NH: Boynton/Cook.

Conference on College Composition and Communication. (2009). *CCCC statement on second language writing and writers.* Retrieved from http://www.ncte.org/cccc/resources/positions/secondlangwriting

CCCC OWI Committee for Effective Practices in Online Writing Instruction. (2013). *A position statement of principles and effective practices for online writing instruction (OWI).* Retrieved from http://www.ncte.org/cccc/resources/positions/owiprinciples

DePew, Kevin Eric. (2011). Social media at academia's periphery: Studying multilingual developmental writers' Facebook composing strategies. *Reading Matrix: An International Online Journal, 11*(1), 54-75.

DePew, Kevin Eric & Miller-Cochran, Susan K. (2009). Social networking in a second language: Engaging multiple literate practices through identity composition. In Michelle Cox, Jay Jordan, Christina Ortmeier-Hooper, & Gwen Grey Schwartz (Eds.), *Inventing identities in second language writing* (pp. 273-295). Urbana, IL: National Council of Teachers of English.

Friedrich, Patricia. (2006). Assessing the needs of linguistically diverse first-year students: Bringing together and telling apart international ESL, resident ESL and monolingual basic writers. *Writing Program Administration, 30*(1.2), 15-35.

Hewett, Beth L. & Lynn, Robert. (2007). Training ESOL instructors and tutors for online conferencing. *The Writing Instructor.* Retrieved from http://www.writinginstructor.com/esol

Hoven, Debra & Palalas, Agnieszka. (2011). (Re)conceptualizing design approaches for mobile language learning. *CALICO Journal, 28*(3), 699-720.

Long, Gary L., Vignare, Karen, Rappold, Raychel P., & Mallory, Jim. (2007). Access to communication for deaf, hard-of-gearing and ESL students in blended learning courses. *International Review of Research in Open and Distance Learning, 8*(3), 1-13.

Matsuda, Paul K. (2006). The myth of linguistic homogeneity in US college composition. *College English, 68*(6), 637-651.

Miller-Cochran, Susan K. (2010). Language diversity and the responsibility of the WPA. In Bruce Horner, Min-Zahn Lu, & Paul Kei Matsuda (Eds.), *Cross-language relations in composition* (pp. 212-220). Carbondale, IL: Southern Illinois University Press.

Moore, Michael G. & Kearsley, Greg. (2004). *Distance education: A systems view* (2nd ed.). Boston: Wadsworth Publishing.

Ortmeier-Hooper, Christina. (2008). "English may be my second language, but I'm not 'ESL.'" *College Composition and Communication, 59*(3), 389-419.

Reid, Joy. (1987). The learning style preferences of ESL students. *TESOL Quarterly, 21*(1), 88-112.

Ruecker, Todd. (2011). Improving the placement of L2 writers: The students' perspective. *Writing Program Administration, 35*(1), 92-118.

Sánchez, Fernando. (2013). Creating accessible spaces for ESL students online. *Writing Program Administration, 37*(1), 161-185.

Shih, Ru-Chu. (2011). Can Web 2.0 technology assist college students in learning English writing? Integrating "Facebook" and peer assessment with blended learning. *Australasian Journal of Educational Technology, 27*(5), 829-845.

Shuck, Gail. (2006). Combating monolingualism: A novice administrator's challenge. *Writing Program Administration, 30*(1.2), 59-82.

Yough, Michael S. & Fang, Ming. (2010). Keeping native languages in ESL class: Accounting for the role beliefs play toward mastery. *Mid-Western Educational Researcher, 23*(2), 27-32.

CHAPTER 10

NONTRADITIONAL STUDENT ACCESS TO OWI

Michael W. Gos
Lee College

This chapter examines difficulties faced by nontraditional students when negotiating online learning in general and OWCs as a particular example of their access challenges. It begins with an identification of populations considered nontraditional and underserved in the realm of online, as opposed to onsite, education. It then examines many of the issues that stand in the way of success for members of these groups as they attempt online learning and OWI particularly. Specific recommendations for OWI are included in the conclusion.

Keywords: African-American, incarcerated, military, older adults, prisons, remotely rural, urban, working class

The CCCC OWI Committee's OWI principles began with what the committee has argued is the overarching principle for effective OWI. OWI Principle 1 reads: "Online writing instruction should be universally inclusive and accessible" (2013, p. 7). This recommendation should be considered at every step of WPA and OWI course planning and implementation processes, as indicated in Chapters 1 and 8.

Access for OWI is not universal today and, even in cases where OWCs are more or less accessible to students, there are factors that affect students' abilities to negotiate them. This lack of inclusiveness tends to be acutely experienced by nontraditional students. This chapter examines several student cohorts generally considered nontraditional and underserved—in that they are not the typical, age 24 and younger, residential students—and it examines the issues they face when negotiating online learning generally and an OWC particularly.

In July, 1995, the National Telecommunications & Information Administration (a division of the Department of Commerce) began a series of reports about what they called the "Have-Nots" with respect to technology access in America. A later report in that series introduced the term "digital divide" (US Department of Commerce, 1998). The term refers to the differences in digital tools and

Internet access among various groups in American society. These reports examined racial, economic, geographic, and educational cohorts and considered their access to technology with respect to each other and to their own earlier status as presented in the previous reports (US Department of Commerce, 1995, 1998, 1999, 2004). The reports noted that young, affluent, white, educated, and especially urban and suburban students were more likely to have access to Internet technology than older, black, Hispanic, Asian, and rural students. Carolyn Haythornthwaite (2007) also found young, urban, suburban, Asian and white users with higher education and income levels to be more likely to be online than black, Hispanic, rural, low-education, or low-income students.

OWI would seem to be a particularly promising venue for serving some difficult-to-reach audiences. Students located so far away from a college center that commuting is impossible would appear to be a perfect fit for a fully online class. Active-duty military and their families often have schedules and sudden deployments that make an onsite writing course impossible. Prison inmates also seem to be a promising audience for OWCs because of the cost and difficulties of setting up onsite programs within the prison itself. Yet, for a variety of reasons, these and other groups like them tend to be underserved by online college and university writing programs.

This chapter first considers where students can access computers, digital technologies, and the Internet generally. Then, it examines the digital divide issue as faced by several nontraditional student groups as they attempt to negotiate OWCs. It concentrates on the following groups:

- Working-class students
- Older adult students
- Remotely rural students
- Urban students
- Military learners: Veteran and active-duty students
- Incarcerated students

While some of the issues faced by students in any one of the above groups tend to be common for all, a few are unique to one cohort. As such, this chapter examines each of the groups separately.

ACCESS AND THE PLIGHT OF THE UNDERSERVED

Access to computers, digital technologies, and the Internet for OWI normally is achieved through one or more of three sources: the home, school, or one's workplace. If none of those sources is available, students often are left to use the local public library as their only resort for finding the tools necessary for access to OWCs.

The first source of computer use—the home—is one that many WPAs and OWI teachers take for granted. Family income is a factor in computer ownership; the US Department of Commerce found that in 2003 just under 50% of the families in the $25,000 to $35,000 income range were Internet users as opposed to nearly 83 percent of those earning $75,000 and above. For very low-income people (under $15,000 a year), just over 31% had access to the Internet at home (Lamb, 2005). For the more desirable high-speed broadband use that is almost a necessity with LMS software, the numbers are 13.4% for the lower income group versus 45.4% for the over $75,000 group (US Department of Commerce, 2004).

In recent years, the situation has not changed significantly. In 2013, children from families with incomes over $75,000 were projected to be twice as likely to have computer access in the home as very low-income families. The numbers for Internet access are even more striking. Ninety three percent of upper-income families were projected to have Internet access versus only 29% for very low-income families. For half of the low and very low-income families, then, access to the Internet typically can only be had at school, the public library, or work (Lamb, 2005).

But even the ability to access the Internet at home is not necessarily sufficient for access to online courses. Of the 50% of people earning under $35,000 a year who do have computer access in the home, many cannot afford to purchase the newer computers needed to remain compatible with current technology and learning strategies (Haythornthwaite, 2007). As educational institutions update their technology, many of the students in online classes are left behind. For example, students with computers without speakers are unable to hear lectures and other audio tools such as Vokis, the small avatars that show on screen and lip-sync messages recorded by the professor. Such students are not able to access any audio-based or audio/video-based asynchronous or synchronous OWI (Elliot, Haggerty, Foster, & Spak, 2008), as outlined in Chapters 2, 3, and 4. For all practical purposes, then, many students with computers and Internet access at home still lack the ability to fully use the Internet or their digital technologies for writing class purposes.

A second source for computer technology that students may access is in the school environment. For many students, their first exposure to computers comes in the classroom. Let us begin with an examination of elementary and secondary schools. A Department of Education study (2010) completed in 2009 found that 97% of teachers had one or more computers located in their classroom every day. Of those, Internet access was available for 93%. This high percentage would suggest that most young students do, indeed, have at least limited access to computers and the Internet as a part of their lower school education process. A limiting factor might be the student-to-computer ratio. The same report identified that ratio as 5.3 students per computer. This ratio indicates that while there is availability, there must be some sharing if all students are to have access. That sharing decreases the likelihood that on any given day all students who need computer and Internet access will have it.

But computers are only helpful if they actually are used. In the same Department of Education study (2010), teachers reported that they or their students used computers in the classroom during instructional time "often" (40%) or "sometimes" (29%). That leaves 31% of students with little access for whatever reasons. In addition to the computers actually located in the classroom, some teachers reported that they or their students used computers in other locations in the school during instructional time "often" (29%) or "sometimes" (43%). Therefore, in the elementary and secondary school environments, most students appear to have computers and the Internet in their classroom environment. Access to the machines, however, is limited by the frequency of teacher use and the ratio of students to computers. And access to the technology is only part of the equation. To have full access to online work, students need to have a degree of experience with and preparation in the use of such tools.

The numbers cited above for current student usage of computers in school seem hopeful for OWI. However, these students are growing up with greater access to digital technologies than currently underserved populations of nontraditional students in postsecondary OWCs. The college situation and (hopefully) access to common technologies of today's average fifth or tenth graders will differ from a contemporary 34-year old worker who returns to college to get a degree that may help her to keep a job, become promoted, or find a new position in a poor economy. To the end of using computers for higher education and OWI, it is helpful to understand that students with less preparation for using computers educationally may have different access challenges once they begin attending college.[1] In some hybrid settings and in most fully online settings, students will need to complete much of their online writing work somewhere other than the actual classroom. Asynchronous courses typically require students to do most or all of their writing on their own. Lack of frequent opportunities to use the computer educationally in postsecondary work, in addition to the potential lack of a home computer—or, at least, an up-to-date computer—can hamper students significantly in feeling comfortable with the levels of work they need to address online for a writing course. To this end, OWI Principle 10 was written to promote adequate preparation for students who take OWI and to prepare them for its unique technological and pedagogical components, thereby increasing students' opportunities to succeed and thrive in the digital setting (pp. 21-22). Even if they have computer access at home, hybrid and fully online writing students will need to seek outside access and assistance.

Finally, using the computer at work, of course, depends entirely on whether one's job calls for computer-based writing. For the most part, service-industry jobs require little-to-no composition on the computer, leaning instead on completing forms and addressing numbers. Positions where written reports and other such communications tend to be in the industries that pay a higher wage.

What happens if someone has no computer access at home, school, or work? Denise Narcisse (2010) reported that nearly 19 million of the US national poor rely on public library computers as their sole source for online work (2010). But public library access, even when available, generally is limited. Many libraries limit screen time, often to 30 minutes particularly when there is a line of potential users. Postsecondary school libraries and computer labs also have time and other use limits; however, the nontraditional student who takes an OWC often does so for geographical and time reasons, which in and of themselves limit students' abilities to use their school's libraries and labs. These time limitations alone create an insufficient scenario for any serious work in an OWC, but they are especially problematic in the writing class where prewriting assignments and drafts must be written, submitted, and revised in response to professors' comments. And they are particularly problematic when students have to rely on access to these technologies to synchronously participate in a class. Some libraries censor Internet sites that might be considered unacceptable for public viewing (Narcisse, 2010), which can limit certain types of research. In addition, most libraries impose printing restrictions or charge for hardcopy printing. Many students still prefer to revise on printed copy, which is a recommended strategy for students with a variety of reading and learning styles (Hewett, 2015a). When printing is banned for any reason, these students are disadvantaged. For students dependent on a library for their computer access, although some access exists, it is limited and may contribute to student frustration, attrition, and failure.

These situations have long-term effects. Samantha Blackmon (2003) found that some underserved students developed attitude issues, thinking there was some kind of a conspiracy that keeps them marginalized by denying them full access to technology. In addition to feeling disadvantaged because of their socio-economic status, they had little or no educational interaction with the technology that would be critical to success in OWCs. Certainly, with lots of time, effort, and practice, once they are able to gain full access to digital technologies (e.g., through work or college computers), low-end users and late adopters might be able to catch up with other, more privileged students regarding experience and educational uses of the technologies. Nonetheless, Haythornthwaite (2007) found that even if late adopters do catch up, the effort to do so causes unequal participation because these students continue to lag behind at the introduction of each new innovation. This difficulty is likely to be the case for working-class students and for less educated and rural people as well.

WORKING-CLASS STUDENTS

Working-class students, for the purposes of this chapter, are defined as those with lower than middle-level incomes, working primarily in service industries, receiving hourly wages, having potentially floating hours, and/or those who work more than one job to stay afloat. Other scenarios that keep these students from economic fluidity or that have not required consistent uses of writing in their work may apply. For these students, some experts have suggested that an OWC—particularly a fully online OWC—may not be their best choice for college writing courses.

Andrew Cavanaugh[2] is Director of Writing for the University of Maryland University College (UMUC), the largest public university in the country, with over 92,000 students worldwide. UMUC also is one of the largest providers of online education in the world with students in 50 states and 22 countries; it has long had a relationship with military organizations. According to Cavenaugh, students who lack a solid background in Internet and computer use have a special need for feedback from the professor in order to be successful. The asynchronous online environment used in many OWI programs makes immediate or regular individualized response to students more difficult than in an onsite or hybrid setting. Often, there are no set office hours during which a distance-based student can meet with the professor through synchronous chat or over a voice medium. End-of-class discussions do not occur in such settings, although hybrid courses make meeting onsite with teachers possible in some configurations (see Chapter 3). In essence, students who may need the most help with technological *and* educational issues are taking a class in the modality and medium least conducive to receiving the needed help (A. Cavanaugh, personal communication, December 7, 2012). Mark Parker, also from UMUC, noted that working-class students largely are unfamiliar with student life in general, right down to simple details such as the definition of plagiarism (M. Parker, personal communication, December 7, 2012). They may never have been on a college campus, are not as involved with the campus activities, and often have families who need their attention when they are not working or taking college courses (Hewett, 2015a). Added to such pressures, the geographic separation from the professor caused by the online environment makes it more difficult for these students to even be aware of the things they do not know about negotiating college. To alleviate this kind of difficulty, Parker recommended that such students should take a "How to be a College Student" type of course (M. Parker, personal communication, December 7, 2012).

Additionally, among other challenges for working-class students, financial viability remains an issue as it connects closely to their success. Allison Butler, also of UMUC, noted that students often are surprised at how difficult college classes are after coming out of high school or working for years, and it takes a while to realize that they are in trouble. Often, they withdraw late from a course and, as a result, find that they owe money to the financial aid program (A. Butler, personal communication, December 7, 2012). As difficult as deciding to return to school may have been to make, events such as failure, fear of failure, or a need to repay a grant because of failure easily can kill a student's desire to continue in school and obtain a college degree.

Providing Accessible OWI for Working-Class Students

The main issues facing working-class students regard Internet access, having current and advanced digital technology, and having sufficient experience to perform at a level where the technology does not become a large part of the learning required for a class. One of the benefits of teaching writing online is the ability to interact with students multiple times a day, seven days a week—provided the students also connect with the teacher and the teacher is willing to make such frequent connections. In my own classes, I receive drafts of planning assignments or sections of large reports often two and occasionally three times a day. A student lacking the access or ability for this frequency of communication with the professor is marginalized from the beginning. In order to participate fully in OWCs, students need to have access to a computer with an Internet connection, the software necessary to open downloaded files, and the expertise to accomplish the necessary tasks of using the LMS and the required software. With these capabilities, they can devote their efforts to the subject matter and not the technology. Without them, educational time is wasted by the technological learning curve, and students become frustrated.

When students work fully online from a geographic distance, the issue of access to the Internet is beyond the control of the professor, the course developer, or the institution itself. UMUC, for example, does not seek to attract students without Internet access for their online courses, offering instead some onsite courses (A. Cavanaugh, personal communication, December 7, 2012). They believe any change in Internet accessibility as a basic requisite for the course will have to be initiated by the government; at the time that students sign up for the course, they should have the necessary connection to do the work. This is an issue of basic access that seems to be particular to students who take fully online courses (as opposed to hybrid courses), where they choose not to (or cannot) use the institution's computer labs and library offerings. This issue is different from access problems discussed in Chapter 8 because fully online students who choose to take a distance-based course would seem to be acknowledging that they can provide their own initial Internet connection to the course if geographically unable to make use of the institution's affordances.

For those who do have Internet access but at a reduced level (e.g., bandwidth limitations or outdated or missing software), other problems arise. Lower bandwidth means that every download takes longer and some files cannot be transferred. Students with limited bandwidth tend to have more challenges when downloading images and audio/video files. Additionally, when students lack a particular piece of software needed to view the downloaded file (e.g., PowerPoint), they also have access issues to the course. Recall that these additional files sometimes are necessary for learning style accessibility per Chapters 1 and 8 even while their use can create access problems for students with particular disabilities. These tend to be problems of socioeconomic access, to which OWI Principle 1 also speaks (pp. 7-11). Per the access guidance suggested in Chapters 1 and 8, OWI teachers can alleviate some of this problem by careful consideration of materials that students genuinely need to download, read, and use for the course.

There are ways to accommodate these students to some degree. In OWCs at my institution (Lee College in Baytown, Texas), for example, module lessons are built in PowerPoint. Upon discovering that many students lacked the Microsoft Office Suite for their home computers, the writing faculty began the practice of routinely converting PowerPoint files to PDF files that open easily in the LMS window. This accommodation accomplishes two things. First, no downloading of files is needed, and all parts of the course stay on the institution's server. Students with reduced bandwidth do not have to wait a long time. Second, students have access to the lesson whether or not they have the software of origination on their computers. By making such simple changes and avoiding the use of more "exotic" bells and whistles such as audio files and Vokis, educators can guarantee that students are not missing integral parts of a class because they lack the technology necessary to access the course material. Relatively speaking, such low band-width documents also tend to be accessible to the users of assistive and adaptive technologies.

Even moderate accommodations of this type are not without drawbacks, however. Once converted to PDF files, slideware files lose the ability to carry voice, external links, and information entry in segments (e.g., line-by-line text entry and pop-up arrows). Not only are some of the flashy attention-grabbers gone, but the pedagogy of the presentation itself is weakened by the necessity of revealing an entire screen's material at once instead of allowing the presentation of a line-by-line explanation or argument.

Accommodating the low-end user also works against some of the key benefits associated with online learning such as interactivity with peers, real-time exchanges, and sophisticated training presentations (Haythornthwaite, 2007). Group discussions through synchronous text-based chats are difficult to follow when a narrow bandwidth shows the student a conversation ten lines behind where it is in real time (and where it is seen by classmates). Any entries posted will appear as non-sequiturs because they refer to sections of the discussion that took place a minute or more before the comment appears on the screen. Teachers may want their students to develop the ability to communicate in real time, but all too often, the technology available to students does not permit that, and real-time communication requires thoughtful decisions about when to use the synchronous and asynchronous modalities. Unfortunately, as those educators advance in technology uses, the lower-income students who lack that technology fall further behind. Every upgrade in equipment, requirements, or technology made at the college end is an added barrier to economically disadvantaged students (Haythornthwaite, 2007).

Finally, there is the issue of limited experience. In every aspect of college life, working-class students begin with far less experience than their managerial-professional class colleagues (Gos, 1996), and the types of experiences they may have (e.g., skills and drills exercises versus lengthy writing opportunities), do not prepare them for the kinds of writing and communicating online (Kynard, 2007) that contemporary rhetoric and composition courses attempt to provide through OWI. The fact that students struggle when facing an OWC is to be expected given the common access issues and potentially insufficient lower school training discussed above.

A problem is created when a working-class student without the ability and experience to operate the technology at a basic level matriculates into an OWC. Either the student is marginalized from the beginning, or the professor must devote learning time to technology education. OWI Principle 2 stated, "An online writing course should focus on writing and not on technology orientation or teaching students how to use learning and other technologies" (p. 11) It is important to understand that this guideline was written (1) to keep the focus on writing over technology in a writing-based course and (2) to free teachers from the belief that their job is to teach new technologies in lieu of writing, as discussed in Chapter 1. Students should receive technology *and* writing-focused training regarding using that technology, however. OWI Principle 10 stated, "Students should be prepared by the institution and their teachers for the unique technological and pedagogical components of OWI" (p. 21). What this means is that even underprepared and previously underserved students with limited economic resources should be given appropriate orientation to OWI and the LMS used in such courses.

For both hybrid and fully online students, such preparation might include an institutionally developed video that demonstrates the affordances of and how to use the LMS as well as that details some of the responsibilities of an online teacher and successful online student. Courses that provide basic computer training and LMS orientation are commonly available from colleges that offer online programs. In many cases, the course will be available both onsite and online. For online orientation courses, students must have enough ability to access an online training package before they can begin learning how to negotiate an online class, which can become the first problem that some students find in their attempts to take an online course. Another option used by many institutions is to require an onsite, initial class session where students meet with the professor to learn about the course and about how to negotiate the LMS. While this type of orientation can be helpful for those who can attend, some of the groups discussed in this chapter—particularly the remotely rural, the deployed military, and prisoners—would find these sessions onerous or impossible to attend.

From the pedagogical perspective, OWI teachers should include some orientation exercises that acquaint students with the basics of the LMS features they will use in support of the course, what writing online means, what successful discussion posts look like (see Chapter 4), as well as how to find and use the OWL (see Chapter 5). In addition to such orientating exercises, there are things of a "first-aid" nature that can be implemented to help students when they reach an obstacle or to assist in preparing themselves for the experience of an OWC. In a discussion about writing centers, Muriel Harris and Michael Pemberton (1995) described student needs for success in accessing and using online writing labs. Each of the items they identify also would help working-class students negotiate OWCs. They list the following student needs that remain important to address:

- Easy access to computer labs
- Training or short courses
- College-provided student computer accounts
- A computer center aggressive in assisting students to become computer literate

To this end, while fully online students may not have access to the campus computer labs, institutions should minimally provide training, online student accounts for accessing the OWL, libraries, and counseling resources (as indicated in OWI Principle 13), and 24/7 computing assistance to enable online students to be independent and efficient in their OWCs.

For a less abrupt transition to OWCs, working-class students might consider taking hybrid classes first. Cavanaugh indicated that some students like this option because they still receive the face-to-face contact with which they are comfortable. Parker, however, noted that any abrupt jumps between communication and learning styles in the two environments of onsite and online meetings may make the hybrid option less attractive (A. Cavanaugh & M. Parker, personal communication, December 7, 2012). I see both things happening in my hybrid courses. In a first-year-level technical writing course that I teach as a hybrid, we meet strictly in the classroom for the first four weeks, an option discussed in Chapter 3. We then meet in the classroom about once a week for the next five or six weeks and do the remainder of the work online. Around the tenth week, I give students the option of finishing the course exclusively online or continuing to meet once a week. The course meets at night and virtually all of the students come to class after a full-days' work in the local oil refineries and chemical plants. One would think they would be vehement about finishing the semester online, but that has never been the case. The vote is always close and on one occasion, they voted to continue the onsite sessions throughout the remainder of the semester. This experience reminds educators of students' differing learning styles and preferences as well as the needs that some students have for familiar interaction (i.e., face-to-face) with instructors.

As faculty, we have little control over student accessibility in terms of their socioeconomic means. However, we should take into consideration and make accommodations for those with reduced computing and Internet capabilities. While faculty cannot provide students with initial Internet access, we can address their limited accessibilities with reasonable accommodations. For students with limited accessibility, software, and experience, WPAs and OWI course designers should avoid requiring downloads of lengthy files, images, and sound and video files when possible. Providing these on the LMS sometimes addresses this problem. Such accommodations can make it easier for students to access the course.

OLDER ADULT STUDENTS

While having a more general meaning today, the term "nontraditional student" was first used as a reference to students over the age of 24 years. This section addresses access needs of students who fall into the above 24-years range and sometimes are much older. These adult learners now account for nearly 40% of the student body at US colleges and universities (American Council on Education, 2013). A factor that separates some members of this group from others is whether or not they are in the work force.

A Department of Commerce (2004) study found that employed adults had a much greater likelihood of having computer technology and Internet access than those who were unemployed. Table 10.1 presents statistics for persons not having access to Internet use:

Table 10.1. Percent lacking Internet access (by age cohort)

Age	In Labor Force	Not in Labor Force
25-49	28.3	50.3
50+	35.6	72.4

Source: (US Department of Commerce, 2004)

In 2011, there remained such a disparity: "People with low incomes, disabilities, seniors, minorities, the less-educated, non-family households, and the non-employed tend to lag behind other groups in home broadband use" (Fact Sheet, 2011).

A lack of Internet access generally translates to a lack of Internet skills. Even when contemporary students are using mobile devices to access the Internet, this access, as explained in Chapter 16, is often different. When access is not there, the basic skills of using the Internet are not developed. If at some later date the adult learner gains access, he begins at a lower skill level than his colleagues. As a result, like the working-class students discussed above, those without access prior to enrolling in college courses may lag behind their classmates long after they have gained full Internet access. As time goes on and new technologies are introduced, those students tend to remain behind (Haythornthwaite, 2007). Students who are trying to do well in an OWC will face serious difficulties if the bulk of study time is spent negotiating the technology.

While employment is a great divider in terms of Internet access and experience, there are difficulties beyond access that seem to be ubiquitous across the older student cohort. One of those, for students who are in middle age, is sensory decline. Aging students often face deteriorating visual and auditory sensitivity as well as the ability to make fine motor movements (Morgan & Morgan, 2007). Some cognitive shifts in memory and determining priorities also may occur. Such decline may result in slower typing and computing, as well as a possible need for reminders about how to access particular parts of the LMS, for example. Building redundancy into the course (per Chapter 4 & 8's recommendations) becomes especially important with these kinds of concerns.

Another issue regarding an older student cohort—outside of technology—is that OWI teachers may need to address the affect connected with the lives students have led prior to coming to our classes. While writing instructors tend to assume that copious life experience is a positive thing for a student in a writing course, it is not always the case that such life experiences have been positive for the students. It is true that traditionally aged students are younger with limited life experience beyond the family to bring to the writing course and that adult learners have been out in the world, in work, in society, and bring with them a richness of experience. Yet, some of that experience can be rather unpleasant, even detrimental to their lives, leading them to see themselves negatively in ways that affect their self-image as student writers. Kristen Welch of Southern Christian University, a small university in central Oklahoma, talked about a few of her older students:

> Some are just out of prison, others have small kids at home, others work full time, some are elderly or disabled. One was a recovering alcoholic. One main challenge is to conquer the negative self-talk that a life of very real failures has brought. One woman wrote her essay about her kids being taken by CPS, for example. (K. Welch, personal communication, November 15, 2012)

While not particular to OWI but an issue that certainly affects students who take hybrid and fully online courses, another effect of being a student over the age of 24 is a time gap between formal writing course experiences. As a result of being years away from their most recent formal English class, many older students find themselves playing catch-up, not only in the areas of critical thinking and idea development, but even in the areas of grammar and syntax. Welch also reported:

> Our biggest challenge has been providing a mix of developmental writing (review of capitalization, using suffixes for words, subject-verb agreement, etc.) and regular English 101 writing assignments. Many of our students come in and don't know the rules for writing a sentence with appropriate punctuation. (K. Welch, personal communication. November 15, 2012)

As a result, she and her colleagues are required to spend a good deal of course time reviewing basic writing skills before beginning the business of a first-year writing (FYW) class (K. Welch, personal communication. November 15, 2012).

Pertinent to OWI and learning through online settings, older adult students may face challenges in terms of their time available for class work. Even though traditional, residential students may work only part-time if at all, many commuter students—which includes some younger ones as well as most older students—are far more likely to work full-time and have other external issues such as family and social activities that make significant claims on their time. These external influences often cause delays in completing assignments, both major (i.e., essay drafts and final papers) and minor (i.e., participation in online discussions). Indeed, online discussions—while asynchronous and often completed over the course of a week or more—require that students log into the system frequently to monitor the discussion and add their comments. Tardiness in posting assignments starts a chain of late activities that often lead to disaster in terms of the student's writing progress and eventual grades. In a writing course, where a series of planning exercises often occur before a draft is attempted, delays in turning in assignments build cumulatively to hinder the students' chances for success and, thus, they deplete the learners' motivation (Blair & Hoy, 2006). Such loss of motivation can lead to the dropping of classes, failure, and/or leaving school altogether.

However, countering all of these negative external factors is the fact that older students tend to adapt more readily to online courses than their younger classmates even though they may do less well than traditional students in face-to-face classes (Community College Research Center, 2013). They also are more likely to be highly motivated, in part because they understand the importance of what they are learning and are making deliberate choices to be in higher education classes. Anecdotal experience suggests that older adult students are ready to learn to write well because they see that life circumstances require that skill. They are especially motivated when the subject matter they are attempting to master will help them solve life problems. Adult learners tend to prefer a problem-solving approach to learning and learn best when materials are presented in a real-life context (Knowles, Holton, & Swanson, 1998) although they also may demonstrate some more adolescent-like needs. These needs would include seeking full independence in choosing research areas while expressing dependence on teachers for showing them step-by-step how to initiate such research, or claiming that the teacher's (sometimes negative) opinion of their writing is not meaningful while also desiring high grades that validate their efforts (Hewett, 2015a). In addition, older adult students tend to prefer learner-centered instruction (McDonald & Gibson, 1998). When the instructor tries teamwork or collaborative learning, these students may demonstrate discomfort. Nonetheless, OWI instructors often are emotionally committed to group work and experience difficulty taking into account these individual learning preferences (Western, 1999).

PROVIDING ACCESSIBLE OWI FOR OLDER ADULT STUDENTS

Like working-class students who are new to the college environment, older adults also often come to higher education with a lack of knowledge on how to take online classes. They sometimes are surprised at how fast things happen. As a result, they may choose several especially time-consuming courses for one semester or may schedule more classes overall than they can handle with their other life responsibilities (A. Cavanaugh, personal communication, December 7, 2012). One helpful policy to help such students online is to require students to contact the professor of an OWC before enrolling. Each time I receive a student request for information or permission to enroll, I send out a copy of a welcome memo that tells them about the course, the textbooks needed, and most important, the time requirements. I find that students may be shocked to learn that the college has an expectation of two minimum hours of outside work for every class hour they take. For OWI students, I make this clearer by converting that formula to the number of hours they are expected to put into the class each week and the ways they might be expected to use this time (e.g., discussion posts, content reading, research, draft writing, and the like). This information is especially helpful in short—in our case, five-week—summer sessions where students need to plan up to 30 hours' work per week for a three-semester credit hour writing course. While having this truth up front sometimes discourages enrollment, it is better for students to make an informed decision about how they will need to function in an OWC than to overcommit, become discouraged, and drop the course—or worse—end their college aspirations entirely because of a sense of inability or failure.

Ideas that professors are emotionally attached to often turn out to be less-than-ideal for student learning in OWI. With older adults, the most important of these may be collaborative work. While faculty have a litany of reasons why collaboration is problematic (e.g., good students carry the poor or dropouts leave groups shorthanded), writing professors still favor collaboration as a key means of teaching. The arguments for group work range from the idea that collaboration often is required at work to a desire to establish a sense of community in the class. There have also been studies that show positive learning results from the practice. Indeed, the online environment would seem to be created perfectly for such collaboration as peer group work and feedback, as well as for collaboratively written projects. But there also are studies that indicate collaboration may be a poor learning tool for older adult learners. One such study was done by Kristine Blair and Cheryl Hoy (2006). They found that adult learners bring a mass of experience, but with it comes a diversity of external influences (e.g., work, family, other courses) that make any kind of scheduled work times problematic. They argued that such exigencies create a need for teaching and learning in private, rather than community spaces (see also Hewett, 2015a). While Blair and Hoy (2006) claimed that adults learn better in more individualized spaces, they indicated that, at the very least, adult students thrive as well in private spaces as in public or community environments. Instead of requiring collaborative activities and group work, they recommended that teachers extend their more public concept of community to a one-to-one relationship (i.e., student-to-student and student-to-teacher) to better acknowledge the students' need for personal, private interaction. In fact, Blair and Hoy found that traditional email between the student and professor and among students themselves to be among the most powerful tools in learning.

One place where group work might prove to be useful for adult learners in OWI is in dealing with the negative life experiences they sometimes carry. Returning to Welch's (2013) description of older adult students as having had difficult life challenges in terms of disability, age, addictions, and even prior incarceration, she found that such issues can be addressed through the use of online discussion boards as a "vent" for frustrations as well as a means to practice writing and responding to others who write. Of course, it is crucial to model different ways for students to disclose their past challenges and to encourage them to think specifically about what they want to disclose in public online spaces and why. One reason that writing teachers may encourage thoughtful self-disclosure involves the powerful writing that can emerge when students take such work begun in the public online space and revise it into more formal writing assignments.

In addition to life experiences, the amount of time since their last writing course is often an issue for adult learners. This issue generally shows itself in sentence-level problems that normally are addressed in developmental English courses. Most courses at the FYW level and above are not geared to teach grammar and punctuation, which especially can be an issue when students opt to take a short online course in a summer or mini-session. To address this issue, Southern Christian University has changed their shorter five-week course to a ten-week course, enabling faculty to incorporate aspects of developmental English into the curriculum and to better accommodate the learning styles of adults (K. Welch, personal communication, November 28, 2012). Also these students may not acknowledge the types of multimodal writing assignments (see Chapter 15) taught in some OWCs as "writing" (see also Hewett, 2015a).

Finally, there is the issue of sensory decline. It is easy to make light of an issue like this, but it needs to be taken as seriously as any other learning challenge or physical disability. The difference with many disabilities is that such sensory decline happens, or will happen, to all of us. For example, before I can read a student draft, I need to use Microsoft Word's zoom feature to increase the viewing size to 150%. While I often can read the body text at the normal size, the labels on the axes of student graphs and the fine print on tables often make those parts of students' technical reports just a blur at the normal viewing level. When developing courses, it is important to take eyesight and hearing difficulties into consideration. Konrad Morgan and Madeline Morgan (2007) recommended making provisions for adult students like using larger typefaces, easy-to-read fonts, and larger interaction spaces (e.g., comments boxes). Volume on audio files should be at the maximum level when recording or the student should be able to increase the volume as needed. The question becomes: When is sensory decline the responsibility of the instructor and when does it lie elsewhere? As Chapters 1 and 8 clearly indicate, the needs of students with disabilities regarding sight and sound should be addressed as part of the institution's responsibility to meet ADA guidelines. But when the circumstance is a decline, and not a full-fledged disability, the course designer/instructor can do much to alleviate students' problems and facilitate access because the disability laws in general expect all institutions of higher education to be ready to accommodate students with a variety of abilities and disabilities. Meeting these elderly students' needs will only move colleges closer to such readiness.

REMOTELY RURAL STUDENTS

If there is any student cohort that seems perfectly suited to online learning, it is the remotely rural. For students living far away from a college campus, the vast physical distance required for a commute is an obstacle in the best of weather. Add ice, snow, whiteout conditions, or heavy rain, and the trip can become impossible. In some parts of the United States, it can be well over 100 miles to the nearest college or university. Online learning appears to be the logical remedy for this situation; yet, in reality, remotely rural students may be just the group that is most disadvantaged when it comes to OWC access.

The study by *A Nation Online* (2004) considered the entire nation and found that, while dial-up still accounted for the majority of Internet connections, in urban areas the higher speed connections were beginning to take over. Not so in rural areas. Table 10.2 presents the contrast in Internet connections between rural and urban areas.

Table 10.2. Percent of households with Internet connection types

Connection Type	Rural	Urban
Broadband	24.7	40.4
Cable Modem	14.3	22.6
DSL	9.2	17.2
Dial-up	74.7	58.9

Source: A Nation Online (2004)

It is important to understand that the category is "rural," not "remotely rural" in this study. If the well-served rural areas were removed from this sample, we would see an even more uneven distribution of Internet access, which does not begin to account for types or age of computers or digital technology through which online students would access their OWCs.

In the same study, 22.1% of rural households that only had dial-up connections reported the lack of high-speed availability from their Internet providers as their reason for having the slower connectivity. Only 4.7% of urban households gave the same response (*A Nation Online*, 2004). Clearly, students living in these remote areas may find their connection options severely constrained. While being limited to dial-up alone is in itself a disadvantage for the user because of low download speeds, even dial-up connections are extremely limited in terms of availability in some rural areas. According to Thomas Davis and Mark Trebian (2001), in 2000, only 8.9% of Native American families on reservations had Internet access. The same year, the national average was 26.2%. Of 185 Bureau of Indian Affairs schools, only 76 had Internet connections. On the Navajo reservation co-located in Utah, Arizona and New Mexico, 80% of the homes—in 2001—still lacked even the most basic phone service (Davis & Trebian, 2001). In 2013, only 53% on the Navajo reservation had wireless broadband service available while the 2013 national average was 98% (Landry, 2013).

These patterns are not limited to Native American reservations but appear to be fairly universal across the rural parts of the United States. In south Texas, for example, colleges like Southwest Texas Junior College in Uvalde have serious limitations when designing online writing programs. With a 16,000 square mile service area, a large portion of the college's district is in areas where home Internet service simply is not available, yet students cannot get to the campus for onsite or hybrid classes given such a broad geographic service area. In many of these places, students are forced to go to local schools or public libraries to gain Internet access. In fact, in some places, even the schools and libraries do not have reliable service (J. Coe, personal communication, November 16, 2012).

While geographic remoteness certainly is one cause of this lack of Internet connectivity, Davis and Trebian (2001) identified additional factors that lead to a lack of access in rural areas, including the following:

- Weak economic base
- Lack of private investment
- Poor targeting of government policies for improving technology infrastructure
- Distrust of new technologies

The situation is so ubiquitous in remotely rural areas that, according to Haythornthwaite (2007), across the country, usable telecommunications infrastructure privileges urban over all rural users. And most rural users are far better served than the remotely rural.

In addition to issues of accessibility, once remotely rural students enroll into an OWC, they also may face issues of "urban bias." This bias suggests that students from rural schools were not properly taught in high school; in other words, their teachers failed to "teach them right." Indeed, both students and their college teachers may believe that the students come to the college writing class already behind their classmates from urban and suburban areas (Done-hower, Hogg, & Schell, 2007). Government policies, educational practices, and even the attitudes of professors and course designers reflect this bias. Kim Do-nehower, Charlotte Hogg, and Eileen Schell (2007) noted the "rural illiteracy stereotype" as something perpetrated not just by the popular media but also especially by academics. Much like the working class student, rural students may feel marginalized and experience being the "other" in the class. Since a large portion of these students also comes from the working classes, the sense of being an outsider is even more acutely felt. These students often have internalized this stereotype.

PROVIDING ACCESSIBLE OWI FOR REMOTELY RURAL STUDENTS

As indicated earlier, many of UMUC's students are located in areas where they cannot get to a college. To offer their courses as widely as possible, UMUC articulates programs with community colleges (M. Parker, personal communication, December 7, 2012). Yet, even an operation of this magnitude cannot reach the truly remote student, who, without Internet connections, cannot access such a broadly reaching institution.

Students in many rural areas can only access OWCs if they can get to a school or library that offers Internet capabilities. When they do find one, there often are limitations in bandwidth and download speed as well as use time limitations, as noted previously. Many libraries also insist the sound be turned off on speakers, so unless the students own and bring their own headphones, they may not have access to sound files. To address this problem, some institutions offer a very "thin" architecture in their courses. For example, UMUC requires minimal downloading to be done by students because files stay on the LMS server. The college's library services also are available online (M. Parker, personal communication, December 7, 2012), a practice supported by OWI Principle 13.

In my own OWCs, which enroll students from across the large state of Texas, I ask one of the college librarians to join the course with full instructor rights in the LMS. Students are encouraged to mail or send discussion notes to her regarding the library research they are doing. In this way, students are enabled to stay within the LMS (also a thin architecture), giving students with limited bandwidth and access to time on the computer as close as possible to full access to the course as their classmates.

Therefore, as with working-class students, postsecondary institutions that cater to students in remotely rural locations have no control over student access and cannot necessarily help those with no Internet access to use their facilities. They should, however, take into consideration and make accommodations for those with reduced computer technology and Internet capabilities wherever possible. As with the working-class student with limited accessibility, software, and experience, access-focused recommendations for remotely rural students include avoiding situations where they need to download large files and audio/video files.

URBAN STUDENTS

As with OWI and multilingual students (see Chapter 9), research is sparse regarding OWI and urban populations, which includes Hispanic students and especially African-Americans. The same can be said regarding general studies about distance education and urban populations although urban households, according to Table 10.2, generally had greater access to most Internet connections types. Yet, even though the urban household tends to fare better than rural households, the numbers demonstrated a dearth of online technologies among the inhabitants of these regions. In addition to this limited access to the capability to participate in online education from one's urban household, serious exigencies that can affect these populations' lives can challenge urban students' access to online education.

As with other populations discussed in this chapter, urban students who want to participate in online education likely are affected by the digital divide; indeed, many may not have computer and Internet access in their household or even in a nearby location that will enable them to participate in online courses. An early focus group conducted by Kelly Ervin and Geoff Gilmore (1999) found that African-American college students had as much access to computer technologies as non-African Americans. However, these results contradicted the US Department of Commerce's (1999) study *Falling Through the Net: Defining the Digital Culture*, which reported that the 23.2% of households with computers among African-Americans trailed all racial and ethnic populations in the United States (p. 18). The number of African-American households using the Internet that year was similarly meager (i.e., 11.2%, p. 26). The rosier picture presented by the US Department of Commerce (2004) in *A Nation Online* showed that Internet access had significantly increased for African-Americans to 45.6%, and broadband use was at 14.2%. Both of these data points were higher than Hispanic populations, an ethnic group that also populates many urban areas. Despite the significantly greater Internet access experienced by African-Americans, they still trailed Caucasian and Asian-Americans by approximately 20% for Internet usage and approximately 10 to 20% for Broadband access. The significant gaps reported in these government reports about computer, Internet, and broadband use among the different racial and ethnic populations raises doubts about Ervin and Gilmore's (1999) findings.

But some researchers have questioned whether simply having access to a computer or various types of Internet access is really the primary access issue for various urban populations, especially African-Americans. Instead, they raised questions about what one might call cultural access, or a feeling that computer technologies were designed to accommodate the needs of primarily hegemonic populations. Blackmon (2003) described how African-American students in her class did not see themselves on the Internet; instead, they were "being asked to see themselves as either rappers and sports stars or as part of the raceless, white majority represented on the Web without ever having the ability to become one of the majority" (p. 93). Similarly, Barbara Monroe (2004) explained that those African-Americans who do not have Internet access are not all "have-nots"; some of these individuals are "don't-wants" who bristle at the marketing strategies technology companies use to target African-Americans. A study conducted by Okwumabua, Walker, Hu, and Watson (2011) regarding online learning and math showed that this cultural access understandably influences how African-American students perceive online education. Almost 65% of their student participants who were between the ages of 7 and 16 "indicated that they did not enjoy using computers to complete school work" (p. 246). While most of the students did not respond that the computer technology made them feel anxious, 67% reported that they did not feel comfortable with the technology (p. 246). Thus, more than a majority of the students had negative impressions about their ability to learn from online tutorials. Overall only 38% of the student respondents believed that online learning and tutoring had any value (p. 246).

PROVIDING ACCESSIBLE OWI FOR URBAN STUDENTS

Many of the issues faced by urban students echo those faced by working class students (discussed above). As noted there, the issue of access to the Internet is beyond the control of the professor or even of the college or university. Any change in Internet accessibility will have to be initiated by the student's family or the government; we must assume students who choose to take an online course are acknowledging that they can provide their own initial Internet connection.

A more addressable issue is what to do about students who have access but at a reduced level due to bandwidth limitations or inadequate software. Symptoms of this issue include slow downloads and the inability to open and manipulate files once downloaded. While urban areas generally have high-bandwidth availability, some families choose slower, less expensive options. Again, as is the case with working class students, teachers can alleviate some of this problem by careful consideration of required course materials. What do students really need to download, read, and use in the course? By making some simple changes and avoiding the use of more exotic bells and whistles such as audio files and Vokis, we can reduce these problems. Audios of lectures can be recorded on such slide-ware as PowerPoint, a software to which even low end users are likely to have access. Low bandwidth documents like PDF files also tend to be accessible to the users with limited software availability. In most LMSs, a PDF file will open in the LMS window, making it available without any additional software.

Then, there is the issue of limited experience. As noted above, African-American students often begin with far less experience than their classmates, and the types of experiences they may have (e.g., skills and drills exercises versus lengthy writing opportunities) do not prepare them for the kinds of writing and communicating that contemporary rhetoric and composition courses attempt to provide through OWI online (Kynard, 2007, MacGillis, 2004; McAdoo, 1994; Sheingold, Martin, & Endreweit, 1987).

The only cure for a lack of experience is more experience. Yet, while students flounder through technology issues, they are using valuable time and energy that could have been spent learning to write. The professor or course designer can simplify the technological challenges by keeping the number of presentation and participation modes to a minimum. The reductions made to alleviate software access problems (as indicated above), when coupled with using a limited number of presentation and activity options available in the LMS, will allow the student to negotiate the class with a reduced amount of pressure from technology issues.

Finally, there is the problem of cultural access. It is here where the problems may be the most daunting. Blackmon (2003) pointed out that African-American students do not see themselves as a part of the world that is involved with the Internet. Monroe (2004) claimed that a substantial number of these students don't want to be involved in the online world. It is not easy to make a dramatic change in a student's view of the world and his place in it. There are some who may argue that it might be unethical to attempt to make such a change. Just as there are those who believe in students' right to their own language, there are also those that believe the same right should extend to the students' worldview. Changes of this type must come from within the family, the community, or the student herself. While the professor can certainly help and encourage those wanting to become online savvy, Monroe's "don't want" students (2004) may be beyond our reach.

Based upon the limited research on urban populations, especially African-Americans, OWI administrators and instructors must understand that they need to help students navigate their way to the technologies that mediate the course. These technologies may not always be in the home; sometimes they are in labs and sometimes they are the mobile devices that these students carry (see Chapter 16). Likewise, WPAs and instructors must consider that not all populations value the technologies that mediate OWI equally, and they need to consider how a distrust of these technologies impacts students' learning. Certainly, the limited research available regarding this population indicates that more studies need to be conducted.

MILITARY LEARNERS

With the increased number of military personnel due to the wars in Iraq and Afghanistan and the availability of new GI bill funds, the numbers of active-duty military and veterans who also are college students have swelled. In the 2007-2008 academic year, 660,000 then-current and former members of the military accounted for 3% of all undergraduate college students in the United States. These students were divided evenly between two- and four-year colleges. Of those students, 215,000 were active-duty military personnel. In that time, 329,000, or 38% of these students, used veteran education benefits.

VETERAN STUDENTS

With the passage of the Montgomery GI Bill, an education tuition program initiated in 2009, that number increased substantially. By January, 2013, more than one million attended American colleges and universities (APSCU, 2013). By then, most of the FYW classes for veterans were taken either online or from two-year colleges. D. Alexis Hart and Roger Thompson (2013) attributed this choice for online and two-year college courses to veterans' desire to quickly and inexpensively fulfill their general education requirements. Under the new GI bill, in 2009 veterans attending school full-time received $1,321 per month for 36 months (Radfors & Wun, 2009); in 2014, the benefit was $1,648 monthly (Military.com, 2014). By 2012, there were two million veterans eligible for $11 billion in federal benefits for education. After four years in existence, the GI bill paid for 800,000 veterans' education (Fain, 2012). This explosion in enrollments has resulted in the founding of veterans' centers and organizations at colleges across the country.

Many students within the class of military veterans, like many nonmilitary adult learners, often bring desirable traits to their college courses. Common attributes include maturity, richness of experience, and an exposure to a well-defined organizational culture. Many also bring strong experience in leadership and possess sound decision-making abilities (Starr-Glasse, 2011). Perhaps most important for success, veterans also possess a high level of motivation. Not only have they come from a culture that values perseverance, tenacity, and positive outcomes, but the Department of Defense reimburses them only for courses that are completed successfully (Starr-Glasse, 2011). This requirement motivates veterans to stay with a course and to do well in it.

Like anyone else, however, veterans also may have traits that are less helpful in academic work. One commonly discussed issue is that military students often face a problem with the flexibility of college, especially the online class. They come from an environment that values, and teaches within, rigid structures. The element of self-pacing that may be comfortable for some other adults often is not appealing for them because it is counter to the culture in which they have operated for years in the military. In dealing with marines, Steven M. Jones, Wanda Mally, Larry A. Blevins, and James E. Munroe (2003) found that to be successful as students, military members must first overcome their resistance to change. A less-structured environment is one of the first changes they encounter. Others agree. Dave Jarrat of Inside Track, a company that works with colleges on student coaching services, indicated that students with military backgrounds sometimes struggle with the relatively flexible schedule of college (Fain, 2012). In a group discussion on a Sloan-C course, Phillip McNair (2013), the Vice-President for Strategic Initiatives at the American Public University System, pointed out that a structured environment is the norm for these students, right down to the position of their socks in a drawer, and they are comfortable with that. Very few OWCs have this kind of rigid structure despite there being a distinct beginning, middle, and end of the course and typically solid assignment due dates. Indeed, asynchronous OWI particularly asks students to develop their own work schedules to meet the course due dates for essays and class participation.

Another difficulty some military veterans (as well as other military students overall) face is a potential lack of acceptance by other students in classes. They may be targets of stereotyping, both political and cultural. In some college environments, military personnel are viewed as suspect and representative of a government whose actions many do not condone. For other classmates, the military is seen as a job of last resort for those unable to find employment in mainstream America. In either case, military students may be marginalized and seen as distanced from contemporary society (Starr-Glasse, 2011). This distancing often makes their experience in a regular classroom—let alone an online class where students make more peripheral contact through how they describe themselves or appear in their posts—more difficult. Writing studies and OWI typically ask students to make connections through group discussions, peer workshops, and other community building activities. When an OWC begins with students introducing themselves via a photograph and biography, as Warnock (2009) recommended, veterans inadvertently may set themselves up for being marginalized by students with biases against the military.

Finally, there is what Hart and Thompson (2013) called the "deficit model." In this perspective, military veterans may be viewed from the standpoint of the deficits and disabilities they bring with them. These include possible Traumatic Brain Injury (TBI) and Post-traumatic Stress Disorder (PTSD). In an association of Higher Education and Disabilities study, Mary Lee Vance and Wayne K. Miller (2009) found that these disorders affect 34% of the male and more than 10% of female veterans. Of all students—military and non-military—identified as having emotional disturbances twenty years ago, 63% attended community colleges (Directory of Disability, 1992), making working with disabled veterans potentially of greater concern at the two-year college level. In her CCCC's Chair's Address, Marilyn Valentino (2010) posed the question of whether faculty would be ready for the anticipated growing influx of such students. Long concerned with emotionally disturbed students, she provided strategies for dealing with these students when they indicate emotional difficulties in their writing (Valentino, 1996); OWI teachers most likely will see any indication of TBI, PTSD, or emotional disturbance in their writing. However, Hart & Thompson (2013) have argued that this "deficit" approach to military students can be harmful. It is important to note that since many veteran students have not served in combat, viewing military students from this perspective can inhibit student success.

ACTIVE-DUTY MILITARY

While veterans may be generally more able to matriculate on a brick-and-mortar campus, or onsite, for their courses, active-duty military personnel often do not have that luxury. Their deployments to remote settings make them like the remotely rural students who cannot access the campus itself. Active-duty military, therefore, often use online courses to continue their education—even from locations as far away as Afghanistan or Japan. Their college experiences are different in other ways as well. For the active-duty or reserve military student, scheduling is a huge issue. Temporary duty work or an unexpected deployment decreases a student's chance for success in a course or, in the worst-case scenario, can end it—requiring a withdrawal or simply leading to the student no longer attending. While the military does encourage education, the culture of "the mission comes first" necessarily dominates (Starr-Glasse, 2011). In many cases, students cannot plan ahead for such occurrences, and they have no choice in needing to stop education temporarily to wait for a new beginning later.

Another issue is Internet accessibility. Active-duty military students often find their access to the Internet sporadic or even unavailable on deployment. When it is available, connection speed and bandwidth are variable and may be problematic. In 1997, fewer than 30% of enlisted men had access to Internet. The situation has improved tremendously since then; according to ArmyMom-Strong.com (2014), deployed soldiers can access the Internet through local Internet cafes, the Morale-Welfare-Recreation Centers, and in their personal living quarters. Personal Internet access, however, can cost upwards of $100.00 per month—costly for low-ranking enlisted soldiers—but this expense can be reduced when shared among roommates. Yet, there still are issues of accessibility and bandwidth. Even simple asynchronous connections and synchronous presentations done in an LMS may be inaccessible depending on the day, time, and deployment. Restrictions on access may be for several days or longer. As more military students in remote locations matriculate to college, this problem of having sufficiently reliable and consistent connectivity to complete an online course is likely to get worse rather than better (Starr-Glasse, 2011).

One Navy veteran (who asked to remain anonymous) expressed that he took a technical writing class online while he was on active duty. He ran into serious problems when he was deployed. He had no Internet access on the ship and was unable to complete the course work. He could not receive an "incomplete" grade because he had not yet completed the required percentage of the course work to qualify for it. His only choices were to withdraw or take a grade of F. He could not get a refund on his tuition and fees because his situation occurred past the deadline. He could not get a reimbursement from GI Bill funds because he had not completed the course (Personal communication, November 26, 2012). Such a situation in an OWI setting can leave the instructor frustrated and the student more so.

Even when deployment is not an issue and students are able to finish a course unimpeded, there is yet another obstacle to be faced. The continuous and sometimes rapid rotation of military personnel makes staying in one duty station for four or more years highly unlikely. In peace time, rotations typically happen on three-year cycles with occasional two- or four-year duties. During wartime, deployments and rotation cycles can be much shorter, causing more disruption in one's school opportunities. Moving and being deployed to war zones can prevent military students from being able to complete a degree program at a single school unless all of the courses are available for online study. Because courses, especially at the upper class level, do not always transfer, military students often find they need to take more courses than their classmates (thus, costing them more money) in order to achieve a degree—if they can finish at all (The Sloan Consortium).

There are other issues faced by military personnel that seldom are considered by colleges. One of those regards textbooks. With class members spread around the world in many cases, the time required to mail textbooks to students can be prohibitive. Printed textbooks must be mailed, and that means student registration must close weeks before classes begin. Even under normal circumstances, receiving a book through the mail could take a week or more, but it often can take considerably more time than that because of the remote location and sporadic mail service to some deployment sites. The use of ebooks might seem to be a reasonable solution. In practice, however, ebooks also can prove to be an unworkable and unreliable option given that deployed military often do not have consistent Internet access and when they do, the bandwidth availability often is poor, making downloading slow and cumbersome. At UMUC, for example, although neither method is completely satisfactory, *both* print and ebooks have been used with many online courses to at least provide more flexibility (M. Parker, personal communication, December 7, 2012). Some publishers are beginning to provide the electronic text of academic titles if the student pays the full cost of the print textbook. These electronic files can be read on various portable ebook readers.

Another issue that colleges face with military students is the handling of learning or physical disabilities. In the military, disability percentages are linked to the individual's ability to participate in a job. In colleges, the process is more complicated. First, the student must self-identify to an office that handles such issues. A costly series of tests and a process of diagnosis sometimes follow that identification. In a culture of self-sufficiency and personal strength, the active-duty military student may see this process as declaring a shortcoming and may consider asking for help as presenting a negative image of himself or getting an advantage other students do not have. As a result, there may be a tendency to resist taking that step, thus leaving the military student without the assistance that a non-military student in the same position would enjoy (A. Butler, personal communication, December 7, 2012).

Providing Accessible OWI for Military Learners

Hart and Thompson (2013) argued that many of the transition issues faced by veterans are the same faced by other older adult students when moving from earlier careers back to college. As such, many of the recommendations presented in that section apply here as well. Others argue, however, that issues unique to veterans are more critical and need special attention.

David Starr-Glasse (2011) identified several traits of the military student that are important to consider when developing an OWC that will be effective for the students' learning styles. First, military students tend to be self-directed. While some students wait to be told what the next move is and when to make it, members of the military have been trained to read available guidance and work with it autonomously, and they may prefer to be treated as autonomous learners. But, in an apparent contradiction that matches adult students who exhibit adolescent traits (Hewett, 2015a), military learners also are used to an environment that is extremely structured (Jones, Mally, Blevins, & Munroe, 2003; McNair, 2013). This dissonance shows up repeatedly in the research literature, and it reveals why military learners may become fixated on the requirements of a syllabus or a particular writing assignment while, perhaps, wanting to accomplish the assignment in their own timeframes. In addition to this learning tendency, military students' issues of deployment require flexibility in assignments, participation requirements, and schedules (Starr-Glasse, 2011) just where they also might crave fixed structure.

In answer to this dilemma, McNair (2013) noted that while a firmly structured course is preferable, there are times when flexibility is important (e.g., times of increased workload or deployment). When it comes to the work requirements and deadlines, the professor's flexibility should not take away from OWC's structure in general. The student's prior experience can be used effectively here. While military life is normally very structured, sudden changes in duty and location have prepared them to some degree, for these abrupt, last-minute changes. Sharing this analogy in an online discussion post or an announcement can help military students make the necessary adjustments more easily.

As noted previously, military students often see themselves as outsiders in the college writing classroom. Attitudes of other students toward members of the military may reinforce that feeling. Indeed, they need to be encouraged to see themselves as legitimate participants in the class community (Starr-Glasse, 2011), and one way to accomplish this is to connect the kinds of work that military learners do with the writing of the class. Discussion threads or early writing assignments that enable such personal revelation may be useful for encouraging the OWC's students to view each other more equitably and from a mutual position of respect. However, because military learners are comfortable with collaborative efforts from their occupational experiences, community-building activities in online courses, when they do not require group projects with group grades, are not only comfortable for military learners but may increase student motivation and reduce attrition (Sadera, Robertson, Song, & Midon, 2009). That said, the fact that they sometimes are forced to disappear from the class at a moment's notice—temporarily or even permanently—and without the ability to explain their absence to classmates, collaborative work can become impractical and military students may once again experience themselves as different. It is a serious "Catch-22" that the OWI teacher must consider when military learners are part of the course. The military is not a "regular" job, yet these learners want a regular education.

Finally, there is the issue of what to do when an otherwise successful student is forced to leave class for a time or permanently due to duty requirements or deployment. Clearly this is an opportunity for flexibility in rules. At UMUC, deployments in mid-semester are handled in one of two ways. If student can return to class by end of the semester, he can complete the course through one-on-one work with the professor. If not, then the student is granted an "administrative withdrawal" for a grade. At many colleges, the grade of incomplete is another option available when the student cannot get back to class before the end of the term. However, rules governing incomplete grades often require the student to have finished a certain percentage of the coursework before becoming eligible for an incomplete, which may not be within the military student's control. At Lee College, the requirement for an incomplete is 70% of the coursework. Colleges that are enrolling active duty members should re-examine such rules to build in flexibility that accommodates the students' needs.

It would appear that online teaching gives the portability and flexibility that military learners so desperately need. An OWC is an ideal venue for these students in many cases. In online programs, students often can finish their degrees at the school they started even if they are re-assigned elsewhere (The Sloan Consortium). With a few minor adjustments, OWI teachers and their institutions can provide a workable way for these learners to earn degrees while still engaged in active duty.

INCARCERATED STUDENTS

If there ever seemed to be a match made in heaven, it is online learning and students in prisons. Somewhat more than two million people currently are incarcerated in prisons and local jails and detention centers (Maeroff, 2003; Wing, 2013). The United States tops all other countries for incarcerated citizens (Wing, 2013). For decades, colleges have sent faculty to prisons around the country to conduct classes within the prison walls. Lee College began sending faculty to teach individual courses at the Texas Department of Criminal Justice's Huntsville Center in 1966. Technical course faculty began to be assigned to the prison the next year, but it was not until 1978 that full-time academic faculty members were located onsite. Throughout those years, academic faculty members made the 190-mile round trip to the center twice a week to teach classes face-to-face. In 1984, the program became a regular branch campus with a full college faculty and administration onsite, complete with labs, greenhouses, and other educational facilities (Lee College).

Prison programs like these are extremely costly, and the students' choice of subjects to study is limited by the number of faculty assigned to the site. Currently, the state of Texas spends about $128 million each year on education programs for inmates. State Senator Florence Shapiro, chair of the Senate Education Committee, has argued that online programs could save the state a substantial amount of money. However, Michelle Lyons with the Texas Department of Criminal Justice indicated that such online courses are not a viable option because most inmates are not allowed to go online for various reasons. In Texas, no inmate has open Internet access although some are allowed to logon in classrooms and certain vocational programs ("Plano Senator," 2011).

Research has revealed that nothing reduces recidivism more than education. Even a simple GED program reduces recidivism by 29% (Steurer, Smith, & Tracy, 2001). Most prison units have such programs. But a study done in New York showed that inmates who complete a college degree while incarcerated are *four* times less likely to reoffend (*Postsecondary*, 2003). Inmates who completed two years of college in the Lee College program at the Huntsville prisons have a 10% recidivism rate compared to 60% for those receiving no additional education. But college offerings are costly and far less common in America's prisons than GED programs. What better way to address this population than through online classes? Students would have a virtually unlimited choice of universities, programs, and classes to choose from. Colleges would be saved the cost of sending faculty or building branch campuses at prison facilities. And what about the thousands of prisoners housed in units that do not currently have college programs to offer? They, too, would have the option of improving their education and earning a degree.

Yet, online programs have been resisted by state prison systems across the country because authorities fear inmates will have Internet contact with persons and groups on the outside that could lead to negative effects on the prisoner's rehabilitation or to criminal activity. Nonetheless, 46 state prison systems (all except Hawaii, Nebraska, Iowa, and Nevada) allow Internet use in supervised educational settings ("Computer Use," 2009). Typical of the policies in most states is this one from Ohio:

> No prisoner in a private correctional facility, county correctional facility, municipal correctional facility, or correctional institution under the control of the department of rehabilitation and correction shall access the Internet through the use of a computer, computer network, computer system, com-

puter services, or information service, unless the prisoner is under direct supervision and is participating in an approved educational program that requires the use of the Internet for training or research purposes, and in accordance with this rule. ("Internet Access for Prisoners," 2005)

Nonetheless, while the exception for "approved educational programs" sounds promising, the problem here is the phrase "under direct supervision." This need for supervision means that, in order for a prisoner to be able to access the Internet, there must be someone in the room watching at all times. While the motivation behind such a rule is understandable, it also defeats the purpose of online education as students can only work when there is a teacher or a guard overseeing their actions. Colleges again are faced with having to place faculty or staff onsite. Granted, the college employee does not have to be a qualified professor, but there still will be requirements for personnel and restrictions on times of availability that local prison officials prefer not to deal with. At Lee College's Huntsville prison campus, for instance, the warden chooses to follow the policy by not allowing Internet use at all. This is a commonly applied solution to the problem, and it denies access to an educational institution's Internet-based LMS as well as to online research options. While there are other options, some of which will be discussed shortly, prison officials who are skeptical of security issues in any new plans will have to be persuaded of the invulnerability of any option under consideration.

Providing Access to OWI for Incarcerated Students

In one sense, the problems facing students in prisons are the easiest to solve. The catch is that while the solutions are simple in themselves, prison administrations must be convinced of their workability, and that is not always possible.

One easy method for allowing online teaching in prisons is for colleges and universities to forget about the traditional Internet offerings and rely instead on a closed-circuit intranet like those common in business and industry. In this way, students would have access to nothing except materials housed on the college LMS server. There need be no connections to the Internet whatsoever. From the standpoint of the student, the course would appear and operate the same as one conducted via the Internet. For the professor and course designer, there is one difference. All files students access in the course of the semester must be housed on the intranet LMS server, which requires significant planning to enable abundant content and research materials—especially for OWCs that require students to learn researched writing strategies. To meet the prison guidelines, there can be no external links to Internet sites and no other physical connection to the Internet.

On the surface, an intranet connection would seem to be a reasonable solution and easy to sell, but prison administrators will need to be convinced (guaranteed, if you will) that it is impossible for prisoners to contact anyone or reach any site except those specifically used in the course and housed on that closed server. Once programs like these are established and tested in a few places, their acceptance is likely to become more universal very quickly. In the meantime, most prisoners in the United States are unlikely to have access to OWI in a hybrid or fully online setting.

CONCLUSION AND RECOMMENDATIONS

This discussion began with the overarching OWI Principle 1 regarding the need for OWI to be inclusive and accessible. It is clear that, at least in the nontraditional student cohorts discussed in this chapter, higher education institutions have not reached that goal. Yet, the CCCC OWI Committee acknowledged inclusivity and access as "the key concern" for faculty as colleges move ahead with OWI (p. 7). There is no question that many of the obstacles faced by nontraditional students negotiating OWCs are formidable. Some, like Internet access for the poor or remotely rural, probably are beyond the scope of colleges and universities given the technology available. Those are issues that will have to be resolved by such others as government, individual communities, businesses, and the individual students themselves. But many of the other obstacles can be addressed and most in a relatively simple way. For example:

- Faculty should become aware of the difficulties nontraditional students face when enrolling in OWCs. Internet-access difficulties may be the most prevalent problem, but underserved students may also be using outdated computer technology and may be less familiar with educational and social uses of digital technology.
- As the population ages, WPAs and OWI teachers need to understand how diminishing sensory or cognitive faculties may be reflected in students' abilities to access OWCs or to respond to writing assignments online.
- WPAs should consider how to provide content through the LMS, textbooks, and ebooks such that remote OWI students have access to the same degree as onsite or geographically local students.
- Policies should be developed that take into consideration the special time-related needs of individuals in particular types of careers, such as the military or other work places where travel and temporary duty is common.
- In the case of prisons, WPAs and OWI teachers should develop intranet-based materials and approaches to OWCs that can reach incarcerated students while still meeting security requirements.

Let me be clear here. I am not suggesting that these underserved nontraditional student populations will have an equal playing field compared to traditional students with years of high tech experience and a relatively uncluttered (or, differently cluttered) private life—students for whom college is their number one or even only career. Nonetheless, online courses and OWI specifically can be made more accessible to the nontraditional students discussed in this chapter, giving them a chance to be successful and to accomplish their learning goals.

NOTES

1. Some research has suggested that when it comes to computer use, working-class students' elementary and secondary school experiences are different from that of the managerial/professional classes (e.g., Anyon, 1980; Bernstein, 1971; Gos, 1995, 1996). One of those differences is in the application of computers in learning. Olsen (1997) and Bowles and Gintis (1976) pointed out long ago that students from different social classes are rewarded for behaviors appropriate for the occupations they are expected to one day fill. Others have argued that working-class students are denied exposure to knowledge and skills—including computer skills—that would allow them to make a successful border crossing (e.g., Anyon, 1980; Apple, 1979; Bernstein, 1971; Kynard 2007; MacGillis, 2004). Indeed, research suggests that the use of computers varies significantly according to class. Schools with higher budgets or that serve primarily middle and upper class populations tend to use computers for collaborative projects and communications as preparation for the professional and managerial roles their students are expected to play as adults. These communication activities require Internet access and extensive writing. Intercity and predominantly working class schools, on the other hand, use computers for drilling lessons, which might have been considered a reasonable preparation for taking orders in the lowest rungs of the service industry (Aronowitz & Giroux, 1993; Cuban, 2001; Monroe, 2004; Moran & Selfe, 1999). As a result, the students in lower budget schools may emerge as only low-end users of computers with little or no experience in writing in the digital environment.

2. Several personal communications are cited in this chapter. A group telephone interview was done with Andrew Cavanaugh, Mark Parker, and Allison Butler from the University of Maryland University College. All conversations with Kristen Welch occurred via emails. The interview with Jill Coe was in-person.

REFERENCES

American Council on Education. (2013). *Adult learners*. Retrieved from http://www.acenet.edu/higher-education/topics/Pages/Adult-Learners.aspx

Anyon, Jean. (1980). Social class and the hidden curriculum of work. *Journal of Education, 162*, 67-92.

Army Mom Strong. (2014). *Internet access for soldiers in Afghanistan and Iraq*. Retrieved from http://armymomstrong.com/internet-access-for-soldiers-in-afghanistan-and-iraq/

Aronowitz, Stanley & Giroux, Henry (1993). *Education still under siege*. Westport, CT. Bergin and Garvey

Association of Private Sector Colleges and Universities. (2013). *Report of the AP-SCU blue ribbon task force for military and veteran education*. Retrieved from http://www.apscu.org/policy-and-issues/federal-issues/military-veterans-ed/blue-ribbon-panel.cfm

Blackmon, Samantha (2003). "But I'm just white" or how "other" pedagogies can benefit all students. In Pamela Takayoshi & Brian Huot (Eds.), *Teaching writing with computers: An introduction* (pp. 92-102). Boston: Houghton Mifflin.

Blair, Kristine & Hoy, Cheryl. (2006). Paying attention to adult learners online: The pedagogy and politics of community. *Computers and Composition, 23*, 32-48.

Bernstein, Basil (1971). Class, codes and control (Vols. 1-3). London: Routledge/K. Paul.

Bowles, Samuel & Gintis, Herbert. (1976). *Schooling in capitalist America: Educational reform and the conditions of economic life*. New York: Basic.

CCCC OWI Committee for Effective Practices in Online Writing Instruction. (2013). *A position statement of principles and effective practices for online writing instruction (OWI)*. Retrieved from http://www.ncte.org/cccc/resources/positions/owiprinciples

CEC (Commission of the European Communities). (2005). *E-inclusion revisited: The local dimensions of the information society*. Retrieved from http://europa.eu.int/comm/employment_social/news/2005/feb/eincllocal_en.pdf

Community College Research Center. (2013, February). *Adaptability to online learning: Differences across types of students and academic subject areas*. (CCRC Working Paper No. 54). New York: Xu, Di & Jaggars, Shanna Smith.

Computer Use for/by Inmates. (2009) *The free library by Farlex*. Retrieved from http://www.thefreelibrary.com/Computer+use+for%2Fby+inmates.-a0208273651

Cuban, L. (2001). *Oversold and underused: Computers in the classroom*. Cambridge, MA: Harvard University Press.

Davis, Thomas & Trebian, Mark. (2001). The digital divide: The nation's tribal colleges and universities. *EDUCAUSE Review, 38*-46.

Donehower, Kim, Charlotte Hogg, & Eileen E. Schell (2007). Constructing rural literacies: Moving beyond the rhetoric's of lack, lag and the rosy past. In

Donehower, Kim, Charlotte Hogg & Eileen E. Schell (Eds.), *Rural literacies* (pp. 1-36). Carbondale, IL: Southern Illinois University Press.

Elliot, Norbert, Haggerty, Blake, Foster, Mary, & Spak, Gale. (2008). Asynchronous training in pharmaceutical manufacturing: A model for university and industrial collaboration. *International Journal on E-Learning, 7*(1), 67-85.

Ervin, Kelly S. & Gilmore, Geoff. (1999). Traveling the superinformation highway: African Americans' perceptions and use of cyberspace technology. *Journal of Black Studies, 29*, 398-407.

Fain, Paul. (2012). Scrambling to understand veterans. *Inside Higher Ed.* Retrieved from http://www.insidehighered.com/news/2012/12/04/colleges-fail-track-performance-student-veterans-survey-finds

Gos, Michael (1995). Overcoming social class markers: Preparing working class students for college [Special issue: Panoramas and vistas: New direction in writing instruction]. *The Clearing House, 69*(1), 30-34.

Gos, Michael (1996). But it's only a pot of iron: Working class students and the core curriculum. In *Selected papers from the Texas seminar on the core curriculum, 1993, 1994, 1995* (pp. 153-158). Houston, TX: University of Houston/ National Endowment for the Humanities.

Harris, Muriel & Pemberton, Michael (1995). Online writing labs (OWLs): A taxonomy of options and issues. *Computers and Composition, 12*, 145-159.

Hart, D. Alexis & Thompson, Roger (2013). *An ethical obligation: Promising practices for veterans in college writing classrooms.* Retrieved from http://www.NCTE.org/library/NCTE files/Groups/CCCC/AnEthicalObligation.pdf

Haythornthwaite, Caroline. (2007). Digital divide and e-learning. In Richard Andrews & Carolyn Haythornthwaite (Eds.), *The Sage handbook of e-learning research* (pp. 97-118). London: Sage.

Hewett, Beth L. (2015a). *Reading to learn and writing to teach: Literacy strategies for online writing instruction.* Boston, MA: Bedford/St. Martin's Press.

Jones, Steven M., Mally, Wanda, Blevins, Larry A., & Munroe, James E. (2003). The US Marine Corps distance learning program. In Michael G. Moore & W. G. Anderson (Eds.), *Handbook of distance education* (pp. 641-654). Mahwah, NJ: Lawrence Erlbaum.

Knowles, Malcom S., Holton III, Elwood, & Swanson, Richard. (1998). *The adult learner: The definitive classic in adult education and human resource development* (5th ed.). Boston, MA: Butterworth-Heinemann.

Kynard, Carmen (2007). Wanted: Some black long distance [writers]': Blackboard flava-flavin and other afrodigital experiences in the classroom. *Computers and Composition 24*, 329-345.

Lamb, Paul. (2005, November 1). Perspective: Technology and the new class divide. *CNET News.* Retrieved from http://news.cnet.com/technology-and-the-new-class-divide/2010-1028_3-5924758.html

Landry, Alysa (2013, April 4). Indian country left on far side of digital dive. *Navajo Times.* Retrieved from http://www.navajotimes.com/news/2013/0413/040413dig.php

Lee College (n.d.). *About LCHC.* Retrieved from http://www.lee.edu/lchc/about-lchc/

MacGillis, A. (September 21, 2004). Law, software fuel new "digital divide." *Baltimore Sun,* 1A.

Maeroff, Gene I. (2003). *A classroom of one: How online learning is changing our schools and colleges.* New York: Palgrave MacMillan.

McAdoo, Maisie. (1994). Equity: Has technology bridged the gap? *Electronic Learning, 13,* 24–39.

McDonald, Jeanette & Gibson, Chere Campbell. (1998). Interpersonal dynamics and group development in computer conferencing. *The American Journal of Distance Education, 12* (1), 6-24.

McNair, Phillip. (2013). Sloan-C Consortium course, *Effective online classrooms: Military students.* Sloan-C Consortium course, live discussion. Retrieved from https://sas.elluminate.com/site/external/launch/native-playback.jnlp?sid=251&psid=2013-03-04.1327.M.DCB17C75F54A-DA5E1429F267BF7A9B.vcr

Military.com, Education. (2014). *Montgomery GI bill.* Retrieved from http://www.military.com/education/gi-bill/montgomery-gi-bill.html

Monroe, Barbara (2004). *Crossing the digital divide: Race, writing and technology in the classroom.* New York: Teachers College Press

Moran, Charlie & Selfe, Cynthia L. (1999). Teaching English across the technology/wealth gap. *English Journal,* 88(6), 48-54.

Morgan, Konrad & Morgan, Madeline. (2007). The challenge of gender, age and personality in e-learning. In Richard Andrews & Carolyn Haythornthwaite, (Eds.), *The Sage handbook of e-learning research* (pp. 328-346). London: Sage.

Narcisse, Denise. (2010). Disconnected, disenfranchised, and poor: Addressing digital inequality in America. *Working Class Perspectives.* Retrieved from http://workingclassstudies.wordpress.com/tag/computer-literacy/

Ohio Department of Correction and Rehabilitation. (2005). *Internet access for prisoners.* Retrieved from http://www.drc.ohio.gov/web/administrative_rules/documents/9-51.pdf

Okwumabua, Theresa M., Walker, Kristin M., Hu, Xiangen, & Watson, Andrea. (2011). An exploration of African American students' attitudes toward online learning (2011). *Urban Education, 46,* 241-250.

Olsen, Laurie. (1997). *Made in America: Immigrant students in our public schools.* New York: The New Press.

Plano senator: Online prison classes could save $$. (2011, March 18) *CBS DFW*. Retrieved from http://dfw.cbslocal.com/2011/03/18/plano-senator-online-prison-classes-could-save/

Postsecondary prison education. (2003, July 25). *Issues & Controversies on File*. Retrieved from http://www.2facts.com.icof/search/i0801650.asp?DBType=ICOF

Radford, Walton, Wun, Jolene, & Weko, Thomas. (2009). *Issue tables: A profile of military service members and veterans enrolled in postsecondary education in 2007-08 (Report #182)*. Washington, DC: National Center for Educational Statistics Sciences. Retrieved from http://nces.ed.gov/pubs2009/2009182.pdf

Reddick, Andrew, Boucher, Christian, & Grosseilliers, Manon. (2000). *The dual digital divide: The information highway in Canada*. The Public Interest Advocacy Centre. Retrieved from http://olt-bta.hrdc-drhc.gc.ca/resources/oltdualdivide_e.pdf

Robinson, Laura. (2009). A taste for the necessary: A Bourdieuian approach to digital inequality [Special issue: Diversity: The second annual special issue of the communication and information technologies section of the American Sociological Association]. *Information, Communication & Society, 12*(4), 488-507.

Sadera, William. A., Robertson, James, Song, Liyan, & Midon, M. Nichelle. (2009). The role of community in online learning success. *Journal of Online Learning and Teaching, 5*(2), 277-284

Sheingold, Karen, Martin, Laura M. W., & Endreweit, Mari E. (1987). Preparing urban teachers for the technological future. In Roy Pea & Karen Scheingold (Eds.), *Mirrors of the mind: Patterns of experience in educational computing* (pp. 67–85). Norwood, NJ: Ablex.

The Sloan Consortium. (n.d.). *Lessons learned from lessons learned: The fit between online education best practices and small school reality*. Retrieved from http://bundlr.com/clips/5107f19f83362c00020016a2

Starr-Glasse, David. (2011). Experience in the design and management of online learning environments. *MERLOT Journal of Online Learning and Teaching, 7*(1).

Steurer, Steven J., Smith, Linda & Tracy, Alice A. (2001). *The three state recidivism study*. Maryland Department of Public Safety and Correctional Services. Retrieved from www.dpscs.state.md.us/doc/pdfs/three-state-recidivism-study-summary.pdf

US Department of Commerce. (1995). *Falling through the net: A survey of the "have-nots" in rural and urban America*. Retrieved from http://www.ntia.doc.gov/ntiahome/fallingthru.html

US Department of Commerce. (1998). *Falling through the net II: Defining the digital divide*. Retrieved from http://www.ntia.doc.gov/ntiahome/net2

US Department of Commerce. (1999). *Falling through the net: Defining the digital divide*. Retrieved from http://www.ntia.doc.gov/report/1999/falling-through-net-defining-digital-divide

US Department of Commerce. (2004). *A nation online: Entering the broadband age*. Retrieved from http://www.ntia.doc.gov/report/2004/nation-online-entering-broadband-age

US Department of Commerce. (2011). *Fact sheet: Digital literacy.* Retrieved from http://www.commerce.gov/news/fact-sheets/2011/05/13/fact-sheet-digital-literacy

US Department of Education, National Center for Education Statistics. (2010). *Teachers' use of educational technology in US public schools: 2009* (NCES 2010-040). Retrieved from http://nces.ed.gov/pubsearch/pubsinfo.asp?pubid=2010040

Vance, Mary Lee, & Miller, Wayne K. II (2009). Serving wounded warriors: Current practices in postsecondary education. *Journal of Postsecondary Education and Disability, 22*(1), 18-28.

Valentino, Marilyn J. (1996). Responding when a life depends on it: What to write in the margins when students self-disclose. *Teaching English in the Two-Year College, 23*(4), 274-283.

Valentino, Marilyn J. (2010). 2010 CCCC chair's address: Rethinking the fourth C: Call to action. *College Composition and Communication, 62*(2), 364-378.

Warnock, Scott. (2009). *Teaching writing online: How and why.* Urbana, IL: National Council of Teachers of English.

Western, Wim. (1999). Paradoxes in open-networked learning environments: Toward a paradigm shift. *Educational Technology, 39*(1), 17-23.

Wing, Nick. (2013). Here are all of the nations that incarcerate more of their population than the US *The Huffington Post*. Retrieved from http://www.huffingtonpost.com/2013/08/13/incarceration-rate-per-capita_n_3745291.html

PART 4. FACULTY AND STUDENT PREPARATION FOR OWI

CHAPTER 11

FACULTY PREPARATION FOR OWI

Lee-Ann Kastman Breuch
University of Minnesota

This chapter, directed primarily to those who will train OWI teachers, examines the importance of training in light of the increase of OWC offerings in colleges and universities nationwide. To this end, the chapter first situates OWI in the larger context of distance learning and identifies characteristics that distinguish OWI from other online courses. Then, the chapter identifies four principles of training teachers for OWI, called the 4-M Training Approach. Using these principles, it then addresses issues specific to helping instructors transition to OWI and offers training suggestions for addressing these issues. Finally, interspersed in the chapter are suggestions for training that involve OWI course planning documents, OWI case study, OWI teaching groups, and assessment activities.

Keywords: accessibility, association, immersion, individualization, investigation, media, migration, modality, model, morale, reflection, social presence, training, usability

As *A Position Statement of Principles and Example Effective Practices for OWI* (CCCC OWI Committee, 2013) noted, the increase in OWCs requires attention toward OWI teacher training and an understanding of effective practices in OWI. The fifteen principles articulated in *A Position Statement of Principles and Example Effective Practices for OWI* provide an excellent basis for OWI training, and two of the 15 OWI principles specifically address training:

> **OWI Principle 7:** "Writing Program Administrators (WPAs) for OWI programs and their online writing teachers should receive appropriate OWI-focused training, professional development, and assessment for evaluation and promotion purposes" (p. 17).

> **OWI Principle 14:** "Online writing lab administrators and tutors should undergo selection, training, and ongoing professional development activities that match the environment in which they will work" (p. 28).

These principles both articulated effective practices as well as a rationale for training. Notably, the rationale for OWI Principle 7 mentioned that OWI teachers need proficiency in three areas: (1) writing instruction experience, (2) ability to teach writing in a digital environment, and (3) ability to teach writing in a text-based digital environment (p. 18). The accompanying effective practices further specified that OWI teachers need training in "modalities, logistics, time management, and career choices" as well as the technological elements of teaching both synchronously and asynchronously (p. 18). As we consider training, we must add accessibility to this list, for accessibility is the overarching principle in *A Position Statement of Principles and Example Effective Practices for OWI* (CCCC OWI Committee, 2013):

> **OWI Principle 1: "Online writing instruction should be universally inclusive and accessible" (p. 7).**

While OWI Principle 1 does not address training specifically, accessibility issues in the development of accessible Web-based content have a critical implication for training. Keeping OWI Principle 1 regarding the need for inclusivity and accessibility in mind, as well as OWI Principles 7 and 14, this chapter addresses OWI training with the goal of helping those who are charged with developing OWI teacher-training programs. Because issues of accessibility are an overarching concern, this chapter begins with an introduction to accessibility relevant to training educators for OWI. Then, this chapter addresses a number of issues associated with OWI training and provides ideas that can contribute to an effective OWI training program.

To ground the training issues provided in this chapter, I use the five educational principles outlined by Beth L. Hewett and Christa Ehmann (2004) in *Preparing Educators for Online Writing Instruction: Principles and Processes*. These principles are investigation, immersion, individualization, association, and reflection. The principle of investigation addresses the need to "rigorously" examine "teaching and learning processes as they occur in *naturalistic* settings" such as the training course (Hewett & Ehmann, 2004, p. 6). Only by investigating our training and OWI practices, asserted Hewett and Ehmann, can we best understand what works and what needs to be approached differently. Immersion is an educational principle that suggests there is no better way to learn something than to be placed within its milieu; language learners are taught in the target language and writers are taught to write by writing. Similarly, learning to teach in an OWC is best accomplished in the online setting. Individualization is a key to helping the learner grasp and make use of the new information and skills being taught. It provides flexibility for the OWI teacher trainee within the structure of a training course. Just as students in OWCs need personalized and individualized attention to their writing, so do new OWI teachers need individual attention from their trainers and from each other. The online setting can be lonely, as OWI Principle 11 (p. 23) recognized by insisting that students need opportunities to develop online communities; similarly, OWI teacher-trainees need to associate with other new learners and their mentors. Providing association is about giving OWI teachers the opportunity to talk with each other—preferably while immersed in the online setting in which they will teach. Finally, learners need the opportunity for a "critically reflexive process of examining notions about teaching and learning in light of one's actual experiences" (p. 20). Such a process is engendered in the principle of reflection, whereby teacher trainees are offered opportunities to both think and talk about their experiences, encouraged to assess these experiences and how they will or will not play into future OWI teaching. Each of these five principles is called upon in the training exercises provided in this chapter.

ACCESSIBILITY

Three high-level accessibility issues and concerns are worth noting because instructors need to learn about them in training: the range of disabilities OWI teachers might encounter, accessible content, and using an LMS in an accessible manner. As well, these accessibility issues can and should be applied to OWI training environments so that instructors have full access to training materials and experiences.

The first is the suggestion to consider the range of disabilities that may affect students in OWCs, or even Web-based environments generally. Thinking about students first helps educators to understand needs students may have and how to help them. My first introduction to accessibility issues in OWI came from reading a graduate student's dissertation on autism and online learning by Christopher Scott Wyatt (2010). Wyatt interviewed 17 autistic adults about their preferences regarding online course interfaces; all students in the study had experience taking online courses. One striking finding was the clear preference among all participants for text-only interfaces, which is to say that uses of color, video, or flashing images were distracting to most of these students and in some cases physically painful. Wyatt offered recommendations for online course design including text-only interfaces. In a similar vein, the collective authors of *Web Accessibility: Web Standards and Regulatory Compliance* suggested considering real people with real challenges as a way to begin thinking about accessibility issues in Web environments. They described people with such challenges as diminished motor control, loss of arms or hands, loss of sight, and loss of hearing. In such cases, individuals may not be able to access a keyboard or mouse, read the screen, or hear audio (Thatcher et al., 2006, pp. 2-3). These authors strongly suggested including disabled persons on Web design teams as a means to improve accessibility.

Web design teams often do not exist for OWI particularly, and instructors largely are on their own as they develop content. This autonomy leads to concerns about accessible content, a second high-level issue regarding OWI accessibility. Instructors may create a variety of documents and media for OWCs such as Microsoft Word and PDF documents, slide show presentations, videos, audio/videos, and podcasts. According to the Web Content Accessibility Guidelines (WCAG) (2012), any file delivered via the Web needs to be accessible in terms of being perceivable, operable, understandable, and robust. WCAG offers extensive details in each of these areas, but generally care must be taken to accommodate screen readers as "text alternatives" for non-text items (e.g., video and images, captions for multimedia, exclusive keyboard functionality sans mouse, avoidance of flashing images that may cause seizures, and use of style guides to help structure reading and information flow in documents). The WCAG guidelines, arising from the Web Accessibility Initiative (WAI), a division of the World Wide Web Consortium (the Web's governing body), have current authority regarding Web accessibility.

For OWI teachers not trained in Web design, the list of accommodations provided by WCAG may feel intimidating, which leads to a third issue to address concerning accessibility: the use of Web-based courseware or LMS packages. An important question is whether or not such courseware systems are designed to address accessibility issues. As Chapter 8 reveals, the answer, unfortunately, is *not completely*. LMSs are not developed to control completely for accessibility issues, in part because they invite content contributions from authors/instructors who typically are able bodied. Instructors ultimately are responsible for making their content accessible, which means that every attachment shared on an LMS must be designed to be accessible in terms of the accommodations listed above. How is this work possible for OWI teachers, given all of the other demands of the job?

If instructors want to make their materials universally acceptable, they must learn to create/author them with accessibility in mind. Using the word processor's "styles" for headings is one example. WCAG advised that information should appear in predictable ways, and consistent headings are one way to structure text-heavy documents. However, this information must be coded into the document so that screen readers can share the information; simply bolding or centering text on its own does not code the text. If authors use the "styles" function in Microsoft Word, for example, headings are coded automatically into documents with consistent font and style structure, enabling screen readers to share that information. Making this simple shift in authoring documents and attachments is one way to create accessible documents. Similarly, Web pages created via LMSs should make use of the "styles" function and "ALT-text" functions available in that courseware package.

Fortunately, those who design LMSs and higher education institutions are beginning to provide specific help and suggestions for accessible and universal design. At my own institution, I examined Moodle (our institution's LMS) for any sign of accessibility suggestions. I could not find it on my own; however, when I contacted the help line, I got an answer in less than 30 minutes with links to suggestions for making content more accessible (Regents, 2014). The suggestions generally followed the WCAG guidelines in terms of adding codes to attachments that would enable screen readers to share descriptions of non-text items and document structures.

With accessibility and OWI Principle 1 in mind, this chapter now addresses specific issues related to OWI training.

FOCAL POINTS FOR OWI TRAINING

Having taught writing online in course settings, tutoring centers, and academic programs for over ten years, and having conducted several training sessions for OWI teachers, I have learned that OWI training must enable instructors to air their concerns and take ownership of their online teaching experience from the very beginning. Instructors rarely come to online instruction training enthusiastically, and they often bring a healthy dose of resistance. An essential part of training involves allowing instructors to articulate their issues and concerns and then to develop suggestions that directly address those concerns. I also have learned that writing instructors—whether tutors, writing faculty, or discipline-specific faculty teaching writing—share many of the same issues and concerns about working with OWI. These issues regard four specific areas for training, a 4-M Training Approach:

1. *Migration*, or decisions about sameness and difference with onsite instruction, is an issue of course design;
2. *Model*, or the conceptual model or mental framework the online course is designed to convey, also is an issue of course design;
3. *Modality and media*, or modality as the form of communication in the course—whether synchronous or asynchronous—and such media as text, visual, audio, or video, are issues of technology choice; and
4. *Morale*, or the sense of community and "social presence" conveyed in the course, is an issue of student engagement in the OWC.

In the remainder of this chapter, I identify and address these recurring issues, and I outline proactive training suggestions to address them. Combined, these training steps allow OWI teachers to develop a design concept for OWI that they can own and tweak as they gain experience with OWI.

MIGRATION

As I use the term in this chapter, *migration* refers to the design elements of OWCs, which is one choice that OWI teacher trainees need to consider as they move to the online setting. One of the interesting things about OWI is that, while it has clear distinctions from other kinds of online courses, it frequently is depicted as having equally clear distinctions from traditional, onsite, face-to-face writing courses despite many discussions about core pedagogies remaining similar. Instructors often ask, "To what extent is OWI different from onsite writing instruction?" and "Is OWI better or worse than onsite writing instruction?" These questions about "sameness" and "difference" are so core and central to discussions about OWI that they demand attention. Scholars address these questions in various ways, but one word often used to address this issue is "migration" as a focal point (see both Chapter 4 & Warnock, 2009, for other perspectives on migration and adaptation of materials, theories, and pedagogical strategies). The issue is whether onsite writing instruction can be migrated effectively to an online writing setting or whether a writing course needs to be entirely redesigned for the online space. When thinking about these concerns, it is useful to recall that hybrid OWCs, while more complex than they may appear at first, exist in both environments (see Chapter 2) and make use of similar pedagogical theories and strategies.

The word *migration* is used frequently to describe OWI, but not always in positive terms. For example, *The State of the Art of OWI* report (2011c) made this overall claim about OWI:

> Teachers and administrators, to include those in writing
> centers, typically are simply migrating traditional face-to-face
> writing pedagogies to the online setting—both fully online
> and hybrid. Theory and practice specific to OWI has yet to be
> fully developed and engaged in postsecondary online settings
> across the United States. (CCCC OWI Committee, 2011c, p.
> 7)

This statement suggests that migration is a negative, or at least neutral, act—almost as if migration is a first step for instructors moving to the online space. Furthermore, in *A Position Statement of Principles and Example Effective Practices for OWI*, OWI Principle 3 stated, "Appropriate composition teaching/learning strategies should be developed for the unique features of the online instructional environment" (p. 12), which might seem to ignore the benefits of migration of onsite to online pedagogies. Yet, the duality of migration—considering whether it is a positive or negative strategy for OWI—can be observed in OWI Principle 4, which stated, "Appropriate onsite composition theories, pedagogies, and strategies should be migrated and adapted to the online instructional environment" (p. 14). The reality is that there is truth to both positions; as Hewett says in Chapter 1. OWI Principle 3 presents a yin to the yang in that most OWCs reflect traditional onsite writing pedagogy, but also that OWI training must prepare instructors for the differences of the online teaching space and potentially lead to new theory for the practice.

On the one hand, many scholars support the notion that OWI shares much in common with traditional, face-to-face writing instruction, and that writing instructors wanting to teach online do not need to start completely from scratch. Scott Warnock (2009) made this point clearly in *Teaching Writing Online*, where he prominently suggested that teachers migrate their face-to-face pedagogies to online environments. He expressed that he disliked the cautionary tales shared by some scholars that techniques used in the onsite classroom may not translate well to online environments. Indeed, Warnock suggested that "these types of cautions plunge new teachers immediately into a zone of uncertainty, where they may feel there is too much to overcome to begin teaching online" (2009, p. xiii). It is true that many instructors freeze at the initial thought of teaching online if it requires rewriting or rethinking every aspect of their teaching. Warnock suggested that teachers should find their core values and work on manifesting those into the online space, and that is, indeed, good advice. Nonetheless, Jason Snart, in Chapter 2, further advised that OWI teachers carefully adapt their writing instructional theories and strategies when migrating them online.

On the other hand, there are unique elements of online spaces, such as the text-only environment most often found in asynchronous settings (see Chapter 3). A text-heavy environment is a drastically different environment from the visual and auditory environment that exists in onsite settings. Hewett (2010, 2015b) acknowledged the challenges of text-based settings in *The Online Writing Conference: A Guide for Teachers and Tutors*. She demonstrated ways that conferencing by text can challenge students' reading skills and teachers' writing practices, and she theorized that semantic integrity (i.e., fidelity between the intended message and the inferred meaning) not only is possible but necessary to strive for in OWI. In *Reading to Learn and Writing to Teach: Literacy Strategies for Online Writing Instruction* (2015a), Hewett further theorized that students need to review and strengthen their reading skills for the cognitive challenges that OWI presents, requiring teachers to rethink their writing strategies for this audience. Warnock (2009) and Hewett's (2010, 2015a, 2015b) positions appear to represent the yin and the yang of OWI Principles 3 and 4.

Hence, concerning migration and OWI, the answer is "both/and." Instructors *both* can borrow strategies from onsite, face-to-face pedagogy *and* continue to adapt and tweak them uniquely for the online environment. Accepting this reality is a bit like straddling a line between sameness and difference: One foot needs to be firmly grounded in writing pedagogy and theory; the other needs to be grounded in online pedagogy. Similar arguments have been made about computers and writing, in which scholars both doubted and celebrated the possibilities of computer technology as they intersect with writing pedagogy. I am fond of citing Cynthia Selfe's (1989) mantra that "pedagogy must drive technology," which is a major theme in *Creating a Computer-Supported Writing Facility: A Blueprint for Action*. In this book, Selfe urged instructors to plan their pedagogy first and integrate technology later, and she adamantly stated that learning objectives need to lead and guide any technological use of computers in the classroom. This advice is repeated in countless treatises of computer-supported pedagogy (Barker & Kemp, 1990; Breuch, 2004; Galin & Latchaw, 1998; Harrington, Rickly, & Day, 2000; Hewett, 2013). This same sentiment is true for OWI: Our pedagogical principles remain strong and consistent, but our techniques and methods may be adapted to suit the online digital environment. In terms of migration, OWI does not operate from a radically different set of pedagogies or ideologies—although new theories may be needed—for it is firmly rooted in writing and composition studies. Yet, OWI teachers need to be open to the nuances introduced by the text-heavy nature of the digital environment.

Training Exercise on Migration

Keeping in mind the five educational principles of investigation, immersion, individualization, association, and reflection, one training exercise on migration might involve a teaching philosophy statement oriented toward OWI. Teaching philosophy statements are an excellent starting point for any OWI training for they ask participants to articulate their pedagogy first and then specify how they might practice that pedagogy through OWI. They also help instructors understand that they can and should exercise control over how they approach OWI. This exercise also is a foundation for professional development in OWI, as instructors can return to and adjust these statements as they become more seasoned OWI teachers.

The example training session, outlined below, engages the training principles of investigation, reflection, and association. It requires teachers to (1) outline key principles that guide one's teaching philosophy and (2) consider how uses of technology might influence or enhance that teaching philosophy.

In completing this activity, it is important to allow people time to hear how others are reconsidering writing instruction in light of OWI so that they may model for and teach each other about their concerns, anxieties, and positive anticipation of this move to the online environment. In the spirit of immersion, trainers can cement the value of this exercise by conducting it in either the asynchronous or synchronous online modality depending on the institution's selected LMS. Trainees can use text in the LMS online discussion board to get a feel for being in the "student" seat or they could create a short video of themselves talking about their statements and guiding principles; these, too, could be posted online to the LMS.

Training Activity

1. Write a brief, 200-word statement to articulate guiding principles that are critical to your writing pedagogy in onsite, face-to-face classrooms. Examples might include such principles as "student-centered writing pedagogy is critical to the success of a writing class" or "writing process is foregrounded in every assignment."

2. Then, write another 200-word statement to articulate how teaching online writing can enhance or mesh with your principles. For example, in terms of student-centered writing pedagogy, you might consider ways online technologies could help foster the goal, such as "students can easily share their writing with one another through electronic means on discussion boards or shared websites." In terms of writing process, you might discuss the use of technologies that allow for visualization of writing process, such as the integration of "comments" and "track changes" tools common to many word processing programs.

3. Discuss in small groups what you are learning about your onsite writing instruction principles and how you imagine they do or do not work in the online setting.

MODEL

Model is the second focal point for training, and it also is an element of design with which OWI teacher trainees should become familiar; they need to understand issues of model in order to make appropriate choices in developing their OWCs. Although there are similarities between online and onsite writing instruction, the text-heavy, digital environment of most asynchronous OWCs requires a different set of expectations regarding the "classroom," as the discussion of hybrid settings in Chapter 2 clearly demonstrates. When synchronous interactions are not available and audio/video rarely is used, what does a text-heavy class look like? How does it function? What are the key activities? How does grading happen? These questions all address issues of conceptual or mental models of the OWC, and interestingly, these questions are very similar to questions that address usability, an interdisciplinary study of how people interact with designs and technology.

Usability studies address how people interact with Web interfaces—often for the first time—and OWI training deals with a similar phenomenon of teacher adaptation to a Web space. In fact, much work in usability studies arose from computer science, specifically interface and software design (Nielsen, 1993). Today, the field of usability studies has grown to include intersections of several disciplines such as psychology, computer science, ergonomics, technical communication, design, and anthropology (Redish, 2004; Quesenbery, n.d.). Usability studies involves the examination of user perspectives to inform design processes, and it is especially concerned with ease-of-use and the ways in which technology helps users achieve their goals (Rubin & Chisnell, 2008, p. 4; Barnum, 2011). Many scholars have further defined usability by articulating attributes such as learnability, satisfaction, effectiveness, efficiency, engagement, and error tolerance (Nielsen, 1993; Rubin & Chisnell, 2008; Quesenbery, n.d.). At its heart, usability is concerned with how people interact with technology.

This concern intersects nicely with OWI in that instructors often worry about how technology affects their instructional goals. Usability studies also intersect with OWI training in that it directly addresses—and values—the anxiety that users may experience in digital environments. One might argue that when taking a course online, both instructors and students experience a degree of anxiety. Much of this anxiety can be attributed to unclear expectations both about how the course will function and student and instructor responsibilities.

It is here that the idea of a *conceptual model* or mental model can be extremely helpful in training for OWI. By conceptual model, I mean an understanding of the expectations of how something works. As Donald Norman (1988) explained in *The Design of Everyday Things*, good design has to do with how we understand what to do with objects (p. 12). Key to his theory of design is the idea of a conceptual or mental model, which he defines as "the models people have of themselves, others, the environment, and the things with which they interact" (p. 17). Using examples of everyday objects, Norman explained how designs can simplify or complicate our actions, resulting in various degrees of satisfaction. One of my favorite examples is his examination of doors in public places. He wondered "how do we know to open the door?" and explained that cues about the design help us understand whether to push or pull a door open (p. 10). For example, I have often observed doors in public buildings that have a large metal plate in the center of the door with a curved handle at the bottom of the plate. The curve, according to Norman, is a visible and physical cue that suggests that users must pull the door open. Without it, users might see the plate and think they must push the door to open it. The point is that design elements can communicate a model of use or intended action. In short, Norman said that conceptual models "allow[s] us to predict the effects of our actions" (13). Jeff Rubin (1996) further explained that conceptual models often are described in terms of metaphors that help users interact with a product or interface (for example, the activity of deleting a document on a computer desktop is symbolized by a trash can icon). Rubin pointed out that conceptual models are always operating, although they are not always explicit. If we can tap into our conceptual models, we have a much better chance of understanding a design and interacting with it successfully. Troubles arise when developer and user conceptual models do not match.

Conceptual models of OWI are always operating, much like Rubin suggested. Unfortunately, time and time again, I have observed that instructors and students bring different conceptual models to the OWI experience, and these clashes often result in attrition and/or student failure in the course. One of the most common clashes I have seen occurs when instructors create an OWC that models a face-to-face class, but students come to the OWC expecting it to be a self-paced, independent study. That is to say, students might expect an OWI to be flexible, negotiable, with a deadline for work at the end of the semester, rather than a large class experience that happens on a weekly schedule online. When this clash happens, students may disappear for weeks at a time and surface when they are ready to complete the work. By the time students realize the consequences of these actions, their only choices might be to drop or fail the course. Keeping this possibility in mind, instructors need to learn to communicate clearly about the overall structure and model of the course before the course even begins. This kind of communication will help ensure that students' and instructor's conceptual models agree and will guide the student's work. As Norman (1988) and Rubin (1996) revealed, successful use is achieved when user and designer conceptual models match one another. The same goal is true for the OWI experience: Student and instructor understandings of OWC model must match.

When this idea of conceptual model is applied further to OWI, it is useful to think about different ways OWC models could be structured in terms of schedules and interactions. To illustrate, three popular models for OWI that I have encountered include an independent study model, a workshop model, or face-to-face class model. Each model structures course schedules and interactions differently.

Independent Study Model

An *independent study model* suggests that individual students take the online course essentially as a one-to-one interaction with the instructor, with no interaction with other students or larger group. The course might be set up with a reading list, specific writing assignments, and deadlines for specific assignments. It might have a great deal of flexibility depending on the schedule constraints of the instructor and student involved; in fact, the instructor and student could refine timelines for work continually and as needed. The conceptual model of an independent study reflects a great deal of flexibility and an expectation that the student will have direct and frequent interaction with the instructor. This model essentially is similar to the *correspondence course* model that characterized distance education courses for decades. While it seems archaic, I mention this model because *it is often the dominant conceptual model that students bring with them to online courses*. Many students sign up for OWCs because of the flexibility an asynchronous course offers (CCCC OWI Committee, 2011c). They might come with the expectation that they can complete the course on their own time.

Registration systems are an important factor in providing information to students about the models used for OWCs. It is helpful to provide detailed information about the course wherever possible. For example, at our institution, we have a Course Guide that allows instructors to provide detailed information about the courses they teach. If the course is online, information about that format can be included. It also is helpful if a syllabus or note from instructor can be shared or accessed on the registration site.

Workshop Model

A second model, the *workshop model*, might create a structure for on-going interactions to occur with instructors and between/among students. A workshop model might be structured around key events that help students practice writing, work in peer review groups to receive feedback on their writing, and revise their work. There are many ways that workshops could be organized; my favorite example of an online writing workshop is from Gotham Writers' Workshop, an organization in New York City that offers hundreds of OWCs for a variety of purposes and contexts. Gotham structures all of their OWCs around sharing individual writers' work, much like a creative writing workshop. They use a strong metaphor to communicate their workshop model, which they call "the booth," which describes the activity of peer review. They visualize the OWC as authors and readers "sitting down" to talk with each other about their work. As it plays out in their online courses, the booth is an interface in which writers copy and paste their work into a split screen. The top of the screen is the author's work, and the bottom of the screen is a space for multiple reviewers to comment. Time in the booth is scheduled carefully through a calendar in which authors meet with reviewers on certain times and dates. Activity in the booth is made visible to the entire class, very much like a creative writing class might handle turn-taking of authors on the hot seat getting review feedback from the rest of the class. In this conceptual model, the booth—workshopped writing—is the primary activity of the course. A similar concept, but different resulting interface, would be the Colorado State University "Writing Studio," which provides students and instructors with the ability to create "rooms" in which they can organize whatever writing activities they wish (Writing@CSU). Like "the booth," the "Writing Studio" carries with it a workshop metaphor in which writing would be reviewed and revised. The studio offers even more robust opportunities for flexible learning environments for instructors and students.

Face-to-Face Writing Class Model

A third model might be simply a *face-to-face writing class*. That is to say, an instructor might say "I want to teach my online class exactly the same way I teach my face-to-face class." This kind of model fully embraces the idea of migration"of face-to-face pedagogies to the online space, which often means that primary activities of the online course involve discussion-based activities organized around assigned readings, peer review workshops, or other course activities. This model implies that online discussions and forums will be key and central to the course, affirming the idea that online experience will be text-intensive. Often, this model requires that all students participate in all discussions, thus creating a heavy reading load for the instructor and students alike (Griffin & Minter, 2013). An important element of the face-to-face model for OWI is the expectation that the course works on a shared schedule involving all students. That is, it is not an independent study in which students can take the course at their own pace. Instructors using this model must consider how the course structure and activities, although migrated, need to be adapted (see Chapters 2 & 4) such that the affordances of the online setting are used fully. OWI teachers should set clear expectation that students will complete assignments and activities as an entire class using the same timeline, and appropriate technologies must be available at the right times to support these activities (e.g., assignment drop box, online discussion forums, synchronous chats, posted reading materials, and the like).

Training for Conceptual Models

In terms of training, integrating different conceptual models into OWI training is a surprisingly fun and innovative exercise. The following exercise is a case study and discussion exercise that engages the training principles of investigation, immersion, and association. Specifically, the exercise asks instructors to identify the possible conceptual models of OWI in the case. The provided case study presents a clash between a teacher and student's understanding of an OWC's conceptual model.

Training Activity

Read the following case study about clashing conceptual models.

Two weeks prior to the end of a summer session, a graduating senior in a technical and professional OWC received an email notice from his instructor that he was failing the course. The news was a big surprise to the student. The instructor noted that the student was failing the course because he did not turn in two major assignments, nor did he participate in several required online discussions throughout the course. The student's reaction was to ask, rather informally and somewhat flippantly, whether the instructor could please cut him a break; he was at his family's cabin for summer vacation, but he needed the course to graduate. He asked the instructor if he could turn in the necessary assignments in one bundle, and would the instructor accept the work? The student suggested he would be happy to do whatever was required to finish the course. In receiving this request, the instructor's initial reaction was to fail the student anyway because the student did not abide by the syllabus requirements. In fact, the student totally disregarded the syllabus requirements by failing to participate in weekly activities and assignments, clearly communicating that he was making up his own rules.

Discuss the following questions with your peers in your online discussion board:

1. How did the conceptual models of this OWC vary between instructor and student?
2. Was the student's disregard for the rules of this online course a reason to fail him and delay his college graduation? Why or why not?
3. In what ways, if at all, do issues of inclusivity and access come into play with this case?
4. What would you decide as an instructor in this situation?
5. What would you do to prevent this situation in future OWCs?

Modality/Media

A third focal point important for OWI training is combined notions of *modality* and *media*, which address crucial choices of technologies for OWCs. In

OWI, modality and media are defined somewhat narrowly. Connie Mick and Geoffrey Middlebrook considered the modes of synchronicity (real time) and asynchronicity (delayed time) in Chapter 3. By media, OWI literature tends to mean the kind of delivery formats that are used for course content such as text, audio, video, or other media (see Hewett, 2013, for example). I discuss these items in the subsections below with the focus of teacher training.

First, however, it is helpful to note the rich connections that OWI should share with digital rhetoric and notions of *multimodality*, particularly given the exigencies of Chapters 14 and 15. Although mode, modality, and media have been defined somewhat differently for OWI and digital rhetoric, multimodality is an important development in writing studies that intersects with OWI and that should enrich an understanding of teaching writing online. Multimodality has received attention in composition studies as a way to expand understanding and definitions of writing. In *Remixing Composition: A History of Multimodal Writing Pedagogy*, Jason Palmeri (2012) noted similarities between multimodal composing and process pedagogy in composition. He asserted that composition has always been a multimodal endeavor, integrating images, text, and speech in ways that contribute to the writing process (p. 25), and he traced the history of composition to demonstrate multimodality. We see even more explicit treatment of multimodality in *Writing New Media*, in which Anne Wysocki (2004) asserted that "new media needs to be opened to writing" (p. 5) and that multimodal compositions allow us to examine the "range of materialities of text" (p. 15). The *Writing New Media* collection illustrated how writing instructors can integrate writing assignments that encourage students to explore and/or create visual, aural, and digital components of their work to enhance the message they want to communicate. Similar examples are found in collections such as *Multimodal Composition* (Selfe, 2007). While these connections illustrate and even justify the view of writing as multimodal, few of these sources address writing instruction as a multimodal endeavor. Instead, these sources are focused on helping *students* create multimodal documents and expand definitions of writing. We might take some of the same lessons of multimodality and apply them to OWI from the teaching perspective.

Synchronous or Asynchronous Modalities

Deciding between the synchronous and asynchronous modalities is one of the first choices an OWI teacher must make when offering a hybrid or fully online OWC, as Chapter 3 describes.

New OWI teachers need to understand that choosing to use a synchronous modality for an OWC means that students must be present (via the Web) at the same time, and the course is scheduled to meet for a regular weekly time and day(s). This modal choice supports the idea of a discussion-oriented writing class, in some ways similar to a traditional face-to-face format. Synchronous courses would require the use of "real-time" conferencing technologies that afford simultaneous audio and text contributions. Webinars are an example of a synchronous modality in which speakers share information and participants speak or write comments or questions; if written, they use chat room or text messaging technology. Images and documents also can be shared during synchronous sessions, and sometimes they can be edited simultaneously. Small groups could be set up to have group chats that supplement course material.

OWI teachers may have a choice in whether to develop a synchronous OWC, although often the LMS dictates their course modality. In making a choice, OWI teachers should consider the advantages and disadvantages of synchronous OWCs. One advantage to a synchronous OWC is the flexibility offered in terms of place and space; students and instructor can participate from any networked computer with the appropriate technology. Another advantage is that a synchronous course immediately communicates the idea that regular attendance and presence are necessary in order to participate, thus removing some of the barriers regarding expectations associated with independent studies or other asynchronous models discussed earlier. A third advantage is the ability to have live question and answer sessions with students, thus providing an opportunity to clear up any confusion about material, assignments, or activities in the class. As well, the synchronous modality has the potential to reinforce the sense and presence of a learning community (rather than individual, asynchronous contributions). One disadvantage of choosing a synchronous OWC regards access. Technological capabilities of synchronous sessions may not always be consistent; sometimes synchronous technologies cannot support a large number of participants at one time. Students may also have a variety of network connections, as Chapter 10 discusses, that may not be sufficient for the synchronous technologies even those that are mobile (see Chapter 16).

In contrast, OWI teachers need to understand that an asynchronous OWC would be offered in a "delayed time" format using non-real time technologies that allow students to participate at any time, around the clock. An asynchronous OWC might provide materials on a course website for review such as presentations, readings, discussion questions, videos, or podcasts. After reviewing material, students might be expected to participate in weekly (or more frequent) online discussions, quizzes, or group work to reinforce what they have learned. Writing assignments might be turned in via a drop box, and instructors would review the material and provide comments individually to students online. Asynchronous comments might be text-based, audio-based, audio/visual. In sum, the asynchronous modal choice reinforces the idea of individual responsibility and drive to participate in an online learning community.

Asynchronous OWCs offer many advantages that OWI teachers need to think about, some of them similar to synchronous courses. Like synchronous courses, flexibility is an advantage for asynchronous courses in that students can participate via distance. However, in asynchronous courses, students participate in their own time rather than a regularly scheduled time. Another advantage of asynchronous courses is that the delayed-time format allows students to think through their contributions, and often students use that opportunity to review and even edit their responses before posting. Some disadvantages of the asynchronous modality are that the sheer volume of textual contributions might be overwhelming and even disengaging for students (as well as their teachers; training should therefore address time management for both). Care needs to be taken to contain reading loads, and one way to address that concern is to make more use of online student group contributions rather than whole-class contributions and to not grade every interaction, as Warnock notes in Chapter 4. Another disadvantage of the asynchronous format is that students need to be highly disciplined to follow deadlines. The absence of a regularly scheduled class may be difficult for some students, and the asynchronous modality for an OWC may convey a stronger sense of flexibility than actually exists.

Whatever choice of modality an instructor makes, there no doubt will be a transition to thinking about "making meaning" in that modality. An important concept in further understanding both modality and shifts in modality is *affordances*, or what Gunther Kress (2012) called "the material 'stuff' of the modality (sound, movement, light and tracings on surfaces, etc.)" (p. 80). He suggested that affordances are "shaped and reshaped in everyday social lives" (p. 80). Affordances are discussed similarly by Norman (1988), where he suggested that affordances manifest in the physical characteristics and capabilities of objects (again, we might reference the curved handle on a metal plate that forms a door handle; the curved handle *affords* users to pull the door open). Continuing this idea of physical or material characteristics, we also might understand affordances by reflecting on Lev Vygotsky's (1986) discussion of tools. In *Thought and Language*, Vygotsky explained affordances as a way to understand "tools that mediate the relationships between students and learning goals" (Castek & Beach, 2013, p. 554). Vygotsky's work often is used to support activity theory, a framework that addresses ways different tools mediate different kinds of activities and resulting meanings (Russell, 1999; Spinuzzi, 1999). Taken together, we might see the synchronous and asynchronous modalities as each having its own "affordances" that support different kinds of meaning making activities. In the next section, I address the OWI counterpart to modality—media—and the opportunities various media present for OWI teachers.

Media: Text, Visuals, Audio, and Video

In OWI, media are the ways through which the learning occurs, not in terms of specific software but in terms of alphabetic text, still visuals and images, audio recordings, and video recordings with and without sound. These media can be used singly or intertwined; digital rhetoric often calls these New Media and their use makes for multimodality. One immediately might think of "tools" in reference to media, or the affordances of material technologies such as online discussion forums, text-based synchronous chats, audio messages, or video chats. But before thinking about tools, it is important to think through media choices more fundamentally in terms of writing pedagogy, which includes teaching goals and strategies, rhetoricity (as Chapter 14 addresses), and the media themselves.

In *Writing New Media*, Anne Wysocki (2004) asserted that "new media needs to be opened to writing" (p. 5) and that multimedia compositions allow us to examine the "range of materialities of text" (p. 15). The *Writing New Media* collection illustrated how writing instructors can integrate writing assignments that encourage students to explore and/or create visual, aural, and digital components of their work to enhance the message they want to communicate. Similar examples are found in such collections as *Multimodal Composition* (Selfe, 2007) and *Remixing Composition* (Palmeri, 2012). Palmeri (2012) noted in particular that composition has always integrated a variety of media such as images, text, and speech, and in ways that contribute to the writing process (p. 25). He advocated the inclusion of various media in composition pedagogy so that students have a broader understanding of the composing process.

These connections illustrate important points about the value of media in writing instruction. For example, including various media can enhance the message of communication, and such inclusion also can help students appreciate and more clearly understand composing processes. In a similar fashion, these lessons can be applied to OWI, which is to say that instructors also must consider the value of multiple media for OWI. For example, integrating multiple media allows OWI teachers to enhance instruction and clarify messages or learning objectives in an online setting; reach students with various learning styles; and make use of the technologies that mirror uses students experience in social interactions, game playing, and the work world. These benefits represent "flexibility in use," a point stated in the justification for OWI Principle 1 regarding inclusion and access and that addresses the variety of preferences and abilities students bring to an online environment (pp. 7-8). The use of multiple media additionally may provide alternative perspectives for students to engage with course material and assignments.

Certainly, different material aspects afford different kinds of meaning-making activities. Applied to OWI, the media choices commonly available provide OWI teachers with a myriad of options involving textual, visual, audio, and video/multimodal tools. The rest of this section details possibilities for OWI in each of these areas. An overlying assertion I forward is that the field of writing studies is filled with accounts of innovative, multimodal writing pedagogies; however, rarely are these accounts placed in the context of OWI. I argue that we can take these insights and connect them more explicitly to OWI.

Text

OWI is characterized as being "text heavy" due in part to the discussion-oriented nature of most OWCs. Alphabetic text, a visual medium unless given shape by Braille or sound by screen readers, is the primary means of communication between students and teacher and among students in contemporary OWI. That prevalence may be an issue of cost or of access, as this book discusses, but often it is not a matter of teacher's choice in that the LMS is developed with text-focused affordances. This textual focus is not a bad thing as it appropriately requires reading and writing literacy skills for a writing or writing-intensive course. Tools that make use of text involve discussion boards, chats, text messaging, email, blogs, Wikis, or course Web pages. OWI teachers need training that includes a rhetorical understanding of these tools, pedagogical uses of them, and familiarity with the technology that engages them. When it comes to text as a medium, it is the writing practice that enhances the writing itself.

A common example of a text-based activity would be a discussion (or message) board, an activity often used in OWCs. Rhetorically, discussion boards allow students to practice writing arguments as well as examine reader responses and perspectives. Discussion boards can be used to support large class discussions about required readings, large class discussions about writing exercises, and small group exercises such as peer review. Typically, an instructor posts a prompt about course material, and students "reply" to the prompt, resulting in one individual message per student; discussions become interactive and more meaningful when students also are expected to respond to each other. The resultant writing practice leads students to produce many more words than they might have otherwise (Warnock, 2009). Online discussions also can be led by students or can be limited to student groups. In any of these formats, discussion prompts are posted, and students respond to the prompt in writing at different times (delayed time).

Despite the prevalence of online discussion boards, it is important to understand that students may not know intuitively how to participate in an online discussion—and instructors may not intuitively know how to mediate (or evaluate) them. Training new OWI teachers to mediate online discussions is one issue that Warnock addressed in Chapter 4 and in *Teaching Writing Online: How and Why* (2009). One instructor shared with me his strategy for structuring online discussion forums. First, he outlined expectations for discussion prompts that included the following elements: (1) the response must directly address the prompt or query, (2) the response must be completed within a word limit (to be determined based on the exercise), (3) the response must include at least one reference to the reading in question, and (4) students must respond to one other student's contribution. This instructor also included a simple, clear 5-point grading structure for online discussions based on the four requirements of the discussion, which clarified for students that these discussions were weighted in the course and were not meant to be personal responses to the readings. This structure meant that the instructor graded each and every response from students—a tall order in an OWC and one that training should consider and debate given the WAC principle that not all writing needs to be graded or formally assessed. However, given a structure like this, perhaps online discussions would be used sparingly, such as once a week rather than two or three times a week.

Another example of text-based activities occurs in chat rooms, a synchronous technology that allows participants to contribute to the same, real-time discussion in a textual environment. Text-based chats may be set up for a large group in a synchronous class setting or in small groups. In either case, the students basically interact about a topic using real-time text messaging. Students can use chats for specific purposes such as discussing a reading, or coming to a group decision, or completing an activity assigned for class. One advantage of textual chats is the sense of community that often develops as students interact with one another. In OWCs that otherwise may be asynchronous, students can miss opportunities to talk with their classmates in real time. Chats sometimes feel informal and encourage informal discussions that students appreciate. Another advantage is that chats can be archived; if students completed important work during a chat, they often can save the archive of the chat for their record (or teacher's record) towards longer written products (see Chapter 4).

Blogs (Weblogs) and journals are other venues that use text in OWI. Using blog technology, instructors can require students to create and maintain their own blog throughout a writing course. The blog software in an LMS typically catalogs entries in reverse chronological order; blogs also afford comments from readers about individual blog entries, in effect creating a "dialogue" among readers. Blogs also afford Web structures; students can create additional links to Web pages that afford students the opportunity to create Web pages for different writing samples. Wikis are another text-based tool designed to create collaborative, living, Web-based documents, but they can be tricky in that often only one writer can work in the Wiki at a time, creating the need for a way to signal other students that the Wiki is open. Instructors have used Wikis to encourage small and large group discussion and projects. Another text-based technology is the OWI Web course page itself—typically located in the LMS—in terms of the textual instructions and material offered by the writing instructor.

As discussed earlier, while there are advantages to a heavy-textual orientation for students, such as increased writing practice, there are also key drawbacks, such as a sense of being overwhelmed by text and experiencing tedium from reading and responding to countless prompts. OWI teachers may find themselves feeling equally overwhelmed with their efforts, which June Griffin and Debbie Minter (2013) called the "literacy load" in keeping with the other loads that teachers carry (see also Chapter 5). Therefore, OWI teachers need training to determine how they can manage this especially heavy literacy load, their own reading of student writing in particular.

Training OWI teachers responsibly would include such recommendations as necessary to make text-based experiences manageable from a sheer reading perspective. High volumes of text on a screen lead to low levels of engagement with text. Research from usability studies provides useful insights on this point, specifically results from eye-tracking studies on how people read online. Jakob Nielsen (2006) asserted, for example, that many studies confirm an "F-Pattern" of reading on the Web in which readers start in the top left-corner, read horizontally, then read down and horizontally at faster increments. Essentially, the F-Pattern suggests that readers on the Web read less as they go along. Eye-tracking research confirms that readers are looking for textual cues, such as headings and key words, and that readers do not tolerate excessive text on the screen (Barnum, 2011). When we consider these confirmed reading habits, we see the importance of making text clear and concise, and as minimal as possible.

To this end, OWI teachers need training in how to make their text readable and manageable. OWI teachers also need training in writing for students, however, as students may struggle themselves with the high literacy load of OWI. *A Position Statement of Principles and Example Effective Practices for OWI* (CCCC OWI Committee, 2013) repeatedly mentioned strategies for clear textual communication, many of which align with technical writing and Web-based writing principles. Some suggestions are found in Effective Practice 3.3, which suggested the following suggestions for OWI in textual modality:

- Writing shorter, chunkier paragraphs
- Using formatting tools wisely to highlight information with adequate white space, colors, and readable fonts
- Providing captioned graphics where useful

- Drawing (when tools allow)
- Striking out words and substituting others to provide clear examples of revision strategies
- Using highlighting strategically (pp. 12-13).

These useful suggestions for writing to students in text-based online settings mesh well with other published recommendations for Web-writing and technical communication (see, for example, Hewett 2015a). For instance, in *Letting Go of the Words*, Janice Redish (2007) offered suggestions for Web-based writing that address typography, color, use of space, and concise writing. One section of her text is actually called "Cut! Cut! Cut! And Cut again!" (p. 132) to reinforce the idea that Web-based writing needs to communicate concisely and clearly. Redish also advised using direct language and thinking strategically about communicating a core message on every page, and this advice resonates with stated effective practices of OWI to use "direct rather than indirect language" (p. 12).

Keeping manageable text in mind, I strongly support training OWI teachers to engage the OWI principles regarding clear and linguistically direct language (part of what Hewett [2015b, 2010] calls semantic integrity). I would add that clear and consistent heading structures also are important to achieve textual clarity in any text-based materials provided by instructors. For example, in our upper-division online course in technical and professional writing, we have structured the course around eight units; each unit has a consistent structure including two main sections: (1) "Read me first" (a section including attachments with an overview of the unit, required readings, and any supplemental materials) and (2) "Activities and assignments" (a section including functions and/or links to discussion forums, assignment drop boxes, Wikis, or blogs). Chunking each unit into these main sections helps students understand the expectations for each unit. An important part of the "Read me first" section is the "overview," a Web page document that provides an introduction of the unit, its learning objectives, and instructor comments about what the unit entails. We have found the "overview" very important as a communication vehicle for students, and we also find that consistent heading structures are imperative. We include the following headings in each unit "overview": Introduction (comment on topic, subject matter, and its importance to the course), learning objectives (specific to that unit with connections to previous and/or future units), readings (the instructor's comments about readings and access can be included here), and assignments and activities (any specific directions can be included here). Figure 11.1 provides an example.

The information in the overview shown in Figure 11.1 provides students with a blueprint about the subject matter and rationale for each unit and its readings, activities, and assignments. Additionally, it aligns with the guidelines of OWI Principle 1 (p. 7) in its uses of "styles," numbers, and bulleted lists that are internally coded for screen readers.

Visuals

Teaching online writing through the Web affords the possibility of including many visuals that can supplement OWI. Visuals also use eyesight; they can be still images such as photographs, diagrams, tables, illustrations, drawings, or other graphics. Training OWI teachers about using visuals well requires some understanding of their relative advantages and challenges for students. Teachers need to learn how to employ visuals in their teaching such that students of all learning styles and abilities can read them; this use typically means providing a text-based caption and, for complete access, a thorough description of the visual.

Students, on the other hand, need to learn both how to read visuals provided by their instructors and to engage and use visuals in their own writing even when it is text-based essay writing. As discussed, many instructors have considered how to help students learn to integrate visuals into their writing, enabling them to explore multimodal aspects of writing (see, for example, Wysocki, Johnson-Eilola, Selfe, & Sirc, 2004). Many online supplemental sites now have a variety of visual materials including charts, graphs, animations, photos, or other images related to writing from which students might choose.

However, an even more immediate use of visuals for purposes of OWI is for students to learn how to visualize writing. Two specific uses of visuals and for which OWI teachers may be trained are well suited to OWI: (1) idea maps that outline writing processes and (2) annotated writing samples.

Idea maps are an often used technique in traditional face-to-face courses to help students outline a writing process or to visualize brainstorming ideas. Idea maps are an assignment that returns this discussion to the straddled line of on-site and OWI; idea maps can be created easily online using a variety of tools, for many software programs and Web-based interfaces now include drawing software that afford idea mapping. Some software programs are especially made for creating visuals and charts of this sort, but simple drawing functions in Microsoft Word work as well, are fairly ubiquitous and accessible (although it must be made clear that not all students use Microsoft Word, and those who do their composing on a mobile device, as described in Chapter 16, will not find it easy to accomplish this kind of technology-enhanced visualization work for educational purposes).

A second type of visual suited to OWI is an *annotated writing sample*. An annotated writing sample is a document that includes callouts (often in color) with explanations or comments about effective or ineffective features of writing. Annotated writing samples often are found in textbooks; when included in an

OWC with real comments from real instructors, annotated samples are excellent ways to provide personalized expectations about writing for students in a given class. Such annotations, however, might not be fully accessible to screen readers and may be unavailable when documents are saved to rich text or other than Microsoft Word formats.

Audio

Sound is an under-used medium in OWI that could be integrated easily and more fully. Sound appeals to a second sense in addition to the heavily used eyesight sense that both text and visuals engage. When more senses are added, it is possible that students will learn differently. Some will find sound to be an appealing and inclusive medium for learning. Therefore, OWI teachers should learn how and when to use sound in their OWCs. Two simple examples of engaging audio whether live or recorded are (1) using the phone and (2) integrating voice messages and/or podcasts to students.

Regarding phone use, I often remind instructors in training sessions that when a writing class is taught online, there is no reason that instructors and students cannot use the phone to communicate. In fact, adding a new medium diversifies communication and can benefit the interaction, while helping students who experience the OWC as distancing to feel more connected (Hewett, 2010, 2015b; Warnock, 2009). Additionally, all instructors and students already know how to use the phone, and it typically is accessible to all. Instructors might set up phone office hours and provide students with a phone number that students can call. Phone office hours provide students the clear benefit of knowing they can contact their instructor at noted times with any questions. It provides assurance that instructors will "be there" to help answer any questions. In-person office visits also are excellent for fully online students who are resident students or for those who are in hybrid OWCs.

Aside from using the phone, other audio methods include voice messages that can be posted asynchronously. Various digital recording devices and software enable voice recording and saving to a file. Sometimes, the software is integrated in an LMS. When the technology also translates voice into text, students can receive a visual text message with their instructor's voice included, increasing accessibility. If provided as part of an LMS, students also can use the technology to communicate with other students, thus skipping the text-heavy need to write for that particular interaction. Podcasts are another audio tool that easily can be implemented in OWCs. Podcasts are audio recordings that are saved, archived, and made accessible via the Web. An effective illustration is the Grammar Girl website by Mignon Fogherty (2009) in which she creates several three-minute podcasts on topics of grammar, punctuation, and mechanics. Each podcast is ac-

Overview:

This unit will introduce you to the concepts of audience (chapter 2), document organization (chapter 16), and the genres of letters and email (chapter 5). You will practice thinking about readers by analyzing an existing letter, writing a letter of complaint, and writing a response to that letter. In the process you will learn about elements of letter writing such as rhetorical analysis, organizational elements of letters, style and usage, and suggested formats. We will conduct our first peer review in this unit. After completing your complaint letter assignment, you will write an email message to your instructor in which you propose an idea for the final analytical report assignment in this class. In addition to helping you think about your final project, the email assignment will help you gain experience thinking about audience and professional correspondence in electronic environments.

Learning Objectives:

After completing this unit, you should be able to
1. Identify and explain a rhetorical situation--including subject, purpose, readers, and context of use--in a correspondence situation.
2. Conduct peer review: write a draft of the assignment and review a peer's draft for rhetorical appeal, organization, style, and format, and summarize your review in a letter to the peer author.
3. Write letters in correct format to two different audiences with different purposes.
4. Write a clear and concise email to your instructor about a potential topic for your final analytical report assignment in this course.

Readings:
- Chapters 2, 16, and 5
- Peer Review Tutorial
- What Else Do Readers Want?
- Downloadable Writer-Centered Analysis Chart
- **Grammar Girl**, "How to Write a Complaint Letter"
- "Writing Effective Email", by Dennis G. Jerz
- Model complaint letter

Figure 11.1. Sample overview of an OWC unit

companied by a text script, so listeners can read as they listen. Podcasts could be used by instructors in a similar way, such as by providing thoughts on an assignment or other class topic; instructors could provide commentary with script. In fact, audio messages have been used in conjunction with writing commentary, as well as to accompany presentations or texts. In sum, audio adds an element of personalization to the OWC in ways that are relatively simple and easy to implement.

Video

Audio/video, called simply *video* here, offers a multimedia option for OWCs that can combine visual, audio, and text productively. It addresses both the senses of sight and sound. With the evolution of common video and streaming technologies often used on the Internet and with social media, video has become a mainstay technology for the Web. As well, video has taken a prominent place in online learning. Many courses that experiment with a "flipped" instructional model include video lectures by instructors enabling more active work time in the class itself; hybrid OWCs can make good use of this model, for example. Video offers many affordances for teaching online writing. In this section, I address three possibilities for which OWI teachers might be trained: (1) asynchronous instructor videos, (2) synchronous video chats with students, and (3) video animations on writing topics (including screen casts).

Asynchronously provided instructor videos are useful tools for sharing course content or simple announcements about the course. Videos offer students a more personal connection with the instructor in that students can hear and see the instructor. Instructors can use simple, often free tools for video announcements. Short videos can be archived and then uploaded as Web links that can be attached to an online course and may even be reused in future OWCs. Instructors also can videotape lectures, although lectures are not a frequent instructional method in most writing courses. Some software affords the combination of visual writing examples or PowerPoint slides, instructor voice, and a picture if desired. Video also offers a promising method for instructors to return feedback to students about their writing. As Elizabeth Vincelette (2013) and Jeff Sommers (2012, 2013) among others have described, instructors can use video capture technology to comment on student papers. Video-capture enables instructors to make use of text, audio, and video to share comments, questions, reader response, and suggestions for revision for students to consider. This multimedia format is helpful to students in providing a diversity of communication that they can replay and integrate at their own speed.

Synchronous video chats are another tool instructors can use in OWCs. Synchronous video using easily accessed and common software can afford the opportunity for instructors to talk with students about their work. Synchronous video chats create opportunities for real-time, one-to-one student conferences; instructors can create a sign-up list and meet with the students at their assigned times. As well, synchronous video chats can be used to foster large or small class discussions. Large-class synchronous discussions might involve an instructor who mediates the discussion and reviews course material and/or readings. In the background, simultaneous written chats enable students present to fuel the large-class discussion. The instructor may field questions by reviewing student contributions to the chat. Synchronous meetings of this sort resemble a Webinar format.

Training is needed, however, because facilitating this kind of discussion can be an overwhelming experience, as OWI teachers must rely on their video and audio while reading simultaneous responses from a variety of students. There also is the issue of technology access and reliability, as synchronous sessions with large groups may experience technical difficulties while supporting multimodal elements such as video, audio, and text simultaneously for 20 people. A variation of synchronous discussions is to have small-group synchronous sessions with the instructor, which can make the interactions more manageable because smaller discussions tend to foster a more close-knit, personal sense of community. The instructor might schedule in advance certain times that students can meet with the instructor to discuss course material. Ideally, an instructor would share presentation slides or other material to the small group and field any questions. In a smaller synchronous discussion, students have the opportunity to each ask questions.

Finally, OWI teachers benefit from knowing about how animated videos can be used to supplement an OWC. Because OWCs often involve the use of various tools, instructors could create screen casts that illustrate different tools. A screen cast might be made to illustrate activities such as peer review (e.g., how to use the "comments" function of Microsoft Word); or a screen cast might be used to illustrate the features of the OWC's Web interface. In addition to screen casts, videos on writing topics might be used. Projects like WRIT VID (2013) used animations to illustrate aspects of writing activities; likewise, many writing programs across the country are including videos with interviews of student and faculty writers. All of these videos can add supplemental material for the writing course.

Training on Modalities and Media

Training workshops offer instructors the important opportunity to investigate different modalities and media, with the goal of becoming more comfortable in the OWC environment. As well, gaining experience with different modalities and media will help instructors better associate with students who also must immerse themselves in the same space. One effective training exercise that engages the training principles of investigation, immersion, association, and reflection involves online peer review among teacher trainees. This activity must be conducted in an online environment, preferably the one teachers will use for the OWC. Teacher trainees should be grouped in pairs. Using the small group venue of the LMS, provide a peer review prompt in which you ask each pair to exchange documents and conduct peer review using a different modality and media. (A document that works well for exchange is the teaching philosophy statement created for the migration training activity shown in this chapter; however, any document could be used.) Assign each pair a different modality and media for their peer review, such as text-only, audio-only, video-only, or multimodal. This activity may require setting up an assignment or discussion prompt to enable their participation as students (rather than as teachers) in the training OWC.

The key to this assignment is not the actual peer review critique but an eventual consideration of the modality and media used. While the textual modality is essential and important for OWI, OWCs easily can make use of multiple modalities of communication and representation such as visual, voice, and video. Using these media from the student position enables immersion into the technology and a pedagogical strategy that can lead to more introspective reflection about one's OWI activities, purposes, and perceived optimal outcomes. It also provides an opportunity for investigating not only different media but also other teacher trainees' experiences of them.

Training Activity

In pairs, engage in online peer review using the teaching philosophy statements from earlier in the training or another suitable text. Each pair should conduct the online peer review using different modalities and media. Exchange your texts and, using the modality and media you've selected, engage in discussion with your peer by articulating any questions, comments, or suggestions about his or her text. Complete this peer review exercise within three days. Prior to the online peer review, you may find it useful to exchange contact information with your peer review partner(s) to set up a plan for technology and timing; this is the kind of engagement that students in the OWC also need to do, making it useful to learn firsthand the challenges of online interactions for assignment completion purposes.

- Pair 1: Text-only peer review (asynchronous)
- Pair 2: Audio-only peer review (asynchronous using voice email or other digital recording technology)
- Pair 3: Audio-only peer review (synchronous using phone)
- Pair 4: Video-only peer review (synchronous using online audio and video technology)
- Pair 5: Multimodal (asynchronous using a screen capture technology— that is, an uploaded document with comments, and voice annotation)
- Pair 6: Multimodal (synchronous using online voice technology and an uploaded document with written comments)

When you have completed the online peer review, engage with the entire training group in an online, text-based discussion about the different peer review modalities and media.

- What did each pair like and dislike about their modality and medium of peer review?
- What were the affordances and what were the constraints of their modality and medium?
- What was the rhetorical effect of each variation of peer review?
- What preparation was needed to set up the peer review?
- How might instructors facilitate such activities for students?

MORALE

The fourth focal area, *morale*, has to do with the level of satisfaction that students and teachers experience regarding a sense of community in an OWC.

Issues of morale help new OWI teachers address ways to help students engage in their OWCs. The questions for OWI teacher trainees that apply here include:

- Are students excited to be in the OWC? How do I know?
- If they are not expressing interest in the course, how can I help to change that?
- What sense of learning community do I observe? What do students express they are experiencing?
- Do I have an interpersonal or educational connection with the students in my OWC? Do they have one with me as instructor?

Morale is incredibly important for OWI teachers and students alike for it can affect attrition rates as well as continued and active student participation in the course. OWI scholarship has acknowledged negative impressions of online courses as potentially cold and isolating spaces (Harris, 1998; Russell, 1999). Ken Gillam and Shannon R. Wooden (2012) referred to OWCs as disembodied, meaning that students lack the physical presence to engage with course material and with the learning process involved in writing. Some writing instructors flatly reject the online space as incapable of fostering warm, inviting, and welcoming spaces for student writers. In fact, online environments may seem like the last place that some writing instructors want to work with students.

This negative sentiment about the apparent impersonal nature of online learning is not unique to OWI. It is a prominent issue in online education, and it also has been studied in terms of isolation in Internet communication and social presence in instructional communication (Aragon, 2003; Turkle, 2012; Whiteside, 2007). One also must consider morale with regard to accessibility issues because if students cannot access online materials or use course technologies, they certainly will be alienated from the rest of the class. The term *social presence* is of particular importance for OWI, as literature has directly addressed it regarding online learning. In "Creating Social Presence in Online Environments," Steven Aragon (2003) wrote that "social presence is one of the most significant factors in improving instructional effectiveness and building a sense of community" (p. 57; see also Hewett & Hewett, 2008). Tracing literature about social presence in education literature, Aragon (2003) credited John Short, Ederyn Williams, and Bruce Christie (1976) for originally defining social presence as the "degree of salience of the other person in the interaction and the consequent salience of the interpersonal relationships" (p. 65). Aragon (2003) further explained social presence through the concepts of "intimacy" and "immediacy" (Guanwardena & Zittle, 1997); the notion of intimacy addresses nonverbal factors whereas immediacy addresses "psychological distance" (Guanwardena & Zittle, 1997, p. 9). The idea of social presence is to foster a sense of shared community that is important to the learning experience. As Aragon (2003) stated, "The overall goal for creating social presence in any learning environment, whether it be online or face-to-face, is to create a level of comfort in which people feel at ease around the instructor and the other participants" (p. 60).

Although social presence is discussed in the literature as mostly under instructor control, Aragon asserted that social presence is the responsibility of all persons involved in an online course. This is an important point for OWI teachers under training because they may worry that all the affect in the OWC is their responsibility. To the contrary, students have responsibilities as well. Aragon therefore offered helpful suggestions for creating social presence among three audiences: instructional designers, teachers, and students (p. 61). For instructional designers, he offered structural suggestions such as limiting class size, incorporating audio as well as text capabilities, building in welcome messages for the start of the class, and structuring several collaborative activities (pp. 62-63). For teachers, he suggested active collaboration from instructors in terms of contributing to discussion boards, providing prompt feedback on email inquiries, and providing frequent feedback on assignments (pp. 63-64). He also suggested that instructors offer personable stories, initiate conversations, address students by name, and use humor and emoticons (pp. 64-65). His suggestions for students are nearly identical to teacher suggestions; students should contribute to online discussions, answer email promptly, and take the initiative to start conversations (pp. 65-66).

In addition to these suggestions, building morale can include establishing social presence by incorporating the "human element" wherever possible by offering students multiple media channels to contact the instructor, such as through email, video, phone, and in-person office visits. In the previous section on modality and media, I shared several suggestions for diversifying communication channels between instructor and student. This diversity is important for establishing instructor presence and boosting morale in online courses. In addition, prompt responsiveness—no matter the modality or media—is critical for maintaining morale. Responding to student queries promptly is important as it reinforces instructor presence and attentiveness, and it helps students to address their own issues on time. If possible, teachers should schedule a regular time when students can be certain to reach them. For example, announcements might be sent out every Monday morning by 9:00 AM, and the instructor may have email, phone, or text-chat office hours Monday-Friday between 3:00 PM and 4:00 PM. The regularity of such open connection times is important to developing a reliable sense of presence.

Building morale also can be achieved through establishing a strong sense of community, which can extend a sense of social presence through engagement

378

with course material and various roles that students and instructors play in an OWC. In *Engaging the Online Learner*, Rita Conrad and J. Ana Donaldson (2004) suggested that establishing a sense of community is essential to encouraging student engagement in online learning. They suggested that one way to enhance engagement is to structure instructor and student roles in such a way that students gradually move from "newbie" to "course planner." Table 11.1 summarizes their approach.

Table 11.1. Phase of engagement (Conrad & Donaldson, 2004)

Time period in course	Instructor Role	Student Role
First quadrant of course	Initiator	Newcomer/Recipient
Second quadrant of course	Leader	Participant
Third quadrant of course	Facilitator	Collaborator
Fourth quadrant of course	Participant	Planner/Organizer

This phase-of-engagement approach essentially endorsed scaffolding, or incrementally integrating units to build skill development. It suggested that instructors build the course structure toward the beginning and allow students to participate and take over building the structure toward the end of the course, essentially empowering students to control their learning environments and further engage them. In terms of OWI, the phase-of-engagement approach could be applied in a variety of ways that trainers can teach to (and model for) OWI teachers. One approach we have been experimenting with is what I call "profiles to portfolios." At the beginning of the course, we encourage students to introduce themselves to the class by creating a brief profile with images that are important to them. Students are encouraged to include photos and descriptions of their interests and hobbies. Throughout the course, students are given a Web space where they can post their written work. Toward the end of the course, students create an ePortfolio of their work, gradually increasing the level of responsibility of student contributions to the online course.

Training on Morale

Building morale in an OWC often involves the concept of social presence, or a sense of interactivity and presence of a learning community. One way to build morale and to strengthen social presence is to establish collaborative activities that demonstrate individual contributions to the whole, encouraging students to experience themselves as important to the working of a potentially faceless OWC. Aragon (2003) suggested incorporating collaborative assignments into the course whenever possible; to that end, I suggest training OWI teachers in whole-class collaboration exercises and activities. One interesting example is the creation of a collaborative annotated bibliography on a common topic. Using features of the LMS, a collaborative database could be established to contribute bibliographic entries with annotations, along with tags that could allow the database to be searchable (see Figure 11.2; also see Breuch, Reynolds, Miller, & Gustafson, 2012). Many other technologies could be used for this activity as well, such as a Wiki or other Web 2.0 technology that allows for multiple authors.

The following training activity engages the training principles of immersion, association, and reflection. It can inform teachers about the experiences students may have in a whole-class activity. In an OWC, a collaborative annotated bibliography not only helps students and writers learn citation practices, but also to understand the multiple affordances of online writing tools, which is a type of rhetorical awareness. For example, using online tools, students can enter citation information, annotations of the sources, and tags to help identify the sources. As more students contribute to the collaborative annotated bibliography, they literally will see the bibliography grow and how their individual citations contribute to a larger bibliographic source. This training exercise also can inform teachers about the preparations needed to organize whole-class activities, such as selecting an accessible tool.

Training Activity

Within your entire teacher trainee group, create a collaborative annotated bibliography using your LMS or other accessible tool. There are four steps to this exercise: (1) establishing parameters for research, (2) selecting a tool, (3) entering bibliographic content, and (4) discussing the experience as a group. These steps are outlined below.

Research Parameters: With your entire group, decide upon the following research parameters:

- Determine a common topic.
- Choose a documentation style (MLA or APA) and recommended resources for consultation.
- Provide suggestions for acceptable sources (e.g., popular versus scholarly).

Tool Selection: With your entire group, select a tool—within the LMS if possible—to facilitate the activity. The following tools outside an LMS are good options:

- Del.icio.us is a social bookmarking tool that accommodates a collection of online sources with tagging functions. It is Web accessible and can be set up for shared access.

- Google Drive allows for shared documents; each contributor could simply add their sources and annotations and use the "comment" function to insert their name on their selections.
- The "database" function of Moodle allows one to set up fields of information. A field could be set up for "bibliographic citation" as well as "annotation." The character limit would need to be specified for each field. As well, tagging options could be selected in advance, giving options for common tags. These may help students search the annotated bibliography later.

Bibliographic entry: As individuals, find and select one source on the common topic that meets the parameters specified by the group. Then, write one bibliographic entry that includes an external citation (using the specified style guide) and a 100-word annotation.

Group discussion: After completing the exercise, contribute to an online discussion in your LMS in which you reflect on the selected parameters and tools—particularly where access is at issue. Possible discussion prompts may include the following questions:

- What pedagogical and/or affective benefits resulted from this collaborative bibliography exercise?
- What pedagogical and/or affective drawbacks appeared from this collaborative bibliography exercise?
- What affordances of the online tools did you most appreciate? Why? How did they benefit (or not) your sense of community, morale, or importance to the OWC?
- What new insights did you learn about bibliographies from this exercise? What do you predict your students might say in response to this question?

CONCLUSION AND RECOMMENDATIONS

This chapter has discussed the importance of training for OWI and some of the training considerations that new OWI teachers should experience. It has reviewed important characteristics of OWCs, such as the interactive nature of the course and the limitations of enrollment due to the text-heavy nature of OWCs. It also has introduced accessibility issues as well as four key issues that new OWI teachers face: migration, model, modality/media, and morale. Throughout, this chapter has introduced strategies for addressing these issues. By taking an issue-driven approach, my intention has been to demonstrate training that helps instructors first make sense of the transition to OWI on a holistic level, which is a critical first step in more fully embracing the possibilities that OWI offers to students and teachers alike.

A Position Statement of Principles and Example Effective Practices for OWI (CCCC OWI Committee, 2013) suggested that OWI training address "modalities, logistics, time management, and career choices" (p. 18), and it also suggested that instructors conduct training in the online modality. The training exercises in this chapter use five training principles of investigation, immersion, individualization, association, and reflection (Hewett & Ehmann, 2004) to help onsite writing instructors transition to hybrid and fully online OWCs.

I end with the following recommendations:

- WPAs and other administrators should provide online writing instructor and tutor training and ongoing professional development as OWI Principles 7 and 14 suggest.
- OWI training must address accessibility issues, with specific attention to course materials that instructors contribute to the LMS.
- The 4-M Training Approach outlined in this chapter offers a strategic way in to such training. Specifically, the 4-M Training Approach introduces central focal points for online writing instructor training: migration, model, modality/media, and morale.
  - Issues of migration and model are central to the design of OWCs.
  - Issues of modality/media address choice of tools and technologies for OWCs.
  - Issues of morale address ways to help students engage in OWCs.
- OWI training programs can address the 4-M Training Approach using the exercises suggested in this chapter, and they can adapt them to their local settings.

Topics	Citation
McCain	McCain 2008. Service to America: 624787.30 Sept. 2008. www.livingroomcandidate.org/commercials/2008/service-to-america-624787.
Obama	Obama for America. Need Education. 30 Sept. 2008. http://www.livingroomcandidate.org/commercials/2008
Obama Television Commercial	Obama Biden 2008. "No Maverick" Ad. 08 Sep 2008. 30 Sep 2008. http://www.youtube.com/watch?v=NBtbG5xjFBY
Obama	Will.i.am and Jesse Dylan. 2008. Yes We Can. 30 Sept. 2008. http://www.livingroomcandidate.org/commercials/2008
Other	Smith, Tovia. "Candidates Mum On Gay Marriage Debate." NPR: All Things Considered. 4 August 2008. 1 October 2008 http://www.npr.org/templates/story/story.php?storyId=93269018.
Palin	Fey, Tina, and Amy Poehler. "Palin/Hillary Open." Video blog post. Saturday Night Live. 13 Sept. 2008. 30 Sept. 2008
Palin	Campbell Brown. Comentary: Sexist treatment of Palin must end. 01 Oct. 2008. http://www.cnn.com/2008/POLITICS/09/24/campbell.brown.palin/index.html#cnnSTCT.ext
McCain	John McCain. McCain-Palin 2008 1 Oct. 2008 [http://www.johnmccain.com/Undecided/WhyMcCain.htm].
Obama	Barack Obama. "Plan For Change"Ad. September 16, 2008. http://www.youtube.com/watch?v=ONM7148cTyc
Obama	Obama Campaign. "Same Ad." YouTube. 30 August 2008. Obama for America. 2 Oct 2008

Page: **1** 2 3 4 5 6 7 8 9 10 (Next)

Figure 11.2. Collaborative annotated bibliography using database function of Moodle

REFERENCES

Allen, I. Elaine & Seaman, Jeff. (2013). *Changing course: Ten years of tracking online education in the United States.* Babson Survey Research Group, Pearson Publishing, and Sloan Consortium. Retrieved from http://www.onlinelearningsurvey.com/reports/changingcourse.pdf

Aragon, Steven R. (2003). Creating social presence in online environments. *New Directions for Adult and Continuing Education, 100,* 57-68.

Barnum, Carol M. (2011). *Usability testing essentials: Ready, set ... test!* New York: Elsevier, Morgan Kaufman.

Barker, Thomas T. & Kemp, Fred O. (1990). Network theory: A postmodern pedagogy for the writing classroom. In Carolyn Handa (Ed.), *Computers and community: Teaching composition in the twenty-first century* (pp. 1-27). Portsmouth, NH: Boynton.

Beaudoin, Michael F. (2002). Learning or lurking? Tracking the "invisible online student." *Internet and Higher Education, 5,* 147-55.

Blair, Kristine & Hoy, Cheryl. (2006). Paying attention to adult learners online: The pedagogy and politics of community. *Computers and Composition, 23,* 32-48.

Blocher, J. Michael., Sujo de Montes, Laura, Willis, Elizabeth M., & Tucker, Gary. (2002). Online learning: Examining the successful student profile. *Journal of Interactive Online Learning 1(2),* 1-12.

Boyd, Patricia Webb. (2008). Analyzing students' perceptions of their learning in online and hybrid first-year composition courses. *Computers and Composition, 25,* 224-43.

Breuch, Lee-Ann Kastman. (2004). *Virtual peer review: Teaching and learning about writing in online environments.* New York: SUNY Press.

Breuch, Lee-Ann Kastman, Reynolds, Thomas J., Miller, Kimberly Schultz, & Gustafson, Tim. (2012). A sociocultural approach to using Web 2.0 technologies in first-year writing. In C. Lutkewitte (Ed.), *Web 2.0 applications for composition classrooms* (pp. 101-120). Southlake, TX: Fountainhead Press X Series.

Brooks, Kevin, Nichols, Cindy, & Priebe, Sybil. (2004). Remediation, genre, and motivation: Key concepts for teaching with Weblogs. In Laura Gurak, Smiljana Antonijevic, Laurie Johnson, Clancy Ratflii, & Jessica Reymann (Eds.), *Into the blogosphere: Rhetoric, community, and culture of Weblogs.* Retrieved from http://www.blog.lib.umn.edu/blogosphere/remediation_genre.html

Brunk-Chavez, Beth & Miller, Shawn J. (2006). Decentered, disconnected, and digitized: The importance of shared space. *Kairos, 11(2),* 1-29. Retrieved from http://kairos.technorhetoric.net/11.2/topoi/brunk-miller/decentered-test/decentered.pdf

Castek, Jill & Beach, Richard. (2013). Using apps to support disciplinary literacy and science learning. *Journal of Adolescent & Adult Literacy, 56*(7), 554-564.

CCCC Committee for Effective Practices in Online Writing Instruction. (2011c). *The state of the art of OWI*. Retrieved from http://www.ncte.org/library/NCTEFiles/Groups/CCCC/Committees/OWI_State-of-Art-Report_April_2011.pdf

CCCC OWI Committee for Effective Practices in Online Writing Instruction. (2013). *A position statement of principles and effective practices for online writing instruction (OWI)*. Retrieved from http://www.ncte.org/cccc/resources/positions/owiprinciples

Colorado State University. (1993-2015). The writing studio. *Writing@CSU*. Retrieved from http://writing.colostate.edu/index.cfm

Conrad, Rita & Donaldson, J. Ana. (2004). *Engaging the online learner: Activities and resources for creative instruction*. San Francisco: Jossey-Bass.

Dabbagh, Nada. (2007). The online learner: Characteristics and pedagogical implications. *Contemporary Issues in Technology and Teacher Education, 7(3)*, 217-226.

Fogarty, Mignon. (2009). *Grammar girl*. Retrieved from http://grammar.quickanddirtytips.com

Galin, Jeffrey & Latchaw, Joan. (Eds.). (1998). *The dialogic classroom: Teachers integrating computer technology, pedagogy, and research*. Urbana, IL: National Council of Teachers of English.

Gillam, Ken & Wooden, Shannon R. (2012). Re-embodying online composition: Ecologies of writing in unreal time and space. *Computers and Composition, 30*, 24-36.

Gotham Writers' Workshop. (2013). Creative writing classes in NYC and online. *Gotham writers' workshop*. Retrieved from http://www.writingclasses.com

Griffin, June & Minter, Deborah. (2013). The rise of the online writing classroom: Reflecting on the material conditions of college composition teaching. *College Composition and Communication, 65*(1), 140-161.

Guanwardena, Charlotte N. & Zittle, Frank J. (1997). Social presence as a predictor of satisfaction within a computer-mediated conferencing environment. *The American Journal of Distance Education, 11*(3), 8-26.

Gurak, Laura, Antonijevic, Smiljana, Johnson, Laurie, Ratliff, Clancy, & Reymann, Jessica. (2004). *Into the blogosphere: Rhetoric, community, and culture of Weblogs*. Retrieved from http://blog.lib.umn.edu/blogosphere/introduction.html

Harrington, Susanmarie, Rickly, Rebecca, & Day, Michael. (Eds.). (2000). *The OWCroom*. Cresskill, NJ: Hampton Press.

Harris, Muriel. (1998). Using computers to expand the role of writing centers. In Donna Reiss, Art Young & Dickie Selfe (Eds.), *Electronic communication across the curriculum* (pp. 3-16). Urbana, IL: National Council of Teachers of English.

Harris, Muriel & Pemberton, Michael. (1995). Online writing labs (OWLs): A taxonomy of options and issues. *Computers and Composition 12(2)*, 145-59.

Haswell, Richard. (2008). Teaching of writing and writing teachers through the ages. In Charles Bazerman (Ed.), *Handbook of research on writing: History, society, school, individual, text*. New York: Lawrence Erlbaum.

Hewett, Beth L. (2010). *The online writing conference: A guide for teachers and tutors*. Portsmouth, NH, Boynton/Cook.

Hewett, Beth L. (2013). Fully online and hybrid writing instruction. In H. Brooke Hessler, Amy Rupiper Taggart, & Kurt Schick (Eds.), *A guide to composition pedagogies* (2nd ed.) (pp. 194-211). Oxford, UK: Oxford University Press.

Hewett, B. L. (2015a). *Reading to learn and writing to teach: Literacy strategies for online writing instruction*. Boston: Bedford/St. Martin's Press.

Hewett, Beth L. (2015b). *The online writing conference: A guide for teachers and tutors*. Boston, MA: Bedford/St. Martin's Press.

Hewett, Beth L. & Ehmann, Christa. (2004). *Preparing educators for online writing instruction: Principles and processes*. Urbana, IL: National Council of Teachers of English.

Hewett, Beth L. & Hewett, Russell J. (2008). Instant messaging (IM) literacy in the workplace. In Pavel Zemlianski & Kirk St. Amant (Eds.), *Virtual workplaces and the new nature of business practices* (pp. 455-572). Hershey, PA: IGI Global.

Howell, Scott L., Williams, Peter B., & Lindsay, Nathan K. (2003). Thirty-two trends affecting distance education: An informed foundation for strategic planning. *Online Journal of Distance Learning Administration, 6*(3). Retrieved from http://www.westga.edu/~distance/ojdla/

Kress, Gunther. (2004). *Reading images: Multimodality, representation, and new media*. Retrieved from http://www.knowledgepresentation.org/BuildingThe-Future/Kress2/Kress2.html

Kress, Gunther. (2010). *Multimodality: A social semiotic approach to contemporary communication*. London: Routledge.

Nielsen, Jakob. (1993). *Usability engineering*. New York: Morgan Kaufmann.

Nielsen, Jakob. (2006). F-shaped pattern for reading Web content. *Jakob Nielsen's alertbox*. Retrieved from http://www.nngroup.com/articles/f-shaped-pattern-reading-web-content/

Norman, Donald. (1988). *The design of everyday things*. New York: Basic Books.

Oblinger, Diana G. & Oblinger, James L. (Eds.). (2005). *Educating the net generation*. EDUCAUSE: Transforming education through information technologies. Retrieved from www.educause.edu/educatingthenetgen/

Palloff, Rena M. & Pratt, Keith. (2003). *The virtual student: A profile and guide to working with online learners.* San Francisco, CA: John Wiley & Sons.

Palmeri, Jason. (2012). *Remixing composition: A history of multimodal writing pedagogy.* Carbondale, IL: Southern Illinois University Press.

Quesenbery, Whitney. (n.d.). *Getting started: Using the 5Es to understand users.* Retrieved from http://www.wqusability.com/articles/getting-started.html

Redish, Janice (Ginny). (2007). *Letting go of the words: Writing Web content that works.* New York: Elsevier, Morgan Kaufman.

Regents of the University of Minnesota. (2014). *Accessibility.* IT@UMN. Retrieved from http://it.umn.edu/services/all/academic-technology-tools/course-management/accessibility/index.htm

Reinheimer, David A. (2005). Teaching composition online: Whose side is time on? *Computers and Composition, 22*(4), 459-470.

Rubin, Jeffrey, Chisnell, Dana, & Spool, Jared. (2008). *Handbook of usability testing: How to plan, design, and conduct effective tests.* New York: Wiley.

Rubin, Jeffrey. (1996). Conceptual design: Cornerstone of usability. *Technical Communication, 43*(2), 130-138.

Russell, David R. (1999). Activity theory and process approaches: Writing (power) in school and society. In Thomas T. Kent (Ed.), *Post-process theory: Beyond the writing-process paradigm* (pp. 80-95). Carbondale, IL: Southern Illinois University Press.

Russell, Scott. (1999). Clients who frequent Madam Barnett's emporium. *Writing Center Journal, 20*(1), 61-72.

Sapp, David Alan & Simon, James. (2005). Comparing grades in online and face-to-face writing courses: Interpersonal accountability and institutional commitment. *Computers and Composition, 22*(4), 471-89.

Selfe, Cynthia L. (1989). *Creating a computer-supported writing facility: A blueprint for action.* Houghton, MI: Computers and Composition.

Selfe, Cynthia. (Ed.). (2007). *Multimodal composition: Resources for teachers.* Cresskill, NJ: Hampton Press.

Short, John E., Williams, Ederyn, & Christie, Bruce. (1976). *The social psychology of telecommunications.* New York: Wiley.

Sommers, Jeff. (2012). Response rethought ... again: Exploring recorded comments and the teacher-student bond. *Journal of Writing Assessment, 5*(1). Retrieved from http://www.journalofwritingassessment.org/article.php?article=59

Sommers, Jeff. (2013). Response 2.0: Commentary on student writing for the new millennium. *Journal of College Literacy and Learning, 39*, 21–37.

Spinuzzi, Clay. (1999). *Designing for lifeworlds: Genre and activity in information systems design and evaluation* (Doctoral dissertation). Retrieved from ProQuest Dissertations and Theses. (Accession Order No. 9940242).

Thatcher, Jim, Burks, Michael R., Heilman, Christian, Henry, Shawn Lawton,

Kirkpatrick, Andrew, Lauke, Patrick H., ... Waddell, Cynthia D. (2006). *Web accessibility: Web standards and regulatory compliance.* New York: Spring-er-Verlag New York.

Turkle, Sherry. (2012). *Alone together: Why we expect more from technology and less from each other.* New York: Basic Books.

University of Minnesota Academic Affairs & Provost. (2013). *eLearning at the University of Minnesota.* Retrieved from http://academic.umn.edu/provost/elearning/index.html

Vincelette, Elizabeth. (2013). Video capture for grading: Multimedia feedback and the millennial student. In Ellen Smyth, & I. John Volker (Eds.), *Enhancing instruction with visual media: Utilizing video and lecture capture* (pp. 107-127). Hershey, PA: IGI-Global.

Vygotsky, Lev. (1986). *Thought and language.* London: MIT Press.

Walker, J. D. & Jorn, Linda. (2009). *Twenty-first century students: Technology survey.* University of Minnesota-Twin Cities. Office of Information Technology. Retrieved from http://stu.westga.edu/~bthibau1/MEDT%208484-%20Baylen/good3.pdf

Warnock, Scott. (2009). *Teaching writing online: how and why.* Urbana, IL: National Council of Teachers of English.

Web Accessibility Initiative. (2012). *Web content accessibility guidelines.* Retrieved from http://www.w3.org/WAI/guid-tech.html

Whiteside, Aimee Lynn. (2007). *Exploring social presence in communities of practice within a hybrid learning environment: A longitudinal examination of two case studies within the school technology leadership graduate-level certificate program* (Doctoral dissertation, University of Minnesota). Retrieved from http://www.academia.edu/2552084/Exploring_social_presence_in_communities_of_practice_within_a_hybrid_learning_environment_A_longitudinal_examination_of_two_case_studies_within_the_School_

WRIT VID. (2013*). Instructional videos about writing.* University of Minnesota. Retrieved from http://www.youtube.com/playlist?feature=c4-feed-u&list=PLRk1rksih9vwfJucx5ViBwxnO4BSY8XXF

Wyatt, Christopher Scott. (2010). *Online pedagogy: Designing writing courses for students with autism spectrum disorders* (Doctoral dissertation, University of Minnesota). Available from ProQuest Dissertations and Theses database. Retrieved from http://search.proquest.com.libproxy.usc.edu/docview/597211269?accountid=14749(597211269)

Wysocki, Anne F., Johnson-Eilola, Johndan., Selfe, Cynthia L., & Sirc, Geoffrey. (2004). *Writing new media: Theory and applications for expanding the teaching of composition.* Logan, UT: Utah State University Press.

CHAPTER 12

FACULTY PROFESSIONALIZATION FOR OWI

Rich Rice
Texas Tech University

WPAs can improve faculty professionalization models for OWI to generate dynamic performance support by examining ways in which application frameworks are created for evolving software systems. Design includes creating ideas and assignments; coding includes methods of presenting, responding, assessing, and supporting. Connecting effective design and coding approaches to OWI effective practices, especially faculty professional development, can improve OWI programs.

Keywords: agile design, code-and-fix design, convergence, course redesign, performance support, predictive design, professional development

Faculty who teach in OWI programs not only need training, as indicated in *A Position Statement of Principles and Example Effective Practices for OWI* (CCCC OWI Committee, 2013) and in Chapter 11 of this book, but they also need ongoing support and professional development opportunities. Given the relative newness of OWI as a disciplinary approach to teaching writing in higher education, professionalization models have yet to be adequately developed in structured ways that may help teachers at a variety of institutional settings, including those that heavily use contingent faculty (see Chapter 7). Yet, professionalization is crucial to developing new OWI teacher pedagogies and also in supporting those who teach in OWCs with fair compensation, including opportunities to remain current with rapidly changing technologies and chances to participate in building programs that use new knowledge and theories being developed for OWI.

In this chapter, I suggest that WPAs and other program administrators can improve faculty professionalization models for OWI to generate dynamic performance support by examining and adopting ways in which application frameworks are created for evolving software systems. The parallel between application frameworks and the work of becoming and remaining up-to-date in OWI suggest a guiding metaphor for professional development. Design in this sense includes creating ideas and assignments, while coding includes methods of presenting, responding, assessing, and supporting faculty. Connecting effective design and coding approaches to OWI principles and effective practices, especially regarding faculty professional development, can improve OWI programs.

CURRENT FACULTY OWI PROFESSIONALIZATION MODELS

CODE-AND-FIX FACULTY PROFESSIONALIZATION DESIGN

The practice of software design has long followed a *code-and-fix* methodology, building programs or websites on successive, layered, quick decisions. If the computer and project application is small, the approach works quite well. Code-and-fix is a way to get or keep moving on a project. But as systems grow, new features or better approaches invariably become challenging to implement. Bugs abound until they are fixed in long testing phases, taxing human resources and frustrating users. If the fix is too time-consuming and the choice regarding user identity and needs is left to programmers, as Jaron Lanier (2011) suggested in *You Are Not a Gadget*, bugs might simply be considered features of the system: *if it is not a bug, it must be a feature.*

Using the code-and-fix method as an analogy, consider the creation of an OWI faculty development plan. Whether they know it or not, most English or writing departments have likely used a code-and-fix methodology to get their OWI programs started. They usually begin by asking faculty to teach a few courses; then they gather comment cards or end-of-semester evaluations to see what students think, figure out which outcomes are met readily and which need more attention, implement strategies to improve those courses, create additional courses, and pepper everyone with occasional workshops or one-on-one support with a tech savvy person in IT or an in-house geek, to spice. The approach may work well to get started, but it is very problematic if it is the only way WPAs know to develop the OWI program. Professionalization also often follows a code-and-fix method: there is a short-term demand to fill OWCs with teachers, so we hire and train (or not) teachers to construct courses and teach online, perhaps calling the courses "betas" or "pilots," fixing problems through implementation. Once courses are going, we copy and paste the original, "fix" courses into additional sections, and hire more instructors and let them teach the content.

This chapter argues that to sustain faculty development in more meaningful ways, certainly *more* than a code-and-fix method is needed. WPAs and other administrators in charge of OWI programs need to be savvy and thoughtful about faculty development and online instruction.

OWI programs evolve. As they evolve, some WPAs may survey faculty and students to prioritize fixing online technology and pedagogical problems, perhaps even creating knowledge bases of frequently-asked questions (FAQs) and solutions. They may ask such questions as:

- How can online teaching enhance pedagogy?
- How should OWI faculty rethink educational approaches and organization overall to better meet online instructional needs?
- How can OWI teachers improve student participation in activities and exercises and discussion?
- How can OWI teachers help students to improve their performance on papers and exams?
- How can OWI teachers give students greater access to the course in terms of flexibility of time and location?
- How can all participants improve their records of interactions between faculty and students and among students?

These more sophisticated questions and the concurrent desire for improved professionalization call for WPAs and OWI teachers alike to move beyond code-and-fix to something more sustainable. At the root of each of these questions and the programmatic development they encourage is access, and access is possible only by conceptualizing accessibility at the level of interface so that our course goals, curriculum, delivery tools, pedagogy, and professionalization also fall in line with this overarching goal.

Chapter 1 shares the rationale for 15 OWI principles for effective OWI practice. The very first principle of *A Position Statement of Principles and Example Effective Practices for OWI* (CCCC OWI Committee, 2013) is an overarching guideline that grounded and supported each of the following 14 principles. OWI Principle 1 strongly suggested that scholars and educators pay close attention to access and inclusivity for students and teachers at every step in the planning and implementing of online classes (pp. 7-11). Code-and-fix approaches to OWI professionalization inadequately follow this principle because universal design for (all) learners and facilitators requires more planning than these approaches allow. Students and teachers should have equal access to content; access to course design; and access to technologies used, assignments prescribed, and assessment measurements planned. It is important to underscore that OWI Principle 1 referred to the access needs of every *teacher* beginning to prepare and teach and assess courses in online environments. The code-and-fix method most likely does not provide such universal access because, as a methodological approach, many potential problems still can remain hidden or unaddressed as simple features of the ongoing program. When professional development includes quick fixes or none at all, there are systemic problems that end up becoming large, crucial, and potentially damaging to the very education that OWI proposes to provide.

Indeed, a few years down the road, important systematic bugs inevitably will arise. Faculty get squeezed. *Who owns the content?* OWI Principle 5 suggested that faculty should retain reasonable control over the content they produce, and doing so can become challenging in this design model (pp. 15-16). *Who is compensated for new course preparation? If the content already is there, is the instructor of record a teacher or merely a facilitator? Can pay for online teaching even be lower than teaching face-to-face?* OWI Principle 8 suggested that faculty should be fairly compensated for creating online course content (pp. 19-20). *Should class sizes be increased because some instructor workload already has been provided, even though increased numbers limit the potential for productive interaction?* OWI Principle 9 recommended online writing classes be capped at 20, and preferably 15 (pp. 20-21). Without strategic planning, class sizes likely will be increased. It is difficult to plan and justify and fight class-size creep in the code-and-fix design method. *Should asynchronous exchange be prioritized over synchronous communication in order to maximize flexible scheduling?* Doing so is code-and-fix professionalization development and support, putting processes into play and then fixing infrastructural concerns as a program proceeds and grows. While there are short-term benefits, the approach causes significant long-term problems for the professionalization of the field where, again, bugs are just bugs.

What are some of the benefits that better, more systematized faculty professionalization design models could provide, benefits that code-and-fix approaches tend to support insufficiently? WPAs need to consider the value of innovative teaching strategies that are not recognized by those in authority in institutions as worthy of productive effort in promotion and tenure cases. If teaching online can create greater time and locational flexibility, consider strategies a department can use to support or incentivize faculty or to help maximize opportunities like conference travel, extended research trips, study abroad work, interdisciplinary or inter-institutional teaching, and the like. These are "integrated scholar" opportunities where faculty can develop their own research, teaching, and service together. Plans for recognizing efforts to design and create effective pedagogy in new modalities is difficult in code-and-fix approaches. Something more systematic should be put into place, too, if faculty members are to be encouraged to package written course content into books or to customize materials in more targeted ways for students and to address programmatic goals. Improving pedagogy and experimenting with new ideas is not encouraged when fixes are too cumbersome to put into place quickly. Faculty who are not supported in smart ways will not innovate and take risks because the cost in terms of human and monetary resources is simply too high.

PREDICTIVE FACULTY PROFESSIONALIZATION DESIGN

There is another approach to software design that works to schedule fixes in more timely ways, saving costs and better supporting system-wide approaches. The goal of this approach is to plan testing and recoding cycles with version updates that are engineered by teams of designers, programmers, and usability testers. Implementing an OWC or set of courses, clearly, will require planned development and growth and support. Predicting the directions that the software should take based on evolving user needs also can be limiting, however. Software, modality, content, access, and other requirements change constantly in effective OWI and not in an easily "scheduled" manner. Design requires much creativity, and prediction for when changes need to be made is difficult, as coding or content construction typically follows design. It often is the case that faculty seek to save time by copying and pasting their course content from one semester to the next without recognizing that student demographics have changed, that content must be updated, and that one size does not fit all—particularly with regard to issues of access and inclusivity. By the time updates or recoding is complete, including a round of design revision, users are likely to demand additional or different features. In this design model, teachers often over-focus on design rather than content, missing the goal of OWI Principle 2, which suggested that the course should not be overburdened by teaching tools (p. 11). The semester already may be under way and content updating becomes superficial. And the move from design to coding to usability often is delayed by more bugs. This model is predictive design, which affords some flexibility for constructing long-term, planned development. For example, it seeks to grow a selection of online courses while planning to upgrade their goals and objectives alongside those of onsite courses.

In terms of using this model as a professionalization analogy, though, this method offers limited recognition for OWI teachers as creative designers and expert pedagogues in online environments. *What are differences in the demands of fully online, hybrid, and face-to-face course deliveries?* OWI Principle 7 called us to focus on adequate training and professional development for OWI specifically (pp. 17-19). *Should different sorts of professional development and support mechanisms be installed and grown based on personnel rather than presumed curricular evolution?* OWI Principles 11, 12, 13, and 14 encouraged us to develop specific support spaces and tools for teachers' and students' online work that may take significant development, such as media labs or OWLs or other virtual or physical thirdspaces (pp. 23-30; see Grego & Thompson, 2007; Lee & Carpenter, 2013). A *thirdspace* is a commonplace where information senders and receivers can construct and transact ideas: "the study of space offers an answer according to which the social relations of production have a social existence to the extent that they have a spatial existence; they project themselves into a space, becoming inscribed there, and in the process producing the space itself" (LeFevre, 1991, p. 129). Other questions emerge: *Do administrators need to analyze teacher and course evaluation assessments with the same or different learning outcomes in mind? How can predictive coding and content creation aid in student and teacher motivation and retention, getting them literally and figuratively plugged-in* (English, 2014)? Again, OWI Principle 7 addressed the needs for fair and educated assessment of OWCs and their teachers (pp. 17-19), while OWI Principle 5 supported trained instructors in autonomous OWC development that might increase both teacher and student motivation as well as retention (pp. 15-16).

Both code-and-fix and predictive design methods are used commonly in developing online courses and teacher-support systems: build and fix as you go, and schedule fixes in between terms or over the summer or next break for the latest academic "version" or customized edition. The first method makes some sense for small programs in order to get started, and the second makes some sense to continue to improve the quality of faculty professionalization as smaller programs grow. And it is possible to bring these two approaches in line with the OWI principles to a certain degree. We should consider, for instance, OWI Principle 4, which suggested that "*appropriate* onsite composition theories, pedagogies, and strategies should be migrated and adapted to the online instructional environment" (pp. 14-15). Follow the move to OWI with a specific analysis of how the onsite and then the online program measures learning objectives. Indeed, these important principles and guidelines can fit well within online writing faculty professionalization.

While these two software development strategies overlap and can build on one another to great benefit, one thing is clear: Because creative processes are difficult to plan and to build into faculty professionalization and because the demand and supply for online teaching and learning fluctuates, fixing is time-consuming and predictability is extraordinarily challenging, often limiting, and still quite time-consuming. It is not enough to transfer existing face-to-face instruction models to OWC development, delivery, and support. There are many professional development design issues, most notably that of access, which require more significant ongoing review and rethinking.

AGILE FACULTY PROFESSIONALIZATION DESIGN MODEL

What if the design stage could include the coding? That is, what if in designing and in redesigning courses OWI program leaders would code and construct content simultaneously, revising and revamping as we use feedback loops to reflect with teachers, students, and WPAs' assessment measuring requirements? How would this approach help faculty professionalization in terms of equal pay for equal work, faculty development, technological support, fair opportunities for contingent faculty, and evidence to support promotion and tenure cases? These are the goals of OWI Principle 7 (pp. 17-19); namely, WPAs overseeing faculty teaching online courses, as well as the faculty themselves, should receive appropriate training, professional development, and credit through evaluation of online instructing and administration work. We can think about the design and construction of courses and professionalization issues synchronously, wherein the synergies of design and construction and support can improve the system as it grows, reprioritizing teaching and scholarship (O'Meara, Rice, & Edgerton, 2005). To this end, there is a third design method that offers guidance to a more effective approach to OWI faculty professionalization: agile faculty professionalization design.

Many software programmers develop code connecting design and construction using agile software design, a third methodology to which people concerned with professionalization should pay attention. The approach is more adaptive than predictive, and more people-oriented than process-oriented. Adaptive methods of building programs welcome and thrive on change. They offer feedback mechanisms at frequent intervals to mitigate the impact of radical change. Requirements always change; we should be more surprised at the people who find *that* surprising. Ultimately, people-oriented methods recognize individual users more than processes (Fowler, 2005)—just as post-process pedagogies might recognize ways to teach and learn writing and achieve outcomes more than process pedagogies. Metaphorically, people are the drivers—albeit transient—not the hardware or software. Systems for how to design and professionalize the teaching of OWCs can generate exigencies for which students and faculty can create their own effective working spaces and opportunities. They can support faculty professionalization, as well.

Let us consider the potential additional benefits of agile faculty OWI professionalization. One benefit connects to the fact that agile software design uses what is called "iterative refactoring," which as a concept also serves as a useful metaphor for principles of productive professionalization. Refactoring, for instance, can be connected theoretically to labor costs and compensation schedules for OWI teachers. The concept is related to problems inherent in providing content-complete course shells rather than enabling instructors to develop unique components that somehow also connect specific learners' needs and teacher expertise. Specifically, code refactoring is a systematic approach to restructuring computer code that alters internal structures without changing external behaviors in order to improve the code's readability, reducing the code's complexity, improving the maintainability, and refining the internal architecture to improve sustainability and future adaptability (Fowler, 2005). Refactoring makes it easier to fix bugs, and the programmers or authors who follow redesigning and recoding more readily can contextualize and shape the code, which is why reducing large routines into concise, well-named, single-sourced processes is important. Although Fowler (2005) does not mention the possibilities of improving access to the software for disabled developers and users, code refactoring can open paths for integrating erstwhile nonexistent accessibility features, and if necessary, can even add interface-level accessibility to the system for users employing adaptive and assistive devices. Using agile faculty OWI professionalization can work to install appropriate online composition teaching and learning strategies (OWI Principle 3, pp. 12-14) without overly focusing on the tools.

Let us also consider the relevance to documenting ongoing authorship of course content that could be used by dozens or hundreds or thousands of students. As Anne Burdick, Johanna Drucker, Peter Lunenfeld, Todd Presner, and Jeffrey Schnapp (2012) pointed out, "The question is no longer 'what is an author?' but what is the author function when reshaped around the plurality of creative design, open compositional practices, and the reality of versioning" (p. 83). With refactoring, comments in the code that may be misleading are removed, and methods that are ambiguous could be moved to a more appropriate class of functions. This is important work that defines much of OWI teachers' processes. It can be likened to single-sourcing, whereby department-critical information is developed, used, and stored for all to reuse and retool. Such work should be documented for professionalization purposes in that individual teachers' knowledge bases can contribute to the entire writing program faculty. It is common lunchroom talk to ask what happens if one person gets hit by a bus and cannot report on or outline the processes of her work or to speculate where the department would be if specific institutional knowledge is lost. WPAs and faculty need to design systems of online courses that capture collective knowledge yet enable and even require unique and personalized content and delivery: converging divergencies. In this way, the potential capabilities of the application are made clear more easily if the "code" or professionalization system is flexible and includes recognizable design patterns that can be replicated or retooled in different ways (Fields et al., 2009). The value of course redesign approaches increases if what is produced is adaptable and includes scaffolding for others. In effect, improving professionalization through agile software design-like methodology involves constantly deconstructing the grammar of what OWI teachers do.

In *The Language of New Media*, Lev Manovich (2002) described the principles of numerical representation, modularity, automation, variability, and transcoding. Flexible or agile creation of valuable professionalization policies embraces these principles. OWI and the teaching of OWCs, for instance, can be considered data objects (numerical representation) that exist both dependently and independently (modularity) of the larger curriculum. They can be created and modified automatically (automation) once they are developed, but they must exist in multiple versions (variability) in order to maximize teacher expertise and student need and disciplinary contextualization. The convergence of layers of media, technology, and culture in OWCs generate new layers of meaning (transcoding). In his more recent work, *Software Takes Command*, Manovich (2013) suggested that "software has become our interface to the world, to others, to our memory and our imagination—a universal language through which the world speaks, and a universal engine on which the world runs" (Manovich, 2013). Software and the production of software, according to Manovich, is taking control over all types of media and organizations. Faculty teaching online are working in (hybrid/fully online) organizations that rely heavily on software and online content production, and "new media proliferates 'programmed visions,' which seek to shape and predict ... a future based on past data. The programmed visions have also made computers, based on metaphor, metaphors for metaphor itself, for a general logic of substitutability" (Chun, 2011, cover). And, as Matt Barton (2008) reasoned in "New Media and the Virtual Workplace" with reference to transcoding and the role of software in virtual organizations and in professionalization, productive virtual workplaces afford room for play and innovation, call attention to space, enable participants to shape identity as creative performance, stimulate simulation opportunities to gain new abilities, and afford meaningful collaboration to work together to solve problems (pp. 389-390). These thirdspaces, which connect the virtual and the real, are situated and contextualized for faculty and students in unique ways, and they require iterative examinations as these spaces or neighborhoods grow and change demographically and experientially. Such online spaces, given time and support, can be optimized for using appropriate onsite composition theories (per OWI Principle 4, pp. 14-15) after experimentation and iterative design (per OWI Principle 6, pp. 16-17).

Our understanding of how online writing faculty professionalization can make effective use of agile design through iterative refactoring becomes clearer by using agile design to newly mediate online learning environments in ever-changing ways, more dynamically responding to plugged-in students and faculty, transcoding cultural and computer layers to maximize play, space, identity, simulation, and collaboration. This new approach is critical and necessary to improve OWI faculty professionalization. In *Because Digital Writing Matters: Improving Student Writing in Online and Multimedia Environments*, Dànielle DeVoss, Elyse Eidman-Aadahl, and Troy Hicks (2010) cited the National Staff Development Council's 2009 standards for professional development: "The kind of high-intensity, job-embedded collaborative learning that is most effective is not a common feature of professional development across most states, districts, and schools in the United States (p. 4)" (p. 116). Their statement is apt, of course. DeVoss et al. related that the "richest conceptions of professional development" must value the idea that people transcend tools, that good praxis transcends technologies, and that designs for learning transcend designs for delivery (p. 118). *A Position Statement of Principles and Example Effective Practices for OWI* (CCCC OWI Committee, 2013) embraced this people-over-technology philosophy. In order to follow OWI Principle 10, students should be prepared for unique technological and pedagogical components of an online class (pp. 21-23). According to OWI Principle 11, personalized and interpersonal online communities can be developed to help foster student and teacher success with online transactional exchange (pp. 23-24). Manipulate the technology to fit the pedagogy, certainly, and at the level of professionalization see where the agile, iterative work and investment behavior of OWI teachers creates value for systems. As the ever-shifting employment structure of college faculty evolves, taking note of investment in the faculty and helping them with stable jobs, promotion, and tenure will be increasingly relevant.

At the center of refactoring is a series of small behavior-preserving transformations wherein each transformation or refactoring does just a little, but together produces significant restructuring, reducing the chances that a system can break during that restructuring (Fowler, 2013). Redesigning classes for hybrid or fully online modalities (see Chapter 2), as well as short- and long-term faculty professionalization and support (see Chapters 7 & 11), should follow a similar approach of micro-assessments while courses are redesigned. Doing so follows OWI Principle 10 (offering student preparation), OWI Principle 11 (providing support communities for teachers and students), OWI Principle 12 (fostering teacher satisfaction as well as programmatic success), OWI Principle 13 (delivering onsite as well as online support mechanisms), and OWI Principle 14 (training for online administrators and tutors) (pp. 21-30). Agile faculty professionalization must include a recursive performance support system, as well, in order to document and recognize the value of that work. It is clear that "because we are in the midst of a transformation in the materiality of information and in the media technologies of communication, things that were once considered 'mere' support systems, transmission media, and conveyance devices are now fundamentally implicated in any meaning-making process" (Burdick et al., 2012, p. 83). Such faculty work should be documented and rewarded.

Before applying a set of refactoring tests and prior to refactoring, software programmers complete unit or smaller module tests to ensure that the behavior of the module is correct. The process involves iterative and recursive testing, and the more the better. Programmers define a number of specific techniques using different amounts of automation, from the abstract to strategies for breaking code into more logical pieces to improving names and code locations. So, too, must effective OWI development engage in refactoring tests in order to support professionalization. What technologies might students see again over multiple online courses? How might instruction be presented over time to teach student populations with differing abilities or learning needs? How might course content be designed in chunks that, together, make a larger picture for students in terms of communication support strategies to help them succeed? Just as students might move from the informal to the formal in their writing, or from one form of expression to another, can they interact in one modality in order to prepare for interaction in another? And in addition to software code refactoring, approaches to hardware refactoring have been used to make complex systems easier to understand in order to increase designer productivity (Fowler, 1999). If software can be likened to teachers designing and constructing course content, hardware can be compared to the administration and infrastructure that enable teachers to work.

We are now rendering a more practical picture of how to build productive and sustainable faculty professionalization. Andrew Hunt and David Thomas' (1999) wisdom in *The Pragmatic Programmer* regarding building maintainable code in this way can help WPAs better understand how to create useful professionalization performance support systems. Here are key approaches that Hunt and Thomas discussed throughout their book applicable to what administrators should consider in building support systems for OWI professionalization:

- avoid knowledge duplication,
- write flexible and dynamic content,
- avoid programming by coincidence,
- bullet-proof code with exceptions,
- capture real requirements,
- test ruthlessly and effectively,
- delight users, build teams of pragmatic programmers, and
- make developments precise with some planned automation. (Hunt & Thomas, 1999)

To this end, effective faculty professionalization practice includes connecting rhizomically throughout a faculty to:

- share resources rather than duplicate efforts,
- create curricula that somehow can be used in successive semesters yet still move in the flexible directions students and faculty need,
- work to meet goals and objectives on the program by design with multiple assignment sets for student options that meet the same goals and objectives,
- apply principles of universal design for learners to ensure access and understanding throughout curriculum design and process of experiencing a course,
- create spaces for reflective practitioners to interact graciously and productively, and
- create a climate of critical reflective praxis.

Effective professionalization, ultimately, is the creation of dynamic electronic performance support systems (EPSSs), which supports the improvement of performance to avoid duplication, increase quality, connect measurements to goals and objectives, and create more reflective practices.

VALUING DIVERGENT CONVERGENCES IN THE OWI PRINCIPLES AND EFFECTIVE PRACTICES

An EPSS is nothing new. Specifically, it is a support mechanism designed to reduce complexity in order to provide employees with unique directions to make effective decisions, thus improving quality and productivity. It is a support approach in line with agile software design and agile faculty professional development design to offer timely and specific (perhaps *kairotic*) flexibly structured support. Building a better system of professionalization begins with strengthening motivation. In *Electronic Performance Support Systems: How and Why to Remake the Workplace Through the Strategic Application of Technology*, Gloria J. Gery (1991) suggested that productive professionalization embraces the "performance zone," a *kairotic*, rhetorical space creating a zone of proximal development between skills and situations. According to Gery, "Individual employees and entire organizations can systematically work and achieve in the performance zone" (p. 13). Further, in *Performance Management Systems: A Global Perspective*, Arup Varma, Pawan S. Budhwar, and Angelo DeNisi (2008) discussed the importance of motivation in project management (PM). "The objective of PM," according to Varma et al., "is to maximize employees' contributions to the organization, which means changing employees' behaviors so that they produce this maximum contribution" (p. 40). They further reasoned that motivation will be high if and only if people see a strong relationship between the energy they devote to something and the results produced, between the results and the favorableness of evaluations, between the level of evaluations and outcomes, and between the outcomes and anticipated satisfactions (pp. 46-47). This trajectory of motivation as a process can lead to what they called "action-to-results" connections. Agile faculty professionalization is about creating just such connections in responsive, nimble ways.

With OWI, motivation as a process is accomplished through retooling old paradigms and re-envisioning how we justify and resist change. An effective, agile professionalization support system must enable people to perform in a system. Every OWI teacher, for instance, has different skills with the content, with the design provided, with new delivery tools, with managing students in online spaces, and with motivating learners individually and in groups in ways that do not overburden the students or the teacher. The ideal performance zone or set of faculty professionalization practices actualizes situated change just-in-time, and affords sound praxis refactored on-demand at any time and in every place. Good professionalization is flexible and dynamic with full faculty buy-in (Light, Chen, & Ittelson, 2012). In "Employee Performance Management," Dennis Briscoe and Lisbeth Claus (2008), for instance, defined Performance Management as, "[T]he system through which organizations set work goals, determine performance standards, assign and evaluate work, provide performance feedback, determine training and development needs, and distribute rewards" (p. 15). Newly mediated OWI and professionalization requires dynamic action to results, which is a situated simulation embracing practical theory. As Joel A. English (2014) opened the Preface to *Plugged In: Succeeding as an Online Learner*:

> We all know that distance learning has become core to the business model of our institutions and the academic model of our programs. However, we have failed to acknowledge collectively that our online students very often require additional technological skills, critical thinking and communication skills, motivation, scheduling and self-administration tools, learning facilities, and financial savvy in order to be successful online. (p. xii)

The same can be said of *the needs of faculty and WPAs* who are working to plug in.

Indeed, limitations of code-and-fix professionalization, as well as predictive professionalization, can be mitigated through agile refactoring to promote effective action, capture and use collective intelligence, create goal-oriented exchanges between administrators and teachers and students, create productive cross-functional teams specializing in action to results, make representations of cultural experience, capture and re-tool the knowledge of first-person experts, and develop smart tools to deal with ranges of complexity. Professionalization can be seen as a process of rewriting, reworking, and re-architecting the grammar or code of online courses and online teaching, thus re-assigning what we value to fix the root of the problem as new contexts and situations arise (Hunt & Thomas, 1999). And the first step is in recognizing that design and content creation by multiple authors (i.e., administrators, teachers, students) is an iterative process. Let us consider crowd-sourced professionalization, for instance:

> crowd-sourced evaluations of scholarly arguments, not to
> mention crowd-sourced production models for generating
> and editing scholarly content, are transforming both the
> authorship function and conventional knowledge platforms,
> [creating] a much more dynamic, iterative, and dialogical
> environment that is predicated on versioning, crowd-sourced
> models of engagement and peer review, and open-source
> knowledge and publication platforms. (Burdick et al., 2012,
> p. 85)

As Daren C. Brabham (2013) wrote in *Crowdsourcing,* "The ability to coordinate and network with one another is at the heart of collective intelligence" (p. 22), and we should move toward professionalization models that value these divergent convergences.

Let us apply some of these ideas about faculty professionalization more directly to the CCCC OWI Committee's *A Position Statement of Principles and Example Effective Practices for OWI* (CCCC OWI Committee, 2013) recommendations through the lens of agile design and refactoring. The OWI principles are categorized by instruction, faculty, institution, and research, with an overarching principle of inclusivity and accessibility. Access is the foundation to each principle, and agile software design that embraces iterative, refactoring decision-making processes supports universal access in effective OWI faculty professionalization practice. Each OWI principle, clearly, is relevant to professionalization as well as to teaching and learning more generally.

OWI PRINCIPLE 1: THE OVERARCHING PRINCIPLE OF ACCESS AND INCLUSIVITY

With OWI Principle 1 as the overarching guideline, just as OWI should be universally inclusive and accessible (pp. 7-11), faculty working online should retain all of the rights and support and pay structure privileges as onsite faculty, especially if following an integrated scholar approach to connecting teaching, research, and service in online learning environments. Working with students online both asynchronously and synchronously is just as intensive as working with students in a classroom and during office hours (see Chapters 2, 4, & 11). To understand this intensive work, consider valuing people-oriented adaptive work rather than process-oriented models, recognizing that every student learns how to read critically and write in developed ways uniquely. As such, faculty who support students in a people-oriented paradigm should be rewarded for the quality of interaction in unique spaces they provide students. And just as a variety of modalities and tools should be made available to different types of learners, faculty should be encouraged to teach in onsite, hybrid, and/or fully online environments to maximize their own teaching skills and integrated scholar needs. Enacting OWI Principle 1, universal access, requires enabling our sensibilities to imagine the real-world audiences as a diverse universe of users with highly divergent needs through converging practices and systematic goals and objectives—and that effort must be considered deeply, taught to one another, researched systematically, written about, and published in scholarly venues. No doubt, it should be rewarded appropriately.

OWI Principles 2 - 6: Instructional Principles

OWI Principles 2 through 6 covered instructional guidelines (p. 11-17). They detailed why OWCs should focus on writing using unique online instructional tools rather than spending too much time teaching technologies. OWI Principle 2, for instance, suggested that OWCs should focus on the writing and not on technology, which means that faculty should be trained to manipulate technology within their pedagogical philosophies rather than vice-versa. In thinking about how students interact with faculty, with each other, and with content online, faculty pedagogy can develop in productive ways. OWI Principle 3 suggested that appropriate teaching and learning strategies should be developed, which means thinking through such issues as how composition instruction in onsite settings may need to change in online ones, how new approaches in online settings need to be employed, and how outcomes can be augmented when students are increasing their technological literacies. OWI Principle 4, similarly, pointed out that appropriate contemporary composition theories should be integrated into online environments. In terms of faculty professionalization, this principle opens new areas of research and training. Faculty should attend campus-wide, local, and national conferences regarding working with learners online, including developing a better understanding of working with adult and nontraditional and visual learners if the demographics warrant (see Chapters 8, 9, & 10). OWI

Principle 5 suggested online teachers should have *reasonable* control over their own content and teaching techniques, and OWI Principle 6 noted that unique and experimental models themselves should, like all OWCs, be required to follow effective practices principles.

Remember that a primary goal of refactoring is to alter internal structures without changing external behaviors. If a teaching load is 4:4 at an institution, that external requirement should be the same even if internal pedagogical shifts in modality are encouraged. If the number of students per section is capped at 20, which is recommended in OWI Principle 9, then the equivalent online course should be similarly capped (although OWI Principle 9 spoke singularly to OWI course caps without considering onsite courses, this recommendation had its origins in the CCCC's *Statement of Principles and Standards for the Postsecondary Teaching of Writing* (1989) and the CCCC's *Statement on Second Language Writing and Writers* (2009), which were written primarily for onsite courses; pp. 20-21). Ultimately, differences between face-to-face, hybrid, and fully online teaching should be an internal matter of teaching styles that increasingly resemble one another rather than demand or call for different teachers with incredibly different skill sets (see Chapter 18). Doing so reduces the complexity of online courses, improves maintainability by enabling teachers to reinforce effective practices in varied delivery modalities, refines the architecture of writing programs to improve sustainability, and develops a model where changes in curriculum or approach or composition theories can be extended readily to all varied course sections in safe and controlled ways.

A significant danger in online writing faculty professionalization is in spending money and time developing a course and then thinking the course is ready to teach term after term without revision or additional thought. Instead, courses should be developed with iterative design in mind in order to breathe, synchronously, with the developing skills and interests and needs of the teacher as well as the increasingly divergent interests of the students. Creating a shared master course or model syllabus with instructors in a program works well in terms of the new media principles of variability and modularity. However, as the OWI instructional principles indicate, writing courses should focus on well-considered content that can make use of online technologies with teachers who are making specific decisions on conveying, teaching, and assessing student writing practices. Adaptable course shells work well if there is teacher ownership, and that should come from teachers' iteratively refactoring design and content so that they can (re)present and transcode the course in their own situated contexts. This room for play and innovation in online learning spaces creates that third-space unique to every shell that is people-based rather than only process-based, so as help teachers to avoid defining students as stock users of class content term after term, year after year.

In *Teaching/Writing in Thirdspaces: The Studio Approach,* Rhonda Grego and Nancy S. Thompson (2008) discussed thirdspaces as being "influenced by institutional politics, preferences, and power relations" (p. 5)—emphasizing local needs and how close attention to the everyday lives of students and teachers in specific locations is important. Researchers need tools to measure the knowledge transfer and benefits of spaces like ePortfolios and online learning systems (see also Lee & Carpenter, 2013; Whithaus, 2013). Students and teachers then participate to shape the classroom as a creative text to stimulate ideas and to work together to solve problems. Refactoring course content and delivery of that content must be assessed for reliability and validity across sections by teams of teachers or administrators, which is essential to OWI Principle 6 (pp. 16-17). Embedding appropriate composition theories and core composition teaching techniques in OWI is critical. Online writing teachers should retain reasonable control over their own content and teaching techniques, and experimental or new models of OWI still should be pedagogically sound, entail adequate preparation, and require valuable oversight.

OWI Principles 7 - 9: Faculty Principles

OWI Principles 7 through 9 covered faculty guidelines, and these are especially significant when considering faculty professionalization (pp. 17-21). OWI Principle 7, for instance, suggested that administrators must receive appropriate OWI-focused training, development, and support for evaluation and promotion. What determines appropriate training varies from place to place and from person to person. At some institutions, a course release is offered to prepare an OWC for the first time. This support may be similar to the time provided to a developer of any course that is taught for the time. At other institutions, such support entails extra compensation for designing and constructing course content in terms of a stipend, additional support for traveling to a conference to present and learn about OWI, opportunities to present development work on campus for additional pay, incentives in terms of useful tools like a scanner or digital camera, or moving to the top of the list of faculty who need a new office computer, and the like. An iterative, agile framework for faculty is needed to support and then recognize the work that is required to create rigorous thought spaces online for students, motivating faculty in development, action, and then action-to-results process. It is vital to encourage faculty to become integrated scholars, connecting teaching to research and service as well as to a sense of investment in the thirdspace culture of the program.

OWI Principle 8 recommended that online writing teachers receive fair and equitable compensation for their work. What is fair is obfuscated sometimes by administrative drive and pressure to increase profit, certainly (see Chapters 6 & 7, for example). We often do not recognize the value in working with students at a distance virtually, for instance, in the same ways that we see faculty work with students physically. There often is less "distance," however, between an online student and faculty member than there is between a faculty lecturer and a student in a face-to-face setting. That is, technologies afford opportunities for highly interactive spaces that, if done well to support students, can be intensive and time-consuming to faculty. And, as the best courses are those that change as needed through agile design, the notion that teachers should only be facilitators is problematic in OWCs. Some higher education models include paying highly trained rhetoricians and compositionists, for instance, to design and create curricula, and then paying less trained and therefore "less expensive" teachers to facilitate the content without iterative refactoring. Good teaching must consider design and content synchronously, however, changing dynamically in directions students take the course in. If teachers in onsite, face-to-face environments are provided offices and classrooms and tools to use, teachers using other delivery systems, too, should be provided the resources they need. Resources may include computers and professional opportunities like holding online office hours, but may also include partial reimbursement for Internet access, phone "minutes," and even more flexible synchronous communication class meeting times.

OWI Principle 9 suggested that OWCs should be capped at 20 students per course with an eye toward 15 if possible. Again, in building an agile design system that highlights interaction and works toward improving types of teacher::-student and student::student interaction using available technologies, a system both can motivate and recognize faculty who excel in building and feeding such spaces. With OWCs, we want students and teachers to "inhabit" these transactional spaces in order to maximize opportunities for learning. Some programs cap online courses at 10% lower than face-to-face courses, others work to keep the same enrollment per class numbers as onsite sections, while still others increase the online course cap, possibly seeing it as less work than onsite courses or knowing that a number of students likely will drop the course. Another model is to lift all caps on OWCs but create small peer groups and asking faculty to manage specific numbers of groups.[1] Ultimately, higher course caps begin to limit adequate motivation to interact to a high degree with one another and with content, thereby creating insufficient opportunities for students to receive teacher and peer feedback. Instructors new to online teaching certainly benefit from lower caps as they work to manage interaction online. Similar to the tendency to cut assignments in onsite courses when student numbers increase or when numbers of sections a teacher is required to teach, online writing teachers with higher course caps may be tempted to cut assignments and to move from synchronous to asynchronous-only models or otherwise to limit interaction or response.

OWI PRINCIPLES 10 - 14: INSTITUTIONAL PRINCIPLES

OWI Principles 10 through 14 cover institutional guidelines (pp. 21-30). OWI Principle 10 suggested that the institution should ensure that both students and teachers are prepared to work using the local tools and approaches employed, which speaks directly to the need for agile training that is revised and updated as newly mediated approaches and tools are put into place. OWI Principle 11 recommended supporting OWI with personalized and interpersonal online communities. For many institutions, such support begins minimally with setting up an FAQ and step-by-step Web page, but this process follows a code-and-fix or predictive design method that leaves many gaps. To create a more useful support mechanism requires generating a knowledge base with feedback offered transactionally by administrators and teachers and students. Institutions and WPAs should enable students and faculty, especially, to create and connect their personal and/or professional identities to this information. OWI Principle 12 suggested that institutions should foster teacher satisfaction with as robust a focus as is given to student satisfaction. To this end, institutions and WPAs should consider designing an electronic performance support system tied to student and programmatic success. OWI Principle 13 suggested that both online and onsite support tools must be in place for students such that online writing students could receive their primary support online and in the modalities and media engaged by their OWCs (see Chapter 5). Creating more media-rich examples, such as screencasts, in addition to text-based keys to success, is important in order to engage divergent learners convergently. Finally, OWI Principle 14 extended support to include OWLs and tutors who must also receive professional development support matching the environment in which they work, which enables OWL administrators and tutors to receive professionalization opportunities in like method and quality as the WPA and online writing teacher.

OWI PRINCIPLE 15: RESEARCH AND EXPLORATION

The final principle, OWI Principle 15, is a research and exploration guideline (p. 31-32). It suggested that administrators and teachers and tutors, as they continue to professionalize their understanding of teaching and learning in online writing environments, must be committed to ongoing action research. That is, again, research requires an agile design refactoring process, where small changes are made and tested in ways that support the larger infrastructure yet make quick, positive improvement. Such an agilely designed refactored research process can significantly restructure approaches over time without breaking the system. Thus, professionalization becomes a process of contact rethinking, rewriting, reworking, and retooling content and approaches through transactional and dialectical exchanges between teachers, tutors, students, content, research in the field, new technological affordances, new motivation through training, and the like.

CONCLUSION AND RECOMMENDATIONS

These OWI principles for effective practices will, to some extent, become more numerous and more nuanced. They will develop as the field of OWI continues to grow and expand, but they also will grow in our own programs as we continue to develop reflective praxis as integrated scholars. Thus, this chapter ends with some general recommendations that WPAs and other administrators of OWI programs should address for dynamic professional development:

- Consider software development methods as models for strengthening and understanding effective OWI practices in local contexts. Take the best of each method and move forward. For instance, get going with code-and-fix strategies as necessary, but then build in predictive updating and assessment to increase support and meet OWI effective practices principles. At the same time, work to progress toward characteristics of more adaptive and agile, people-oriented professionalization performance support system models and frameworks.
- Recognize that improving the quality of teaching online takes a great deal of time. What seems to be there or what knowledge appears to be transferring may not be and the work may require a sort of triangulation of understanding that may not be necessary in onsite, face-to-face modalities. Be sure of equal access to content, course design, technologies, and tools used in fulfilling assignments for all students.
- Work to meet instructional, institutional, and overarching effective OWI practices through iterative refactoring in order to develop a more flexible allocation of time and talent that can build productive teaching and learning spaces.
- Think though ways to build and sustain a healthy digital economy of proactive attention. Our students have diverse needs, a changing level of experience and comfort with technologies, and a wide range of access. Think *kairotically*.
- In addition to working with students in unique ways, recognize that teachers have an even greater diversity of experience, skill, motivation, and aptitude toward using technology effectively. Our goal should be

"teach-nology"; that is, we should seek to optimize teaching and learning and knowledge transfer with each instructor's individual teaching situation in mind. Adaptability and scalability can work against one another—and thus need repeated attention—with professional development and principles of numerical representation, modularity, automation, variability, and transcoding.

NOTES

1. Additionally, see the National Center for Academic Transformation's 6 models for course redesign at http://www.thencat.org/PlanRes/R2R_ModCrsRed.htm.

REFERENCES

Barton, Matt. (2008). New media and the virtual workplace. In Pavel Zemlianski & Kirk St.Amant. *Virtual workplaces and the new nature of business practices.* (pp. 382-394). Hershey, PA: IGI Global.

Brabham, Daren C. (2013). *Crowdsourcing.* Cambridge, MA: MIT Press.

Briscoe, Dennis R. & Clause, Lisbeth M. (2008). Employee performance management: Policies and practices in multinational enterprises. In Arup Varma, Pawan S. Budhwar & Angelo DeNisi, *Performance management systems: A global perspective* (pp. 15-39). New York: Routledge.

Burdick, Anne, Drucker, Johanna, Lunenfeld, Peter, Presner, Todd, & Schnapp, Jeffrey. (2012). *Digital humanities.* Cambridge, MA: MIT Press.

CCCC Committee for Principles and Standards for the Postsecondary Teaching of Writing. (1989). *Statement of principles and standards for the postsecondary teaching of writing.* Retrieved from http://www.ncte.org/cccc/resources/positions/postsecondarywriting

CCCC OWI Committee for Effective Practices in Online Writing Instruction. (2013). *A position statement of principles and effective practices for online writing instruction (OWI).* Retrieved from http://www.ncte.org/cccc/resources/positions/owiprinciples

Conference on College Composition and Communication. (2009). *CCCC statement on second language writing and writers.* Retrieved from http://www.ncte.org/cccc/resources/positions/secondlangwriting

Chun, Wendy Hui Kyong. (2011). *Programmed visions: Software and memory.* Cambridge, MA: MIT Press.

DeVoss, Dànielle Nicole, Eidman-Aadahl, Elyse, & Hicks, Troy. (2010). *Because digital writing matters: Improving student writing in online and multimedia environments.* San Francisco, CA: Jossey-Bass.

English, Joel. (2014). *Plugged in: Succeeding as an online learner.* Boston, MA: Wadsworth.

Fields, Jay, Harvie, Shane, Fowler, Martin, & Beck, Kent. (2009). *Refactoring: Ruby edition.* New York: Addison-Wesley.

Fowler, Martin. (1999). *Refactoring: Improving the design of existing code.* New York: Addison-Wesley.

Fowler, Martin. (2005). *The new methodology.* MartinFowler.com. Retrieved from http://martinfowler.com/articles/newMethodology.html

Fowler, Martin. (2013). Refactoring home page. *ThoughtWorks.* Retrieved from http://refactoring.com

Gery, Gloria J. (1991). *Electronic performance support systems: How and why to remake the workplace through the strategic application of technology.* Cambridge, MA: Ziff Institute.

Grego, Rhonda & Thompson, Nancy S. (2007). *Teaching/Writing in thirdspaces: The Studio Approach.* Carbondale, IL: Southern Illinois University Press.

Hunt, Andrew, & David Thomas. (1999). *The pragmatic programmer: From journeyman to master.* New York: Addison-Wesley.

Lanier, Jaron. (2011). *You are not a gadget: A manifesto.* New York: Vintage.

Lee, Sohui, & Carpenter, Russell G. (2013). *The Routledge reader on writing centers and new media.* New York: Routledge.

LeFevre, Karen Burke. (1987). *Invention as a social act.* (Studies in Writing and Rhetoric Series). Carbondale, IL: Southern Illinois University Press.

Light, Tracy Penny, Chen, Helen L., & Ittelson, John C. (2012). *Documenting learning with eportfolios: A guide for college instructors.* San Francisco, CA: Jossey-Bass.

Manovich, Lev. (2002). *The language of new media.* Boston, MA: MIT Press.

Manovich, Lev. (2013). *Software takes command.* New York: Bloomsbury Academic. Retrieved from http://lab.softwarestudies.com/p/softbook.html

National Center for Academic Transformation. (2005). *Six models for course redesign.* Retrieved from http://www.thencat.org/PlanRes/R2R_ModCrsRed.htm

O'Meara, Kerry Ann, Rice, Eugene, & Edgerton, Russell. (2005). *Faculty priorities reconsidered: Rewarding multiple forms of scholarship.* San Francisco: Jossey-Bass.

Varma, Arup, Budhwar, Pawan S., & DeNisi, Angelo. (2008). *Performance management systems: A global perspective.* New York: Routledge.

Whithaus, Carl. (2013). ePortfolios as tools for facilitating and assessing knowledge transfer from lower division, general education courses to upper division, discipline-specific courses. In Kathy Wills & Rich Rice (Eds.), *ePortfolio performance support systems: Constructing, presenting, and assessing portfolios.* Fort Collins, CO: The WAC Clearinghouse/Parlor Press. Retrieved from http://wac.colostate.edu/books/eportfolios/chapter11.pdf

CHAPTER 13

PREPARING STUDENTS FOR OWI

Lisa Meloncon
University of Cincinnati

Heidi Harris
University of Arkansas, Little Rock

This chapter examines how institutions and instructors can prepare students for OWCs. Integrating the latest research across fields with the work of the CCCC OWI Committee, this chapter provides effective practices and strategies for adequately preparing students for technology-based courses and for learning to write in such settings.

Keywords: community building, online orientation, online readiness, online teaching strategies, student preparation, student support

Students, particularly nontraditional ones, increasingly seek online educational opportunities as they juggle the constraints and demands of families, part- or full-time jobs, and other social and financial responsibilities (Noel-Levitz, 2013; see also Chapters 9 & 10). With college enrollments declining overall (US Census Bureau, 2013), colleges and universities are seeking additional enrollment in online courses as a part of their long-term strategies (Allen & Seaman, 2013, p. 4) while state governments increasingly seek evidence not just of enrollment, but also of retention and graduation when funding colleges and universities (Harnish, 2011). Retention rates in online classes were noted as an "important or very important barrier to the growth of online education" by 73.5% of chief academic officers in the most recent Babson survey of higher education administrators (Allen & Seaman, 2013, p. 30).

Students continue to seek online educational opportunities because of flexibility in scheduling, the perception of online courses as "time-saving," and the ability to attend to family responsibilities while taking courses (Harris & Martin, 2012; Leh, 2002; Shea, Swan, Fredricksen & Pickett, 2002; Young, 2006). However, once students select online education, they must then be assisted by educational institutions to become successful in online courses, particularly in OWCs, where students must engage much more fully with both reading and producing written texts and navigating the technologies to do so. While students taking online courses in content-heavy subjects might watch lectures, read a textbook, and take multiple-choice or other objective exams, students in OWCs more frequently might be asked to engage in collaborative activities (i.e., discussion boards, small group projects), complete writing tasks (i.e., written essays), and interact with students and faculty (i.e., peer-writing groups, synchronous conferences with faculty). Any of these activities require successfully navigating a variety of LMS components as well as uploading digital files, accessing and evaluating written feedback, and participating in course activities that require them to engage and interact with peers and with the instructor (see OWI Principles 3, 4, 11, & 13).

Literature reviews across a number of fields (Future of State Universities 2011; Lack, 2013; Warnock, 2013) have illustrated the wide variety of research about how learning outcomes in online courses compare to onsite or face-to-face courses. While writing studies has been developing its understanding of instructor-related issues regarding online teaching (Hewett, 2010, 2015b; Hewett & Ehmann, 2004; McGrath, 2008; Meloncon, 2007), time it takes to teach online (Worley & Tesdell, 2009), and general issues related to online learners (Cargile-Cook & Grant-Davie, 2005, 2103; special issues of *Computers and Composition* 2001, 18.4 and 2006, 23.1; *Technical Communication Quarterly,* 1999, 8.1 and 2007, 16.1), research in OWI has not adequately addressed the issue of student preparation and student success for OWCs.

In March, 2013, the CCCC OWI Committee published *A Position Statement of Principles and Example Effective Practices for OWI*, which provided 15 OWI principles. Three of the OWI principles related directly to students and student preparation:

- **OWI Principle 10: Students should be prepared by the institution and their teachers for the unique technological and pedagogical components of OWI** (pp. 21-23).
- **OWI Principle 11: Online writing teachers and their institutions should develop personalized and interpersonal online communities to foster student success** (pp. 23-24).
- **OWI Principle 13: OWI students should be provided support components through online/digital media as a primary resource; they should have access to face-to-face support components as a secondary set of resources** (pp. 26-28).

These three principles dealing most directly with student preparation are included within the institutional principles category. One of the reasons for their inclusion in this category rather than in a category specific to students is that remarkably little research has been conducted with students on their preparation for online courses (see Chapter 17). Thus, this chapter highlights what we know about student preparation for online courses in general and for OWI in particular, and it offers recommendations and effective practices addressing student preparation for OWI. This information is drawn from the research work of the committee, the CCCC OWI Committee Expert/Stakeholder Panel, and consistent themes in published research, much of which is described in the Introduction and Chapter 1.

THE NECESSITY OF STUDENT PREPARATION FOR OWI

Ivan L. Harrell's (2008) multi-disciplinary review of the existing literature on student preparation offered suggestions to increase success involving student readiness, student orientation, and student support. His study foreshadowed many of the principles and effective practices of the OWI policy statement, which demonstrates that the OWI principles are not radical or unknown to educators working with onsite and online students. However, in writing studies in general and in rhetoric and composition in particular, little-to-no work has been done specifically on how students select online classes, how to prepare students for OWCs, and what characteristics of online learners help them succeed in online classes. To help them understand the current state of affairs in OWI, the CCCC OWI Committee administered two nationwide surveys—one for fully online courses and the other for hybrid ones (CCCC OWI Committee, 2011a & 2011b, respectively) that resulted in *The State of the Art of OWI* report (2011c). This survey was, in part, an attempt to learn about student preparation and preferences from the instructor's point of view. One issue that emerged from the CCCC OWI Committee surveys is the need to understand more about students' apparent readiness for online education.

Over the past decade and more, research in online education across the disciplines, particularly in education and psychology, has considered student readiness for online learning. In particular, this research has focused on the use of student surveys and other diagnostic instruments (McVay, 2000, 2001; Parnell & Carraher, 2003; Smith, 2005; Smith, Murphy, & Mahoney, 2003; Watkins, Leigh, & Triner, 2004) and identifying the characteristics of students who are successful online learners (Dabbagh, 2007; Tallent-Runnels et al., 2006). In relation to identifying online student characteristics, Nada Dabbagh (2007) predicted that "the profile of the online learner population is changing from one that is older, mostly employed, place bound, goal oriented, and intrinsically motivated, to one that is diverse, dynamic, tentative, younger, and responsive to rapid technological changes" (p. 224); these traits indicate that online education appeals not only to so-called nontraditional learners but increasingly to younger learners as well. Current consensus in online education is that successful student learners are self-motivated, goal-oriented, and efficient at time management. However, OWI teachers are likely to find the full range of students in their classrooms; mingling in classes with the dynamic, tentative, and younger students are students who are returning to school with full-time jobs, reconsidering their first careers for second (or even third) careers, and/or juggling family responsibilities with school. Some have poor technology skills, others have excellent skills with social media but no skills with educational technology, and others easily use technology in any setting (Hewett, 2015a). Additionally, students have a wide range of access needs—often masked by the online setting—that include physical disabilities, learning challenges, multilingual language learning traits, and socioeconomic disadvantages as described in Chapters 1, 8, 9, & 10 & OWI Principle 1 (pp. 7-11). It is challenging for writing studies educators to ensure that support is in place for this range of students with varying access needs and technological, writing, and life skills to complete OWCs successfully.

Recent research, such as that by Moon-Heum Cho (2012), has shown that online orientations to the LMS or the course are useful for students and their success in online courses. However, in the CCCC OWI Committee's surveys, only 19% of survey respondents agreed or strongly agreed that "students have completed an instrument, which [sic] has indicated that their learning preferences are conducive to success in an online environment" (CCCC OWI Committee, 2011c, p. 82). Thus, even if the research indicated that online orientations are highly reliable and valid (Dray, Lowenthal, Miszkiewicz, Ruiz-Primo, & Marczynski, 2011), the majority of students are more than likely enrolling in online courses regardless of their readiness for online learning. As institutions seek to boost online enrollments, they are unlikely to require students to participate in mandatory institutional readiness assessments prior to enrollment and to exclude students from enrolling for online courses. Even those students who do take recommended readiness exams may believe that they will be successful in online courses despite the results of these surveys.

Once students enroll in online courses, whether or not they are offered formal preparation for online learning, they face a number of challenges. One of the CCCC OWI Committee's (2011a, 2011b) survey questions asked, "What do students report are the most problematic aspects of the [writing] courses?" Compiled results from the two surveys showed participants indicating that once students enroll in online classes, regardless of their preparation, the most common challenges they face are "keeping up with the class" (75%), "technical problems with the student interface" (58%), "lack of motivation" (50%), and "getting started in the course" (39%) (CCCC OWI Committee, 2011c, p. 84).

Instructors indicated that they most frequently dealt with student issues through "community building activities early in the semester" (66%), "informal portions of discussion board" (60%), "communicating a reasonable amount of flexibility for the larger, more sophisticated projects (acknowledging that things do/can go wrong)" (54%), and "work[ing] closely with the IT department to correct technical problems quickly" (52%) (CCCC OWI Committee, 2011c, p. 84). Overall, the survey results indicated that student issues early in the term might be linked, at least in part, to unfamiliarity with the course requirements and lack of understanding of the online interface or problems with the online interface itself. Faculty responses to problematic aspects of online courses frequently were communication-based: setting up opportunities for questions in the LMS and communicating with students and with IT staff in a timely manner.

How students perceive online courses is a second aspect of student readiness for OWI that is slightly less tangible than gauging student readiness via a survey or instrument. Noel-Levitz's (2013) surveys regarding student readiness for online instruction indicated that the top five challenges students face in online courses relate to their perceptions of student/faculty interaction and the quality of the course. Respondents were asked to rate the following statements:

- The quality of instruction is excellent.
- Student assignments are clearly defined in the syllabus.
- Faculty are responsive to student needs.
- Tuition paid is a worthwhile investment.
- Faculty provide timely feedback about student progress. (Noel-Levitz, 2013, p. 9)

These factors are related to student perception because, whether or not the elements listed above are true objectively (i.e., a faculty member might indeed be responsive but the students do not consider her to be responsive because they do not share the same definition for "responsive" in this context), students in the survey perceived these five factors to be challenges to success in online classes. At least three of the above-stated factors (i.e., clearly defined assignments, faculty responsiveness to student needs, and timely feedback about student progress) relate directly to potentially effective practices in OWI (OWI Principles 3 and 4, pp. 12-15; also see Chapters 3, 4, 5, & 11). A better understanding of students' motivation and their reasons for choosing online classes as well as their perceptions of whether and how online courses meet their interpersonal and intellectual needs can provide institutions and instructors much needed information in developing OWI that will help students succeed. Instructor perceptions and anecdotal data, when combined and triangulated with other data sources such as retention rates (see Chapter 6) and student perception and experience studies (see Chapter 17), can offer important insights into what institutions and faculty can do to better prepare students and help them succeed in OWCs.

. The lessons from the CCCC OWI Committee surveys of fully online and hybrid OWI educators and from other research into student preparation and success are three fold: (1) student readiness for online courses cannot always be directly measured, (2) student perception of the online course plays a role in their success in online courses, and (3) what instructors believe students need to be successful in an online course has little to do with being successful in an online *writing* course. According to the "State-of-the-Art Report" (CCCC OWI Committee, 2011c):

> The differences between online courses, online writing courses, between online training and online writing instruction training, and online teaching and online writing teaching blur throughout this report, indicating that traditional ideas and strategies simply have migrated to online setting without sufficient consideration of what specific media mean for learning in a particular disciplinary area like writing. (p. 10)

In the remainder of this chapter, we recommend strategies at the institutional and instructor levels that keep in mind the challenges associated with OWI and highlight the unique qualities of OWI that make student support challenging.

RECOMMENDATIONS FOR STUDENT PREPARATION

The OWI principles and accompanying example effective practices provided a variety of recommendations for institutions and instructors regarding OWI in general. In this section, we focus on the factors that relate to student preparation and success first at the institutional level and then the instructor level.

INSTITUTIONAL LEVEL

Orientation Modules/Models

While an onsite, face-to-face writing class might rely on little more than the technology of books, chalkboards, pens, and papers—and possibly a computer-powered projector—the online class usually relies on a functioning LMS, an accessible IT professional or student help desk, a working computer, and reliable access to the Internet (see Chapter 10). In addition to these external factors, students need technological capabilities and preparation before beginning an online class.

Individual institutions offer a wide range of technology training, support, development, and mentoring for students (and instructors). Some institutions or their writing programs make a concerted effort to standardize their online courses so that students can have similar experiences across courses. Other institutions provide minimal technology training, support, development and mentoring, relying on faculty and students to be motivated to troubleshoot their own problems. OWI Principle 7 called for both technology and pedagogical preparation for taking an OWC, making such minimal support unacceptable for preparing students or teachers for success in OWI (p. 17).

In conjunction with instructors within the disciplines, general orientation opportunities should be provided to students enrolling in online classes. These orientations need to include three specific areas:

1. An overview of required technologies and technological skills necessary to complete the course, including an introduction to the LMS;
2. Self-awareness assessments to help students gauge their own efficacy for completing the course; and
3. Disciplinary-specific information on what particular elements the course will include (i.e., small group work, synchronous meeting sessions, and the like).

Technology-related orientations should be twofold. First, they should include general information regarding the hardware, software, and applications that will be required in the class. For example, students need to know whether a netbook computer, tablet, or mobile device like a smart phone is suitable for the types and kinds of activities they will perform (see Chapter 16) or whether they need to access more powerful or otherwise different technology. Students also need to know whether they can access the LMS through the Internet alone or whether they also need access to such software as Adobe Acrobat or plug-ins as an updated version of Java to access course content. These technological needs are issues of access addressed in OWI Principle 1 (pp. 7-11) and discussed in Chapters 8 and 10. Second, students need an in-depth overview of the LMS that will be used in the course with respect to how it will be used in an OWC particularly. Moreover, students with disabilities require additional instruction on how they will interface their assistive technology—screen readers, Braille Displays, voice input software, and the like—with the institutional LMS, library, and other student services websites. OWI Principle 10 encouraged institutions and instructors to provide OWI preparation that includes familiarization with the interface and provides explicit instruction on where to find assignments, post and retrieve writing, and participate in interactive components of the class (i.e., discussion board, group work, and the like) (pp. 21-23). OWI Effective Practice

10.7 advocated for the OWC use of the institutionally approved software or LMS (pp. 22-23). One rationale for this effective practice is that instructors and students will need to have an outside resource for help with technological support that may arise, taking the onus for technology training and problem-solving assistance off the OWI teachers' shoulders. Another rationale, discussed in Chapter 1, is the notion that for some issues of student access, using a common LMS and foregoing outside software and programs levels the playing field and avoids requiring OWI teachers to teach technology over writing itself (see also OWI Principle 2, p. 7, and Chapters 4, 8, & 14 regarding this somewhat sticky issue).

Joel English (2014) highlighted four fundamentals for students to succeed as online learners: motivation, self-discipline, communication, and commitment. English underscored what OWI teachers already know: an online course is not easier than an onsite, face-to-face course and success requires time and engaged commitment (p. 85). While these seem obvious to the experienced instructor, these concepts can often be daunting for college students, especially first and second-year students. Student self-assessment often is included as part of orientations to online learning to enable them to self-gauge their preparation for taking an online class. The lack of preparation and readiness for online learning is one of the primary reasons students drop out of the courses. OWI Effective Practice 10.2 recommended that information be provided to students to help with study habits and skills (p. 22). One way to provide this information is through self-assessments that students can complete to help them understand their own habits. Students need to be encouraged to perform a self-assessment to determine whether their motivation and self-discipline are sufficient to keep them on track while taking an online course.

Such an intake also can provide the instructor with valuable data about the special needs of any disabled students enrolled in the course. Numerous self-assessment orientation modules are available online. One of the most widely used and adapted instruments is TOOLS (http://www.txwescetl.com/test-of-online-learning-success-tools/), which was created by Marcel Kerr of Texas Wesleyan College. It measures students' strengths and weaknesses regarding online learning including self-assessment information. (See Kerr, Rynearson & Kerr, 2006, for more information). This sort of detailed orientation affords students the opportunity to start the course better prepared technologically. Thus, they can spend their time and effort on the content of the course.

Finally, a key facet of online orientation for OWCs is an overview of the assignments, activities, and requirements in a class in addition to a list of minimal technological skills and personal skills necessary to succeed in OWCs (see Appendix for a Student Preparation Checklist). In the CCCC OWI Committee national surveys (2011a, 2011b), only 6% of respondents reported that students need to be able to read or write well to succeed in an OWC. That is not to say that such basic literacy skills are not needed; indeed, according to Beth L. Hewett (2015a), these are especially crucial skills for learning to writing in online settings because of the heavy text-based literacy loads (see also Griffin & Minter, 2013 & Chapter 6). It seems possible that the survey respondents simply were not thinking in terms of such basic literacies or that the survey worded the questions poorly regarding this aspect of student preparedness. Since much of an OWC is mediated through texts, students need to be able to read and to be able to communicate their questions and concerns. Discipline-specific orientations may ask questions about how much students are willing to read and other concerns geared particularly to online writing. For OWI orientation, students should be asked to identify how they take in information best: aurally through audio; visually through images and text; and/or aurally and visually through audio/visual sound, images, and text (see Chapter 11 for teaching strategies engaging these media). OWI carries the capability to use both synchronous and asynchronous modalities (see Chapter 3) and multiple media; when students identify their learning preferences, they are better able to voice their learning needs in an orientation to the OWC, better enabling the teacher to meet those needs—again, an issue of access.

One concern of particular importance in OWCs is time commitment. Students will need to schedule time to read and write assignments, possibly view videos, and participate in collaborative activities such as class discussion and peer feedback, in addition to their other writing tasks. Jane Bozarth, Diane Chapman, and Laura LaMonica (2004) asked online students, "If you could have learned something about online learning prior to beginning an online course, what would have been helpful?" The most common response was knowledge of the time commitment required (p. 95). To ensure student success, Effective Practice 10.2 suggested that specific information be provided to students about the time needed for drafting, revising, and working with peer group members (p. 22). While provided time estimates do not need to be exact, anecdotally students often miscalculate the amount of time needed to read, study, and do assignments. They may have a misinformed belief that online courses—OWCs included—take less time than onsite courses. Offering a range of time, such as suggested in Chapter 10, can help students visualize their time commitment in real terms instead of something that somehow gets done in cyberspace.

Gather and Leverage Existing Data

Every postsecondary institution now can collect reams of data about students from a myriad of internal systems. With the ease of computing technologies that can analyze and make sense of "big data," institutions are beginning to tap their own data assets to learn more about students and programs. According to Alyse Hachey, Katherine Conway, and Claire Wladis (2013), "Course and institutional management systems today collect a wealth of data on student characteristics, enrollment patterns and course outcomes that are not being utilized but are readily available for faculty and administrators to study ... to make thoughtful program improvement" (para. 1). WPAs and writing program faculty may be able to take advantage of such data to understand their student population and its learning needs better. For example, Di Xu & Shanna Smith Jaggers (2013) of the Community College Research Center compiled a dataset of nearly 500,000 courses take by over 40,000 students in the Washington State Community College system. This dataset is a prime example of leveraging existing data to find important trends and provide empirically based information on which to base decisions. Xu and Jaggers found that certain students (males, Black students, and younger students) had lower performance in online courses, and they extrapolated from these data the provocative suggestion that institutions could "redefine online learning as a student privilege rather than a right" in ways that would limit the types and kinds of courses a student could take online until the student proves they are ready (Community College Research Center, 2013, p. 25). In the context of OWI, using existing data (and gathering consistent data) could provide programs and instructors the leverage to make claims about student success and access to online learning, making more realistic decisions about who takes an OWC possible.

Most WPAs already are skilled in gathering student-generated data to facilitate assessment and program review in face-to-face courses, but as Virginia Tucker (2012) acknowledged, "Assessment in distance education is a topic of relatively recent study" (para. 2). Tucker explained that a distance writing program administrator (dWPA) needs a specific assessment strategy for online courses that is different from face-to-face strategies: "Understanding the particular assessment needs of a distance writing program allows a dWPA to better lead a conversation about programmatic assessment strategies" (para. 3; see also Chapter 6). While the dWPA should be able to gather information about assignments, exercises, and other pedagogical information from instructors, she most likely will need to ask for data about students and their accessing of the online platform from another location on campus. By leveraging institutional data in meaningful ways, institutions, WPAs, and instructors can provide necessary support structures that can increase student success in OWCs.

Limit Class Sizes to a Reasonable Number

OWI Principle 9 recommended that "OWCs should be capped responsibly at 20 students per course with 15 being a preferable number" (p. 20). Smaller OWC sizes offer significant benefits to both students and instructors (see Chapter 6 for more detail). Perhaps the greatest benefit is that lower course caps provide instructors the opportunity to offer more frequent (and possibly more substantive or more helpful) formative feedback on student writing. Respondents to the CCCC OWI Committee surveys (2011a, 2011b) indicated that responding to student writing does not change when moved to an online environment—the work still is there. The same grading and feedback demands exist. If student numbers increased, then feedback would decrease, which would undermine the effectiveness of the course.

However, respondents overwhelmingly also cited time and grading/responses/feedback as the primary reasons for keeping course caps low. Indeed, many open-ended responses pointed to the extra written communication that is necessary when teaching online as a quantifiable way to justify smaller class sizes. However, other than grading- or assessment-related feedback, many respondents also indicated that interacting to students in other ways also increases their workload (e.g., commenting on discussion posts, crafting class announcements, responding to emails and questions). For example, one respondent wrote, "Online teaching requires a lot of intense email communication in the evenings—the more students I have, the longer this takes each night." Quite simply, OWI is a text-heavy teaching venue with teachers teaching primarily through their writing and not their oral capabilities (Hewett, 2015a). They are stretched by the literacy load in ways similar to students.

While WPAs and administrators initially might balk at what are perceived as relatively low course caps, they need to consider the importance of online student retention not only in OWCs but across the university. Just as onsite, face-to-face writing courses help universities with retention, so, too, can online courses—but only if students complete them successfully. Appropriate enrollments allow students to succeed long term at the university, thus paying dividends in the future as opposed to simply meeting short-term enrollment goals.

Provide and Fund Training for OWI Teachers

OWI Principle 8 advocated for OWI teachers to receive fair and equitable compensation for their work. Compensation needs to match the additional effort required to develop, teach, and revise online courses, as indicated in Chapters 6, 7, and 12. The literature has suggested that creating a new online course takes more time and research (Worley & Tesdell, 2009). However, only 44.7% of chief academic officers in the Babson survey agreed that online courses require more faculty time and effort (Allen & Seaman, 2013, p. 22). When this time and effort is not acknowledged and provided for by the institution, student preparation is cheated, potentially leading to attrition and failure.

A consistent theme in the research that underscored the OWI principles was the need for instructors to participate in training before teaching online. Instructors also need ongoing professional development to keep up with new pedagogies and technology. To attend to these issues involves time and commitment that must come from other areas of faculty lives; thus to encourage faculty to participate in additional training and to compensate them for their time and efforts, OWI teachers need to be trained and funded for their professional commitment to teaching online. In Laura McGrath's (2008) national survey of OWI teachers, one instructor wrote that she could be better supported in her online teaching if her institution would "make it financially worthwhile to train to teach online." Hewett and Christa Ehmann (2004) similarly acknowledged that "precious few dollars are spent on teacher training, particularly on training that supersedes learning how to navigate a specific electronic platform and that addresses, instead, the pedagogy of online teaching and learning" (p. xiii). The trickle-down effect of professional training for OWI to improve student OWC experiences cannot be overstated. If the teachers are insufficiently prepared for OWI, the students lose.

Create More Support Structures for Students

Two particular areas of institutional support can facilitate student success. First, students need technology support throughout the course. OWI Effective Practice 10.4 stated that "the institution should provide 24/7, accessible technical support for any LMS or other approved software or technology used for meeting with or participating in the OWC. Teachers should not be considered the primary IT expert for the OWC" (p. 22). For some faculty this practice is, and will be for the foreseeable future, more dream than reality. Yet, if in essence the institution takes responsibility for IT orientation and support for all online courses, including OWCs, and if OWI teachers require students to complete an institution-driven orientation for the LMS when available, there will be fewer basic questions about using the LMS. If faculty further determine not to add unnecessary outside software to the course outside the LMS—and it is up to them to determine what is necessary or not—then another layer of technology frustration may be eliminated, thus enhancing inclusivity and accessibility (see OWI Principles 1, 2 & 10, as well as Chapter 14, to complicate the meaning of "necessary"). Writing faculty then will be left with a writing program-based necessity of helping students understand how the technology use changes in an OWC setting (OWI Principle 10). Of course, faculty should be cognizant that students might have limited access to and success with IT support systems, technology can fail, and that their job is to provide "accessible back-up plans for when technology fails, either on their end or the institution's end," according to Effective Practice 10.6 (p. 22).

Second, students need access to online tutoring if they are to succeed, and ultimately, this provision of tutoring is an institutional consideration (unless the institution's Writing Center is purely driven and funded by the writing program, in which case responsibility for this provision belongs to the writing program). Errin Heyman (2010) noted that a key factor in relation to student retention is "student support and student connection with the institution" (para. 16). OWI Principle 13 underscored the need for online writing students to have support components that include tutoring and other online resources typically found onsite. It stated, "OWI students should be provided support components through online/digital media as a primary resource; they should have access to onsite support components as a secondary set of resources" (p. 26). Moreover, given Xu & Jaggers' (Community College Research Center, 2013) recent research suggesting that males, Black students and students who are in basic writing may need more support services to help them succeed (p. 23), it is incumbent on writing programs to provide it. Students with disabilities likely require additional support in all of these matters. Support services include tutoring, writing centers that have virtual components, and OWLs. Chapter 5 outlines these necessary components of OWI that helps to enable student success. In preparing *A Position Statement of Principles and Example Effective Practices for OWI*, the CCCC OWI Committee believed that online writing students are best supported by online writing tutoring; such tutoring needs to be funded, staffed with trained administrators and tutors (see OWI Principle 14, pp. 28-30), and advertised to students for their use.

INSTRUCTOR LEVEL

Accessibility

In recent research, Sushil Oswal and Lisa Meloncon (2014) discussed the need for instructors to "pay attention" to accessibility and disability in OWCs. This need is necessitated by the fact that there are a growing number of students with disabilities (Newman Wagner, Cameto, Knokey, & Shaver., 2010; Snyder & Dillow, 2010). Some estimate students reporting a disability at 11% of undergraduates and 8% of graduate students (US Department of Education, 2012). Indeed, these numbers likely are low since many students with disabilities have a desire to forge an identity that is not related to their disability (Lightner, Kipps-Vaughan, Schulte, & Trice, 2012; Marshak, Van Wieren, Ferrell, Swiss, & Dugan, 2009). Other research has found that between 60-80% of students with disabilities choose not to disclose their challenges for any number of reasons (Schelly, Davies, & Spooner, 2011; Wagner, Newman, Cameto, Garza, & Levine, 2005). In terms of the OWI principles, these numbers certainly are low given that the CCCC OWI Committee included among students needing inclusivity and access attention not only those who are physically disabled, but also those with identified learning challenges, those with multilingual language concerns, and those with socioeconomic disadvantages. To this end, the CCCC OWI Committee strongly believes that OWI Principle 1 should ground all of OWI—from the WPA to individual teachers. Oswal and Meloncon (2014) provided instructors with strategies for creating accessible online courses, including adequate preparation for instructors, incorporating universal design into the course structure, selecting an appropriate delivery tool, and building capacity within writing programs. The authors indicated that "The strategies provided are ways to get started because for accessibility to be effectively implemented across programs requires a fundamental shift in ideology; it requires starting with accessibility as a parallel to learning outcomes" (p. 294).

Course design and navigation are related intimately with accessibility concerns. Faculty and students are familiar with the materiality of the onsite writing classes where discussions, meetings, and instructor interaction have, for the most part, clear and sometimes tacit expectations. In onsite writing classes, students generally understand that teachers will be speaking from particular places in the classroom, that teachers take responsibility for beginning and ending class sessions, that the projector or chalkboard will contain important information, that students might be working in peer-review groups and how to do so, that they will be asked to write and hand in papers and how to do so, and what to expect in terms of teacher comments on those papers (although the content of comments may vary, they often still will be returned on hardcopy papers). In the online class, however, navigational structures replace the chairs, chalkboard, and projector of the classroom, and the structure of each online class has to be learned and interpreted. Courtney Shivetts (2011), who has written a comprehensive literature review on the importance of the learner in online learning, found that while student motivation is an important factor for student success, students are also highly dependent on course layout and accessibility. While these two findings will not surprise many readers—especially those readers who have taught online—they do afford educators the opportunity to reconsider the materiality of the online classroom in order to motivate and prepare students for OWI and make OWCs more accessible.

Because students encounter each new online class as if they were encountering a new online *classroom*, design issues are of paramount concern in OWCs. Cheng-Yuan Lee, Jeremy Dickerson, and Joe Winslow (2012) offered three organizational philosophies of online course structure: the fully autonomous approach, the basic guidelines approach, and the highly specified approach. Online rubrics, such as the Chico State Rubric for Online Instruction, make general, research-based recommendations about course design. Whatever the approach one takes, students may need various levels of assistance from the OWI teacher. For example, the OWC might be structured much like an onsite course in that there are a set number of major and minor writing assignments that will be graded, class discussion is expected about reading and writing strategies (albeit through text in the common OWC), and some peer work is anticipated. In this case, students would benefit from an analogy with onsite writing classes indicating similarities and differences, drawing on their past knowledge. They also would benefit from understanding where and how to access the syllabus, whether there is any changeability to the course calendar (and when and they might find out about changed schedules), where the assignments are provided, where to post formal assignments, where to post writing to peers, and where to post personal communications with the teacher, and the like. If the OWC is differently structured—such as in a fully workshop setting where different students receive whole-class feedback each week—students would benefit from a different sort of explanation regarding the class expectations and where and how to access course materials. Given the hundreds of variations that an OWC can take, it behooves teachers to keep inclusion and access in mind; students who do not know what to do may choose to do nothing at all, failing to ask the questions to which they believe others automatically know the answers. Students with visual impairments and learning disabilities in general struggle to keep up with course readings and might need direct communications via email about schedule revisions and other last minute changes.

The scholarship of teaching and learning has advocated consistently for course creation that is transparent. Transparency involves not only providing clear learning outcomes but also information about how those outcomes will be achieved and what is required of students. In one pilot study, the most frequent answer that students gave to the question, "if you could have learned something about online learning prior to beginning an online courses, what would have been helpful?" was that they needed to know instructor expectations (Bozarth, Chapman, & LaMonica, 2004, p. 95). For online classes, students need to have a clear understanding of instructor expectations, and this can be accomplished by consistent communication through multiple channels that reminds students of expectations and course objectives, according to OWI Effective practice 11.3 (p. 23; see also Warnock, 2009 & Chapter 4). These channels should be designed into the structure of the course, regardless the course structure.

These multiple channels with built-in redundancies are a crucial lifeline for students with learning disabilities for surviving in online environments. Online courses not only need to provide students clear navigational pathways, instructions, and assignments, but online educators also need to be aware that students must relearn new patterns of navigation and systems for organization for each online class they encounter, meaning that the writing instruction might, at first, be slowed down as students learn to navigate a new online class. To this end, OWI teachers can provide basic, initial assignments designed to help students navigate the LMS while also beginning a purposeful reading and/or writing assignment.

Research the Profiles and Demographics of Students in OWCs

Closely related to the recommendation that institutions should access and leverage available data to understand online students better, instructors, too, should use institutional data to their advantage. These data can provide important insights to assist in course planning, development, and design. Resources, pedagogical approaches, and assignments that appeal to the unique characteristics of the students who gravitate toward online and technology-mediated course delivery in one's home institution (or in similar institutions regarding student population and levels offered) can only help those students succeed. For example, at the University of Cincinnati, the student body is comprised of 31% first-generation college students (University of Cincinnati, 2012, p. 73). Many online writing students are first generation and these students have particular issues that have been well documented such as lack of an understanding of college experience (Thayer, 2000; Vargas 2004) and lack of educational expectations and encouragement (Choy, 2001; Schmidt, 2003). Characteristics of such students may include pride in attempting college work and anxiety or fear of failing the family; when combined, these attributes may cause these students to take too many classes, not knowing what to expect from any one. In terms of taking online courses, first-generation students may come from impoverished or under-supported educational backgrounds, may have minimal Internet connection, and may be unfamiliar with using technology or with using it for educational purposes. With institutional data and a little research, OWI teachers can address the needs of such students when designing courses and throughout the term, all of which also applies to accessibility.

Building Community

The lack of a specified time and place to meet physically is one of the biggest barriers students must overcome when taking online courses. While instructors cannot control student motivation, they can encourage students to engage in an online course in a consistent manner. Even an asynchronous course that is built around an any time/anywhere learning philosophy can be aided by asking students to login at particular times each week or informing them that teacher messages or updates will occur on a regular and predictable schedule. A recent study by Hilde Patron and Salvador Lopez (2011) has shown that consistency is a key factor to student success: "Students who log in more frequently and with less variation of minutes per day tend to get higher grades" (p. 6). One way to help students develop consistent practices in completing online course work can be accomplished by applying OWI Principle 11, which advocated for the construction of an online community to foster student success (pp. 23-24). Research has shown that online students who feel a sense of community are more likely to continue with the course (Ludwig-Harman & Dunlap, 2003; McCracken, 2004). Some ways that OWI faculty can inspire online community follow:

- Create ice breaker exercises that allow students to get comfortable with each other as they explore the online environment or new tasks associated with the online environment.
- Incorporate options such as blogging and expanded discussions that allow students to continue conversations begun in discussion boards; doing so also may give them a more active voice in the course and encourage them to take control of their learning.
- Provide students with an area where they can answer each other's questions and/or share information in their own community of practice.

An integral part of building community is for the instructor to be present, demonstrate personal desire to interact with students, and model what online interaction looks like. Unlike an onsite or hybrid class, where the instructor is clearly present or not present, obviously interacting with students or maintaining a distance from them, instructor presence is not always evident online. In the OWC, students "see" their instructors through online profiles, participation in discussion boards, announcements and other general communications, emails to students, audio/video files, and in synchronous activities (e.g., online chats, voice and video activities, synchronous lectures, or asynchronous sessions in the LMS). These activities—plus evaluated writing—are the only ways that students know the teacher is present and actively working with them; uncertainty about teacher-student connections may create anxiety or discomfort for some students, which might prompt excessive emails as students seek connection and instruction.

Margaret Edwards, Beth Perry, and K. Katherine Janzen (2011) found that students believed the best online instructors were those that engaged, demonstrated interaction, and intervened at strategic moments. Embedded in OWI Principle 11's effective practice examples is the concept of interactivity; teachers should take "full advantage of the flexibility of electronic communications" in helping students both effectively navigate the course and effectively become writers (p. 13). Effective Practice 10.8 further recommended that "Students should be apprised of the time teachers will require for formal or informal conferences with teachers" (p. 23). Thus, teachers, as much as possible, should find ways to be present with students through student teacher conferences and office hours much as instructors would be in a face-to-face class.

The difference in "presence" in an online class comes to the forefront here. Not all OWI teachers are comfortable using the affordances of the LMS and other online applications that allow synchronous communication with students. Faculty who are present through asynchronous, written discussion boards and comments or feedback on students papers rely on students accessing those forms. In other words, in the asynchronous OWC, a student will only know if a professor is present in the class if s/he reads discussion boards, accesses and reads feedback, and checks his or her email or course messaging system. Changing this dynamic is not difficult. From an anecdotal perspective, OWI teachers may not realize how pleasantly surprising it can be to a student to receive even a very brief chat communication when both happen to be online. Reaching out with a friendly "hello" and "how is the class going for you?" on a synchronous text chat can open the student to an interpersonal relationship with the teacher that can be the difference between just surviving the term and thriving in the OWC.

Prepare Students for the Online Experience and for Academic Writing

Most of us have heard instructors indicate that students are not prepared for their online classes or that they believe that online courses will be less time-consuming or less difficult than onsite classes. Instructors also have reported that there is a "misperception among students that online courses would demand only that they log in once a week to get an assignment or provide a posting; instructors reported that students often seem surprised at the level of interaction and frequency of contact demanded by many courses" (Bozarth et al., 2004, p. 91). Often, students conflate online courses with independent study, self-paced, or correspondence courses (see Chapter 12). Students also might have experiences with introductory courses in other disciplines where assessment was a multiple-choice exam and courses required little writing or engagement. It is all too easy for students to extrapolate a similar situation for OWI; indeed, anecdotally speaking, we know that some teachers do teach their OWCs in just that manner with papers substituting for exams and little-to-no interpersonal connection developed. OWI Principle 7 was written to help OWI teachers move decidedly away from such OWC structures (CCCC OWI Committee, 2013).

Research has shown that students often do not realize the time and effort that is involved in taking an online *writing* course. According to Heyman (2010), while such concerns as student motivation may be outside of the control of instructors and institutions, factors such as course structure and faculty support can have positive impacts on student satisfaction and retention (see also Street, 2010). A way to mitigate competing expectations is to employ Effective Practice 10.5, which encourages instructors to complete "trial runs" to help students get comfortable with the online environment (p. 22). These trial runs could be as simple as sending out announcements encouraging students to complete either the institutional- or instructor-created online orientations or as complex as asking students to post introductions and ask questions about the syllabus prior to the first day of class. These sorts of exercises and expectations help to introduce students to the online environment, the LMS, and the rigors of an online community that is essential in a writing course.

One of the first class periods and exercises should focus on the demands of an OWC. For example, many onsite writing courses provide a writing prompt for in-class writing exercises. Students could be asked to read a short text, locate additional information on the same topic, and then generate a short response text that needs to be posted to the discussion board. This same work of a sample writing prompted by a specific thought or question can be imported to the online environment. Hybrid courses may do this kind of writing in the onsite setting or fully online depending on the teacher's goals. Such an assignment migration can help to illustrate how difficult writing on the fly can be and encourage students to set aside focused time for reading and writing for other course assignments. This sort of immediate exercise helps to prepare students for the rigors of the course and allows them to better assess whether they are ready for an OWC.

In addition to preparing students before or in the early stages of the course, following are some examples of effective practices that enable students to be successful throughout the term. These examples build on Effective Practices 11.5 and 11.7 (p. 24). See Appendix 13.A directly following this chapter for an additional Student Preparation Checklist.

- Incorporate elements into the course that reinforce information that students either should have learned in an orientation and/or that instructors believe students must know before they can take the course.
- Include links to expand the syllabus.
- Provide multiple and redundant entry points into assignments or little nuggets of information to which students can hyperlink, giving them individualized experience. Recycle these assignments and information as useful in the course.
- Include multiple types and genres of assignments such a choose-your-own adventure, buffet-style learning that works really well online.
- Use the course materials as a model for expectations of student perfor-

mance (e.g., short video or audio that comments on their assignments that students can use as a model for peer review; commenting on a discussion thread in the same way that you would want students to comment)

- Create short exercises within the drop/add timeframe at your institution that can help identify whether students are ready for the OWC. For example, students can be asked to find a specific article in the library databases, download it, attach it to an email, and submit it through a particular portal in the LMS. Then, they can be asked to write a summary of the article in the discussion board. Or, students can be asked to submit a short biography and post it to a specific place on the discussion board or class roster.
- Create a short video that shows students where the pertinent information is on the course website and follow up with a short quiz in the LMS on information on the course structure and outcomes.
- Create and post a page in the LMS that lists contact information for technological problems. Most institutions have an IT office that deals with technology problems for the LMS or for student email. Locate resources either within your institution or that are available online outside the institution that can help students with common problems. For example, it is likely that librarians have a tutorial on how to locate research resources (and it is possible that a librarian will agree to meet your class virtually).
- Keep the technology as streamlined as possible. Students like multiple communicative channels, but they should be accessible without multiple logins or a series of different tools. Even if the LMS is not the perfect solution, it may be the best solution since students may have more familiarity with it—particularly if the institution has done a good job of orienting them to the LMS or if they are online course frequent fliers.
- Develop task-based or goal-oriented assignments and exercises.
- Vary or add use of synchronous sessions in peer editing, OWLs, or office hours to appeal to students' different learning styles.

Many of these examples are derived from advice offered by the CCCC OWI Committee Expert/Stakeholders' Panel (CCCC OWI Committee, 2011d, 2012a, & 2012b).

CONCLUSION AND RECOMMENDATIONS

No one-size-fits-all model exists for preparing students to take an OWC because students come from a wide variety of backgrounds, experiences, and ability levels. Student diversity means that OWI teachers have little control over being fully prepared to address each student's past experiences and current motivation.

WPAs and their OWI teachers need to be vigilant in creating courses and program environments that prepare students to be successful. We can say with some confidence that being a successful online learner actually is not terribly different from being a successful face-to-face learner, yet there are areas of concern that must be addressed. To that end, to ensure students' success in online courses, institutions and instructors must prepare students for this experience (OWI Principle 10); they must create a sense of community (OWI Principle 11); and they must provide adequate support structures and resources (OWI Principle 13) (pp. 21-24, 26-28). Moreover, course design and content always should start with accessibility (OWI Principle 1, p. 7). Practices that we have found to be most successful at preparing online students include:

- Reaching out to students prior to the start of class to ensure that they understand the type of course and the workload of the course.
- Providing students with a technological and a personal self-assessment so they can adequately gauge their own preparation for an OWC.
- Providing students an online orientation to the technology, which should be done both at the institutional level (for technology and general online learning strategies) and the course level (for OWI-specific learning strategies). In both of these orientations, the specialized needs of students with disabilities must be covered.
- Offering students a detailed view of the structure of the course and course expectations.
- Creating a course that adheres to accessibility guidelines (see Chapters 8, 9, & 10)

Finally, writing studies needs additional empirical research (OWI Principle 15, pp. 31-32) across multiple institutions that bring students' expectations, experiences, and needs into the research process. In the evolution of OWCs, writing studies badly needs additional information in order to answer the question of how to prepare and empower students with a range of abilities to succeed in OWCs.

REFERENCES

Allen, I. Elaine & Seaman, Jeff. (2013). *Changing course: Ten years of tracking online education in the United States.* Retrieved from www.onlinelearningsurvey.com/reports/changingcourse.pdf

Blakelock, Jane & Smith, Tracy E. (Eds.). (2006) Distance learning: Evolving perspectives [Special issue]. *Computers and Composition, 23*(1).

Bozarth, Jane, Chapman, Diane, & LaMonica, Laura. (2004). Preparing for distance learning: Designing an online student orientation. *Educational Technology and Society, 7*(1), 87-106.

Brown, Robert M. & McMurrey, David A. (Eds.). (1999). Technical communication, distance learning, and the World Wide Web [Special issue]. *Technical Communication Quarterly, (8)*1.

CCCC Committee for Effective Practices in Online Writing Instruction. (2011a). *Fully online distance-based courses survey results.* Retrieved from http://s.zoomerang.com/sr.aspx?sm=EAupi15gkwWur6G7egRSXUw8k-pNMu1f5gjUp01aogtY%3d

CCCC Committee for Effective Practices in Online Writing Instruction. (2011b). *Hybrid/blended course survey results.* Retrieved from http://s.zoomerang.com/sr.aspx?sm=%2fPsFeeRDwfznaIyyz4sV0qxkkh5Ry7O1NdnGH-CxIBD4%3d

CCCC Committee for Effective Practices in Online Writing Instruction. (2011c). *The state of the art of OWI.* Retrieved from http://www.ncte.org/library/NCTEFiles/Groups/CCCC/Committees/OWI_State-of-Art_Report_April_2011.pdf

CCCC OWI Committee for Effective Practices in Online Writing Instruction. (2011d). [Transcript of expert/stakeholders' panel virtual meeting of 10/27/2011.] Unplublished raw data.

CCCC OWI Committee for Effective Practices in Online Writing Instruction. (2012a). [Transcript of expert/stakeholders' panel virtual meeting of 01/12/2012.] Unpublished raw data.

CCCC OWI Committee for Effective Practices in Online Writing Instruction. (2012b). [Transcript of expert/stakeholders' panel virtual meeting of 02/17/2012.] Unpublished raw data.

CCCC OWI Committee for Effective Practices in Online Writing Instruction. (2013). *A position statement of principles and effective practices for online writing instruction (OWI).* Retrieved from http://www.ncte.org/cccc/resources/positions/owiprinciples

California State University, Chico. (2011). *Rubric for online instruction.* Retrieved from http://www.csuchico.edu/roi/the_rubric.shtml

Cargile-Cook, Kelli & Grant-Davie, Keith (Eds.). (2005). *Online education: Global questions, local answers.* Amityville, NY: Baywood Publishing.

Cargile-Cook, Kelli & Grant-Davie, Keith (Eds.). (2013). *Online education 2.0: Evolving, adapting, and reinventing online technical communication.* Amityville, NY: Baywood Publishing.

Cho, Moon-Heum. (2012). Online student orientation in higher education: A developmental study. *Educational Technical Research and Development, 60*(6),

1051-1069.

Choy, Susan P. (2001). Students whose parents did not go to college: Postsecondary access, persistence, and attainment (NCES 2001-126). Washington, DC: US Department of Education, National Center for Education Statistics.

Community College Research Center. (2013, February). *Adaptability to online learning: Differences across types of students and academic subject areas.* (CCRC Working Paper No. 54). New York: Xu, Di & Jaggars, Shanna Smith.

Dabbagh, Nada. (2007). The online learner: Characteristics and pedagogical implications. *Contemporary Issues in Technology and Teacher Education, 7*(3), 217-226.

Dray, Barbara J., Lowenthal, Patrick R., Miszkiewicz, Melissa J., Ruiz-Primo, Maria Araceli, & Marczynski, Kelly. (2011). Developing an instrument to assess student readiness for online learning: A validation study. *Distance Education, 32*(1), 29-47.

Edwards, Margaret, Perry, Beth, & Janzen, K. Katherine. (2011). The making of an exemplary online educator. *Distance Education, 32*(1), 101-118.

English, Joel. (2014). *Plugged in: Succeeding as an online learner.* Boston, MA: Wadsworth, Cengage.

Future of State Universities. (2011). *Research on the effectiveness of online learning: A compilation of research on online learning.* Retrieved from http://www.academicpartnerships.com/sites/default/files/Research%20on%20the%20Effectiveness%20of%20Online%20Learning.pdf

Griffin, June & Minter, Deborah. (2013). The rise of the online writing classroom: Reflecting on the material conditions of college composition teaching. *College Composition and Communication, 65*(1), 140-161.

Hachey, Alyse, Conway, Katherine, & Wladis, Claire. (2013). Community colleges and underappreciated assets: Using institutional data to promote success in online learning. *Online Journal of Distance Learning Administration, 16*(1).

Harnish, Thomas. (2011). *Performance-based funding: A reemerging strategy in public higher education funding.* Retrieved from http://www.aascu.org/uploadedFiles/AASCU/Content/Root/PolicyAndAdvocacy/PolicyPublications/Performance_Funding_AASCU_June2011.pdf

Harrell II, Ivan L. (2008). Increasing the success of online students. *Inquiry, 13*(1), 36-44.

Harris, Heidi, & Martin, Elwyn. (2012). Student motivations for choosing online classes. *International Journal for the Scholarship of Teaching and Learning, 6*(2), 1-8.

Hawisher, Gail & Selfe, Cindy. (Eds.). (2001). Distance education: Promises and perils of teaching and learning online [Special issue]. *Computers and Composition, 18*(4).

Hewett, Beth L. (2010). *The online writing conference: A guide for teachers and tutors.* Portsmouth, NH, Boynton/Cook.

Hewett, Beth L. (2015a). *Reading to learn and writing to teach: Literacy strategies for online writing instruction.* Boston, MA: Bedford/St. Martin's Press.

Hewett, Beth L. (2015b). *The online writing conference: A guide for teachers and tutors.* (Updated). Boston, MA: Bedford/St. Martin's Press.

Hewett, Beth L. & Ehmann, Christa. (2004). *Preparing educators for online writing instruction: Principles and processes.* Urbana, IL: National Council of Teachers of English.

Hewett, Beth L. & Ehmann, Christa. (Eds.). (2007). Online teaching and learning: Preparation, development, and organizational communication [Special issue]. *Technical Communication Quarterly, 16*(1).

Heyman, Errin. (2010). Overcoming student retention issues in higher education online programs. *Online Journal of Distance Learning Administration, 8*(4).

Kerr, Marcel S., Rynearson, Kimberly, & Kerr, Marcus C. (2006). Student characteristics for online learning success. *The Internet and Higher Education, 9*(2), 91-105.

Lack, Kelly A. (2013). *Current status of research on online learning in postsecondary education.* Retrieved from http://www.sr.ithaka.org/research-publications/current-status-research-online-learning-postsecondary-education

Lee, Cheng-Yuan, Dickerson, Jeremy, & Winslow, Joe. (2012). An analysis of organizational approaches to online course structures online. *Journal of Distance Learning Administration, 15*(1).

Leh, Amy S. C. (2002). Action research on hybrid courses and their online communities. *Education Media International, 39*, 31-39.

Lightner, Kirsten, Kipps-Vaughan, Deborah, Schulte, Timothy, & Trice, Ashton (2012). Reasons university students with a learning disability wait to seek disability services. *Journal of Postsecondary Education and Disability, 25*(2), 145-159.

Ludwig-Hardman, Stacy, & Dunlap, Joanna C. (2003). Learner support services for online students: Scaffolding for success. *International Review of Research in Open and Distance Learning, 5*(1).

Marshak, Laura, Van Wieren, Todd, Ferrell, Diane Raeke, Swiss, Lindsay, & Dugan, Catherine (2010). Exploring barriers to college student use of disability services. *Journal of Postsecondary Education and Disability, 22*(3), 151-165.

McCracken, Holly. (2004). Extending virtual access: Promoting engagement and retention through integrated support systems. *Online Journal of Distance Learning Administration, 7*(1).

McGrath, Laura. (2008). In their own voices: Online writing instructors speak out on issues of preparation, development, & support. *Computers and Composition Online, Spring.*

McVay, Maggie. (2000). *Developing a Web-based distance student orientation to enhance student success in an online bachelor's degree completion program* (Doctoral dissertation, Nova Southeastern University). Retrieved from http://web.pdx.edu/~mmlynch/McVay-dissertation.pdf

McVay, Maggie. (2001). *How to be a successful distance education student: Learning on the Internet.* New York: Prentice Hall.

Meloncon, Lisa. (2007). Exploring electronic landscapes: Technical communication, online learning, and instructor preparedness. *Technical Communication Quarterly, 16*(1), 31-53.

Newman, L., Wagner, M., Cameto, R., Knokey, A-M., & Shaver, D. (2010). *Comparisons across time of the outcomes of youth with disabilities up to 4 years after high school. A report of findings from the national longitudinal transition study (NLTS) and the national longitudinal transition study-2 (NLTS-2)(NCSER 2010-3008).* Menlo Park, CA: SRI International. Retrieved from http://files.eric.ed.gov/fulltext/ED512149.pdf

Noel-Levitz. (2013). *2013 National online learners priorities report.* Coralville, IA: Noel-Levitz.

Oswal, Sushil & Meloncon, Lisa. (2014). Paying attention to accessibility when designing online courses in technical and professional communication. *Journal of Business and Technical Communication, 28*(3), 271-300.

Parnell, John A. & Carraher, Shawn. (2003). The management education by Internet readiness (Mebir) scale: Developing a scale to assess personal readiness for internet-mediated management education. *Journal of Management Education, 27*(4), 431-446.

Patron, Hilde & Lopez, Salvador. (2011). Student effort, consistency, and online performance. *The Journal of Educators Online, 8*(2), 1-11.

Schelly, Catherine, Davies, Patricia, & Spooner, Craig. (2011). Student perceptions of faculty implementation of universal design for learning. *Journal of Postsecondary Education and Disability, 24*(1), 17-30.

Schmidt, Peter. (2003). Academe's Hispanic Future: The nation's largest minority group faces big obstacles in higher education, and colleges struggle to find the right ways to help. *The Chronicle of Higher Education, 50*(14), A8.

Shea, Peter J., Swan, Karen, Fredericksen, Eric E., & Pickett, Alexandra M. (2002). Student satisfaction and reported learning in the SUNY Learning Network. In J. Bourne & J. C. Moore (Eds.), *Elements of quality online education* (pp. 145-155). Needham, MA: The Sloan Consortium.

Shivetts, Courtney. (2011). E-learning and blended learning: The importance of the learner: A research literature review. *International Journal on E-learning, 10*(3), 331-337.

Smith, Peter J. (2005). Learning preferences and readiness for online learning.

Educational Psychology, 25(1), 3-12.

Smith, Peter J., Murphy, Karen L., & Mahoney, Sue E. (2003). Towards identifying factors underlying readiness for online learning: An exploratory study. *Distance Education, 24*(1), 57-67.

Snyder, Thomas D. & Dillow, Sally A. (2010). Digest of Education Statistics 2009 (NCES 2010-013), (Table 231). Washington, DC: National Center for Education Statistics, Institute of Education Sciences, US Department of Education.

Street, Hannah. (2010). Factors influencing a learner's decision to drop-out or persist in higher education distance learning. *Online Journal of Distance Learning Administration, 13*(4).

Tallent-Runnels, Mary K., Thomas, Julie A., Lan, William Y., Cooper, Sandi, Ahern, Terence C., Shaw, Shana M., & Liu, Xiaoming. (2006). Teaching courses online: A review of the research. *Review of Educational Research, 76*(1), 93-135.

Thayer, Paul B. (2000). Retention of students from first generation and low income backgrounds (ERIC ED446633). *Opportunity Outlook, May,* 2-8.

Tucker, Virginia M. (2012). Listening for the squeaky wheel: Designing distance writing program assessment. *Online Journal of Distance Learning Administration, 15*(3).

US Department of Education, National Center for Education Statistics. (2012). *Table 285. Students reported disability status by selected characteristics 2007 to 2008.* Retrieved from https://www.census.gov/compendia/statab/2012/tables/12s0285.pdf

US Census Bureau. (2013). *After a recent upswing, college enrollment declines.* Census Bureau reports. Retrieved from http://www.census.gov/newsroom/press-releases/2013/cb13-153.html

University of Cincinnati. (2012). *Student fact book.* University of Cincinnati Institutional Research. Retrieved from http://www.uc.edu/content/dam/uc/provost/docs/institutional_research/student_reports/student_fact_book/UC_Student_Factbook_portfolio.pdf

Vargas, Joel H. (2004). *College knowledge: Addressing information barriers to college.* Boston, MA: College Access Services: The Education Resources Institute (TERI). Retrieved from www.teri.org

Wagner, Mary, Newman, Lynn, Cameto, Renee, Garza, Nicolle, & Levine, Phyliss. (2005). *After high school: A first look at the postschool experience of youth with disabilities.* Menlo Park, CA: SRI International.

Warnock, Scott. (2013). Studies comparing outcomes among onsite, hybrid, and fully-online writing courses. *WPA-CompPile Research Bibliographies, 21.* Retrieved from https://docs.google.com/file/d/0BygwPfTKm-RqSUtqcllyX-

3RQeEE/edit
Warnock, Scott. (2009). *Teaching writing online: How and why*. Champaign, IL: National Council of Teachers of English.

Watkins, Ryan, Leigh, Doug, & Triner, Don. (2004). Assessing readiness for e-learning. *Performance Improvement Quarterly, 17*(4), 66-79.

Worley, Wanda L. & Tesdell, Lee S. (2009). Instructor time and effort in online and face-to-face teaching: Lessons learned. *IEEE PCS, 52*(2), 138-151.

Young, Suzanne (2006). Student views of effective online teaching in higher education. *The American Journal of Distance Education, 20*(2), 65-77.

APPENDIX: STUDENT PREPARATION CHECKLIST

Instructors can adapt this checklist for their own purposes. We recommend sending it to students prior to the first day of class.

- Know yourself and how you learn.
  - Are you able to accomplish tasks and assignments with little oversight?
  - Are you using any adaptive or assistive technology to access your online courses that require additional help from your instructor?
  - Do you need consistent reminders?
  - Are you able to manage your time well so you're not waiting until the last minute?
- Know your technology.
  - Do you know what kind of hardware and software that you have and what you may need?
  - Who is your ISP provider?
  - Is it reliable?
  - Is your Internet access "high speed"?
  - If you are using wireless Internet access, is it secure and reliable enough to download and upload files for this course?
  - Do you have current browsers and plug-ins?
  - Does the course LMS work well with your assistive technology (if applicable)?
- Know your LMS.
  - Are you familiar with the LMS? Take time to complete an orientation (if available), attend a training session, schedule a time with someone at the technology center, or schedule a time with your instructor to walk through the particulars of the system.
  - If you use assistive technology, does the course LMS work well with it?
- Know the basics of technological literacy.
  - Do you know how to upload a file? How to download a file?

- ◦ Do you know how to attach a file to an email?
- ◦ Do you understand how to use "commenting" and "track changes" features in Microsoft Word?
- ◦ Do you know how to change the margins in a Word document?
- ◦ Do you feel comfortable using "commenting" and "track changes" features if you access Word with assistive technology?
- Know your own comfort levels with reading and writing—both online and using hardcopy books and articles. Online courses are mediated through technology but rely in large part on the use of texts.
  - ◦ How confident are you in your ability to read and understand complex but general reading material?
  - ◦ How confident are you in your ability to communicate via writing?
- Know how to ask a good question.
  - ◦ What are good questions? They are questions that show the student has done some of the thinking required but needs additional help and guidance.
  - ◦ How comfortable are you in asking questions of the professor publicly?
  - ◦ How comfortable are you in asking questions of the professor privately?
- Know where to go for help.
  - ◦ Do you know the contact information for technology support (IT) on campus?
  - ◦ Do you know the contact information for the writing center?
  - ◦ Do you know how the online writing center can help you with your writing?

CHAPTER 14

PREPARING FOR THE RHETORICITY OF OWI

Kevin Eric DePew
Old Dominion University

This chapter, directed to both instructors and students, addresses OWI as a digital rhetoric with all of the political and ideological dimensions of a rhetoric. As instructors and students prepare for OWI, they need to look beyond the functionality of the technologies used to teach the class and learn how to read them rhetorically. For instructors and students, digital rhetoric is applied in the production of instructional communication (i.e., the strategies these individuals use to communicate about policies and course content through the mediating technologies) and course content (i.e., what students are learning to produce in OWI classes). This chapter addresses the rhetorical features that OWI instructors should be aware of and how they can reasonably impart this awareness upon their students, particularly in light of OWI Principles 1 and 2.

Keywords: applied rhetoric, digital rhetoric, functional literacy, critical literacy, rhetorical literacy

To describe the practices of teaching and learning in OWI as applications of digital rhetoric would hardly be provocative to many stakeholders and observers of these courses. However, I argue that the uncontroversial nature of this description correlates with the way the term *digital rhetoric* typically is applied to any practice using digital tools, such as the computers and—increasingly—mobile devices (see Chapter 16) commonly used to mediate OWI. While such an application of this term acknowledges that all communication can be rhetorically construed, it often de-emphasizes the potentially persuasive and ideological nature of this communication. In other words, *rhetoric* almost becomes synonymous with *use* in these situations. But digital rhetoric—or *applied rhetoric* using digital technologies as it often is connoted in this chapter—should signify how an interlocutor considers to use digital tools when choosing the best available means of persuasion (to draw upon the Aristotelian definition) and how to use their affordances. Or, even in the absence of digital technologies, the interlocutor considers how digital tools can still influence one's means to be persuasive.

Indeed, OWCs—to include FYW—should be perceived and taught as applied rhetoric courses that use digital technology to mediate interaction between instructors and students.

Others who have examined the rhetorical nature of digital communication echoed the sentiments of this definition. James P. Zappen (2005), rather than define digital rhetoric, acknowledged that it is "an amalgam of more-or-less discrete components rather than a complete and integrated theory in its own right. These discrete components nonetheless provide at least a partial outline for such a theory, which has potential to contribute to the larger body of rhetorical theory and criticism and the rhetoric of science and technology in particular" (p. 323). To understand digital rhetoric is to understand the relationship between many different technologies and the myriad of ways that arguments get made. Because there are so many different ways that these components can be put together to create both effective and ineffective arguments, it becomes difficult to identify what exactly digital rhetoric is. Furthermore, the technological components have expanded writers' capabilities to communicate multimodally, and thus argue in new ways (see Chapter 15). As a result, the emphasis of digital rhetoric seems to be shifting toward an emphasis on the digital writing tools that afford the capability to compose multimodally. In a special issue of *Computers & Composition* entitled "Digital Rhetoric, Digital Literacy, Computers and Composition," guest editor Carolyn Handa (2001) also did not define digital rhetoric, but she argued, "incorporating digital elements into writing—especially in the form of Web pages and multimedia projects—demands that we draw on our knowledge of rhetoric perhaps even more than our knowledge of HTML, design issues, or graphics software. Images and sounds are rhetorical" (p. 2). For Handa, the technology is less important than both the message and the deliberate strategies one adopts to compose said message. However, recognizing the rapid rise of technologies that somewhat easily allow writers to incorporate visuals and sounds into their text, Handa emphasized that writers cannot lose sight of these elements' rhetorical nature. In short, "digital rhetoric" is not just about the *use* of digital communicative technologies.

In instructional contexts, the art of persuasion is prevalent, not just in the work students do in their writing courses but in their everyday interactions. Both instructors and students are constantly persuading each other. Among the many arguments that instructors make, they typically want to convince students that the subject matter is important, that their version of the subject matter is more accurate than competing theories, and that they are using the best approaches to help students understand the subject matter. Students, likewise, want to persuade instructors; they mostly argue for their capabilities to retain and apply what they have learned with hopes of leveraging this argument for a favorable assessment and/or recommendation. Moreover, if writing instruction is understood to be the teaching of applied rhetoric, the students, whether they understand it or not, are learning how to make such arguments in the courses they take. James Berlin (1982) wanted writing studies to accept that, "[i]n teaching writing, we are not simply offering training in useful technical skill that is meant as a simple complement to the more important studies of other areas. We are teaching a way of experiencing the world, a way of ordering and making sense of it" (p. 776). Writing instructors are teaching students how to interact with the world around them using various semiotic systems—how they are shaped by others' use of these semiotics and how they can shape others.

In the context of OWI, especially in fully online OWCs, the means by which instructors and students make arguments mostly is mediated by digital technologies and delivered through writing, even though the multimodal nature of many Web technologies does expand one's repertoires for making these arguments. Whether instructors and students choose to communicate textually with linguistic symbols or through other modalities, the actual technologies they use to communicate impacts the ways they can and do communicate. These contextual conditions positions the first two principles of *A Position Statement of Principles and Example Effective Practices for OWI*s (CCCC OWI Committee, 2013) as crucial guidelines for what instructors do in their courses. OWI Principle 1 reminds course designers to consider who will be taught and OWI Principle 2 reminds them about what needs to be taught. While administrators and instructors should clearly want OWCs to be accessible to all students, deciding the role the technology will play in the course is less straightforward and has to be context-dependent. OWI Effective Practice 7.2 stated that those who teach OWI should be hired for their expertise in writing because *they are teaching a writing course* (p. 18). However, when most writing in our contemporary age is composed and delivered with digital technologies, can instruction ignore the material conditions of our writing practices? This is not an easy question to answer, especially when an OWI technology's role often depends upon local institutional and programmatic resources, including, but not limited to what technologies are available, the OWI faculty's competencies with various digital technologies, and the knowledge of the rhetorical connections between writing and writing technologies.

Each of these technologies has affordances, or programmer-designed capabilities, that prescribe how the user *should* use it (see Chapter 11). The problem is that these programmer-designed features become transparent to many users—instructors and students alike—who naturalize them as inherent parts of the technology rather than the product of other people's decisions—an individual or an organization with ideological worldviews (Stone, 2001). Specifically the influences on designers and users range from Hollywood to the mass media to government agencies to educational institutions (Selber, 2004, p. 150). Unfortunately, many instructors and students are unaware how the rhetorical decisions of the corporations, teams, and individuals who write and design their digital technologies shape the ways they can communicate and, therefore, construct arguments. It is only when they experience a cryptic error message meant to be deciphered by "computer experts" that they become hyper-aware of these decisions that others have made (Selber, 2004). Arguably, the digitally mediated interaction between OWI participants, predominantly writing, is high stakes and has consequences to both the students' well-being (e.g., the ways that success in class can be leveraged for institutional and/or career success) and instructors' well-being (e.g., the ways that instructional success can be leveraged for job security, promotion, and/or financial reward). Making these arguments sometimes becomes more complicated for instructors and students who have physical or learning disabilities, who have a non-native command of English, who can only access technologies for OWI during certain times and at certain places, or whose technologies' limited capabilities provides diminished access to the OWC. Even those who rarely or never experience these issues should understand that individuals with these challenges will comprise a segment of their audience. Therefore, instructors and students alike can benefit from developing an awareness of the digital technology's influence on their communication. The question becomes where and when in the program and course design do the stakeholders incorporate this metacognition? To cover the widest swath of OWI participants, the teaching of digital rhetoric should start with instructor preparation because they, in turn, have the opportunity to impart this wisdom on their students.

To build upon the work of the three previous chapters in this section (see Chapters 11, 12, & 13), especially those that focus on instructor preparation, I position teacher preparation, and by extension student preparation, as primarily a response to *A Position Statement of Principles and Example Effective Practices for OWI*'s first two principles, respectively OWI Principle 2 about designing curricula that emphasizes that OWCs are *primarily* about learning how to write rather than learning how to use the technology and OWI Principle 1 about making OWCs accessible and inclusive. Discussing Principle 2 before Principle 1 does not deprioritize issues of inclusivity and accessibility; instead it helps to frame these access concerns as practical and rhetorical issues about connecting with one's audience. Using an Aristotelian foundation for writing instruction, I juxtapose the institutional realities that many writing programs face with the ideals the field advocates as a way to address what we should be preparing faculty and students for before and during the OWI course. Stuart Selber's (2004) theories of multiliteracy, especially his treatment of the concepts *functional literacy* and *rhetorical literacy*, provide useful vocabulary for discussing and contextually prioritizing the lessons that need to be learned to make OWI successful and the lessons that educators want instructors and students to learn in order to foster an outcome of rhetorically aware students and citizens. In the second part of the chapter, I highlight the principles in the OWI Statement that help to justify developing a rhetorical understanding of the technology among the OWI faculty and students, as well as exemplifying possible practices for developing these understandings.

FUNCTIONAL AWARENESS VERSUS RHETORICAL AWARENESS

A Position Statement of Principles and Example Effective Practices for OWI's (CCCC OWI Committee, 2013) second principle stated that "an online writing course should focus on writing and not on technology orientation or teaching students how to use learning and other technologies" (p. 11). As Beth L. Hewett acknowledges in Chapter 1, this principle is a strained union between two schools of thought. One school of thought prioritizes protecting both instructors and students. These advocates acknowledge the OWI should be more about "writing" than about being "online" and mediated through computer technologies. As a result, the curricular goals should be teaching students how to "invent the university" (Bartholomae, 1985) in the introductory (FYW) writing courses and teaching them how to communicate within their discipline's discourse in more advanced and writing-intensive disciplinary courses. Therefore, WPAs, when recruiting from a pool of highly qualified writing instructors (OWI Principle 7, Effective Practice 7.2), should not expect these instructors also to be digital technology experts. Rather these instructors should be taught how to use the computer technologies they need to competently manage the course and fulfill their institution's guidelines for writing instruction. The students, similarly, should be expected to learn the conventions of various discourse communities rather than how to use an array of applications, many they may never use again. Furthermore, students should not be asked to make potentially burdensome financial or time expenditures related to technology to participate in their writing courses.

The other school of thought contends that writing instruction is the teaching of applied rhetoric. Therefore, the instructor is responsible for extensively teaching students the available means of persuasion. Included among these means is the canon of delivery, so increasing both the writing students' repertoire of delivery modes, or writing technologies, and expanding their understanding of these writing tools' affordances increases the available means for them.[1] A writer with a vast array of rhetorical strategies can best approximate their audiences' expectations, and, arguably, have a greater chance of being successfully persuasive. Students in these types of classes, as a result, are prepared in their writing courses how to respond to different types of rhetorical situations rather than having finite amount of prescribed strategies.

Although scholars, instructors, and administrators who subscribe to these schools of thought can become very entrenched in their positions, the schools of thought, of course, are not mutually exclusive and can overlap in practice in many ways. Writing programs can design courses that teach students how to meet the expectations of their discourse communities through the writing and pre-writing that they do with various digital technologies. Also, some scholars maintain that instructors can use some multimodal composing technologies as a scaffold for teaching students rhetorical strategies they can use to participate in academic and disciplinary discourse communities, especially when working with multilingual writers (DePew, 2011; DePew & Miller-Cochran, 2010).

Resources, especially when limited, often prevent these positions from being reconciled. While some institutions can keep pace with the latest hardware and software innovations, other institutions do not have a lot of technology, have old and/or poorly maintained hardware and software, and/or experience incompatibility between the hardware and software. Some of these issues can be addressed with free software, but only if the applications are compatible with the computers and the institution will allow these applications to be placed on their computers. There is also the question as to whether among an institution's resources are faculty who have been appropriately prepared to use the technology and then to teach students how to compose with an expanded repertoire of writing technologies (see OWI Principle 7). Institutions also must negotiate how to address instructor preparation with the technology. Some institutions have robust IT departments, but they may cater to "sage-on-the-stage" paradigms that are discouraged for writing courses (DePew & Lettner-Rust, 2009, p. 180) or they may be focused strictly on the LMS that may or may not be appropriate for OWI. Other institutions will customize this technology preparation within the writing program. But even if instructors are learning how to operate various applications to teach OWCs, they may not be learning how to think about the rhetorical implication of these writing technologies—an issue that can be exacerbated when technologies, like the present generation of LMSs, provide little contextual information for blind users who cannot adequately access the technology to understand its rhetorical nature. Anecdotally, there are many institutions that offer OWI populated with faculty who think about the technology much more functionally than rhetorically. If the administrators and the OWI faculty do not value a rhetorical knowledge, then it cannot be imparted upon the students. And this state of writing pedagogy, arguably, precipitates from institutional attitudes that writing itself is a functional rather than a rhetorical technology.

While most would perceive that advantages of expertise and resources would favor four-year institutions over two-year institutions and private institutions over public institutions, the realities are sometimes different. These issues that institutions with very limited resources face are not just challenges for various types of hybrid OWCs that help provide student access to OWI (see Chapter 2), but in the fully online OWC these issues can limit how instructors learn how to teach and how they can mediate their course. So, due to these limited resources, two positions that seemingly can reach a compromise often remain contested. The student body also needs to be considered. Just as some campuses have more students who have developed adept literate practices, others have significant student populations who struggle with various aspects of reading and writing; the same can be said about students and their technology skills. And the students who excel or struggle with their literate behaviors are not necessarily the same ones who excel or struggle with the technology. Furthermore, the resources to help these disparate students at different campuses are rarely equal. *A Position Statement of Principles and Example Effective Practices for OWI* has been written to create the most effective literacy learning conditions for all students taking an OWC, whether they are honors students at a well-funded, well-regarded, research-rich, four-year institution or developmental writers at an underfunded, provincially known, single-building community college. Since these clearly are different contexts, individual institutions have to work within their given parameters to create the most effective experiences for all students. In other words, student populations also have to be an important indicator of the appropriateness of an "ideal" digital rhetoric approach.

Due to all of these factors, the space to create this compromise often feels as big as the eye of a needle—a narrow space in which administrators and instructors invested in OWI have to negotiate between designing practices that are most pedagogically sound for an applied rhetoric course and designing practices based upon the resources, knowledge, and culture that comprise their institutional realities. In many instances, it is difficult to thread this needle, and institutions often do the best they can to offer sound writing instruction with the realities that their institutions offer. When all-types of higher educational institutions—four-year, two-year, public, private, and for-profit institutions—are considered, a functional approach to writing and digital technologies appears to dominate the OWI landscape. Therefore, to provide a different, and maybe ideal, perspective, this chapter primarily advocates for strategies to design OWI as applied rhetoric courses using digital technologies.

Selber's (2004) descriptions of functional and rhetorical approaches to technologies help to explain the functional/rhetorical tension that is inherent in *A Position Statement of Principles and Example Effective Practices for OWI*s (CCCC OWI Committee, 2013) second principle. In *Multiliteracies for a Digital Age*, Selber (2004) challenged his audience to understand that technological education entails more than learning the tools' operational functions. Supporting Neil Postman's (1995) argument that teaching technologies is a humanities-based endeavor, Selber (2004) warned that "simply understanding the mechanics of computing, particularly in decontextualized ways, will not prepare students and teachers for the challenges of literacy in the twenty-first century" (p. 2). He stated that although this mechanical approach to teaching technology will foster "some extremely useful skills" within these students, he believed they "will have a much more difficult time thinking critically, contextually, and historically about the ways that computer technologies are developed and used within our culture, and how such use, in turn, intersects with writing and communication practices in the classroom" (p. 9). And one also can include contexts outside of the classroom. The situation Selber described is exacerbated in the OWC context because whether the course is hybrid or fully online (see Chapter 2), the students not only have to interact with the digital technologies, but they *must* interact with other people—especially those who have authority over them—through the technologies. Therefore, through this critical, contextual, and historical analysis of one's digital writing tools, writers may begin to understand how they can adapt the tools for their own purposes, which in the OWC can have immediate communicative consequences.

To paraphrase Selber, those who subscribe to the perspective that technologies are simply instruments also tend to fully embrace them as panaceas or reject them as a social cancer. These digital technologies, according to Selber, are much more complex than overblown pronouncement of their potential. The "hype," whether supporting or vilifying these tools, ignores that "computer technologies are aligned with competitive and oppressive formations that tend to shore up rather than address existing social inequalities" (p. 12). The stakeholders, too immersed in the commonplaces about technology, rarely are prompted to challenge these ubiquitous arguments. But, as Andrew Feenberg (1991) taught, the digital technologies are never neutral. And despite the "kumbaya rhetoric" of global equality that digital corporations use to sell their wares, at the end of the day these companies need to turn a profit, so they design their hardware and write their applications to appeal to hegemonic values and aesthetics (Selfe & Selfe, 1994; Stone, 2001). Therefore, any adoption of these products by higher education institutions to mediate online instruction—often through long-term contracts perceived to be lucrative investments—positions instructors as agents of these inequalities. For example, instructors at my institution were asked to participate in a pilot of three different LMSs. Two were corporate products and one was freeware, and my institution's IT department, based upon a confluence of factors, chose to retain the ubiquitous LMS program it had already been using. Despite this decision, the institution responsibly gave the instructors from across the curriculum an opportunity to test the different programs with their respective courses and decide which was the most effective product for their curricular goals. But many institutions, based upon my conversations with peers in field, do not solicit this type of feedback and choose programs for their instructors respective of how conducive they are for writing instruction.

Even though some instructors will use or supplement instruction with other digital applications, instructors and students—in some instructional contexts—can make choices about how they use these technologies. For example, given the choice, should an instructor ask students to build a blog with the institutional LMS or using another online program? From one perspective, using an LMS complies with *A Position Statement of Principles and Example Effective Practices for OWI*'s Effective Practice 10.7: "In most cases, teachers should make use of the institutionally approved software and/or LMS on which students are prepared for the OWC" (p. 22). The CCCC OWI Committee privileged colleges' and universities' LMS because these programs, built into the institutional infrastructure, often are widely employed and supported by IT in their contexts, which, therefore, reifies their presence and accessibility. In effect, when the institution's LMS is used, the playing field is level for all students—except those for whom access to the LMS has not been provided adequately—a critical issue that always needs attention, as Chapter 8 details. Examined from another perspective, the CCCC OWI Committee also recognized that LMSs, for some students and instructors, can limit inclusivity and accessibility insofar as they may be poorly designed. My students have described our campus' LMS as not being as intuitive as popular program's interfaces, and my peers complain about its inefficiency. Indeed, writing instructors often realize quickly that the LMS was not developed with writing instruction in mind. Furthermore, because other blogging programs exist outside the LMS, the instructor for many good pedagogical reasons (as suggested by Effective Practice 7.2), may prefer these programs because they afford students the potential of a real audience for their writing.

The CCCC OWI Committee also understood that some "composition teachers may desire to bring additional, often free, software into the OWC," but if they choose to do this, "they should: (1) have a clear pedagogical rationale for doing so; (2) have appropriate permission to do so; (3) make sure that it is accessible to all students; and (4) prepare students adequately for the change and/or addition to the LMS" (pp. 22-23). OWI instructors, and in some cases their WPAs, have to balance many challenges to make difficult decisions. In the case of choosing between the LMS and an outside software, should the instructor create a course in which all course features are contained within a LMS, a single and presumably familiar program? Or should OWI instructors choose the non-LMS programs with affordances that support their pedagogical goals (e.g., using outside software that is not password-protected like an LMS and allows writers to push their works to outside, more "real" audiences) differently? These stakeholders also have to weigh other considerations. With both programs, students concede ownership of their texts to the institution or corporation. Does the instructor or do the students know the implications of this often unspoken requirement? Also, do these stakeholders consider the pedagogical and ethical implications of the privacy the LMS affords versus the access to outside audiences that outside software affords? And do the instructors understand how making these decisions disadvantages some students and privileges others? Answering these questions and making these decisions are not easy, but that is exactly why administrators and instructors need to understand the implications of these issues and be involved in the decision-making process for selecting OWI technologies.

These arguments often go unchallenged in courses that teach students how to use these technologies. Citing Don Byrd and Derek Owens (1998), Selber (2004) emphasized how the technologies' potential for generating hybrid forms often goes unrealized; instead, the technologies often are used to reify entrenched ideological positions (pp. 137-138). Considering that most higher education computer literacy requirements are "monolithic and one-dimensional" and ignore "the fact that computer technologies are embedded in a wide range of constitutive contexts, as well as entangled in value systems" (p. 22), it is understandable that students simply accept these commonplaces as truth. In other words, when institutions present digital technologies to students, they also need to provide students with heuristics, yet these questions need to move beyond "How do I use this technology?" to "What does this technology want me to do?" and "Why?" Selber contended that "critique is certainly one crucial aspect of any computer literacy program, for it encourages a cultural awareness of power structures. But students must also be able to use computers effectively as well as participate in the construction and reconstruction of technological systems" (p. 7). This is the pivot point where function and rhetoric merge. By understanding how an application's affordances reifies certain social values, such as the hierarchical structure of most meeting software or the playful applications in social media, the users, whether instructors or students, can understand who the application designer thinks they are or who they want them to be. Only with this knowledge can users then accept the affordances on their own terms or appropriate the affordances for their own purposes.

Therefore, a complete rhetorical education of computer technologies entails the operational functions, an understanding of the technology as an artifact of power dynamics, and the opportunity to conceptualize new ways to design these technologies—arguably an act of empowerment. To this end, Selber proposed a multiliteracy education that covers functional, critical, and rhetorical literacies. One of the ways that Selber defined these literacies is through how each respectively positions the individual: "students as users of technologies, students as questioners of technology, and students as producers of technology" (p. 25). Although the students' agencies seem to increase favorably as one moves from functional literacy through critical literacy to rhetorical literacy, Selber clearly argued that there is no hierarchy among these different computer literacies and students need to be competent in all three (p. 24).

Selber (2004) came closest to defining rhetorical literacy when he said, "Rhetorical literacy concerns the design and evaluation of online environments; thus students who are rhetorically literate can effect change in technological systems. Students should not just be effective users of computers, nor should they be just informed questioners" (p. 182). *A Position Statement of Principles and Example Effective Practices for OWIs* (CCCC OWI Committee, 2013) OWI Principle 2 warned administrators and instructors about designing "writing courses" that focus on functional literacy to the exclusion of writing, that require OWI teachers to become technology specialists, or that focus the course curriculum on teaching how to compose with an array of writing technologies rather than how to effectively communicate within various discourse communities, especially those valued in the academy. Yet, a rhetorical literacy corresponds with this principle by teaching students how to use and adapt the technologies most effectively to produce desired texts. To help his audience understand rhetorical literacy, Selber (2004) established its parameters. Where functional literacy aims at effective practice and critical literacy aims at informed critique, rhetorical literacy aims at reflective praxis or a "thoughtful integration" between the two former literacies (pp. 25, 145). Additionally, Selber presented four other terms—persuasion, deliberation, reflection, social action—that round out the rhetorical literacies' parameters. As one uses these concepts to sketch an outline for what rhetorical literacy can be, it becomes apparent that rhetorically literate students see the devices' and applications' interfaces as not only texts produced by ideological bodies that need to be read and negotiated, but such interfaces also are potential entry points for users to become social actors in the design and use of interfaces. For example, Selber explained that hypertext was supposed to empower its readers by giving them choices about how they will read a text. Yet, despite the affordances that allow readers to choose their own path through a site, or, for that matter, compose multiple paths through a site, the metaphor of the linear text still guides most production and reception practices. Selber advocated teaching students how to read the metaphor that guide one's practices paying attention to both the "presences" and the "absences" (pp. 179-182).

An example of the praxis Selber advocated can be found in the "Tech" section of *Time* magazine from August 2013. Elinia Dockterman (2013) described the different ways that mobile technology users in specific contexts are "appjacking," or finding "presences" to repurpose applications for local and potentially unintended purposes. Examples Dockterman included were using Instagram to sell sheep in Kuwait, using LinkedIn for promoting prostitution, and employing Vine to create six-second video résumés (p. 16). While these activities range from the illegal to the practical, they demonstrate what a user can do if they understand what a digital technology allows them to do (critical), knows how to do it (functional), and adapts the digital technology for the argument (i.e., "Buy my product," "Hire me") the users wants to make (rhetorical). These users essentially have "hacked" these applications by reading their affordances and successfully adopting them for purposes that programmers may not have originally intended.

To adapt this type of learning to the writing classroom does not mean that the instructor is forgoing the teaching of linguistic-based writing to have students play with social media sites and mobile phone apps. Instead, particularly when this type of exploration is part-and-parcel of the writing course objectives, such adaptation means that instructors are designing writing pedagogies that allow students to choose the purposes for their own texts and they are helping their students choose the best available means (i.e., digital technologies) to achieve that purpose. While, I am not arguing that OWC instructors should be teaching their students how to be hackers, I believe instructors—because students have to use digital technologies to communicate with their instructors and the institution—need to learn how to teach students how to use the sanctioned technologies of the course to compose successful arguments, which may take varied forms. With many students taking courses online, there is a good chance that the strategies they learn for making arguments to their instructors will not just be applied to the general education writing course; ideally they will also be used for courses in the students' major or certificate programs, as well as contexts outside the academy.

Advocating that instructors learn how the technological tools' design influences a writer's composition would seem to contradict the OWI Principle 2—"an online writing course should focus on writing and not on technology orientation or teaching students how to use learning and other technologies" (p. 13). This principle, however, was written to guide instructors away from using their own and the students' resources, particularly time (and possibly money), just to teach students how to use the technologies that they need to participate in the class or to provide a plethora of outside technologies that reflect teachers' preferences over the LMS. In the latter case particularly, teachers risk a relatively leveled playing field through common and presumably accessible LMS technology for additional technologies that can be unnecessary in an OWC, as addressed in OWI Principle 1. In other words, the instructor should not need to begin a course with a unit about how to use the campus' LMS or ask students to use outside technologies that an LMS would address unless a similar technology's affordances facilitate an instructor's pedagogical goals to teach specific rhetorical applications (see earlier discussion about LMS blogs versus non-LMS blogs). OWI Principle 10 placed that responsibility of basic LMS student-preparation on the institution's IT unit even though the same principle indicated that OWI instructors should reify and repeat LMS skills and strategies relevant to using it for *writing* and *learning to write* in the course.

Instead, OWI Principle 2 made clear that the course should remain focused on writing instruction—of which rhetorical understanding certainly is key. The rationale for OWI Principle 2 (further explained in Chapter 1) also stated, "Unlike a digital rhetoric course, an OWC is not considered to be a place for stretching technological skills as much as for becoming stronger writers in various selected genres" (p. 11). A digital rhetoric course, narrowly defined, often teaches students a wide array of writing technologies (e.g., Web authoring, image editing, video editing) with a focus on how each technology taught can help students make the arguments they are composing or will compose for a specific purpose. For example, in such a course, one might want to teach students how to code a Web page so that they have more control over the outcome's design than if they chose to use a pre-designed template. But an applied rhetoric course, such as FYW, that is mediated by digital technologies (i.e., OWI), takes advantage of the course's material conditions, whether fully online or hybrid, to teach students real lessons about writing with digital technologies. Unlike the narrowly defined digital rhetoric course, learning methods of digital delivery is secondary to learning how to negotiate one's purpose with one's target audience.

OWI Principle 2 did not indicate, however, that instructors and students should not develop a meta-awareness of the ways that writing technologies influence the messages they compose. If all writing courses are applied rhetoric courses, then teaching digital rhetoric, more broadly defined as a way to get students to think about how writing technologies influence the message they compose—for both course assignments and course communication—is appropriate in online writing-focused courses. In such OWCs, allowing students to use templates is a suitable pedagogical method; however, instructors also may fold into their lessons a critical reading of these templates, urging students to analyze what these prescribed designs allow and do not allow them to compose. Likewise students can be taught to speculate why they think such templates were designed in particular ways and who the designers think their audiences are.

While some might argue that the writing classroom should be more focused on linguistic productions than cultural readings of the world or of digital technology, I argue that the instructors and students can learn to be better producers of texts when they, like the technology designers, have a better understanding of their audience. Instructors and students often produce texts for homogeneous audiences assuming that those with whom they are communicating have an idealized standard of linguistic and technological access to the texts they produce (e.g., assignments sheets, assignments submitted, communication between the instructor or students). This resonates with Paul Kei Matsuda's (2006) myth of linguistic homogeneity that Susan Miller Cochran describes in Chapter 9. Therefore, by prompting instructors and students to anticipate different audiences with diverse needs, it becomes an imperative that they understand how the technologies they use also impact their audiences' access to and understanding of their texts.

A Position Statement of Principles and Example Effective Practices for OWI's (CCCC OWI Committee, 2013) OWI Principle 1 addressed this imperative. This overarching principle—"Online writing instruction should be universally inclusive and accessible" (p. 7)—exemplified the need for OWI instructors' work to be grounded in digital rhetoric; this principle reminds them that they have to consider all audiences while communicating through digital technologies. More specifically the principle's rationale argued that issues of inclusivity and accessibility should "supersede[s] and connect[s] to every principle" in *A Position Statement of Principles and Example Effective Practices for OWI*, which makes disability, linguistic, and socioeconomic difference primary considerations when courses are designed and delivered (p. 7). The CCCC OWI Committee rationalized that "addressing the accessibility needs of the least confident readers increases the potential to reach all types of learners" (p. 7). As with the onsite, face-to-face classroom, the presence of these diverse student audiences means that the instructor cannot simply prepare for a homogeneous audience that one can expect will experience the course the same way: "given [OWI's] inherent connection to technology; patterns of exclusion have too often resulted from an uncritical adoption of digital technology and an indifference to how it could be used by persons with various disabilities and learning challenges" (p. 8). Instead, instructors have to think about the impact their strategies for communicating with students, especially the technologies that they choose, has on these diverse student populations. Because this principle guides all of *A Position Statement of Principles and Example Effective Practices for OWI* principles and example effective practices, it demonstrates the importance of reaching a wide student audience. While each OWI course will have general pedagogical goals, "OWI teachers should determine their uses of modality and media based not only on [these] goals but also on their students' likely strengths and access" (p. 9). However, to connect to this audience, the OWI instructor needs to know (1) how students expect to experience the texts they produce, (2) what technologies they, as faculty, have access to when communicating with and teaching this audience, and (3) how they best can use the technologies to meet their audiences' needs. Again, instructors who develop strategies for implementing these practices are better positioned to teach them to their students.

Students, likewise, have to consider similar heuristics when communicating with instructors, other students, and audiences beyond the classroom. These strategies should be adopted both when communicating with the diverse student body of the class en masse and when interacting with diverse individuals on a one-to-one basis. In an OWC designed to promote interaction among the students, they not only will have to learn effective strategies for communicating with each other; many also will need to learn how to use the same or similar technologies effectively to communicate with people with whom they work (and *play*) outside of the academic context. Many homogeneous and diverse FYW students, based upon the assumptions I have heard them articulate about their peers, believe that the student audiences they write for are just like them. It is only when students are physically marked by their disability, such as with blindness or limited motor skills, that their peers tend to acknowledge and try to accommodate their different audiences. Indeed, students tend to be less aware or sympathetic about how "invisible" disabilities (e.g., dyslexia, Asperger's Disorder), multilingual issues, and socioeconomic problems might affect their audiences. Although these can be difficult and touchy conversations to have with students—particularly online where asynchronous text or audio/video might lead teachers to feel like they are lecturing students rather than talking with them—the instructor can design research and writing assignments that ask students to understand issues of access and inclusivity in the class or in other writing contexts as a way to raise their consciousness regarding how the technologies help or hinder with the ways they digitally communicate with others (see the appendix to this chapter for more details about such assignments).

INSTRUCTOR PREPARATION

Instructors clearly need to take the lead in understanding the rhetorical nature of writing technologies in order to use their knowledge to teach students to develop such awareness. Therefore, faculty preparation is a writing program's best opportunity for inserting elements of digital rhetoric into the OWI curriculum. Faculty preparation for writing instruction, in its many forms (e.g., pre-semester orientations, in-service meetings and workshops, and graduate coursework), often occupies the more practical side of the theory/practice continuum. Due to limited resources and time, those who lead and design instructor preparation must decide which strategies and what knowledge instructors most need to soundly teach students strategies for effective written communication as well as how to manage a classroom environment. As I can attest from my conversations with professors and administrators who prepare writing faculty, they—given the limited time, and sometimes new instructor's inexperience—sometimes choose to emphasize helping the instructors get through the daily business even though they strongly believe that all instructors teaching their own courses should learn how to theorize the curriculum and policies they design or have assigned to them. In-service instructors are begging for this level of help in order to get through the next class session. Similarly, for OWI courses, those who prepare the faculty, in addition to teaching faculty how to impart the curriculum and manage the course, have to ready these instructors for the digital technologies that will mediate all of this work (see Chapters 11 & 12). To answer why instructors and, by extension, students are not learning a rhetorical digital literacy, the answer emerges primarily from the decisions WPAs and others who prepare faculty make regarding expending resources, especially time (see Chapters 6 & 7, for example). Unfortunately often, when resources are limited, teaching instructors about the rhetorical theories that inform their literacy education practices seems extra-curricular. Yet, if administrators would emphasize that any writing course is an applied rhetoric course, then those WPAs who prepare OWI instructors to teach writing and the instructors who teach the student strategies for effective writing can fold these practices into preparation and curricular design that anticipate the rhetorical nature of writing technologies. Several principles from *A Position Statement of Principles and Example Effective Practices for OWI* (CCCC OWI Committee, 2013) justify this preparation.

OWI Principle 7 specifically considered instructor and administrator preparation; it stated, "Writing Program Administrators (WPAs) for OWI programs and their online writing teachers should receive appropriate OWI-focused training, professional development, and assessment for evaluation and promotion purposes" (p. 17). As previously mentioned, when most OWI training, especially preparation in technology management, is handled outside the writing program, instructors often receive only a functional knowledge of the technology, usually with an emphasis on how to distribute knowledge to the students. A writing program that prepares its own faculty—or supplements the preparation of its faculty—can teach them how to use the technologies in ways that best support the field's preferred practices for writing instruction. Therefore, a WPA or assistant WPA who is well-versed in OWI and digital rhetoric can provide OWI teachers with effective strategies for using the technology to make the arguments that instructors are most concerned about.

While it is important for those who administrate writing programs to be immersed in all of the mediated practices that they ask their faculty to practice, this preparation arguably is more necessary for the writing instructors who interact with the students on a regular basis. From the design of the course to the final assignment's assessment (or possibly through addressing a grading grievance), the instructor is constantly communicating with the students in terms of articulating curricula, establishing and managing policies, and providing feedback. Because of this work and the subject matter of the writing course, the instructor needs to be both a skilled rhetor and rhetorician. OWI Principle 7 also advocated that OWI instructors be chosen from a pool of experienced writing instructors who already have demonstrated capabilities to teach a soundly designed writing course (p. 18). Writing instructors, as teachers of applied rhetoric, should be familiar with the potential argumentative nature of communication. Therefore, OWI instructors should be drawn from a pool of teachers already familiar with teaching argumentation. When the technologies that mediate OWI are added to the rhetorical strategies already taught, these instructors who are well-versed in applying rhetoric and teaching the application of rhetoric will have a stronger foundation for strategizing and applying how these OWI technologies can be used best to produce desired results with their communication, including effectively teaching students argumentation.

Again, WPAs may argue that developing instructors' rhetorical literacy during OWI faculty preparation is superfluous in light of the instructors' concerns about managing the technology and the day-to-day practices of the OWC. As with a WAC workshop, prompting new OWI instructors to write and reflect *briefly* on their future practices during faculty preparation can frame how they think about the functional elements they learn about their campus' OWI technologies. Instructors new to OWI always should start with the question, "What are your curricular goals for your writing course?" so that they are reminded that the teaching of writing supersedes the teaching of the technology. This is a question that can and should be addressed even if the program asks or requires faculty to teach a prescribed syllabus for the course. Other questions that might be posed throughout the faculty preparation process include:

- Why have you chosen to teach OWI?
- What are your expectations for what the technology can do for you in teaching your writing course?
- What excites you about teaching with these technologies?

- What are your concerns about the technologies you are expected to use?
- Are any of these technologies unsuitable for your anticipated student audience given issues of access or inclusivity?
- What are your questions and concerns about the assistive and adaptive technologies your students with disabilities might use?
- What do you expect the technology to do for you in this course? Or, what would the ideal technology be able to do for you?
- What do you want these technologies to allow you to do that they currently do not?
- What worries you about potential technology problems? How will you address any technology challenges that you have?

These are not questions that instructors have to spend a lot of time responding to. But giving them five to ten minutes to write about these OWI issues offers the instructors a critical and rhetorical frame for thinking about the technological functions they are learning. Furthermore, as Selber (2004) argued, functional literacy cannot be separated from critical and rhetorical literacy. Therefore, administrators, WPAs or other staff preparing the faculty for OWI have the opportunity to develop many instructors' understanding of what OWI-relevant applications can do. This development certainly includes addressing issues of access and inclusivity to open and maintain avenues of communication to one's entire student audience.

First, it is useful to teach instructors that interfaces are rhetorical texts. Scholarly articles like those by Cynthia Selfe and Richard Selfe (1994) and Tim McGee and Patricia Ericsson (2002) detailed how users can read these texts rhetorically. Moreover, many people, writing instructors included, only know the most basic functions of an application like Microsoft Word. Thus, for example, by teaching the faculty about the comment function in Microsoft Word, an OWI teacher, by virtue of knowing the possibilities of the application, may choose to use this relatively efficient and nonintrusive commenting approach rather than inserting bracketed or multicolored comments into the student's text (keeping readability to various student populations in mind, of course). Or, to go one step further, OWI faculty could be taught how to use a freeware application to provide audio/ video comments on students' papers, a strategy that some students have said they preferred over written comments alone (Vincelette, 2013; Vincelette & Bostic, 2013). Bearing in mind and attending to the access problems outlined in Chapters 8, 9, and 10, such additional software uses may increase access by blind students; multilingual writers who have grown accustomed to the instructors' accent; and overcommitted students, who because of having to balance family, work, and education, can now take advantage of watching these videos on various mobile devices during their bus commute to or from work. While I can see the first two commenting methods being taught in faculty preparation for OWI, the third option probably would not make many faculty preparation schedules. But the video option does give the instructors another method for a specific type of communication with their students. By expanding OWI faculty understanding of a feedback applications' functionality, for example, they receive different opportunities to decide the most effective ways to make arguments about revision (e.g., "These are the issues you will want to address with your writing") to the student audience in their OWI class. Ultimately, the goal is not to make instructors "power users" of the digital technologies; instead, it is to increase their competency with OWI-relevant applications and functions so that they have reasonable accessible options when they are choosing the most effective ways to communicate with their students in a given situation. Then, ideally, OWI teachers can use this knowledge responsibly to help students develop the same meta-awareness of the technology.

By incorporating digital rhetoric into instructor preparation, writing programs can use the completion of the OWI Principle 7 to fulfill OWI Principle 12: "Institutions should foster teacher satisfaction in online writing courses as rigorously as they do for student and programmatic success" (p. 24). Implementing OWI Principle 12 helps to justify why digital rhetoric should be part of instructor preparation. In the rationale for this OWI principle, the CCCC OWI Committee (2013) wrote, "Teacher satisfaction is dependent on a number of affective factors, including being personally suited to teaching online and being comfortable communicating with students using digital/electronic means" (p. 24). By preparing instructors to go beyond teaching the technological nuts and bolts of the digital tools they use and to critically examine the technologies in order to consider the best means of adopting them for their own rhetorical purposes, instructors receive the means to adapt their teaching as their rhetorical situations shift kairotically. These shifts inevitably happen. They can happen in the space of a fifty-minute hybrid class when an application suddenly will not launch, or they can happen as the student body changes from class to class and semester to semester. Certainly, they happen when technology producers design new (and not necessarily better) applications or when new versions of existing applications suddenly become inaccessible to certain groups of students.

Preparing OWI instructors for their work as digital rhetoricians also responds to OWI Principle 12's rationale that instructors should be taught "relative advantages and disadvantages of teaching an OWC in their institution" (p. 24). While these discussions should include such factors as institutional policies and compensation, they also need to address the rewards and challenges of teaching OWCs. One of the rewards that also is quite challenging is that instructors put themselves in a position to learn how to use new writing and communication technologies that they may not otherwise have used. In teacher training, this reward can be extended to include not only a functional knowledge of these technologies, but also a rhetorical understanding of them. With this preparation, instructors should learn specific "pedagogical factors as understanding how communication in the OWC environment differs and learning the benefits and challenges of the asynchronous and the synchronous modalities" (p. 24). Learning the course environment (see Chapter 2), affordances of modalities (see Chapter 3), and various media made available to all students enables OWI teachers to choose the best ones to make arguments to their students (as with the comment example), and by extension to their administrators about their OWCs and their own competency as instructors. *A Position Statement of Principles and Example Effective Practices for OWI* (CCCC OWI Committee, 2013) emphasized that "teaching writing online involves focused teacher responses that are crafted to specific student compositions" (p. 25). Unlike other courses in which automated feedback, such as instantaneous grades provided by the click of a mouse after taking a LMS-mediated quiz or an exam graded by an optical scanner, is an acceptable disciplinary pedagogical strategy, sound writing instruction requires the instructor to provide individual feedback to the writing and discussion board or other communications. Although automated messages can be, and have been, composed anticipating general rhetorical situations, individualized interaction requires responses crafted to specific rhetorical situations. Moreover, developing strategies for reading and working with the technologies' affordances helps OWI instructors not only to efficiently and effectively interact with students, but it also helps them to teach their students these same strategies for their own online mediation.

STUDENT PREPARATION

Just as this rhetorical meta-knowledge about the technology helps OWI teachers to make arguments to students, students who learn to understand the technology they use as a rhetorical tool can develop effective communicative strategies for the OWI course and beyond. As with the faculty, the purpose of teaching students the rhetorical reading of digital tools is not to turn them into power users but to make them more aware of the potential outcomes for the rhetorical choices they make and potentially can make, especially regarding the technologies they use to write. Furthermore, the focus for this instruction should be on technologies relevant to the OWC, both in terms of how the students' compose their assignments and how they communicate with their instructor and peers. Several of the principles in *A Position Statement of Principles and Example Effective Practices for OWI* (CCCC OWI Committee, 2013) help to rationalize this instructional practice.

OWI Principle 10 stated, "Students should be prepared by the institution and their teachers for the unique technological and pedagogical components of OWI" (p. 21). Students in OWI courses inevitably become practitioners of digital rhetoric because of the assignments they submit and the ways they communicate with their instructors and peers, but their practice can be (more) purposeful and consciously developed if they receive adequate preparation. Although contemporary students often are assumed to be "digital natives" (Prensky, 2001), or individuals of a generation that has developed an adeptness with the technology because of a perceived constant exposure to it and use of it, real users have proven that there are individuals of this generation who struggle to use these technologies and need assistance from the institution and instructors to learn how to use the technologies that mediate and manage the course (Hewett, 2015a; also see Chapters 8 & 10). Moreover, even for the so-called "digital natives," the rationale for OWI Principle 10 explained that "the kind of online communicating that tech-savvy students do in their personal lives often is fast, frequent, and informal, which typically is not the kind of communicating they will need to do regularly to be successful in OWCs" (p. 22). OWI teachers are positioned ideally to design writing assignments that teach students composing strategies that effectively use technologies to meet situational ends. During this process, OWI teachers also need to teach students how to write and use the applications typically used in OWI (e.g., email, word-processing shortcuts, and blogs). Although some students may have had experience with these technologies in the past, few will have used them for academic writing (Hewett, 2010, 2015a, 2015b). Hence, many students will not only need to learn how to use new technologies, but they also will need to learn new expectations (i.e., academic) for what they produce using already familiar technologies.

While the institution primarily should be responsible for preparing students to use technologies commonly employed in its courses, OWI Principle 10 also advocated that individual instructors "support and/or repeat elements of that training in the OWC to assist with student success" in that specific writing class. In short, instructors should familiarize students with the ways that they will be using the technologies for writing instruction. To this end, "appropriate OWI preparation should begin with interface familiarization and experiential exercises that make clear the public (i.e., communication to/from the teacher and among all students in the course) and private (i.e., communication between the teacher and individual student) spaces" (p. 22). Such communications provide an exigency for instructors to help students examine how these interfaces can influence their real communications with real audiences, such as the instructor and peer students. These are useful lessons that students may not receive from writing assignments alone because the writing contexts are real.

This understanding of how to communicate effectively with peers is crucial for building community among the students—an important feature of OWI. OWI Principle 11 stated, "Online writing teachers and their institutions should develop personalized and interpersonal online communities to foster student success" (p. 23). This principle mirrored the most effective social constructivist practices already endorsed for the onsite, face-to-face classroom. Communities are not an outcome that instructors simply can create by using a specific digital technology or adopting a specific pedagogical practice. Instead, creating community is a rhetorical act deliberately attempted (DePew, Spangler, & Spiegel, 2013). In the onsite classroom, this process requires the instructor to convince students that working together has benefits that are worth their time and effort. Similarly, students need to compose arguments to their peers demonstrating that they agree with the instructor's belief that working together will benefit all involved; to support this argument, they also have to convince their peers that working with them is worthwhile. Unless students are taking a hybrid OWC (see Chapter 2), these arguments can be made only through the digital technologies, and having a metacognitive approach to do this communication can help instructors and students make such arguments.

Essentially, the last three effective practices for OWI Principle 11 support the "hows" and "whys" of both instructors and students needing to understand their digital tools' rhetorical nature. The first of these, Example Practice 11.5, recommended that instructors design informal writing assignments that "elicit meaningful responses among class participants" (p. 24). Thus the instructor's focus should be more on the type of writing that will achieve these goals, not the technology the class participants will use. The type of writing and the media cannot be mutually exclusive decisions, but if the instructor's primary goal is for the students to engage the class content and in doing so to engage each other, then the instructor needs to use writing genres that allow students to make the necessary arguments to each other and the instructor. Although this decision belongs to instructors, they can make their decisions transparent to their students helping them understand why particular genres and the digital technologies that support them are most conducive for the desired rhetorical outcomes.

With Effective Practice 11.6, *A Position Statement of Principles and Example Effective Practices for OWI* (CCCC OWI Committee, 2013) recommended that instructors use the course mediating technologies to collect anonymous and secure feedback about the course at regular intervals. Although this type of course feedback has been a typical practice in many onsite and online classrooms alike, for the OWC, evaluations can become an especially important teaching moment (Hewett, 2010, 2015b). As OWI teachers ask students to compose arguments that can produce real consequences for the course, they can highlight how various features of their digital tools used to elicit feedback—especially those that foster anonymity but maybe also the interface (i.e., radio buttons or pull-down menus for closed-ended questions or text boxes for open-ended questions)—encourage certain types of feedback from the students and might influence how they create arguments.

Similarly, Effective Practice 11.7 argued, "Teachers should develop forums, threads, and assessments in which students can have open discussions, either with or without teacher involvement, about course dynamics" (p. 24). More specifically:

> If students are given opportunities to express their experiences and to vent their frustrations, perhaps in threads like "Lounge" or "Comments about our learning platform" or in an anonymous midterm course evaluation, that might engender a greater willingness to persevere in a new or different learning setting. Additionally, such communications enable OWI teachers to make adjustments and provide feedback to their administrators. (CCCC OWI Committee, 2013, p. 24)

As with the formal feedback, this practice offers students an opportunity to affect genuine change through a given digital writing tool used to argue how the course can best serve one's own needs. When coupled with anonymous formal feedback, students are given rhetorical choices about the best delivery methods for their praise and/or grievances. They can consider which digital option might produce the most significant impact while also providing the best personal security. Given these different opportunities to engage in discussions about the course's infrastructure, the strategies OWI teachers develop for students to assert agency in the OWC arguably can transfer to contexts beyond that writing course.

A common concern about teaching technology in the writing course is that these lessons take time away from the teaching of writing, often defined as the teaching of grammar and rhetorical techniques that masquerade as genres (e.g., narrative essay, persuasive essay, definition essay, compare/contrast essay). But the challenge for instructors should be to consider how they can design assignments and activities that fold lessons about the technology into the students' understanding of applied rhetoric. This focus means that as OWI instructors teach students how to compose linguistic or multimodal texts (see Chapter 15), they are raising the students' awareness of how the technology influences the texts they want to compose. This lesson is not a separate or extra-curricular topic; instead, it helps to make the rhetorical lessons of writing instruction conscious and metacognitive, especially in the context of OWI where each digitally composed interaction can have implications.

CONCLUSIONS AND RECOMMENDATIONS

As WPAs who prepare OWI instructors, as OWI instructors who design and implement their courses, or as OWI students who are learning how to negotiate their education through increasing ubiquitous digital tools, it is useful to reflect upon Selber's (2004) wisdom: "Not only are teachers obligated to prepare students responsibly for a digital age in which the most rewarding jobs will require multiple literacies, but students will be citizens and parents as well as employees, and in these roles they will also need to think in expanded ways about computer use" (p. 4). OWI, by its very nature, creates a situation in which instructors can teach students skills and strategies they will need for various roles they will occupy throughout their lives. Nonetheless, when the technology is not taught at all, this opportunity is missed. When the technology is just taught operationally, this opportunity is missed. When the teaching of the technology is completely separated from the teaching of applied rhetoric, this opportunity is missed. When writing is taught without acknowledging the material conditions of writing, this opportunity is missed.

Administrators and instructors can seize these opportunities by using the inherent features of OWI—online communication and writing instruction—to teach OWI students how to be effective digital rhetoricians, not necessarily master programmers, but people who can potentially shape their world with the digital writing tools at their disposal. The OWI principles in *A Position Statement of Principles and Example Effective Practices for OWI* (CCCC OWI Committee, 2013) recognized this exigency.

The following recommendations can assist WPAs and OWI teachers in preparing students for the rhetoricity of OWI technologies:

- OWI courses should be perceived and taught as applied rhetoric courses that use digital technology to mediate interaction between instructors and students. Therefore, the course's material conditions give instructors and students opportunities to practice what they are learning.
- As an applied rhetoric course, audience is a primary concern in the OWC, and instructors and students should make concerted efforts to make their course communication accessible to all audiences. Therefore, these digital writers need to be taught how to address the communicative needs of students with disabilities, multilingual students, and other students who cannot easily access a course through digital technologies.
- Instructors should pose any real challenges that the technology creates as

a real rhetorical problem and teachable moment.

- WPAs and others who prepare OWI faculty need to teach instructors how to be functionally, critically, and rhetorically literate with the courses' technologies, as well as how to teach any digital technologies that students will use to compose assignments.
- Instructors need to teach students how to be functionally, critically, and rhetorically literate with the courses' technologies, as well as any digital technologies students will use to compose assignments. To this end, instructors might use the example lessons found in Appendix 14.A directly following this chapter.

NOTES

1. I want to acknowledge the works of Paul Prior et al. (2007) and James Porter (2009), both of whom argued that the ways people communicate today (and, in the case of Prior et al., even in Ancient Greece) are too complex for an oversimplified understanding of the canon of "delivery."

REFERENCES

Bartholomae, David. (1985). Inventing the university. In Mike Rose (Ed.) *When a writer can't write: Studies in writer's block and other composing-process problems*. New York: Guilford.

Berlin, James. (1982). Contemporary composition: The major pedagogical theories. *College English, 44*(8), 765-777.

Byrd, Don & Owens, Derek. (1998). Writing in the hivemind. In Todd Taylor & Irene Ward (Eds.), *Literacy theory in the age of the internet* (pp. 47-58). New York: Columbia University Press.

CCCC OWI Committee for Effective Practices in Online Writing Instruction. (2013). *A position statement of principles and effective practices for online writing instruction (OWI)*. Retrieved from http://www.ncte.org/cccc/resources/positions/owiprinciples

DePew, Kevin E. & Lettner-Rust, Heather. (2009). Mediating power: Distance learning interfaces, classroom epistemology, and the gaze. *Computers & Composition, 26*(3), 174-189. doi:10.1016/j.compcom.2009.05.002

DePew, Kevin E. & Miller-Cochran, Susan. (2010). Social Networking in a second language: Engaging multiple literate practices through identity composition. In Michelle Cox, Jay Jordan, Christina Ortmeier-Hooper, Gwen Gray Schwartz (Eds.), *Reinventing identities in second language writing* (pp. 273-295). Urbana, IL: National Council of Teachers of English.

DePew, Kevin E., Spangler, Sarah, & Spiegel, Cheri L. (2013). Getting past our assumptions about Web 2.0 and community building: How to design research-based literacy pedagogy. In Marohang Limbu & Binod Gurung (Eds.), *Emerging pedagogies in the networked knowledge society: Practices integrating social media and globalization* (pp. 120-143). Hershey, PA: IGI Global.

Dockterman, Eliana. (2013, August) Appjacked! *Time. 182*(7), 16.

Feenberg, Andrew. (1991). *Critical theory of technology.* Oxford, UK: Oxford University Press.

Handa, Carolyn. (2001). Letter from the guest editor: Digital rhetoric, digital literacy, computers, and composition. *Computers & Composition, 18*(1), 1-10.

Hewett, Beth L. (2010). *The online writing conference: A guide for teachers and tutors.* Portsmouth, NH, Boynton/Cook.

Hewett, Beth L. (2015a). *Reading to learn and writing to teach: Literacy strategies for online writing instruction.* Boston, MA: Bedford/St. Martin's Press.

Hewett, Beth L. (2015b). *The online writing conference: A guide for teachers and tutors* (Updated). Boston, MA: Bedford/St. Martin's Press.

Matsuda, Paul Kei. (2006). The myth of linguistic homogeneity in US college composition. *College English, 68*(6), 637-651.

McGee, Tim & Ericsson, Patricia. (2002). The politics of the program. MS Word as the invisible grammarian. *Computers & Composition, 19*(4), 453-470.

Prensky, Marc. (2001). Digital natives, digital immigrants. *On the Horizon, 9*(5), 1-6.

Prior, Paul, Solberg, Janine, Berry, Patrick, Bellwoar, Hannah, Chewing, Bill, Lunsford, Karen K., ... Walker, Joyce. (2007). Re-situating and re-mediating the canons: A cultural-historical remapping of rhetorical activity. *Kairos: A Journal of Rhetoric, Technology, and Pedagogy, 11*(3). Retrieved from http://kairos.technorhetoric.net/11.3/index.html

Porter, James. (2009). Recovering delivery for digital rhetoric. *Computers & Composition, 26*(4), 207-224.

Postman, Neil. (1995). *The end of education: Redefining the value of school.* New York: Knopf.

Selber, Stuart A. (2004). *Multiliteracies for a digital age.* Carbondale, IL: Southern Illinois University Press.

Selfe, Cynthia L. & Selfe, Richard, Jr. (1994). The politics of the interface: Power and its exercise in electronic contact zones. *College Composition and Communication, 45*(4), 480-504.

Stone, Allucquère R. (2001). *The war of desire and technology at the close of the mechanical age.* Cambridge, MA: The MIT Press.

Vincelette, Elizabeth. (2013). Video capture for grading: Multimedia feedback and the millennial student. In Ellen Smyth and John Volker (Eds.), *Enhanc-*

ing instruction with visual media: Utilizing video and lecture capture (pp. 107-127). Hershey, PA: IGI-Global.

Vincelette, Elizabeth Jackson & Bostic, Timothy. (2013). Show and tell: Student and instructor perceptions of screencast assessment. *Assessing Writing*, *18*(4), 257-277.

Zappen, James P. (2005). Digital rhetoric toward an integrated theory. *Technical Communication Quarterly*, *14*(3), 319-325.

APPENDIX: SAMPLE LESSONS

OWI teachers can introduce students to rhetorical literacy as they teach about audience. For example, in the first few weeks of the course, students can be assigned a short assignment with the purpose of learning about their peers as audience for the course. Assigned to groups of three to four, students would begin by composing a 500-750 word literacy narrative that they post in a group discussion board or on a blog. Each student in a group would read these narratives, paying attention to how the author self-identifies as a writer and a reader. Using this information to work together, the group would collaboratively compose a survey to distribute to the rest of the class about their reading and writing practices; students could be asked to use such tools as a discussion board, a Wiki, or digitally shared document that enables real-time co-writing depending on whole-class accessibility. After students collect data from their survey, they would collaboratively compose an essay, memo, or report about the audience needs that students should consider when writing to the class. The collective knowledge created by the students' research and writing is intended to help them throughout the course to select which technologies to use and which functions on those technologies to use when writing to others in the class. From these data, students may learn that a few of their peers are dyslexic or do most of their technological work on their cell phone (per Chapter 16), which—with the OWI teacher's assistance—should prompt them to consider how to communicate most effectively with these audiences. While this example assignment gives students an opportunity to wrestle productively with digital rhetoric issues, it also entails many of the lessons that educators want students to learn in writing classes (i.e., audience awareness, collaborative writing, research skills, and such genres as memos and reports). By collecting these data themselves, students learn to make sound decisions about how to communicate with their peers based upon data rather than assumptions; such an assignment also makes the lessons about digital rhetoric and audience accommodation a concrete reality rather than a seemingly liberal abstraction supported by the instructor.

For another assignment of activity, instructors can use the applications commonly found on the LMS as a text they ask students to learn how to read rhetorically. The goal of this activity is to teach students how to understand what an application demands of users and what it prevents or obscures from users based upon the application's interface design. In other words, students learn to examine how writing technologies shape what the writer can or cannot do. Essentially, the instructor would prompt students to analyze three different texts using text-specific modifications to the following heuristics:

- How did you respond to this text? Why?
- What is the argument the text's author makes? What does the author want the audience to do or think after engaging with the text?
- What evidence does the author use to support this argument? Or, what leads you to the conclusion that such is the argument?
- Who do you think the target audience is for this text? Do you think the text effectively connects with that audience? Why or why not? Is the author excluding certain members of this intended audience by overlooking their needs?
- How do you think other audiences will respond to this text? Why? Name one of these different audiences.
- What is your opinion of the author(s) based upon this text? Why?
- How would you design this text differently? Would you use the same or different media? What features would you redesign and why?

OWI teachers can begin this lesson with the first text, an editorial from a local news organization. Regardless of whether it is available online, the instructor needs to provide students with either a hardcopy text or an accessible PDF of the hardcopy text. In this case, a hyperlink will not do. For example, in a hybrid OWC in which the instructor has face-to-face time with the students, the instructor can provide a hardcopy of the editorial; in either the fully online or hybrid OWC, the instructor can use the LMS or email to send students a PDF of the text and ask them to print it because they will need to work from hardcopy. Given the selected genre, the editorial argument should be overt and relatively easy to identify. The difficult task will be getting the students to think about the text's interface because most people take paper and ink media for granted and do not necessarily think of it *as* an interface.

The second text would be a commercial website, such as Amazon.com (or if one wants to gender the assignment, ESPN.com or Forever21.com); the students should be provided a link to that website. While the argument "Buy our products/services!" is pretty overt on any of these sites, they are not presented in ways that many students, especially in the early sequence of writing courses, think about an argument. Thus, such sites help to develop students' understanding of what an argument is and how it can be presented. Unlike the editorial, the students would engage the website through something that they recognize as an "interface" and one that the students, once they identify the argument, will believe should be user-friendly and easy to navigate. However, it is at the places where these texts are not easy to use that students may begin to see design decisions. For example, how easy is it to access items on clearance sale versus featured items? Or, how easy or possible is it to find the statistics for a female athlete versus a male athlete in the same sport?

Finally, the instructor should ask the students to read the institution's LMS relative to how their own course is presented. The analysis of the editorial as an interface and the commercial website as an argument should have prepared students to see the LMS itself as an argumentative text and to consider whether and how the interface design supports the argument it appears to make. Through this exercise of analyzing the LMS, the students may become more critical consumers of the applications they will need to use to make arguments in their OWC. Moreover, the students would be provided with strategies to become rhetorically literate with the LMS and to use their understanding of the LMS as text/tool to fulfill their desired purposes as writers throughout the course of the semester, and into future courses. Combined with the previously described assignment in this section regarding learning about their class' student audience, students could be empowered. They can synthesize their understanding of the LMS's argumentative potential with what they know about their peer audience and then use this knowledge through their writing to persuade their peers—the outcome can be mutually beneficial.

If writing courses are applied rhetoric courses, then these applications of rhetorical awareness comply with programmatic outcomes. Such exercises can be a series of stand-alone activities or they can be scaffolded in support of the students' later analysis of an individually chosen interface.

PART 5. NEW DIRECTIONS IN OWI

CHAPTER 15

TEACHING MULTIMODAL ASSIGNMENTS IN OWI CONTEXTS

Kristine L. Blair
Bowling Green State University

This chapter provides effective practices for instructors who want to transform alphabetic text-centric assignments into multimodal ones in OWI contexts. By focusing on needs assessments, assignment options, tools selection, and assessment, the chapter advocates a shift from migrating and adapting onsite writing instruction to instead transforming it through a broadened definition of writing as multimodal composing that enables students to produce content as twenty-first century learners and citizens.

Keywords: access, assessment, ePortfolios, learning management systems, multiliteracies, multimodality, New Media, professional development, visual rhetoric

The 2013 film *The Internship* featured Vince Vaughn and Owen Wilson as two recently unemployed salespeople, downsized as a result of changing marketing and purchasing trends that have migrated from face-to-face and door-to-door to the online marketplace of point, click, and purchase. As part of their efforts to retool, they sought a coveted internship at Google and participated in a pre-interview at a local library computer with Web-cam access. The site of two middle-aged men hovering over Webcam technology to which they had not had access as users is endemic to the movie's theme. Technology has changed the rules of interpersonal engagement in all contexts, including the classroom, as many students (regardless of the millennial stereotype) and instructors are not any more prepared than the characters in the film. Just as the protagonists are accustomed to a face-to-face as opposed to video chat interview, we are accustomed in writing classrooms to a primarily alphabetic as opposed to a multimodal text.

Nevertheless, *A Position Statement of Principles and Example Effective Practices for OWI* (CCCC OWI Committee, 2013) offered OWI Principle 3 as, "Appropriate composition teaching/learning strategies should be developed for the unique features of the online instructional environment" (p. 12). The rationale accompanying this principle noted that "some changes in traditional composition pedagogy are necessary for teaching writing in the OWI setting, an environment that is by nature text-centric and reading-heavy and that requires intensive written communication" (p. 12). Yet, as the larger writing studies discipline challenges the operational definition of "writing" in light of a Web 2.0 era of digital literacy and composing processes, June Griffin and Deborah Minter (2013) contended that "the proliferation of online classrooms raises the field's stake in emerging technologies not only for the impact of those technologies on course design and students' literacies, but also for their capacity to help us see more clearly changes on the horizon for our profession and to mine those changes for opportunities to improve student learning" (p. 145). Thus, they appropriately aligned themselves with Cynthia Selfe's (2009) longstanding call to "pay attention" and how that call "is now extricably linked to literacy and literacy education in this country" (quoted at p. 141). Certainly, technology has been an impetus for constant change, and in the context of online writing pedagogies, this change has impacted not only the spaces in which we teach writing as process but also the increasingly diverse students we serve. Despite the emphasis on the range of new media literacy practices and the tools and technologies that enable those practices, what we teach in the writing classroom, both hybrid and fully online, has remained unchanged: we teach alphabetic writing meant to be produced and consumed on an 8.5 x 11 piece of paper, accessed onscreen or in-hand.

There are a number of factors that contribute to this ongoing privileging of the alphabetic, including a typical emphasis on print-based learning outcomes within higher education writing programs that favor the production of the academic essay and are aligned with larger university general education outcomes, as well as a lack of training and faculty development for the ever-growing contingent of adjunct faculty and graduate students who typically teach undergraduate writing courses. This lack of training and professional development also impacts full-time non-tenure track faculty for whom professional development is not a guarantee and, given the academic labor of teaching writing fulltime, does not always allow for maintaining currency in the field as it evolves its understanding of writing to include a more inclusive, integrated range of modalities and media (see, for example, Chapters 7, 8, 11, 12, & 14). Sometimes these issues are generational; for instance, the composition director at my own institution, Bowling Green State University, recently confessed concern about the lack of interest on the part of some faculty to integrate more visual rhetoric into the curriculum while graduate students, because of their recent training and often generational status as millennials, are eager to integrate technologies that exceed the readiness of the curriculum and the training available. Thus, despite our field's ongoing multimodal turn in twenty-first century composing theories, if we do not heed that call to pay attention to both the possibilities and the constraints as we develop online writing curriculum, the identities students develop in such virtual writing spaces will continue to be as alphabetic as ever.

I have noted elsewhere (Blair, 2007) that this text-centricity also is due to the spaces in which OWI typically occurs (i.e., LMSs). As Scott Warnock (2009) recommended to new online instructors, "In your initial efforts to teach an OWcourse, simplify things by using your campus CMS [aka LMS], and learn only the tools you will need" (p. 23). Although Warnock appropriately and effectively encouraged important experimentation with a range of tools such as blogs, Wikis, and SecondLife and acknowledged the potential for audiovisual tools and alternatives to text-based assessment, the underlying assumption of the "hows" and "whys" of his book *Teaching Writing Online* is that these tools enhance alphabetic writing processes. Warnock overviewed the ability of various tools to foster a more dialogic approach to writing, emphasizing tools that foster peer review, student-centered interaction, and personalized interactions between students and teachers. Thus, another useful guideline Warnock included among his eighteen guidelines was, "Initially, you want to think migration, not transformation, when teaching online. Think about what you do well, and then think about how you use various resources to translate those skills to the OWcourse" (p. xvii.). For novice teachers of online writing, this advice undoubtedly is sound, particularly because of the need to align any use of technology with larger curricular objectives at both the program and course level. But the emphasis on *migration* as opposed to *transformation* has the potential to create an inadvertent gap between larger theoretical discussions of multimodal composing and practical implementation of multimodal composing pedagogies in hybrid and online writing classrooms, a gap described in Chapter 14. Indeed, these apparently opposing needs reveal why the CCCC OWI Committee wrote both OWI Principle 3 (outlined earlier; pp. 12-14) and OWI Principle 4 (regarding migrating and adapting appropriate contemporary composition pedagogy to OWI; pp. 14-15), which are, as Hewett indicated in Chapter 1, yin and yang principles.

Undoubtedly, there exist numerous challenges to integrating multimodal production into fully online OWCs—perhaps more so than in hybrid OWCs—and the ability to "transform" the curriculum. Such challenges include:

1. the ideological presumption that writing remains a "text-based" process, and thus OWI may not align with the field's emphasis on literate practices (see Chapters 14 & 16);
2. the limited/inconsistent access to digital composing tools for both students and teachers (see Chapters 1, 8, 9, 10 & 16);
3. the ableistic nature of some of the multimodal technologies and their denial of bodily and neural diversity among users (see Chapter 8);

4. the lack of faculty training for multimodal curriculum development (see Chapters 11, 12, & 16); and

5. the course design logistics within LMSs that have few internal options for multimodal composing (see Chapters 8 & 14).

Given these challenges, my particular focus is upon the whats, hows, and whys of transforming OWI from a text-centric composing space for our students to one that integrates multimodal elements for students and instructors in as viable, accessible, and introductory a way as possible. This focus meshes with OWI Principle 2: *"An online writing course should focus on writing and not on technology orientation or teaching students how to use learning and other technologies"* (p. 11). Thus, I include a series of effective practices for new and more experienced OWI teachers, as well as for administrators who develop OWI initiatives in both hybrid and fully online contexts. These practices focus on needs assessment, assignment design, and assessment processes that foster multimodality in progressive ways that begin to bridge the gap between migration and transformation, ultimately helping instructors ground multimodal composing in rhetorical contexts and positively impacting the evolving identities that online students must develop as twenty-first century composers.

THE TENSION BETWEEN OWI AND MULTIMODAL COMPOSING

Just as Warnock (2009) provided useful advice to new OWI instructors for migrating existing composition curricula, contributors to Selfe's (2007) collection *Multimodal Composition* provided similar practical strategies for transforming that same curricula, calling for writing teachers to acknowledge "multiple semiotic channels" and agree that "literacy pedagogies must account for the multiplicity of texts allowed and encouraged by digital technologies" (Takayoshi & Selfe, 2007, p. 2). For Takayoshi and Selfe, the multimodal turn is more than moving students away from composing practices that are all too similar to those of their parents and grandparents. They align themselves—as most multimodal theorists do—with the New London Group's 1996 "Pedagogy of Multiliteracies," in which literacy is not only technological but cultural, material, and political. In this way, the writing studies field needs to rethink its goal of migrating writing to instead transforming our understanding of writing as multimodal composing that better prepares undergraduates to communicate successfully within professional and social contexts outside the academy.

The distinction between "writing" versus "composing" frequently is positioned as an either/or argument—that in privileging one over the other, we do a disservice to students *either* in not sufficiently introducing them to more traditional print-based discourse crucial to their academic success *or* in not bridging the gap between how students use technologies to compose outside the classroom and how we use (or do not use) those same technologies. As Selfe (2009) powerfully argued:

> My argument is not *either/or* but *both/and*. I am not arguing against writing, the value we place on writing, or an understanding of what writing—and print—contribute to the human condition that is vitally important... . I do want to argue that teachers of composition need to pay attention to, and come to value, the multiple ways in which students compose and communicate meaning. (p. 642)

Similarly, I am not recommending the elimination of alphabetic texts in OWI; rather, I embrace Jay David Bolter's (2001) longstanding position that digital text does not signal "the end of print; it is instead the remediation of print" (p. 46). This remediated process stresses print as one modality among many, and as I shall stress in the OWI effective practices section of this chapter, the relationship among these modalities must be flexible, to address the existing skill sets of both students and instructors as well as the access issues and learning styles our students may bring to OWI per OWI Principle 1: "Online writing instruction should be universally inclusive and accessible" (p. 7).

Even as I attempt to bridge the gap between migration and transformation, however, it is equally crucial to interrogate some assumptions we may hold about students as multimodal composers, the most common being our students' generational status as "digital natives" (Prensky, 2001). As many of us who have taught OWCs have discovered, our students can be anything but typical in such environments: working adults, military personnel, transfer and international students, and even high school age students enrolled in post-secondary programs. Such diversity calls into question the presumption of equal access (see OWI Principle 1 and Chapters 8 & 10). For example, consider the current controversy surrounding the shift of the General Education Development (GED) from a paper-based to online process as a result of the profit-bearing partnership between The American Council on Education and Pearson Vue (Tran, 2013), leading to concerns about the affordability of the exam and the concerns about the lack of computing skills among the unemployed, the working poor, and the incarcerated. Similar presumptions of access to and comfort with the array of tools needed to compose in multimodal form can be a false one that rather than empower online learners actually may disenfranchise them, as in the case of the GED. Indeed, such presumptions often ignore issues of age and socioeconomic status, given that just as Takayoshi and Selfe (2007) may lament writing curricula that promotes the pedagogies of our parents, the reality is that students the age of our parents are, of course, more and more common, particularly in online learning environments. This concern inevitably resonates with OWI Principle 1 (pp. 7-11).

Because of these tensions, it is not enough to reconsider our definition of *writing* but also our definition of *multimodality*, understanding that, just as with text-based assignments, it is important to integrate genres and modes in progressively complex ways. And just as a typical FYW course would not automatically begin with the extended research paper assignment, multimodal assignments should begin where both students and teacher are regarding their composing expertise, allowing a point of entry that fosters early success and develops skills and aptitudes over time. Such a process also should account for a definition of multimodality that is not purely digital, recognizing the many print-based genres that have multimodal components, from scrapbooks to posters to zines. Equally important is that our understanding of multimodality should acknowledge the redefinition of "literacy" as the more nuanced "multiliteracies" that Stuart Selber (2004) outlined as (1) functional, which views computers as tools and students as users of technology; (2) critical, which views computers as cultural artifacts and students as questioners of technology; and (3) rhetorical, which views computers as hypertextual media (i.e., multimodality) and as students as producers of technology (p. 25; see Chapter 14). Thus, a multiliteracies framework has just as much potential to foster critical thinking, reading, and composing as our traditional text-based writing processes.

My goal in outlining a range of effective practices for integrating, producing, and assessing multimodal assignments is to bridge the gap not only between migration and transformation of OWI content but also between the either/or, both/and positions in order to emphasize a twenty-first century model of online writing. The goal in doing so is to acknowledges, as Selfe concluded(2009), "*all available means of persuasion,* all available dimensions, all available approaches, not simply those limited to the two dimensional space of the printed page" (p. 645).

OWI EFFECTIVE PRACTICES FOR MULTIMODAL COMPOSITION

NEEDS ASSESSMENTS

OWI Principle 1 included a range of effective practices that address access issues by making OWI a more multimodal process, specifically OWI Effective Practice 1.9, "Teachers must become acquainted with multimodal means for distributing and assessing learning materials" (p. 10), and OWI Effective Practice 1.10, "OWI teachers should offer instructional materials in more than one medium" (p. 10). Undoubtedly, these practices help to ensure equitable access for students with a range of abilities and learning preferences. The greatest challenge to integrating multimodal assignments in the OWC is the lack of consistent access to hardware and software that afford students the opportunity to not just consume digital material but produce it themselves, something frequently tied to fully online students' place bound status as well as their inevitable differences in sensory ability and socioeconomic status.

For these reasons, it is important to conduct needs assessments prior to the start of a class. Needs assessments are not new to online curricula; standard practice at both the postsecondary institution and course level encourages feedback prior to the start of an online program about the types of technology students to which student have access and the types of skills students possess, from the ability to upload an attachment to the ability to edit digital images or record audio (see Chapter 13 for other student assessment advice). Such assessments are consistent with OWI principle 1 and the need to ask students "to confirm that they have the required technology at the beginning of an online course ... and advise students regarding how to meet course requirements through, for example, institutional computing equipment" (p. 9). This guideline is particularly significant in light of the high-end digital tools that simply cost more than the average student can afford, a consideration that aligns with OWI Effective Practice 1.3 (p. 9) and that calls for instructors to familiarize themselves with both free and open-source alternatives to proprietary, institutionally supported software applications. Admittedly, the time and effort required for such work is both an academic labor and a professional development issue, particularly in institutional settings where there is not a training program for new and continuing OWI teachers across the disciplines.

Another important assessment involves students' learning styles. According to Neil Fleming and David Baume (2006),

> Much education is either mono- or at the most bi-modal.
> Teaching often reflects the teacher's preferred teaching style
> rather than the students' preferred learning styles. Managed or
> Virtual Learning Environments may not change that as much
> as we hoped—they simply implement old teaching styles in
> new technologies. (p. 6)

Fleming's research has included the development of VARK, a learning styles questionnaire that allows students to self-assess their preferences for visual, aural, read-write, or kinesthetic approaches to academic tasks. While this issue resonates with OWI Principle 1 and the need to develop and deliver course content in multiple modalities and with varied media, acknowledging students' learning styles also connects to their communication strengths as well. Within the context of an OWC, it is clearly important to focus on writing genres that ensure success in both academic and non-academic venues, thus mandating that instructors balance more text-centric assignments with those that allow a broader range of modalities with which students are familiar.

Regardless of that familiarity, students often come to OWI with even more traditional expectations than their instructors: writing equals print essays; writing equals grammar. Thus, another aspect of needs assessment includes determining the expectations students have about the course, about what they will be learning, and about their own motivation to be successful. For writing instructors, some of the initial icebreaking activities used within face-to-face writing courses, such as asking students to share their definitions and attitudes about writing, and what tools they use to "write," are critical in an OWI environment. Students may not see the texting, Facebooking, Tweeting, Instagraming, and YouTubing (many of these tasks have become action verbs in the larger Web 2.0 culture) they do as a form of either writing or multimodal composing, but helping them to see the way technology transforms our collective definitions and assumptions of what a writing course is supposed to be is as crucial to their success as to the instructor's.

ASSIGNMENTS AND ACTIVITIES

One key to success in multimodal assignment construction is to allow organic opportunities for multimodal composing—that is, to not integrate new media technology for its own sake but because the development of a visual argument or an audio essay represents a rhetorically appropriate response to the assignment context. As the following assignment options suggest, these genres are not necessarily new to OWI but may involve transforming an alphabetic-only option to one that provides students the opportunity to meaningfully assemble digital artifacts to compose a multimodal response for a specific purpose and audience. In the spirit of a both/and model, as opposed to either/or, OWI teachers could develop such representative activities to mesh with existing assignment contexts, or even to introduce multimodal elements as part of particular stages of the writing process, from invention to showcase, ensuring that they can maintain alignment of these assignments with existing rhetorical learning outcomes.

Literacy Narratives

Asking students to reflect on their reading and writing practices has become a standard genre in undergraduate writing course, and it often has involved discussions of various writing technologies that students use to communicate.

In OWI, such a literacy narrative is an equally significant task, particularly at the beginning of the term when students need opportunities to self-assess their comfort level and its impact on their success in the course. Such narratives can serve multiple purposes. On one hand, they offer that critical opportunity for reflection on growth as writers and composers and ground their access in cultural and material conditions that may include such issues as age, gender, and class. On the other hand, the literacy narrative offers a significant opportunity for multimodal composing in that instructors, even if using a word-processing tool such as Microsoft Word, can encourage the inclusion of images—located online or created by students themselves through a basic cell phone camera—that relate to textual content. Another important aspect of this assignment is its ability to serve as a representation of progress throughout the course, with students' updating the document and enhancing its design and development over time, even shifting from a basic tool to a more advanced one as their skills grow.

Visual Arguments

Given the multimodal possibilities of the literacy narrative assignment, it is clear that this particular genre has the potential to be represented visually. Students encounter visual arguments on a daily basis: on billboards, online, and perhaps without realizing it, they both create and circulate these images through an array of Web 2.0 genres that we did not have names for just a few years ago, including memes, tag clouds, comics, and the remediation of infographics in social media. Because of this proliferation of visual rhetorical culture, OWI teachers have ample opportunity to engage students in analysis of these visuals as arguments and, in many cases, as parody and social commentary. This analysis should move inevitably from consumption to production, and while it is not necessary for the instructor to teach students to use the range of tools designed to construct a visual argument, students should be allowed to select a tool that suits that audience and purpose for their visual themes. For instance, memes and comics may resonate more with some audiences than others, though such literacy practices are indeed prevalent, as most recently represented in Jonathan Alexander's and Elizabeth Losh's (2013) composition textbook *Understanding Rhetoric: A Graphic Guide to Writing (2013)*. Similar to the literacy narrative assignment, students are equally able to create a visual argument with an image pasted into a word-processed document, rather than to be expected to use such higher end and expensive tools as Adobe Photoshop.

Storyboards

Students and teachers are accustomed to the concept of outlining as an organizational plan for an alphabetic essay. While common invention strategies also may include more visual elements such as clustering, storyboarding is a standard process for both print and digital media projects where composers are aligning image, text, and other modes to craft a persuasive message. The beauty of storyboarding is that it applies across genres, from websites to photo and video essays, allowing students to consider where elements will be placed and how they will work together rhetorically. In addition to serving as a pre-writing or invention activity, such an activity is itself a form of multimodal composing that need not be digital, thus allowing students to reflect upon the relationship among modes.

Digital Demos

It is virtually impossible for an instructor or a student to be aware of the wide range of applications that enable multimodal composing. One way to encourage students to view themselves as co-equal participants in the course and collaborative knowledge-makers is to share the labor of developing technological expertise. Assigning students either individually or collaboratively to develop a brief demonstration (if hybrid) that includes an online handout has the potential not only to teach a particular tool's multimodal function but also, in designing the handout, doing so allows teachers to balance alphabetic and multimodal texts as students develop a viable set of instructions for completing the task. For instance, an initial multimodal strategy that is common to the instructional genre is a screen capture, an easy task on both Mac and PC platforms, that could then be pasted into a basic word-processed document to be augmented with the use of, in the case of Microsoft Office, word art that includes arrows and other useful directional features. What makes this activity so useful to the course is the ability to collectively develop an archive of multimodal composing tips that students can refer to as they create upcoming projects and take with them as they move forward to other courses in the curriculum.

Audio Essays

Perhaps the greatest technology we have at our disposal is the technology of the human voice, whether it be in the form of a personal narrative or an interview. On one level, audio essays are manageable migrations of alphabetic content into digital form with the most basic preparation being the text/script itself; certainly, a necessary part of the audio process is the emphasis on accessibility through including alphabetic transcripts. An important preparatory activity is to have students review some of the powerful audio commentary available online, including "This I Believe" [thisibelieve.org] and other related commentary from sites like the National Public Radio, also known as NPR. Such essays often are brief, engage the personal, and stress the powerful role of

narrative and storytelling in the larger culture. There are both high-end proprietary and low-end inexpensive tools that make the audio recording process more
accessible to students (i.e., including the use of smartphones apps or free Web-
based or other sound-editing tools). As students' skills advance, they potentially
can layer in music and other sound effects similar to professional podcasts to
create a range of genres: arguments, debates, reviews, and interviews. Despite
the writing studies discipline's historical shift from teaching speech to teaching
writing, an emphasis on aural composing helps to ground the writing curriculum within a rhetorical tradition that has emphasized the connection between
oratorical education and civic rhetoric. Indeed, instructors should offer these
media as options to students but also give them comparable credit in assessment,
particularly since not all students will be equally competent at employing certain
media. Moreover, Ann-Marie Pedersen and Carolyn Skinner (2007) acknowledged the challenges of developing audio (and video) assignments in distance
learning settings where students may not have opportunities to advance their
skills; for that reason, they advocate collaboration in ways that allow students to
pool their knowledge and encourage instructors to pre-assess student expertise
before forming group project teams.

Research Exhibitions/Virtual Poster Sessions

Admittedly, when we think of student presentations, the focus tends to be
on the use of slideware tools like Microsoft PowerPoint, which, despite being a
robust tool that fosters multimodal composing, conjures up all too many tem-
plate-driven bulleted lists of alphabetic text. As a result, students often view such
presentations as the mere copying and pasting of information, rather than taking
advantage of its affordances to shape and align visual and textual information
to communicate effectively and rhetorically to virtual and onsite, face-to-face
audiences. Fostering more rhetorically aware presentations also involves reconsidering how we label such genres; as the field evolves its definition of writing,
we have borrowed language and formats from other disciplines, including concepts of the exhibit (from art and museum studies, for example) and poster
sessions, that while common to social and physical science disciplines are less
typical within the humanities. Regardless of what we label them, these projects
represent significant forms of professionalization for students and an opportunity to share the results of their efforts in public ways that often align with university-level emphases on "undergraduate research." Depending on where these
projects are housed and the tools used to create them, an exhibition and interactive commenting space can evolve in the LMS or other instructional space (e.g.,
blog, Wiki, Google drive, and the like).

Multimodal Writing Journal

One of the major problems with many LMSs is that the students have very little control over ownership of the real estate; that is, there are few spaces that are their own to customize in terms of format and to populate in terms of content (or even to keep in months or years after the course). Their role is that of consumer rather than that of producer. Using a blog, for example, can allow students to practice integrating visual images, links, videos and other resources into their responses to course readings and writing tasks. Thus—once access concerns have been identified and addressed—the multimodal journal has as much potential to serve as an invention or prewriting tool as its more alphabetic counterpart, particularly if similar to providing guidance for discussion or chat forum posts in OWI, expectations are clarified with regard to the relationship between and amount of both textual and multimodal content. Although a separate part from the course/LMS, instructors can provide links to the journals in the event the spaces are meant to be shared with other students for commentary and potential collaboration. Overall, the key for instructors is to be flexible to the students' preferences and access needs regarding the tools that would enable this activity to be successful.

Certainly, as Rochelle Rodrigo's Chapter 16 suggests, the plethora of mobile and tablet devices students use make it impossible to address all the possibilities for multimodal composing given the numerous apps, free Web 2.0 tools, and proprietary software available for both hybrid and fully online courses. But success in integrating multimodal assignments is enabled through the recognition that the curriculum must allow for composing flexibility, not requiring that students use a particular tool unless is it genuinely available and accessible to all. Inevitably, we also must recognize that our students, because of differences in access, may not be interacting with the course content in the same way: some using smartphones, some using tablets, some using desktops, and the like. Likewise, for many, this access is possible through the mediation of screen readers, Braille displays, voice input systems, and other assistive devices. Despite this potential, it also is important that, depending on the nature of the assignment and on both instructor/student comfort and access, it is just as possible to compose multimodally with ubiquitous word-processing and slideware applications. While I do not focus on these specific applications within this chapter, helping students to move beyond the more traditional alphabetic uses of these applications is a progressive first step in (1) integrating visual and other modalities into their composing processes and (2) understanding that text is one modality among several that may not be the optimal choice based on an assignment's rhetorical context. Although my breakdown of assignments and activities discusses multimodal composing in discrete terms (e.g., image editing, audio), it is important to remember that many of these assignment genres enable more complex integration of the aural, visual, and verbal. This integration has strong implications for accessibility, particularly because of the need to provide multiple versions of texts for differently-abled users, such as a textual transcript for an audio essay or either transcripts or screen captions for video. This multiple versioning is just one way multimodal composing can be as accessible as its print, alphabetic, text-only counterpart.

Assessment

The concerns about integrating multimodal composing projects into onsite and OWCs are similar. Although instructors may have experience offering online feedback in the form of email response, textual comments in word-processed and PDF files, or even audio comments through a digital voice recorder or audio, these same instructors typically have limited experience evaluating the multimodal deliverables and production processes of their own students. A common perspective is that the very same assessment criteria instructors use to assess alphabetic texts can be applied to multimodal projects, given the emphasis of those criteria on standard rhetorical concerns that apply across modalities: purpose, audience, development, organization, style and editing. In "Evaluating Academic Hypertexts," Anne Herrington and Charles Moran (2002) documented the elements of assessment that remain consistent between print and online texts, including "Focus and Central Claim," "Evidence of Constructive Thinking," and "Organization/Coherence" (p. 249). Herrington and Moran advised that teachers new to hypertext and mixed media genres review as many samples as possible, and as they reflect on their initial efforts:

> Reading hypertext with non-hypertext in mind not only
> serves to familiarize you with the various ... genres and
> approaches to composing ... it also helps to bring into relief
> our expectations for ... academic writing and some of the
> conventions and evaluation criteria we take for granted. We
> believe such self-reflection is valuable for any teacher. For us,
> it prompted critical examination of the ways of thinking and
> shaping of information that we value and ... the conventions
> for composing which we value. (p. 253).

Understanding what we value in terms of assessment, as Bob Broad (2003) has articulated, involves a process "by which instructors and administrators in writing programs discover, negotiate, and publicize the rhetorical values they employ when they judge student writing" (p. 14) for internal and external stakeholders. Contemporary discussions of multimodal assessment have stressed the need to share and shape those values with input from students themselves. Sonya Borton and Brian Huot (2007) urged teachers to view assessment as a way of teaching production and design to go beyond the functional skills and technical affordances of various media tools and genres. They advised teachers to collaborate with students in developing formative assessment criteria that ensures multimodal projects are grounded in processes; they further suggested including rubrics that allow students to assess their own texts and make rhetorical decisions about when, why, and how to compose in various modalities. By doing this assessment work together, multimodal composing becomes a sustainable process, not something done for a singular class or a more teacher-centered audience; rather, it involves an ongoing set of critical and rhetorical literacies for students to deploy throughout their academic and professional careers. The following assessment strategies are designed to help students make those choices.

Multimodal "Norming"

Although neither teachers nor students have extensive experience evaluating multimodal compositions, there are some aspects of design that can be intuitive even for novice composers. For example, students often can assess levels of accessibility and readability on a basic slideware presentation, whether color schemes or font sizes are more or less readable on a website, or whether visuals are aligned appropriately in both design and theme with their textual counterparts. One strategy for tapping these intuitive assessment criteria is to ask students to find websites, slideshows, and other multimodal genres that they find rhetorically appealing in terms of organization, design, and creativity and to share those models electronically with other members of the class. As the class reviews these artifacts, the instructor can facilitate interactive discussion about why the students view these examples as effective, generating shared criteria.

The "Ugly" Composition

Such multimodal design experts as Kristin Arola (2010) have stressed that despite the "death" of the personal homepage coded and designed in HTML, "in a Web 2.0 world, composition teachers need to engage, along with our students, the work of design" (p. 4) to understand its affordances in fostering students' writerly identities. And scholars such as James Inman (2004) and Dánielle De-Voss (2013) have focused on multimodal design don'ts as a way to teach multimodal design do's. Having students collaboratively engage in an ugly slideware design contest, as DeVoss has done in a number of her visual rhetoric courses, can teach students a great deal about document design elements in making visual presentations more rhetorically aware. These elements include typography, color-scheme, and overall consistency, as well as the relationship among image, text, color, and audio. Inman (2004) developed similar activities with websites, using the activity to not only enhance students' understanding of design but also to enhance their recognition that professional-quality design presumes access to both tools and expertise (p. 216) and can equalize skills among students who have had such access and those who have not. In addition, the emphasis on design do's would offer an opportunity to emphasize accessible design strategies, such as ALT Tags on Web-based images and the need for textual descriptions of visual content in the content of the site.

Collaborative Rubric Development

Despite the potential of intuitive knowledge to guide initial discussions of multimodal assessment, OWI teachers should be prepared to work with students to shape these conversations into detailed discussions of criteria to be formalized in rubric form, ideally for each multimodal assignment given the differing technical affordances and skills required for composing with video, audio, or Web-design tools. As many of us who have developed multimodal assignments can attest, rubrics and other forms of assessment must include a strong balance between product and process. This balance may include completion of invention activities such as storyboards, participation in peer review activities, self-assessments and other forms of progress reporting, Above all, the rubric should function as a form of "instructive evaluation" that establishes a relationship between the use of technology to compose in a particular medium and, according to Borton and Huot (2007), "a course's specific instructional goals and a contextual understanding of other rhetorical constraints and possibilities having to do with purpose, audience, content, genre, circulation, and organization, as well" (p. 103).

Peer Studio Review

Often, our discussion of peer review presumes assessment of print-based products, even in fully online settings. While we may use free digital collaboration tools or small-group discussion forums in the LMS, formative multimodal assessment calls for a broader range of feedback options, ideally customized to each type of assignment genre, whether it is a website or a video essay. A common approach for multimodal assignments is the studio review, once again relying upon interdisciplinary language about production and assessment that involves the presentation and review by a larger group. Because students have less familiarity responding to multimodal texts, a good strategy is to have them respond to sample genres prior to such a studio review. Because not all students may have the same level of access or comfort with a particular technology, it is important to design activities that allow all students to participate regardless of how complete their projects are. In my own hybrid courses, I often have provided in-class studio time to first work on aspects of the project prior to a formal studio review; when it is time for review, students call up work on the screen and craft a series of questions for fellow classmates to address about the project as the group migrates around to different student stations. Assessment then becomes a co-equal process, with both students and instructor providing frequently consistent advice about next steps for revision, based on shared assessment criteria. Such a studio review process may not be as logistically viable in a fully online asynchronous course; nevertheless, it is possible to assign students to peer review based on similarities in genre, or relative strengths in certain aspects of composing process, including alphabetic skills, to ensure a rich review of the various modalities at work in a single artifact.

Revision Plans

Given the substantial amount of feedback students could receive during a studio review as described above, the need for synthesis and summary helps to prioritize next steps in the revision process. As Kara Poe Alexander (2007) has suggested, the revision process for multimodal texts is far more complex than the standard alphabetic essay. Regardless of the useful content and format suggestions students receive, the normative timeframes for multimodal assignments do not always allow for complete overhaul of work. Therefore, having students create a revision plan summary of the general feedback received, decisions on what to prioritize, and a general timeline for completion can serve as a useful self-assessment strategy for both individual and group projects. Additionally, it helps to have students share these plans publicly in a discussion forum or other course space (indeed, I have even used social media-based groups for this purpose), as very often, the types of feedback and necessary revisions can help other students to see that they are not alone in their multimodal composing challenges and also to get additional strategies for enhancing their own work.

Student Conferences

Not unlike student discussion board posts where it would be unrealistic—and not necessarily student-centered—to expect an instructor to respond to each and every post in every thread throughout the term, it may not be as possible to respond to every multimodal artifact each student produces in a studio review environment. For that reason, ensuring one-to-one interaction is crucial in order to clarify instructor expectations and alleviate students' concerns that they are making progress toward achieving assignment outcomes. The importance of instructor-student interaction on multimodal work in progress mandates the flexibility on the instructor's part to communicate in whatever modality or media are most accessible for individual students. While in hybrid OWCs, this communication strategy may include face-to-face and even telephone conferences, in fully online formats, the possibilities are bountiful depending on access and comfort level. Free video conferencing software can expedite the conferencing process, although access might make text-based chat forums a more viable alternative. Undoubtedly, student conferences are a significant part of an instructors' academic labor; some ways to consolidate efforts may include group conferences organized around genre or other aspects of the composing process.

Electronic Portfolios

Undoubtedly, electronic portfolios, or ePortfolios, have the potential to play a vital role in the multimodal composing process in their ability to serve similar functions to their paper-based counterparts of development over time, self-reflection, self-assessment of progress, and summative showcase of rhetorical accomplishments. An ePortfolio, as Kathleen Yancey (2004) has suggested, helps to "remediate" the self, allowing the student designer to use multimodal literacies to construct a relationship between technology and identity. For Darren Cambridge (2010), "fully embracing them requires finding ways to make ePortfolios simultaneously serve individual self-actualization and institutional transformation. Excellence in lifelong learning and assessment are inextricably linked" (p. 11). Cambridge's latter point makes ePortfolios a strong assessment option for multimodal composing, connecting to Borton and Huot's (2007) emphasis on instructive assessment. Of course, ePortfolios can be an "easier said than done" strategy for a lone instructor, and ideally any portfolio initiative for hybrid and fully online OWC will represent a programmatic collaboration among the WPA and the instructors. With careful planning, however, instructors and programs can develop an ePortfolio space even within common LMSs, as Christine Tulley (2013) documented, although Tulley conceded that these systems are likely to be augmented with other open source and Web 2.0 tools.

CONCLUSION AND RECOMMENDATIONS

At the conclusion of *The Internship*, the film I used to introduce this chapter, there existed both a predictable happy ending common to the comedy genre and an important message. The two middle-age protagonists helped their team and themselves to land the coveted future job at Google, not only as a result of their emerging tech savvy but also as a result of their strong communication and rhetorical skills that made them good salespeople in the first place. The message is not one of either/or but both/and, and as we look to transform our understanding of writing, we must maintain an understanding of our goal of equipping students with all available means of persuasion in our OWCs and their communicative lives beyond them.

Much of this chapter has focused on the whats and the hows of integrating multimodality into the online curriculum. But like Warnock's (2009) powerful emphasis on the whys of OWI, it is equally important to consider, in this case, the whys of multimodal composing. Moving beyond a functional view of multimodal literacy not only aligns technology with rhetoric to foster a critical citizenry that communicate in a range of media, but in the case of OWI, also allows students to deploy multimodal genres to critically and rhetorically explore identity and the role that various tools play in shaping and representing that identity through a broadened definition of writing.

Even as I recognize the whys of multimodal composing, in the spirit of both/and, I concede it is not always possible for programs, instructors, and students to make every assignment multimodal. What I hope I have provided in this chapter are starting points and options given the access needs, specific curriculum, instructor expertise, student population, and delivery options unique to readers' individual OWI contexts. Similar to Warnock's advice, I would begin with the tools you need and what you can do well. That may mean transforming one single alphabetic assignment to a visual argument instead, or including a virtual poster session as part of a collaborative research project. It does not mean making each and every assignment a high-end technological endeavor for students and instructors, but it may mean making assignments flexible enough so that students have technological and rhetorical choices. Future success for OWI teachers also involves establishing a professional development plan in which they outline multimodal composing goals for their students, determining what education and training is needed on their end to achieve those goals, and seeking out those resources both on and off campus and both onsite and online. This need not be an isolated process, however. Dickie Selfe (2007) has advocated "communities of practice" to ensure that such multimodal initiatives are sustainable over time and across the writing curriculum and that include instructional support specialists for instructors and students.

In attempting to address Griffin and Minter's (2013) important call to pay attention to the material and ideological conditions of OWI, I have addressed the possibilities and constraints of integrating multimodal assignments, selecting tools and resources, and assessing student success. These efforts are aligned with Selfe's (2009) point that:

> Composition classrooms can provide a context not only for
> *talking about* different literacies, but also *practicing* different
> literacies, learning to create texts that combine a range of mo-
> dalities as communicative resources: exploring their affordanc-
> es, the special capabilities they offer to authors; identifying
> what audiences expect of texts that deploy different modalities
> and how they respond to such texts. (p. 643)

Several of the OWI principles stress the ongoing need for instructors and tutors to communicate with students across modalities and to use digital tools in developing content for students to consume—clearly transformative processes. Granted, no one text, regardless of modality, is accessible to all, and instructors should consider the ways that students can produce multiple versions of texts (e.g., audio transcripts, video captions, rich description of images, and the like) to enable critical awareness of audience access needs. Thus, my goal in this chapter has been to suggest representative multimodal writing contexts that enable students to produce content as twenty-first century composers and to experiment with multiple modes as much as possible to provide access to as many users as possible. To this end, OWI teachers, in collaboration with WPAs and other university stakeholders have a vital advocacy role to play to transform learning outcomes in OWI and face-to-face writing instruction that continue to privilege alphabetic textual production as the singular mode of rhetorical effectiveness.

A summary of recommendations toward these goals include:

- Integrate multimodal assignments at a pace where you and your students seem most ready to begin. For example, piloting a visual essay in a partic-ular course will help you determine existing challenges and future skills required the next time around.
- Align multimodal assignment genres with rhetorical outcomes of pur-pose, audience, development, organization, and style; help students un-derstand why an audio essay, for instance, is a more viable choice with some audiences (and for some rhetors).
- Make assignments flexible enough that students could complete multi-modal composing tasks using a range of tools to which they may have more consistent access than the ones you initially suggest.
- Develop flexible assessment processes, understanding that because of the learning curve involved, students' initial multimodal efforts may be messy and may not represent the ideal response you had in mind.
- Provide as many resources, websites, campus IT services, and other forms of documentation and training to students who will be completing these assignments independently and from a distance.

- Include opportunities for student self-assessment of their progress, as such opportunities that not only help them to reflect on their growth in aptitude and attitude but that also help instructors to understand the assignment difficulties and any resulting need for modifications.
- Begin your own professional development plan for integrating multimodality. What do you need to know to effectively align the technological and the rhetorical? How are you going to get there?

REFERENCES

Alexander, Jonathan & Losh, Elizabeth. (2013). *Understanding rhetoric: A graphic guide to writing.* Boston, MA: Bedford St. Martin's Press.

Alexander, Kara Poe. (2007). More about reading, responding, and revising: The three Rs of peer review and revision. In Cynthia Selfe (Ed.), *Multimodal composition: Resources for teachers* (pp. 113-131). Cresskill, NJ: Hampton.

Arola, Kristin. (2010). The design of Web 2.0: The rise of the template, the fall of design. *Computers and Composition, 27*(1), 4-14.

Blair, Kristine. (2007). Course management tools as "gated communities": Expanding the potential of distance learning spaces through multimodal tools. In E. Bailey (Ed.), *Focus on distance education developments* (pp. 441-454). New York: Nova Science.

Bolter, Jay David. (2001). *Writing space: Computers, hypertext, and the remediation of print.* Mahwah, NJ: Erlbaum.

Borton, Sonya & Huot, Brian. (2007). Responding and assessing. In C. Selfe (Ed.), *Multimodal composition: Resources for teachers* (pp. 99-111). Cresskill, NJ: Hampton.

Broad, Bob. (2003). *What we really value: Beyond rubrics in teaching and assessing writing.* Logan: UT, Utah State University Press.

Cambridge, Darren. (2010). *Eportfolios for lifelong learning and assessment.* San Francisco, CA: Jossey Bass.

CCCC OWI Committee for Effective Practices in Online Writing Instruction. (2013). *A position statement of principles and effective practices for online writing instruction (OWI).* Retrieved from http://www.ncte.org/cccc/resources/positions/owiprinciples

Fleming, Neil, and Baume, David. (2006). Learning styles again: VARKing up the right tree!, *Educational Developments, SEDA Ltd, 7*(4), 4-7.

Griffin, June & Minter, Deborah. (2013). The rise of the online writing classroom: Reflecting on the material conditions of college composition teaching. *College Composition and Communication, 65*(1), 140-161.

Inman, James. (2004). *Computers and writing: The cyborg era.* Mahwah, NJ: Erlbaum.

Levine, Dan (Producer), & Levy, Shawn (Director). (2013). *The Internship* [Motion picture]. USA: Twentieth Century Fox.

Moran, Charles & Herrington, Anne. (2003). Evaluating academic hypertexts. In Pamela Takayoshi & Brian Huot (Eds.), *Teaching writing with computers: An introduction* (pp. 247-257). Boston: Houghton Mifflin.

New London Group. (1996). A pedagogy of multiliteracies: Designing social futures. *Harvard Educational Review, 66,* 60-92.

Pederson, Anne-Marie & Skinner, Carolyn. (2007). Collaborating on multimodal projects. In Cynthia Selfe (Ed.), *Multimodal composition: Resources for teachers* (pp. 39-47). Cresskill, NJ: Hampton.

Prensky, Marc. (2001). Digital natives, digital immigrants. *On the Horizon 9*(5), 1-6.

Selber, Stuart. (2004). *Multiliteracies for a Digital Age.* Carbondale, IL: Southern Illinois University Press.

Selfe, Cynthia L. (2009). The movement of air: The breath of meaning: Aurality and multimodal composing. *College Composition and Communication, 60*(4), 616-663.

Selfe, Richard. (2007). Sustaining multimodal composition. In Cynthia Selfe (Ed.), *Multimodal composition: Resources for teachers* (pp. 167-179). Cresskill, NJ: Hampton.

Takayoshi, Pamela & Selfe, Cynthia. (2007). Thinking about multimodality. In Cynthia Selfe (Ed.), *Multimodal composition: Resources for teachers* (pp. 1-12). Cresskill, NJ: Hampton.

Tran, Mai. (2013). National debate on 2014 GED changes. *The Council of State Governments Justice Center.* Retrieved from http://csgjusticecenter.org/reentry/posts/national-debate-on-2014-ged-changes/

Tulley, Christine. (2013). Migration patterns: A status report on the transition from paper to ePortfolios and the effect on multimodal composition initiatives within first-year composition. *Computers and Composition, 30*(2), 101-114.

Warnock, Scott (2009). *Teaching writing online: How and why.* Urbana, IL: National Council of Teachers of English.

Yancey, Kathleen Blake. (2004). Postmodernism, palimpsest, and portfolios: Theoretical issues in the representation of student work. *College Composition and Communication, 55*(4), 738-761.

CHAPTER 16

OWI ON THE GO

Rochelle Rodrigo
Old Dominion University

A growing number of students own smartphones and tablets, some of whom use those devices as their primary Internet connection. To account for this trend, OWI administrators and instructors need to support students accessing and completing OWCs through their mobile devices. OWI WPAs should research the students of their own programs and dialogue with IT administrators to learn how to support students on their mobile devices. OWI programs need to develop an ongoing professional development community that helps faculty and staff explore and understand the various devices students bring to their learning endeavors. OWC instructors need to design instructional content for delivery on the typically smaller screens of mobile devices. To this end, they might use the need for supporting a myriad of hardware and software as well as the affordances of mobile connectivity as an exigency for designing both low-stakes and major course assignments using or about mobile devices.

Keywords: digital divide, mobile, multimodal, professional development, smartphone, support, tablet

In September 2013, EDUCAUSE's annual Study of Undergraduate Students and Information Technology stated that "ownership of smartphones and tablets jumped the most (among all devices from 2012-13)" (Dahlstrom, Walker, & Dziuban, 2013, p. 24) and that students' "ownership of laptops and smartphones exceeds that of the general adult population" (p. 25). In short, undergraduate students in higher education are already mobile; therefore, OWI Principle 1, with its call for universal inclusivity and accessibility (pp. 7-11), requires that OWI WPAs and instructors start going mobile as well. Knowing who owns smartphones is not enough; OWI Principle 2 reminds us that OWI should focus on writing, not teaching the technology unless the rhetoric of technology is part of the course outcomes (pp. 7-11; also see Chapter 14). Indeed, OWI WPAs and faculty need to understand how smartphone owners use the devices as well. A recent Pew Internet-focused study has noted a "mobile difference":

Once someone has a wireless device, she becomes much more

active in how she uses the Internet–not just with wireless connectivity, but also with wired devices. The same holds true for the impact of wireless connections and people's interest in using the Internet to connect with others. (Zichuhr & Smith, 2012, p. 14)

WPAs and OWI teachers deserve credit for all the hard work they already do; however, the shift to smaller, Internet-connecting mobile devices will need both groups to remain committed to *writing* instruction (OWI Principle 2) while *adapting* to and *adopting* strategies for the growing number of students using mobile devices (OWI Principle 1). This chapter uses the discussion of mobile devices—their prevalence in higher education, the ways in which they complicate OWI, and suggestions for ways to incorporate mobile learning into OWI—to continue complicating the tension between OWI Principle 1 and OWI Principle 2, as discussed in Chapters 1, 4, 8, 9, 10, and 14 (pp. 7-11).

ON THE GO: MOBILE DEVICES IN HIGHER EDUCATION

In *The Mobile Academy*, Clark N. Quinn (2012) discussed four capabilities of mobile devices to consider when thinking about teaching and learning in online settings: storing and accessing *content, capturing* materials, *computing* and manipulating digital data, and *communicating* (pp. 17-18). These affordances emphasize the core communicative—dare I say, rhetorical—nature of mobile devices. As smartphones and tablets become increasingly popular for day-to-day business and personal communications through the Internet, why wouldn't composition instructors be teaching mobile communication strategies in writing courses generally and accounting for mobile learning strategies in OWCs particularly?

This call is not new; in 2009, Amy Kimme Hea, the editor of *Going Wireless,* claimed that composition teachers and researchers needed to pay attention to mobile devices and their quickly evolving nature. However, as the iPhone had just been released in 2007, most of the chapters within Hea's collection discussed the impact of laptops, as well as cellphones and/or PDAs occasionally. Although many of the critical arguments found in *Going Wireless* are relevant to smartphones, smartphones are impacting our culture in slightly different ways that make investigating them separately or differently from how we examine laptops, especially in terms of OWI, a required endeavor.

The New Media Consortium's (NMC) and the National Learning Infrastructure Initiative's (a group within EDUCAUSE) second *Horizon Report* (2005) projected "ubiquitous wireless" as a technology within the one year or less time-to-adoption within higher education. Although they were discussing laptops, handhelds, and cell phones (p. 9)—not explicitly discussing smartphone or tablet usage—it is quickly becoming obvious that the NMC and EDUCAUSE have had a clear view of the importance of mobile devices in higher education long before many OWI-focused WPAs and teachers; they particularly considered devices ranging from "larger" laptops to more personalized and smaller cell phones, tablets, and smartphones.

Thinking about mobile devices in higher education is no longer about looking forward to change; instead, it is about reconciling with technological changes that have been occurring over the past decade as Internet connection devices have become smaller, more personalized, and more prevalent—currently stabilizing in the shape of the smartphone (a cell phone with its own operating system and Internet connectivity through both cellular and Wi-Fi networks). This reconciliation with mobile technologies is at the heart of OWI Principle 1, making sure OWI is designed and delivered in a way to include participants accessing OWCs with dominant technologies—which now includes mobile devices (pp. 7-11).

Aaron Smith's (2012a) March, 2012 Pew Internet and American Life report announced a tipping point: Suddenly, there were more smartphone than regular cell phone users; 46% of Americans owned smartphones with 41% owning other phones (p. 2). Since then, the numbers have only increased. The Nielsen Company (2013b) announced in March, 2013 that 59% of Americans owned smartphones (p. 17). Ownership numbers are higher among traditional college-aged people: 66% ownership 18-29 year olds (Smith, 2012a, p. 5). Additionally, income and educational attainment are not as significant with this younger-aged group; in other words, individuals under 30 years of age are more likely to own smartphones whether or not they make more than $30,000 and/or have some college experience (p. 5). Although these numbers are outdated even as I write this chapter (e.g., as soon as September 2012, six months after Smith's report above, Lee Rainie's (2012a) September, 2012 report from the Pew Foundation emphasized both youth and higher income brackets as markers of smartphone ownership), and definitely by the time this book is published, the data still demonstrate important trends for faculty and administrators of OWI programs.

OWI Principle 1 specifically addressed the digital divide with concerns about "technological equality" and the financial accessibility of technologies required by an OWC. Ownership statistics about smartphones flip some common assumptions about technological equality and accessibility. Age and education are not the only markers of smartphone ownership. In March, 2013, The Nielsen Company (2013b) announced the following smartphone ownership patterns by ethnicity: White 55%, African American 68%, Hispanic 68%, and Asian 74% (p. 17). One of the Pew studies (Zickuhr & Smith, 2012) more eloquently stated:

> Groups that have traditionally been on the other side of the digital divide in basic Internet access are using wireless connections to go online. Among smartphone owners, young adults, minorities, those with no college experience, and those with lower household income levels are more likely than other groups to say that their phone is their main source of Internet access. (p. 2)

A few months later in June, A. Smith (2012b) claimed that "55% cell phone users use their phone to go online" and 17% "go online *mostly* on cell phone" (p. 2). By March 2013, a Pew report claimed that 74% of teens ages 12-17 access the Internet on mobile devices "at least occasionally" and "one in four teens are 'cell-mostly' Internet users" (Zickuhr, Rainie, Purcell, Madden & Brenner, 2013, p. 2). In October 2012, Rainie's (2012c) report from Pew discussed Pew's need to change how they ask about and define Internet usage. Although they added a question that "counts" mobile Internet usage, it did not increase the number of American Internet users in a statistically significant manner (p. 2). However, Rainie acknowledged that there are "demographic differences when mobile connectivity is added" (p. 2).

Studies of undergraduate smartphone ownership generally parallel national studies of technology ownership. During their 2008 annual national study of undergraduate students and information technology, EDUCAUSE stopped asking about basic cell phone ownership (Smith, Salaway & Caruso, 2009, p. 87). As of 2012, 62% of undergraduate students owned smartphones and "nearly twice as many in 2012 (67%) than in 2011 (37%) reported using their smartphone for academic purposes" (Dahlstrom, 2012, p. 14). In 2012, students also reported a growth in tablet ownership and a leveling off of e-reader ownership (p. 15) with many using the devices for academic work—67% and 47% respectively (p. 14). According to Eden Dahlstrom and Stephen diFilipo (2013), in 2012, students brought on average at least two Internet-capable devices to campuses; they projected that by 2014, students would be bringing more than three devices (p. 10).

Although studies from Pew and Nielsen may reveal data that can overturn how most faculty understand the socio-economic digital divide, EDUCAUSE's data remind scholars that a digital divide still exists. In 2011, "students at associate's colleges and other two-year programs [were] more likely to own 'stationary' technologies, such as desktop computers" (Dobbin, Dahlstrom, Arroway, &

Sheehan, 2011, p. 9). The 2012 report specifically discussed smartphone ownership:

> There are some significant differences in the demographics or institution type of undergraduate students who own smartphones but the field is equal for age and gender. Students who said they use their smartphones for academics, however, tended to be non-white (p <0.0001>), were not freshman/first-year or sophomore/second-year students (p <0.0001) and were presently attending four-year institutions as opposed to an AA institution (p<0.0001). (Dahlstrom, 2012, p. 15)

Whereas all the data demonstrate an increased trend of smartphone ownership across all demographics, knowing specific populations within specific contexts obviously is important.

Although student ownership of smartphones and other Internet capable mobile devices is up, Gartner's 2012 Hype Cycle[1] report for Education (Lowendahl, 2012) put both "mobile-learning" and "mobile-learning smartphones" in the "sliding into the trough of disillusionment" portion of the chart (i.e., as people have spent more time with the technology, they now have overcome the "peak of inflated expectations" and have lower expectations about what, how, and why the technology will work successfully). Based on almost ten years of predictions in The New Media Consortium's *Horizon Reports* (2005-2013), faculty in higher education should not be surprised with Gartner's placement of mobile-learning—small screens and tiny keyboards are not surprisingly challenging tools for writing lengthy papers, for example. However, just because mobile-learning is not new and people have adjusted their expectations does not mean we should be ignoring mobile technologies when discussing online learning. The statistics from Pew, Nielsen, and EDUCAUSE above demonstrate that a majority of our students have smartphones and a growing number own e-readers and tablets as well. As mobile-learning moves towards Gartner's "slope of enlightenment" and the "plateau of productivity," now is the perfect time to critically strategize mobile-learning in relation to OWI.

Both Pew studies as well as reports from The Nielsen Company emphasized the rise of the "connected viewer" (Smith & Boyles, 2012) who moves between screens "watching across different platforms including both mobile and tablet devices" (The Nielsen Company, 2013b). These are the same type of habits scholars already have tracked with students doing academic work (e.g., Dodd & Antonenko, 2012; Ihanainen & Moravec, 2011; Laffey, Amelung, & Goggins, 2009). However, whereas much of the scholarship about teaching and learning implies a distracted student, especially by social media (e.g., Fewkes & McCabe,

2012), A. Smith and Jan Lauren Boyles (2012) discussed how television viewers were checking data or websites introduced on television, as well as discussing and see what others had to say about a particular program (p. 2)—these evaluative processes and informed communications are some of the many behaviors we ask of "information literate" students (Association of College and Research Libraries, 2000). Kathryn Zickuhr and A. Smith's Pew study (2012) emphasized how Black, non-Hispanic, and Hispanic groups are more likely to use various functionalities of their smartphones like accessing the Internet; taking, sending, and receiving photos; playing music, games, and videos; as well as doing online "business" like social networking, banking, or video calling/chatting (p. 21). Rainie's (2012b) Pew report also discussed similar differences across race/ethnicity; however, the gap was quickly closing even then. Again, these mobile communicative activities speak to both OWI Principle 1 (accessibility) and OWI Principle 2 (focus on writing) and can be included as part of the content covered in OWI courses (pp. 7-11).

EDUCAUSE's annual reports of undergraduate and information technology also documented how and why students use their devices. As early as 2009, over 50% of the owners of Internet-capable handheld devices were checking information, e-mailing, using social networking sites, and instant messaging (Smith et al., 2009, p. 95). Over 20% of the undergraduates polled were also conducting personal business, downloading/streaming music, and downloading/watching videos (p. 95). By 2010, using maps via satellite had jumped to over 50%, and those activities that had been at 20% usage increased to over 30% (Smith & Caruso, 2010, p. 60). In 2010, students rated the following mobile technologies as "extremely valuable" for academic success: laptop computer at 81%, netbook at 46%, smartphone at 33%, e-reader at 33%, mobile/cell phone at 32%, tablet (not iPad) at 26%, and iPad at 24% (p. 16).

When the CCCC OWI Committee conducted their surveys about fully online and hybrid/blended writing instruction (CCCC OWI Committee, 2011a & 2011b, respectively), they did not list mobile technologies as an option in their question about "which virtual tools and online teaching strategies" instructors use; however, the survey was conducted in 2010, only two years after ED-UCAUSE stopped asking about cell phone ownership. Although the surveys shortsightedly did not provide the option, one individual wrote in "mobile blogging" while many short answers to open-ended questions discussed using phone calls and conferences as a strategy.

In short, mobile devices—especially handheld, personalized devices like smartphones and tablets—are here to stay, and they are used for educational purposes. With their general functionalities that emphasize various literate practices (e.g., reading, writing, image and video viewing), as well as the growing number of individuals that use mobile devices as their primary access to the Internet, WPAs and OWI teachers should be planning for mobile-learning now.

READY, SET, GO: MOBILE DEVICES AND OWI

As indicated, the basis for this chapter is OWI Principle 1, which stated, "Online writing instruction should be universally inclusive and accessible" (p. 7) Specifically, Effective Practice 1.6, an example strategy for providing that access and inclusivity, reminded instructors that students *may* use mobile devices to access OWCs; however, the statistics above demonstrate that students *may* be doing more than just accessing the course materials. While a growing number of individuals use their mobile devices as their primary means of accessing the Internet, instructors need to be prepared for students who both may want, even need, to access and actively participate in the class from their mobile device. And OWI instructors are not alone because the institution and any student support service (i.e., IT, LMS, OWL, advising, and the like) also should be prepared to support students accessing their online resources and services through mobile devices (see OWI Principle 13, pp. 26-28; and Chapters 5 & 8). In other words, the digital divide works both ways; educators need to support the "haves" as well as the "have nots."

There are a variety of ways that student uses of mobile devices impact the understanding and interpretations of the different OWI principles. Although OWC instructors should focus on writing, not the technologies, as explained in OWI Principle 2 (p. 11), the reality is many instructors still need to support their student's technological interface with the course, which is primary to putting access first, as advocated in OWI Principle 1 (pp. 7-11). For example, many experienced OWI teachers probably have scripts of texts reminding students that the current version of the LMS works better in a particular browser. With the rise of mobile use, instructors—ideally through their institutions—will need to make students aware of whether or not their institution's LMS has a mobile application as well as on which mobile operating systems that application runs. Studies have shown that students greatly prefer accessing their course materials from a native mobile app versus the mobile Web browser (Bowen & Pistilli, 2012, p. 7). Many companies first develop their applications for the iOS, Apple's mobile operating system, since it does not run Flash; they leave Android, and now Windows, mobile users working through the mobile device's regular Web browser. Indeed, just because the LMS has a mobile application does not mean that the application includes all of the functionality required to complete an OWC course. Many first attempts at LMS mobile applications result in functionality that only allows the students to access and consume course material, as opposed to producing and uploading their writing. Many institutions have labeled "facilitating anytime, anywhere access to course materials for students [as] a high or essential priority" (Dahlstrom & diFilipo, 2013, p. 33); however, that does not necessarily mean students would be able to use the various interactive functionalities like posting and responding in discussion boards and/or uploading assignments. Verifying an LMS's mobile app does not take into consideration whether the app itself is accessible, in the more traditional sense of the term, to students with different auditory or visibility abilities. Just as with computers, there is hardware and software that makes various applications more accessible in mobile environment; does the OWI LMS and course materials interface with those apps?

Even if the LMS or other required course applications are available in a mobile environment, it does not necessarily mean that a student's mobile device is prepared to handle the application. Just as with software, different applications and media have different hardware, software, and Internet connectivity requirements. OWCs that require accessing videos or synchronous meetings might require large amounts of bandwidth. Students may not have access to a robust enough Wi-Fi network or they may not have purchased a large enough data plan from their mobile service provider. Writing programs will need to warn students in advance of the technological requirements, not only in terms of hardware and software, but also in terms of bandwidth and media/modalities.

Especially after trying to access their own courses from within a mobile environment, instructors may find that they need to be even more careful about course design and delivery for smaller screens. Not only should OWI instructors think about alphabetic text delivery, writing shorter, chunky paragraphs (OWI Effective Practice 3.3, pp. 12-13); they also might think about the ability, or lack thereof, for mobile device users to move back and forth between different sections of the course or assigned texts. Mobile devices might not allow students to move easily between tabbed browser pages or have two word processing documents open, one with notes and the other with drafted text. In looking to a future of more mobile devices and students accessing higher education through them, instructors and scholars would do well to start thinking about, experimenting with, and sharing strategies for composing in different environments, including the affordances and constraints found with mobile hardware and software.

Onsite and OWI teachers also need to consider that if a student's primary computer is, in fact, her mobile device, she might be drafting entire papers with her thumbs. Similarly, although the word processing programs on mobile devices are becoming increasingly sophisticated, students still might struggle to handle more complex formatting requirements like hanging indents for bibliographic citations. Whereas OWI teachers traditionally have not been as concerned with students finding proctored computer labs to take high stakes tests, faculty need to help students realize that final formatting of papers likely needs to happen on a "regular" computer with a fully functional word processing program. As with the nontraditional students discussed in Chapter 10, the solution for these students may be the public library if they do not have alternate access at home or work and if the campus is geographically too distant. Although this may require more work on the student's part and creative, patient support from the instructor (especially at a distance), it also represents an opportunity to emphasize core instructional principles about teaching and learning writing—in this case, emphasizing multiple drafts as a productive part of a writing process.

Although there may have been the illusion that instructors could somehow "know" all of the interface possibilities with their online courses while students were primarily using full-function computers (e.g., desktops or laptops), the various makes, models, and operating systems within the world of mobile devices definitely makes it impossible for any individual instructor to know how a student's device will interface with the course material. The CCCC OWI Committee certainly is not asking such an impossibility of teachers. Although OWI Principles 2 and 10 emphasize that institutions should be the ones supporting student technology use (pp. 7, 21-23), respondents to the surveys about fully online and hybrid/blended OWI emphatically agreed about the need for "providing reasonable support to students for succeeding in the online environment" (CCCC OWI Committee, 2011a, 2011b). To provide this type of support to the growing number of students using mobile devices, or at least having faculty reasonably aware of some of the major issues that might occur when their OWC interacts with popular mobile devices and operating systems, WPAs will need to advocate for institutional support of students, faculty, and programs per OWI Principle 12 (pp. 24-26).

One final problem—for now—regarding the issue of OWI in mobile environments is the WPAs' and OWI teachers' general lack of awareness of mobile computing with respect to OWCs. Since many of these individuals cannot imagine taking an online course and/or writing an entire paper on a mobile device, especially a small-screened device, they disavow the fact that students actually are doing a lot of work, sometimes a majority of their work, on mobile devices. Even with evidence like that presented at the beginning of this chapter, many faculty and administrators cannot imagine that *their* students fit into this category. Hence, WPAs and their OWI faculty cannot begin to discuss what might constitute "reasonable" support for online learners using mobile devices if they are not aware of the students in their programs. Just as *A Position Statement of Principles and Example Effective Practices for OWI* concluded that folks in an

OWC should be committed to ongoing research (OWI Principle 15, pp. 31-32), this chapter now ends the discussion of potential problems and starts the discussion of solutions and recommendations, beginning with the suggestion that writing programs specifically research the types of hardware and software students are using in their OWCs—and, in many cases, may be using in their onsite courses as well.

AWAY WE GO: OWI AND MOBILE DEVICES

Organizations like Pew, Nielsen, and EDUCAUSE are regularly collecting and publishing data about mobile device ownership and usage patterns. These organizations, as well as higher education administrators, instructors—even this author—can get caught up in the positivistic rhetoric produced by business and industry. WPAs and instructors of OWCs should collect similar data so that they can talk more precisely about the mobile needs of their program, per the research suggestions of OWI Principle 15 (pp. 31-32). Writing programs (again, students use these devices in onsite courses, too) probably should collect more than just ownership and basic usage data; *access* is more than just having the hardware and software, but also entails knowing how to use it flexibly. Researchers can begin identifying students with whom they might conduct more robust, even longitudinal, studies and about how students learn and write in a mobile environments. Beyond researching and exploring the specific contextual needs of their program so that they are universally inclusive and accessible, administrators and instructors of OWCs should think about how to engage with pedagogical, professional development, and institutional support issues related to mobile learning.

Good to Go: OWI and Mobile Pedagogy

Most of the pedagogical suggestions below attempt to balance the need to make OWI inclusive and accessible, as stated in OWI Principle 1 (pp. 7-11), while still staying focused on the instruction of writing, per OWI Principle 2, over teaching technology or attempting to become versatile in all of the technologies students may use (p. 11). In many cases, the pedagogical suggestions fall within OWI Principle 3 by taking unique features of mobile learning to design OWI instructional materials and activities (pp. 12-14).

Michael G. Moore and Greg Kearsley (1996) claimed that in distance learning there are different types of interaction: learner-to-content, learner-to-instructor, and learner-to-learner. When instructors of OWCs acknowledge that a growing number of students will be accessing and participating in the course via a mobile device with a smaller screen and probably slower connection speeds

(Cheon, Lee, Crooks, & Song, 2012, p. 1060), they need to plan these interactions accordingly. If the majority of the interactions are asynchronous, speed is not as high of a concern; however, in a culture that privileges speed and efficiency, having a "slow" course reflects poorly upon both the instructor and the institution. To meet the needs of students accessing the course via mobile devices, instructors need to make sure course content is downloadable in bite-size chunks. To facilitate learner-to-instructor and learner-to-learner interaction, instructors should try to work with the methods and applications that are more streamlined on the students' mobile devices; this workaround implies that instructors will survey students at the beginning of the semester to find out what hardware *and* software or applications they are using to access and participate in the course.

In other words, as students continue to use a growing variety of hardware and software options to access the online course, they will need help understanding and reflecting upon their individualized learning experience. Besides individuality, Eric Klopfer, Kurt Squire, and Henry Jenkins (2002) identified four more properties of mobile devices that can impact teaching and learning writing online: portability, social interactivity, context sensitivity, and connectivity. These characteristics describe certain affordances and constraints of designing OWCs with mobile learning in mind. Considering portability means that not only can online learning take place anywhere, instructors specifically can require that OWI take place in a multitude of locations; instructors can ask students to identify context-specific examples of different rhetorical acts and/or other communicative texts (e.g., advertisements on billboards, pamphlets in medical offices). Many mobile devices are geo-spatially aware; faculty might include reflections of analyzing (as well as producing) texts that account for specific geo-spatial coordinates or other information. For example, faculty might have students collaboratively construct maps with content that is tagged with specific location information. Mobile devices allow OWI teachers not only to design for distance learning but for location-specific composition as well. And, since the devices are connected, instructors can ask for students to interact asynchronously or synchronously from within different environments, especially using social media or document-sharing applications; while discussing mobile composition, Olin Bjork and John Pedro Schwartz (2009) reminded us that "*where* students write determines not only *what* they write but also what they write *with*" (p. 225). Now, more than ever, this thinking is apt.

Ultimately, the online writing instructor should be focusing on teaching writing, not teaching technology (OWI Principle 2, p. 11); however, as students use an increasingly diverse set of hardware and software to access and engage course materials, OWI instructors do need to account for technical support. Effective practices emphasize that institutional IT staff should help support students' learning and using the required course technologies; however; OWI faculty might want to incorporate low-stakes learn-the-technology assignments where students safely can explore how they will interact in a specific course with their individual devices. These types of activities will help all students practice accessing course materials with their specific hardware, like smaller screened mobile devices, and/or software, like screen readers. And although students may appear to know how to work their mobile devices, they may only know how to send text messages and post Facebook updates. The 2012 EDUCAUSE undergraduate students and IT report explicitly claimed that "even though most students felt prepared to use technology upon entry, most also said they need or want more technology training or skills" (Dahlstrom, 2012, p. 22). Although it is not the explicit responsibility of OWI teachers to increase their students' techno-literacies, doing so can be considered within their purview as writing-as-rhetoric teachers (see Chapter 14, for example). On a practical level, historically, writing instructors have had to accept this task in terms of educating their students about specific communications technologies, especially concerning advanced formatting features in word processing programs, which is one reason that OWI teachers asked for a guideline such as OWI Principle 2 to begin with (p. 11). Providing low-stakes opportunities to understand better how a student's device interacts with the different course technologies and materials, and then repeating the activities (OWI Effective Practice 3.6, p. 13), can help to avoid major crises during later high-stakes assignments. It is helpful, therefore, to make sure students understand that testing technologies in advance is a techno-literacy skill with learning benefits for students and instructors alike. For example, should the mobile device fail to be usable for a particular assignment, the students who tested their technologies will know that they need to access a different device to complete the work. More importantly, testing technologies in advance is a techno-literacy administrators need to understand as well. The first day of class is too late for students to realize the computer they plan to use for their OWC will not suffice. Administrators need to construct a system that makes students aware of the technological requirements of OWCs *and* allows students to test their computers and mobile devices *prior* to enrolling in the OWC per OWI Principle 10 (pp. 21-23; see also Chapter 13).

Learn-the-technology assignments need not only be low-stakes or assigned to individual students; OWI teachers can design major assignments that ask all students to take responsibility for learning and supporting their own computing devices. Based on the course modality, OWI students already will be more aware about how they interface with different technologies—or, their teachers can endeavor to make them so. Minimally, faculty can adapt typical technical or professional writing "instructions" assignment for OWI learn-the-technology assignments. Grouping students who own similar devices would allow them to share resources and support one another as well as to develop support communities that foster student success per OWI Principle 11 (pp. 23-24). This type of activity by no means excuses instructors and institutions from supporting students' technology issues (i.e., they can share resources located and developed by instructors and/or the institution); instead, it makes online technology support per OWI Principle 13 (pp. 26-28) a collaborative endeavor—the way it often is in business and industry.

Beyond merely being prepared for students using mobile devices in OWCs (OWI Principle 1, pp. 7-11), mobile devices offer certain affordances that positively support writing instruction (OWI Principle 2, p. 11). Mobile devices already are multimodal pocket notebooks that should be leveraged so that students can record images, sounds, video, and traditional alphabetic text while they are out and about in the world. Instructors can ask students to find and record examples of course concepts or to accumulate a digital pile of multimodal invention or research notes. Clay Spinuzzi (2009) stated that the "genie's out of the bottle" and students already are using their mobile devices to record "news" in the real world; OWI should prompt students to use mobile devices to "record" and write the world as well.

As it is likely that many-to-most students in the OWC own mobile devices of some kind—despite their choice to use more traditional and potentially more manageable technologies for their classes—some assignments can ask the entire class to consider and use a mobile device. For example, mobile devices might be used to help emphasize different possible steps in any given writing process and/or different canon of rhetoric. Johndan Johnson-Eilola and Stuart A. Selber (2009) proposed the "3CT" framework to help students analyze and reflect production processes in terms of context, change, content, and tools. As indicated in Chapter 14, students and instructors can use the variety of production, publication, and consumption devices as a way to discuss the rhetorical appropriateness of a composition process and/or product. Discussing with students how final formatting might require a different environment, maybe even a different hardware and/or software application, helps to emphasize the distinction between drafting and global level revision with final formatting, editing, and delivery or publication. Asking students to write in different environments can help to "foster awareness of their social, cultural, and historical locations" (Bjork & Schwartz, 2009, p. 231).

Mobile devices are, at their core, communication environments where an increasing amount of "business," both inside and outside of higher education, gets done. Having students compose and deliver mobile-friendly genres (i.e., emails, social media posts and responses, even digital images and videos with basic editing) from their devices in a critically sound and reflective manner promotes a variety of twenty-first century and multimedia literacies (National Council of Teachers of English, 2013). Students might even conduct research on how communication practices in their field, discipline, and/or future profession have been impacted by mobile devices. In other words, with mobile devices student might both *take* the OWI course as well as *complete* the OWI writing assignments.

Considering that many smartphone users access the Internet from their smartphones for information, especially just-in-time and location/activity specific (Dahlstrom, 2012; The Nielsen Company, 2013a; Rainie & Fox, 2012; Smith & Boyles, 2012), it makes sense to add a layer of discussions and activities around accessing, evaluating, and using electronic resources. The Pew study "How Teens Do Research in the Digital World" (Purcell et al., 2012) claimed that both "teachers and students alike report that for today's students, 'research' means 'Googling'" (p. 3). In that same report, 42% of the instructors who said they had their students use cell phones in the classroom said that they had students look up information during class (p. 32). Beyond teaching mobile-adapted information literacy skills, OWC instructors that require students to access and use library databases for their research projects might need to verify that the institution's databases are adequately designed for mobile interfaces and/or suggest that students find alternative Internet access (e.g. institutional and library computer labs) for such work.

Many of the social media applications readily available for mobile devices promote community building per OWI Principle 11 (pp. 23-24) as well as sharing and providing feedback on specific texts. There are a multitude of mobile applications that promote sharing and communicating about texts; these applications easily could support both peer and instructor reviews and comments of works in progress as well as final drafts. In discussing major methods for incorporating social media (most of which have at least one mobile application) into teaching and learning, Tanya Joosten (2012) specifically mentioned increasing communication and encouraging contact, developing a richer learning environment, and building cooperation and feedback through dialogue.

Learning from a mobile device has some challenges, as one could easily surmise. A. Smith (2012c) reported that survey participants said mobile phones can make "it harder to give people your undivided attention" and more difficult "to focus on a single task without being distracted." Some scholarship about distance learning already has discussed the need for students to be highly focused, extremely motivated, and self-regulated learners (e.g., Artino & Jones, 2012; Briggs & Wagner, 1997; Harnet, St. George, & Dron, 2011; see also Chapter 13); and it appears that distance students participating in their online courses through mobile devices may need to be even more focused. Requiring that students monitor and reflect upon their own time management may help with these issues; there are mobile applications that students can use to help manage and monitor time management.

GOTTA GO: OWI PROFESSIONAL DEVELOPMENT AND MOBILE DEVICES

These pedagogical suggestions cannot simply be added on top the responsibilities of an OWI teacher. While the following discussion begins to add to faculty professional development workload, it also provides suggestions for how OWI WPAs and faculty might start learning about mobile learning per OWI Principle 7 (pp. 17-19). According to data collected by the CCCC OWI Committee (2011c), most instructors of fully online and blended/hybrid courses have participated in some formal training for online teaching and online course design; however, most have not worked with instructional technology specialists or collaborated with colleagues to help design a course. Respondents also mentioned some of the following types of activities as "essential" for faculty training: sharing/interaction with peers and colleagues, training taught by other faculty, informal/group discussions, faculty mentorship and collaboration, and support network. Developing collegial and casual faculty and staff learning communities can provide the continual professional development opportunities OWI need, especially to adapt to continuously changing technologies like the variety of mobile devices (Harrington, Rickly, & Day, 2000; Hewett & Ehmann, 2004; Rodrigo, 2009).

Based on the need to be universally inclusive and accessible, WPAs and faculty in OWI programs need to become increasingly aware of how any of the required technologies function in different types of mobile environments. Instead of passively waiting to see how the LMS or packaged textbook website will manage mobile devices, OWI administrators and faculty need to engage actively in discussions with representatives from IT and the LMS companies. Faculty and staff from the institution can consider combining the need to aggressively test and engage different types of mobile devices with faculty professional development. Faculty with different makes and models of mobile devices can test the various applications and share the results with the rest of the writing program and institution.

Instructors, even institutional IT departments, cannot possibly know and support every make, model, and operating system of mobile devices; instead, administrators, WPAs, and faculty, as well as other technical and student support personal, should embrace the diversity of devices. To help increase awareness regarding the functionality of different devices, institutions might develop faculty and staff learning communities that continuously explore pedagogical affordances as well as other topics, issues, and policies related to mobile learning. Within a large enough group, faculty and staff hopefully will own different models of devices. They can play within online course environments and share the results of working within specific LMSs and other learning applications. Similarly, meeting and dialoging as a group allows faculty to share not only experiences and instructions on how to function within a given device or application but the opportunity to discuss pedagogical reasons and ideas for critically incorporating and supporting mobile devices. The group can start to collect, develop, and share resources collaboratively.

In short, most of these ideas about building community to support OWI faculty learning about and incorporating mobile learning into their pedagogical strategies, suggest a twist of OWI Principle 11: *Online writing teachers and their institutions should develop personalized and interpersonal online communities to foster student* and faculty *success* (pp. 23-24).

HERE GOES: INSTITUTIONS SUPPORTING MOBILE DEVICES AND OWI

In an EDUCAUSE report discussing how to best support mobile growth on campuses, Eden Dahlstrom, Tom de Boor, Peter Grunwalk, and Martha Vockley (2011) emphasized the need for a "balanced approach to mobile development" that accounts for developing resources for the mobile Web, native apps, and/or mobile frameworks (p. 5). In a Gartner report about Bring Your Own Device (BYOD) strategies in the workplace, David A. Willis (2012) similarly emphasized a balanced approach that goes beyond just the technology that includes "policy, software, infrastructure controls and education in the near term, and with application management and appropriate cloud services in the longer term" (p. 2). Especially if OWI administrators have collected data about mobile device ownership and usage patterns in their specific programs, they will be prepared to have meaningful conversations with the Chief Information Officer (CIO) and other IT administrators at their institutions. CIOs in higher education know that mobility matters and to continue moving forward they must collaborate with administrators and faculty. In a discussion about IT in higher education in 2020, symposium participants most commonly identified faculty as institutional stakeholders (p. 6) and that CIO's need to be "date-maker[s]" to facilitate productive collaborations (Grajek & Pirani, 2012). To help the institution develop mobile learning support mechanisms so that OWI instructors can focus on the teaching of writing per OWI Principle 2 (p. 7), OWI administrators and instructors should reach out to the IT leaders on their campus to proactively start these discussions.

No matter what, if campuses are sincerely promoting a BYOD environment, they need to make sure that student introductions to LMS environments do not assume the use of any given device, browser, or application. Instead, institutional introductory materials should promote both the teaching and learning of the environment by both demonstrating what the environment should generally look and function like, and, more importantly, provide learning activities that prompt students to engage in the environment from and with their own devices. When asked about the delivery format of student orientation for fully online and/or hybrid/blended courses, the respondents to the CCCC OWI Committee's surveys implied that most of the options, especially those offered by the institution, were extremely static, lacking any opportunity for students to interact and play with the online learning environments (CCCC OWI Committee, 2011c). Students needed time and prompting to explore how to use the specific online learning environment with their specific devices per OWI Principle 10 (pp. 21-23). Students should have the opportunity to test their individual devices and receive feedback and any required support prior to the start of a specific course per OWI Principle 10. Institutions or OWI programs might even want to start device-specific users groups that invite faculty, staff, and students to explore and support one another; the user groups would also need to reach out to and support the truly geographically distant online students as well.

OWI WPAs and faculty need to talk about mobile learning beyond just understanding how it impacts their OWCs; they also need to be in serious discussions with institutional LMS decision makers. If the online writing program theoretically and pedagogically privileges student-student interaction, OWI administrators and faculty need to emphasize heavily the need for LMS mobile applications that do more than access online course materials. Students definitely prefer working within native mobile applications in comparison to mobile Web browsers, primarily because the mobile applications are generally faster and easier to use (Bowen & Pistilli, 2012). Although experts may worry about the lack of diversity or "closed gardens" that will emerge if apps dominate the access and use of the Internet (Anderson & Rainie, 2012, p. 7), they acknowledge that apps make it more streamlined for people to do what they want to do and, therefore, they will continue to be preferred and grow as a favored method for accessing the Internet (p. 6).

Not only will OWI administrators and faculty want to participate in discussions about campus-wide technology adoptions, they also will want to be in on discussions about supporting students, as well as a growing number of faculty, who use mobile devices to teach and learn in online environments.

CONCLUSION AND RECOMMENDATIONS

Alan K. Livingston (2009) claimed that no one noticed the "revolution" of mobile phones and multimobile services in higher education. Specifically, he claimed the Internet "changed everything" while the mobile revolution "changed nothing," especially because faculty and staff in higher education have not realized what is going on. Instructors in and administrators of OWI programs cannot ignore the growing use of mobile devices. Instead, OWI programs must acknowledge mobile devices are here to stay, students are using them to access and interact in OWCs, and there will be no streamlining of the mobile platforms and/or applications. Dialogs with IT administrators, professional development, support of OWI faculty and students, and OWC material and assignment designs all must consider the various affordances and constraints associated with mobile learning.

The following recommendations may help OWI WPAs and teachers to integrate mobile devices into their thinking and OWCs:

- Student technological access is no longer just divided by Macs and PCs or different browser applications. As such, instructors, WPAs, and institutions need to be thinking about students both accessing *and* completing work (i.e., writing papers) on smartphones and tablets with different operating systems.
- Check OWCs for usability, or at least check the institutional LMSs, with all major brands of devices and interface operating systems. Develop faculty and staff learning communities to share this work and its results.
- Research your own student population to develop appropriate course, programmatic, and/or institutional support materials (especially to help students test and prepare their devices for working in the online course environment *before* the term begins).
- Take advantage of students' access to mobile devices when designing assignments. Emphasize process; have students reflect on the affordances and constraints of production and consumption of texts in mobile environments.
- Help students support one another with "teach/learn the technology" assignments. Also take advantage of mobility with space- and location-aware assignments. In keeping with the advice offered in Chapter 15, there is no need to give up multimodal assignments; many mobile platforms include robust multimodal recording and editing applications as well.

NOTES

1. Gartner is a prominent information technology company. Gartner's Hype Cycle for technology adoption includes the following phases: Technology Trigger, Peak of Inflated Expectations, Trough of Disillusionment, Slope of Enlightenment, and Plateau of Productivity.

REFERENCES

Anderson, Janna Quitney & Rainie, Lee. (2012). *The Web is dead? No. Experts expect apps and the Web to converge in the cloud; but many worry that simplicity for users will come at a price.* Retrieved from http://www.pewinternet.org/files/old-media/Files/Reports/2012/PIP_Future_of_Apps_and_Web.pdf

Artino, Anthony R. & Jones, Kenneth D. (2012). Exploring the complex relations between achievement emotions and self-regulated learning behaviors in online learning. *Internet and Higher Education, 15,* 170-175. doi:10.1016/j.iheduc.2012.01.006

Association of College and Research Libraries. (2000). *Information literacy competency standards for higher education.* ACRL: Association of Colleges & Research Libraries; A Division of the American Library Association. Retrieved from http://www.ala.org/acrl/standards/informationliteracycompetency

Bjork, Olin & Schwartz, John Pedro. (2009). Writing in the wild: A paradigm for mobile composition. In Amy C. Kimme Hea (Ed.), *Going wireless: A critical exploration of wireless and mobile technologies for composition teachers and researchers* (pp. 223-237). Cresskill: NJ: Hampton Press.

Bowen, Kyle & Pistilli, Matthew D. (2012). *Student preferences for mobile app usage (Research bulletin).* Retrieved from http://www.educause.edu/library/resources/student-preferences-mobile-app-usage

Briggs, Lowell A. & Wagner, Dale. (1997). Factors of distraction in a one-way-video, two-way-audio distance learning setting. *PAACE Journal of Lifelong Learning, 6,* 67-75. Retrieved from http://www.iup.edu/ace/publications/default.aspx

CCCC OWI Committee for Effective Practices in Online Writing Instruction. (2011a). *Fully online distance-based courses survey results.* Retrieved from http://s.zoomerang.com/sr.aspx?sm=EAupi15gkwWur6G7egRSXUw8k-pNMu1f5gjUp01aogtY%3d

CCCC OWI Committee for Effective Practices in Online Writing Instruction. (2011b). *Hybrid/blended course survey results.* Retrieved from http://s.zoomerang.com/sr.aspx?sm=%2fPsFeeRDwfznaIyyz4sV0qxkkh5Ry7O1NdnGHCxIBD4%3d

CCCC OWI Committee for Effective Practices in Online Writing Instruction. (2011c). *The state of the art of OWI.* Retrieved http://www.ncte.org/library/NCTEFiles/Groups/CCCC/Committees/OWI_State-of-Art_Report_April_2011.pdf

CCCC OWI Committee for Effective Practices in Online Writing Instruction. (2013). *A position statement of principles and effective practices for online writing instruction (OWI).* Retrieved from http://www.ncte.org/cccc/resources/positions/owiprinciples

Cheon, Jongpil, Lee, Sangno, Crooks, Steven M., & Song, Jaeki. (2012). An investigation of mobile learning readiness in higher education based on the theory of planned behavior. *Computers & Education, 50,* 1054-1064. doi: 10.1016/j.compedu.2012.04.015

Dahlstrom, Eden. (2012). *ECAR study of undergraduate students and information technology, 2012 (Research report).* Retrieved from http://www.educause.edu/library/resources/ecar-study-undergraduate-students-and-information-technology-2012

Dahlstrom, Eden, de Boor, Tom, Grunwalk, Peter, & Vockley, Martha. (2011). *The ECAR national study of undergraduate students and information technology, 2011 (Research report).* Retrieved from https://net.educause.edu/ir/library/pdf/ERS1103/ERS1103W.pdf

Dahlstrom, Eden, de Boor, Tom, Grunwalk, Peter, & Vockley, Martha. (2011). *Mobile IT in higher education, 2011 (Research report).* Retrieved from https://net.educause.edu/ir/library/pdf/ers1104/ERS1104W.pdf

Dahlstrom, Eden & diFilipo, Stephen. (2013). *The consumerization of technology and the bring-your-own-everything (BYOE) era of higher education (Research report).* Retrieved from http://www.educause.edu/discuss/constituent-groups-about-information-technology-management-and-leadership/cio-constituent-group/consumerization-techn

Dahlstrom, Eden, Walker, J. D., & Dziuban, Charles. (2013). *ECAR study of undergraduate students and information technology, 2013 (Research report).* Retrieved from http://www.educause.edu/library/resources/ecar-study-undergraduate-students-and-information-technology-2013

Dodd, Bucky J. & Antonenko, Pavlo D. (2012). Use of signaling to integrate desktop virtual reality and online learning management systems. *Computers & Education, 59,* 1099-1108. Retrieved from http://dx.doi.org/10.1016/j.compedu.2012.05.016

Fewkes, Aaron M. & McCabe, Mike. (2012). Facebook: Learning tool or distraction? *Journal of Digital Learning in Teacher Education, 28*(3), 92-98. Retrieved from http://www.iste.org/learn/publications/journals/jdlte

Grajek, Susan & Pirani, Judith A. (2012). *Through a glass, brightly: IT's impact on higher education by 2020 (Research bulletin).* Retrieved from https://net.educause.edu/ir/library/pdf/ERB1209.pdf

Harnet, Maggie, St. George, Alison, & Dron, John. (2011). Examining motivation in online distance learning environments: Complex, multifaceted, and situation-dependent. *The International Review of Research in Open and Distance Learning, 12*(6), 20-38. Retrieved from http://www.irrodl.org/index.php/irrodl/issue/view/48

Harrington, Susanmarie, Rickly, Rickly, & Day, Michael. (Eds.). (2000). *The online writing classroom*. Cresskill, NJ: Hampton Press.

Hewett, Beth L. & Ehmann, Christa. (2004). *Preparing educators for online writing instruction: Principles and processes*. Urbana, IL: National Council of Teachers of English.

Ihanainen, Pekka & Moravec, John W. (2011). Pointillist, cyclical, and overlapping: Multidimensional facets of time in online learning. *The International Review of Research in Open and Distance Learning, 12*(7), 27-39. Retrieved from http://www.irrodl.org/index.php/irrodl/issue/view/49

Johnson, Larry, Adams, Samantha, & Cummins, Michele. (2012). *The NMC horizon report: 2012 higher education edition*. The New Media Consortium. Retrieved from http://www.nmc.org/pdf/2012-horizon-report-HE.pdf

Johnson, Larry, Adams Becker, Samantha, Cummins, Michelle, Estrada, Victoria, Freeman, Alex, & Ludgate, Holly. (2013). *NMC horizon report: 2013 higher education edition*. The New Media Consortium. Retrieved from http://www.nmc.org/pdf/2013-horizon-report-HE.pdf

Johnson, Larry, Levine, Alan, & Smith, Rachel. (2009). *The 2009 horizon report*. The New Media Consortium. Retrieved from http://www.nmc.org/sites/default/files/pubs/1316814843/2009-Horizon-Report.pdf

Johnson, Larry, Levine, Alan, Smith, Rachel, & Stone, Sonja. (2010). *The 2010 horizon report*. The New Media Consortium. Retrieved from http://www.nmc.org/sites/default/files/pubs/1316815357/2010-Horizon-Report.pdf

Johnson, Larry, Smith, Rachel, Willis, Holly, Levine, Alan, & Haywood, Keene. (2011). *The 2011 NMC horizon report*. The New Media Consortium. Retrieved from http://www.nmc.org/sites/default/files/pubs/1316814265/2011-Horizon-Report%282%29.pdf

Johnson-Eilola, Johndan & Selber, Stuart A. (2009). The changing shapes of writing: Rhetoric, new media, and composition. In Amy C. Kimme Hea (Ed.), *Going wireless: A critical exploration of wireless and mobile technologies for composition teachers and researchers* (pp. 15-34). Cresskill: NJ: Hampton Press.

Joosten, Tanya. (2012). *Social media for educators: Strategies and best practices*. San Francisco, CA: Jossey-Bass.

Kimme Hea, Amy C. (2009). Introduction. In Amy C. Kimme Hea (Ed.), *Going wireless: A critical exploration of wireless and mobile technologies for composition teachers and researchers* (pp. 1-11). Cresskill: NJ: Hampton Press.

Klopfer, Eric, Squire, Kurt, & Jenkins, Henry. (2002, August). Environmental detectives: PDAs as a window into a virtual simulated world. *Proceedings of IEEE International Workshop on Wireless and Mobile Technologies in Education*.

Vaxjo, SE: IEEE Computer Society, 95-98. Abstract retrieved from http://ieeexplore.ieee.org/xpl/articleDetails.jsp?arnumber=1039227&sortType%-3Dasc_p_Sequence%26filter%3DAND%28p_IS_Number%3A22273%29

Laffey, James, Amelung, Chris, & Goggins, Sean. (2009). A context awareness system for online learning: Design based research. *International Journal on E-Learning, 8*(3), 313-330.

Livingston, Alan K. (2009). The revolution no one noticed: Mobile phones and multimobile services in higher education. *EDUCAUSE Quarterly/EDUCAUSE Review Online*. Retrieved from http://www.educause.edu/ero/article/revolution-no-one-noticed-mobile-phones-and-multimobile-services-higher-education

Lowendahl, Jan-Martin. (2012). *Hype cycle for education, 2012: Summary*. Retrieved from http://gartner.com/doc/2094815/hype-cycle-education-

Moore, Michael G. & Kearsley, Greg. (1996). *Distance education: A systems view*. Belmont, CA: Wadsworth Publishing Co.

National Council of Teachers of English. (2013). *The NCTE definition of twenty-first century literacies*. Retrieved from http://www.ncte.org/positions/statements/21stcentdefinition

New Media Consortium & EDUCAUSE Learning Initiative. (2006). *The horizon report: 2006 edition*. Retrieved from http://www.nmc.org/publication/nmc-horizon-report-2006-higher-ed-edition/

New Media Consortium & EDUCAUSE Learning Initiative. (2007). *The horizon report: 2007 edition*. Retrieved from http://www.nmc.org/sites/default/files/pubs/1316813966/2007_Horizon_Report.pdf

New Media Consortium & EDUCAUSE Learning Initiative. (2008). *The horizon report: 2008 edition*. Retrieved from http://www.nmc.org/sites/default/files/pubs/1316816013/2008-Horizon-Report.pdf

New Media Consortium & National Learning Infrastructure Initiative. (2005). *The horizon report: 2005 edition*. Retrieved from http://www.nmc.org/sites/default/files/pubs/1316813462/2005_Horizon_Report.pdf

Purcell, Kristen, Rainie, Lee, Heaps, Alan, Buchanan, Judy, Friedrich, Linda, Jacklin, Amanda, Chen, Clara, & Zickuhr, Kathryn. (2012). *How teens do research in the digital world*. Retrieved from http://www.pewinternet.org/2012/11/01/how-teens-do-research-in-the-digital-world/

Quinn, Clark N. (2012). *The mobile academy: mLearning for higher education*. San Francisco, CA: Jossey-Bass.

Rainie, Lee. (2012a). *Two-thirds of young adults and those with higher income are smartphone owners*. Retrieved from http://www.pewinternet.org/2012/09/11/smartphone-ownership-update-september-2012/

Rainie, Lee. (2012b). *25% of American adults own tablet computers*. Retrieved from http://www.pewinternet.org/2012/10/04/25-of-american-adults-own-tablet-computers/

Rainie, Lee. (2012c). *Changes to the way we identify internet users*. Retrieved from http://www.pewinternet.org/2012/10/03/changes-to-the-way-we-identify-internet-users/

Rainie, Lee & Fox, Susannah. (2012). *Just-in-time information through mobile connections*. Retrieved from http://www.pewinternet.org/2012/05/07/just-in-time-information-through-mobile-connections/

Rodrigo, Rochelle. (2009). *Motivation and play: How faculty continue to learn new technologies* (Doctoral dissertation). Available from ProQuest Digital Dissertations (3354462).

Smith, Aaron. (2012). *Nearly half of American adults are smartphone owners*. Retrieved from http://www.pewinternet.org/2012/03/01/nearly-half-of-american-adults-are-smartphone-owners/

Smith, Aaron. (2012a). *Cell Internet use 2012*. Retrieved from http://www.pewinternet.org/2012/06/26/cell-internet-use-2012/

Smith, Aaron. (2012b). *The best (and worst) of mobile connectivity*. Retrieved from http://www.pewinternet.org/2012/11/30/the-best-and-worst-of-mobile-connectivity/

Smith, Aaron. (2012c). *The rise of the "connected viewer.* Retrieved from http://www.pewinternet.org/2012/07/17/the-rise-of-the-connected-viewer/

Smith, Shannon & Caruso, Judy B. (2010). *The ECAR study of undergraduate students and information technology, 2010 (Research report)*. Retrieved from http://www.educause.edu/library/resources/ecar-study-undergraduate-students-and-information-technology-2010

Smith, Shannon, Salaway, Gail, & Caruso, Judy B. (2009). *The ECAR study of undergraduate students and information technology, 2009 (Research report)*. Retrieved from http://www.educause.edu/library/resources/ecar-study-undergraduate-students-and-information-technology-2009

Spinuzzi, Clay. (2009). The genie's out of the bottle: Leveraging mobile and wireless technologies in qualitative research. In Amy C. Kimme Hea (Ed.), *Going wireless: A critical exploration of wireless and mobile technologies for composition teachers and researchers* (pp. 255-273). Cresskill: NJ: Hampton Press.

The Nielsen Company, The. (2013a). *The mobile consumer: A global snapshot*. Retrieved from http://www.nielsen.com/us/en/insights/reports/2013/mobile-consumer-report-february-2013.html

The Nielsen Company, The. (2013b). *Free to move between screens: The cross-platform report*. Retrieved from http://www.nielsen.com/us/en/insights/reports/2013/the-nielsen-march-2013-cross-platform-report--free-to-move-betwe.html

Willis, David A. (2012) *Bring your own device: New opportunities, new challenges.* Retrieved from http://gartner.com/doc/2125515/bring-device-new-opportunities-new

Zickuhr, Kathryn, Rainie, Lee, Purcell, Kristen, Madden, Mary, & Brenner, Joanna. (2013). *Teens and technology 2013.* Retrieved from http://www.pewinternet.org/2013/03/13/teens-and-technology-2013/

Zickuhr, Kathryn & Smith, Aaron. (2012). *Digital differences.* Retrieved from http://www.pewinternet.org/2012/04/13/digital-differences/

CHAPTER 17

OWI RESEARCH CONSIDERATIONS

Christa Ehmann
Smarthinking, Inc.

Beth L. Hewett
CCCC Committee for Effective Practices in OWI
Defend & Publish, LLC

This chapter examines strategies for researching distance education in the OWI context. It considers overall methodological research approaches that can be employed to engage in consistent and useful investigation of one's program whether it has a writing course or writing center focus. The chapter also addresses key factors related to choice of research instruments, sample selection, data collection, and analysis, as well as issues of reporting and information dissemination post-research.

Keywords: automated writing evaluation (AWE), data collection, empirical research, mobile technology, MOOC, methodological design, outcomes, practice, RAD research, replicable, qualitative, quantitative, stakeholder, theory

A significant challenge facing online education is committing to a deeper understanding of the efficacy, values, and inner workings of OWI (both classroom- and tutor-based); its innumerable, rapidly changing modalities; its distinctive nature; and how it functions in a pedagogical sense. The writing studies discipline awaits viable theories of OWI as a philosophy of writing *and* as a series of strategies for teaching and learning to write in digital settings. To these ends, the CCCC OWI Committee has reasoned that ongoing research is crucial. OWI Principle 15 stated, "OWI/OWL administrators and teachers/tutors should be committed to ongoing research into their programs and courses as well as the very principles in this document" (CCCC OWI Committee, 2013, p. 31).

This chapter focuses on how useful, ongoing research into OWI might be developed by examining and highlighting the crucial need for a deeper understanding of OWI; it offers suggestions for developing a rigorous framework of investigation when engaging in OWI. Methodological strategies for researching distance education in the OWI context also are considered. Specifically, the chapter examines overall methods and research approaches that can be employed to engage in consistent and useful investigation of one's program whether it has a writing course or writing center focus. The chapter analyses key factors related to choice of research instruments, sample selection, data collection, and analysis. In a final section, the chapter discusses reporting and information dissemination post-research.

A NEED FOR RESEARCH INTO OWI

The Internet has had a profound impact across educational contexts with the teaching and learning of writing among the most primary. There are innovative and exciting writing models that are linked inextricably to the online modalities that power them. The education landscape is marked by rapid growth and expansion of online technologies that are used to construct and deliver education and instruction—including writing instruction.

Systematic and broad scale national and international data specifically targeting OWI trends do not exist. Overall, however, US higher education has seen considerable enduring growth with online education. For example, the National Center for Education reported that over 200 fully accredited online higher education institutions currently operate in the United States (Radford, 2011)—these institutions all provide high-enrollment, core courses that include composition. Further, Eduventures—a leading research and consulting firm for higher education institutions—estimated that in the fall of 2010, 2.78 million students enrolled in fully online programs. This number represents 14% of all higher education enrollments (Aslanian & Clinefelter, 2012). Along these lines, 77% of all four-year university presidents reported that their institutions offered some type of online or hybrid classes (Parker, Lendard, & Moore, 2011). Worldwide trends are similar; both online programs and enrolled students are increasing yearly. Indeed, even students in traditional onsite courses can expect to access some of their course materials and/or communicative experiences in online settings such as an institution's LMS or, minimally, email.

These statistics reflect online learning overall. As this book demonstrates, when we consider OWI alone, there is much that remains unknown. Undoubtedly, there is much to learn about how the changing digital landscape affects writing instruction in online settings. Among a wide variety of possible concerns are issues of accessibility, mobile technologies, and experimental learning formats. We provide the following examples to ground the exigency of developing appropriately sound and potentially helpful OWI research.

Accessibility, for instance, received primary importance in *A Position Statement of Principles and Example Effective Practices for OWI* (CCCC OWI Committee, 2013). OWI Principle 1 concerned the need for inclusivity and accessibility in OWI for all students and teachers. Where inclusivity has been more or less retrofitted (Oswal & Hewett, 2013) to online settings in the past, it is provided a paramount position in this position statement. With OWI Principle 1, it becomes clear that every activity in an OWI setting and the technology choices for those activities should be determined with accessibility as a priority for both students and teachers (pp. 7-11). Student audiences, for example, are masked in online settings, making it difficult to know whether they are physically disabled, intellectually challenged, struggling with multilingual needs, and/or socioeconomically disadvantaged. Some students may have none of these specific problems but may be poor or slow readers with challenges in online educational settings (Hewett, 2015a). Without self-disclosure of such vital concerns, teachers may be unaware of particular student needs yet somewhat aware of their struggles as revealed in the student's writing. Indeed, given a potential for difficulties in handling the increased literacy load of a common OWC (Griffin & Minter, 2013), all students might be considered somewhat disadvantaged in OWI settings (Hewett, 2015a). Too little research has been produced to assist with understanding this phenomenon although scholars are beginning to address this stark need (see, for example, Meloncon, 2013). Even though Chapters 8, 9, and 10 address many access and inclusivity concerns, it is useful to consider here some of the most pressing areas to be researched:

- Regarding teacher/tutor training for accessibility:
  - What kinds of training, if any at all, do teachers and professional and peer tutors currently receive to provide universally accessible and inclusive OWI?
  - What training, if any, from different college disciplines or other online systems would support writing teachers/tutors in providing more accessible and inclusive OWI?
  - What attitudes do teachers/tutors need to acknowledge, address, and/or overcome to develop more accessible and inclusive OWI?
- Regarding self-disclosure:
  - How many students self-disclose some type of disability before, during, or after their OWCs? What types of disabilities do student disclose?
  - Under what situations (e.g., pre-course preparatory materials or general encouragement from teachers) do students tend to self-disclose accessibility needs for OWCs?
  - Given legal restrictions from the Family Education Rights and Privacy Act (FERPA) and the ADA, how can students be provided helpful guidance about self-disclosure?
  - What sort of research partnerships are possible between OWI pro-

grams and campus disability services to learn about disabled students' technological needs, learning styles, and other academic preferences?

- ○ How, if at all, do teachers (or tutors) modify their work with online writing students to meet access needs?

- Regarding students who may not previously have been considered as needing particular access:

  - ○ What kinds of accessibility and/or inclusivity needs do multilingual students have in an OWC?
  - ○ Under what conditions should multilingual students receive accessibility assistance in an OWC or with an online tutor?
  - ○ What do we know about the accessibility of online tutoring systems for students with disabilities?
  - ○ What are the socioeconomic factors that teachers/tutors must consider when providing accessibility OWI for students?
  - ○ What are the socioeconomic factors that administrators must consider when preparing OWI teachers and tutors?

In the field of writing studies, there is a wealth of scholarship about multilingual student writers as well as students whose literacy performances are affected by their socioeconomic conditions. But there is a dearth of scholarship about how these student populations perform in OWI contexts.

As a second example of the need for continued OWI research, the trend of using mobile devices and cell phone technology for OWI is among the changes in digital technologies, which is discussed in Chapter 16 of this book. Using such technology in writing courses undoubtedly will have an impact on writing instruction and student competency (Ehmann, 2012) as well as on student reading literacy (Hewett, 2015a). There is growing evidence to suggest that a growing population of students is using tablet and even mobile phone technology for educational purposes. Apple alone counts 1.5 million iPads in use by students in K-12 US schools (Kessler, 2012). In early October 2012, Piper Jaffray analyst Gene Munster released survey results showing that iPhone ownership also is growing at a rapid rate. According to Munster's findings, 34% of surveyed high school students now own an iPhone, and 40% said they planned to buy one in the next month (CourseSmart, 2012). A May 2012 survey released by CourseSmart estimated that 93% of university students own laptops, 57% own smartphones, and 22% own tablets (CourseSmart, 2012). As students become ever-more attached to their mobile technology, online learning opportunities via mobile devices undoubtedly will expand. A 2011 Pearson Foundation study on US students and tablets reported the following findings:

- Seventy percent of high school seniors and university students would like to own a tablet device.

- Twenty percent of college students and 7% of university-bound high school seniors planned to purchase one in the next six months.
- Sixty-nine percent of university-level students reported that they think tablet computing will change education in the future.
- Sixty-three percent of students surveyed reported that tablets can enhance education.
- Almost half of the surveyed students expect digital textbooks to replace paper textbooks within the next five years (p. 2).

In theory, there are some interesting opportunities for learner engagement with mobile devices and the development of writing skills. For example, students can easily and collaboratively share information and ideas with each other through this very social technology—as well as enjoy easy access to peer reviews. Research questions surrounding such mobile technology choices for OWI include:

- Regarding flipped classrooms:
  - Contemporary composition courses typically are taught in "flipped" manner—with lecture rejected for in-class practice and peer workshops—because it makes sense to have students perform the hands-on or direct engagement aspects of the learning process in the presence of the teaching professional. Given this scenario, how can mobile devices facilitate the flipped classroom?
  - Are mobile devices the best or just one of several tools for such activities?
  - What are their best uses in a writing instruction context?
  - How do these technologies enable or inhibit accessibility and inclusion?
- Regarding anywhere/anytime learning:
  - In what ways, if at all, do students actually use such mobile devices for educational writing experiences?
  - What is student satisfaction level with such uses?
  - In what ways, if at all, does the use of these devices hinder or support writing improvement from the teacher's perspective? From the student's perspective?
  - To what extent and in what ways do these technological tools promote learning and engage participants?
- Regarding writing conventions:
  - In what ways, if any, do students follow or reject traditional writing conventions, to include Standard Academic English, when they use mobile devices for educational writing experiences?

- ○ What kind of writing skills do students need and use for texting, tweeting, and other types of instant messaging modes that are twenty-first century skills necessary both in the work place and daily life?
- ○ How do (or can) writing teachers address and/or support such writing skills?
- ○ In what real contexts do the discourses of the academy and online discourse overlap, and how are these facilitated (or not) by mobile technology in writing course settings?

Houghton-Mifflin Harcourt conducted a US study from 2010 to 2011 on one of their mobile applications that teaches Algebra I and reported positive results. Although very small, this study is widely cited as evidence for the efficacy of mobile learning within the sciences (HMHEducation.com, 2012). Such a study for writing has yet to be published.

Another relatively recent movement that is gaining attention and points to the significant growth of online learning with potential impact on writing instruction is that of MOOCs. Targeting learners world-wide, MOOCs are an experimental form of online courses available to large audiences of learners through open Web access. MOOCs developed out of the open educational resources movement as "a response to the challenges faced by organizations and distributed disciplines in a time of information overload" (Cormier, 2010). According to Dave Cormier (2010), the most important feature of a MOOC is that it "builds on the active engagement of several hundred to several thousand 'students' who self-organize their participation according to learning goals, prior knowledge and skills, and common interests." Structurally, MOOCs may be similar to some college-level programs. Typically, MOOCs do not offer the college credits that paying students at colleges and universities receive although some colleges have done so (Koller, 2012).

The CCCC OWI Committee's *A Position Statement of Principles and Example Effective Practices for OWI* currently lists MOOCs as an experimental use of educational technology and OWI Principle 6 suggested that they "should be subject to the same principles of pedagogical soundness, teacher/designer preparation, and oversight detailed in this document" (p. 16). A study of such experimental uses of educational technology has not yet been published for composition or writing-enhanced disciplinary courses, although data have been collected on the four institutions (i.e., Duke University, Georgia Technological Institute, San Jacinto Community College, The Ohio State University) that won Gates Fellowship Grants to establish MOOCs for writing courses. Questions for such research on MOOCs, adaptable to other experimental OWCs, might be:

- Regarding the philosophies driving contemporary composition:

- In what ways, if at all, do MOOCs, support core writing studies philosophies?
- In what ways do they not support core philosophies?
- How, if at all, do writing MOOCs extend core writing studies philosophies and/or develop new strategies helpful to student writers?
- The four writing MOOCs piloted in 2013 enrolled a large number of students from around the world. What potential does such global reach of MOOCs offer to writing studies pedagogy?
- Regarding accessibility, enrollment, retention, and persistence:
  - What student accessibility challenges exist surrounding OWI? How and to what extent can such challenges can be addressed?
  - What types of students most benefit from the MOOC environment? In what ways do they benefit?
  - What types of students are most challenged by the environment? In what ways are they challenged?
  - What qualities of MOOCs encourage writing students to enroll?
  - Why do some students persist and others drop out?
  - What measures, if any at all, would encourage greater retention?
- Regarding the written products that students develop from learning in a MOOC:
  - In what ways, if any, is peer review supportive of a student's writing development in a MOOC?
  - In what ways, if any, would such students benefit from experienced writers' (e.g., teaching assistants, teachers, and professional writers) review and response in a MOOC?
  - How, if at all, should student writing be evaluated for course credit when the student has completed a writing MOOC?

The rapid expansion of such technologies and trends as those listed above and the growing sphere of instructors who engage in digitally enhanced and Internet-based education are evidence that online education in general and OWI specifically are becoming significant within the higher education landscape (Ehmann, 2012; Krause & Lowe, 2014; see also Chapter 18). Although actual technologies, formats, and procedures may change, the Internet has transformed education and the teaching of writing in meaningful ways. Within this exciting context of change and transformation, however, few individuals have investigated the outcomes, processes, and procedures of online teaching and learning in rigorous and empirical ways. This reality also holds true for OWI specifically. Indeed, the empirically based learning science surrounding online writing contexts has a long way to go before replicable results yield convincing learning theories in connection with writing.

Certainly, the understanding has developed that digitally enhanced or hosted writing instruction is not a replacement for onsite courses but rather a complement to them. Educators have begun to recognize that providing writing instruction in multiple modalities supports writing instruction rather than limits it (Hewett, 2010, 2015a, 2015b; Snart, 2010; Warnock, 2009), making OWI a substantial tool in a large toolbox that we use to make learning more accessible to a more diverse population of learners throughout the world, with some students benefiting from online learning and writing instruction more than others (Hewett & Ehmann, 2004). Nonetheless, even the anecdotal literature that exists often avoids the question of *what* really works and *why*.

Many experts have discussed the need to understand more deeply the various pedagogies related to OWI. As seen in the CCCC OWI Committee's *Annotated Bibliography on Online Writing Instruction* (2008) that gathered, reviewed, and annotated Web texts, articles, and books from 1980 to 2008, still much about what we know of OWI, what those processes look like, how students learn, and how teachers teach in the online writing environment is not comprehensive and does not account fully for the intricacies or complexities of participants and contexts (CCCC OWI Committee, 2008). Another annotated bibliography, "Studies Comparing Outcomes among Onsite, Hybrid and Fully Online Writing Courses" compiled by Scott Warnock (2013), studied the notion of difference between traditionally onsite and online (fully online and hybrid) composition courses. Warnock stated, "While generally few differences have been found in terms of educational outcome based on course modality, some studies identify nuanced differences in course experiences" (p. 2). Such nuances tend to affect retention and persistence as well as "student behaviors or performances in online courses in ways that lend themselves to comparison with onsite courses" (p. 2). Yet, such comparisons may be inappropriate for various reasons including that OWI often is scrutinized more than or differently from onsite writing courses, as Warnock indicates in Chapter 4.

Nonetheless, essential questions as to what distinguishes OWI from composition instruction and learning in onsite settings remain. Such distinctions, reported anecdotally and experientially by practitioners and researchers alike, strongly suggest that OWI may need its own theories unique to student cognition, teacher instruction, and affective dimensions of learning when working online (Hewett & Ehmann, 2004). The most obvious difference from onsite learning is in the affective realm from the loss of real-time body/face/voice connections where researchers have suggested that such loss interferes with developing classroom community (DePew & Lettner-Rust, 2009; Ehmann, 2010; Gouge, 2009). To some degree, these ideas are comprised of teacher impressions that require thoughtful research to test their veracity. On the other hand, in a few studies that questioned student experiences (see Warnock, 2013, for example), students have reported that their interactions with instructors and peers were similarly satisfactory when compared to those in onsite settings and that their satisfaction was connected in part from frequency of interactions and prompt feedback from instructors (Boyd, 2008; Johnson & Card, 2008). These issues would benefit from additional research. In particular, affective loss, student progress and retention, and the notion of leveling classroom power would be useful topics for further research.

Beyond concerns of affective connection, Beth L. Hewett (2010, 2015b) theorized in *The Online Writing Conference: A Guide for Teachers and Tutors* that OWI requires an increased clarity of written language, what she calls semantic integrity—response to students that recognizes fidelity between what teachers and tutors say in their writing and what they mean. This fidelity enables instructors to express themselves with clear intention and students to interpret their intentions as accurately as possible. Semantic integrity involves using straightforward language that is linguistically direct rather than indirect or suggestive and avoiding such conditional language as rhetorical questions and yes/no closed questions. In *Reading to Learn and Writing to Teach: Literacy Strategies for Online Writing Instruction,* Hewett (2015a) theorized that the decreased connection of body/face/voice in OWI reflects most strongly in lost cognition. When writing is taught primarily through reading and writing, an increased literacy load (Griffin & Minter, 2013)—where reading and writing are text-heavy *and* text-rich—taxes students who must make cognitive connections among what they read about writing generally, their writing specifically, and how to apply that information to their own writing-in-progress. Such reading challenges students, but it also challenges teachers who must understand that they are responsible for writing comprehensible instructional text that is straightforward and clear, leading directly back to a need for semantic integrity (Hewett, 2010, 2013, 2015a, 2015b). Indeed, according to David Alan Sapp and James Simon (2005), "Though many writing teachers may have the skills to communicate content and assignment instructions to students online, few have the sophisticated communication skills necessary to connect with students interpersonally, to build trust and rapport in unfamiliar virtual environments" (p. 478). Hewett's (2015a) literacy-cognition theory of OWI requires additional research both for confirmation and mitigation of its effects on students with various learning needs and styles.

Although composition theories and some teaching strategies can be migrated and adapted to online settings as described in OWI Principle 4 (also see Warnock, 2009), institutional writing programs cannot simply move or transfer traditional educational methods online in a wholesale manner (pp. 14-15).

Rather, new techniques and pedagogies unique to digital environments must be discerned and employed, as revealed in OWI Principle 3, to address the heavily text-based nature of OWI and the myriad of technological devices available for educational uses (pp. 12-14). However, what educators believe are the best online *teaching* strategies are not always the best *learning* strategies for students, which means that research must address that aspect of OWI as well. As described in the Introduction, the CCCC OWI Committee's weakest area of research in terms of its field visits, surveys, and work with the CCCC OWI Committee Expert/Stakeholder Panel was in its consideration of student learning experiences. The discipline needs to step back and understand what works for students and then consider how to marry that with overall pedagogical approaches—particularly given students' accessibility needs. Depending on local institutional constraints, that marriage may look different within and across various contexts.

With these points in mind, there is a strong need for open-ended research into overarching areas of interest surrounding OWI as it occurs in naturalistic settings across institutions and student and teacher cohorts. To be sure, close-ended, tightly controlled experimental studies that, for example, test pre-determined theories or hypotheses about such issues as how students learn in this environment can serve an important role and can address various research questions about quantitative benefits and measurable outcomes (Ehmann, 2003). These we recommend as well. From a pedagogically driven perspective and in light of the *current* landscape of OWI knowledge, however, we believe strongly that more interpretive open-ended research should be a leading priority in any study of OWI. Given existing questions about participant experiences and OWI processes, therefore, a primary need is to explore the phenomenon of OWI—with individual cases across various institutions and learning contexts being viewed as opportunities to investigate overall trends and patterns that can lead to a deeper understanding of OWI as a phenomenon in and of itself. Based on previous exploratory research, compelling areas for empirical, theory-generating research are related to literacy and cognition, processes, participant perceptions and experiences, and outcomes. Because much of OWI is text-based, scholars are well positioned to delve into archives of teacher and learner work to explore short-term/one-off moments as well as longitudinal evidence of learning. In addition to deepening our understanding of the literacy and cognition challenges of OWI and pedagogical inner-workings and processes of OWI, it is essential that student outcomes also are assessed. Outcomes include student grades and other performance measures, course retention, and persistence. Although the analysis of such outcomes in relation to student achievement and learning has its pitfalls, it is undeniable that such information is useful as a baseline for both faculty and administrators who require such data as a means of quantitative efficacy.

This background strongly suggests that program and course design should be developed to allow such information to be captured and analyzed. Within an interpretative framework, both qualitative and quantitative methodological designs can be employed to address key questions surrounding OWI and OWL outcomes, processes, and participant perspectives. These areas will be discussed in the next sections of this chapter with particular focus on how they relate to planning for a postsecondary program that includes OWI and designing an OWI course; however, readers may adapt these discussions particularly to OWLs where the focus seems relevant.

PERSPECTIVES FOR OWI RESEARCH

As indicated in the previous section, the urgent call for OWI educators in assessing their current courses/programs and in contemplating the outlook of future development is, minimally, fourfold:

- Establishing opportunities within courses to investigate the phenomenon of OWI through an interpretive, process-oriented research framework;
- Using the analytic data available through LMSs to study students' assistive technology use and learning patterns;
- Establishing opportunities to collect and study a baseline of performance-related student outcomes that can be analyzed by internal and external third parties; and
- Establishing opportunities to collect and study instructional strategies pertinent to both composition and the OWI-environment that also can be analyzed internally and externally for quality measures.

This need for research is highlighted in OWI Principle 15 of *A Position Statement of Principles and Example Effective Practices for OWI* (p. 31). Specifically, the CCCC OWI Committee's statement reported on a common theme from leaders in the field about the need for professional development in the area of OWI and OWLs. The CCCC OWI Committee expressed a pressing need to "educate the writing community on OWI and OWLs and to help direct the teaching and learning of our students with what is known about state of the art and effective practices" (p. 31). Moreover, the statement called for developments in OWI and OWLs to be rooted in "valid and reliable research findings and systematic information dissemination" (p. 31). In other words, of paramount importance is the knowledge sharing that occurs pre-, mid-, and post-research.

As in other contexts, the challenge for undertaking the type of aforementioned research resides in the time and funding resources for accomplishing such work. For an obvious example, student writing appropriately is one measure of any writing program's efficacy. Studying that writing, however, is time and labor intensive. With that in mind, some computer programs or automated writing evaluation (AWE, a term that appears to have been coined by Warschauer and Paige [2006]) tools potentially may be used for research purposes to determine writing differences by, for example, indicating linguistic changes across drafts and revisions—provided the AWE tool is adequately trained and normed to specific prompts informed by human-directed parameters of strong and weak writing. At this time, such AWE programs typically cannot accurately synthesize *within individual contexts* (i.e., for individual students and their unique essay writing) whether and how those changes represent an individual's specific rhetorical strengths and weaknesses, content accuracy and depth, and overall writing maturity (NCTE Position Statement on Machine Scoring, 2013; Perelman, 2013). Indeed, this work requires trained human instructors and readers. Given the need to balance the requirements of human expertise with the time and resources necessary for research into OWI, it is worth considering how markers of writing change may be quantitatively assessed via AWE technology *in conjunction with* human efforts related to the qualitative understanding, teaching, and assessment of writing.

To be sure, there is much controversy surrounding the use of AWE for placement, assessment, and instruction—let alone as a potential analysis tool to aid research of OWI. Earlier critiques of AWE have (1) typically focused on scoring rather than integration of AWE into the writing classroom and (2) relied more on composition theory than on empirical classroom studies of AWE's impact on student learning (Ericsson & Haswell, 2006; Grimes & Warshauer, 2006; Shermis, Burstein, & Bliss, 2004). More recent studies have investigated the impact of AWE on student scores on standardized tests, teachers' impressions of AWE, student impressions of AWE, impact on student writing, and student behavior as they use AWE applications (Chen & Cheng, 2008; Cotos, 2011; Grimes & Warshauer, 2010; Holman, 2011; Perelman, 2013; Schroder, Grohe, & Pogue, 2008; Shermis & Burstein, 2013; Shermis & Hammer, 2013). The point we wish to make here is that whether or not AWE is positioned as an optimal *instructional or evaluative* tool for complex and unique writing challenges and development issues that individual learners face, it may be leveraged for *research into OWI* if done with its strengths and limitations in mind. These items certainly warrant further consideration.

The human labor involved in OWI research requires training, developed experience, allotted time, and funding, all of which have been an impediment to OWI and other writing researchers who typically are not expected, encouraged, or educated to seek grants for such research. Indeed, writing studies scholars— whether focused on onsite or OWI—often are not prepared for such research generally. And, when it is developed, venues for publishing it can be scarce.

In 2005, Richard Haswell's "NCTE/CCCC's Recent War on Scholarship" cogently argued for RAD research in composition studies. His argument for empirical research in the field serves as a counterpoint to Stephen M. North's (1987) popular and helpful *The Making of Knowledge in Composition: Portrait of an Emerging Field*—in that the field no longer is emerging and that assumptions drawn from research ought to be validated and, to some degree, comparable across studies. Janice M. Lauer and J. William Asher's (1988) *Composition Research: Empirical Designs* provided solid advice toward RAD research, but Haswell (2005) speculated that because the key NCTE/CCCC journals for the writing studies field (e.g., *College English* and *College Composition and Communication*) failed to publish sufficient RAD research, it discouraged publishing scholars from conducting it. To the field's benefit, some scholars have taken up Haswell's call to action with powerful critiques of current non-RAD research and practices based on it; Rebecca Day Babcock and Terese Thonus' (2012) *Researching the Writing Center: Toward an Evidence-based Practice* comprises one such critique. In support of OWI, a few scholars have taken up such research (Hewett, 2000, 2004-2005, 2006; Jones, Georghiades, & Gunson, 2012; Wolfe & Griffin, 2013), which has helped to ground practice-based OWI development. Nonetheless, few researchers actually have replicated previous studies—using prior research methods, taxonomies, or other analytical tools—allowing the research to become part of a growing body of knowledge where comparisons might be made. Hewett (1998, 2000), where previously used methods and taxonomies were adapted to a new setting (2003-2005, 2006), provided one example of an attempt at RAD research based on earlier used talk and revision taxonomies (Faigley & Witte, 1981; Gere & Abbott, 1985, Gere & Stevens, 1985).

RAD research into OWI presents considerable challenges that we are not dismissing in this chapter. However, given these challenges, a strong case can be made to apply an action research approach to the overall study of OWI—such that educators can leverage their own practices as scholarly investigation. Grounded in an action research approach that is designed to ask educators to investigate, reflect, and report on their own practices, the CCCC OWI Committee's explication of this research-focused principle encouraged practitioners to research their own courses, students, and programs (also see Hewett, 2010, 2015b; Hewett & Ehmann, 2004). As co-creators and/or participant observers, OWI and OWL administrators and teachers/tutors alike are situated ideally to commit to continuous research of their courses, students, and programs—with the overall intention of building and strengthening the theoretical and pedagogical frameworks for OWI and OWLs. Pepperdine University's Center for Collaborative Action Research advocated a similar version of action research.

They explained that action research:

> is the systematic, reflective study of one's actions, and the
> effects of these actions, in a workplace context. As such, it in-
> volves deep inquiry into one's professional practice.... . Action
> research is a way of learning from and through one's practice
> by working through a series of reflective stages that facilitate
> the development of a form of "adaptive" expertise. Over time,
> action researchers develop a deep understanding of the ways
> in which a variety of social and environmental forces interact
> to create complex patterns. Since these forces are dynamic,
> action research is a process of living one's theory into practice.
> (Reil, 2010)

As emphasized in OWI Principle 15 of *A Position Statement of Principles and Example Effective Practices for OWI*, "Empirical, repeatable, and longitudinal research that addresses questions regarding the phenomena of OWI and OWLs will drive a deeper understanding of OWI and OWLs, ultimately benefiting students and the teaching and learning of writing in online contexts" (p. 31). Similarly, follow-up reporting and information dissemination are important phases in the strategy of "progressive inquiry" (Reil, 2010) for action research. The intention is for research findings to be critiqued and validated by peers as well as the scholarly community and administrators in composition studies. As the CCCC OWI Committee's *A Position Statement of Principles and Example Effective Practices for OWI* advocated under OWI Principle 15:

> OWI and OWL administrators and teachers/tutors should en-
> gage actively in the scholarly conversation by sharing research
> findings at regional and national conferences and through
> peer-reviewed journals and other academic publications. OWI
> and OWL administrators and teachers/tutors should share
> research findings with the general public in suitable venues
> to assist with setting appropriate expectations for and under-
> standing of OWI and OWLs. (p. 31)

Perhaps most importantly, such research can be used to inform and ultimately improve one's own practice within a cyclical, phased approach.

As indicated earlier in this chapter, there are numerous main areas that, in light of the current state of knowledge about OWI, can be considered research priorities. For the purposes of this chapter, we categorize these priorities into three overarching areas pertinent to OWI/OWLs: processes and interactions, participant perceptions and experiences, and outcomes. Although a myriad of potential research topics related to these broad areas exist, the point here is to highlight *examples* of research questions and methodological choices that can serve to deepen understanding and knowledge of processes, participant experiences, and outcomes of OWI for both teaching and tutoring practices.

PROCESSES AND INTERACTIONS

Effective Practice 15.1 of the CCCC OWI Committee's *A Position Statement of Principles and Example Effective Practices for OWI* articulated the need to design and deploy empirical investigations surrounding "the processes of asynchronous and/or synchronous OWI or OWL interactions" and "student and teacher/tutor behaviors, actions, and relationships within the context of the actual exchanges" (p. 31). Processes and interactions in an OWI context can be taken to mean one-to-one and group interactions that occur among teachers/tutors and learners.

Within these areas, there are multiple subsets of OWI that warrant investigation including asynchronous and synchronous modalities, fully online and hybrid contexts, effects of medium on learning, feedback and response strategies using different technologies, and overall approaches to online learning where writing is the focus. Common examples include fully online or hybrid classroom exchanges among individuals, one-to-one exchanges in an online tutorial or conference setting, online conversations that occur in peer revision groups, and email exchanges. Moreover, these interactions occur in asynchronous and synchronous modalities such as delayed, multi-textual, correspondence exchanges; one-way or two-way audio and audio/video messages; and voice and/or text chat-based messaging. Above and beyond the specific context, the primary point here is that the focus on processes and interaction relies on studying the nature of the human-to-human interactions and exchanges among participants in digital, educational settings—all of which, in most settings, can be captured and accessed with consent via online archiving and records. Following an interpretive strategic methodological approach, open-ended research questions about processes can address broader, descriptive notions about the OWI phenomenon (Ehmann, 2003, 2012). Such questions include but are not limited to the following areas:

- What happens in fully online OWI courses, online conferences (course-based and/or tutorial), and associated text-based exchanges?
- Similarly, what happens in hybrid courses and conferences?
- What is the overall structure and format of these online teaching and learning environments—in both fully online and hybrid contexts?
  - What is the length of engagement for a class?
  - What is the frequency, length, and nature of one-to-one conferences,

group interaction, and any peer interaction?
- What is the substantive focus of participant exchanges in these contexts?
- What topics do teachers/tutors initiate and how do students respond?
- What topics do students initiate and how do teachers/tutors respond?
- How do participants "talk" in text about the topics they initiate?
- What pedagogical strategies do instructors employ in their teaching of writing?
- What strategies do students employ in their learning of writing?
- How do these strategies compare with those of students with learning disabilities?
- What strategies can develop to suit these students' learning needs?
- What indications or evidence of understanding and progress do participants demonstrate in their participation, written work, and revision?

The kinds of data required to address these types of process/interaction-focused questions point to artifacts that are inherent to OWI. Specifically, *A Position Statement of Principles and Example Effective Practices for OWI* reported that the OWI and OWL environments are "particularly well positioned as sites of on-going research in that almost all interactions are saved and archived ... enabling empirical analysis" (p. 31) Indeed, the inherent characteristics and qualities of OWI and OWLs can be leveraged in meeting this call and commitment for on-going research. Key records of interaction among teachers/tutors and learners can involve such texts as email, various modes of online platform communication, online group discussion, and a portfolio of longitudinal writing drafts and revisions. These records can serve as artifacts available for investigating the deep pedagogical processes of OWI in meaningful ways.

When considering meaningful analysis methods for the interaction data collected, an approach that remains true to the open-ended intent of the research is paramount. With the intention of exploring what individuals actually are doing rather than what existing sentiment says they *should* or *could* do, analysis methods need to support the desire to produce findings that accurately reflect participant practices and to build on previous research where applicable and appropriate (Ehmann, 2003). Options for analyzing interactions can involve fine-grained scrutiny of participant talk such as linguistic or discourse analysis of participant talk which entails the detailed and systematic investigation of functional structures and hierarchies potentially related to student revision (see, for example, Hewett, 2006, 2003-2005, 2000, 1998).

Broader brush-stroke approaches include the identification of thematic activity, behaviors, or writing development within or potentially connected to such learning exchanges. Regardless of the level of granularity, however, a unit of analysis within an interaction must be identified and justified for the investigation's purposes—whether the unit is a conversation move, an episode, or some other discreet chunk within social and instructional exchanges. Depending on the research objectives, both quantitative and qualitative methods can be used in the analysis of largely qualitative talk or text-based data—for example, using numeric analysis to describe the actions that individuals take in teaching and learning exchanges. Units of analysis can be counted and presented; such an approach may lend external credibility to findings depending on the audience. Based on actual conferencing interactions, Hewett's (2004-2005, 2006) research is among the most relevant empirical scholarship regarding OWI interactions to date. In her work, Hewett found that students' revised writing demonstrated linguistic connections to the online conferences in which they participated; where the connections did not exist, however, the students' open-ended survey responses provided interesting evidence toward her theory that instructors' semantic integrity is crucial in a text-based setting (Hewett, 2010, 2015a, 2015b). Some of these findings have been replicated in recent research into uses of metaphor in online tutoring (Thonus & Hewett, 2015). Moving forward, new empirical studies might build upon this work, which can ground adaptations and changes in instructional approaches for both asynchronous and synchronous settings.

STAKEHOLDER PERCEPTIONS AND EXPERIENCES

The importance of deepening our understanding of OWI/OWL interactions and learning exchanges is clear. An additional area that requires investigation is that of participant perceptions and experiences. The CCCC OWI Committee's example Effective Practice 15.1 called attention to this point, suggesting that "Studies might examine participant perceptions of OWI or OWLs (e.g., benefits, challenges, experiences) via interviews with students, teachers/tutors, and administrators" (p. 31).

Students are primary stakeholders in the OWI endeavor. As such, their first-hand experiences warrant exploration in addition to their reasons for engaging in OWI and their views about its purpose and value in the postsecondary context. A priority of this approach is to seek descriptive responses that are rooted in respondents' actual experiences rather than evaluative responses about what OWI should or should not be. Both Nancy Sommers (2006) and Jane Mathison Fife and Peggy O'Neil (2001) have indicated how important it is to understand how students believe they have benefitted from feedback and essay response, for example. The student experience helps to triangulate what researchers see in the many texts that OWI makes archivally available.

Similarly, with teachers/tutors, a priority is to explore descriptive accounts of OWI experiences as well as observations about OWI beyond the scope of single instances or courses. It is crucial to understand notions about the purpose and value of what they are doing as teachers/tutors within the OWI context as well as why and how are they doing it.

A third OWI stakeholder includes administrators and non-faculty decision-makers about OWI programs. Exploring their views of OWI also is important, with the primary objectives being to discern their perceptions about the purpose and value of OWI and how OWI fits into other ways of teaching and learning writing at the institution.

With attention to these stakeholders and their needs in mind, the following types of research questions can be formulated:

- Why do stakeholders engage in and with OWI/OWLs?
- What are the perceived purposes of OWI/OWLs—from all participant perspectives?
- What approaches to practice do participants see themselves taking?
  - What pedagogical strategies do they view as most effective?
  - What pedagogical strategies do they view as least effective?
  - What evidence do they look for in terms of efficacy and student learning?
- What is the perceived value of OWI/OWLs for students, faculty, and administrators?
- What are the perceived benefits for students, faculty, and administrators?
- What are the perceived challenges for students, faculty, and administrators?
- What approaches to practice do stakeholders see themselves taking?
- What approaches to learning do students see themselves taking?
- What training and professional development opportunities do instructors and administrators view as most helpful, least helpful, and most necessary?
  - What delivery mechanisms are best for such training and professional development?
  - How can training and professional development best be evaluated for potential efficacy?
- What orientation and support services do students, in particular, view as most helpful, least helpful, and most necessary?

Furthermore, regarding students as stakeholders, it is paramount to understand which populations of learners are served better online than others. While ADA law is clear, institutions may not have equipped themselves to support students online who have learning disabilities and/or physical challenges. While their needs may be connected more to ethical rather than legal exigency, students with multilingual issues, limited socioeconomic resources, or who are ill-prepared for college also have access and inclusivity needs. Institutional responsibility includes preparing teachers/tutors for developing their online instruction inclusively. In its early days, online learning was lauded as a new way to help those students who could not get to campus for whatever reason. Ironically, however, the CCCC OWI Committee's research strongly suggested that writing studies educators really do not know how to support those who are, perhaps, most in need of the access-based opportunities that OWI can afford—such as the blind, the dyslexic, and auditory learners, for example. There is little anecdotal literature and even less research on the matter, making it a crucial area for future research.

From the instructor perspective, we must determine the strategies, skills, and understandings needed in orientation, training, and on-going professional development—for new teachers as well as veteran onsite teachers entering into the online environment, perhaps for the first time. As is commonly documented in the OWI literature (Hewett & Ehmann, 2004; McGrath, 2012), many have seen firsthand that the best face-to-face teachers and subject matter experts do not always make the best online teachers—this reality crosses international as well as subject-area boundaries. The instructional skills needed in the OWI environment do not transfer directly or straightforwardly from physical contexts, and online instructors need training as well as ongoing professional development to orient them to the most effective strategies for teaching writing in online settings. In addition to comfort and fluency with the online technologies, instructors need to be strong teachers and tutors of writing. Attracting, training, and retaining good teachers to use technology as well as implementing and advancing online writing-specific pedagogies *together* provide the cornerstone for any online writing program's success. How to accomplish this twofold goal definitely warrants further study and can be explored via collecting participant perceptions.

The kinds of data required to access and to investigate individuals' views and perspectives about OWI can be collected effectively via interviews and surveys (both open- and closed-ended). As an interpretive starting point, semi-structured, open-ended interviews can focus on issues deemed important to an OWI/OWL study and provide an opportunity to understand how respondents make sense of those issues as well as other topics they believe are important within the OWI context. Such perspectives can be captured with individual students in pre-course surveys, mid-course feedback sessions, and exit-interviews after the course. They also can be captured in student and professor course evaluations. In the analytical process, it is possible to explore themes surrounding, for example, approaches to OWI practice, attitudes towards OWI and students in the online environment, and perceived benefits and challenges of OWI. Employing appropriate sampling techniques and using findings from and empirical analysis conducted on interview data can then inform closed-ended surveys and questionnaires that ultimately can be administered on a larger scale. Based on initial open-ended interviews with identified OWI leaders in the field, the CCCC OWI Committee administered two larger scale surveys regarding hybrid and fully online OWI environments (CCCC OWI Committee, 2011a, 2011b), as described in the Introduction to this book. *The State of the Art of OWI* (CCCC OWI Committee, 2011c) report indicated important contextual background and trends for the OWI landscape including:

- the lack of a common pedagogical framework grounded in theory and practice specifically related to OWI,
- the urgent need for training and professional development of educators and supplemental support (such as online writing centers) involved in OWI,
- the lack of knowledge about ELL students and those with disabilities in the OWI environment, and,
- the challenges associated with instructors' professional satisfaction with OWI in terms of adequate institutional support for training and technology needs.

From the report, it is clear that more work in the aforementioned areas is warranted.

OUTCOMES

Quantitative studies that investigate student performance in terms of learning outcomes or benchmarks, grades, and course retention should be designed and deployed for OWI and OWL settings. From an administrative perspective, return on investment studies also can be deployed to help understand the financial impact—and potential benefits and challenges—of OWI or of an OWL to institutions. Where possible, longitudinal research should be designed and institutionally funded to understand the differing complexities of learning to read and write in digital, online, and distributed online educational settings. Retention is one of the greatest challenges for institutions and students; this certainly is true in the United States, and other countries face the same challenge (Boston, Ice, & Gibson, 2011). With that challenge in mind, experts must pursue targeted, strategic research, and administrators must implement newfound effective practices surrounding the support of online writing students in terms of the expectations and modes of interaction those students encounter in online learning environments. The following types of questions can be formulated to address student and institutional outcomes:

- What are demographics of the students who participate in OWI/OWLs?
- What are demographics of the instructors who participate in OWI/OWLs?
- What quantifiable measures of student engagement can be tracked and reported on—such as attendance, assignment completion, participation levels, and student-to-student and/or instructor-to-student contacts?
- What are student grades in these settings?
- What are OWI course pass rates?
- What are OWI course completion rates?
- What are the OWI course retention and persistence rates?
- What are the overall institutional retention rates and how are they affected by the OWI courses and/or OWL presence?
- What other standardized and/or high stakes competency or skills testing gains do OWI students achieve?
- What is the fiscal and/or human investment for OWI to a department and/or institution and what is the return on this investment?

The kind of data required to address the aforementioned research questions involves student demographic information that is typically collected in standard institutional database systems. The questions also require course-level information typically collected in an LMS. Data analytics regarding student usage, activity, and other such behavior also can be used to triangulate and provide a fuller picture of outcomes in the OWI environment.

With an eye toward understanding these key areas of interactions, experiences, and outcomes, practitioners and administrators alike would do well to design courses with these factors in mind. When designing research, using data that already may have been collected by the institution for any given course (e.g., student demographic information or performance) can help to achieve optimal efficiency for research. Finally, there must be a commitment on behalf of the institution to allow practitioners the crucial time to organize, analyze, reflect, present, refine, and disseminate their research and findings. This commitment to time and timing is an important element in course design that must be negotiated in the design process. Additionally, such a commitment to practitioner time for research reflects attention to the needs for appropriate compensation for OWI development work, as suggested by OWI Principle 8.

RECOMMENDATIONS

This section of the chapter summarizes key points and recommendations for designing an appropriate research strategy for OWI, which includes the uses of OWLs. Table 17.1 provides a sample research memo that can be adapted to gain institutional, administrator, and faculty support and resources for the endeavor. It may be used as well to encourage buy-in for a course/OWL design that can accommodate on-going research.

Table 17.2 (Ehmann, 2013) further summarizes research strategy options and illustrates: key relationships between dependent and explanatory variables, an array of possible data collection methods with corresponding analysis techniques for quantitative and qualitative data, and final reporting and action steps. It succinctly encapsulates research options, and it can be used as a starting point for discussion with various audiences.

The ultimate credibility of any research will rely on the goals, justifications, articulated limitations, and overall transparency of the projects. Addressing the following areas can serve to provide such credibility in the dissemination of research findings:

- A plan for researching OWI
- Research questions
- Overall research strategy
- Choice of research instruments
- Role of researcher
- Ethical considerations
- Selecting the sample
- Conduct of and lessons learned during piloting
- Data collection
- Conduct of the interviews and/or surveys, if used
- Analysis of the interactions
- Analysis of the interview data
- Findings
- Conclusions
- Recommendations for additional research

CONCLUSION

Rhetoric and composition educators understand the need for OWI research and evidence that supports OWI teaching and learning strategies. As indicated, there are many areas open for research where scholars and practitioners can contribute to the knowledge of this field. Among such areas are:

- Outcomes on quantitatively measurable OWI student gains (e.g., grades, course retention, and sequence persistence) to justify overall course success to, for example, administrators and institutional leadership for funding purpose, and

Table 17.1: Example research proposal memo for OWI

Introduction
With the pervasiveness of Internet-based education (and paucity of data and analysis), questions abound surrounding teaching and learning in online writing instructional contexts, instructor preparation, student gains, and the administration and delivery of online programs. This memo outlines potential research options for the exploration of online writing processes and the relationships between student participation in online writing and student performance in academic courses. It encourages the investigation of student usage data and OWI session archives generated via the course platform.
Institutional Background
[Insert key contextual information about the institution]
Research Concept
While many factors, such as faculty effort or student demographics, can have an impact on grades, course pass rates, and retention, online writing instructional courses are an important margin in schools' administrative decisions and budgets. Understanding the potential links between OWI services and various measures of student satisfaction and student academic success is an important step in designing OWI programs that improve overall institutional performance. To reach a better understanding of this intersection, research into OWI is well suited to focus on high-risk attrition courses such as math, chemistry, and writing. Findings from such a study could facilitate an institution's assessment of OWI as it relates to student experience and learning, retention, and ultimately return on investment.
Methods
Depending on specific research questions, the project can be designed in various ways that can lead to a largely instructor-driven initiative. Potential data sets, a summary of potential options for research design and methods, and timeline guidelines are outlined in Chart A below.
Data Sets
Outcomes: Institution X's system tracks student course performance, usage, activity, and grades. These data provides contextual information about how and when students use the service. Overall student performance (grades, retention etc.), demographic information, and other needed data would be required from the institution. Student perspectives: Students' perspectives of their experience engaging in OWI qualify the extent to which and ways in which they view this type of online instruction as beneficial to their learning and potentially to other aspects of their education. Course evaluations, interviews and online surveys could provide cost-effective means of collecting such perspectives. Faculty perspectives: Via interviews and online surveys, faculty could provide feedback on the effect of OWI on student learning and participation as well as how OWI has an impact on their teaching and pedagogical approaches and understandings. Similarly, administrators could provide feedback on the level of understanding and impact of OWI on overall departmental and institutional advances. Interactions: Via archives of student work, peer collaboration/communication/engagement, and faculty-student interaction, the processes and procedures of OWI can be studied. A detailed analysis of such interactional data can yield deep insights into the pedagogical strategies and approaches that are most beneficial to students and can assist with training and professional of faculty members.

Table 17.2: OWI in fully-online and hybrid contexts (Ehmann, 2013)

Dependent variables	Explanatory variables	Data collection methods	Analysis techniques	Reporting & action steps
• Student grades • Course pass & completion rates • Institution retention and persistence rates • Measures of student and faculty satisfaction (for example, faculty or course evaluations)	Student work and usage patterns; writing, communication, participation and other interactional indicators, tutorial frequency and duration Student, faculty, administrator perspectives Teaching and learning processes	Data analytics via reporting tools (available as a part of most course management systems) In-depth, semi-structured-ended interviews, online surveys, pre-, mid-, and post- course evaluations or course exit interviews Teacher / tutor / learner interactions captured in asynchronous and synchronous modalities	**Quantitative analysis** • Descriptive statistics • Correlation/ co-variation between different quantitative or qualitative measures of student success • Probabilistic models (i.e. logit or probit) that link various binary outcomes (pass/fall or retention) to explanatory variables (unit of analysis: student) **Qualitative analysis** • Discourse analysis; content analysis; or rhetorical analysis of human-to-human interactions to explore patterns of pedagogy, behavior and learning activity. • Comparing outputs of student work • Tracking types of student participation on tutorial sessions • Correlating types of student participation to student work.	• Written reports & publications • Conferences • Other peer reviewed scholarship • Social media activity • Web logs, blogging, other • User group meetings

- The more qualitatively, interpretative, theory-generating work needed to understand the success and value of various strategies, techniques, and pedagogies associated with OWI.

A significant challenge exists in meeting both ends of this research spectrum. This chapter has outlined strategic investigative approaches and methodologies that can address quantitatively as well as qualitatively focused questions within an action research paradigm. When planning for a postsecondary program that includes OWI and designing an OWI course or that involves the intricacies of tutoring in an OWL, these recommendations can incorporate and ultimately be used to strengthen and fortify the teaching of writing and student learning in online and onsite settings alike.

REFERENCES

Aslanian, Carol B. & Clinefelter, David L. (2012). *Online college students 2012: Comprehensive data on demands and preferences.* Retrieved from http://www.learninghouse.com/files/documents/resources/Online%20College%20Students%202012.pdf

Boston, Wallace E., Ice, Phil, & Gibson, Angela (2011). Comprehensive assessment of student retention in online learning environments. *Online Journal of Distance Learning Administration, 4*(1). Retrieved from http://www.westga.edu/~distance/ojdla/spring141/boston_ice_gibson141.pdf

Boyd, Patricia Webb. (2008). Analyzing students' perceptions of their learning in online and hybrid first-year composition courses. *Computers and Composition, 25,* 224-243.

CCCC OWI Committee for Effective Practices in Online Writing Instruction. (2008). *Annotated bibliography on online writing instruction 1980-2008.* Committee for Best Practices on Online Writing Instruction (Keith Gibson & Beth L. Hewett, Eds.). Retrieved from http://www.ncte.org/library/NCTEFiles/Groups/CCCC/Committees/OWIAnnotatedBib.pdf

CCCC OWI Committee for Effective Practices in Online Writing Instruction. (2011a). *Fully online distance-based courses survey results.* Retrieved from http://s.zoomerang.com/sr.aspx?sm=EAupi15gkwWur6G7egRSXUw8k-pNMu1f5gjUp01aogtY%3d

CCCC OWI Committee for Effective Practices in Online Writing Instruction. (2011b). *Hybrid/blended course survey results.* Retrieved from http://s.zoomerang.com/sr.aspx?sm=%2fPsFeeRDwfznalyyz4sV0qxkkh5Ry7O1NdnGH-CxIBD4%3d

CCCC Committee for Effective Practices in Online Writing Instruction. (2011c). *The state of the art of OWI.* Retrieved from http://www.ncte.org/library/NCTEFiles/Groups/CCCC/Committees/OWI_State-of-Art_Report_April_2011.pdf

CCCC OWI Committee for Effective Practices in Online Writing Instruction. (2013). *A position statement of principles and effective practices for online writing instruction (OWI).* Retrieved from http://www.ncte.org/cccc/resources/

positions/owiprinciples

Chen, Chi-Fen Emily & Cheng, Wei-Yuan Eugene. (2008). Beyond the design of automated writing evaluation: Pedagogical practices and perceived learning effectiveness in EFL writing classes. *Language Learning & Technology 12*(2), 94-112.

Cormier, Dave. (2010). *What is a MOOC?* Retrieved from https://www.youtube.com/watch?v=eW3gMGqcZQc

Cotos, Elena. (2011). Potential of automated writing evaluation feedback. *CALICO Journal, 28*(2), 420-459.

CourseSmart & Wakefield Research. (2012). *CourseSmart survey.* Retrieved from http://www.coursesmart.com/media#pr10

DePew, Kevin Eric & Lettner-Rust, Heather. (2009). Mediating power: Distance learning interfaces, classroom epistemology, and the gaze. *Computers and Composition, 26,* 174–189.

Ehmann, Christa. (2003). *A study of peer tutoring in higher education* (Doctoral thesis, The University of Oxford, Oxford, UK).

Ehmann, Christa. (2010). A study of online writing instructor perceptions. In Beth L. Hewett (Ed.), *The online writing conference: A guide for teachers and tutors* (pp. 163-171). Portsmouth, NH: Heinemann.

Ehmann, Christa (2012, December). Online teaching and learning: Past, present, and future. Conference on e-Learning & e-Libraries Wellington College, UK.

Ehmann, Christa (2013). OWI in fully-online & hybrid contexts [Chart]

Ericsson, Patricia. F. & Haswell, Richard. (Eds.). (2006). *Machine scoring of student essays: Truth and consequences.* Logan, UT: Utah State University Press.

Faigley, Lester & Witte, Stephen. (1981). Analyzing revision. *Computers and Composition, 32*(4), 400-414.

Fife, Jane Mathison & O'Neill, Peggy. (2001). Moving beyond the written comment: Narrowing the gap between response practice and research. *College Composition and Communication, 53*(2), 300-321.

Gere, Ann Ruggles & Abbott, Robert D. (1985). Talking about writing: The language of writing groups. *Research in the Teaching of Writing, 19*(4), 362-381.

Gere, Ann Ruggles & Ralph S. Stevens. (1985). The language of writing groups: How oral response shapes revision. In Sarah Warshaur Freedman (Ed.), *The acquisition of written language: Response and revision* (pp. 85-105). NJ: Ablex.

Gouge, Catherine. (2009). Conversation at a crucial moment: Hybrid courses and the future of writing programs. *College English, 71*(4), 338-362.

Griffin, June & Minter, Deborah. (2013). The rise of the online writing classroom: Reflecting on the material conditions of college composition teaching. *College Composition and Communication, 65*(1), 140-161.

Grimes, Douglas & Warschauer, Mark. (2006, April). *Automated essay scoring in the classroom*. Paper presented at the American Educational Research Association (AERA) Annual Conference, San Francisco, CA.

Grimes, Douglas & Warschauer, Mark. (2010). Utility in a fallible tool: A multi-site case study of automated writing evaluation. *Journal of Technology, Learning, and Assessment, 8*(6). Retrieved from http://ejournals.bc.edu/ojs/index.php/jtla/article/view/1625/1469

Hewett, Beth L. (1998). *The characteristics and effects of oral and computer-mediated peer group talk on the argumentative writing process* (Doctoral dissertation). Retrieved from http://www.defendandpublish.com/Diss_Characteristics.pdf

Hewett, Beth L. (2000). Characteristics of interactive oral and computer-mediated peer group talk and its influence on revision. *Computers & Composition, 17*, 265-288.

Hewett, Beth L. (2001). Generating new theory for online writing instruction. *Kairos: Rhetoric, Technology, and Pedagogy, 6.2*. Retrieved from http://english.ttu.edu/kairos/6.2/index.html

Hewett, Beth L. (2004-2005). Asynchronous online instructional commentary: A study of student revision. *Readerly/Writerly Texts: Essays in Literary, Composition, and Pedagogical Theory (Double Issue), 11 & 12*(1 & 2), 47-67.

Hewett, Beth L. (2006). Synchronous online conference-based instruction: A study of whiteboard interactions and student writing. *Computers and Composition, 23*(1), 4-31.

Hewett, Beth L. (2010). *The online writing conference: A guide for teachers and tutors*. Portsmouth, NH, Boynton/Cook.

Hewett, Beth L. (2013). Fully online and hybrid writing instruction. In Gary Tate, Amy Rupiper Taggart, Kurt Schick, & H. Brooke Hessler (Eds.), *A guide to composition pedagogies* (2nd ed.) (pp. 194-211). New York: Oxford University Press.

Hewett, Beth L. (2015a). *Reading to learn and writing to teach: Literacy strategies for online writing instruction*. Boston: Bedford/St. Martin's Press.

Hewett, Beth L. (2015b). *The online writing conference: A guide for teachers and tutors* (Updated). Boston: Bedford/St. Martin's Press.

Hewett, Beth L. & Ehmann, Christa. (2004). *Preparing educators for online writing instruction*. Urbana, IL, National Council of Teachers of English.

HMHEducation.com (2012). *Results of a year-long algebra pilot in Riverside, California*. Retrieved from http://www.hmheducation.com/fuse/pdf/hmh-fuse-riverside-whitepaper.pdf

Holman, Lester Donnie. (2011). *Automated writing evaluation program's effect on student writing achievement* (Doctoral dissertation). Available from ProQuest Dissertations and Theses database. (913400137)

Johnson, E. Janet & Card, Karen. (2008). The effects of instructor and student immediacy behaviors in writing improvement and course satisfaction in a Web-based undergraduate course. *MountainRise, 04*(2). Retrieved from http://mountainrise.wcu.edu/index.php/MtnRise/article/view/81/36

Kessler, Sarah. (2012). *Why the iPad won't transform education just yet.* Retrieved from http://www.cnn.com/2012/01/20/tech/innovation/ipad-wont-trans-form-education/index.html Mashable.com

Koller, Daphne. (2012, June). *What we're learning from online education.* [Talk presented at the TEDGlobal 2012, Edinburgh, Scotland, UK]. Retrieved from http://www.ted.com/talks/daphne_koller_what_we_re_learning_from_online_education.html

Krause, Steven D. & Lowe, Charles (Eds.). (2014). *Invasion of the MOOCs: The perils and promises of massive open online courses.* Anderson, SC: Parlor Press.

Marquis, Justin W. & Rivas, K. (2012, June 26). Eight nations leading the way in online education [Web log post]. Retrieved from http://www.onlineuniversities.com/blog/2012/06/8-nations-leading-way-online-education/

Meloncon, Lisa. (Ed.). (2013). *Rhetorical access-ability: At the intersection of technical communication and disability studies.* Amityville, NY: Baywood Publishing.

McGrath, Laura. (2008). In their own voices: Online writing instructors speak out on issues of preparation, development, & support. *Computers and Composition Online* (Spring). Retrieved from http://www.bgsu.edu/departments/english/cconline/OWIPDS/index.html

NCTE Task Force on Writing Assessment. (2013). *Machine scoring fails the test. NCTE Position Statement on Machine Scoring.* Retrieved from http://www.ncte.org/positions/statements/machine_scoring

Oswal, Sushil K. & Hewett, Beth L. (2013). Accessibility challenges for visually impaired students and their OWI teachers. In Lisa Meloncon (Ed.), *Rhetorical access-ability: At the intersection of technical communication and disability studies* (pp. 135-156). Amityville, NY: Baywood Publishing.

Parker, Kim, Lenhard, Amanda, & Moore, Kathleen. (2011). *The digital revolution and higher education.* Pew Research Center Internet & American Life Project. Retrieved from http://www.pewsocialtrends.org/files/2011/08/online-learning.pdf

Pearson Foundation. (2011). *Survey on students and tablets.* Retrieved from http://www.pearsonfoundation.org/downloads/PF_Tablet_Survey_Summary.pdf

Perelman, Les C. (2013). Critique of Mark D. Shermis & Ben Hammer, "Contrasting state-of-the-art automated scoring of essays: Analysis." *Journal of Writing Assessment, 6.* Retrieved from http://www.journalofwritingassessment.org/article.php?article=69

Radford, Alexandria W. (2011). *Learning at a distance: Undergraduate enrollment in distance education courses and degree programs.* National Center for Education Statistics. Retrieved from: http://nces.ed.gov/pubs2012/2012154.pdf

Reil, Margaret (2010). *Understanding action research.* University of Pepperdine, Center for Collaborative Action Research. Retrieved from http://cadres.pepperdine.edu/ccar/define.html

Sapp, David Alan & Simon, James. (2005). Comparing grades in online and face-to-face writing courses: Interpersonal accountability and institutional commitment. *Computers and Composition, 22*(4), 471-489.

Schroeder, Julie, Grohe, Bonnie, & Pogue, Rene. (2008). The impact of criterion writing evaluation technology on criminal justice student writing skills. *Journal of Criminal Justice Education 19(8), 432–445.*

Shermis, Mark D., Burstein, Jill. C., & Bliss, Larry. (2004, April). *The impact of automated essay scoring on high stakes writing assessments.* Paper presented at the annual meetings of the National Council on Measurement in Education, San Diego, CA.

Shermis, Mark D. & Burstein, Jill C. (Eds.). (2013). *Handbook of automated essay evaluation: Current applications and new directions.* New York: Routledge.

Thonus, Terese & Hewett, Beth L. (2015). Follow this path: Conceptual metaphors in writing center online consultations. Manuscript in preparation.

CHAPTER 18

THE FUTURE OF OWI

Beth L. Hewett
CCCC Committee for Effective Practices in OWI
Defend & Publish, LLC

Scott Warnock
Drexel University

This chapter asks readers to consider future trends in OWI by understanding its contemporary nature. Given the rise of online, computer-mediated technologies such as an LMS for many writing courses, we argue that more and more in the near future writing instruction will be hybrid in nature—if it is not already so. We further suggest that OWI can influence composition writ large for the better in the twenty-first century if we use its principles to set the pace for teacher training, work with and beyond text, rethinkthe student, teach with technology thoughtfully, share resources openly, reframe research and assessment, and always keep access in the forefront.

Keywords: access, alphabetic writing, assessment, collaboration, composition writ large, ethics, "good" OWI, hybrid, literacy, multimedia, reading, House of Lore, MOOC; MOOEE, OWI Online Resource, research, WPA, writing pedagogy;

Throughout this book, the authors have provided detailed explanations of principles that emerged from research about OWI. But as these writers mention repeatedly, the OWI principles also are good *writing instruction* principles in general. Thus, as we look to the future of OWI, we must address the nature of composition instruction itself. How much of what we say about OWI is the same for all composition/writing courses? In our travels to conferences and other institutions and in our many virtual interactions, educators are telling us that the OWI principles can be applied broadly to the motivations and the exigencies for composition writ large.

We believe that OWI *is* composition writ large because OWI enables teaching students to write with, through, and about the next wave of writing technologies. Dennis Baron (1999) explained that writing itself is a technology, and Michael Halloran (1990) detailed some of the tools with which writing became a common technology in the nineteenth century, leading to a rise in the American middle class and a postsecondary focus on writing as well as oral declamation. When writing then superseded the once-primary orality for the citizen rhetor, institutions and teachers sought to teach it both in person *and* at a distance using such tools as US mail correspondence, television broadcasts, and audio/video tapes; now, of course, we continue this trend digitally (Declair, 2012; Hewett, 2013). This cycle of shifting educational technologies will continue. As with writing technologies of times past, those used for OWI also will change—particularly in terms of mobile devices, as detailed in Chapter 16. Indeed, some technologies have returned us, not coincidentally, to orality through audio/video technologies. In fact, OWI Principle 1's access requirements remind us—because both educators and the general public may forget about textual literacy in the face of visual communication—that written transcripts must accompany those more oral and visual productions to ensure inclusive communication. Walter Ong (1982) said, "Writing can never dispense with orality" (p. 8), and we are seeing that orality cannot dispense with writing in OWI.

We believe one major change in OWI will be the gradual—but not necessarily slow—diminishment of distinctive features between a hybrid OWC and one that traditionally has been considered onsite and face-to-face. Such a change will emerge naturally as digital devices infiltrate onsite writing courses—by individual instructor initiative, institutional decree, and a trickle-down cultural effect—and as teachers rely more often on the Internet and an LMS of some kind to distribute content, collect writing, and provide feedback. As evidenced through what many now call *Web-enabled* onsite courses, teachers increasingly will learn to develop their courses with interactions mediated both physically onsite and through Internet technologies (see Chapters 1 & 2), which is a key aspect of hybridity regardless of designated seat time. Although there certainly will remain core differences regarding geographical presence when considering the interactions of face-to-face and fully online meetings, we go one step further in this prediction: In time, many differences among teaching in onsite, hybrid, and fully online classrooms will begin to disappear, creating a fluid transition from one educational environment to the other. For example, almost all composing will be accomplished digitally through keyboard and even voice-recognition technology, so pen and paper will become, if not old fashioned, then simply a different way of approaching the technological problem of composing texts; these digital tools will be invisible technology-wise in the same ways that we do not now differentiate composing by pencil (e.g., wooden, disposable, and refillable mechanical) versus pen (e.g., fountain pen, ballpoint, and rollerball). Many contemporary students are not taught cursive handwriting—or even keyboarding—as they grow up pecking and swiping on hand-held devices (Shapiro & Voisin, 2013). They are interacting—albeit more socially than educationally—via computer technology (Hewett 2015a). Educational computing certainly will become the norm rather than the choice that it now is, and educators and students alike will need to work with it as education all too slowly aligns with the cultural attraction to digital technologies. The culture will then move inexorably ahead of education, as it always seems to do (Jukes, McCain, & Crocket, 2010), leaving educators to keep what is the best of what we now know as OWI and to attend to ever new technological advances requiring pedagogical adaptation.

The future of OWI is not down the road. It is *now*. Even a book that purports to be up-to-date reflects the past more than the future. The publication of this book is like any other book in that it leaves a time gap from its inception to when it is in the hands of readers. However, that future of OWI also is now because digital technologies will not wait on educators to catch up. Digital technology's nature requires continuing change, and the strategies that teachers and tutors can and should use to teach students online must follow, albeit a few steps behind. Indeed, we hope we will see composition studies use OWI to elbow its way to the financial and production tables and participate in necessary conversations about the development of technological innovations. As Christina Haas (1996) once indicated, the changes in technologies inevitably change the landscape and nature of composition itself, which is the primary theme of this final chapter.

Interestingly, perhaps, the kind of broader disciplinary absorption of OWI practices and approaches into what we just generally think of as composition means a re-thinking of our terminology. The term *OWI* may end up being reserved for the *administrative* side of composition and for the logistical and material considerations of teaching via computer and online technologies instead of in an onsite classroom. As Jason Snart demonstrates in Chapter 2, logistics and place still matter in terms of how courses are designed and deployed. But pedagogically, the term *OWI* may mean less and less to us. We will need a new way of thinking about the ubiquity of digital tools, a new term—and we wonder whether maybe that term is simply *composition*. Thus, OWI is and will continue to be about composition—not just composition taught in an online setting but, we argue, composition writ large. In this sense, we smile to think that the CCCC OWI Committee as it currently is named and conceived is moving toward obsolescence given that its specialized online work is becoming that of writing instruction more generally.

"GOOD" OWI

At the end of this book, we find ourselves trying to articulate what we believe comprises "good" OWI. For those who have paid attention to OWI itself as merely a supplemental educational approach for composition writ large, the ongoing, global march of digital technology into all composing processes and educational venues offers the potential to revitalize composition instruction overall—to enable new views of composition, some subtle, some overt. OWI offers all writing educators a new lens for framing our work. To that end, good OWI extends the potential to revisit what we think about composition overall and how we, as a discipline, want to move forward.

Good OWI Means Being a Good Teacher

Good OWI means that one first must be a good teacher. To this end, we strongly believe that OWI Principle 7 rightly grounds OWI teacher preparation. One first should be a good teacher of text-based composition—remember that alphabetic writing is not going away—then a teacher who can teach composition through text as well as image and video, and then a teacher who knows how to do these things using digital technologies. The writing studies field, perhaps through re-designed graduate training, will need to prepare new teachers by painstakingly and methodically addressing all three of those needs.

To expound on these three needs, first, it seems clear that knowledge of writing studies with respect to teaching writing is crucial. There are fundamental concepts without which teachers of writing cannot proceed. Some scholars (Meyer & Land, 2006; Wardle, 2012) have explored writing studies' "threshold concepts," which are crucial to teachers' understanding of what they do as well as helpful for students who strive to make sense of what they are being taught and why. The notion that "conceptions of writing matter, come from somewhere, and various conceptions of writing are more or less accurate and helpful" is important for grounding the teaching of writing in a stable body of knowledge. Such concepts also include "text mediates human activity; people don't write in a vacuum" and "'composing' goes far beyond our usual conceptions of it as related to alphabetic/print-based writing. What counts as composing changes as our world and technologies change" (Wardle, 2012). These concepts underscore the commonality of this field of study, recognize its challenges for pinning down a single theory of writing, and validate its flexible nature.

The second aspect—the ability to convey that knowledge through text, images, and video—is a newer factor, however. In years past, writing primarily has been conveyed through textbook content and oral lecture. In OWI, composing knowledge is conveyed asynchronously through thousands of teacher's words and students' written responses (Warnock, 2009). Hewett (2010, 2015a, 2015b) theorized that some students fail to persist and/or succeed in OWCs because writing is taught through teacher writing and student reading of that writing. Students' basic reading literacy skills particularly need to be strong in OWI because much of their understanding of writing strategies is gained primarily by reading *text-based* instruction. Where their literacy skills are weak—and we think many contemporary students have suboptimal traditional literacy skills—they can become lost in what often is an effort to teach themselves how to write through comprehending and applying to their own writing what they are reading about writing (see, for example, Fleischer, 2010; Hewett, 2015a; Rose, 2012). Where teacher writing skills have not been developed with instructing through text as the goal—and most contemporary teachers have been prepared primarily for oral instruction and the use of others' professional, edited textbooks (see, for example, Britton & Gűlgőz, 1991; Hewett, 2015a)—then teachers strain to make themselves understood (to fully-online students particularly); they may find themselves frustrated with their OWI students. These situations must change with focused teacher preparation for primarily text-based instruction.

The third need for good OWI teachers is that all teachers, not just the select few OWI pioneers, should understand how to use digital technologies effectively and flexibly to reach the wide variety of student learners matriculated into contemporary postsecondary institutions. This means teachers need training and support in an access-friendly LMS through which the teaching of writing is stressed over how to use the technology acontextually, and they need to use their writing studies knowledge to benefit a wider variety of learners than ever before. To foster teacher satisfaction, Effective Practice 12.1 suggests that only teachers who are best suited to OWI should be assigned OWCs. That practice makes sense given that some educators have taught onsite for decades and may find online teaching to be so different or off-putting as to hurt their effectiveness and to damage students' writing course experiences. Consider that even today many teachers have no model of online instruction from a participant view: They have never taken such a course. However, in what might seem like an unfair turn-about, we believe that in the OWI future that is now, all new teachers should be being prepared to teach writing in hybrid and fully online settings. The future of OWI as composition writ large will not be able to accommodate teachers who function well only onsite where technology does not intrude or does so in merely a Web-enhanced manner. When digital technology is part of all writing instruction, as we believe it will be, every writing teacher should be able to function in that milieu.

GOOD OWI MEANS THAT COMPOSITION IS BOTH *ABOUT* AND *BEYOND* TEXT

Good OWI also encourages and enables the field of writing studies to continue the redefinition of what it means by "composition" beyond text and then to use the digital strategies, such as those described in this book and articulated through research with other experienced instructors, to help students learn how to produce both traditionally text-based writing and digitally and multimedia-enhanced products. Rhetoric and composition educators have long thought in terms of alphabetic, text-based writing; while we strongly believe this is a necessary literacy focus that needs continuing attention, as technorhetoricians point out (see Chapter 14, for example), however crucial textual literacy remains, multimodal composition also is important. Undoubtedly, composition is about a broader digitally produced, image- and audio-based type of writing that integrates with text to convey a message, and composition researchers have looked at composition in terms broader than text for some time. For example, Mary Hocks and Michelle Kendrick (2003) said we need to move beyond stark binaries and instead focus on the "complex, interpenetrating relationships between word and images" (p. 5). In the opening chapter of her co-edited anthology, *Writing New Media*, Anne Wysocki (2004) said she need not even argue "that we need to open writing classes to new media" because so many similar arguments had already been made; instead, she stated, "I want to argue that *new media needs to be opened to writing*" (p. 5, emphasis in original). Indeed, because OWI naturally is connected to digital tools, multimodal composing processes may be reinvigorated and strengthened in this learning environment—although significant differences remain when teaching such composing processes *as ways to engage digital technologies* versus *teaching those processes online, at a distance, and through digital technologies*. OWI platforms are almost always digital and thus invite new communication media into the writing process and product because all media forms are arguably more easily accessible, reproducible, and shareable online.

Textual, visual, and oral/aural literacies are, of course, increasingly necessary to communicate in the globally digital world that is home to us and our students. Teaching these literacies means rethinking the types of texts, genres, styles, purposes, and audiences on which a composition course focuses. It means, as well, reconsidering the notion of literacy in the face of text, image, and audio/video media. Is the expository or argumentative researched essay that students have been taught in FYW and supported in upper-level writing courses still the most viable or crucial genre to teach? If so, why? If not, what elements of that genre should be carried into the instruction of new or different genres? These questions represent a miniscule part of the conversation that writing studies educators should address broadly because OWI is not only a tool, style, or strategy for teaching writing. Writing online *is* the essence of composing for the many students and teachers who have grown up with digital tools.

Contemporary students certainly must supplement their traditional reading and writing skills with the additional rhetorical strategies of visual and oral/audio literacy. However, students often are not getting this instruction because many instructors resist learning how to use these technologies, perhaps thinking that teaching how to compose with them is optional, and many administrators directly or tacitly support this perspective. With OWI, instructors minimally will need to learn different technologies and how they support pedagogical goals. This task perhaps is not easy or intuitive, yet as digital tools become inherent components to all writing instruction, we should become more able to incorporate these approaches into what we do. If students are to develop highly critical literacy skills in written, visual, and oral/aural venues, then composition writ large must change. In addressing that need, we believe teachers will become better by teaching with and through digital technology.

Good OWI Means Rethinking Our Students

Suppose that writing teachers really can be better at what we do because we use technology throughout our instruction. If this is the case, how can we help students become better students because they learn to write with and through the same technologies?

The CCCC OWI Committee believes the OWI principles fundamentally hold regardless of modality, media, or digital device, but we recognize that we—we as a committee as well as the writing studies field—will have opportunities to refine teaching practices, and some of these refinements no doubt will be based on our student populations. The question then becomes one of understanding our student populations, perhaps in new ways. Does OWI lead us to the creation of different approaches for thinking about the types of students in our courses?

For certain, educators must continue to improve how we work with underserved populations, as OWI Principle 1 stated. These populations include, but are not limited to, first-in-the-family college students, those who work full time, those who return to college after previous postsecondary failure or attrition, and those who leverage their future through student loans. They include, as Part 3 of this book indicates, students with physical disabilities; both significant and minor learning differences; multilingual backgrounds; socioeconomic disadvantages; and access concerns inherent to remotely rural, urban, incarcerated, and military populations. The committee's overarching drive in including access front-and-center is to help us think more about who is in our courses and work creatively to address them, using a generosity of spirit that accommodates all.

GOOD OWI MEANS TEACHING WITH TECHNOLOGY IN THOUGHTFUL WAYS

As we mentioned, the time may be upon us to move from the dichotomy between onsite and OWI and into the frame that all writing instruction is now taught through/with digital technology and students in all settings share the promises, challenges, and responsibility of writing in the technology-centric twenty-first century. "Computers simply are not going to go away," said Tim Mayers and Kevin Swafford (1998; see also Hewett & Ehmann, 2004), arguing that we need to put them to good use (p. 146). From the perspective of 2015, we argue that digital tools are even more ingrained.

Luddites might rankle at the idea of digital ubiquity, but think about how such technological commonality might advance several educational causes. For example, educational technology is siloed in writing studies. At the CCCC conference, those who teach OWI can choose to submit or attend a panel from the "Information Technology" cluster. At other venues, the conferences of NCTE or MLA, the "computer people" (or people who think about teaching literacy skills through digital technologies) are off to the side. (Think how ridiculous it would be to have a "cluster" about pencil-based writing!). So-called computer people may only be the majority at the Computers and Composition conference. If we begin to think about digital technologies as woven into the writing and communication experiences of all teachers and students and as an essential part of composition writ large, the conversation about OWI will change. OWI suddenly will be less a colorful addition to writing studies' tapestry and more the weft to the warp with every OWI line, shape, and color becoming just as important as traditional onsite writing instruction. Just as OWI Principles 3 and 4 offer a yin and yang position between developing theory and practice for OWI and migrating appropriate onsite theory and pedagogy to online settings, a more integrated sense of OWI into composition will enable teachers to provide ways for students to learn that occur on a continuum of sorts. Teachers and tutors then will have techniques to teach with their best selves and strategies while they also engage innovative digital strategies based *on what they want to do in a class[room]*.

The perspective that *OWI = alphabetic text* remains locked into the mindset of many institutions, and, again, we strongly believe alphabetic writing remains important. But as we mentioned above, the exciting—and access-based—ways that OWI encourages multimodality and other experimental or newer permutations of composing will continue to demand attention as new digital developments appear and writing evolves (or, by ancient standards) returns to composing in varying media. The premise of such work might be, although it does not have to be, technologically deterministic: How do learning technologies shift pedagogy and philosophy? For example, as work by Jeff Sommers (2002) and others (e.g., Warnock, 2008) have shown, using audiovisual commentary to respond to student writing may alter students' interactions with their own writing because the medium may shift how they understand the feedback and apply it to their composing processes; these shifts are beyond the platform and form of commentary yet also related to them. As we continue to explore the ways that OWI inspires us to use multimodality for teaching and learning, we will have to think about how we communicate with and teach our students and how those approaches shift in varying environments—as well as how what we teach as composing and process change. In line with Sommers (2013), how might different means of communicating with students about their writing change those very conversations? How might technologies that link students and provide easy spaces to share and comment on peer texts? What might that mean for teaching? Other fundamental questions arise, such as how does multimodal OWI alter relationships between teachers and students and among students themselves? As Gail Hawisher (1992) pointed out, asynchronous dialogue can be liberating in its reduction or outright elimination of barriers based on identity. How will multimodal OWI change that dynamic in both positive and negative ways? Thoughtful answers to such questions certainly emerge from a well-considered research agenda and sharing of both empirical and experiential studies, as we discuss next.

GOOD OWI MEANS CATALOGING THE *HOUSE OF LORE*

Who has the next killer app to help students access course material? Is that app really wonderful for students or just interesting to technologically sophisticated teachers? How can we create, as part of our fundamental course structures, environments that provide access—and opportunity—for all learners? Will opportunities for us to use big data tools help us not just know our students demographically but also understand their writing profiles in new ways? What can we learn about writing from these tools? What is the best support in terms of online tutoring, library access, and counseling access for online writing students? Why do we think so? What do we need to know? The fields that comprise writing studies could do a lot more to design research that helps us think through how particular applications, technologies, and technology-facilitated approaches affect student populations.

Stephen North's (1987) *House of Lore* is oft cited because it is an enduring and endearing metaphor of composition teaching knowledge—"a rambling, to my mind delightful old manse" (p. 27)—but we have wandered that house for too long without cataloging it. Writing instruction in general needs a better collective memory so we are not all reinventing student interactions, pedagogical strategies, and assignments (Haswell, 2005). Composition itself, if for no other reason than the widely varied number and types of offered writing courses coupled with the quasi-professional status rendered upon so many writing teachers, has a large, specific problem in this way. Writing teachers who meet each other annually at professional meetings may not realize that they are inventing the same innovative teaching practices. To help end this serious problem for OWI, the CCCC OWI Committee has undertaken the major work of developing an OWI Online Resource. We hope that writing educators who teach online will submit their own OWI effective practices for possible publication. This peer-reviewed, open-source, community-themed resource is designed to assist all OWI instructors in sharing, developing, and refining teaching practices that are connected to the OWI principles and effective practices. Of course, in line with the broader point we are making here, this endeavor will evolve into an open, free resource for *all* writing instructors.

GOOD OWI MEANS RE-FRAMING WRITING RESEARCH AND ASSESSMENT

As Chapter 17 indicates, one of the most prominent obstacles in the way of advancing powerful writing education is a dearth of empirical research. Consequently, many people in positions of community, state, federal, and corporate power—people who do not know anything about teaching writing—have been given the opportunity to dictate how teachers generally and writing teachers specifically teach and assess our classes. Again, OWI can help reverse engineer the entire field of writing instruction and influence composition writ large by tapping into the campus and national curiosity that online learning engenders to develop strong, concrete research that demonstrates what students are learning, how they are learning, and, perhaps, what methods are most effective for helping particular student populations learn. Our humanistic work does not require scientific reproducibility, but the lack of concrete markers for success undoubtedly has contributed to the disciplinary respect issues of writing studies.

Viewed from this perspective, this book does not merely provide methods for teaching writing online more effectively but also a map for launching into empirical research not just for OWI, not just for composition writ large, but for teaching in general. As the Introduction asserts, the CCCC OWI Committee made such strides by engaging in data gathering and research that otherwise does not exist regarding real teachers conducting real OWCs. To this end, good OWI certainly requires quality and kairotic writing research.

Writing assessment itself has too long had its own place as an uncatalogued branch of composition's House of Lore and needs to be addressed more straightforwardly and even eagerly. To that end, good OWI requires an understanding of teaching effectiveness through assessment, which should be developed based on OWI principles and effective practices. Both teachers' work and students' learning need such evaluation badly because we know too little about how to effect genuine and lasting change in student writing in online settings. OWI's fundamental connection to technology through AWE opens up many assessment opportunities, as described in Chapter 17. We need to know *what* students are learning in their composing and whether and how their writing looks and changes over time. The digital technologies inherent to OWI capture and archive student writing in connection to teachers' assignments, content, and feedback. And if we open our minds to the possibilities of technology-assisted assessment, we can harness the wealth of available data to describe writing characteristics and qualities, learning empirically the nature of writing in our time.

Why should researchers, WPAs, and OWI teachers be aggressive here? We might view our OWI assessment prospects with AWE as analogous to how composition treated the machine grading of student writing: The field did not act, and now these types of applications have spread like kudzu (Haswell, 2006), yet they do little to help teaching and learning. If we do not design assessment measures that make sense based on writing class and program outcomes—as well as on the characteristics inherent in genuine student writing—without question such measures will be defined for us and implemented upon us. Going forward, OWI teachers need to construct and pilot ways of measuring their courses and student writing growth in terms of change that allow sensible, applicable results. We also need to study and share such assessment measures with students, whose feedback is essential to refining these assessment tools. To this end, we should consider how OWI provides entrée into empirical ways of research; *such research should inform our assessments going forward.*

OWI's inherently technical nature meshes naturally with AWE, corpus analysis, and data mining because digital platforms provide unprecedented ways of helping writing researchers get at tough questions about writing instruction and its effects. In fact, we envision a continuing shift in graduate programs to help those who want to specialize in composition toward hybrid-type research methodologies that involve statistics, social science, ethnography, linguistics, and rhetorical and textual analysis. In their introduction to a special issue of *College English*, "The Digital Humanities and Historiography in Rhetoric and Composition," Jessica Enoch and David Gold (2013) discussed how the invention by digital scholars of "tools to mine and make sense of this archival infinitude," in the context of the digital humanities, "is breeding a new type of scholarship:

digital historiography" (pp. 106-107). There are, in short, new research methods and tools that will be developed as we deal not only with the newness of these texts but also with their sheer volume and our need for ways to access and assess them. (The rest of the issue addresses specifics for how to do just that.) Again, because of the inherent digital nature of the teaching, learning, interactions, and community of OWI, these approaches, we believe, are a natural part of the overall composition endeavor.

While the teaching of writing undoubtedly will change by virtue of OWI, we worry that without the kind of conscious actions discussed in this book that composition itself, in fact, will not change the way it needs to. We worry that digital technologies simply will be used as a mechanism to replicate the troubled structures of traditional, onsite writing instruction: bad pay, no respect, few full-time professional opportunities, and lack of shared development, among others. If that happens, our CCCC OWI Committee is concerned it will have served no one. June Griffin and Deborah Minter (2013) talked about Cynthia Selfe (2009, 1999), to whom we return here: We must pay attention to not allowing OWI to worsen education and social inequities, both larger and within the field writ large. The danger certainly exists (Griffin & Minter, 2013, p. 141). Our hope resides in the fact that the artifacts of writing revealed and presented so beautifully via OWI can help us; the "digital classroom record can be mined for information," and it can help change the material conditions of teaching for the better because the "intellectual work" of the class "might be more easily documented now that online classrooms have the long memory of the digital" (Griffin & Minter, 2013, p. 153). One thing is for certain: We have always been confident that if external audiences and stakeholders could see and understand what we do in composition courses with students, they would be amazed and come to understand the incredible complexity of teaching composing.

GOOD OWI MEANS ETHICAL AND MORAL WRITING INSTRUCTION

It is appropriate for us to end this chapter, and thus the book, where *A Position Statement of Principles and Example Effective Practices for OWI* begins: The fundamental responsibility we have is to make sure that OWCs are inclusive of and accessible to all learners. As education, especially higher education, continues to ask difficult questions about accessibility, OWI educators now find ourselves at the forefront—a place where composition itself also should be. Based on our committee's research, unfortunately the overall field of writing studies is not at the forefront of access issues. As OWI Principle 1 insists and all the chapters of this book support, ethical and moral composition instruction means being thoughtfully inclusive and providing willing, flexible, and generous access at all stages of the writing instructional process and with any tools necessary. To put access first—to be proactive and not retroactive—changes the nature of every administrative and pedagogical decision that follows (see, for example, Part 3 of this book and Oswal & Hewett, 2013). Every question asked of or by a WPA is changed in light of proactive access policies. Every student need should be considered in light of whether inclusivity and access are at issue, and not just for the sake of legality but because such consideration is a reflection of who we are as rhetorician/compositionists and as human beings

The OWI principles in *A Position Statement of Principles and Example Effective Practices for OWI* stress genuinely fair treatment of OWI students and teachers. These OWI principles, if applied, suggest practical approaches to experimental, online, educational venues such as the massification of writing courses involved in MOOCs. We would not, as a committee, try to undermine the extraordinary openness that computers can represent (as described so optimistically by those like Bonk, 2008), but composition never has been and never will be able to be represented by a massive dumping of content. It cannot be leveraged with approaches of massiveness. For example, if 15 to 20 students are the maximum any OWI teacher should have in any one course, as OWI Principle 9 stated, obvious mathematics indicate how many teachers and/or set of tutor-teachers need to be involved if a MOOC counts as a credit-worthy writing course where students receive individual, learned feedback. Principle-generated thinking encourages such creative options as designating the MOOC to be more a writing lab or other supplementary or non-credit bearing educational experience, what Warnock calls a MOOEE in Chapter 4. OWI Principle 13 also calls for online tutoring that matches the OWC's modality and medium, creating a smoother technological transition for students from OWC to OWL assistance. Indeed, applying the OWI principles to online tutoring clarifies that *providing* accessible learning support is more crucial than *how* that support is provided or paid for—enabling administrators a different way into the problem. We treat students ethically and morally when we provide them with appropriate preparation and sufficiently well-prepared teachers and tutors. The OWI principles call for fair and appropriate compensation for teachers' work, class sizes that enable genuine instruction to occur, and professional development that helps teachers fit the teaching modality to themselves rather than the other way around.

Thus, good OWI that is composition writ large means using the intentions of the OWI principles to foreground all of our teaching with access and inclusivity no matter how much doing so might require changing our personal teaching strategies. Accessible OWI means rethinking the very nature of writing by enabling and encouraging students to write with both text *and* voice (e.g., using computer or cell-phone voice recognition software for drafting) to compose their ideas and perhaps even to deliver them. Access-focused OWI means letting go of some habits of thinking about composing and recognizing that being straightforward, using linguistically direct language, and providing students flexibly varied entry points into writing are not cheating but rather teaching them to use the best available means for their composition purposes. It means modeling how to write, re-teaching reading strategies that some never learned well, and thinking differently about collaboration and plagiarism worries (Hewett, 2015a, 2015b, 2010). Such changes can enhance the moral and ethical practices for writing instruction overall.

Good OWI inevitably will—*must*—change the face of composition by its ethical and moral practice. This future that is now offers an invitation we should accept, and we should try not to step back into the mass of colleagues who teach online in rote ways that ignore the complexities of writing and writing through and with digital technologies. Students at all levels of education and with all kinds of backgrounds take writing courses. They all need our attention no matter how challenging their backgrounds make them as writing students.

CONCLUSION

Good OWI should help the field of composition be better. We believe that OWI will—if allowed—change how people in our profession view their work as writing teachers overall and ultimately change how outsiders view us. Good OWI should move composition—the whole structure—forward. As we discussed earlier, our terminology may not be keeping up with the pedagogical approaches of composition now, approaches that draw from and fundamentally use not just the actual tools but also concepts of digitality and virtuality. A challenge going forward for our committee may be to re-frame the term OWI, separating conceptually the logistical offering of courses in different modalities (online, onsite, hybrid/blended) from the composition pedagogies that all use digital tools—no matter whether teachers breathe the same air as their students once a term, once a week, or never. For now, though, we see OWI as merging into a compositional future when digital composition and creation will be inherent.

Many scholars have labored to study the effects of the computer and other digital technology on composition, teaching, and learning. In fact, this book is dedicated in honor of their work and contributions. Without them, there could be no principled study of OWI. Over 25 years ago, Lisa Gerrard (1989) said that we must remember that the computer is an additional tool, not the primary one (p. 107). Perhaps that reality has changed in that the computer has become—if not a *must* in postsecondary institutions (as well as in most places of business)—then at least a transparent part of the cultural and communications landscape: We are one with these devices; they are part of our lives. Those without adequate access to OWI continue to suffer from the resulting digital illiteracies much as those who cannot read or write do (Selfe, 1999, 2009). In fact, all of their literacies necessary to navigating their world suffer by extension. The future of OWI is composition in flux. It is composition in tension where traditional literacies and digital composing strategies must learn to collaborate in the digital production of messages. As technology becomes ubiquitous—even to those who currently are denied adequate access—and as it changes to become increasingly common, OWI necessarily and repeatedly will return to a need for textual, alphabetic literacy.

OWI indeed offers composition writ large the opportunity to supplement traditional reading and writing skills just as it requires higher levels of attention to those same traditional literacy skills. OWI takes the worn-out role of *teacher* we are used to and forces us to rethink it as well as notions of *literacy, student, reading, writing, composition, collaboration,* and *course.* OWI offers us opportunities to reconstruct not only our roles but how we go about teaching—and *treating*—students of all physical abilities, ages, learning styles, languages, and economic backgrounds as humans who want to learn how to use reading, writing, images, and oral/aural means to think.

Using the OWI principles to guide online writing instructional work is what this book has been about; yet, as this chapter suggests, these OWI principles can help to guide composition to a new place. The future of OWI is now. How shall we take it on?

REFERENCES

Baron, Dennis. (1999). From pencils to pixels: The stages of literacy technologies. In Gail E. Hawisher & Cynthia L. Selfe (Eds.), *Passions, pedagogies, and twenty-first century technologies* (15-33). Logan, UT: Utah State University Press.

Bonk, Curtis. (2009). *The world is open.* San Francisco: Jossey-Bass.

Britton, Bruce K. & Gűlgőz, Sami. (1991). Using Kintsch's computational model to improve instructional text: Effects of repairing inference calls on recall and cognitive structures. *Journal of Educational Psychology, 83*(3), 329-345.

CCCC OWI Committee for Effective Practices in Online Writing Instruction. (2013). *A position statement of principles and effective practices for online writing instruction (OWI).* Retrieved from http://www.ncte.org/cccc/resources/positions/owiprinciples

Declair, D. P. (2012). *History.* Retrieved from http://iml.jou.ufl.edu/projects/spring01/declair/history.html

Enoch, Jessica & Gold, David. (2013). Digital humanities and historiography. *College English, 76*(2), 105-114.

Fleischer, Cathy. (2010). *Reading & writing & teens: A parent's guide to adolescent literacy.* Champaign, IL: National Council of Teachers of English.

Gerrard, Lisa. (1989). Computers and basic writers: A critical view. In Gail Hawisher & Cindy Selfe (Eds.), *Critical perspectives on computers and composition instruction* (94-108). New York: Teachers College Press.

Griffin, June & Minter, Deborah. (2013). The rise of the online writing classroom: Reflecting on the material conditions of college composition teaching. *College Composition and Communication, 65*(1), 140-61.

Haas, Christina. (1996). *Writing technology: Studies on the materiality of literacy.* Mahwah, NJ: Erlbaum.

Halloran, S. Michael. (1990). From rhetoric to composition: The teaching of writing in America to 1900. In James J. Murphy (Ed.), *A short history of writing instruction: From ancient Greece to twentieth-century America* (pp. 151-182). Mahwah, NJ: Hermagoras Press.

Haswell, Richard H. (2006). Automatons and automated scoring: Drudges, black boxes, and dei ex machina. In Patricia Freitag Ericsson & Richard Haswell (Eds.), *Machine scoring of student essays: Truth and consequences* (pp. 57-78). Logan, UT: Utah State University Press.

Haswell, Richard. (2005). NCTE/CCCC's recent war on scholarship. *Written Communication, 22*(2), 198-223.

Hawisher, Gail E. (1992). Electronic meetings of the minds: Research, electronic conferences, and composition studies. In Gail E. Hawisher & Paul LeBlanc (Eds.), *Re-imagining computers and composition: Teaching and research in the virtual age* (pp. 81-101). Portsmouth, NH: Boynton.

Hewett, Beth L. (2013). Fully online and hybrid writing instruction. In Gary Tate, Amy Rupiper Taggart, Kurt Schick, & H. Brooke Hessler, (Eds), *A guide to composition pedagogies* (2nd ed.) (pp. 194-211). Oxford, UK: Oxford University Press.

Hewett, Beth L. (2015a). *Reading to learn and writing to teach: Literacy strategies for online writing instruction.* Boston, MA: Bedford/St. Martin's Press.

Hewett, Beth L. (2015b). *The online writing conference: A guide for teachers and tutors* (Updated). Boston, MA: Bedford/St. Martin's Press.

Hocks, Mary E. & Kendrick, Michelle. (2003). Eloquent images. Introduction. In Mary Hocks & Michelle Kendricks (Eds.), *Eloquent images: Word and image in the age of new media* (pp. 1-18). Cambridge, MA: MIT Press.

Jukes, Ian, McCain, Ted, & Crockett, Lee. (2010). *Understanding the digital generation: Teaching and learning in the new digital landscape.* Kelowna, BC, CA: 21st Century Fluency Project.

Mayers, Tim & Swafford, Kevin. (1998). Reading the networks of power: Rethinking "critical thinking" in computerized classrooms. In Todd Taylor & Irene Ward (Eds.), *Literacy theory in the age of the Internet* (pp. 146-157). New York: Columbia University Press.

Meyer, Jan & Land, Ray. (2006). *Overcoming barriers to student understanding: Threshold concepts and troublesome knowledge.* New York: Routledge.

North, Stephen M. (1987). *The Making of knowledge in composition: Portrait of an emerging field.* Portsmouth, NH: Boynton/Cook Heinemann.

Ong, Walter. (1982). *Orality and literacy: The technologizing of the word.* London: Metheun.

Oswal, Sushil K. & Hewett, Beth L. (2013). Accessibility challenges for visually impaired students and their OWI teachers. In Lisa Meloncon (Ed.), *Rhetorical accessibility: At the intersection of technical communication and disability studies* (135-156). New York: Baywood Publishing.

Rose, Mike. (2012). The missing element in student success. *Inside Higher Ed.* Retrieved from http://www.insidehighered.com/advice/2012/09/07/advice-using-classroom-teaching-enhance-student-success-essay

Shapiro, T. Rees & Voisin, Sarah L. (2013, April 4). Cursive handwriting disappearing from public schools. *The Washington Post.* Retrieved from http://www.washingtonpost.com/local/education/cursive-handwriting-disappearing-from-public-schools/2013/04/04/215862e0-7d23-11e2-a044-676856536b40_story.html

Sommers, Jeff. (2002). Spoken response: Space, time, and movies of the mind. In Pat Belanoff, M. Dickson, S. I. Fontaine, & Charles Moran (Eds.), *Writing with Elbow* (pp. 172-186). Logan, UT: Utah State Press.

Sommers, Jeff. (2013). Response 2.0: Commentary on student writing for the new millennium. *Journal of College Literacy and Learning, 39*: 21-37.

Warnock, Scott. (2008). Responding to student writing with audio-visual feedback. In Terry Carter & Maria A. Clayton (Eds.), *Writing and the iGeneration: Composition in the computer-mediated classroom* (pp. 201-227). Southlake, TX: Fountainhead Press.

Warnock, Scott. (2009). *Teaching writing online: How and why.* Urbana, IL: National Council of Teachers of English.

Wysocki, Anne Frances. (2004). Opening new media to writing: Openings and justifications. In Anne Frances Wysocki, Johndan Johnson-Eilola, Cynthia L. Selfe, & Geoffrey Sirc (Eds.), *Writing new media: Theory and applications for expanding the teaching of composition* (pp. 1-42). Logan, UT: Utah State University Press.

AUTHOR BIOGRAPHIES

Kristine Blair is Professor of English at Bowling Green State University, Ohio, where she teaches courses in digital rhetoric and scholarly publication in the Rhetoric and Writing doctoral program. The author of numerous publications on gender and technology, online learning, electronic portfolios, and the politics of technological literacy acquisition, Dr. Blair serves as editor of both *Computers and Composition* and *Computers and Composition Online*. In 2007, she received the national Technology Innovator Award from the CCCC, and in 2010, she received the national Charles Moran Award for Distinguished Contributions to the Field of Computers and Composition. In 2014, she will begin a two-year term as Chair of the CCCC Consortium of Doctoral Programs in Rhetoric and Composition. Dr. Blair is a member of the CCCC OWI Committee Expert/Stakeholder Panel.

Lee-Ann Kastman Breuch is an Associate Professor in the Department of Writing Studies at the University of Minnesota, where she is the Director of Undergraduate Studies. She teaches courses in first-year writing, technical communication, computer and online pedagogy, and usability evaluation of online interfaces. Dr. Breuch enjoys conducting research on writers in action and the texts they produce, whether in the workplace, university, or in writing groups. Her research addresses writing theory and pedagogy in composition, technical communication, writing centers, and writing across the curriculum. Dr. Breuch is a member of the CCCC OWI Committee Expert/Stakeholder Panel.

Kevin Eric DePew is an Associate Professor and the Graduate Program Director of Old Dominion University's English Ph.D. program, which has an online component. He has authored and co-authored works about OWI in *Computers and Composition*, as well as the *Handbook of Research on Computer Mediated Communication* and *Emerging Pedagogies in the Networked Knowledge Society*. Dr. DePew's research about OWI is one component of his larger project of designing better writing instruction. Other works examine how to advocate for social justice through writing instruction, how to raise instructors' awareness of effective strategies for teaching multilingual writers, and how to design writing curriculum that encourages students to transfer what they learn in their writing courses to other contexts. He is a current member of the CCCC's Committee for Effective Practices in Online Writing Instruction.

Christa Ehmann (Senior Vice President & Chief Education Officer of Smarthinking, Inc.–A Pearson Company) is a leader in the development of online tutoring and mentoring in the United States and internationally, having

565

headed the education department of Smarthinking since its founding in 1999. She initially developed the unique protocols and mechanisms for online tutoring, and thereafter implemented the operational systems to manage the growth of Smarthinking, which now tutors hundreds of thousands of students each year. Dr. Ehmann earned her master's and doctorate degrees from Oxford University and has taught and worked worldwide in the field of online tutoring and education. Involved in various non-profit education organizations, Dr. Ehmann sits on the Washington D.C. board of directors of Learning Ally—a nonprofit organization dedicated to giving individuals equal access to learning by making reading accessible for all K-12, high school, college and graduate students, veterans and lifelong learners with blindness, visual impairment, dyslexia or other learning disabilities through digital recordings and assistive technology devices. She is a past member of the CCCC's Committee for Effective Practices in Online Writing Instruction.

Michael W. Gos is a professor at Lee College in Baytown, Texas, where he teaches technical writing, composition, and humanities studies. He received his Ph.D. in Rhetoric and Composition from Purdue University. Dr. Gos has served eight years on the executive board and three years as president of the Two-Year College English Association's Southwest region. He is currently the State of Texas policy analyst for NCTE. His research interests include writing instruction in computer environments, working class students and the difficulties they face negotiating college, and Texas writers and cowboy poets. Dr. Gos is also the author of a Texas-centered philosophy column for *Bay Area Houston Magazine*. He loves dogs, the outdoors, photography, and writing about Texas. He is a past member of the CCCC's Committee for Effective Practices in Online Writing Instruction.

Elif Guler is an Assistant Professor of Rhetoric and Professional Writing at Longwood University, where she teaches courses and conducts research in cultural rhetoric and professional writing. She previously taught both face-to-face and distance education writing courses at Old Dominion University (ODU). She is the recipient of a shining star faculty award from ODU and has co-authored an article on the use of online tools for assessment in the writing classroom.

Heidi Skurat Harris is an Assistant Professor of Rhetoric and Writing at the University of Arkansas at Little Rock where she teaches technical writing, digital rhetoric, grant writing, and rhetorical theory both face-to-face and online. Her primary research interest involves student experiences in and perceptions of online courses, including the relationship between student satisfaction in online courses and the incorporation of principles and effective practices from *A Position Statement of Principles and Example Effective Practices for OWI*. Dr. Harris has presented the results of her research at the CCCC, Distance Learning Administration National Conference, and at the United States Distance Learning

Association Conference. Her work appears in the *International Journal for the Scholarship of Teaching and Learning, The Next Digital Scholar, WAC,* and the book *Disrupting Pedagogies: Teaching the Knowledge Society.* Dr. Harris is a member of the CCCC's Committee for Effective Practices in Online Writing Instruction and a past member of the CCCC OWI Committee Expert/Stakeholder Panel.

Beth L. Hewett is a leading expert in online writing instruction. She has chaired or co-chaired the CCCC Committee for Effective Practices in Online Writing Instruction for seven years and remains an active member with special interests in research. She was the initial developer of the OWI program at Smarthinking, Inc., and later redesigned the TutorVista OWI program from the ground up. For seven years she was a co-editor at *Kairos,* first for CoverWeb and then for the journal as a whole. Her individual publications on online writing include: *Reading to Learn and Writing to Teach: Literacy Strategies for Online Writing Instruction* (Bedford/St. Martin's Press, 2015) and *The Online Writing Conference: A Guide for Teachers and Tutors* (Heinemann, 2010; updated, Bedford/St. Martin's Press, 2015). She has co-edited/co-authored additional publications: *Virtual Collaborative Writing in the Workplace: Computer-Mediated Communication Technologies and Processes* (IGI Global, 2010), *Preparing Educators for Online Writing Instruction: Principles and Processes* (NCTE, 2004), and *Technology and English Studies: Innovative Career Paths* (LEA, 2005). Dr. Hewett is an Educational Consultant and Dissertation Coach who specializes in practical problems of online writing and teaching. She also is a bereavement coach, facilitator, facilitator trainer, and author of the *Good Words for Grief* book series (WestBow Press, 2014; Grief Illustrated Press, 2010-2013).

Diane Martinez is an assistant professor of professional communication at Western Carolina University. Previously, she worked as a writing specialist in an online writing center and developed and taught online composition and technical writing courses. Dr. Martinez also developed and conducted an online training program to teach faculty and graduate students effective strategies for online teaching and learning. Currently co-chair of the CCCC's Committee for Effective Practices in Online Writing Instruction, she has been a member since 2011 and was a consultant to the Committee from 2009-2010.

Mahli Xuan Mechenbier is an Associate Lecturer in the Department of English at Kent State University: Geauga. She teaches Technical Writing, Business & Professional Writing, and Introduction to LGBT Literature. She is a certified Quality Matters Master Reviewer and APPQMR Facilitator. Her research interests include asynchronous online tone and communication methods; how academic administrations manage and budget distance learning; the unionization of professors; and employment conditions of contingent faculty members. Dr. Mechenbier serves on the MLA Executive Committee of the Discussion Group on Part-Time Faculty Members and the Modern Language Association Liaison Committee for the Association for Business Communication. She was adopted from South Vietnam through Operation Babylift, and she has two cats and one hamster. Dr. Mechenbier is a current member of the CCCC's Committee for Effective Practices in Online Writing Instruction and serves on the editorial board for the Online Writing Instruction Open Resource.

Lisa Meloncon is an associate professor of technical and professional communication in the Department of English at the University of Cincinnati and Director of the McMicken Health Research Center in the College of Arts and Sciences. Dr. Meloncon specializes in medical and health communication, programmatic issues in technical and professional communication, and online learning. Her work has appeared in journals such as *Technical Communication Quarterly, Technical Communication,* and the *Journal of Technical Writing and Communication.* She is editor of *Rhetorical Accessibility: At the Intersection of Technical Communication and Disability Studies* (2013). She is a current member of the CCCC's Committee for Effective Practices in Online Writing Instruction.

Connie Synder Mick is an Associate Special Professional Faculty member at the University of Notre Dame. Dr. Mick is Director of Community-Based Learning and Co-Director of the Poverty Studies Interdisciplinary Minor through the Center for Social Concerns. She teaches community-based courses on writing, rhetoric, poverty, gender, and ethical leadership. She presents nationally and publishes on a wide range of topics, such as teaching writing through technology, teaching poverty and privilege through writing, and the development of multiple literacies in English language learners through service-learning and civic engagement. She directed university writing centers for ten years. Dr. Mick has two composition textbooks forthcoming from Oxford University Press: a reader for writers called *Poverty/Privilege* and a rhetoric and reader on writing for social change called *Good Writing.* She is a past member of the CCCC's Committee for Effective Practices in Online Writing Instruction.

Geoffrey Middlebrook is a Teaching Professor in the Writing Program, Director of the Writing Center, and Distinguished Faculty Fellow in the Center for Excellence in Teaching at the University of Southern California (USC). Dr. Middlebrook has established himself as an authority on writing in digital environments and is the recipient of grants and recognition at USC, including the Provost's Prize for Teaching with Technology and the Advanced Writing Teaching Award. He presents his work frequently at national conferences, has published in journals and books, and is a past member of the CCCC's Committee for Effective Practices in Online Writing Instruction.

Susan Miller-Cochran is Professor of English and Director of First-Year Writing at North Carolina State University. Her research focuses on technology,

ESL writing, and writing program administration. Her work has appeared in *College Composition and Communication, Composition Studies, Computers and Composition, enculturation*, and *Teaching English in the Two-Year College*, and she is an editor of *Rhetorically Rethinking Usability* (Hampton Press, 2009) and *Strategies for Teaching First-Year Composition* (NCTE, 2002). Additionally, she is a co-author of *The Wadsworth Guide to Research* (Cengage, 2014) and *Keys for Writers* (Cengage, 2014). Before joining the faculty at NC State, Dr. Miller-Cochran was a faculty member at Mesa Community College (AZ). She has served on the Executive Committee of the Conference on College Composition and Communication and the Executive Board of the Council of Writing Program Administrators. She currently serves as Vice President of the Council of Writing Program Administrators. Dr. Miller-Cochran is a past member of the CCCC's Committee for Effective Practices in Online Writing Instruction.

Deborah Minter is Associate Professor of English and Associate Dean of the University of Nebraska–Lincoln's College of Arts and Sciences with responsibility for undergraduate education. She has served as Coordinator of UNL's Composition Program and Vice Chair of the English Department. Dr. Minter teaches graduate and undergraduate composition courses in onsite and online classrooms. She co-edited *Composition, Pedagogy and the Scholarship of Teaching* (Boynton/Cook, 2002) with Amy Goodburn. Her work also has appeared in several edited collections and such journals as *College Composition and Communication, Pedagogy*, and *College English*. She is a past member of the CCCC's Committee for Effective Practices in Online Writing Instruction.

Webster Newbold has been teaching and developing courses in computer-based writing instruction and digital literacy at Ball State University since the 1980s. He has published in *Kairos* and made numerous conference presentations on teaching FWY in online settings. Dr. Newbold has most recently concentrated on online-only writing instruction in LMS environments, and he was a member of the CCCC's Committee for Effective Practices in Online Writing Instruction from 2010 to 2014. He is now retired.

Leslie Olsen is an adjunct English instructor at Excelsior College, teaching composition, business writing, and professional communications online. She received an MA in English from the University of Washington, where her research interests included genre studies, discourse analysis, and writing center pedagogy. She spent eight years as the Writing Center Coordinator at the University of Washington, Bothell campus, before becoming the first Writing Center Coordinator at Capella University, overseeing both face-to-face and online tutoring, as well as developing onsite and online writing centers. She is a current member of the CCCC's Committee for Effective Practices in Online Writing Instruction and served on the editorial board for the Online Writing Instruction Open Resource.

Sushil K. Oswal is a Technical Communication and Environmental Studies faculty at the University of Washington, Tacoma, and a faculty of Disability Studies at the University of Washington, Seattle. He received the C. R. Anderson Award for the work on his doctoral study of an Environmental Taskforce in a Japanese-owned corporation. As a newly-minted Ph.D. from the University of Cincinnati, where he was also a Taft Doctoral Fellow, he led the founding of a Writing Portfolios Program at Middle Tennessee State University. Later, as the director of a Technical Communication program at a private university in Connecticut, he was the winner of a six figure joint grant from the United Technologies Corporation for designing a fully-accessible computer writing lab. Dr. Oswal's present research focuses on human-centered design and the accessibility of multimodal digital communication (see *Communication Design Quarterly, Journal of Business and Technical Communication, Kairos: A Journal of Rhetoric, Technology, and Pedagogy,* and *Work: a Journal of Prevention, Assessment, and Rehabilitation*). As a member of the CCCC's Committee for Effective Practices in Online Writing Instruction since its inception, he has led its accessibility efforts.

Rich Rice is Associate Professor at Texas Tech University where he teaches new media, rhetoric, grant writing, intercultural communication, and composition in the Technical Communication and Rhetoric program. He directs the TTU Department of English Media Lab. Dr. Rice's most recent book is *ePortfolio Performance Support Systems: Constructing, Presenting, and Assessing Portfolios* (2013) with Parlor Press and the WAC Clearinghouse. Recent book chapters and journal articles include topics addressing faculty professionalization, intercultural competence, teaching philosophies, mobile medicine, convergence theory, problem-based universal design for learning, photo essays, media labs, and study abroad models. His research seeks to make connections between new media, communication, and teaching. Dr. Rice currently is developing sustainable study abroad models in India. He is a Fulbright-Nehru Scholar, and he is a member of the CCCC OWI Committee Expert/Stakeholder Panel.

Rochelle (Shelley) Rodrigo is Assistant Professor of Rhetoric & (New) Media at Old Dominion University. She was a full time faculty member for nine years in English and film studies at Mesa Community College in Arizona. Dr. Rodrigo researches how "newer" technologies better facilitate communicative interactions, more specifically teaching and learning. As well as co-authoring the first and second editions of *The Wadsworth Guide to Research*, she also was co-editor of *Rhetorically Rethinking Usability* (Hampton Press). Her work also has appeared in *Computers and Composition, Teaching English in the Two-Year College, EDUCAUSE Quarterly, The Journal of Interactive Technology & Pedagogy,*

Flow, as well as various edited collections. Dr. Rodrigo is a member of the CCCC OWI Committee Expert/Stakeholder Panel.

Jason Snart is a Professor of English at College of DuPage, in Glen Ellyn, Illinois. He earned his Ph.D. from the University of Florida. His books include *Making Hybrids Work* (NCTE, forthcoming), *Hybrid Learning: The Perils and Promise of Blending Online and Face-to-Face Instruction in Higher Education* (Praeger, 2010) and *The Torn Book: UnReading William Blake's Marginalia* (Susquehanna University Press, 2006). He currently is working in the areas of curricular, faculty, and administrative development to support effective hybrid learning. His teaching includes writing and literature courses delivered face-to-face, fully online, and in hybrid settings. Dr. Snart, is a member of the CCCC's Committee for Effective Practices in Online Writing Instruction's, leads the editorial board for the Online Writing Instruction Open Resource, and is a past member of the CCCC OWI Committee Expert/Stakeholder Panel.

Robbin Zeff Warner is a Senior Writing Coach at Defend & Publish, LLC, and an educational consultant in OWI. Previously she was an Assistant Professor of Writing, Professional Technology Fellow, and WID Studio Director at George Washington University (GWU). She also is a Teacher Consultant with the Northern Virginia Writing Project. Dr. Warner's interest in online technology was launched in writing the landmark book *The Nonprofit Guide to the Internet* in 1996 when there were so few nonprofits online one could actually count them. This book initiated a series of books on Internet use for the nonprofit community by John Wiley & Sons. She then wrote the first book on online advertising back in 1997 (*Advertising on the Internet*), which eventually was translated into six languages. Recently, Dr. Warner lived in Brussels, Belgium, for four years where she studied chocolate making; she is now writing novels that showcase artisan chocolate.

Scott Warnock is an associate professor of English at Drexel University and Director of the University Writing Program. He is the author of *Teaching Writing Online: How and Why* and numerous book chapters and journal articles on a range of writing-related concerns. Dr. Warnock has presented and conducted workshops about teaching and technology issues and opportunities at national conferences and many institutions. He is co-chair of the CCCC Committee for Effective Practices in Online Writing Instruction.

INDEX

A

ableism, 279

ability, 294, 311, 315-318, 320, 329, 335, 337, 350, 361, 402, 430, 473, 477, 479-480, 550

access (accessible), 8, 12-13, 20, 23-28, 37-45, 47-48, 53-54, 56-57, 59, 62, 64-66, 69, 72, 75, 78-82, 85, 87, 95, 99-100, 102-104, 119, 125, 129, 131, 133-134, 138, 146-141, 145, 153-155, 158-159, 170-171, 173, 178, 184-190, 190-194, 196-197, 203, 205-207, 211-2 214, 216-218, 221, 223-224, 229-233, 234, 238-241, 246-247, 253-254, 256-262, 264, 266-283, 291, 293, 298, 300, 302-303, 305, 311-313, 314-318, 318-320, 322, 325, 327-330, 334-335, 338-341, 350-353, 362, 364, 366-367, 370-372, 374, 377, 380-382, 391, 393-394, 396, 400, 402-403, 406, 408, 412, 416-420, 422-426, 428, 430-431, 437-438, 441-442, 445, 447-448, 451-453, 456-457, 462-463, 471-477, 479-483, 485-486, 488-489, 504, 506, 510, 518-524, 526, 531, 535, 548, 551-552, 554-555, 558-561

adapt (adaptation of theory or practice), 10, 53, 72, 98, 99, 118, 136, 167, 259, 354, 358, 450, 533, 549

adjunct, 56, 60, 103, 174, 227-230, 232-246

adjunct faculty, 25, 228, 229, 233-247, 472

African-American, 328, 329

agile design, 397, 402, 406

agile faculty professionalization, 395, 396, 397, 398, 400, 401, 405

agile refactoring, 401, 402, 407, 408

agile software (design), 395, 397, 400, 402

agile training, 406

alphabetic assignment, 488

alphabetic essay, 47, 480,54

alphabetic writing, 472-473, 550, 560

Americans with Disabilities Act (ADA), xiii, 19, 40-42, 62, 189, 264, 266, 276-277, 325, 534

applied rhetoric, 152, 439-441, 443, 445, 451, 454-455, 461-462, 467

Aristotle, 9

Aristotelian rhetoric, 53

Asperger's, 453

assessment, xiv, 6, 24, 40, 56-56, 60-63, 78, 135, 151, 153, 160, 173, 176-177, 199, 211-212, 219-221, 230, 236-237, 240, 260, 299, 302, 349, 391, 394-395, 398, 408, 414, 417-418, 420-421, 428, 431, 441, 454-455, 461, 473-474, 477, 481, 483-487, 489-490, 528, 539, 556-557

association, 55, 73, 75, 200, 233, 350-351, 356, 361, 375, 380, 382

CPSIA information can be obtained at www.ICGtesting.com
Printed in the USA
LVOW10s1519190315

431114LV00004B/4/P